MASTERPIECES OF THE DRAMA

MASTERPIECES OF THE DRAMA

second edition

Edited by

Alexander W. Allison

Arthur J. Carr

Arthur M. Eastman

University of Michigan

The Macmillan Company New York

Fourth Printing, 1968

Library of Congress catalog card number: 66–16702

THE MACMILLAN COMPANY, NEW YORK
COLLIER-MACMILLAN CANADA, LTD., TORONTO, ONTARIO

Printed in the United States of America

ACKNOWLEDGMENTS

THE OEDIPUS REX OF SOPHOCLES, *An English Version* by Dudley Fitts and Robert Fitzgerald, copyright 1949 by Harcourt, Brace & World, Inc., New York, and reprinted with their permission. THE BACCHAE by Euripides, translated by Philip Vellacott, reprinted from *The Bacchae and Other Plays* by permission of Penguin Books, Limited, Baltimore, Md. THE MISER by Molière, translated by and used with the permission of Lloyd Parks, who gratefully acknowledges the assistance of Eric Bentley. All rights whatsoever in this translation are strictly reserved, and applications for performances, excerpts, and so on, should be made to Mr. Parks, Department of English, Ohio State University, Columbus, Ohio. HEDDA GABLER by Henrik Ibsen, translated by Edmund Gosse and William Archer. From *The Collected Works of Henrik Ibsen,* Volume X, entirely revised and edited by William Archer, copyright 1907 by Charles Scribner's Sons, New York, 1935 by Frank Archer. Reprinted by permission of the publishers. THE CHERRY ORCHARD by Anton Chekhov, translated by Constance Garnett, reprinted by permission of the publishers, Chatto & Windus Ltd., London. RIDERS TO THE SEA by J. M. Synge. Reprinted by permission of the publishers, Random House, Inc., New York, and George Allen & Unwin, Limited, London. JUNO AND THE PAYCOCK by Sean O'Casey, copyright 1928 by The Macmillan Company, 1953 by Sean O'Casey, reprinted by permission of Macmillan and Co., Ltd., London, and St. Martin's Press, Inc., New York. THE HOUSE OF BERNARDA ALBA by Federico Garcia Lorca, translated by James Graham-Luján and Richard L. O'Connell, copyright 1947 by New Directions and reprinted with their permission. THE MADWOMAN OF CHAILLOT by Jean Giraudoux, translated by Maurice Valency, copyright 1949 by Maurice Valency. Reprinted by permission of Random House, Inc. THE CAUCASIAN CHALK CIRCLE by Bertolt Brecht, translated by Eric Bentley, copyright © by him, 1947, 1948, 1961, 1963; prologue copyright © 1959 by Eric Bentley; originally published in *Parables for the Theatre* by the University of Minnesota Press, and used with their permission. ALL THAT FALL and ACT WITHOUT WORDS I by Samuel Beckett, reprinted from *Krapp's Last Tape and Other Dramatic Pieces* by Samuel Beckett, copyright © 1957 by Samuel Beckett, copyright © 1958, 1959, 1960 by Grove Press Incorporated, and used with their permission.

INTRODUCTION

THIS INTRODUCTION DETAILS some matters of fact and some articles of theory which it is hoped students will find serviceable and teachers less than meddlesome.

A play is a work of literary fiction enacted by living persons before the eyes of an audience. A literary study of the drama postulates an ideal performance of each work, assuming that the mind's eye will apprehend living persons and the mind's ear the intonations of speech. If one wants to appeal more particularly than this to the plays as theater pieces, as it will profit him to do from time to time, he must distinguish different kinds of theatrical performance.

He may conceive the Greek plays in this book as performed in a large outdoor amphitheater before the façade of a supposed palace or temple. This stage has no curtain; the actors either come out of the palace gates or enter in plain sight from the sides. They wear masks accentuating their dominant character traits, and high-soled boots which increase their stature. In front of the stage, in the focal area of the semicircular theater, is the circular "orchestra" or dancing place, and in the center of that, at the theater's focal point, stands an altar to Dionysus, the god in whose honor the plays are given. A chorus of fifteen men enters the orchestra during the first ode ("párodos") and remains there until the end of the play. This ode and the others they chant melodically, supporting their chant by the motions and poses of a highly stylized form of dancing. Sometimes they divide into semichoruses of seven and seven and chant responsively. Their leader performs sometimes with the rest of them and sometimes singly. At times he takes part in spoken interchanges with the actors. At times, also, one or more of the actors chant responsively with the chorus. Taken together, the absence of particular setting and the stylized character of the whole performance kept the Greek plays from seeming representative of any special time and place, leaving their audience free to consider their universal implications.

One may conceive the Elizabethan play (*Volpone*) as performed in the courtyard of a three-tiered theater, on a stage which juts out into the courtyard. Spectators sit in the three tiers of balconies or stand around the stage. There is no curtain; actors begin scenes by walking on and end them by walking off. Set into the wall behind the stage, however, are two small curtained acting areas, one at stage level and the other in the theater's second story. The lower one of these usually represents a ground-floor interior (*e.g.*, Volpone's bedchamber); the upper, an upstairs room or balcony; the whole backdrop, the front of a house. All major features of the Elizabethan theater were built into it and hence remained constant, but stage properties and costumes were changed. In general, theatrical performances of the time were less severely formal than those of the Greeks but not so literally representative as modern performances.

The subsequent plays in this volume were written for a stage of which three essential features are familiar to us all: it is recessed into one wall of an indoor theater, it is curtained, and it is illuminated by footlights. Such a stage lends itself to a very literal form of illusion. As the curtain rises, the audience may imagine that the fourth wall of a room has been removed, revealing real people within. Molière's *The Miser* and Sheridan's *The Rivals,* to be sure, were still written with highly artificial stage conventions in view. But the five plays which follow these show to the audience for the most part the physical face of external reality. The construction of the modern theater, like the constitution of the modern mind in one of its aspects, fosters somewhat literal representations of life as it is illumined by the light of common day.

In another of its aspects, the modern mind harbors doubts as to whether any reality beyond itself can be clearly distinguished and whether, in particular, the order of things apparent in dramatic art answers to an order in the world "out there" or is solely a figment of the playwright's imagination. A fancifulness mirroring such hesitations has been conspicuous in the theater of the past few decades. The plays in this volume by Giraudoux, Brecht, and Beckett manifestly deviate from so-called "fourth-wall realism" into suggestiveness once more, and invite performances in varying degrees formal and conventional.

The whole body of plays, however, in this volume or any other, may be abstracted from modes of performance and examined for those features which they have in common. They obey the laws which govern all literary fictions; ideally each one is single and complete, each is free from any sort of irrelevance, each traces a necessary or probable sequence of events.

The most rigid dramatic theory actually prescribes a single structure to which all plays must conform; and while no intelligent students of drama find exclusive virtue in this pattern, almost all of them grant its generality of application and use at least some of the terms which it has made current. According to this strict theory, the audience is first given enough general information so that it will be able to understand the action which follows; this initial imparting of knowledge is called the *exposition*. Then the leading character (*protagonist*) becomes involved in an action which will materially affect his future well-being; this involvement is called the *complication*. There presently follows in the natural course a happening which decides whether the whole action will turn out well or ill; this critical happening is called the *crisis*. The play then moves toward its inevitable conclusion, variously called the *denouement* ("unravelling") or the *catastrophe*—the latter word being now reserved for an adverse outcome.

There is, finally, a general recognition of two sharply opposed dramatic kinds, tragedy and comedy, and a partly independent body of theory for each of these. The most influential body of tragic theory remains Aristotle's *Poetics,* and the section of it most often alluded to reads as follows:

> A perfect tragedy should imitate actions which excite pity and fear, this being the distinctive function of tragic imitation. It follows plainly, in the first place, that the change of fortune presented must not be the spectacle of virtuous man brought from prosperity to adversity, for this moves neither pity nor fear; it merely shocks us. Nor, again, that of a bad man passing from adversity to prosperity, for nothing can be more alien to the spirit of Tragedy; it possesses no single tragic quality; it neither satisfies the moral sense nor calls forth pity or fear. Nor, again, should the downfall of an utter villain be exhibited. A plot of this kind would doubtless satisfy the moral sense, but it would inspire neither pity nor fear; for pity is aroused by unmerited misfortune, fear by the misfortune of a man like ourselves. Such an event, therefore, will be neither pitiful nor terrible. There remains, then, the character between these two extremes—that of a man who is not eminently good and just, yet whose misfortune is brought about not by vice or depravity, but by some error or frailty. He must be one who is highly renowned and prosperous—a personage like Oedipus, Thyestes, or other illustrious men of such families. (Trans. S. H. Butcher)

Aristotle's theory strongly emphasizes the sense of release ("purgation") which the audience experiences upon the completion of a tragedy. Variants of this theory substitute admiration for fear as a component of the tragic emotion and emphasize the hero's ethical growth as a result of his misfortune.

There is no single theory of comedy which is as widely accepted, even with qualification, as is Aristotle's theory of tragedy. But there is considerable agreement on the nature of comedy at its most frankly satiric. It is agreed that a chief source of humor is incongruity, and that in satiric comedy some norm of just and reasonable behavior is assumed, departures from which impress us as incongruous and therefore amusing. To respond to satire, it logically follows, we must retain a measure of detachment. And no comedy asks for either the kind or degree of emotional commitment which tragedy demands.

It is, however, hard to generalize concerning comedy or any other literary form—both hard and less than wholly rewarding. One of the delights of literary study, indeed, is the discovery that while great works conform in part to the same great patterns, each one also takes a shape distinctively its own.

A NOTE ON ANNOTATION

Notes are supplied only to forestall misunderstanding or to present relevant information which is not common knowledge. Annotation is generally avoided when the pertinent information can be found in the standard college dictionaries.

CONTENTS

MASTERPIECES OF THE DRAMA

SOPHOCLES
496?–406 B.C.

OEDIPUS REX
430 B.C.

In oedipus rex Sophocles endows the figures of a legend with such distinctive yet universal traits that we seem to know them as well as our own acquaintances. We recognize his Oedipus as a mighty and benevolent man who turns rashly tyrannical when crossed, who out of pride and a need for self-assertion imposes his own character on his community, and who from an honesty more compelling than pride destroys himself in a quest for truth. "I am on the brink of dreadful speech!" says the shepherd, and Oedipus replies, "And I of dreadful hearing. Yet I must hear."

Sophocles develops his plot with the same profound fidelity to universal human experience that governs his characterization. From Oedipus' opening assertion of authority to Creon's final rebuff ("Think no longer That you are in command here"), we witness a sequence of events recognizably true in even their smallest elements to the motives, feelings, and temperaments of the characters involved. We understand, for example, why Oedipus responds to Teiresias' silence with irritation mounting to wrath, why Teiresias finally tells his secret, and why Oedipus cannot begin to apprehend it. The importance of plot rendered thus true to human experience is that it gives intelligible form to that experience. As we understand merely one character or another, one act or another, we understand only the accidents of human nature, the unrelated particulars of life. But when we see one act lead naturally to another and that to another, as in Sophocles' linked chain of causation from glorious beginning to infamous end, we have seen through accident to form, through experience to the laws which govern experience.

To understand Oedipus and the laws which govern him, we must understand more than psychology. We must apprehend the world in which he acts and reacts. This world, as the religious festival which gives the play its occasion suggests, is one which the gods govern. And the gods, be it said, are no mere collection of superstitious oddities. They are the embodiments of a profound conviction that the universe, however mysterious, is governed by an agency which takes moral cognizance of man. The play begins in religious supplication; Teiresias speaks with supernatural authority; the chorus repeatedly prays to the gods; and when Oedipus makes his final discovery, it is that he and his parents, in their desperate efforts to escape the oracles, have lived out, against their own wills, the wills of the gods.

This conflict between Oedipus and the oracles, between the pride of self-sufficient man and the authority of divine law, gives the play its form, which is based on a separation between human will and divine will, a separation rhythmically narrowing with each accession of knowledge until the two merge. The units of rhythm are the individual scenes, each of which shows an Oedipus who is convinced of his own innocence seeking a knowledge which, as he approaches it, turns ironically into an evidence of his own guilt.

The irony of the play deserves particular mention. That it informs the plot is already evident. It also throws its oblique light on every character. Teiresias means to keep his secret but tells it; Iocastê cheers Oedipus with her tale of a false oracle that turns out to be deadly true; the messenger brings good news but finds it most evil. Even the shepherd thought to save a child but committed him to an unspeakable destiny. The irony enters, too, into scores of lines which mean one thing to the speaker, another to the audience. "Poor children," says Oedipus, "I know that you are deathly sick; and yet, Sick as you are, not one is as sick as I." The importance of this pervading irony is that it gives us a dual vision, a view of things as seen by mortal man and a view of the same things under the aspect of eternity. It catches in its duality the play's conflict and the play's theme.

Oedipus and the chorus ultimately discover what the irony keeps making us see—that the individual mind, self-sufficient in its ignorance, responds in fact to control beyond its ken, gives unknown allegiance to a will which unites the infinity of the world's separate wills into a single harmony. Before that greater will man can only do what Creon does—submit himself—and say with the chorus:

> Let me be reverent in the ways of right,
> Lowly the paths I journey on;
> Let all my words and actions keep
> The laws of the pure universe
> From highest Heaven handed down.

OEDIPUS REX : *SOPHOCLES*

AN ENGLISH VERSION
BY DUDLEY FITTS AND ROBERT FITZGERALD

Characters

OEDIPUS	*King of Thebes*
A PRIEST	
CREON	*brother of Iocastê*
TEIRESIAS	*a blind seer*
IOCASTÊ	*the Queen, wife of Oedipus*
MESSENGER	
SHEPHERD OF LAÏOS	
SECOND MESSENGER	
CHORUS OF THEBAN ELDERS	

THE SCENE. *Before the palace of Oedipus, King of Thebes. A central door and two lateral doors open onto a platform which runs the length of the façade. On the platform, right and left, are altars; and three steps lead down into the* "orchestra," *or chorus-ground. At the beginning of the action these steps are crowded by suppliants who have brought branches and chaplets of olive leaves and who lie in various attitudes of despair.* OEDIPUS *enters.*

PROLOGUE

OEDIPUS. My children, generations of the living
In the line of Kadmos, nursed at his ancient hearth:
Why have you strewn yourselves before these altars
In supplication, with your boughs and garlands?
The breath of incense rises from the city
With a sound of prayer and lamentation.
Children,
I would not have you speak through messengers,
And therefore I have come myself to hear you—
I, Oedipus, who bear the famous name.
[*to a* PRIEST]
You, there, since you are eldest in the company,
Speak for them all, tell me what preys upon you,
Whether you come in dread, or crave some blessing:
Tell me, and never doubt that I will help you
In every way I can; I should be heartless
Were I not moved to find you suppliant here.
PRIEST. Great Oedipus, O powerful King of Thebes!
You see how all the ages of our people
Cling to your altar steps: here are boys
Who can barely stand alone, and here are priests
By weight of age, as I am a priest of God,
And young men chosen from those yet unmarried;
As for the others, all that multitude,
They wait with olive chaplets in the squares,
At the two shrines of Pallas, and where Apollo

Prologue This play consists of a prologue, a párodos, four scenes—each followed by an ode—and an éxodos. The **párodos** is the ode sung by the chorus as it enters; the **éxodos** is that part of the play which follows the last ode. The play, then, is composed of a beginning (prologue and párodos) in which the situation is defined and explored; a middle (the four scenes and their terminal odes) in which the plot develops, with choral commentary, to the catastrophic discovery; and an end (the éxodos) in which the consequences of the discovery are explored and, in part, realized.

3 **Kadmos** founder of Thebes, great-great-grandfather of Oedipus. Cf. ll. 280–81.

Speaks in the glowing embers.
Your own eyes
Must tell you: Thebes is in her extremity
And can not lift her head from the surge of death.
A rust consumes the buds and fruits of the earth;
The herds are sick; children die unborn,
And labor is vain. The god of plague and pyre
Raids like detestable lightning through the city,
And all the house of Kadmos is laid waste,
All emptied, and all darkened: Death alone
Battens upon the misery of Thebes.

You are not one of the immortal gods, we know;
Yet we have come to you to make our prayer
As to the man of all men best in adversity
And wisest in the ways of God. You saved us
From the Sphinx, that flinty singer, and the tribute
We paid to her so long; yet you were never
Better informed than we, nor could we teach you:
It was some god breathed in you to set us free.

Therefore, O mighty King, we turn to you:
Find us our safety, find us a remedy,
Whether by counsel of the gods or men.
A king of wisdom tested in the past
Can act in a time of troubles, and act well.
Noblest of men, restore
Life to your city! Think how all men call you
Liberator for your triumph long ago;
Ah, when your years of kingship are remembered,
Let them not say *We rose, but later fell—*
Keep the State from going down in the storm!
Once, years ago, with happy augury,

43 **Sphinx** monster that settled near Thebes and slew all passers-by who failed to solve the riddle she asked of them: "What being has four feet in the morning, two at noon, and three at night?" Years before the play's opening Oedipus had rescued Thebes by solving the riddle ("Man"), whereupon the Sphinx killed herself, and the Thebans made **Oedipus their king**

You brought us fortune; be the same again!
No man questions your power to rule the land:
But rule over men, not over a dead city!
Ships are only hulls, citadels are nothing,
When no life moves in the empty passageways.

OEDIPUS. Poor children! You may be sure I know
All that you longed for in your coming here.
I know that you are deathly sick; and yet,
Sick as you are, not one is as sick as I.
Each of you suffers in himself alone
His anguish, not another's; but my spirit
Groans for the city, for myself, for you.

I was not sleeping, you are not waking me.
No, I have been in tears for a long while
And in my restless thought walked many ways.
In all my search, I found one helpful course,
And that I have taken: I have sent Creon,
Son of Menoikeus, brother of the Queen,
To Delphi, Apollo's place of revelation,
To learn there, if he can,
What act or pledge of mine may save the city.
I have counted the days, and now, this very day,
I am troubled, for he has overstayed his time.
What is he doing? He has been gone too long.
Yet whenever he comes back, I should do ill
To scant whatever hint the god may give.

PRIEST. It is a timely promise. At this instant
They tell me Creon is here.

OEDIPUS. O Lord Apollo!
May his news be fair as his face is radiant!

PRIEST. It could not be otherwise: he is crowned with bay,
The chaplet is thick with berries.

OEDIPUS. We shall soon know;
He is near enough to hear us now.

[*Enter* CREON.]

89 **bay** the laurel, sacred to Apollo and, when worn in wreaths or crowns, symbolic of victory

O Prince:
Brother: son of Menoikeus:
What answer do you bring us from the god?
CREON. It is favorable. I can tell you, great afflictions
Will turn out well, if they are taken well.
OEDIPUS. What was the oracle? These vague words
Leave me still hanging between hope and fear.
CREON. Is it your pleasure to hear me with all these
Gathered around us? I am prepared to speak,
But should we not go in?
OEDIPUS. Let them all hear it.
It is for them I suffer, more than for myself.
CREON. Then I will tell you what I heard at Delphi.

In plain words
The god commands us to expel from the land of Thebes
An old defilement that it seems we shelter.
It is a deathly thing, beyond expiation.
We must not let it feed upon us longer.
OEDIPUS. What defilement? How shall we rid ourselves of it?
CREON. By exile or death, blood for blood. It was
Murder that brought the plague-wind on the city.
OEDIPUS. Murder of whom? Surely the god has named him?
CREON. My lord: long ago Laïos was our king,
Before you came to govern us.
OEDIPUS. I know;
I learned of him from others; I never saw him.
CREON. He was murdered; and Apollo commands us now
To take revenge upon whoever killed him.
OEDIPUS. Upon whom? Where are they? Where shall we find a clue
To solve that crime, after so many years?
CREON. Here in this land, he said.
If we make enquiry,
We may touch things that otherwise escape us.
OEDIPUS. Tell me: Was Laïos murdered in his house,
Or in the fields, or in some foreign country?
CREON. He said he planned to make a pilgrimage.
He did not come home again.

OEDIPUS. And was there no one,
No witness, no companion, to tell what happened?
CREON. They were all killed but one, and he got away
So frightened that he could remember one thing only.
OEDIPUS. What was that one thing? One may be the key
To everything, if we resolve to use it.
CREON. He said that a band of highwaymen attacked them,
Outnumbered them, and overwhelmed the King.
OEDIPUS. Strange, that a highwayman should be so daring—
Unless some faction here bribed him to do it.
CREON. We thought of that. But after Laïos' death
New troubles arose and we had no avenger.
OEDIPUS. What troubles could prevent your hunting down the killers?
CREON. The riddling Sphinx's song
Made us deaf to all mysteries but her own.
OEDIPUS. Then once more I must bring what is dark to light.
It is most fitting that Apollo shows,
As you do, this compunction for the dead.
You shall see how I stand by you, as I should,
To avenge the city and the city's god,
And not as though it were for some distant friend,
But for my own sake, to be rid of evil.
Whoever killed King Laïos might—who knows?—
Decide at any moment to kill me as well.
By avenging the murdered king I protect myself.

Come, then, my children: leave the altar steps,
Lift up your olive boughs!
One of you go
And summon the people of Kadmos to gather here.
I will do all that I can; you may tell them that.
[*Exit a* PAGE.]
So, with the help of God,

163 **God** Apollo, god of music, archery, healing, light (***Phoibos,*** as he is called at l. 167, means *light* or *pure*), and truth. Through his oracle he mediates between man and the gods.

We shall be saved—or else indeed we are lost.

PRIEST. Let us rise, children. It was for this we came,
And now the King has promised it himself.
Phoibos has sent us an oracle; may he descend
Himself to save us and drive out the plague.

[*Exeunt* OEDIPUS *and* CREON *into the palace by the central door. The* PRIEST *and the* SUPPLIANTS *disperse R. and L. After a short pause the* CHORUS *enters the orchestra.*]

PÁRODOS

CHORUS. What is the god singing in his profound — STROPHE 1
Delphi of gold and shadow?
What oracle for Thebes, the sunwhipped city?

Fear unjoints me, the roots of my heart tremble.

Now I remember, O Healer, your power, and wonder:
Will you send doom like a sudden cloud, or weave it
Like nightfall of the past?

Ah no: be merciful, issue of holy sound:
Dearest to our expectancy: be tender!

ANTISTROPHE 1

Let me pray to Athenê, the immortal daughter of Zeus,
And to Artemis her sister
Who keeps her famous throne in the market ring,
And to Apollo, bowman at the far butts of heaven—

O gods, descend! Like three streams leap against
The fires of our grief, the fires of darkness;
Be swift to bring us rest!

As in the old time from the brilliant house
Of air you stepped to save us, come again!

Now our afflictions have no end. — STROPHE 2

Now all our stricken host lies down
And no man fights off death with his mind;

The noble plowland bears no grain,
And groaning mothers can not bear—

See, how our lives like birds take wing,
Like sparks that fly when a fire soars,
To the shore of the god of evening.

The plague burns on, it is pitiless, ANTISTROPHE 2
Though pallid children laden with death
Lie unwept in the stony ways,

And old gray women by every path
Flock to the strand about the altars

There to strike their breasts and cry
Worship of Zeus in wailing prayers:
Be kind, God's golden child!

There are no swords in this attack by fire, STROPHE 3
No shields, but we are ringed with cries.

Send the besieger plunging from our homes
Into the vast sea-room of the Atlantic
Or into the waves that foam eastward of Thrace—

For the day ravages what the night spares—

Destroy our enemy, lord of the thunder!
Let him be riven by lightning from heaven!

Phoibos Apollo, stretch the sun's bowstring, ANTISTROPHE 3
That golden cord, until it sing for us,
Flashing arrows in heaven!

207 **God's golden child** Athena, daughter of Zeus

Artemis, Huntress,
Race with flaring lights upon our mountains!

O scarlet god, O golden-banded brow,
O Theban Bacchos in a storm of Maenads,
[*Enter* OEDIPUS, *center*.]
Whirl upon Death, that all the Undying hate!
Come with blinding cressets, come in joy!

SCENE I

OEDIPUS. Is this your prayer? It may be answered. Come,
Listen to me, act as the crisis demands,
And you shall have relief from all these evils.

Until now I was a stranger to this tale,
As I had been a stranger to the crime.
Could I track down the murderer without a clue?
But now, friends,
As one who became a citizen after the murder,
I make this proclamation to all Thebans:
If any man knows by whose hands Laïos, son of Labdakos,
Met his death, I direct that man to tell me everything,
No matter what he fears for having so long withheld it.
Let it stand as promised that no further trouble
Will come to him, but he may leave the land in safety.

Moreover: If anyone knows the murderer to be foreign,
Let him not keep silent: he shall have his reward from me.
However, if he does conceal it; if any man
Fearing for his friend or for himself disobeys this edict,
Hear what I propose to do:

I solemnly forbid the people of this country,

221 **scarlet** flushed with wine
222 **Theban** born in Thebes and descended on his mortal side from Kadmos

Where power and throne are mine, ever to receive that man
Or speak to him, no matter who he is, or let him
Join in sacrifice, lustration, or in prayer.
I decree that he be driven from every house,
Being, as he is, corruption itself to us: the Delphic
Voice of Zeus has pronounced this revelation.
Thus I associate myself with the oracle
And take the side of the murdered king.

As for the criminal, I pray to God—
Whether it be a lurking thief, or one of a number—
I pray that that man's life be consumed in evil and
  wretchedness.
And as for me, this curse applies no less
If it should turn out that the culprit is my guest here,
Sharing my hearth.
  You have heard the penalty.
I lay it on you now to attend to this
For my sake, for Apollo's, for the sick
Sterile city that heaven has abandoned.
Suppose the oracle had given you no command:
Should this defilement go uncleansed for ever?
You should have found the murderer: your king,
A noble king, had been destroyed!
  Now I,
Having the power that he held before me,
Having his bed, begetting children there
Upon his wife, as he would have, had he lived—
Their son would have been my children's brother,
If Laïos had had luck in fatherhood!
(But surely ill luck rushed upon his reign)—
I say I take the son's part, just as though
I were his son, to press the fight for him
And see it won! I'll find the hand that brought
Death to Labdakos' and Polydoros' child,
Heir of Kadmos' and Agenor's line.

280–81 **Labdakos' . . . line** The child is Laïos, whose male ancestry Oedipus traces back: Laïos-Labdakos-Polydoros-Kadmos-Agenor

And as for those who fail me,
May the gods deny them the fruit of the earth,
Fruit of the womb, and may they rot utterly!
Let them be wretched as we are wretched, and worse!

For you, for loyal Thebans, and for all
Who find my actions right, I pray the favor
Of justice, and of all the immortal gods.
CHORAGOS. Since I am under oath, my lord, I swear
I did not do the murder, I can not name
The murderer. Might not the oracle
That has ordained the search tell where to find him?
OEDIPUS. An honest question. But no man in the world
Can make the gods do more than the gods will.
CHORAGOS. There is one last expedient—
OEDIPUS. Tell me what it is.
Though it seem slight, you must not hold it back.
CHORAGOS. A lord clairvoyant to the lord Apollo,
As we all know, is the skilled Teiresias.
One might learn much about this from him, Oedipus.
OEDIPUS. I am not wasting time:
Creon spoke of this, and I have sent for him—
Twice, in fact; it is strange that he is not here.
CHORAGOS. The other matter—that old report—seems useless.
OEDIPUS. Tell me. I am interested in all reports.
CHORAGOS. The King was said to have been killed by highwaymen.
OEDIPUS. I know. But we have no witnesses to that.
CHORAGOS. If the killer can feel a particle of dread,
Your curse will bring him out of hiding!
OEDIPUS. No.
The man who dared that act will fear no curse.

[*Enter the blind seer* TEIRESIAS, *led by a* PAGE.]

CHORAGOS. But there is one man who may detect the criminal.
This is Teiresias, this is the holy prophet
In whom, alone of all men, truth was born.
OEDIPUS. Teiresias: seer: student of mysteries,

289 CHORAGOS leader of the chorus

Of all that's taught and all that no man tells,
Secrets of Heaven and secrets of the earth:
Blind though you are, you know the city lies
Sick with plague; and from this plague, my lord,
We find that you alone can guard or save us.

Possibly you did not hear the messengers?
Apollo, when we sent to him,
Sent us back word that this great pestilence
Would lift, but only if we established clearly
The identity of those who murdered Laïos.
They must be killed or exiled.
Can you use
Birdflight or any art of divination
To purify yourself, and Thebes, and me
From this contagion? We are in your hands.
There is no fairer duty
Than that of helping others in distress.

TEIRESIAS. How dreadful knowledge of the truth can be
When there's no help in truth! I knew this well,
But did not act on it: else I should not have come.

OEDIPUS. What is troubling you? Why are your eyes so cold?

TEIRESIAS. Let me go home. Bear your own fate, and I'll
Bear mine. It is better so: trust what I say.

OEDIPUS. What you say is ungracious and unhelpful
To your native country. Do not refuse to speak.

TEIRESIAS. When it comes to speech, your own is neither temperate
Nor opportune. I wish to be more prudent.

OEDIPUS. In God's name, we all beg you—

TEIRESIAS. You are all ignorant.
No; I will never tell you what I know.
Now it is my misery; then, it would be yours.

OEDIPUS. What! You do know something, and will not tell us?
You would betray us all and wreck the State?

TEIRESIAS. I do not intend to torture myself, or you.
Why persist in asking? You will not persuade me.

OEDIPUS. What a wicked old man you are! You'd try a stone's
Patience! Out with it! Have you no feeling at all?

TEIRESIAS. You call me unfeeling. If you could only see
The nature of your own feelings . . .
OEDIPUS. Why,
Who would not feel as I do? Who could endure
Your arrogance toward the city?
TEIRESIAS. What does it matter!
Whether I speak or not, it is bound to come.
OEDIPUS. Then, if "it" is bound to come, you are bound to tell me.
TEIRESIAS. No, I will not go on. Rage as you please.
OEDIPUS. Rage? Why not!
And I'll tell you what I think:
You planned it, you had it done, you all but
Killed him with your own hands: if you had eyes,
I'd say the crime was yours, and yours alone.
TEIRESIAS. So? I charge you, then,
Abide by the proclamation you have made:
From this day forth
Never speak again to these men or to me;
You yourself are the pollution of this country.
OEDIPUS. You dare say that! Can you possibly think you have
Some way of going free, after such insolence?
TEIRESIAS. I have gone free. It is the truth sustains me.
OEDIPUS. Who taught you shamelessness? It was not your craft.
TEIRESIAS. You did. You made me speak. I did not want to.
OEDIPUS. Speak what? Let me hear it again more clearly.
TEIRESIAS. Was it not clear before? Are you tempting me?
OEDIPUS. I did not understand it. Say it again.
TEIRESIAS. I say that you are the murderer whom you seek.
OEDIPUS. Now twice you have spat out infamy. You'll pay for it!
TEIRESIAS. Would you care for more? Do you wish to be really angry?
OEDIPUS. Say what you will. Whatever you say is worthless.
TEIRESIAS. I say that you live in hideous love with her
Who is nearest you in blood. You are blind to the evil.
OEDIPUS. It seems you can go on mouthing like this for ever.
TEIRESIAS. I can, if there is power in truth.
OEDIPUS. There is:
But not for you, not for you,
You sightless, witless, senseless, mad old man!

TEIRESIAS. You are the madman. There is no one here
Who will not curse you soon, as you curse me.
OEDIPUS. You child of endless night! You can not hurt me
Or any other man who sees the sun.
TEIRESIAS. True: it is not from me your fate will come.
That lies within Apollo's competence,
As it is his concern.
OEDIPUS. Tell me:
Are you speaking for Creon, or for yourself?
TEIRESIAS. Creon is no threat. You weave your own doom.
OEDIPUS. Wealth, power, craft of statesmanship!
Kingly position, everywhere admired!
What savage envy is stored up against these,
If Creon, whom I trusted, Creon my friend,
For this great office which the city once
Put in my hands unsought—if for this power
Creon desires in secret to destroy me!

He has bought this decrepit fortune-teller, this
Collector of dirty pennies, this prophet fraud—
Why, he is no more clairvoyant than I am!
Tell us:
Has your mystic mummery ever approached the truth?
When that hellcat the Sphinx was performing here,
What help were you to these people?
Her magic was not for the first man who came along:
It demanded a real exorcist. Your birds—
What good were they? or the gods, for the matter of that?
But I came by,
Oedipus, the simple man, who knows nothing—
I thought it out for myself, no birds helped me!
And this is the man you think you can destroy,
That you may be close to Creon when he's king!
Well, you and your friend Creon, it seems to me,
Will suffer most. If you were not an old man,
You would have paid already for your plot.
CHORAGOS. We can not see that his words or yours
Have been spoken except in anger, Oedipus,

And of anger we have no need. How can God's will
Be accomplished best? That is what most concerns us.
TEIRESIAS. You are a king. But where argument's concerned
I am your man, as much a king as you.
I am not your servant, but Apollo's.
I have no need of Creon to speak for me.

Listen to me. You mock my blindness, do you?
But I say that you, with both your eyes, are blind:
You can not see the wretchedness of your life,
Nor in whose house you live, no, nor with whom.
Who are your father and mother? Can you tell me?
You do not even know the blind wrongs
That you have done them, on earth and in the world below.
But the double lash of your parents' curse will whip you
Out of this land some day, with only night
Upon your precious eyes.
Your cries then—where will they not be heard?
What fastness of Kithairon will not echo them?
And that bridal-descant of yours—you'll know it then,
The song they sang when you came here to Thebes
And found your misguided berthing.
All this, and more, that you can not guess at now,
Will bring you to yourself among your children.

Be angry, then. Curse Creon. Curse my words.
I tell you, no man that walks upon the earth
Shall be rooted out more horribly than you.
OEDIPUS. Am I to bear this from him?—Damnation
Take you! Out of this place! Out of my sight!
TEIRESIAS. I would not have come at all if you had not asked me.
OEDIPUS. Could I have told that you'd talk nonsense, that
You'd come here to make a fool of yourself, and of me?
TEIRESIAS. A fool? Your parents thought me sane enough.
OEDIPUS. My parents again!—Wait: who were my parents?
TEIRESIAS. This day will give you a father, and break your heart.

446 **Kithairon** mountain near Thebes where the infant Oedipus was left to die. Cf. ll. 762–63

OEDIPUS. Your infantile riddles! Your damned abracadabra!
TEIRESIAS. You were a great man once at solving riddles.
OEDIPUS. Mock me with that if you like; you will find it true.
TEIRESIAS. It was true enough. It brought about your ruin.
OEDIPUS. But if it saved this town?
TEIRESIAS [*to the* PAGE]. Boy, give me your hand.
OEDIPUS. Yes, boy; lead him away.
—While you are here
We can do nothing. Go; leave us in peace.
TEIRESIAS. I will go when I have said what I have to say.
How can you hurt me? And I tell you again:
The man you have been looking for all this time,
The damned man, the murderer of Laïos,
That man is in Thebes. To your mind he is foreign-born,
But it will soon be shown that he is a Theban,
A revelation that will fail to please.
A blind man,
Who has his eyes now; a penniless man, who is rich now;
And he will go tapping the strange earth with his staff.
To the children with whom he lives now he will be
Brother and father—the very same; to her
Who bore him, son and husband—the very same
Who came to his father's bed, wet with his father's blood.

Enough. Go think that over.
If later you find error in what I have said,
You may say that I have no skill in prophecy.
[*Exit* TEIRESIAS, *led by his* PAGE. OEDIPUS *goes into the palace.*]

ODE I

CHORUS. The Delphic stone of prophecies STROPHE 1
Remembers ancient regicide
And a still bloody hand.
That killer's hour of flight has come.

491 **Delphic stone of prophecies** platform of rock on which stood the temple of the Delphic oracle

He must be stronger than riderless
Coursers of untiring wind,
For the son of Zeus armed with his father's thunder
Leaps in lightning after him;
And the Furies follow him, the sad Furies.

Holy Parnassos' peak of snow ANTISTROPHE 1
Flashes and blinds that secret man,
That all shall hunt him down:
Though he may roam the forest shade
Like a bull gone wild from pasture
To rage through glooms of stone.
Doom comes down on him; flight will not avail him;
For the world's heart calls him desolate,
And the immortal Furies follow, for ever follow.

But now a wilder thing is heard STROPHE 2
From the old man skilled at hearing Fate in the wingbeat of a bird.
Bewildered as a blown bird, my soul hovers and can not find
Foothold in this debate, or any reason or rest of mind.
But no man ever brought—none can bring
Proof of strife between Thebes' royal house,
Labdakos' line, and the son of Polybos;
And never until now has any man brought word
Of Laïos' dark death staining Oedipus the King.

Divine Zeus and Apollo hold ANTISTROPHE 2
Perfect intelligence alone of all tales ever told;
And well though this diviner works, he works in his own night;
No man can judge that rough unknown or trust in second sight,
For wisdom changes hands among the wise.
Shall I believe my great lord criminal

497 **son of Zeus** Apollo
500 **Parnassos** mountain, sacred to Apollo, on the side of which Delphi and its oracle stood
516 **son of Polybos** Oedipus. Cf. ll. 829–30

At a raging word that a blind old man let fall?
I saw him, when the carrion woman faced him of old,
Prove his heroic mind! These evil words are lies.

SCENE II

CREON. Men of Thebes:
I am told that heavy accusations
Have been brought against me by King Oedipus.

I am not the kind of man to bear this tamely.

If in these present difficulties
He holds me accountable for any harm to him
Through anything I have said or done—why, then,
I do not value life in this dishonor.
It is not as though this rumor touched upon
Some private indiscretion. The matter is grave.
The fact is that I am being called disloyal
To the State, to my fellow citizens, to my friends.
CHORAGOS. He may have spoken in anger, not from his mind.
CREON. But did you not hear him say I was the one
Who seduced the old prophet into lying?
CHORAGOS. The thing was said; I do not know how seriously.
CREON. But you were watching him! Were his eyes steady?
Did he look like a man in his right mind?
CHORAGOS. I do not know.
I can not judge the behavior of great men.
But here is the King himself.
[*Enter* OEIDPUS.]
OEDIPUS. So you dared come back.
Why? How brazen of you to come to my house,
You murderer!
Do you think I do not know
That you plotted to kill me, plotted to steal my throne?
Tell me, in God's name: am I coward, a fool,
That you should dream you could accomplish this?

A fool who could not see your slippery game?
A coward, not to fight back when I saw it?
You are the fool, Creon, are you not? hoping
Without support or friends to get a throne?
Thrones may be won or bought: you could do neither.

CREON. Now listen to me. You have talked; let me talk, too.
You can not judge unless you know the facts.

OEDIPUS. You speak well: there is one fact; but I find it hard
To learn from the deadliest enemy I have.

CREON. That above all I must dispute with you.

OEDIPUS. That above all I will not hear you deny.

CREON. If you think there is anything good in being stubborn
Against all reason, then I say you are wrong.

OEDIPUS. If you think a man can sin against his own kind
And not be punished for it, I say you are mad.

CREON. I agree. But tell me: what have I done to you?

OEDIPUS. You advised me to send for that wizard, did you not?

CREON. I did. I should do it again.

OEDIPUS. Very well. Now tell me:
How long has it been since Laïos—

CREON. What of Laïos?

OEDIPUS. Since he vanished in that onset by the road?

CREON. It was long ago, a long time.

OEDIPUS. And this prophet,
Was he practicing here then?

CREON. He was; and with honor, as now.

OEDIPUS. Did he speak of me at that time?

CREON. He never did;
At least, not when I was present.

OEDIPUS. But . . . the enquiry?
I suppose you held one?

CREON. We did, but we learned nothing.

OEDIPUS. Why did the prophet not speak against me then?

CREON. I do not know; and I am the kind of man
Who holds his tongue when he has no facts to go on.

OEDIPUS. There's one fact that you know, and you could tell it.

CREON. What fact is that? If I know it, you shall have it.

OEDIPUS. If he were not involved with you, he could not say

That it was I who murdered Laïos.
CREON. If he says that, you are the one that knows it?—
But now it is my turn to question you.
OEDIPUS. Put your questions. I am no murderer.
CREON. First, then: You married my sister?
OEDIPUS. I married your sister.
CREON. And you rule the kingdom equally with her?
OEDIPUS. Everything that she wants she has from me.
CREON. And I am the third, equal to both of you?
OEDIPUS. That is why I call you a bad friend.
CREON. No. Reason it out, as I have done.
Think of this first: Would any sane man prefer
Power, with all a king's anxieties,
To that same power and the grace of sleep?
Certainly not I.
I have never longed for the king's power—only his rights.
Would any wise man differ from me in this?
As matters stand, I have my way in everything
With your consent, and no responsibilities.
If I were king, I should be a slave to policy.

How could I desire a scepter more
Than what is now mine—untroubled influence?
No, I have not gone mad; I need no honors,
Except those with the perquisites I have now.
I am welcome everywhere; every man salutes me,
And those who want your favor seek my ear,
Since I know how to manage what they ask.
Should I exchange this ease for that anxiety?
Besides, no sober mind is treasonable.
I hate anarchy
And never would deal with any man who likes it.

Test what I have said. Go to the priestess
At Delphi, ask if I quoted her correctly.
And as for this other thing: if I am found
Guilty of treason with Teiresias,
Then sentence me to death! You have my word

It is a sentence I should cast my vote for—
But not without evidence!
You do wrong
When you take good men for bad, bad men for good.
A true friend thrown aside—why, life itself
Is not more precious!
In time you will know this well:
For time, and time alone, will show the just man,
Though scoundrels are discovered in a day.
CHORAGOS. This is well said, and a prudent man would ponder it.
Judgments too quickly formed are dangerous.
OEDIPUS. But is he not quick in his duplicity?
And shall I not be quick to parry him?
Would you have me stand still, hold my peace, and let
This man win everything, through my inaction?
CREON. And you want—what is it, then? To banish me?
OEDIPUS. No, not exile. It is your death I want,
So that all the world may see what treason means.
CREON. You will persist, then? You will not believe me?
OEDIPUS. How can I believe you?
CREON. Then you are a fool.
OEDIPUS. To save myself?
CREON. In justice, think of me.
OEDIPUS. You are evil incarnate.
CREON. But suppose that you are wrong?
OEDIPUS. Still I must rule.
CREON. But not if you rule badly.
OEDIPUS. O city, city!
CREON. It is my city, too!
CHORAGOS. Now, my lords, be still. I see the Queen,
Iocastê, coming from her palace chambers;
And it is time she came, for the sake of you both.
This dreadful quarrel can be resolved through her.
[*Enter* IOCASTÊ.]
IOCASTÊ. Poor foolish men, what wicked din is this?
With Thebes sick to death, is it not shameful
That you should rake some private quarrel up?
[*to* OEDIPUS]

Come into the house.
—And you, Creon, go now:
Let us have no more of this tumult over nothing.
CREON. Nothing? No, sister: what your husband plans for me
Is one of two great evils: exile or death.
OEDIPUS. He is right.
Why, woman I have caught him squarely
Plotting against my life.
CREON. No! Let me die.
Accurst if ever I have wished you harm!
IOCASTÊ. Ah, believe it, Oedipus!
In the name of the gods, respect this oath of his
For my sake, for the sake of these people here!

STROPHE 1

CHORAGOS. Open your mind to her, my lord. Be ruled by her, I beg you!
OEDIPUS. What would you have me do?
CHORAGOS. Respect Creon's word. He has never spoken like a fool,
And now he has sworn an oath.
OEDIPUS. You know what you ask?
CHORAGOS. I do.
OEDIPUS. Speak on, then.
CHORAGOS. A friend so sworn should not be baited so,
In blind malice, and without final proof.
OEDIPUS. You are aware, I hope, that what you say
Means death for me, or exile at the least.

STROPHE 2

CHORAGOS. No, I swear by Helios, first in Heaven!
May I die friendless and accurst,
The worst of deaths, if ever I meant that!
It is the withering fields
That hurt my sick heart:
Must we bear all these ills,
And now your bad blood as well?
OEDIPUS. Then let him go. And let me die, if I must,

697 **Helios** the sun-god

Or be driven by him in shame from the land of Thebes.
It is your unhappiness, and not his talk,
That touches me.
As for him—
Wherever he is, I will hate him as long as I live.

CREON. Ugly in yielding, as you were ugly in rage!
Natures like yours chiefly torment themselves.

OEDIPUS. Can you not go? Can you not leave me?

CREON. I can.
You do not know me; but the city knows me,
And in its eyes I am just, if not in yours.

[*Exit* CREON.]

ANTISTROPHE 1

CHORAGOS. Lady Iocastê, did you not ask the King to go to his chambers?

IOCASTÊ. First tell me what has happened.

CHORAGOS. There was suspicion without evidence; yet it rankled
As even false charges will.

IOCASTÊ. On both sides?

CHORAGOS. On both.

IOCASTÊ. But what was said?

CHORAGOS. Oh let it rest, let it be done with!
Have we not suffered enough?

OEDIPUS. You see to what your decency has brought you:
You have made difficulties where my heart saw none.

ANTISTROPHE 2

CHORAGOS. Oedipus, it is not once only I have told you—
You must know I should count myself unwise
To the point of madness, should I now forsake you—
You, under whose hand,
In the storm of another time,
Our dear land sailed out free.
But now stand fast at the helm!

IOCASTÊ. In God's name, Oedipus, inform your wife as well:
Why are you so set in this hard anger?

OEDIPUS. I will tell you, for none of these men deserves

My confidence as you do. It is Creon's work,
His treachery, his plotting against me.

IOCASTÊ. Go on, if you can make this clear to me.

OEDIPUS. He charges me with the murder of Laïos.

IOCASTÊ. Has he some knowledge? Or does he speak from hearsay?

OEDIPUS. He would not commit himself to such a charge,
But he has brought in that damnable soothsayer
To tell his story.

IOCASTÊ. Set your mind at rest.
If it is a question of soothsayers, I tell you
That you will find no man whose craft gives knowledge
Of the unknowable.
Here is my proof:

An oracle was reported to Laïos once
(I will not say from Phoibos himself, but from
His appointed ministers, at any rate)
That his doom would be death at the hands of his own son—
His son, born of his flesh and of mine!
Now, you remember the story: Laïos was killed
By marauding strangers where three highways meet;
But his child had not been three days in this world
Before the King had pierced the baby's ankles
And had him left to die on a lonely mountain.

Thus, Apollo never caused that child
To kill his father, and it was not Laïos' fate
To die at the hands of his son, as he had feared.
This is what prophets and prophecies are worth!
Have no dread of them.
It is God himself
Who can show us what he wills, in his own way.

OEDIPUS. How strange a shadowy memory crossed my mind,
Just now while you were speaking; it chilled my heart.

IOCASTÊ. What do you mean? What memory do you speak of?

OEDIPUS. If I understand you, Laïos was killed
At a place where three roads meet.

IOCASTÊ. So it was said;

We have no later story.
OEDIPUS. Where did it happen?
IOCASTÊ. Phokis, it is called: at a place where the Theban Way
Divides into the roads toward Delphi and Daulia.
OEDIPUS. When?
IOCASTÊ. We had the news not long before you came
And proved the right to your succession here.
OEDIPUS. Ah, what net has God been weaving for me?
IOCASTÊ. Oedipus! Why does this trouble you?
OEDIPUS. Do not ask me yet.
First, tell me how Laïos looked, and tell me
How old he was.
IOCASTÊ. He was tall, his hair just touched
With white; his form was not unlike your own.
OEDIPUS. I think that I myself may be accurst
By my own ignorant edict.
IOCASTÊ. You speak strangely.
It makes me tremble to look at you, my King.
OEDIPUS. I am not sure that the blind man can not see.
But I should know better if you were to tell me—
IOCASTÊ. Anything—though I dread to hear you ask it.
OEDIPUS. Was the King lightly escorted, or did he ride
With a large company, as a ruler should?
IOCASTÊ. There were five men with him in all: one was a herald;
And a single chariot, which he was driving.
OEDIPUS. Alas, that makes it plain enough!
But who—
Who told you how it happened?
IOCASTÊ. A household servant,
The only one to escape.
OEDIPUS. And is he still
A servant of ours?
IOCASTÊ. No; for when he came back at last
And found you enthroned in the place of the dead king,
He came to me, touched my hand with his, and begged
That I would send him away to the frontier district
Where only the shepherds go—
As far away from the city as I could send him.

I granted his prayer; for although the man was a slave,
He had earned more than this favor at my hands.

OEDIPUS. Can he be called back quickly?

IOCASTÊ. Easily.
But why?

OEDIPUS. I have taken too much upon myself
Without enquiry; therefore I wish to consult him.

IOCASTÊ. Then he shall come.
But am I not one also
To whom you might confide these fears of yours?

OEDIPUS. That is your right; it will not be denied you,
Now least of all; for I have reached a pitch
Of wild foreboding. Is there anyone
To whom I should sooner speak?

Polybos of Corinth is my father.
My mother is a Dorian: Meropê.
I grew up chief among the men of Corinth
Until a strange thing happened—
Not worth my passion, it may be, but strange.

At a feast, a drunken man maundering in his cups
Cries out that I am not my father's son!

I contained myself that night, though I felt anger
And a sinking heart. The next day I visited
My father and mother, and questioned them. They stormed,
Calling it all the slanderous rant of a fool;
And this relieved me. Yet the suspicion
Remained always aching in my mind;
I knew there was talk; I could not rest;
And finally, saying nothing to my parents,
I went to the shrine at Delphi.

The god dismissed my question without reply;
He spoke of other things.
Some were clear,
Full of wretchedness, dreadful, unbearable:

As, that I should lie with my own mother, breed
Children from whom all men would turn their eyes;
And that I should be my father's murderer.

I heard all this, and fled. And from that day
Corinth to me was only in the stars
Descending in that quarter of the sky,
As I wandered farther and farther on my way
To a land where I should never see the evil
Sung by the oracle. And I came to this country
Where, so you say, King Laïos was killed.

I will tell you all that happened there, my lady.

There were three highways
Coming together at a place I passed;
And there a herald came towards me, and a chariot
Drawn by horses, with a man such as you describe
Seated in it. The groom leading the horses
Forced me off the road at his lord's command;
But as this charioteer lurched over towards me
I struck him in my rage. The old man saw me
And brought his double goad down upon my head
As I came abreast.
He was paid back, and more!
Swinging my club in this right hand I knocked him
Out of his car, and he rolled on the ground.
I killed him.

I killed them all.
Now if that stranger and Laïos were—kin,
Where is a man more miserable than I?
More hated by the gods? Citizen and alien alike
Must never shelter me or speak to me—
I must be shunned by all.
And I myself
Pronounced this malediction upon myself!

Think of it: I have touched you with these hands,
These hands that killed your husband. What defilement!

Am I all evil, then? It must be so,
Since I must flee from Thebes, yet never again
See my own countrymen, my own country,
For fear of joining my mother in marriage
And killing Polybos, my father.
Ah,
If I was created so, born to this fate,
Who could deny the savagery of God?

O holy majesty of heavenly powers!
May I never see that day! Never!
Rather let me vanish from the race of men
Than know the abomination destined me!

CHORAGOS. We too, my lord, have felt dismay at this.
But there is hope: you have yet to hear the shepherd.

OEDIPUS. Indeed, I fear no other hope is left me.

IOCASTÊ. What do you hope from him when he comes?

OEDIPUS. This much:
If his account of the murder tallies with yours,
Then I am cleared.

IOCASTÊ. What was it that I said
Of such importance?

OEDIPUS. Why, "marauders," you said,
Killed the King, according to this man's story.
If he maintains that still, if there were several,
Clearly the guilt is not mine: I was alone.
But if he says one man, singlehanded, did it,
Then the evidence all points to me.

IOCASTÊ. You may be sure that he said there were several;
And can he call back that story now? He cán not.
The whole city heard it as plainly as I.
But suppose he alters some detail of it:
He can not ever show that Laïos' death
Fulfilled the oracle: for Apollo said
My child was doomed to kill him; and my child—
Poor baby!—it was my child that died first.

No. From now on, where oracles are concerned,
I would not waste a second thought on any.

OEDIPUS. You may be right.
But come: let someone go
For the shepherd at once. This matter must be settled.

IOCASTÊ. I will send for him.
I would not wish to cross you in anything,
And surely not in this.—Let us go in.
[*Exeunt into the palace.*]

ODE II

CHORUS. Let me be reverent in the ways of right, STROPHE 1
Lowly the paths I journey on;
Let all my words and actions keep
The laws of the pure universe
From highest Heaven handed down.
For Heaven is their bright nurse,
Those generations of the realms of light;
Ah, never of mortal kind were they begot,
Nor are they slaves of memory, lost in sleep:
Their Father is greater than Time, and ages not.

The tyrant is a child of Pride ANTISTROPHE 1
Who drinks from his great sickening cup
Recklessness and vanity,
Until from his high crest headlong
He plummets to the dust of hope.
That strong man is not strong.
But let no fair ambition be denied;
May God protect the wrestler for the State
In government, in comely policy,
Who will fear God, and on His ordinance wait.

Haughtiness and the high hand of disdain STROPHE 2
Tempt and outrage God's holy law;
And any mortal who dares hold
No immortal Power in awe

Will be caught up in a net of pain:
The price for which his levity is sold.
Let each man take due earnings, then,
And keep his hands from holy things,
And from blasphemy stand apart—
Else the crackling blast of heaven
Blows on his head, and on his desperate heart;
Though fools will honor impious men,
In their cities no tragic poet sings.

ANTISTROPHE 2

Shall we lose faith in Delphi's obscurities,
We who have heard the world's core
Discredited, and the sacred wood
Of Zeus at Elis praised no more?
The deeds and the strange prophecies
Must make a pattern yet to be understood.
Zeus, if indeed you are lord of all,
Throned in light over night and day,
Mirror this in your endless mind:
Our masters call the oracle
Words on the wind, and the Delphic vision blind!
Their hearts no longer know Apollo,
And reverence for the gods has died away.

SCENE III

[*Enter* IOCASTÊ.]

IOCASTÊ. Princes of Thebes, it has occurred to me
To visit the altars of the gods, bearing
These branches as a suppliant, and this incense.
Our King is not himself: his noble soul
Is overwrought with fantasies of dread,
Else he would consider
The new prophecies in the light of the old.
He will listen to any voice that speaks disaster,
And my advice goes for nothing.
[*She approaches the altar, R.*]

To you, then, Apollo,
Lycean lord, since you are nearest, I turn in prayer.
Receive these offerings, and grant us deliverance
From defilement. Our hearts are heavy with fear
When we see our leader distracted, as helpless sailors
Are terrified by the confusion of their helmsman.

[*Enter* MESSENGER.]

MESSENGER. Friends, no doubt you can direct me:
Where shall I find the house of Oedipus,
Or, better still, where is the King himself?
CHORAGOS. It is this very place, stranger; he is inside.
This is his wife and mother of his children.
MESSENGER. I wish her happiness in a happy house,
Blest in all the fulfillment of her marriage.
IOCASTÊ. I wish as much for you: your courtesy
Deserves a like good fortune. But now, tell me:
Why have you come? What have you to say to us?
MESSENGER. Good news, my lady, for your house and your husband.
IOCASTÊ. What news? Who sent you here?
MESSENGER. I am from Corinth.
The news I bring ought to mean joy for you,
Though it may be you will find some grief in it.
IOCASTÊ. What is it? How can it touch us in both ways?
MESSENGER. The people of Corinth, they say,
Intend to call Oedipus to be their king.
IOCASTÊ. But old Polybos—is he not reigning still?
MESSENGER. No. Death holds him in his sepulchre.
IOCASTÊ. What are you saying? Polybos is dead?
MESSENGER. If I am not telling the truth, may I die myself.
IOCASTÊ [*to a* MAID-SERVANT]. Go in, go quickly; tell this to your master.

O riddlers of God's will, where are you now!
This was the man whom Oedipus, long ago,
Feared so, fled so, in dread of destroying him—
But it was another fate by which he died.

[*Enter* OEDIPUS, *center*.]

988 **Lycean lord** lord of light. Cf. l. 163n.

OEDIPUS. Dearest Iocastê, why have you sent for me?
IOCASTÊ. Listen to what this man says, and then tell me
What has become of the solemn prophecies.
OEDIPUS. Who is this man? What is his news for me?
IOCASTÊ. He has come from Corinth to announce your father's death!
OEDIPUS. Is it true, stranger? Tell me in your own words.
MESSENGER. I can not say it more clearly: the King is dead.
OEDIPUS. Was it by treason? Or by an attack of illness?
MESSENGER. A little thing brings old men to their rest.
OEDIPUS. It was sickness, then?
MESSENGER. Yes, and his many years.
OEDIPUS. Ah!
Why should a man respect the Pythian hearth, or
Give heed to the birds that jangle above his head?
They prophesied that I should kill Polybos,
Kill my own father; but he is dead and buried,
And I am here—I never touched him, never,
Unless he died of grief for my departure,
And thus, in a sense, through me. No. Polybos
Has packed the oracles off with him underground.
They are empty words.
IOCASTÊ. Had I not told you so?
OEDIPUS. You had; it was my faint heart that betrayed me.
IOCASTÊ. From now on never think of those things again.
OEDIPUS. And yet—must I not fear my mother's bed?
IOCASTÊ. Why should anyone in this world be afraid,
Since Fate rules us and nothing can be foreseen?
A man should live only for the present day.

Have no more fear of sleeping with your mother:
How many men, in dreams, have lain with their mothers!
No reasonable man is troubled by such things.
OEDIPUS. That is true; only—
If only my mother were not still alive!
But she is alive. I can not help my dread.
IOCASTÊ. Yet this news of your father's death is wonderful.

1035 **Pythian hearth** Delphic oracle, where Apollo slew the serpent *Python*

OEDIPUS. Wonderful. But I fear the living woman.
MESSENGER. Tell me, who is this woman that you fear?
OEDIPUS. It is Meropê, man; the wife of King Polybos.
MESSENGER. Meropê? Why should you be afraid of her?
OEDIPUS. An oracle of the gods, a dreadful saying.
MESSENGER. Can you tell me about it or are you sworn to silence?
OEDIPUS. I can tell you, and I will.
  Apollo said through his prophet that I was the man
  Who should marry his own mother, shed his father's blood
  With his own hands. And so, for all these years
  I have kept clear of Corinth, and no harm has come—
  Though it would have been sweet to see my parents again.
MESSENGER. And is this the fear that drove you out of Corinth?
OEDIPUS. Would you have me kill my father?
MESSENGER. As for that
  You must be reassured by the news I gave you.
OEDIPUS. If you could reassure me, I would reward you.
MESSENGER. I had that in mind, I will confess: I thought
  I could count on you when you returned to Corinth.
OEDIPUS. No: I will never go near my parents again.
MESSENGER. Ah, son, you still do not know what you are doing—
OEDIPUS. What do you mean? In the name of God tell me!
MESSENGER. —If these are your reasons for not going home.
OEDIPUS. I tell you, I fear the oracle may come true.
MESSENGER. And guilt may come upon you through your parents?
OEDIPUS. That is the dread that is always in my heart.
MESSENGER. Can you not see that all your fears are groundless?
OEDIPUS. How can you say that? They are my parents, surely?
MESSENGER. Polybos was not your father.
OEDIPUS. Not my father?
MESSENGER. No more your father than the man speaking to you.
OEDIPUS. But you are nothing to me!
MESSENGER. Neither was he.
OEDIPUS. Then why did he call me son?
MESSENGER. I will tell you:
  Long ago he had you from my hands, as a gift.
OEDIPUS. Then how could he love me so, if I was not his?
MESSENGER. He had no children, and his heart turned to you.

OEDIPUS. What of you? Did you buy me? Did you find me by chance?
MESSENGER. I came upon you in the crooked pass of Kithairon.
OEDIPUS. And what were you doing there?
MESSENGER. Tending my flocks.
OEDIPUS. A wandering shepherd?
MESSENGER. But your savior, son, that day.
OEDIPUS. From what did you save me?
MESSENGER. Your ankles should tell you that.
OEDIPUS. Ah, stranger, why do you speak of that childhood pain?
MESSENGER. I cut the bonds that tied your ankles together.
OEDIPUS. I have had the mark as long as I can remember.
MESSENGER. That was why you were given the name you bear.
OEDIPUS. God! Was it my father or my mother who did it?
Tell me!
MESSENGER. I do not know. The man who gave you to me
Can tell you better than I.
OEDIPUS. It was not you that found me, but another?
MESSENGER. It was another shepherd gave you to me.
OEDIPUS. Who was he? Can you tell me who he was?
MESSENGER. I think he was said to be one of Laïos' people.
OEDIPUS. You mean the Laïos who was king here years ago?
MESSENGER. Yes; King Laïos; and the man was one of his herdsmen.
OEDIPUS. Is he still alive? Can I see him?
MESSENGER. These men here
Know best about such things.
OEDIPUS. Does anyone here
Know this shepherd that he is talking about?
Have you seen him in the fields, or in the town?
If you have, tell me. It is time things were made plain.
CHORAGOS. I think the man he means is that same shepherd
You have already asked to see. Iocastê perhaps
Could tell you something.
OEDIPUS. Do you know anything
About him, Lady? Is he the man we have summoned?
Is that the man this shepherd means?
IOCASTÊ. Why think of him?

1108 **the name you bear** *Oedipus* means *swollen-foot*

Forget this herdsman. Forget it all.
This talk is a waste of time.

OEDIPUS. How can you say that,
When the clues to my true birth are in my hands?

IOCASTÊ. For God's love, let us have no more questioning!
Is your life nothing to you?
My own is pain enough for me to bear.

OEDIPUS. You need not worry. Suppose my mother a slave,
And born of slaves: no baseness can touch you.

IOCASTÊ. Listen to me, I beg you: do not do this thing!

OEDIPUS. I will not listen; the truth must be made known.

IOCASTÊ. Everything that I say is for your own good!

OEDIPUS. My own good
Snaps my patience, then; I want none of it.

IOCASTÊ. You are fatally wrong! May you never learn who you are!

OEDIPUS. Go, one of you, and bring the shepherd here.
Let us leave this woman to brag of her royal name.

IOCASTÊ. Ah, miserable!
That is the only word I have for you now.
That is the only word I can ever have.
[*Exit into the palace.*]

CHORAGOS. Why has she left us, Oedipus? Why has she gone
In such a passion of sorrow? I fear this silence:
Something dreadful may come of it.

OEDIPUS. Let it come!
However base my birth, I must know about it.
The Queen, like a woman, is perhaps ashamed
To think of my low origin. But I
Am a child of Luck; I cannot be dishonored.
Luck is my mother; the passing months, my brothers,
Have seen me rich and poor.
If this is so,
How could I wish that I were someone else?
How could I not be glad to know my birth?

ODE III

CHORUS. If ever the coming time were known — STROPHE
To my heart's pondering,
Kithairon, now by Heaven I see the torches
At the festival of the next full moon,
And see the dance, and hear the choir sing
A grace to your gentle shade:
Mountain where Oedipus was found,
O mountain guard of a noble race!
May the god who heals us lend his aid,
And let that glory come to pass
For our king's cradling-ground.

Of the nymphs that flower beyond the years, — ANTISTROPHE
Who bore you, royal child,
To Pan of the hills or the timberline Apollo,
Cold in delight where the upland clears,
Or Hermês for whom Kyllenê's heights are piled?
Or flushed as evening cloud,
Great Dionysos, roamer of mountains,
He—was it he who found you there,
And caught you up in his own proud
Arms from the sweet god-ravisher
Who laughed by the Muses' fountains?

1177–78 **And let that glory . . . cradling-ground** i.e., let this wonderful thing which I prophesy come true for Kithairon

1183 **Kyllenê** highest mountain in the Peloponnesus, sacred to Hermes

1188 **god-ravisher** nymph whom the chorus conjecture to have been Oedipus' mother

1189 **Muses' fountains** springs of Helicon, sacred to Apollo and the Muses

SCENE IV

OEDIPUS. Sirs: though I do not know the man,
I think I see him coming, this shepherd we want:
He is old, like our friend here, and the men
Bringing him seem to be servants of my house.
But you can tell, if you have ever seen him.
[*Enter* SHEPHERD *escorted by servants.*]
CHORAGOS. I know him, he was Laïos' man. You can trust him.
OEDIPUS. Tell me first, you from Corinth: is this the shepherd
We were discussing?
MESSENGER. This is the very man.
OEDIPUS [*to* SHEPHERD]. Come here. No, look at me. You must answer
Everything I ask.—You belonged to Laïos?
SHEPHERD. Yes: born his slave, brought up in his house.
OEDIPUS. Tell me: what kind of work did you do for him?
SHEPHERD. I was a shepherd of his, most of my life.
OEDIPUS. Where mainly did you go for pasturage?
SHEPHERD. Sometimes Kithairon, sometimes the hills near-by.
OEDIPUS. Do you remember ever seeing this man out there?
SHEPHERD. What would he be doing there? This man?
OEDIPUS. This man standing here. Have you ever seen him before?
SHEPHERD. No. At least, not to my recollection.
MESSENGER. And that is not strange, my lord. But I'll refresh
His memory: he must remember when we two
Spent three whole seasons together, March to September,
On Kithairon or thereabouts. He had two flocks;
I had one. Each autumn I'd drive mine home
And he would go back with his to Laïos' sheepfold.—
Is this not true, just as I have described it?
SHEPHERD. True, yes; but it was all so long ago.
MESSENGER. Well, then: do you remember, back in those days,
That you gave me a baby boy to bring up as my own?
SHEPHERD. What if I did? What are you trying to say?
MESSENGER. King Oedipus was once that little child.
SHEPHERD. Damn you, hold your tongue!

OEDIPUS. No more of that!
It is your tongue needs watching, not this man's.
SHEPHERD. My King, my Master, what is it I have done wrong?
OEDIPUS. You have not answered his question about the boy.
SHEPHERD. He does not know . . . He is only making trouble . . .
OEDIPUS. Come, speak plainly, or it will go hard with you.
SHEPHERD. In God's name, do not torture an old man!
OEDIPUS. Come here, one of you; bind his arms behind him.
SHEPHERD. Unhappy king! What more do you wish to learn?
OEDIPUS. Did you give this man the child he speaks of?
SHEPHERD. I did.
And I would to God I had died that very day.
OEDIPUS. You will die now unless you speak the truth.
SHEPHERD. Yet if I speak the truth, I am worse than dead.
OEDIPUS. Very well; since you insist upon delaying—
SHEPHERD. No! I have told you already that I gave him the boy.
OEDIPUS. Where did you get him? From your house? From somewhere else?
SHEPHERD. Not from mine, no. A man gave him to me.
OEDIPUS. Is that man here? Do you know whose slave he was?
SHEPHERD. For God's love, my King, do not ask me any more!
OEDIPUS. You are a dead man if I have to ask you again.
SHEPHERD. Then . . . Then the child was from the palace of Laïos.
OEDIPUS. A slave child? or a child of his own line?
SHEPHERD. Ah, I am on the brink of dreadful speech!
OEDIPUS. And I of dreadful hearing. Yet I must hear.
SHEPHERD. If you must be told, then . . .
They said it was Laïos' child;
But it is your wife who can tell you about that.
OEDIPUS. My wife!—Did she give it to you?
SHEPHERD. My lord, she did.
OEDIPUS. Do you know why?
SHEPHERD. I was told to get rid of it.
OEDIPUS. An unspeakable mother!
SHEPHERD. There had been prophecies . . .
OEDIPUS. Tell me.
SHEPHERD. It was said that the boy would kill his own father.
OEDIPUS. Then why did you give him over to this old man?

SHEPHERD. I pitied the baby, my King,
And I thought that this man would take him far away
To his own country.
He saved him—but for what a fate!
For if you are what this man says you are,
No man living is more wretched than Oedipus.
OEDIPUS. Ah God!
It was true!
All the prophecies!
—Now,
O Light, may I look on you for the last time!
I, Oedipus,
Oedipus, damned in his birth, in his marriage damned,
Damned in the blood he shed with his own hand!
[*He rushes into the palace.*]

ODE IV

CHORUS. Alas for the seed of men. STROPHE 1

What measure shall I give these generations
That breathe on the void and are void
And exist and do not exist?

Who bears more weight of joy
Than mass of sunlight shifting in images,
Or who shall make his thought stay on
That down time drifts away?

Your splendor is all fallen.

O naked brow of wrath and tears,
O change of Oedipus!
I who saw your days call no man blest—
Your great days like ghosts gone.

That mind was a strong bow. ANTISTROPHE 1

Deep, how deep you drew it then, hard archer,
At a dim fearful range,
And brought dear glory down!

You overcame the stranger—
The virgin with her hooking lion claws—
And though death sang, stood like a tower
To make pale Thebes take heart.

Fortress against our sorrow!

Divine king, giver of laws,
Majestic Oedipus!
No prince in Thebes had ever such renown,
No prince won such grace of power.

And now of all men ever known STROPHE 2
Most pitiful is this man's story:
His fortunes are most changed, his state
Fallen to a low slave's
Ground under bitter fate.

O Oedipus, most royal one!
The great door that expelled you to the light
Gave at night—ah, gave night to your glory:
As to the father, to the fathering son.

All understood too late.

How could that queen whom Laïos won,
The garden that he harrowed at his height,
Be silent when that act was done?

But all eyes fail before time's eye, ANTISTROPHE 2
All actions come to justice there.
Though never willed, though far down the deep past,
Your bed, your dread sirings,
Are brought to book at last.

Child by Laïos doomed to die,
Then doomed to lose that fortunate little death,
Would God you never took breath in this air
That with my wailing lips I take to cry:

For I weep the world's outcast.

Blind I was, and cannot tell why;
Asleep, for you had given ease of breath;
A fool, while the false years went by.

ÉXODOS

[*Enter, from the palace,* SECOND MESSENGER.]

2ND MESSENGER. Elders of Thebes, most honored in this land,
What horrors are yours to see and hear, what weight
Of sorrow to be endured, if, true to your birth,
You venerate the line of Labdakos!
I think neither Istros nor Phasis, those great rivers,
Could purify this place of the corruption
It shelters now, or soon must bring to light—
Evil not done unconsciously, but willed.

The greatest griefs are those we cause ourselves.

CHORAGOS. Surely, friend, we have grief enough already;
What new sorrow do you mean?

2ND MESSENGER. The Queen is dead.

CHORAGOS. Iocastê? Dead? But at whose hand?

2ND MESSENGER. Her own.
The full horror of what happened you cannot know,
For you did not see it; but I, who did, will tell you
As clearly as I can how she met her death.

When she had left us,
In passionate silence, passing through the court,

1338 **Istros . . . Phasis** the Danube and the Rion, conventional types of great rivers

She ran to her apartment in the house,
Her hair clutched by the fingers of both hands.
She closed the doors behind her; then, by that bed
Where long ago the fatal son was conceived—
That son who should bring about his father's death—
We heard her call upon Laïos, dead so many years,
And heard her wail for the double fruit of her marriage,
A husband by her husband, children by her child.
Exactly how she died I do not know:
For Oedipus burst in moaning and would not let us
Keep vigil to the end: it was by him
As he stormed about the room that our eyes were caught.
From one to another of us he went, begging a sword,
Cursing the wife who was not his wife, the mother
Whose womb had carried his own children and himself.
I do not know: it was none of us aided him,
But surely one of the gods was in control!
For with a dreadful cry
He hurled his weight, as though wrenched out of himself,
At the twin doors: the bolts gave, and he rushed in.
And there we saw her hanging, her body swaying
From the cruel cord she had noosed about her neck.
A great sob broke from him, heartbreaking to hear,
As he loosed the rope and lowered her to the ground.

I would blot out from my mind what happened next!
For the King ripped from her gown the golden brooches
That were her ornament, and raised them, and plunged them down
Straight into his own eyeballs, crying, "No more,
No more shall you look on the misery about me,
The horrors of my own doing! Too long you have known
The faces of those whom I should never have seen,
Too long been blind to those for whom I was searching!
From this hour, go in darkness!" And as he spoke,
He struck at his eyes—not once, but many times;
And the blood spattered his beard,
Bursting from his ruined sockets like red hail.

So from the unhappiness of two this evil has sprung,
A curse on the man and woman alike. The old
Happiness of the house of Labdakos
Was happiness enough: where is it today?
It is all wailing and ruin, disgrace, death—all
The misery of mankind that has a name—
And it is wholly and for ever theirs.

CHORAGOS. Is he in agony still? Is there no rest for him?

2ND MESSENGER. He is calling for someone to lead him to the gates
So that all the children of Kadmos may look upon
His father's murderer, his mother's—no,
I can not say it!
And then he will leave Thebes,
Self-exiled, in order that the curse
Which he himself pronounced may depart from the house.
He is weak, and there is none to lead him,
So terrible is his suffering.
But you will see:
Look, the doors are opening; in a moment
You will see a thing that would crush a heart of stone.

[*The central door is opened;* OEDIPUS, *blinded, is led in.*]

CHORAGOS. Dreadful indeed for men to see.
Never have my own eyes
Looked on a sight so full of fear.

Oedipus!
What madness came upon you, what daemon
Leaped on your life with heavier
Punishment than a mortal man can bear?
No: I cannot even
Look at you, poor ruined one.
And I would speak, question, ponder,
If I were able. No.
You make me shudder.

OEDIPUS. God. God.
Is there a sorrow greater?

Where shall I find harbor in this world?
My voice is hurled far on a dark wind.
What has God done to me?
CHORAGOS. Too terrible to think of, or to see.
OEDIPUS. O cloud of night, STROPHE 1
Never to be turned away: night coming on,
I can not tell how: night like a shroud!

My fair winds brought me here.
O God. Again
The pain of the spikes where I had sight,
The flooding pain
Of memory, never to be gouged out.
CHORAGOS. This is not strange.
You suffer it all twice over, remorse in pain,
Pain in remorse.

OEDIPUS. Ah dear friend ANTISTROPHE 1
Are you faithful even yet, you alone?
Are you still standing near me, will you stay here,
Patient, to care for the blind?
The blind man!
Yet even blind I know who it is attends me,
By the voice's tone—
Though my new darkness hide the comforter.
CHORAGOS. Oh fearful act!
What god was it drove you to rake black
Night across your eyes?

OEDIPUS. Apollo. Apollo. Dear STROPHE 2
Children, the god was Apollo.
He brought my sick, sick fate upon me.
But the blinding hand was my own!
How could I bear to see
When all my sight was horror everywhere?
CHORAGOS. Everywhere; that is true.
OEDIPUS. And now what is left?
Images? Love? A greeting even,

Sweet to the senses? Is there anything?
Ah, no, friends: lead me away.
Lead me away from Thebes.
Lead the great wreck
And hell of Oedipus, whom the gods hate.
CHORAGOS. Your fate is clear, you are not blind to that.
Would God you had never found it out!

ANTISTROPHE 2

OEDIPUS. Death take the man who unbound
My feet on that hillside
And delivered me from death to life! What life?
If only I had died,
This weight of monstrous doom
Could not have dragged me and my darlings down.
CHORAGOS. I would have wished the same.
OEDIPUS. Oh never to have come here
With my father's blood upon me! Never
To have been the man they call his mother's husband!
Oh accurst! Oh child of evil,
To have entered that wretched bed—
the selfsame one!
More primal than sin itself, this fell to me.
CHORAGOS. I do not know how I can answer you.
You were better dead than alive and blind.
OEDIPUS. Do not counsel me any more. This punishment
That I have laid upon myself is just.
If I had eyes,
I do not know how I could bear the sight
Of my father, when I came to the house of Death,
Or my mother: for I have sinned against them both
So vilely that I could not make my peace
By strangling my own life.
Or do you think my children,
Born as they were born, would be sweet to my eyes?
Ah never, never! Nor this town with its high walls,
Nor the holy images of the gods.
For I,
Thrice miserable!—Oedipus, noblest of all the line

Of Kadmos, have condemned myself to enjoy
These things no more, by my own malediction
Expelling that man whom the gods declared
To be a defilement in the house of Laïos.
After exposing the rankness of my own guilt,
How could I look men frankly in the eyes?
No, I swear it,
If I could have stifled my hearing at its source,
I would have done it and made all this body
A tight cell of misery, blank to light and sound:
So I should have been safe in a dark agony
Beyond all recollection.
Ah Kithairon!
Why did you shelter me? When I was cast upon you,
Why did I not die? Then I should never
Have shown the world my execrable birth.

Ah Polybos! Corinth, city that I believed
The ancient seat of my ancestors: how fair
I seemed, your child! And all the while this evil
Was cancerous within me!
For I am sick
In my daily life, sick in my origin.

O three roads, dark ravine, woodland and way
Where three roads met: you, drinking my father's blood,
My own blood, spilled by my own hand: can you remember
The unspeakable things I did there, and the things
I went on from there to do?
O marriage, marriage!
The act that engendered me, and again the act
Performed by the son in the same bed—
Ah, the net
Of incest, mingling fathers, brothers, sons,
With brides, wives, mothers: the last evil
That can be known by men: no tongue can say
How evil!
No. For the love of God, conceal me

Somewhere far from Thebes; or kill me; or hurl me
Into the sea, away from men's eyes for ever.

Come, lead me. You need not fear to touch me.
Of all men, I alone can bear this guilt.

[*Enter* CREON.]

CHORAGOS. We are not the ones to decide; but Creon here
May fitly judge of what you ask. He only
Is left to protect the city in your place.

OEDIPUS. Alas, how can I speak to him? What right have I
To beg his courtesy whom I have deeply wronged?

CREON. I have not come to mock you, Oedipus,
Or to reproach you, either.
[*to* ATTENDANTS]—You, standing there:
If you have lost all respect for man's dignity,
At least respect the flame of Lord Helios:
Do not allow this pollution to show itself
Openly here, an affront to the earth
And Heaven's rain and the light of day. No, take him
Into the house as quickly as you can.
For it is proper
That only the close kindred see his grief.

OEDIPUS. I pray you in God's name, since your courtesy
Ignores my dark expectation, visiting
With mercy this man of all men most execrable:
Give me what I ask—for your good, not for mine.

CREON. And what is it that you would have me do?

OEDIPUS. Drive me out of this country as quickly as may be
To a place where no human voice can ever greet me.

CREON. I should have done that before now—only,
God's will had not been wholly revealed to me.

OEDIPUS. But his command is plain: the parricide
Must be destroyed. I am that evil man.

CREON. That is the sense of it, yes; but as things are,
We had best discover clearly what is to be done.

OEDIPUS. You would learn more about a man like me?

CREON. You are ready now to listen to the god.

OEDIPUS. I will listen. But it is to you

That I must turn for help. I beg you, hear me.

The woman in there—
Give her whatever funeral you think proper:
She is your sister.
—But let me go, Creon!
Let me purge my father's Thebes of the pollution
Of my living here, and go out to the wild hills,
To Kithairon, that has won such fame with me,
The tomb my mother and father appointed for me,
And let me die there, as they willed I should.
And yet I know
Death will not ever come to me through sickness
Or in any natural way: I have been preserved
For some unthinkable fate. But let that be.

As for my sons, you need not care for them.
They are men, they will find some way to live.
But my poor daughters, who have shared my table,
Who never before have been parted from their father—
Take care of them, Creon; do this for me.
And will you let me touch them with my hands
A last time, and let us weep together?
Be kind, my lord,
Great prince, be kind!
Could I but touch them,
They would be mine again, as when I had my eyes.
[*Enter* ANTIGONE *and* ISMENE, *attended.*]
Ah, God!
Is it my dearest children I hear weeping?
Has Creon pitied me and sent my daughters?

CREON. Yes, Oedipus: I knew that they were dear to you
In the old days, and know you must love them still.

OEDIPUS. May God bless you for this—and be a friendlier
Guardian to you than he has been to me!

Children, where are you?
Come quickly to my hands: they are your brother's—

Hands that have brought your father's once clear eyes
To this way of seeing–
Ah dearest ones,
I had neither sight nor knowledge then, your father
By the woman who was the source of his own life!
And I weep for you–having no strength to see you–,
I weep for you when I think of the bitterness
That men will visit upon you all your lives.
What homes, what festivals can you attend
Without being forced to depart again in tears?
And when you come to marriageable age,
Where is the man, my daughters, who would dare
Risk the bane that lies on all my children?
Is there any evil wanting? Your father killed
His father; sowed the womb of her who bore him;
Engendered you at the fount of his own existence!

That is what they will say of you.

Then, whom
Can you ever marry? There are no bridegrooms for you,
And your lives must wither away in sterile dreaming.

O Creon, son of Menoikeus!
You are the only father my daughters have,
Since we, their parents, are both of us gone for ever.
They are your own blood: you will not let them
Fall into beggary and loneliness;
You will keep them from the miseries that are mine!
Take pity on them; see, they are only children,
Friendless except for you. Promise me this,
Great Prince, and give me your hand in token of it.
[CREON *clasps his right hand.*]
Children:
I could say much, if you could understand me,
But as it is, I have only this prayer for you:
Live where you can, be as happy as you can–
Happier, please God, than God has made your father!

CREON. Enough. You have wept enough. Now go within.
OEDIPUS. I must; but it is hard.
CREON. Time eases all things.
OEDIPUS. But you must promise—
CREON. Say what you desire.
OEDIPUS. Send me from Thebes!
CREON. God grant that I may!
OEDIPUS. But since God hates me . . .
CREON. No, he will grant your wish.
OEDIPUS. You promise?
CREON. I can not speak beyond my knowledge.
OEDIPUS. Then lead me in.
CREON. Come now, and leave your children.
OEDIPUS. No! Do not take them from me!
CREON. Think no longer
That you are in command here, but rather think
How, when you were, you served your own destruction.

[*Exeunt into the house all but the* CHORUS; *the* CHORAGOS *chants directly to the audience.*]

CHORAGOS. Men of Thebes: look upon Oedipus.
This is the king who solved the famous riddle
And towered up, most powerful of men.
No mortal eyes but looked on him with envy,
Yet in the end ruin swept over him.

Let every man in mankind's frailty
Consider his last day; and let none
Presume on his good fortune until he find
Life, at his death, a memory without pain.

EURIPIDES
485?–406? B.C.

THE BACCHAE
406? B.C.

In a narrow sense, *The Bacchae* is a play about Dionysus' revenge upon Thebes for denying his divine paternity and present deity. It is a well-made play and builds unrelentingly to its catastrophe. From the beginning, when Dionysus manifests his identity and purpose, the conclusion is foregone. Pentheus, king of Thebes, *thinks* that he is the hunter, tracking down the stranger to destroy him. We *know,* in a metaphor the play repeats, that the hunter is the hunted, that each step he makes toward the kill is toward his own destruction. We see Pentheus flout Dionysus and plan to destroy the god's converts among the Theban women. We hear, too, that Pentheus' mother, Agauë, one of those who once repudiated the god, has become one of his converts and leads the Theban Bacchae on the side of Mt. Cithaeron. Son and mother, we apprehend with ironic certainty, are moving toward a fatal convergence. And when they come, in their agonies, to the knowledge of what Dionysus has willed for them, they discover indeed that a god insulted does not forgive.

Thus seen, the play has about it the special if chilly gratification that comes from dramas of intrigue, in which the schemer is hoist with his own petard. But Euripides so manipulates the audience's feelings that the promised gratification is not attained. At first we are attracted to Dionysus, the injured deity concerned for his mother's honor and his own. The chorus of Asian women, his devotees who have followed him into this land, compellingly testifies to his power and appeal. Even Cadmus and Teiresias, submitting their withered limbs to the Bacchic dance, add their witness. And Pentheus so fatuously refuses to hear reason, so disgustingly reveals the obscene shape of his own imaginings, that we side with Dionysus and look forward to his revenge. When the god enters Pentheus, however, metamorphosing his blunt masculinity into horrid effeminacy, our pleasure may begin to pall. At length Euripides forces on us the full horror of Pentheus' destruction, the man crying out as his body is torn asunder, "O Mother, have mercy on me; I have sinned, but I am your son: do not kill me!" We are further made to behold Agauë's agony as her eyes clear and she sees what it is that she has held aloft in ecstatic triumph. So terrible is this suffering, so terrible the god ruthlessly exacting it, that our allegiances shift—from the injured god to the more cruelly injured mortals. In their plight we experience our own.

The Bacchae is about Dionysus, not Apollo. No character raises the great questions, as Oedipus does, or arrives at the great answers. We appear to be in a diminished universe where the gods are gods not because they are wise and good, but because they are powerful. Here there is feeling, not thought, and the Dionysian feeling operates with the ambiguity of wine. Wine frees man from what diminishes him and releases his powers. "If there were no more wine," says the herdsman, "why, there's an end of love, and of every other pleasure in life." The god-intoxicated Theban women sing and decorously dance on the mountain side; they feed the animal young and ride joyful children on their shoulders. Dionysus is genial, benign—a savior. But wine liberates in another way; it rids man of that which keeps him human, and surrenders him to his lusts. The Bacchae tear the flesh of heifers, bulls, human beings. They glut themselves with blood and triumph in kindless savagery. Dionysus is violent, brutal—a destroyer.

Euripides visits upon us the meaning of the Dionysian spirit, whether the intoxication be that of grape, religious enthusiasm, or political cult. He preaches no lesson of abstinence, certainly, or even of moderation. But, making Dionysus manifest both to the dying eyes of the Theban king and to the living eyes of the audience, he compels us at once to acknowledge and to fear this ambiguous power, demonic or divine.

THE BACCHAE ⁝ *EURIPIDES*

TRANSLATED BY PHILIP VELLACOTT

Characters

DIONYSUS	
CHORUS	*of Oriental women, devotees of Dionysus*
TEIRESIAS	*a blind Seer*
CADMUS	*founder of Thebes, and formerly king*
PENTHEUS	*his grandson, now king of Thebes*
A GUARD	*attending Pentheus*
A HERDSMAN	
A MESSENGER	
AGAUË	*daughter of Cadmus and mother of Pentheus*

THE SCENE. *Before the palace of Pentheus in Thebes. At one side of the stage is the monument of Semele; above it burns a low flame, and around it are the remains of ruined and blackened masonry.*

PROLOGUE

[*Enter* DIONYSUS *on stage right. He has a crown of ivy, a thyrsus in his hand, and a fawnskin draped over his body. He has long flowing hair and a youthful, almost feminine beauty.*]

DIONYSUS. I am Dionysus, son of Zeus. My mother was Semele, daughter of Cadmus; I was delivered from her womb by the fire of a lightning-flash. To-day I have laid aside the appearance of a god,

Prologue See p. 4 note. *The Bacchae* has five scenes with accompanying odes, instead of four; otherwise its structure parallels that of *Oedipus Rex*.

2 **thyrsus** a light stick of reed or fennel, with fresh strands of ivy twined round it. It was carried by every devotee of Dionysus; and the action of the play illustrates the supernatural power that was held to reside in it. (Translator's note.)

and have come disguised as a mortal man to this city of Thebes, where flow the two rivers, Dirce and Ismenus. Here by the palace I see the monument recording my mother's death by lightning; here are the smouldering ruins of her house, which bear the still living flame of Zeus's fire—the undying token of Hera's cruelty to my mother. Cadmus does well to keep this ground untrodden, a precinct consecrated to his daughter; and I now have decked it round with sprays of young vine-leaves.

From the fields of Lydia and Phrygia, fertile in gold, I came to the sun-beaten Persian plains, the walled towns of Bactria, harsh Media, wealthy Arabia, and the whole of that Asian sea-board where Greeks and Orientals live side by side in crowded magnificent cities; and before reaching this, the first city of Hellas I have seen, I had already, in all those regions of the East, danced my dance and established my ritual, to make my godhead manifest to mortal men.

And the reason why Thebes is the first place in Hellas where, at my command, women have raised the Bacchic shout, put on the fawnskin cloak, and taken my weapon in their hands, the thyrsus wreathed with ivy—the reason is this: my mother's sisters said—what they should have been the last to say—that I, Dionysus, was not the progeny of Zeus; but that Semele, being with child by some mortal, at her father's suggestion ascribed to Zeus the loss of her virginity; and they loudly insisted that this lie about the fatherhood of her child was the sin for which Zeus had struck her dead.

Therefore I have plagued these same sisters with madness, and driven them all frantic out of doors; now their home is the mountains, and their wits are gone. And I made them carry the emblems of my mysteries; and the whole female population of Thebes, every woman there was in the town, I drove raving from their homes; now they have joined the daughters of Cadmus, and there they are, sitting roofless on the rocks under the silver fir-trees. Thebes must learn, unwilling though she is, that my Bacchic revels are something beyond her present knowledge and understanding; and I must vindicate the honour of my mother Semele, by manifesting myself before the human race as the god whom she bore to Zeus.

Now Cadmus has handed over his kingly honours and his throne to his daughter's son Pentheus. And this Pentheus is a fighter against God—he defies me, excludes me from libations, never names me in prayer. Therefore I will demonstrate to him, and to all Thebes, that I am a god.

When I have set all in order here, I will pass on to some other place, and manifest myself. Meanwhile, if the Theban city in anger tries to bring the Bacchae home from the mountains by force, I will join that army of women possessed and lead them to battle. And this is why I have changed my divine form to human, and appear in the likeness of a man.

Come, my holy band of revellers, women I have brought from lands of the East, from the slopes of Tmolus, bastion of Lydia, to be with me and share my travels! Raise the music of your Phrygian home, the timbrels invented by Rhea the Great Mother and by me; surround the palace of Pentheus and strike up such a peal of sound as shall make Thebes turn to look! I will go to the glens of Cithaeron where my Bacchae are, and join their dances.

[DIONYSUS *goes out towards the mountain; the* CHORUS *enter where* DIONYSUS *entered, from the road by which they have travelled.*]

PÁRODOS

CHORUS.

From far-off lands of Asia, STROPHE 1
From Tmolus the holy mountain,
We run with the god of laughter;
Labour is joy and weariness is sweet,
And our song resounds to Bacchus!

Beware of the interloper! ANTISTROPHE 1
Indoors or out, who listens?
Let every lip be holy;
Stand well aloof, be silent, while we sing
The appointed hymn to Bacchus!

Blest is the happy man STROPHE 2
Who knows the mysteries the gods ordain,
And sanctifies his life,
Joins soul with soul in mystic unity,

And, by due ritual made pure,
Enters the ecstasy of mountain solitudes;
Who observes the mystic rites
Made lawful by Cybele the Great Mother;
Who crowns his head with ivy,
And shakes aloft his wand in worship of Dionysus.

On, on! Run, dance, delirious, possessed!
Dionysus comes to his own;
Bring from the Phrygian hills to the broad streets of Hellas
The god, child of a god,
Spirit of revel and rapture, Dionysus!

Once, on the womb that held him ANTISTROPHE 2
The fire-bolt flew from the hand of Zeus;
And pains of child-birth bound his mother fast,
And she cast him forth untimely,
And under the lightning's lash relinquished life;
And Zeus the son of Cronos
Ensconced him instantly in a secret womb
Chambered within his thigh,
And with golden pins closed him from Hera's sight.

So, when the Fates had made him ripe for birth,
Zeus bore the bull-horned god
And wreathed his head with wreaths of writhing snakes;
Which is why the Maenads catch
Wild snakes, nurse them and twine them round their hair.

O Thebes, old nurse that cradled Semele, STROPHE 3
Be ivy-garlanded, burst into flower
With wreaths of lush bright-berried bryony,
Bring sprays of fir, green branches torn from oaks,
Fill soul and flesh with Bacchus' mystic power;
Fringe and bedeck your dappled fawnskin cloaks
With woolly tufts and locks of purest white.
There's a brute wildness in the fennel-wands—
Reverence it well. Soon the whole land will dance
When the god with ecstatic shout

Leads his companies out
To the mountain's mounting height
Swarming with riotous bands
Of Theban women leaving
Their spinning and their weaving
Stung with the maddening trance
Of Dionysus!

ANTISTROPHE 3

O secret chamber the Curetes knew!
O holy cavern in the Cretan glade
Where Zeus was cradled, where for our delight
The triple-crested Corybantes drew
Tight the round drum-skin, till its wild beat made
Rapturous rhythm to the breathing sweetness
Of Phrygian flutes! Then divine Rhea found
The drum could give her Bacchic airs completeness;
From her, the Mother of all,
The crazy Satyrs soon,
In their dancing festival
When the second year comes round,
Seized on the timbrel's tune
To play the leading part
In feasts that delight the heart
Of Dionysus.

EPODE

O what delight is in the mountains!
There the celebrant, wrapped in his sacred fawnskin,
Flings himself on the ground surrendered,
While the swift-footed company streams on;
There he hunts for blood, and rapturously
Eats the raw flesh of the slaughtered goat,
Hurrying on to the Phrygian or Lydian mountain heights.
Possessed, ecstatic, he leads their happy cries;
The earth flows with milk, flows with wine,

122 **Curetes** Demigods who cared for the infant Zeus.

139 **celebrant** Dionysus and the Chorus comprise the typical group of Bacchic worshipers, a male leader with a devoted band of women and girls. The leader *flings himself on the ground* in the climax of ecstasy, when the power of the god enters into him and he becomes possessed. (Translator's note.)

Flows with nectar of bees;
The air is thick with a scent of Syrian myrrh.
The celebrant runs entranced, whirling the torch
That blazes red from the fennel-wand in his grasp,
And with shouts he rouses the scattered bands,
Sets their feet dancing,
As he shakes his delicate locks to the wild wind.
And amidst the frenzy of song he shouts like thunder:
'On, on! Run, dance, delirious, possessed!
You, the beauty and grace of golden Tmolus,
Sing to the rattle of thunderous drums,
Sing for joy,
Praise Dionysus, god of joy!
Shout like Phrygians, sing out the tunes you know,
While the sacred pure-toned flute
Vibrates the air with holy merriment,
In time with the pulse of the feet that flock
To the mountains, to the mountains!'
And, like a foal with its mother at pasture,
Runs and leaps for joy every daughter of Bacchus.

SCENE I

[*Enter* TEIRESIAS. *Though blind, he makes his way unaided to the door, and knocks.*]

TEIRESIAS. Who keeps the gate? [*A servant is heard answering from inside.*] Call out Cadmus, the son of Agenor, who came from Sidonia to build these walls of Thebes. Go, someone, tell him Teiresias is looking for him. He knows why I have come—the agreement I made with him—old as I am, and he older still—to get myself a Bacchic wand, put on the fawnskin cloak, and wear a garland of young ivy-shoots.

[*Enter* CADMUS.]

CADMUS. O my dear friend, I knew your voice, although I was indoors, as soon as I heard it—the wise voice of a wise man. Look, I am ready, I have everything the god prescribes. Dionysus is my own daughter's son; and now he has shown himself to the world as a god, it is right that I should do all I can to exalt him. Where should we go to dance, and take our stand with the rest, tossing our old grey beards? You must guide me in this, Teiresias—you're nearly as old as I am, and you understand such matters. No, it won't be too much for me; I can beat time with my thyrsus night and day! It's a happy thing to forget one's age.

TEIRESIAS. Then you feel just as I do. I am young too; I'll make an attempt at the dance.

CADMUS. You don't think we should make our way to the mountains in a carriage?

TEIRESIAS. No, no, that would not show the same respect for the god.

CADMUS. I'll be your guide then—two old men together.

TEIRESIAS. The god will guide us there, and without weariness.

CADMUS. Shall we be the only men in Thebes who dance to Bacchus?

TEIRESIAS. We are the only men right-minded; the rest are perverse.

CADMUS. We are wasting time. Now, take my hand.

TEIRESIAS. There; hold firmly, with a good grip.

CADMUS. Mortals must not make light of the gods—*I* would never do so.

TEIRESIAS. We entertain no theories or speculations in divine matters. The beliefs we have received from our ancestors—beliefs as old as time—cannot be destroyed by any argument, nor by any ingenuity the mind can invent. No doubt I shall be criticized for wearing an ivy-wreath and setting off for the dance; they will say I have no sense of what befits my age. They will be wrong: the god has drawn no distinction between young and old, which should dance and which should not. He wishes to receive honour alike from all; he will not have his worship made a matter of nice calculation.

CADMUS. Teiresias, since you are blind I must be your prophet. I see Pentheus the son of Echion, to whom I have resigned my rule in Thebes, hurrying towards the palace. He looks thoroughly upset! What is he going to tell us?

[*Enter* PENTHEUS. *He addresses the audience, without at first noticing* CADMUS *and* TEIRESIAS, *who stand at the opposite side of the stage.*]

PENTHEUS. I've been away from Thebes, as it happens; but I've heard the news—this extraordinary scandal in the city. Our women,

I discover, have abandoned their homes on some pretence of Bacchic worship, and go gadding about in the woods on the mountain side, dancing in honour of this upstart god Dionysus, whoever he may be. They tell me, in the midst of each group of revellers stands a bowl full of wine; and the women go creeping off this way and that to lonely places and there give themselves to lecherous men, under the excuse that they are Maenad priestesses; though in their ritual Aphrodite comes before Bacchus.

Well, those that I've caught, my guards are keeping safe; we've tied their hands, and lodged them at State expense. Those still at large on the mountain I am going to hunt out; and that includes my own mother Agauë, and her sisters Ino and Autonoe. Once I have them secure in iron chains I shall soon put a stop to this outrageous Bacchism.

I understand too that some Oriental magician or conjurer has arrived from Lydia, a fellow with golden hair flowing in scented ringlets, the flush of wine in his face and the charm of Aphrodite in his eyes; and that he entices our young girls with his Bacchic mysteries, and spends day and night in their company. Only let me get that fellow inside my walls—I'll cut his head from his shoulders; that will finish his thyrsus-waving and hair-tossing. *He* is the one—this foreigner—who has spread stories about Dionysus, that he is a god, that he was sewn up in Zeus's thigh. The truth about Dionysus is that he's dead, burnt to a cinder by lightning along with his mother, because she lied about Zeus—said that Zeus had lain with her. But whoever this man may be, does not his insufferable behaviour merit the worst of punishments, hanging?

[*He turns to go, and sees* CADMUS *and* TEIRESIAS.]

Why, look! Another miracle! Here's the prophet Teiresias, and my mother's father, playing the Bacchant, in dappled fawnskin and carrying fennel-wands! Well, there's a sight for laughter! [*But he is raging, not laughing.*] Sir, I am ashamed to see two men of your age with so little sense of decency. Come, you are my grandfather: throw away your garland, get rid of that thyrsus. *You* persuaded him into this, Teiresias. No doubt you hope that, when you have introduced this new god to the people, you will be his appointed seer, you will collect the fees for sacrifices. Your grey hairs are your protection; otherwise you should sit with all these crazy females in prison, for encouraging such pernicious performances.

As for women, my opinion is this: when the sparkle of sweet wine appears at their feasts, no good can be expected from their ceremonies.

CHORUS. What profanity! Sir, do you not revere the gods, or Cadmus, who sowed the seed of the earth-born men? Echion your father was one of them—will you shame your own blood?

TEIRESIAS. When a clever man has a plausible theme to argue, to be eloquent is no great feat. But though you seem, by your glib tongue, to be intelligent, yet your words are foolish. Power and eloquence in a headstrong man can only lead to folly; and such a man is a danger to the state.

This new divinity whom you ridicule—no words of mine could adequately express the ascendancy he is destined to achieve through the length and breadth of Hellas. There are two powers, young man, which are supreme in human affairs: first, the goddess Demeter; she is the Earth—call her by what name you will; and she supplies mankind with solid food. Second, Dionysus the son of Semele; the blessing he provides is the counterpart to the blessing of bread; he discovered and bestowed on men the service of drink, the juice that streams from the vine-clusters; men have but to take their fill of wine, and the sufferings of an unhappy race are banished, each day's troubles are forgotten in sleep—indeed this is our only cure for the weariness of life. Dionysus, himself a god, is poured out in offering to the gods; so that through him mankind receives blessing.

Now for the legend that he was sewn up in Zeus's thigh—do you mock at it? Then I will explain to you the truth that lies in the legend. When Zeus snatched the infant Dionysus away from the fire of the lightning, and brought him to Olympus as a god, Hera wanted to cast him out of heaven; so, to prevent her, Zeus—as you would expect—devised a plan. He broke off a piece of the sky that envelops the earth, made it into the likeness of a child, and gave it to Hera as a pledge, to soothe her jealousy. He entrusted the true Dionysus to others to bring up. Now the ancient word for a *pledge* is very similar to our word 'thigh'; and so in time the word was mistaken, and

265 **earth-born men** By Athena's advice Cadmus sowed the teeth of a dragon he had slain; the harvest was armed men who fought and slew each other until only five were left—the ancestors of the Theban nobility.

293 **the ancient word for a pledge** The translation necessarily expands the original. *Homeros* means "pledge," and *meros* "thigh." (Translator's note.)

men said Dionysus was saved by Zeus's *thigh,* instead of by Zeus's *pledge,* because a pledge was given to Hera in his likeness.

And this god is a prophet; for the Bacchic ecstasy and frenzy contain a strong element of prophecy. When Dionysus enters in power into a human body, he endows the possessed person with power to foretell the future. He also in some degree shares the function of Ares, god of war. It has happened that an army, equipped and stationed for battle, has fled in panic before a spear has been raised. This too is a madness sent by Dionysus.

Ay, and the day will come when you shall see him on the very rocks of Delphi, amidst flaring torches bounding over the twin-peaked ridge, hurling and brandishing his Bacchic staff, honoured by all Hellas.

Come, Pentheus, listen to me. You rely on force; but it is not force that governs human affairs. If you think otherwise—beware of mistaking your perverse opinion for wisdom. Welcome Dionysus to Thebes; pour libations to him, garland your head and celebrate his rites. Dionysus will not compel women to control their lusts. Self-control in all things depends on our own natures. This is a fact you should consider; for a chaste-minded woman will come to no harm in the rites of Bacchus. And think of this too: when crowds stand at the city gates, and the people glorify the name of Pentheus, you are filled with pleasure; so, I think, Dionysus is glad to receive honour.

So then I, and Cadmus, whom you mock, will wear the ivy-wreath and join in the dancing—we are both old men, but this is our duty; and no words of yours shall persuade me to fight against the gods. For your mind is most pitifully diseased; and there is no medicine that can heal you. Yet . . . there is one remedy for your madness.

CHORUS. What you have said, Teiresias, means no dishonour to Phoebus, whose prophet you are; and shows your wisdom in honouring Dionysus as a great god.

CADMUS. My son, Teiresias has advised you well. Do not venture outside the customary pieties; stay with us. Just now your wits are scattered; you think you are talking sense, but it is not sense at all. And even if you are right, and this god is not a god, at least let him have your word of acknowledgment; lie for a good purpose, so that Semele may be honoured as mother of a god, and I and our whole family may gain in dignity. Remember Actaeon—his tragic end; he boasted, out in these valleys, that he was a better hunter than

Artemis, and was torn to pieces and devoured by the very hounds he had bred. Don't invite the same fate! Come, let me put this ivy-wreath on your head. Join us in worshipping Dionysus.

PENTHEUS. Keep your hands off! Go to your Bacchic rites; and don't wipe off your crazy folly on me! But I will punish this man who has taught you your lunacy. Go, one of you, immediately to the place of augury where Teiresias practises, smash it with crowbars, knock down the walls, turn everything upside down, fling out his holy fripperies to the winds. That will sting him more than anything else. The rest of you, comb the city and find this effeminate foreigner, who plagues our women with this strange disease and turns them into whores. If you catch him, bring him here in chains, and I'll have him stoned to death. He shall be sorry he ever came revelling in Thebes.

[*Exit* PENTHEUS.]

TEIRESIAS. Foolhardy man, you don't know what you are saying. You were out of your mind before; now you are raving mad.

Come, Cadmus; let us go and pray both for this man, brutish as he is, and for Thebes, and entreat Dionysus to be forbearing. Come, take your thyrsus and follow. Try to support me—there, we will help each other. It would be a pity for us both to fall; but never mind that. We must pay our service to Dionysus the son of Zeus.

Cadmus: the name *Pentheus* means *grief*. Let us hope he is not going to bring grief on your house. I am not speaking by inspiration; I judge by his conduct. The things he has said reveal the depth of his folly.

[*Exeunt* TEIRESIAS *and* CADMUS.]

ODE I

CHORUS.

STROPHE 1

Holiness, Queen of heaven,
Holiness, golden-winged ranging the earth,
Do you hear his blasphemy?
Pentheus dares—do you hear?—to revile the god of joy,
The son of Semele, who when the gay-crowned feast is set
Is named among gods the chief;
Whose gifts are joy and union of soul in dancing,
Joy in music of flutes,

Joy when sparkling wine at feasts of the gods
Soothes the sore regret,
Banishes every grief,
When the reveller rests, enfolded deep
In the cool shade of ivy-shoots,
On wine's soft pillow of sleep.

The brash, unbridled tongue, ANTISTROPHE 1
The lawless folly of fools, will end in pain.
But the life of wise content
Is blest with quietness, escapes the storm
And keeps its house secure.
Though blessed gods dwell in the distant skies,
They watch the ways of men.
To know much is not to be wise.
Pride more than mortal hastens life to its end;
And they who in pride pretend
Beyond man's limit, will lose what lay
Close to their hand and sure.
I count it madness, and know no cure can mend
The evil man and his evil way.

O to set foot on Aphrodite's island, STROPHE 2
On Cyprus, haunted by the Loves, who enchant
Brief life with sweetness; or in that strange land
Whose fertile river carves a hundred channels
To enrich her rainless sand;
Or where the sacred pastures of Olympus slant
Down to Pieria, where the Muses dwell—
Take me, O Bromius, take me and inspire
Laughter and worship! There our holy spell
And ecstasy are welcome; there the gentle band
Of Graces have their home, and sweet Desire.

Dionysus, son of Zeus, delights in banquets; ANTISTROPHE 2
And his dear love is Peace, giver of wealth,
Saviour of young men's lives—a goddess rare!

398 **Bromius** another name for Dionysus.

In wine, his gift that charms all griefs away,
Alike both rich and poor may have their part.
His enemy is the man who has no care
To pass his years in happiness and health,
His days in quiet and his nights in joy,
Watchful to keep aloof both mind and heart
From men whose pride claims more than mortals may.
The life that wins the poor man's common voice,
His creed, his practice—this shall be my choice.

SCENE II

[*Some of the guards whom* PENTHEUS *sent to arrest* DIONYSUS *now enter with their prisoner.* PENTHEUS *enters from the palace.*]

GUARD. Well, sir, we went after this lion you told us to hunt, and we have been successful. But—we found the lion was tame! He made no attempt to escape, but freely held out his hands to be bound. He didn't even turn pale, but kept the fresh colour you see in his face now, smiling, and telling us to tie him up and run him in; waited for me, in fact—gave us no trouble at all. Naturally I felt a bit awkward. 'You'll excuse me, sir,' I said, 'I don't want to arrest you, but it's the king's orders.'

And there's another thing, sir. Those women you rounded up and put in fetters and in prison, those religious maniacs—why, they're all gone, let loose to the glens; and there they are, dancing and calling on Bacchus. The fetters simply fell from their limbs, the bolts flew back without the touch of any mortal hand, and let the doors open. Master, this man has come to our city of Thebes with a load of miracles. What is going to happen next is your concern, not mine.

PENTHEUS. Untie his hands. [*The guard does so.*] He is in the trap, and he's not nimble enough to escape me now.

Well, my man: you have a not unhandsome figure—for attracting women, which is your object in coming to Thebes. Those long curls of yours show that you're no wrestler—cascading close over your cheeks, most seductively. Your complexion, too, shows a carefully-preserved whiteness; you keep out of the sun and walk in the shade, to use your lovely face for courting Aphrodite. . . .

Ah, well; tell me first what country you were born in.

DIONYSUS. That is easily told without boasting. Doutbless you have heard of the flowery mountain, Tmolus.

PENTHEUS. Yes, the range that curves round the city of Sardis.

DIONYSUS. That was my home; I am a Lydian.

PENTHEUS. And why do you bring these rituals to Hellas?

DIONYSUS. Dionysus the son of Zeus instructed me.

PENTHEUS. Is there a Lydian Zeus, then, who begets new gods?

DIONYSUS. No; I speak of your Zeus, who made Semele his bride here in Thebes.

PENTHEUS. And when Dionysus took possession of you, did he appear in a dream by night, or visible before your eyes?

DIONYSUS. I saw him face to face; and he entrusted to me these mysteries.

PENTHEUS. What form do these mysteries of yours take?

DIONYSUS. That cannot be told to the uninitiated.

PENTHEUS. What do the worshippers gain from it?

DIONYSUS. That is not lawful for you to hear—yet it is worth hearing.

PENTHEUS. A clever answer, baited to rouse my curiosity.

DIONYSUS. Curiosity will be useless; the rites of the god abhor an impious man.

PENTHEUS. If you say you saw Dionysus clearly—what was his appearance?

DIONYSUS. It was what he wished it to be. I had no say in that.

PENTHEUS. Another clever evasion, telling nothing.

DIONYSUS. *A wise speech sleeps in a foolish ear.*

PENTHEUS. Is this the first place where you have introduced Dionysus?

DIONYSUS. No; every Eastern land dances these mysteries.

PENTHEUS. I believe it. Oriental standards are altogether inferior to ours.

DIONYSUS. In this point they are superior. But their customs are different.

PENTHEUS. Do you celebrate your mysteries by night or by day?

DIONYSUS. Chiefly by night. Darkness induces religious awe.

PENTHEUS. For women darkness is treacherous and impure.

DIONYSUS. Impurity can be practised by daylight too.

PENTHEUS. It is time you were punished for your foul, slippery tongue.

DIONYSUS. And you for your crass impieties.

PENTHEUS. How bold his Bacchic inspiration makes him! He knows how to argue too.

DIONYSUS. Tell me my sentence. What punishment are you going to inflict?

PENTHEUS. First I'll cut off your scented silky hair.

DIONYSUS. My hair I keep for the god; it is sacred to him.

PENTHEUS. Next, hand over that thyrsus.

DIONYSUS. Take it from me yourself. I carry it for Dionysus, whose it is.

PENTHEUS. And I shall keep you safe in prison.

DIONYSUS. The god himself will set me free whenever I wish.

PENTHEUS. Set you free? When you stand among those frenzied women and pray to him—no doubt!

DIONYSUS. He is here, close by me, and sees what is being done to me.

PENTHEUS. Oh, indeed? Where? To my eyes he is quite invisible.

DIONYSUS. Here at my side. You, being a blasphemer, cannot see him.

PENTHEUS [*to the guards*]. Get hold of him. He is laughing at me and the whole city.

DIONYSUS [*to the guards*]. I warn you not to bind me. . . . [*To* PENTHEUS.] I am sane, you are mad.

PENTHEUS [*to* DIONYSUS]. My orders overrule yours. [*To the guards.*] Bind him, I tell you.

DIONYSUS. You do not know what life you live, or what you do, or who you are.

PENTHEUS. Who I am? Pentheus, son of Echion and Agauë.

DIONYSUS. *Pentheus* means 'sorrow.' The name fits you well.

PENTHEUS. Take him away. Imprison him over there in the stables; he'll have all the darkness he wants.—You can dance in there! As for these women you've brought to aid and abet you, I shall either send them to the slave market, or retain them in my own household to work at the looms; that will keep their hands from drumming on tambourines!

DIONYSUS. I will go. Nothing can happen to me that is not my destiny. But Dionysus, who you say is dead, will pursue you and take his revenge for this sacrilege. You are putting *him* in prison, when you lay hands on me.

[*Guards take* DIONYSUS *away to the stables;* PENTHEUS *follows.*]

ODE II

CHORUS.

STROPHE

Dirce, sweet and holy maid,
Acheloüs' Theban daughter,
Once the child of Zeus was made
Welcome in your welling water,
When the lord of earth and sky
Snatched him from the undying flame,
Laid him safe within his thigh,
Calling loud the infant's name:
'Twice-born Dithyrambus! Come,
Enter here your father's womb;
Bacchic child, I now proclaim
This in Thebes shall be your name.'
Now, divine Dirce, when my head is crowned
And my feet dance in Bacchus' revelry—
Now you reject me from your holy ground.
Why should you fear me? By the purple fruit
That glows in glory on Dionysus' tree,
His dread name yet shall haunt your memory!

ANTISTROPHE

O what anger lies beneath
Pentheus' voice and sullen face—
Offspring of the dragon's teeth,
And Echion's earth-born race,
Brute with bloody jaws agape,
God-defying, gross and grim,
Slander of his human shape!
Soon he'll chain us limb to limb—
Bacchus' servants! Yes, and more.
Even now our comrade lies
Deep on his dark prison floor.
Dionysus! do your eyes

See us? O son of Zeus, the oppressor's rod
Falls on your worshippers; come, mighty god,
Brandish your golden thyrsus and descend
From great Olympus; touch this murderous man,
And bring his violence to a sudden end!

Where are you, Dionysus? Leading your dancing bands — EPODE
Over the mountain slopes, past many a wild beast's lair,
Or upon rocky crags, with the thyrsus in their hands?
Or in the wooded coverts, maybe, of Olympus, where
Orpheus once gathered the trees and mountain beasts,
Gathered them with his lyre, and sang an enchanting air.
Happy vale of Pieria! Bacchus delights in you;
He will cross the flood and foam of the Axius river, and there
He will bring his whirling Maenads, with dancing and with feasts,—
Cross the father of waters, Lydias, generous giver
Of wealth and luck, they say, to the land he wanders through,
Whose famous horses graze by the rich and lovely river.

SCENE III

[*Suddenly a shout is heard from inside the building—the voice of* DIONYSUS.]

DIONYSUS.
Io, Io! Do you know my voice, do you hear?
Worshippers of Bacchus! Io, Io!

CHORUS. Who is that? Where is he? The voice of Dionysus calling to us!

DIONYSUS. Io, Io! Hear me again: I am the son of Semele, the son of Zeus!

CHORUS.
Io, Io, our lord, our lord!
Come, then, come to our company, lord of joy!

DIONYSUS. O dreadful earthquake, shake the floor of the world!

CHORUS [*with a scream of terror*].
Pentheus' palace is falling, crumbling in pieces! [*They continue severally.*]

575 **Io** an ecstatic cry.

Dionysus stands in the palace; bow before him!
We bow before him. See how the roof and pillars
Plunge to the ground! God from the inner prison
Will shout the shout of victory.

[*The flame on Semele's tomb grows and brightens.*]

DIONYSUS.

Fan to a blaze the flame the lightning lit;
Kindle the conflagration of Pentheus' palace!

CHORUS.

Look, look, look!
Do you see, do you see the flame of Semele's tomb,
The flame that remained when she died of the lightning-stroke?

[*A noise of crashing masonry is heard.*]

Down, trembling Maenads! Hurl yourselves to the ground!
Your god is wrecking the palace, roof to floor;
He heard our cry—he is coming, the son of Zeus!

[*The doors open and* DIONYSUS *appears.*]

DIONYSUS. Women of Asia, why are you cowering terrified on the ground? You heard Bacchus himself shattering Pentheus' palace; come, stand up! Stop this trembling! Courage!

CHORUS. Oh, what a joy to hear your Bacchic shout! You have saved us. We were deserted and alone: how happy we are to see you!

DIONYSUS. Were you plunged in despair, when I was sent inside to be thrown into Pentheus' dark dungeon?

CHORUS. How could we help it? Who was there to protect us, if you were taken? But tell us how you escaped from the clutches of this wicked man.

DIONYSUS. I alone with effortless ease delivered myself.

CHORUS. But did he not bind your arms with knotted ropes?

DIONYSUS. Ha, ha! There I made a mockery of him. He thought he was binding me; but he fed himself on delusion—he neither took hold of me nor even touched me. Near the stall where he took me to shut me in, he found a bull; and he was tying his rope round the bull's knees and hooves, panting with rage, dripping sweat, and biting his lips; while I sat quietly by and watched him. And it was then that Bacchus came and shook the building and made the flame on his mother's tomb flare up. When Pentheus saw this, he imagined the place was on fire, and went rushing this way and that, calling to the servants to bring water, till the whole household was in commotion—all for nothing.

Then he thought I had escaped. He left throwing water, snatched up his murderous sword and darted into the palace. Thereupon Dionysus—or so it seemed to me; I tell what I thought—made a phantom figure appear in the palace courtyard; and Pentheus flew at it, and kept stabbing at the sunny air, imagining he was killing *me*.

But the god had further humiliation in store for him: he laid the stable-buildings in ruins on the ground—there they lie, a heap of rubble, to break his heart as he looks at my prison. Now he is helpless with exhaustion. He has dropped his sword. He, a mortal man, dared to take arms against a god. I walked quietly out of the palace, and here I am. Pentheus does not disturb me. But I hear his heavy tread indoors; I think he will be out here in a moment. What will he say after this? For all his rage, he shall not ruffle me. The wise man preserves a smooth-tempered self-control.

[*Enter* PENTHEUS.]

PENTHEUS. This is outrageous. That foreigner was locked up and in chains a little while ago; now he has escaped me. [*He sees* DIONYSUS *and gives an excited shout.*] That's the man! What's going on? How did you get out? How dare you show yourself here before my very doors?

DIONYSUS. Stay where you are. You are angry. Now control yourself.

PENTHEUS. You were bound and locked in: how did you escape?

DIONYSUS. Did you not hear me say that I should be set free by—

PENTHEUS. By whom? Everything you say is strange.

DIONYSUS. By him who plants for mortals the rich-clustered vine.

PENTHEUS. The god who makes men fools and women mad.

DIONYSUS. A splendid insult, that, to Dionysus!

PENTHEUS [*to attendant guards*]. Close the gates all round—every gate in the city wall.

DIONYSUS. And why? Cannot gods pass even over walls?

PENTHEUS. Oh, you know everything—except the things you ought to know.

656 **The god who makes** This is conjecturally supplied in place of a missing line. (Translator's note.)

DIONYSUS. The things one ought to know most of all, those things I know.

But first listen to what this man has to tell you; he comes from the mountains with news.—I will stay here; I promise not to run away.

[*Enter a* HERDSMAN.]

HERDSMAN. Pentheus, ruler of Thebes! I come from Cithaeron, where the ground is never free from dazzling shafts of snow.

PENTHEUS. And what urgent news do you bring me?

HERDSMAN. I have seen the holy Bacchae, who in madness went streaming bare-limbed out of the city gates. I have come with the intention of telling you, my lord, and the city, of their strange and terrible doings—things past all wonder. But I would like to know first if I may speak freely of what is going on there, or if I should trim my words. I am afraid of your hastiness, my lord, your hot temper; you are too much like a king.

PRENTHEUS. Say all that you have to say; fear nothing from me. The more terrible your story about the Bacchae, the more certainly will I execute justice upon this man, the instigator of their wickedness.

HERDSMAN. Just when the sun's rays first beamed out to warm the earth, I was pasturing my cattle and working up towards the high ground; when I saw three groups of women who had been dancing together. The leader of one group was Autonoe; your mother Agauë was at the head of the second, and Ino of the third. They were all sleeping, stretched out and quiet. Some rested on beds of pine-needles, some had pillows of oak-leaves; they lay just as they had thrown themselves down on the ground,—but with modesty in their posture; they were not drunk with wine, as you told us, or with music of flutes; nor was there any love-making there in the loveliness of the woods.

As soon as your mother Agauë heard the lowing of the horned cattle, she stood up among the Bacchae and called loudly to them to rouse themselves from sleep. And they threw off the strong sleep from their eyes and leapt to their feet. They were a sight to marvel at for modesty and comeliness—women old and young, and girls still unmarried. First they let down their hair over their shoulders; those whose fawnskins had come loose from their fastenings tied them up; and they girdled the dappled fur with snakes which licked their cheeks. And some would have in their arms a young gazelle, or wild wolf-cubs, and give them their own white milk—those who had infants at home recently born, so that their breasts were still full. And they wreathed their heads with garlands of ivy and oak and flowering bryony.

And one of them took her thyrsus and struck it on the rock; and from the rock there gushed a spring of limpid water; another struck her wand down into the earth, and there the god made a fountain of wine spring up; and any who wanted milk had only to scratch the earth with the tip of her fingers, and there was the white stream flowing for her to drink; and from the ivy-bound thyrsus a sweet ooze of honey dripped. Oh! if you had been there and seen all this, you would have entreated with prayers this god whom you now accuse.

Well, we herdsmen and shepherds gathered and stood talking together, and arguing about these strange and extraordinary doings. And one fellow, a gadder up to town, and a good speaker, addressed the rest of us. 'You who live on the holy mountain heights,' he said, 'how if we should hunt down the king's mother, Agauë, bring her away from these orgies, and do the king a service?' We thought it was a good suggestion; so we hid ourselves among the leafy bushes and waited our chance.

When the set time came, the women began brandishing their wands and preparing to dance, calling in unison on the son of Zeus, 'Iacchus! Bromius!' And the whole mountain, and the wild beasts too, became a part of their joyful dance—there was nothing that was not roused to leap and run.

Now Agauë as she ran happened to pass close to me; so I sprang out of the ambush where we lay hidden, meaning to capture her. But she cried out, 'Oh, my swift hounds, we are being hunted by these men. Come, then, and follow; arm yourselves with the thyrsus, and follow me!'

So we fled, and escaped being torn in pieces by these possessed women. But our cattle were feeding there on the fresh grass; and the Bacchae attacked them, with their bare hands. You could see Agauë take up a bellowing young heifer with full udders, and hold it by the legs with her two arms stretched wide. Others were tearing our cows limb from limb, and you could see perhaps some ribs or a cleft hoof being tossed high and low; and pieces of bloody flesh hung dripping on the pine-branches. And bulls, which one moment were savagely looking along their horns, the next were thrown bodily to the ground, dragged down by the soft hands of girls—thousands of them; and they stripped the flesh off their bodies faster than you could wink your royal eyes.

Then, like birds, skimming the ground as they ran, they scoured the plain which stretches by the river Asopus and produces a rich harvest for Thebes; and like an enemy army they bore down on the villages of Hysiae and Erythrae, which lie on the low slopes of Cithaeron, and ransacked them. They snatched up children out of the houses; all the plunder they laid on their shoulders stayed safely there without any fastening; nothing fell to the dark earth, not bronze or iron even; they carried fire on their heads, and their hair was not burnt.

The villagers, of course, were furious at being plundered by the Bacchae, and they resisted with weapons; and then, my lord, was an astonishing sight to behold. The spears cast by the villagers drew no blood; but the women, hurling the thyrsus like a spear, dealt wounds; those women turned the men to flight. There was the power of a god in that.

Then they went back to the place they had started from, to those fountains the god had made flow for them. And they washed off the blood, and the snakes licked the stains clean from their cheeks.

So, master, whoever this god may be, receive him in our city. He has great power in many ways; but especially, as I hear, it was he who gave men the gift of the vine as a cure for sorrow. And if there were no more wine, why, there's an end of love, and of every other pleasure in life.

CHORUS. I hesitate to speak freely before the king; yet I will say it: there is no greater god than Dionysus.

PENTHEUS. This outrageous Bacchism advances on us like a spreading fire, disgracing us before all Hellas. We must waste no time. [*To the* HERDSMAN.] Go at once to the Electran gate; tell all my men who bear shields, heavy or light, all who ride fast horses or twang the bowstring, to meet me there in readiness for an assault on the Bacchae. This is past all bearing, if we are to let women so defy us.

DIONYSUS. You refuse, Pentheus, to listen to what I say or to alter your behaviour. Yet, in spite of all I have suffered at your hands, I warn you to stay where you are and not to take arms against a god. Dionysus will not stand quietly by and see you drive his Bacchae from their mountain rites.

PENTHEUS. I want no instruction from you. You have escaped from your fetters—be content; or I will punish you again.

DIONYSUS. You are a mortal, he is a god. If I were you I would control my rage and sacrifice to him, rather than kick against the pricks.

PENTHEUS. Sacrifice! I will indeed—an offering of women's blood, slaughtered as they deserve in the glens of Cithaeron.

DIONYSUS. You will all be put to flight. It would be disgraceful for the wands of Bacchic women to rout your brazen shields.

PENTHEUS. This foreigner is an impossible man to deal with; in prison or out, he will not hold his tongue.

DIONYSUS. My friend! A happy settlement may still be found.

PENTHEUS. How? By making me a slave to my own slaves?

DIONYSUS. I will bring those women here, without use of weapons.

PENTHEUS. Heaven help us, you are plotting some trick.

DIONYSUS. A trick? If I use my power to save you?

PENTHEUS. This is something you have arranged with the women, so that the revelling may continue.

DIONYSUS. This is something, certainly, that I have arranged—not with them, but with the god.

PENTHEUS. That is enough from you.—Bring out my armour, there!

DIONYSUS [*with an authoritative shout*]. Wait! [*Then, quietly.*] Would you like to *see* those women, sitting together, there in the mountains?

PENTHEUS. Yes, indeed; I would give a large sum of gold to see them.

[*From now on* DIONYSUS *gradually establishes a complete ascendancy over* PENTHEUS.]

DIONYSUS. And what has betrayed you into this great eagerness?

PENTHEUS. I am not eager to see them drunk; that would be a painful sight.

DIONYSUS. Yet you would be glad to see a sight that would pain you?

PENTHEUS. I would, yes; if I could sit quietly under the pine-trees and watch.

DIONYSUS. However secretly you go they will track you down.

PENTHEUS. You are quite right. I will go openly.

DIONYSUS. Shall I show you the way, then? You will venture on this?

PENTHEUS. Lead me there at once; I am impatient.

DIONYSUS. Then, first dress yourself in a fine linen gown.

PENTHEUS. Why a linen gown? Must I change my sex?

DIONYSUS. They will kill you if you are seen there dressed as a man.

PENTHEUS. You are quite right; you think of everything!

DIONYSUS. It was Dionysus who inspired me with that thought.

PENTHEUS. How can your suggestion best be carried out?

DIONYSUS. I will come indoors with you and dress you.

PENTHEUS. Dress me? Not in woman's clothes? I would be ashamed.

DIONYSUS. You have lost your enthusiasm for watching the Maenads.

PENTHEUS. What kind of dress do you say you will put on me?

DIONYSUS. I will cover your head with long, flowing hair.

PENTHEUS. And after that? What will my costume look like?

DIONYSUS. A robe falling to your feet; and a snood on your head.

PENTHEUS. Anything else?

DIONYSUS. A thyrsus in your hand, and a dappled fawnskin round you.

PENTHEUS. I could never wear woman's clothes.

DIONYSUS. If you join battle with the Bacchae there will be bloodshed.

PENTHEUS. You are right; I must first go to spy on them.

DIONYSUS. That is wiser than inviting violence by using it.

PENTHEUS. And how shall I get through the streets of Thebes without being seen?

DIONYSUS. We will go by lonely ways; I will guide you.

PENTHEUS. I must not be laughed at by the Bacchae—anything rather than that. Now I will go in, and decide how best to act.

DIONYSUS. You may. My own preparations are all made.

PENTHEUS. I will go, then; and I will either visit the mountains armed—or else I will follow your advice.

[*Exit* PENTHEUS.]

DIONYSUS. Women, this man is walking into the net. He will visit the Bacchae; and there he shall be punished with death.

Dionysus (for you are not far away), all is now in your hands. Let us be revenged on him! And—first assail him with fantastic madness and drive him out of his mind; for while he is sane he will never consent to put on a woman's clothes; but once he has broken from the rein of reason he will put them on. I long to set Thebes laughing at him, as I lead him dressed like a woman through the streets; to humble him from the arrogance with which he threatened me at first.

Now I will go, to array Pentheus in the dress which he will take down with him to the world of the dead, slaughtered by his own mother's hands. And he shall know the son of Zeus, Dionysus; who, though most gentle to mankind, can prove a god of terror irresistible.

[DIONYSUS *follows* PENTHEUS *into the palace.*]

ODE III

CHORUS.

O for long nights of worship, gay STROPHE
With the pale gleam of dancing feet,
With head tossed high to the dewy air—
Pleasure mysterious and sweet!
O for the joy of a fawn at play
In the fragrant meadow's green delight,
Who has leapt out free from the woven snare,
Away from the terror of chase and flight,
And the huntsman's shout, and the straining pack,
And skims the sand by the river's brim
With the speed of wind in each aching limb,
To the blessed lonely forest where
The soil's unmarked by a human track,
And leaves hang thick and the shades are dim.

What prayer should we call wise? REFRAIN
What gift of Heaven should man
Count a more noble prize,
A prayer more prudent, than
To stretch a conquering arm

Over the fallen crest
Of those who wished us harm?
And what is noble every heart loves best.

ANTISTROPHE

Slow, yet unfailing, move the Powers
Of Heaven with the moving hours.
When mind runs mad, dishonours God,
And worships self and senseless pride,
Then Law eternal wields the rod.
Still Heaven hunts down the impious man,
Though divine subtlety may hide
Time's creeping foot. No mortal ought
To challenge Time—to overbear
Custom in act, or age in thought.
All men, at little cost, may share
The blessing of a pious creed;
Truths more than mortal, which began
In the beginning, and belong
To very nature—these indeed
Reign in our world, are fixed and strong.

REFRAIN

What prayer should we call wise?
What gift of Heaven should man
Count a more noble prize,
A prayer more prudent, than
To stretch a conquering arm
Over the fallen crest
Of those who wished us harm?
And what is noble every heart loves best.

EPODE

Blest is the man who cheats the stormy sea
And safely moors beside the sheltering quay;
So, blest is he who triumphs over trial.
One man, by various means, in wealth or strength
Outdoes his neighbour; hope in a thousand hearts
Colours a thousand different dreams; at length
Some find a dear fulfilment, some denial.
  But this I say,
  That he who best

Enjoys each passing day
Is truly blest.

SCENE IV

[*Enter* DIONYSUS. *He turns to call* PENTHEUS.]

DIONYSUS. Come, perverse man, greedy for sights you should not see, impatient for deeds you should not do—Pentheus! Come out of the palace and show yourself to me, wearing the garb of a frenzied Bacchic woman, ready to spy on your mother and all her company! [*Enter* PENTHEUS *dressed as a Bacchic devotee. He is dazed, and entirely subservient to* DIONYSUS.] Ah! You look exactly like one of Cadmus' daughters.

PENTHEUS. Why—I seem to see two suns; I see a double Thebes, and the city wall with its seven gates—double! I see you leading me forward—you are like a bull, you have horns growing on your head. Tell me, were you an animal a little while ago? You have certainly become a bull.

DIONYSUS. The god did not favour us before; now he is with us, and we have made our peace with him. Now you see as you ought to see.

PENTHEUS. Well, how do I look? Do you think I stand like Ino or like my mother Agauë?

DIONYSUS. I think you are their very image. Wait—this curl of hair is out of place, not as I arranged it under your snood.

PENTHEUS. I must have shaken it loose indoors, tossing my head up and down like a Bacchic reveller.

DIONYSUS. Come, it is for me to look after you; I will set it straight. Now, lift your head.

PENTHEUS. There, *you* put it right. I depend entirely on you.

DIONYSUS. And your girdle is loose; and the folds of your gown are not hanging straight to your ankles.

PENTHEUS. I agree, they are not—at least, here by the right foot. But on the other side the gown hangs well to the heel.

DIONYSUS. I think you will reckon me the chief of your friends, when you see the Bacchae and find to your surprise how well they are behaving—will you not?

[*But* PENTHEUS *is not listening.*]

PENTHEUS. Ought I to hold my thyrsus in this hand or in the right, to look more like a Bacchanal?

DIONYSUS. Hold it in your right hand, and raise it at the same time as you raise your right foot. [PENTHEUS *attempts it.*] I am glad you are so—changed in mind.

PENTHEUS. Do you think I could lift up on my shoulders the glens of Cithaeron, with all the women revelling there?

DIONYSUS. You could, if you wished. Before, your mind was diseased; now, it is as it should be.

PENTHEUS. Shall we take crowbars? Or shall I simply set my shoulder, or my arm, against the mountain peaks, and tear them up with my hands?

DIONYSUS. No, you must not destroy the homes of the Nymphs, and the haunts where Pan sits piping.

PENTHEUS. You are right. Women are not to be subdued by brute force. I will hide among the pine-trees.

DIONYSUS. Hide? Yes! You shall find the right hiding-place to hide you—coming like a crafty spy to watch the Maenads!

PENTHEUS. Yes, I can picture them—like birds in the thickets, wrapped in the sweet snare of love.

DIONYSUS. That is the very thing you are going to look for; and perhaps you will catch them—if you are not first caught yourself.

PENTHEUS. Now lead me through the central streets of Thebes. There is no one dares to do this—I am the only *man* among them.

DIONYSUS. You alone suffer for the whole city—you alone; and the struggle that awaits you is your destined ordeal. Come; I will see you safely there; another shall bring you home.

PENTHEUS. You mean my mother?

DIONYSUS. A sight for all to see.

PENTHEUS. It is for that I am going.

DIONYSUS. You will be carried home—

PENTHEUS. What splendour that will be!

DIONYSUS. —in your mother's arms.

PENTHEUS. Why, you make a weakling of me!

DIONYSUS. That is—one way of putting it.

PENTHEUS. Yet it is what I deserve.

[*Exit* PENTHEUS.]

DIONYSUS. Pentheus, you are a man to make men fear; and fearful will be your end—an end that shall raise your fame to the height of heaven. Stretch out your hands, Agauë, and you her sisters, daughters of Cadmus! I am bringing the young man to his battle; and I and Dionysus shall be victors. [*then he adds quietly*] What more shall happen, the event will show.

[*Exit* DIONYSUS.]

ODE IV

CHORUS.

Hounds of Madness, fly to the mountain, fly STROPHE
Where Cadmus' daughters are dancing in ecstasy!
Madden them like a frenzied herd stampeding,
Against the madman hiding in woman's clothes
To spy on the Maenad's rapture!
First his mother shall see him craning his neck
Down from a rounded rock or a withered trunk,
And shout to the Maenads, 'Who is the man, you Bacchae,
Who has come to the mountain, come to the mountain spying
On the swift wild mountain-dances of Cadmus' daughters?
Which of you is his mother?
No, that lad never lay in a woman's womb;
A lioness gave him suck, or a Libyan Gorgon!'

Justice, now be revealed! Now let your sword
Thrust—through and through—to sever the throat
Of the godless, lawless, shameless son of Echion,
Who sprang from the womb of Earth!

See! With contempt of right, with a reckless rage ANTISTROPHE
To combat your and your mother's mysteries, Bacchus,
With maniac fury out he goes, stark mad,
For a trial of strength against *your* invincible arm!
The sober and humble heart
That accords the gods their due without carp or cavil,
And knows that his days are as dust, shall live untouched.
I have no wish to grudge the wise their wisdom;
But the joys *I* seek are greater, outshine all others,
And lead our life to goodness and loveliness:
The joy of the holy heart

That night and day is bent to honour the gods
And disown all custom that breaks the bounds of right.

Justice, now be revealed! Now let your sword
Thrust—through and through—to sever the throat
Of the godless, lawless, shameless son of Echion,
Who sprang from the womb of Earth!

[*Then with growing excitement, shouting in unison, and dancing to the rhythm of their words.*]

EPODE

Come, Dionysus!
Come, and appear to us!
Come like a bull or a
Hundred-headed serpent,
Come like a lion snorting
Flame from your nostrils!
Swoop down, Bacchus, on the
Hunter of the Bacchae;
Smile at him and snare him;
Then let the stampeding
Herd of the Maenads
Throw him and throttle him,
Catch, trip, trample him to death!

SCENE V

[*Enter a* MESSENGER.]

MESSENGER. O house once glorious throughout Hellas, house of the old Sidonian king who sowed in this soil the dragon's earth-born crop! How I weep for you! I am a slave; but a good slave feels the blow that strikes his master.

CHORUS. What has happened? Have you news from the mountains?

MESSENRER. Pentheus, the son of Echion, is dead.

CHORUS. Dionysus, god of rapture! Your power is revealed!

MESSENGER. What? What did you say? Do you even exult at the cruel end that has overtaken my master?

CHORUS. I am no Greek; I sing for joy in a foreign tune. Now I've no need to cower in terror of prison.

MESSENGER. Do you suppose Thebes has no men left to take command?

CHORUS. Dionysus commands *me;* not Thebes, but Dionysus.

MESSENGER. Allowance must be made for you; yet, when irreparable wrong has been done, it is shameful to rejoice.

CHORUS. Tell me what happened; tell me, how did he die—this tyrant pursuing his tyranny?

MESSENGER. When we had left the houses of Thebes behind, and crossed the river Asopus, we began climbing the foothills of Cithaeron, Pentheus and I—I was attending my master—, and that foreigner who was showing us the way to what we were to see.

Well, first we sat down in a grassy glade; we kept our footsteps and our talk as quiet as possible, so as to see without being seen. We were in a valley full of streams, with cliffs on either side; and there, under the close shade of pine-trees, the Maenads were sitting, their hands busy at their happy tasks. Some of them were twining with fresh leaves a thyrsus that had lost its ivy; others, like foals let loose from the painted yokes, were singing holy songs to each other in turn.

But the ill-fated Pentheus did not see these women; and he said, 'From where we are standing, my friend, I cannot clearly make out these pretended worshippers, these Maenads; if I climbed a towering pine-tree on the cliff-side I could have a proper view of their shameful behaviour.'

And then—I saw that foreigner do an amazing thing. He took hold of the topmost skiey branch of a pine and dragged it down, down, down to the dark earth. It was bent in a circle as a bow is bent, as the curve of a wheel, drawn with peg and line, bends the running rim to its own shape; so the foreigner took that mountain-pine in his hands and bent it to the ground—a thing no mortal man could do. Then he set Pentheus on the top branches, and began letting the tree spring upright, slipping it steadily through his grip, and taking care not to unseat him; and the pine-trunk straightened itself and soared into the soaring sky with the King sitting astride; so that he was more plainly visible to the women than they were to him.

1090 **holy songs** The Greek word is *Bacchic* songs. In English this adjective is too often associated with the "profane" drinking of wine, whereas in this play it always has a religious, or at least a ritualistic, meaning. In translation I have been deliberately inconsistent, using both *Bacchic* and *holy* for the sake of keeping both ideas operative. (Translator's note.)

And he was just coming into view on his lofty perch,—the foreigner was nowhere to be seen—when a voice—I suppose it was Dionysus—pealed out from heaven: 'Women! I bring you the man who made a mockery of you, and of me, and of my holy rites. Now punish him.' And in the very moment the voice spoke, a flash of unearthly fire stretched between the sky and the ground.

The whole air fell silent. The wooded glade held every leaf silent. You could hear no cry of any beast. The women had not caught distinctly what the voice said; they stood up and gazed around. Then came a second word of command. As soon as Cadmus' daughters recognized the clear bidding of Bacchus, they darted forward with the speed of doves on the wing, and all the Bacchae after them. Up the valley, along by the stream, over the rocks they went leaping on, possessed with the very breath of the god. When they saw the King sitting in the tree, first they climbed the cliff where it rose up like a battlement, and with all their strength pelted him with pieces of rock, or aimed pine-branches at him like javelins. Some were hurling the thyrsus at their pitiable target; but the shots fell short—the height was too great for all their efforts; while the wretched man sat there trapped and helpless.

At last, with a force like lightning, they tore down branches of oak, and used these as levers, trying to tear out the tree's roots. All their struggles were useless. Then Agauë spoke to them: 'Come, you Maenads, stand round the tree and grip it. We must catch this climbing beast, or he will reveal the secret dances of Dionysus.' A thousand hands grasped the tree; and they tore it from the earth. Then from his high perch plunging and crashing to the ground came Pentheus, with one incessant scream as he understood what end was near.

First his mother, as priestess, began the ritual of death, and fell upon him. He tore off the headband from his hair, that his wretched mother might recognize him and not kill him. 'Mother!' he cried, touching her cheek, 'it is I, your son, Pentheus, whom you bore to Echion. O mother, have mercy on me; I have sinned, but I am your son: do not kill me!'

Agauë was foaming at the mouth, her eyes were rolling wildly. She was not in her right mind; she was under the power of Dionysus; and she would not listen to him. She gripped his right arm between wrist and elbow; she set her foot against his ribs; and she tore his arm off by the shoulder. It was no strength of hers that did it; the god was in her fingers and made it easy. Ino was at him on the other side, tearing at his flesh; and now Autonoe joined them, and the whole pack of raving women. There was a single continuous yell—Pentheus shrieking as long as life was left in him, the women howling in triumph. One of them was carrying an arm, another had a foot with the shoe still on it; the ribs were stripped—clawed clean. Every hand was thick red with blood; and they were tossing and catching, to and fro, like a ball, the flesh of Pentheus.

His body lies scattered, some under hard rocks, some in the deep green woods; it will not be easy to find. His poor head—his mother is holding it; she has fixed it on the point of her thyrsus, and carries it openly over the mountain-side, leaving her sisters dancing with the Maenads. And she is coming here to the palace, exulting in her fearful and horrible prey, shouting to Bacchus as her fellow-hunter, calling him her partner in the kill, her comrade in victory. But Bacchus gives her tears for her reward.

I am going; I want to be far away from this horror before Agauë comes.

The noblest thing a man can have is a humble and quiet heart that reveres the gods. I think that is also the wisest thing for a man to possess, if he will but use it.

[*Exit.*]

ODE V

CHORUS.

Let us dance a dance to Bacchus, shout and sing
For the fall of Pentheus, heir of the dragon's seed,
Who hid his beard in a woman's gown,
And sealed his death with the holy sign
Of ivy wreathing a fennel-reed,
When bull led man to the ritual slaughter-ring.
Frenzied daughters of Cadmus, what renown
Your victory wins you—such a song
As groans must stifle, tears must drown!
Emblem of conquest, brave and fine!—
A mother's hand, defiled
With blood and dripping red

Caresses the torn head
Of her own murdered child!

But look! I see Pentheus' mother, Agauë, running towards the palace, with eyes wildly rolling. Welcome the worshipping company of Dionysus!

ÉXODOS

[AGAUË *appears, frenzied and panting, with* PENTHEUS' *head held in her hand. The rest of her band of devotees, whom the* CHORUS *saw approaching with her, do not enter; but a few are seen standing by the entrance, where they wait until the end of the play.*]

AGAUË. Women of Asia! Worshippers of Bacchus!
[AGAUË *tries to show them* PENTHEUS' *head; they shrink from it.*]
CHORUS. Why do you urge me? Oh!
AGAUË. I am bringing home from the mountains
A vine-branch freshly cut,
For the gods have blessed our hunting.
CHORUS. We see it . . . and welcome you in fellowship.
AGAUË. I caught him without a trap,
A lion-cub, young and wild.
Look, you may see him: there!
CHORUS. Where was it?
AGAUË. On Cithaeron;
The wild and empty mountain—
CHORUS. Cithaeron!
AGAUË. . . . spilt his life-blood.
CHORUS. Who shot him?
AGAUË. I was first;
All the women are singing,
'Honour to great Agauë!'
CHORUS. And then—who next?
AGAUË. Why, Cadmus' . . .
CHORUS. What—Cadmus?
AGAUË. Yes, his daughters—
But after me, after me—
Laid their hands to the kill.

To-day was a splendid hunt!
Come now, join in the feast!

CHORUS. What, wretched woman? *Feast?*

AGAUË [*tenderly stroking the head as she holds it*].
This calf is young: how thickly
The new-grown hair goes crisping
Up to his delicate crest!

CHORUS. Indeed, his long hair makes him
Look like some wild creature.

AGAUË. The god is a skilled hunter;
And he poised his hunting women,
And hurled them at the quarry.

CHORUS. True, our god is a hunter.

AGAUË. Do you praise me?

CHORUS. Yes, we praise you.

AGAUË. So will the sons of Cadmus . . .

CHORUS. And Pentheus too, Agauë?

AGAUË. Yes, he will praise his mother
For the lion-cub she killed.

CHORUS. Oh, fearful!

AGAUË. Ay, fearful!

CHORUS. You are happy?

AGAUË. I am enraptured;
Great in the eyes of the world,
Great are the deeds I've done,
And the hunt that I hunted there!

CHORUS. Then, poor Agauë, show this triumphant spoil of yours that you've carried home—show it to the people of Thebes.

AGAUË. Come, then, all you Thebans who live in this lofty and lovely city, come and see the beast we have caught and killed—we, Cadmus' daughters; caught not with nets or thonged Thessalian javelins, but with our own white arms and fingers. After this, should huntsmen boast, who buy their paltry tools from the armourer? We with our bare hands caught this quarry, then tore it limb from limb.

Where is my father? Let him come here! And my son Pentheus, where is he? Let him get a strong ladder, and take this head, and climb up and nail it to the top of the palace wall, this lion that I hunted and brought home!

[*Enter* CADMUS *with attendants bearing the body of* PENTHEUS.]

CADMUS. Come, men. Bring your sad burden that was Pentheus; bring him to his home. I found the fragments of his body scattered in a thousand places, no two together, about the glens of Cithaeron, or hidden in thick woods; and with weary search I gathered them, and have brought them here.

I had already returned with old Teiresias from the Bacchic dance, and was inside the walls of the city, when news was brought me of my daughters' terrible deed. I turned straight back to the mountain; and here I bring my son, killed by the Maenads. I saw Autonoe, who bore Actaeon to Aristaeus, and her sister Ino, there among the copses, still in their unhappy frenzy; but I understand that Agauë came raving towards the palace—it is true, there she is! Oh, what a terrible sight!

AGAUË. Father! You may boast as loudly as you will, that no man living is so blest in his daughters; I mean all three, but myself especially. I have left weaving at the loom for greater things—for hunting wild beasts with my bare hands. See here what I carry in my arms; this is the prize I won; I have brought it to hang on your palace wall. Take it, Father; hold it. Be proud of my hunting, and call your friends to a banquet; let them all envy and congratulate you, for the splendour of my deed.

CADMUS. O anguish unmeasured, intolerable! O pitiful hands—your splendid deed is murder! What victim is this you would lay at the gods' feet, calling Thebes, and me, to a banquet? Your suffering is worst, but mine is next. Dionysus, god of joy, has been just, but too cruel. He was born of my blood, and he has destroyed my house.

AGAUË. How ill-humoured old age makes a man! How he scowls at me! I wish that my son were a great hunter, like his mother, pursuing wild beasts with all the young men of Thebes; but he can only fight against gods. Father, you must reason with him. Let someone call him here before me, to see my good fortune.

CADMUS. Oh, my daughters! If you come to understand what you have done, how terrible your suffering will be! But if you remain always as you are now, though you could not be called happy, at least you will not know your own misery.

AGAUË. Misery? What is wrong? Where is my cause for misery?

CADMUS. First, turn your eyes this way—look at the sky.

AGAUË. I am looking. Why do you tell me to look at it?

CADMUS. Is it still the same, or does it seem to you to have changed?

AGAUË. It is brighter than before—more luminous.

CADMUS. And this madness you suffered from—is it still with you?

AGAUË. I do not know what you mean. But I feel a change in my mind; my thoughts are somehow clearer.

CADMUS. Can you now hear and answer clearly?

AGAUË. Yes . . . I have forgotten what we said just now, Father.

CADMUS. When you were married, whose house did you come to?

AGAUË. You gave me to Echion, who was said to have been sown in the ground.

CADMUS. Then, Echion had a son born to him—who was he?

AGAUË. Pentheus—my son and his father's.

CADMUS. Yes: and whose head is that you hold in your arms?

AGAUË. A lion's—or so the women said who hunted it.

CADMUS. Now look straight at it; it is not much trouble to look.

[AGAUË *looks at the head in silence; then cries out.*]

AGAUË. Oh! What am I looking at? What am I holding?

CADMUS. Look at it steadily, and understand more clearly.

AGAUË. I see—O gods, what horror! What torture!

CADMUS. Does this seem to you like a lion?

AGAUË. No, it is Pentheus' head I hold in my accursed hand.

CADMUS. Tears have been shed for him already—before you knew it was he.

AGAUË. Who killed him? How did he come into my hands?

CADMUS. O bitter truth, revealed in a cruel hour!

AGAUË. Tell me—my heart is bursting—I must know the rest.

CADMUS. You killed him—you and your sisters.

AGAUË. Where was it done? At home? Or where else?

CADMUS. Where Actaeon was torn by hounds.

AGAUË. Cithaeron? What evil fate brought Pentheus there?

CADMUS. He went in scorn of Dionysus and your frenzied worship.

AGAUË. But how was it we were all there?

CADMUS. You were mad; the whole city was possessed by Dionysus.

AGAUË. Now I understand: Dionysus has destroyed us.

CADMUS. He was insulted and abused. You did not acknowledge his godhead.

AGAUË. Where is the dear body of my son, Father?

CADMUS. It is here. I searched long for it, and brought it.

AGAUË. Is it decently composed, limb to limb?

CADMUS. Not yet; we came here as quickly as possible.

AGAUË. I will do it myself, if I may be allowed to touch him.

CADMUS. You will be allowed; your guilt is not greater than his.

AGAUË. But what part had Pentheus in my madness?

CADMUS. He was like you in not reverencing Dionysus. Therefore the god has joined all in one destruction, you and your sisters, and Pentheus, to strike down my house and me. I have no son; and now I see the child of your womb, my unhappy daughter, cut off by a shameful and horrible death. Pentheus, dear boy, my daughter's child, this house looked to you as its head; you were its bond of strength; and Thebes feared you. No man would slight your old grandfather if he saw you near; you would give him his deserts. Now I, Cadmus the Great, who sowed in the ground the seed of the Theban race, and reaped a glorious harvest, shall live, a dishonoured exile, far from my home.

O dearest son—yes, even in death you shall be held most dear to me—never again will you touch my beard, and call me Grandfather, and put your arm round me and say, 'Who has wronged you, or insulted you? Who is unkind to you or vexes you? Tell me, Grandfather, that I may punish him.' . . . Never again. Now there is only misery for me, suffering for you, tears for your mother, torment for all our family.

If there be any man who derides the unseen world, let him consider the death of Pentheus, and acknowledge the gods.

CHORUS. Cadmus, I grieve for you. Your grandson suffered justly, but you most cruelly.

AGAUË. [Father, you see how one terrible hour has shattered my whole life, and turned my pride to shame; my happiness to horror. Now I long only to compose my son's body for burial, and lament for him; and then to go away and die. But I do not know if this is lawful; my hands are filthy with a pollution of their own making. When I have spilt the blood that is my own, torn the flesh that grew in my own womb, how can I, without offence to the gods, clasp him to my breast, or chant his ritual dirge? Yet I beg you, if

1364 **Father, you see** This long bracketed passage is a conjectural reconstruction of missing lines.

you think it not blasphemous, let me touch my son, and say farewell to that dear body which I loved, and destroyed unknowing. It is right that you should pity, for you suffer too, although you have not sinned.

CADMUS. My daughter, you and I and our whole house are crushed and broken by the anger of Dionysus. It is not for me to keep you from your son. Only I would warn you to steel your heart against a sight that must be fearful to any eyes, but most of all to a mother's. [*to his attendants*] Lay your burden here before her, and remove the covering, that Agauë may see her son.

[*The coffin is laid on the ground before* AGAUË, *who kneels beside it.*]

AGAUË. O dearest child, how unnatural are these tears, that should have fallen from your eyes upon my dead face. Now I shall die with none to weep for me. I am justly punished; for in pride I blasphemed the god Dionysus, and did not understand the things I ought to have understood. You too are punished for the same sin; and I cannot tell whether your fate or mine is the more terrible. But since you have suffered with me, you will forgive me both for what I did, not knowing what I did, and for what I do now, touching you with unholy hands—at once your cruellest enemy and your dearest lover.

Now I place your limbs as they should lie; I kiss the flesh that my own body fed, my own care reared to manhood. Come, Father, help me; lay his poor head here; as far as we can, make all exact and seemly.

O dearest face, O young fresh cheek; O kingly eyes, your light now darkened! O my son! See, with this veil I now cover your head, your torn and bloodstained limbs.

Now take him up and carry him to burial—a king lured to a shameful death by the anger of a god.

[DIONYSUS *appears above the wall of the palace.*]

CHORUS. But look! what is this? It is he, our lord Dionysus himself, no longer disguised as mortal, but in the glory of his godhead!

DIONYSUS. Behold me, a god great and powerful, Dionysus, immortal son of Zeus and Semele!

I come to the City of Seven Gates, to Thebes, whose men and women mocked me, denied my divinity, and refused to receive my holy rites. Now they see clearly the result of impious folly. The royal house is overthrown; the city's streets are full of guilty fear, as every Theban repents too late for his blindness and blasphemy. First and chief in sin was this man Pentheus, who not only rejected my just claims, but put me in fetters and insulted me. Therefore death came to him in the most shameful way of all, at the hands of his own mother. This fate he has justly suffered; for no god can see his worship scorned, and hear his name profaned, and not pursue vengeance to the utmost limit; that mortal men may know that the gods are greater than they.

Now listen further, while I reveal what is destined for the people of Thebes. The day will come when they will be driven from their city to wander East and West over the earth; for Zeus will not suffer a godless city to remain.

Agauë and her sisters must leave Thebes this very day; their exile will prove a full and just penance for the foul pollution they have incurred in this bloodshed. Never again shall they see their native land; for it is an offence to piety that hands so defiled should remain to take part in the city's sacrifices.

Now, Cadmus, I will tell you what suffering you yourself are destined to fulfill.] You shall change your form to a serpent; and your wife Harmonia, whom you, though mortal, received from her divine father Ares, shall likewise change to a beast of the earth, and become a snake. Thus says the oracle of Zeus: You, at the head of a barbaric army, shall with your wife drive a pair of oxen yoked to a wagon; with your innumerable host you shall destroy many cities; but when they plunder the temple of Apollo's oracle, their reward shall be sorrow at their home-coming. But you yourself and Harmonia shall be saved by Ares, who shall bestow on you immortal life among the blessed ones.

I, who tell you this, am Dionysus, son of no mortal father, but of Zeus. If you all had chosen wisdom, when you would not, you would have found the son of Zeus your friend, and you would now be happy.

CADMUS. Dionysus, have mercy on us; we have sinned.

DIONYSUS. You recognize me too late; when you should have known me, you did not.

CADMUS. All this we have realized; but your vengeance is too heavy.

DIONYSUS. I am a god; and you insulted me.

CADMUS. Gods should not be like men, keeping anger for ever.

DIONYSUS. Zeus my father ordained this from the beginning.

AGAUË. All hope is gone, Father. Our sentence is passed: we are exiles.

DIONYSUS. Why then put off what is inevitable?

[*Exit* DIONYSUS.]

CADMUS. O my daughter, what utter misery and horror has overtaken us all—you, and your sisters, and me your unhappy father. In my old age I must leave my home and travel to strange lands. Further than that, it is foretold that I shall lead a mixed barbarian horde against Hellas. Both I and my wife, Harmonia, child of Ares, must take the brute form of serpents, and thus I am to lead her, at the head of an armed force, to desecrate the altars and tombs of the Hellenes. And I am to find no respite from suffering; I may not even cross the deep-flowing stream of Acheron to find peace in death.

AGAUË. And I shall live in exile, separated from you, Father.

CADMUS. Poor child! Why do you throw your arms round me, cherishing my white hair as a swan cares for its old and helpless ones?

AGAUË. Where am I to turn, driven from my home and country?

CADMUS. I do not know, child; your father is little help to you.

AGAUË.

Farewell, my home; farewell the land I know.
Exiled, accursed and wretched, now I go
Forth from this door where first I came a bride.

CADMUS.

Go, daughter; find some secret place to hide
Your shame and sorrow.

AGAUË. Father, I weep for you.

CADMUS. I for your suffering, and your sisters' too.

AGAUË.

There is strange tyranny in the god who sent
Against your house this cruel punishment.

CADMUS.

Not strange: our citizens despised his claim,
And you, and they, put him to open shame.

AGAUË. Father, farewell.

CADMUS. Poor child! I cannot tell
How you can *fare well;* yet I say, Farewell.

AGAUË.

I go to lead my sisters by the hand
To share my wretchedness in a foreign land.

[*She turns to the Theban women who have been waiting at the edge of the stage.*]

Come, see me forth.
Gods, lead me to some place
Where loath'd Cithaeron may not see my face,
Nor I Cithaeron. I have had my fill
Of mountain-ecstasy; now take who will
My holy ivy-wreath, my thyrsus-rod,
All that reminds me how I served this god!

[*Exit, followed by* CADMUS.]

CHORUS.

Gods manifest themselves in many forms,
Bring many matters to surprising ends;
The things we thought would happen do not happen;
The unexpected God makes possible:
And that is what has happened here to-day.

[*Exeunt.*]

BEN JONSON
1573?–1637

VOLPONE, OR THE FOX
1606

THE THEATER-GOER who saw Ben Jonson's new comedy of *Volpone, or the Fox* for the first time may well have been reminded of Shakespeare's recent tragedy, *Othello, the Moor of Venice*. Both plays are set against the background of a city noted alike for its magnificence and its vice. Both present characters of "rare ingenious knavery" (Shakespeare's Iago resembling both Volpone and Mosca). And both exhibit the dramatic inventiveness and varied eloquence of the finest Elizabethan drama. At the center of Jonson's satiric comedy, however, there stands not an heroic Othello but Volpone, a genius in crime, incapable of either generosity or self-knowledge. His fall reveals not the mystery of the human lot but the tendency of vice to overreach itself.

Although the satire is ultimately moral, its immediate perspective is largely social and legal. It traces the features of vice under the masks of respectability, exposing the manipulations of the hypocrites without altogether excusing the imperceptiveness of their victims. Against scoundrels cloaked in propriety and skilled in legal dodging, the mainly passive virtuous characters are practically defenseless. Even the good-natured guardians of the law are dull-witted, and the true innocents, Bonario and Celia, finally get free only because the knaves ensnare themselves in their own subtleties. The laws of the state are vindicated, but only at long last and in tones of slightly hollow self-congratulation.

Despite its consistently satiric purpose, *Volpone* at first appears bewilderingly diverse. A seemingly irrelevant academic skit is enacted by a dwarf, a eunuch, and an hermaphrodite. Disguised as a mountebank, Volpone makes a long-winded spiel aimed as much at burlesquing itinerant quacks as at advancing his designs on Celia. The English travelers play out an almost independent farce of their own. And in the unraveling of the main plot Jonson risks anticlimax by launching, as late as the fifth act, a brilliant new series of complications. Such fertility of dramatic device may well leave an impression of rich disorder.

The play is rich but it is not disordered. Volpone, flanked by the indefatigable Mosca, draws all events and characters into his orbit. Around him circle the lesser predators—a "Vulture," a "Raven," a "Crow"—impelled by avarice and dragging in their train others less guilty, merely foolish, or altogether innocent. Even Sir Politic Would-be, with his little schemes for getting rich, his pretentious misinformation, and his empty suspicions, is in some ways a parody of Volpone and has an equally appropriate come-uppance.

Beyond these adroit elaborations of plot and character a principle of thematic integration is at work. From Volpone's first speech, in idolatry of gold, to the final plain-spoken summary of the magistrate, Jonson tirelessly explores the idea of hypocrisy as the mask of lust and of lust as perversion of human nature. Lust in the guise of avarice is thematically developed in references to possessions, possessing, and—at length—to being possessed. That lust is perverse and deceptive is expressed by emphasis on tricks and transformations. The themes interlace. Volpone's lust for gold fires his imagination to feats of deception and rhetoric beyond the reach of his victims. Mosca, touched with the same fire, caters to Volpone's lust for Celia, which in turn leads him to impersonate a mountebank, the very emblem of greed and falsehood. Lust for Volpone's possessions makes a husband eager to prostitute his wife and a father to disown his son. In the oddly relevant academic skit the deformed and mutilated servants of Volpone's household make sport of greed, hypocrisy, and perversion to gratify their master's taste.

Throughout the play the figures of speech and the historical and classical allusions embroider these themes of possession and transformation. They concur most explicitly in Volpone's attempt to transform Celia, the object of his lust, into a prize possession. That is the turning point of his fortunes. Thereafter his brilliance decays as he becomes more and more visibly what he is. In the last three scenes of the play the word *possession,* echoed by almost every character, attains a culminating definition: *possessed by demons.*

The final transformations reveal the truth. Volpone's last stratagem is to remove his last disguise and to pull all the hypocrites down in his own ruin. Virtue is barely saved as the virtuosity of Ben Jonson triumphs.

VOLPONE, OR THE FOX : *JONSON*

TO THE MOST NOBLE AND MOST EQUAL SISTERS, THE TWO FAMOUS UNIVERSITIES, FOR THEIR LOVE AND ACCEPTANCE SHOWN TO HIS POEM IN THE PRESENTATION, BEN JONSON, THE GRATEFUL ACKNOWLEDGER, DEDICATES BOTH IT AND HIMSELF.

Characters

VOLPONE	*a magnifico*
MOSCA	*his parasite*
VOLTORE	*an advocate*
CORBACCIO	*an old gentleman*
CORVINO	*a merchant*
BONARIO	*a young gentleman*
POLITIC WOULD-BE	*a knight*
PEREGRINE	*a gentleman traveler*
NANO	*a dwarf*
CASTRONE	*a eunuch*
ANDROGYNO	*an hermaphrodite*
GREGE	*mob*
COMMANDADORI	*officers*
MERCATORI	*three merchants*
AVOCATORI	*four magistrates*
NOTARIO	*the register*
SERVITORE	*a servant*
MADAM WOULD-BE	*the knight's wife*
CELIA	*Corvino's wife*
WOMEN	

SCENE. *Venice.*

Characters: **Mosca** the fly **Voltore** the vulture **Corbaccio** the raven **Corvino** the crow **Bonario** the well-favored man **Politic Would-be** the professed man of the world **Celia the heavenly** one

THE ARGUMENT

V OLPONE, childless, rich, feigns sick, despairs,
O ffers his state to hopes of several heirs,
L ies languishing; his parasite receives
P resents of all, assures, deludes; then weaves
O ther cross plots, which ope themselves, are told.
N ew tricks for safety are sought; they thrive: when, bold,
E ach tempts th' other again, and all are sold.

ACT I

SCENE I. *A room in Volpone's house.*

[*Enter* VOLPONE *and* MOSCA.]

VOLPONE. Good morning to the day; and next, my gold.
Open the shrine, that I may see my saint.—
Hail the world's soul, and mine. More glad than is
The teeming earth to see the long'd-for sun
Peep through the horns of the celestial Ram,
Am I, to view thy splendor darkening his;
That, lying here, amongst my other hoards,
Show'st like a flame by night, or like the day
Struck out of chaos, when all darkness fled
Unto the center. O thou son of Sol,
But brighter than thy father, let me kiss,

ARGUMENT: **sold** defrauded
8 **Ram** zodiacal sign, Aries, which the sun enters in late March
11–13 **day . . . center** the first day of the Creation, when darkness fled to the center of the earth. In this speech Volpone also alludes to the Golden Age (**that age**), the golden goddess (**Venus**), the adage that Silence is Golden (**the dumb god**), and the old belief that gold ore was imprisoned sunlight and was plentiful in the soil of hell.

With adoration, thee, and every relic
Of sacred treasure in this blessed room.
Well did wise poets, by thy glorious name,
Title that age which they would have the best;
Thou being the best of things, and far transcending
All style of joy, in children, parents, friends,
Or any other waking dream on earth.
Thy looks when they to Venus did ascribe,
They should have giv'n her twenty thousand Cupids;
Such are thy beauties and our loves! Dear saint,
Riches, the dumb god, that giv'st all men tongues,
That canst do nought, and yet mak'st men do all things;
The price of souls; even hell, with thee to boot,
Is made worth Heaven. Thou art virtue, fame,
Honor, and all things else! Who can get thee,
He shall be noble, valiant, honest, wise—

MOSCA. And what he will, sir. Riches are in fortune
A greater good than wisdom is in nature.

VOLPONE. True, my beloved Mosca. Yet I glory
More in the cunning purchase of my wealth
Than in the glad possession, since I gain
No common way; I use no trade, no venture;
I wound no earth with ploughshares, fat no beasts
To feed the shambles; have no mills for iron,
Oil, corn, or men, to grind 'em into powder;
I blow no subtle glass, expose no ships
To threat'nings of the furrow-faced sea;
I turn no monies in the public bank,
No usure private—

MOSCA. No, sir, nor devour
Soft prodigals. You shall ha' some will swallow
A melting heir as glibly as your Dutch
Will pills of butter, and ne'er purge for 't;
Tear forth the fathers of poor families
Out of their beds, and coffin them alive

34 **purchase** acquisition
40 **subtle glass** fine Venetian glassware
43 **usure** usury

In some kind clasping prison, where their bones
May be forthcoming, when the flesh is rotten.
But your sweet nature doth abhor these courses;
You loathe the widow's or the orphan's tears
Should wash your pavements, or their piteous cries
Ring in your roofs, and beat the air for vengeance.

VOLPONE. Right, Mosca; I do loathe it.—

MOSCA. And, besides, sir,
You are not like the thresher that doth stand
With a huge flail, watching a heap of corn,
And, hungry, dares not taste the smallest grain,
But feeds on mallows, and such bitter herbs;
Nor like the merchant, who hath fill'd his vaults
With Romagnía, rich and Candian wines,
Yet drinks the lees of Lombard's vinegar.
You will not lie in straw, whilst moths and worms
Feed on your sumptuous hangings and soft beds.
You know the use of riches, and dare give now
From that bright heap, to me, your poor observer,
Or to your dwarf, or your hermaphrodite,
Your eunuch, or what other household trifle
Your pleasure allows maintenance.—

VOLPONES. Hold thee, Mosca;
Take of my hand; thou strik'st on truth in all,
And they are envious term thee parasite.
Call forth my dwarf, my eunuch, and my fool,
And let 'em make me sport. [*Exit* MOSCA.]
What should I do,
But cocker up my genius, and live free
To all delights my fortune calls me to?
I have no wife, no parent, child, ally,
To give my substance to; but whom I make
Must be my heir; and this makes men observe me.
This draws new clients daily to my house,

68 **observer** servant
74 **they** those who
78 **cocker up** indulge
82 **observe** be attentive to

Women and men of every sex and age,
That bring me presents, send me plate, coin, jewels,
With hope that when I die (which they expect
Each greedy minute) it shall then return
Tenfold upon them; whilst some, covetous
Above the rest, seek to engross me whole,
And counter work the one unto the other,
Contend in gifts, as they would seem in love;
All which I suffer, playing with their hopes,
And am content to coin 'em into profit,
And look upon their kindness, and take more,
And look on that; still bearing them in hand,
Letting the cherry knock against their lips,
And draw it by their mouths, and back again.—
How now!

SCENE II

[*Enter* MOSCA *with* NANO, ANDROGYNO, *and* CASTRONE.]

NANO. Now, room for fresh gamesters, who do will you to know
They do bring you neither play nor university show,
And therefore do entreat you that whatsoever they rehearse
May not fare a whit the worse for the false pace of the verse.
If you wonder at this, you will wonder more ere we pass;
For know, here is enclos'd the soul of Pythagoras,
That juggler divine, as hereafter shall follow,
Which soul, fast and loose, sir, came first from Apollo,
And was breath'd into Aethalides, Mercurius his son,
Where it had the gift to remember all that ever was done.

8 **here** in Androgyno, the "man-woman." This scene, in the style of an academic skit, refers especially to Lucian's dialogue between a cobbler who longs for riches and a cock who embodies the soul of the Greek philosopher, Pythagoras. The soul recounts its transmigrations through the lives of men and women famous for the pursuit of wealth (e.g., **Aethalides,** herald of the Argonauts who found the Golden Fleece; **Aspasia,** the noted courtesan, mistress of Pericles) and of philosophers who, it is implied, prostituted their talents. By alluding to the Pythagorean Brotherhood, a mystic society that strictly forbade the eating of flesh and beans and employed an esoteric symbolism of numbers, Jonson also satirizes some of the religious extremists of his time.

From thence it fled forth, and made quick transmigration
To goldy-lock'd Euphorbus, who was kill'd, in good fashion,
At the siege of old Troy, by the cuckold of Sparta.
Hermotimus was next (I find it in my charta);
To whom it did pass, where no sooner it was missing,
But with one Pyrrhus of Delos it learn'd to go a-fishing;
And thence did it enter the sophist of Greece.
From Pythagore, she went into a beautiful piece,
Hight Aspasia, the meretrix; and the next toss of her
Was again of a whore—she became a philosopher,
Crates the cynic, as itself doth relate it.
Since, kings, knights, and beggars, knaves, lords, and fools gat it,
Besides ox and ass, camel, mule, goat, and brock,
In all which it hath spoke, as in the cobbler's cock.
But I come not here to discourse of that matter,
Or his one, two, or three, or his great oath, "By QUATER!"
His musics, his trigon, his golden thigh,
Or his telling how elements shift; but I
Would ask, how of late thou hast suffered translation,
And shifted thy coat in these days of reformation.

ANDROGYNO. Like one of the reformed, a fool, as you see,
Counting all old doctrine heresy.

NANO. But not on thine own forbid meats hast thou ventur'd?

ANDROGYNO. On fish, when first a Carthusian I enter'd.

NANO. Why, then thy dogmatical silence hath left thee?

ANDROGYNO. Of that an obstreperous lawyer bereft me.

NANO. O wonderful change! When sir lawyer forsook thee,
For Pythagore's sake, what body then took thee?

ANDROGYNO. A good dull mule.

NANO. And how! by that means
Thou wert brought to allow of the eating of beans?

ANDROGYNO. Yes.

28–29 **Or his . . . thigh** or of Pythagorean practices and traditions: the number-symbolism; the oath **By Quater!** on the "triangle of four"; the abstruse theory of musical intervals; the symbolic triangular harp (**trigon**); and the legend that the thigh of Pythagoras was all of gold

33 **reformed** extreme Protestants

37 **silence** vowed by Pythagoreans as well as, later, by Carthusians, who were members of a rigorous monastic order

NANO. But from the mule into whom didst thou pass?
ANDROGYNO. Into a very strange beast, by some writers call'd an ass;
By others a precise, pure, illuminate brother
Of those devour flesh—and sometimes one another;
And will drop you forth a libel, or a sanctifi'd lie,
Betwixt every spoonful of a nativity-pie.
NANO. Now quit thee, 'fore Heaven, of that profane nation;
And gently report thy next transmigration.
ANDROGYNO. To the same that I am.
NANO. A creature of delight,
And, what is more than a fool, an hermaphrodite!
Now, pray thee, sweet soul, in all thy variation,
Which body wouldst thou choose to take up thy station?
ANDROGYNO. Troth, this I am in; even here would I tarry.
NANO. 'Cause here the delight of each sex thou canst vary?
ANDROGYNO. Alas, those pleasures be stale and forsaken;
No, 'tis your fool wherewith I am so taken,
The only one creature that I can call blessed;
For all other forms I have prov'd most distressed.
NANO. Spoke true, as thou wert in Pythagoras still.
This learned opinion we celebrate will,
Fellow eunuch, as behoves us, with all our wit and art,
To dignify that whereof ourselves are so great and special a part.
VOLPONE. Now, very, very pretty. Mosca, this
Was thy invention?
MOSCA. If it please my patron,
Not else.
VOLPONE. It doth, good Mosca.
MOSCA. Then it was, sir.
[*Sings.*]
Fools they are the only nation
Worth men's envy or admiration;

47 **precise . . . brother** hair-splitting, self-righteous Puritan who claims to be divinely enlightened

50 **nativity-pie** Christmas pie (another dig at the "precise" Puritan who shrank from saying "Christmas" to avoid the "Popish" reference to "Christ's Mass")

55 **fool** jester, not necessarily a simpleton

Free from care or sorrow taking,
Selves and others merry making:
All they speak or do is sterling.
Your fool he is your great man's dearling,
And your ladies' sport and pleasure;
Tongue and bauble are his treasure.
E'en his face begetteth laughter,
And he speaks truth free from slaughter;
He's the grace of every feast,
And sometimes the chiefest guest;
Hath his trencher and his stool,
When wit waits upon the fool.
O, who would not be
He, he, he?

[*One knocks without.*]

VOLPONE. Who's that? Away! Look, Mosca.

MOSCA. Fool, begone!

[*Exeunt* NANO, CASTRONE, *and* ANDROGYNO.]

'Tis Signior Voltore, the advocate;
I know him by his knock.

VOLPONE. Fetch me my gown,
My furs, and nightcaps; say my couch is changing,
And let him entertain himself awhile
Without, i' th' gallery. [*Exit* MOSCA.] Now, now my clients
Begin their visitation! Vulture, kite,
Raven, and gorcrow, all my birds of prey,
That think me turning carcass, now they come;
I am not for 'em yet.

[*Re-enter* MOSCA, *with the gown, etc.*]

How now! the news?

MOSCA. A piece of plate, sir.

VOLPONE. Of what bigness?

MOSCA. Huge,
Massy, and antique with your name inscrib'd,
And arms engraven.

VOLPONE. Good! and not a fox

84 **slaughter** punishment
107 **plate** dish of gold or silver

Stretch'd on the earth, with fine delusive sleights,
Mocking a gaping crow? ha, Mosca?
MOSCA. Sharp, sir.
VOLPONE. Give me my furs.—Why dost thou laugh so, man?
MOSCA. I cannot choose, sir, when I apprehend
What thoughts he has without now, as he walks:
That this might be the last gift he should give,
That this would fetch you; if you died today,
And gave him all, what he should be tomorrow;
What large return would come of all his ventures;
How he should worshipp'd be, and reverenc'd;
Ride with his furs and footcloths, waited on
By herds of fools and clients; have clear way
Made for his mule, as letter'd as himself;
Be call'd the great and learned advocate!
And then concludes there's nought impossible.
VOLPONE. Yes, to be learned, Mosca.
MOSCA. O, no! rich
Implies it. Hood an ass with reverend purple,
So you can hide his two ambitious ears,
And he shall pass for a cathedral doctor.
VOLPONE. My caps, my caps, good Mosca. Fetch him in.
MOSCA. Stay, sir; your ointment for your eyes.
VOLPONE. That's true;
Dispatch, dispatch; I long to have possession
Of my new present.
MOSCA. That, and thousands more,
I hope to see you lord of.
VOLPONE. Thanks, kind Mosca.
MOSCA. And that, when I am lost in blended dust,
And hundred such as I am, in succession—
VOLPONE. Nay, that were too much, Mosca.
MOSCA. You shall live
Still to delude these harpies.
VOLPONE. Loving Mosca!

120 **fetch you** persuade you to make him your heir
124 **footcloths** decorative trappings of a horse
133 **cathedral doctor** university professor

'Tis well; my pillow now, and let him enter. [*Exit* MOSCA.]
Now, my feign'd cough, my phthisic, and my gout,
My apoplexy, palsy, and catarrhs,
Help, with your forced functions this my posture,
Wherein, this three year, I have milk'd their hopes.
He comes; I hear him— Uh, uh, uh, uh!—Oh!

SCENE III

[*Enter* MOSCA *with* VOLTORE.]

MOSCA. You still are what you were, sir. Only you,
Of all the rest, are he commands his love,
And you do wisely to preserve it thus,
With early visitation and kind notes
Of your good meaning to him, which, I know,
Cannot but come most grateful. Patron! sir!
Here's Signior Voltore is come—
VOLPONE. What say you?
MOSCA. Sir, Signior Voltore is come this morning
To visit you.
VOLPONE. I thank him.
MOSCA. And hath brought
A piece of antique plate, bought of St. Mark,
With which he here presents you.
VOLPONE. He is welcome.
Pray him to come more often.
MOSCA. Yes.
VOLTORE. What says he?
MOSCA. He thanks you, and desires you see him often.
VOLPONE. Mosca.
MOSCA. My patron!
VOLPONE. Bring him near. Where is he?
I long to feel his hand.
MOSCA. The plate is here, sir.
VOLTORE. How fare you, sir?

15 **Help . . . posture** help with your simulated actions this my (im)posture

15 **St. Mark** St. Mark's Square

VOLPONE. I thank you, Signior Voltore.
Where is the plate? mine eyes are bad.
VOLTORE. I'm sorry
To see you still thus weak.
MOSCA [*aside*]. That he is not weaker.
VOLPONE. You are too munificent.
VOLTORE. No, sir; would to Heaven
I could as well give health to you, as that plate.
VOLPONE. You give, sir, what you can. I thank you. Your love
Hath taste in this, and shall not be unanswer'd.
I pray you see me often.
VOLTORE. Yes, I shall, sir.
VOLPONE. Be not far from me.
MOSCA. Do you observe that, sir?
VOLPONE. Hearken unto me still; it will concern you.
MOSCA. You are a happy man, sir; know your good.
VOLPONE. I cannot now last long—
MOSCA [*aside*]. You are his heir, sir.
VOLTORE [*aside*]. Am I?
VOLPONE. I feel me going—uh, uh, uh, uh!—
I'm sailing to my port—uh, uh, uh, uh!—
And I am glad I am so near my haven.
MOSCA. Alas, kind gentleman; well, we must all go—
VOLTORE. But, Mosca—
MOSCA. Age will conquer.
VOLTORE. 'Pray thee, hear me.
Am I inscrib'd his heir, for certain?
MOSCA. Are you!
I do beseech you, sir, you will vouchsafe
To write me i' your family. All my hopes
Depend upon your Worship. I am lost
Except the rising sun do shine on me.
VOLTORE. It shall both shine, and warm thee, Mosca.
MOSCA. Sir,
I am a man that hath not done your love
All the worst offices: here I wear your keys,

57 **write . . . family** regard me as a servant of your household

See all your coffers and your caskets lock'd,
Keep the poor inventory of your jewels,
Your plate, and monies; am your steward, sir,
Husband your goods here.

VOLTORE. But am I sole heir?

MOSCA. Without a partner, sir; confirm'd this morning;
The wax is warm yet, and the ink scarce dry
Upon the parchment.

VOLTORE. Happy, happy me!
By what good chance, sweet Mosca?

MOSCA. Your desert, sir;
I know no second cause.

VOLTORE. Thy modesty
Is loth to know it; well, we shall requite it.

MOSCA. He ever lik'd your course, sir; that first took him.
I oft have heard him say how he admir'd
Men of your large profession, that could speak
To every cause, and things mere contraries,
Till they were hoarse again, yet all be law;
That, with most quick agility, could turn,
And return; make knots, and undo them;
Give forked counsel; take provoking gold
On either hand, and put it up; these men,
He knew, would thrive with their humility.
And, for his part, he thought he should be blest
To have his heir of such a suffering spirit,
So wise, so grave, of so perplex'd a tongue,
And loud withal, that would not wag, nor scarce
Lie still, without a fee; when every word
Your Worship but lets fall, is a *cecchine!*
[*Another knocks.*]
Who's that? One knocks; I would not have you seen, sir.
And yet—pretend you came and went in haste;

85 **provoking gold** a legal fee
86 **put it up** pocket it
89 **suffering** tolerant
90 **so . . . tongue** such devious utterance
93 **cecchine** gold coin

I'll fashion an excuse. And, gentle sir,
When you do come to swim in golden lard,
Up to the arms in honey, that your chin
Is borne up stiff with fatness of the flood,
Think on your vassal; but remember me:
I ha' not been your worst of clients.

VOLTORE. Mosca—

MOSCA. When will you have your inventory brought, sir?
Or see a copy of the will?—Anon.—
I'll bring 'em to you, sir. Away, begone,
Put business i' your face. [*Exit* VOLTORE.]

VOLPONE. Excellent Mosca!
Come hither, let me kiss thee.

MOSCA. Keep you still, sir.
Here is Corbaccio.

VOLPONE. Set the plate away.
The vulture's gone, and the old raven's come.

SCENE IV

[MOSCA *and* VOLPONE *remain.*]

MOSCA. Betake you to your silence, and your sleep.—
[*to the plate*] Stand there and multiply.—[*aside*] Now shall we see
A wretch who is indeed more impotent
Than this can feign to be; yet hopes to hop
Over his grave.—
[*He admits* CORBACCIO.]
Signior Corbaccio!
You're very welcome, sir.

CORBACCIO. How does your patron?

MOSCA. Troth, as he did, sir; no amends.

CORBACCIO. What? mends he?

MOSCA. No, sir: he is rather worse.

CORBACCIO. That's well. Where is he?

4 **impotent** infirm

MOSCA. Upon his couch, sir, newly fall'n asleep.
CORBACCIO. Does he sleep well?
MOSCA. No wink, sir, all this night,
Nor yesterday; but slumbers.
CORBACCIO. Good! he should take
Some counsel of physicians. I have brought him
An opiate here, from mine own doctor—
MOSCA. He will not hear of drugs.
CORBACCIO. Why? I myself
Stood by while 'twas made, saw all th' ingredients,
And know it cannot but most gently work.
My life for his, 'tis but to make him sleep.
VOLPONE [*aside*]. Ay, his last sleep, if he would take it.
MOSCA. Sir,
He has no faith in physic.
CORBACCIO. Say you? say you?
MOSCA. He has no faith in physic; he does think
Most of your doctors are the greater danger,
And worse disease, t' escape. I often have
Heard him protest that your physician
Should never be his heir.
CORBACCIO. Not I his heir?
MOSCA. Not your physician, sir.
CORBACCIO. O, no, no, no;
I do not mean it.
MOSCA. No, sir, nor their fees
He cannot brook; he says they flay a man
Before they kill him.
CORBACCIO. Right, I do conceive you.
MOSCA. And then they do it by experiment;
For which the law not only doth absolve 'em,
But gives them great reward; and he is loth
To hire his death so.
CORBACCIO. It is true, they kill
With as much license as a judge.
MOSCA. Nay, more;

20 **slumbers** dozes
34 **your** the

For he but kills, sir, where the law condemns,
And these can kill him too.

CORBACCIO. Ay, or me,
Or any man. How does his apoplex?
Is that strong on him still?

MOSCA. Most violent.
His speech is broken, and his eyes are set,
His face drawn longer than 'twas wont—

CORBACCIO. How? how?
Stronger than he was wont?

MOSCA. No, sir; his face
Drawn longer than 'twas wont.

CORBACCIO. O good.

MOSCA. His mouth
Is ever gaping, and his eyelids hang.

CORBACCIO. Good.

MOSCA. A freezing numbness stiffens all his joints,
And makes the color of his flesh like lead.

CORBACCIO. 'Tis good.

MOSCA. His pulse beats slow, and dull.

CORBACCIO. Good symptoms still.

MOSCA. And from his brain—

CORBACCIO. Ha? How? Not from his brain?

MOSCA. Yes, sir, and from his brain—

CORBACCIO. I conceive you; good.

MOSCA. Flows a cold sweat, with a continual rheum,
Forth the resolved corners of his eyes.

CORBACCIO. Is 't possible? Yet I am better, ha!
How does he with the swimming of his head?

MOSCA. O, sir, 'tis past the scotomy; he now
Hath lost his feeling, and hath left to snort;
You hardly can perceive him, that he breathes.

CORBACCIO. Excellent, excellent; sure I shall outlast him;
This makes me young again, a score of years.

MOSCA. I was a-coming for you, sir.

79 **resolved** decomposing
82 **scotomy** giddiness
83 **left** ceased

CORBACCIO. Has he made his will?
What has he giv'n me?

MOSCA. No, sir.

CORBACCIO. Nothing? ha?

MOSCA. He has not made his will, sir.

CORBACCIO. Oh, oh, oh.
What then did Voltore, the lawyer, here?

MOSCA. He smelt a carcass, sir, when he but heard
My master was about his testament;
As I did urge him to it for your good—

CORBACCIO. He came unto him, did he? I thought so.

MOSCA. Yes, and presented him this piece of plate.

CORBACCIO. To be his heir?

MOSCA. I do not know, sir.

CORBACCIO. True;
I know it too.

MOSCA [*aside*]. By your own scale, sir.

CORBACCIO. Well,
I shall prevent him yet. See, Mosca, look,
Here I have brought a bag of bright *cecchines*,
Will quite weigh down his plate.

MOSCA. Yea, marry, sir.
This is true physic, this your sacred medicine;
No talk of opiates to this great elixir!

CORBACCIO. 'Tis *aurum palpabile,* if not *potabile*.

MOSCA. It shall be minister'd to him in his bowl!

CORBACCIO. Ay, do, do, do.

MOSCA. Most blessed cordial!
This will recover him.

CORBACCIO. Yes, do, do, do.

MOSCA. I think it were not best, sir.

CORBACCIO. What?

MOSCA. To recover him.

96 **about his testament** planning his will
106 **prevent** get ahead of
112 **aurum . . . potabile** gold tangible, if not drinkable. Elixir of gold was an esteemed restorative
116 **recover him** recover his favor
120 **recover** cure

CORBACCIO. O, no, no, no; by no means.
MOSCA. Why, sir, this
Will work some strange effect, if he but feel it.
CORBACCIO. 'Tis true; therefore forbear. I'll take my venture;
Give me 't again.
MOSCA. At no hand; pardon me,
You shall not do yourself that wrong, sir. I
Will so advise you, you shall have it all.
CORBACCIO. How?
MOSCA. All, sir; 'tis your right, your own; no man
Can claim a part; 'tis yours without a rival,
Decreed by destiny.
CORBACCIO. How, how, good Mosca?
MOSCA. I'll tell you, sir. This fit he shall recover—
CORBACCIO. I do conceive you.
MOSCA. And, on first advantage
Of his gain'd sense, will I re-importune him
Unto the making of his testament,
And show him this. [*Points to the money.*]
CORBACCIO. Good, good.
MOSCA. 'Tis better yet,
If you will hear, sir.
CORBACCIO. Yes, with all my heart.
MOSCA. Now would I counsel you, make home with speed;
There, frame a will; whereto you shall inscribe
My master your sole heir.
CORBACCIO. And disinherit
My son?
MOSCA. O, sir, the better; for that color
Shall make it much more taking.
CORBACCIO. O, but color?
MOSCA. This will, sir, you shall send it unto me.
Now, when I come to enforce, as I will do,
Your cares, your watchings, and your many prayers,
Your more than many gifts, your this day's present,
And last, produce your will; where (without thought

126 **At no hand** by no means
149 **color** pretense

Or least regard unto your proper issue,
A son so brave, and highly meriting)
The stream of your diverted love hath thrown you
Upon my master, and made him your heir;
He cannot be so stupid or stone-dead,
But, out of conscience and mere gratitude—

CORBACCIO. He must pronounce me his?

MOSCA. 'Tis true.

CORBACCIO. This plot
Did I think on before.

MOSCA. I do believe it.

CORBACCIO. Do you not believe it?

MOSCA. Yes, sir.

CORBACCIO. Mine own project.

MOSCA. Which, when he hath done, sir—

CORBACCIO. Publish'd me his heir?

MOSCA. And you so certain to survive him—

CORBACCIO. Ay.

MOSCA. Being so lusty a man—

CORBACCIO. 'Tis true.

MOSCA. Yes, sir—

CORBACCIO. I thought on that too. See, how he should be
The very organ to express my thoughts!

MOSCA. You have not only done yourself a good—

CORBACCIO. But multiplied it on my son!

MOSCA. 'Tis right, sir.

CORBACCIO. Still, my invention.

MOSCA. 'Las, sir! Heaven knows,
It hath been all my study, all my care,
(I e'en grow gray withal) how to work things—

CORBACCIO. I do conceive, sweet Mosca.

MOSCA. You are he
For whom I labor here.

CORBACCIO. Ay, do, do, do.
I'll straight about it.

MOSCA [*aside*]. Rook go with you, raven.

CORBACCIO. I know thee honest.

MOSCA. You do lie, sir—

178 **he should be** Mosca is

CORBACCIO. And–
MOSCA. Your knowledge is no better than your ears, sir.
CORBACCIO. I do not doubt to be a father to thee.
MOSCA. Nor I to gull my brother of his blessing.
CORBACCIO. I may ha' my youth restor'd to me, why not?
MOSCA. Your Worship is a precious ass–
CORBACCIO. What say'st thou?
MOSCA. I do desire your Worship to make haste, sir.
CORBACCIO. 'Tis done, 'tis done; I go. [*Exit.*]
VOLPONE [*leaping from his couch*]. Oh, I shall burst!
Let out my sides, let out my sides–
MOSCA. Contain
Your flux of laughter, sir; you know this hope
Is such a bait, it covers any hook.
VOLPONE. O, but thy working, and thy placing it!
I cannot hold; good rascal, let me kiss thee;
I never knew thee in so rare a humor.
MOSCA. Alas, sir, I but do as I am taught;
Follow your grave instructions, give 'em words,
Pour oil into their ears, and send them hence.
VOLPONE. 'Tis true, 'tis true. What a rare punishment
Is avarice to itself!
MOSCA. Ay, with our help, sir.
VOLPONE. So many cares, so many maladies,
So many fears attending on old age.
Yea, death so often call'd on, as no wish
Can be more frequent with 'em, their limbs faint,
Their senses dull, their seeing, hearing, going,
All dead before them; yea, their very teeth,
Their instruments of eating, failing them.
Yet this is reckon'd life! Nay, here was one,
Is now gone home, that wishes to live longer!
Feels not his gout, nor palsy; feigns himself
Younger by scores of years, flatters his age
With confident belying it, hopes he may
With charms like Aeson have his youth restor'd;
And with these thoughts so battens, as if fate

202 **haste** pronounced h*ass*t
230 **Aeson** a legendary Greek king

Would be as easily cheated on as he;
And all turns air! Who's that there, now? a third?
[*Another knocks.*]
MOSCA. Close; to your couch again; I hear his voice.
It is Corvino, our spruce merchant.
VOLPONE [*lying down*]. Dead.
MOSCA. Another bout, sir, with your eyes. [*anointing them*]—Who's there?

SCENE V

[*Enter* CORVINO.]
Signior Corvino! come most wish'd for! Oh,
How happy were you, if you knew it, now!
CORVINO. Why? what? wherein?
MOSCA. The tardy hour is come, sir.
CORVINO. He is not dead?
MOSCA. Not dead, sir, but as good;
He knows no man.
CORVINO. How shall I do then?
MOSCA. Why, sir?
CORVINO. I have brought him here a pearl.
MOSCA. Perhaps he has
So much remembrance left as to know you, sir.
He still calls on you; nothing but your name
Is in his mouth. Is your pearl orient, sir?
CORVINO. Venice was never owner of the like.
VOLPONE. Signior Corvino!
MOSCA. Hark!
VOLPONE. Signior Corvino.
MOSCA. He calls you; step and give it him.—H' is here, sir.
And he has brought you a rich pearl.
CORVINO. How do you, sir?—
Tell him it doubles the twelfth carat.
MOSCA. Sir,
He cannot understand: his hearing's gone;
And yet it comforts him to see you—

CORVINO. Say
I have a diamond for him, too.
MOSCA. Best show 't, sir;
Put it into his hand; 'tis only there
He apprehends; he has his feeling yet.
See, how he grasps it!
CORVINO. 'Las, good gentleman!
How pitiful the sight is!
MOSCA. Tut, forget, sir.
The weeping of an heir should still be laughter
Under a visor.
CORVINO. Why, am I his heir?
MOSCA. Sir, I am sworn, I may not show the will
Till he be dead. But here has been Corbaccio,
Here has been Voltore, here were others too–
I cannot number 'em, they were so many–
All gaping here for legacies; but I,
Taking the vantage of his naming you,
"Signior Corvino, Signior Corvino," took
Paper, and pen, and ink, and there I ask'd him
Whom he would have his heir! "Corvino." Who
Should be executor? "Corvino." And
To any question he was silent to,
I still interpreted the nods he made,
Through weakness, for consent; and sent home th' others,
Nothing bequeath'd them, but to cry and curse.
CORVINO. Oh, my dear Mosca. [*They embrace.*] Does he not perceive us?
MOSCA. No more than a blind harper. He knows no man,
No face of friend, nor name of any servant,
Who 'twas that fed him last, or gave him drink;
Not those he hath begotten, or brought up,
Can he remember.
CORVINO. Has he children?
MOSCA. Bastards,
Some dozen, or more, that he begot on beggars,
Gypsies, and Jews, and black-moors, when he was drunk.
Knew you not that, sir? 'Tis the common fable.

The dwarf, the fool, the eunuch, are all his;
H' is the true father of his family,
In all save me. But he has giv'n 'em nothing.
CORVINO. That's well, that's well. Art sure he does not hear us?
MOSCA. Sure, sir! Why, look you, credit your own sense. [*Shouts in* VOLPONE'S *ear.*]
The pox approach, and add to your diseases,
If it would send you hence the sooner, sir;
For your incontinence it hath deserv'd it
Throughly and throughly, and the plague to boot!—
You may come near, sir.—Would you would once close
Those filthy eyes of yours, that flow with slime
Like two frog-pits; and those same hanging cheeks,
Cover'd with hide instead of skin—Nay, help, sir—
That look like frozen dishclouts set on end.
CORVINO. Or like an old smok'd wall, on which the rain
Ran down in streaks.
MOSCA. Excellent, sir! speak out;
You may be louder yet; a culverin
Discharged in his ear would hardly bore it.
CORVINO. His nose is like a common sewer, still running.
MOSCA. 'Tis good! And what his mouth?
CORVINO. A very draught.
MOSCA. O, stop it up—
CORVINO. By no means.
MOSCA. Pray you, let me;
Faith, I could stifle him rarely with a pillow
As well as any woman that should keep him.
CORVINO. Do as you will; but I'll be gone.
MOSCA. Be so;
It is your presence makes him last so long.
CORVINO. I pray you use no violence.
MOSCA. No, sir? why?
Why should you be thus scrupulous, 'pray you, sir?
CORVINO. Nay, at your discretion.
MOSCA. Well, good sir, begone.

92 **rarely** exceedingly well
93 **keep** attend

CORVINO. I will not trouble him now to take my pearl?
MOSCA. Pooh, nor your diamond. What a needless care
Is this afflicts you? Is not all here yours?
Am not I here, whom you have made, your creature,
That owe my being to you?
CORVINO. Grateful Mosca!
Thou art my friend, my fellow, my companion,
My partner, and shalt share in all my fortunes.
MOSCA. Excepting one.
CORVINO. What's that?
MOSCA. Your gallant wife, sir.
[*Exit* CORVINO.]
Now is he gone; we had no other means
To shoot him hence but this.
VOLPONE. My divine Mosca!
Thou hast today outgone thyself. Who's there?
[*Another knocks.*]
I will be troubled with no more. Prepare
Me music, dances, banquets, all delights;
The Turk is not more sensual in his pleasures
Than will Volpone. [*Exit* MOSCA.] Let me see; a pearl!
A diamond! plate! *cecchines!* Good morning's purchase.
Why, this is better than rob churches, yet;
Or fat, by eating, once a month, a man—
[*Re-enter* MOSCA.]
Who is 't?
MOSCA. The beauteous Lady Would-be, sir,
Wife to the English knight, Sir Politic Would-be—
This is the style, sir, is directed me—
Hath sent to know how you have slept tonight,
And if you would be visited.
VOLPONE. Not now.
Some three hours hence—
MOSCA. I told the squire so much.
VOLPONE. When I am high with mirth and wine; then, then.
'Fore Heaven, I wonder at the desperate valor
Of the bold English, that they dare let loose
Their wives to all encounters!

MOSCA. Sir, this knight
Had not his name for nothing: he is politic,
And knows, howe'er his wife affect strange airs,
She hath not yet the face to be dishonest.
But had she Signior Corvino's wife's face—
VOLPONE. Hath she so rare a face?
MOSCA. O, sir, the wonder,
The blazing star of Italy! a wench
Of the first year! a beauty ripe as harvest!
Whose skin is whiter than a swan, all over!
Than silver, snow, or lilies! a soft lip,
Would tempt you to eternity of kissing!
And flesh that melteth in the touch to blood!
Bright as your gold! and lovely as your gold!
VOLPONE. Why had not I known this before?
MOSCA. Alas, sir,
Myself but yesterday discover'd it.
VOLPONE. How might I see her?
MOSCA. Oh, not possible;
She's kept as warily as is your gold;
Never does come abroad, never takes air
But at a window. All her looks are sweet,
As the first grapes or cherries, and are watch'd
As near as they are.
VOLPONE. I must see her—
MOSCA. Sir,
There is a guard of ten spies thick upon her,
All his whole household; each of which is set
Upon his fellow, and have all their charge,
When he goes out, when he comes in, examin'd.
VOLPONE. I will go see her, though but at her window.
MOSCA. In some disguise then.
VOLPONE. That is true; I must
Maintain mine own shape still the same; we'll think.

[*Exeunt.*]

141 **politic** worldly wise, devious and urbane

ACT II

SCENE I. *Before Corvino's house in St. Mark's Square.*

[*Enter* SIR POLITIC WOULD-BE, *and* PEREGRINE.]

POLITIC. Sir, to a wise man, all the world's his soil:
It is not Italy, nor France, nor Europe,
That must bound me, if my fates call me forth.
Yet I protest, it is no salt desire
Of seeing countries, shifting a religion,
Nor any disaffection to the state
Where I was bred, and unto which I owe
My dearest plots, hath brought me out; much less
That idle, antic, stale, grey-headed project
Of knowing men's minds and manners, with Ulysses!
But a peculiar humor of my wife's
Laid for this height of Venice, to observe,
To quote, to learn the language, and so forth—
I hope you travel, sir, with license?

PEREGRINE. Yes.

POLITIC. I dare the safelier converse.—How long, sir,
Since you left England?

PEREGRINE. Seven weeks.

POLITIC. So lately!
You ha' not been with my Lord Ambassador?

PEREGRINE. Not yet, sir.

POLITIC. Pray you, what news, sir, vents our climate?
I heard last night a most strange thing reported
By some of my Lord's followers, and I long
To hear how 'twill be seconded!

PEREGRINE. What was 't, sir?

15 **Laid for** headed for **height of** highly fashionable
16 **quote** note
17 **license** government authorization

POLITIC. Marry, sir, of a raven that should build
In a ship royal of the king's.
PEREGRINE [*aside*]. This fellow,
Does he gull me, trow? or is gull'd?—Your name, sir?
POLITIC. My name is Politic Would-be.
PEREGRINE [*aside*]. O, that speaks him.—
A knight, sir?
POLITIC. A poor knight, sir.
PEREGRINE. Your lady
Lies here in Venice, for intelligence
Of tires and fashions and behavior,
Among the courtesans? The fine Lady Would-be?
POLITIC. Yes, sir; the spider and the bee ofttimes
Suck from one flower.
PEREGRINE. Good Sir Politic!
I cry you mercy; I have heard much of you.
'Tis true, sir, of your raven.
POLITIC. On your knowledge?
PEREGRINE. Yes, and your lion's whelping in the Tower.
POLITIC. Another whelp!
PEREGRINE. Another, sir.
POLITIC. Now Heaven!
What prodigies be these? The fires at Berwick!
And the new star! These things concurring, strange!
And full of omen! Saw you those meteors?
PEREGRINE. I did, sir.
POLITIC. Fearful! Pray you, sir, confirm me,
Were there three porpoises seen, above the Bridge,
As they give out?
PEREGRINE. Six, and a sturgeon, sir.
POLITIC. I am astonish'd!
PEREGRINE. Nay, sir, be not so;

30 **raven** This reference, like the following ones to lion's whelps, the new star (a famous nova, of 1604), porpoises, and a whale, indicates both the ready credulity of Sir Politic and the widespread interest in omens associated with the wars and negotiations between the Protestants (of Great Britain and the Low Countries) and the Catholics (of Austria, Italy, and Spain).

52 **fires** meteors

I'll tell you a greater prodigy than these—
POLITIC. What should these things portend?
PEREGRINE. The very day,
Let me be sure, that I put forth from London,
There was a whale discover'd in the river,
As high as Woolwich, that had waited there,
Few know how many months, for the subversion
Of the Stode fleet.
POLITIC. Is 't possible? Believe it,
'Twas either sent from Spain, or the Archdukes!
Spinola's whale, upon my life, my credit!
Will they not leave these projects? Worthy sir,
Some other news.
PEREGRINE. Faith, Stone, the fool, is dead,
And they do lack a tavern fool extremely.
POLITIC. Is Mas' Stone dead?
PEREGRINE. He's dead, sir; why, I hope
You thought him not immortal?—[*aside*] Oh, this knight,
Were he well known, would be a precious thing
To fit our English stage. He that should write
But such a fellow, should be thought to feign
Extremely, if not maliciously.
POLITIC. Stone dead!
PEREGRINE. Dead.—Lord! how deeply, sir, you apprehend it!
He was no kinsman to you?
POLITIC. That I know of.
Well! that same fellow was an unknown fool.
PEREGRINE. And yet you knew him, it seems?
POLITIC. I did so. Sir,
I knew him one of the most dangerous heads
Living within the state, and so I held him.
PEREGRINE. Indeed, sir?

69 **Stode fleet** vessels of the English Merchant Adventurers, a trading company with a base at Stade, near Hamburg, Germany

71 **Archdukes** Archduke Albert of Austria and his wife, the Spanish Infanta Isabella, jointly the governors of the Netherlands and titled "the Archdukes"

72 **Spinola** commander of Spanish forces in the Netherlands

88 **unknown** unrecognized

POLITIC. While he liv'd, in action,
He has receiv'd weekly intelligence,
Upon my knowledge, out of the Low Countries;
For all parts of the world, in cabbages;
And those dispens'd again to ambassadors,
In oranges, muskmelons, apricots,
Lemons, pome-citrons, and such like; sometimes
In Colchester oysters, and your Selsey cockles.

PEREGRINE. You make me wonder!

POLITIC. Sir, upon my knowledge.
Nay, I have observ'd him, at your public ordinary,
Take his advertisement from a traveller
(A conceal'd statesman) in a trencher of meat;
And instantly, before the meal was done,
Convey an answer in a toothpick.

PEREGRINE. Strange!
How could this be, sir?

POLITIC. Why, the meat was cut
So like his character, and so laid as he
Must easily read the cipher.

PEREGRINE. I have heard
He could not read, sir.

POLITIC. So 'twas given out,
In polity, by those that did employ him;
But he could read, and had your languages,
And to 't, as sound a noddle—

PEREGRINE. I have heard, sir,
That your baboons were spies, and that they were
A kind of subtle nation near to China.

POLITIC. Ay, ay, your Mamaluchi. Faith, they had
Their hand in a French plot or two; but they
Were so extremely given to women, as
They made discovery of all: yet I

104 **ordinary** tavern
105 **advertisement** information
117 **In polity** for political reasons
123 **Mamaluchi** Mamelukes, a powerful group of Mohammedan white slaves, noted for their machinations

Had my advices here, on Wednesday last,
From one of their own coat, they were return'd,
Made their relations, as the fashion is,
And now stand fair for fresh employment.

PEREGRINE [*aside*]. Heart!
This Sir Pol will be ignorant of nothing.—
It seems, sir, you know all.

POLITIC. Not all, sir. But
I have some general notions. I do love
To note and to observe. Though I live out,
Free from the active torrent, yet I'd mark
The currents and the passages of things
For mine own private use; and know the ebbs
And flows of state.

PEREGRINE. Believe it, sir, I hold
Myself in no small tie unto my fortunes,
For casting me thus luckily upon you,
Whose knowledge, if your bounty equal it,
May do me great assistance, in instruction
For my behavior, and my bearing, which
Is yet so rude and raw—

POLITIC. Why? came you forth
Empty of rules for travel?

PEREGRINE. Faith, I had
Some common ones, from out that vulgar grammar,
Which he that cri'd Italian to me, taught me.

POLITIC. Why, this it is that spoils all our brave bloods,
Trusting our hopeful gentry unto pedants,
Fellows of outside, and mere bark. You seem
To be a gentleman of ingenuous race.—
I not profess it, but my fate hath been
To be where I have been consulted with,
In this high kind, touching some great men's sons,
Persons of blood and honor.—

PEREGRINE. Who be these, sir?

SCENE II

[*Enter* MOSCA *and* NANO *disguised, with workmen who erect a stage.*]

MOSCA. Under that window, there 't must be. The same.

POLITIC. Fellows to mount a bank! Did your instructor
In the dear tongues never discourse to you
Of the Italian mountebanks?

PEREGRINE. Yes, sir.

POLITIC. Why,
Here shall you see one.

PEREGRINE. They are quacksalvers,
Fellows that live by venting oils and drugs!

POLITIC. Was that the character he gave you of them?

PEREGRINE. As I remember.

POLITIC. Pity his ignorance.
They are the only knowing men of Europe!
Great general scholars, excellent physicians,
Most admir'd statesmen, profess'd favorites
And cabinet counsellors to the greatest princes!
The only languag'd men of all the world!

PEREGRINE. And, I have heard, they are most lewd impostors;
Made all of terms and shreds; no less beliers
Of great men's favors, than their own vile med'cines;
Which they will utter upon monstrous oaths;
Selling that drug for twopence, ere they part,
Which they have valu'd at twelve crowns before.

POLITIC. Sir, calumnies are answer'd best with silence.
Yourself shall judge.—Who is it mounts, my friends?

MOSCA. Scoto of Mantua, sir.

POLITIC. Is 't he? Nay, then

2 **bank** a small platform
11 **venting** vending
20 **lewd** ignorant
23 **utter** dispense

I'll proudly promise, sir, you shall behold
Another man than has been phant'sied to you.
I wonder yet, that he should mount his bank
Here in this nook, that has been wont t' appear
In face of the Piazza! Here he comes.

[*Enter* VOLPONE, *disguised as a mountebank doctor, and followed by a crowd of people.*]

VOLPONE [*to* NANO]. Mount, zany.

GREGE. Follow, follow, follow, follow, follow.

POLITIC. See how the people follow him! he's a man
May write ten thousand crowns in bank here. Note,
Mark but his gesture— I do use to observe
The state he keeps in getting up!

PEREGRINE. 'Tis worth it, sir.

VOLPONE. Most noble gentlemen, and my worthy patrons, it may seem strange that I, your Scoto Mantuano, who was ever wont to fix my bank in the face of the public Piazza, near the shelter of the portico to the Procuratia, should now, after eight months' absence from this illustrious city of Venice, humbly retire myself into an obscure nook of the Piazza.

POLITIC. Did not I now object the same?

PEREGRINE. Peace, sir.

VOLPONE. Let me tell you: I am not, as your Lombard proverb saith, cold on my feet; or content to part with my commodities at a cheaper rate than I accustomed—look not for it. Nor that the calumnious reports of that impudent detractor, and shame to our profession (Alessandro Buttone, I mean), who gave out, in public, I was condemn'd *a' sforzato* to the galleys, for poisoning the Cardinal Bembo's cook, hath at all attached, much less dejected me. No, no, worthy gentlemen; to tell you true, I cannot endure to see the rabble of these ground *ciarlitani* that spread their cloaks on the pavement, as if they meant to do feats of activity, and then come in lamely, with their mouldy tales out of Boccaccio, like stale Tabarin, the fabulist; some of

31 **phant'sied** represented
57 **a' sforzato** to hard labor
60 **ground ciarlitani** cheap entertainers

them discoursing their travels, and of their tedious captivity in the Turk's galleys, when, indeed, were the truth known, they were the Christian's galleys, where very temperately they ate bread, and drunk water, as a wholesome penance, enjoin'd them by their confessors, for base pilferies.

POLITIC. Note but his bearing, and contempt of these.

VOLPONE. These turdy-facy-nasty-paty-lousy-fartical rogues, with one poor groat's-worth of unprepar'd antimony, finely wrapp'd up in several *scartoccios,* are able, very well, to kill their twenty a week, and play; yet these meagre, starv'd spirits, who have half stopp'd the organs of their minds with earthy oppilations, want not their favorers among your shrivell'd salad-eating artisans, who are overjoy'd that they may have their half-pe'rth of physic; though it purge 'em into another world, 't makes no matter.

POLITIC. Excellent! ha' you heard better language, sir?

VOLPONE. Well, let 'em go. And, gentlemen, honorable gentlemen, know that for this time our bank, being thus remov'd from the clamors of the *canaglia,* shall be the scene of pleasure and delight; for I have nothing to sell, little or nothing to sell.

POLITIC. I told you, sir, his end.

PEREGRINE. You did so, sir.

VOLPONE. I protest I and my six servants are not able to make of this precious liquor so fast as it is fetch'd away from my lodging by gentlemen of your city, strangers of the terra-firma, worshipful merchants, ay, and senators, too, who, ever since my arrival, have detained me to their uses, by their splendidous liberalities. And worthily. For what avails your rich man to have his magazines stuff'd with *moscadelli,* or of the purest grape, when his physicians prescribe him, on pain of death, to drink nothing but water cocted with aniseeds? O health! health! the blessing

65 **the truth** i.e., that they were criminals being properly punished rather than slaves of the Turkish infidels
72 **scartoccios** twists of paper
74 **oppilations** obstructions
76 **half-pe'rth** halfpenny's worth
82 **canaglia** rabble
92 **magazines** storage vaults **moscadelli** muscatel

of the rich! the riches of the poor! who can buy thee at too dear a rate, since there is no enjoying this world without thee? Be not then so sparing of your purses, honorable gentlemen, as to abridge the natural course of life—

PEREGRINE. You see his end.

POLITIC. Ay, is 't not good?

VOLPONE. For, when a humid flux, or catarrh, by the mutability of air, falls from your head into an arm or shoulder, or any other part, take you a ducat, or your *cecchine* of gold, and apply to the place affected; see what good effect it can work. No, no; 'tis this blessed *unguento,* this rare extraction, that hath only power to disperse all malignant humors that proceed either of hot, cold, moist, or windy causes—

PEREGRINE. I would he had put in dry too.

POLITIC. 'Pray you, observe.

VOLPONE. To fortify the most indigest and crude stomach, ay, were it of one that, through extreme weakness, vomited blood, applying only a warm napkin to the place, after the unction and fricace;—for the *vertigine* in the head, putting but a drop into your nostrils, likewise behind the ears, a most sovereign and approv'd remedy; the *mal caduco,* cramps, convulsions, paralyses, epilepsies, *tremor cordia,* retir'd nerves, ill vapors of the spleen, stoppings of the liver, the stone, the strangury, *hernia ventosa, iliaca passio;* stops a *dysenteria* immediately; easeth the torsion of the small guts; and cures *melancholia hypochondriaca,* being taken and applied according to my printed receipt. [*Pointing to his bill and his glass*] For this is the physician, this the medicine; this counsels, this cures; this gives direction, this works the effect; and, in sum, both together may be term'd an abstract of the theoric and practic in the Aesculapian art. 'Twill cost you eight crowns.—And, Zan Fritada, pray thee sing a verse, extempore, in honor of it.

POLITIC. How do you like him, sir?

106 **humors** in medieval physiology, the four kinds of body-fluid, corresponding to the traditional four elements, that determined both health and temperament

112–13 **unction and fricace** ointment and massage. In the rest of this speech Volpone makes a flourish of medical terminology not to inform but to impress

PEREGRINE. Most strangely, I!

POLITIC. Is not his language rare?

PEREGRINE. But alchemy,
I never heard the like, or Broughton's books.

NANO [*sings*].

Had old Hippocrates, or Galen,
That to their books put med'cines all in,
But known this secret, they had never
(Of which they will be guilty ever)
Been murderers of so much paper,
Or wasted many a hurtless taper;
No Indian drug had e'er been famed,
Tobacco, sassafras, not named;
Ne yet of guacum one small stick, sir,
Nor Raymund Lully's great elixir.
Ne had been known the Danish Gonswart,
Or Paracelsus, with his long-sword.

PEREGRINE. All this, yet, will not do; eight crowns is high.

VOLPONE. No more.—Gentlemen, if I had but time to discourse to you the miraculous effects of this my oil, surnamed *oglio del Scoto,* with the countless catalogue of those I have cured of th' aforesaid, and many more diseases; the patents and privileges of all the princes and commonwealths of Christendom; or but the depositions of those that appear'd on my part, before the signiory of the Sanitâ and most learned College of Physicians; where I was authorized, upon notice taken of the admirable virtues of my medicaments, and mine own excellency in matter of rare and unknown secrets, not only to disperse them publicly in this famous city, but in all the territories that happily joy under the government of the most pious and magnificent states of Italy. But may some other gallant fellow say, "Oh, there be divers that make profession to have as good, and as experimented receipts as yours." Indeed, very many have assay'd, like apes, in imitation of that which is really and essen-

130 **But** except for
131 **Broughton** an eccentric English theologian
142 **great elixir** of youth
152 **signiory . . . Sanitâ** governors of the hospital

tially in me, to make of this oil; bestow'd great cost in furnaces, stills, alembics, continual fires, and preparation of the ingredients (as indeed there goes to it six hundred several simples, besides some quantity of human fat, for the conglutination, which we buy of the anatomists); but when these practitioners come to the last decoction—blow, blow, puff, puff, and all flies in fumo. Ha, ha, ha! Poor wretches! I rather pity their folly and indiscretion, than their loss of time and money; for those may be recovered by industry; but to be a fool born, is a disease incurable. For myself, I always from my youth have endeavor'd to get the rarest secrets, and book them, either in exchange or for money; I spared nor cost nor labor where anything was worthy to be learned. And, gentlemen, honorable gentlemen, I will undertake, by virtue of chemical art, out of the honorable hat that covers your head, to extract the four elements; that is to say, the fire, air, water, and earth, and return you your felt without burn or stain. For, whilst others have been at the *balloo* I have been at my book; and am now past the craggy paths of study, and come to the flow'ry plains of honor and reputation.

POLITIC. I do assure you, sir, that is his aim.

VOLPONE. But, to our price.

PEREGRINE. And that withal, Sir Pol.

VOLPONE. You all know, honorable gentlemen, I never valu'd this *ampulla,* or vial, at less than eight crowns; but for this time, I am content to be depriv'd of it for six; six crowns is the price, and less in courtesy I know you cannot offer me; take it or leave it, howsoever, both it and I am at your service. I ask you not as the value of the thing, for then I should demand of you a thousand crowns; so the Cardinals Montalto, Fernese, the great Duke of Tuscany, my gossip, with divers other princes, have given me; but I despise money. Only to show my affection to you, honorable gentlemen, and your illustrious state here, I have neglected the messages of these princes, mine own offices, fram'd my journey hither, only to present you with the fruits of my travels.—Tune your voices once more to the touch of

179 **balloo** a game of ball
192 **gossip** close friend

your instruments, and give the honorable assembly some delightful recreation.

PEREGRINE. What monstrous and most painful circumstance
Is here, to get some three or four gazets,
Some threepence i' the whole! for that 'twill come to.

NANO [*sings*].

You that would last long, list to my song;
Make no more coil, but buy of this oil.
Would you be ever fair, and young?
Stout of teeth, and strong of tongue?
Tart of palate? quick of ear?
Sharp of sight? of nostril clear?
Moist of hand? and light of foot?
Or (I will come nearer to 't)
Would you live free from all diseases?
Do the act your mistress pleases,
Yet fright all aches from your bones?
Here's a med'cine for the nones.

VOLPONE. Well, I am in a humor, at this time, to make a present of the small quantity my coffer contains; to the rich in courtesy, and to the poor for God's sake. Wherefore now mark: I ask'd you six crowns; and six crowns, at other times, you have paid me; you shall not give me six crowns, nor five, nor four, nor three, nor two, nor one; nor half a ducat; no, nor a *moccinigo*. Sixpence it will cost you, or six hundred pound—expect no lower price, for, by the banner of my front, I will not bate a bagatine,—that I will have, only, a pledge of your loves, to carry something from amongst you, to show I am not contemn'd by you. Therefore, now, toss your handkerchiefs, cheerfully, cheerfully; and be advertised, that the first heroic spirit that deigns to grace me with a handkerchief, I will give it a little remembrance of something beside, shall please it better than if I had presented it with a double pistolet.

201 **gazets** small coins
215 **nones** purpose
221 **moccinigo** small Venetian coin
223 **banner of my front** flag of my profession
224 **bagatine** trivial coin
230 **pistolet** gold coin

PEREGRINE. Will you be that heroic spark, Sir Pol?
[CELIA, *at the window, throws down her handkerchief.*]
O, see! the window has prevented you.

VOLPONE. Lady, I kiss your bounty; and, for this timely grace you have done your poor Scoto of Mantua, I will return you, over and above my oil, a secret of that high and inestimable nature, shall make you for ever enamor'd on that minute wherein your eye first descended on so mean, yet not altogether to be despis'd an object. Here is a powder conceal'd in this paper, of which, if I should speak to the worth, nine thousand volumes were but as one page, that page as a line, that line as a word; so short is this pilgrimage of man, which some call life, to the expressing of it. Would I reflect on the price? Why, the whole world is but as an empire, that empire as a province, that province as a bank, that bank as a private purse, to the purchase of it. I will only tell you: it is the powder that made Venus a goddess, given her by Apollo, that kept her perpetually young, clear'd her wrinkles, firm'd her gums, fill'd her skin, color'd her hair; from her deriv'd to Helen, and at the sack of Troy unfortunately lost; till now, in this our age, it was as happily recover'd, by a studious antiquary, out of some ruins of Asia, who sent a moiety of it to the court of France (but much sophisticated), wherewith the ladies there now color their hair. The rest, at this present, remains with me, extracted to a quintessence; so that, wherever it but touches, in youth it perpetually preserves, in age restores the complexion; seats your teeth, did they dance like virginal jacks, firm as a wall; makes them white as ivory, that were black as—

SCENE III

[*Enter* CORVINO.]

CORVINO. Spite o' the devil, and my shame! Come down here;
Come down!—No house but mine to make your scene?
Signior Flaminio, will you down, sir? down?

257 **virginal jacks** activating levers, or keys, of a small harpsichord
3 **Signior Flaminio** "Mr. Leading Actor"

What, is my wife your Franciscina, sir?
No windows on the whole piazza, here,
To make your properties, but mine? but mine?
[*He beats away the mountebank, etc.*]
Heart! ere tomorrow I shall be new christen'd,
And called the *Pantalone di Bisognosi;*
About the town.

PEREGRINE. What should this mean, Sir Pol?

POLITIC. Some trick of state, believe it; I will home.

PEREGRINE. It may be some design on you.

POLITIC. I know not.
I'll stand upon my guard.

PEREGRINE. It is your best, sir.

POLITIC. This three weeks, all my advices, all my letters,
They have been intercepted.

PEREGRINE. Indeed, sir?
Best have a care.

POLITIC. Nay, so I will.

PEREGRINE [*aside*]. This knight.
I may not lose him, for my mirth, till night. [*Exeunt*].

SCENE IV. A room in Volpone's house.

[*Enter* VOLPONE *and* MOSCA.]

VOLPONE. O, I am wounded.

MOSCA. Where, sir?

VOLPONE. Not without;
Those blows were nothing; I could bear them ever.
But angry Cupid, bolting from her eyes,
Hath shot himself into me like a flame;
Where now he flings about his burning heat,
As in a furnace some ambitious fire
Whose vent is stopp'd. The fight is all within me.
I cannot live, except thou help me, Mosca;

6 **Franciscina** cute little maidservant (a type in the Italian popular plays)
11 **Pantalone di Bisognosi** the doting old fool (another such type)

My liver melts, and I, without the hope
Of some soft air from her refreshing breath,
Am but a heap of cinders.

MOSCA. 'Las, good sir,
Would you had never seen her.

VOLPONE. Nay, would thou
Hadst never told me of her.

MOSCA. Sir, 'tis true;
I do confess I was unfortunate,
And you unhappy; but I am bound in conscience,
No less than duty, to effect my best
To your release of torment, and I will, sir.

VOLPONE. Dear Mosca, shall I hope?

MOSCA. Sir, more than dear,
I will not bid you to despair of aught
Within a human compass.

VOLPONE. O, there spoke
My better angel. Mosca, take my keys,
Gold, plate, and jewels, all 's at thy devotion;
Employ them how thou wilt—nay, coin me too—
So thou in this but crown my longings, Mosca!

MOSCA. Use but your patience.

VOLPONE. So I have.

MOSCA. I doubt not
To bring success to your desires.

VOLPONE. Nay, then,
I not repent me of my late disguise.

MOSCA. If you can horn him, sir, you need not.

VOLPONE. True.
Besides, I never meant him for my heir.
Is not the color o' my beard and eyebrows
To make me known?

MOSCA. No jot.

VOLPONE. I did it well.

MOSCA. So well, would I could follow you in mine,
With half the happiness; and yet I would

40 **horn** cuckold. Folk tradition had it that a deceived husband grew horns

Escape your epilogue.

VOLPONE. But were they gull'd
With a belief that I was Scoto?

MOSCA. Sir,
Scoto himself could hardly have distinguish'd!
I have not time to flatter you now; we'll part,
And as I prosper, so applaud my art. [*Exeunt.*]

SCENE V. *A room in Corvino's house.*

[*Enter* CORVINO, *with his sword in his hand, dragging in* CELIA.]

CORVINO. Death of mine honor, with the city's fool!
A juggling, tooth-drawing, prating mountebank!
And at a public window! where, whilst he,
With his strain'd action, and his dole of faces,
To his drug-lecture draws your itching ears,
A crew of old, unmarried, noted lechers,
Stood leering up like satyrs; and you smile
Most graciously! and fan your favors forth,
To give your hot spectators satisfaction!
What, was your mountebank their call? their whistle?
Or were you enamor'd on his copper rings,
His saffron jewel, with the toad-stone in 't,
Or his embroid'red suit, with the cope-stitch,
Made of a hearse cloth, or his old tilt-feather,
Or his starch'd beard? Well! you shall have him, yes.
He shall come home, and minister unto you
The fricace for the mother. Or, let me see,
I think you'd rather mount! Would you not mount?
Why, if you'll mount, you may; yes, truly, you may.
And so you may be seen, down to th' foot.
Get you a cittern, Lady Vanity,
And be a dealer with the virtuous man;
Make one. I'll but protest myself a cuckold,

19 **fricace . . . mother** literally, massage to cure hysteria
23 **Lady Vanity** character representing worldly pleasure in the old morality plays

And save your dowry. I am a Dutchman, I!
For if you thought me an Italian,
You would be damn'd ere you did this, you whore.
Thou 'dst tremble to imagine that the murder
Of father, mother, brother, all thy race,
Should follow, as the subject of my justice!

CELIA. Good sir, have patience!

CORVINO. What couldst thou propose
Less to thyself, than in this heat of wrath,
And stung with my dishonor, I should strike
This steel into thee, with as many stabs
As thou wert gaz'd upon with goatish eyes?

CELIA. Alas, sir, be appeas'd! I could not think
My being at the window should more now
Move your impatience than at other times.

CORVINO. No? not to seek and entertain a parley
With a known knave? before a multitude?
You were an actor with your handkerchief!
Which he most sweetly kiss'd in the receipt,
And might, no doubt, return it with a letter
And 'point the place where you might meet; your sister's,
Your mother's, or your aunt's might serve the turn.

CELIA. Why, dear sir, when do I make these excuses,
Or ever stir abroad, but to the church?
And that so seldom—

CORVINO. Well, it shall be less;
And thy restraint before was liberty,
To what I now decree; and therefore mark me.
First, I will have this bawdy light damm'd up;
And till 't be done, some two or three yards off
I'll chalk a line; o'er which if thou but chance
To set thy desp'rate foot, more hell, more horror,
More wild remorseless rage shall seize on thee
Than on a conjuror that had heedless left
His circle's safety ere his devil was laid.
Then here's a lock which I will hang upon thee,

54 **light** window

And, now I think on 't, I will keep thee backwards;
Thy lodging shall be backwards, thy walks backwards,
Thy prospect—all be backwards, and no pleasure,
That thou shalt know but backwards. Nay, since you force
My honest nature, know it is your own
Being too open, makes me use you thus.
Since you will not contain your subtle nostrils
In a sweet room, but they must snuff the air
Of rank and sweaty passengers—[*Knock within.*] one knocks.
Away, and be not seen, pain of thy life;
Nor look toward the window; if thou dost—
Nay, stay, hear this—let me not prosper, whore,
But I will make thee an anatomy,
Dissect thee mine own self, and read a lecture
Upon thee to the city, and in public.
Away!— [*Exit* CELIA.]

[*Enter* SERVITORE.]

Who's there?

SERVITORE. 'Tis Signior Mosca, sir.

SCENE VI

[CORVINO *and* SERVITORE *remain.*]

CORVINO. Let him come in. [*Exit* SERVITORE.]—His master's dead! There's yet
Some good to help the bad.—[*Enter* MOSCA.] My Mosca, welcome;
I guess your news.

MOSCA. I fear you cannot, sir.

CORVINO. Is 't not his death?

MOSCA. Rather the contrary.

CORVINO. Not his recovery?

MOSCA. Yes, sir.

CORVINO. I am curs'd;

62 **backwards** in the back rooms of the house
70 **passengers** passers-by

I am bewitch'd; my crosses meet to vex me.
How? how? how? how?

MOSCA. Why, sir, with Scoto's oil!
Corbaccio and Voltore brought of it,
Whilst I was busy in an inner room—

CORVINO. Death! that damn'd mountebank! but for the law,
Now, I could kill the rascal. 'T cannot be
His oil should have that virtue. Ha' not I
Known him a common rogue, come fiddling in
To th' *osteria,* with a tumbling whore,
And, when he has done all his forc'd tricks, been glad
Of a poor spoonful of dead wine, with flies in 't?
It cannot be. All his ingredients
Are a sheep's gall, a roasted bitch's marrow,
Some few sod earwigs, pounded caterpillars,
A little capon's grease, and fasting spittle:
I know 'em to a dram.

MOSCA. I know not, sir;
But some on 't, there, they pour'd into his ears,
Some in his nostrils, and recover'd him;
Applying but the fricace.

CORVINO. Pox o' that fricace.

MOSCA. And, since, to seem the more officious
And flatt'ring of his health, there, they have had,
At extreme fees, the college of physicians
Consulting on him, how they might restore him;
Where one would have a cataplasm of spices,
Another a flay'd ape clapp'd to his breast,
A third would ha' it a dog, a fourth an oil,
With wildcats' skins. At last, they all resolv'd
That, to preserve him, was no other means
But some young woman must be straight sought out,
Lusty, and full of juice, to sleep by him;
And to this service most unhappily,
And most unwillingly, am I now employ'd,
Which here I thought to pre-acquaint you with,

23 **osteria** hostelry
35 **Pox** a plague

For your advice, since it concerns you most;
Because I would not do that thing might cross
Your ends, on whom I have my whole dependence, sir.
Yet, if I do not they may delate
My slackness to my patron, work me out
Of his opinion; and there all your hopes,
Ventures, or whatsoever, are all frustrate.
I do but tell you, sir. Besides, they are all
Now striving who shall first present him. Therefore—
I could entreat you, briefly, conclude somewhat:
Prevent 'em if you can.

CORVINO. Death to my hopes!
This is my villainous fortune! Best to hire
Some common courtesan!

MOSCA. Ay, I thought on that, sir;
But they are all so subtle, full of art—
And age again doting and flexible,
So as—I cannot tell—we may, perchance,
Light on a quean may cheat us all.

CORVINO. 'Tis true.

MOSCA. No, no; it must be one that has no tricks, sir,
Some simple thing, a creature made unto it;
Some wench you may command. Ha' you no kinswoman?
Gods so—Think, think, think, think, think, think, think, sir.
One o' the doctors offer'd there his daughter.

CORVINO. How!

MOSCA. Yes, Signior Lupo, the physician.

CORVINO. His daughter!

MOSCA. And a virgin, sir. Why, alas,
He knows the state of 's body, what it is:
That naught can warm his blood, sir, but a fever,
Nor any incantation raise his spirit;
A long forgetfulness hath seiz'd that part.
Besides, sir, who shall know it? Some one or two—

CORVINO. I pray thee give me leave.—[*stepping aside*] If any man
But I had had this luck—The thing in 't self,
I know, is nothing.—Wherefore should not I

73 **Gods so** on God's oath

As well command my blood and my affections
As this dull doctor? In the point of honor,
The cases are all one of wife and daughter.

MOSCA [*aside*]. I hear him coming.

CORVINO [*aside*]. She shall do 't; 'tis done.
'Slight! if this doctor, who is not engag'd,
Unless 't be for his counsel, which is nothing,
Offer his daughter, what should I, that am
So deeply in? I will prevent him. Wretch!
Covetous wretch!—Mosca, I have determin'd.

MOSCA. How, sir?

CORVINO. We'll make all sure. The party you wot of
Shall be mine own wife, Mosca.

MOSCA. Sir, the thing,
But that I would not seem to counsel you,
I should have motion'd to you, at the first;
And make your count, you have cut all their throats.
Why! 'tis directly taking a possession!
And in his next fit, we may let him go.
'Tis but to pull the pillow from his head,
And he is throttled; it had been done before
But for your scrupulous doubts.

CORVINO. Ay, a plague on 't;
My conscience fools my wit! Well, I'll be brief,
And so be thou, lest they should be before us.
Go home; prepare him; tell him with what zeal
And willingness I do it. Swear it was
On the first hearing, as thou mayst do, truly,
Mine own free motion.

MOSCA. Sir, I warrant you,
I'll so possess him with it, that the rest
Of his starv'd clients shall be banish'd all;
And only you receiv'd. But come not, sir,
Until I send, for I have something else
To ripen for your good—you must not know 't.

CORVINO. But do not you forget to send, now.

MOSCA. Fear not. [*Exit.*]

92 **'Slight** by God's light

SCENE VII

[CORVINO *remains.*]

CORVINO. Where are you, wife? My Celia! Wife!

[*Enter* CELIA.]

—What, blubbering?
Come, dry those tears. I think thou thought'st me in earnest;
Ha? By this light I talk'd so but to try thee.
Methinks, the lightness of the occasion
Should ha' confirm'd thee. Come, I am not jealous.

CELIA. No?

CORVINO. Faith I am not, I, nor never was;
It is a poor, unprofitable humor.
Do not I know, if women have a will,
They'll do 'gainst all the watches o' the world,
And that the fiercest spies are tam'd with gold?
Tut, I am confident in thee, thou shalt see 't;
And see I'll give thee cause, too, to believe it.
Come, kiss me.—Go, and make thee ready straight,
In all thy best attire, thy choicest jewels,
Put 'em all on, and, with 'em, thy best looks:
We are invited to a solemn feast,
At old Volpone's, where it shall appear
How far I am free from jealousy or fear. [*Exeunt.*]

ACT III

SCENE I. A street.

[*Enter* MOSCA.]

MOSCA. I fear I shall begin to grow in love

With my dear self and my most prosp'rous parts;
They do so spring and burgeon. I can feel
A whimsy i' my blood—I know not how—
Success hath made me wanton. I could skip
Out of my skin now, like a subtle snake,
I am so limber. Oh! your parasite
Is a most precious thing, dropp'd from above,
Not bred 'mongst clods and clotpolls, here on earth.
I muse the mystery was not made a science,
It is so liberally profess'd! Almost
All the wise world is little else, in nature,
But parasites or sub-parasites. And yet
I mean not those that have your bare town-art,
To know who's fit to feed 'em; have no house,
No family, no care, and therefore mold
Tales for men's ears, to bait that sense; or get
Kitchen-invention, and some stale receipts
To please the belly, and the groin; nor those,
With their court dog-tricks, that can fawn and fleer,
Make their revenue out of legs and faces,
Echo my Lord, and lick away a moth:
But your fine, elegant rascal, that can rise
And stoop, almost together, like an arrow;
Shoot through the air as nimbly as a star;
Turn short as doth a swallow; and be here,
And there, and here, and yonder, all at once;
Present to any humor, all occasion;
And change a visor swifter than a thought!
This is the creature had the art born with him;
Toils not to learn it, but doth practise it
Out of most excellent nature; and such sparks
Are the true parasites, others but their zanies.

2 **parts** abilities
12 **clotpolls** blockheads
13 **muse the mystery** wonder that the trade
24 **legs and faces** bows and smiles
32 **a visor** his expression

SCENE II

[*Enter* BONARIO.]

MOSCA. Who's this? Bonario, old Corbaccio's son?
The person I was bound to seek. Fair sir,
You are happ'ly met.

BONARIO. That cannot be by thee.

MOSCA. Why, sir?

BONARIO. Nay, 'pray thee know thy way, and leave me.
I would be loth to interchange discourse
With such a mate as thou art.

MOSCA. Courteous sir,
Scorn not my poverty.

BONARIO. Not I, by Heaven;
But thou shalt give me leave to hate thy baseness.

MOSCA. Baseness!

BONARIO. Ay; answer me, is not thy sloth
Sufficient argument? thy flattery?
Thy means of feeding?

MOSCA. Heaven be good to me.
These imputations are too common, sir,
And eas'ly stuck on virtue, when she's poor.
You are unequal to me, and howe'er
Your sentence may be righteous, yet you are not,
That, ere you know me, thus proceed in censure.
St. Mark bear witness 'gainst you, 'tis inhuman. [*Weeps.*]

BONARIO [*aside*]. What! does he weep? the sign is soft and good!
I do repent me that I was so harsh.

MOSCA. 'Tis true, that, sway'd by strong necessity,
I am enforc'd to eat my careful bread
With too much obsequy; 'tis true, beside,
That I am fain to spin mine own poor raiment
Out of my mere observance, being not born
To a free fortune; but that I have done

22 **unequal** (1) of superior rank (2) unjust
30 **obsequy** obsequiousness

Base offices, in rending friends asunder,
Dividing families, betraying counsels,
Whispering false lies, or mining men with praises,
Train'd their credulity with perjuries,
Corrupted chastity, or am in love
With mine own tender ease, but would not rather
Prove the most rugged and laborious course,
That might redeem my present estimation,
Let me here perish, in all hope of goodness.

BONARIO [*aside*]. This cannot be a personated passion!—
I was to blame, so to mistake thy nature;
'Pray thee forgive me; and speak out thy bus'ness.

MOSCA. Sir, it concerns you; and though I may seem
At first to make a main offence in manners,
And in my gratitude unto my master,
Yet for the pure love which I bear all right,
And hatred of the wrong, I must reveal it.
This very hour your father is in purpose
To disinherit you—

BONARIO. How!

MOSCA. And thrust you forth,
As a mere stranger to his blood; 'tis true, sir.
The work no way engageth me, but as
I claim an interest in the general state
Of goodness and true virtue, which I hear
T' abound in you; and for which mere respect,
Without a second aim, sir, I have done it.

BONARIO. This tale hath lost thee much of the late trust
Thou hadst with me; it is impossible.
I know not how to lend it any thought
My father should be so unnatural.

MOSCA. It is a confidence that well becomes
Your piety; and form'd, no doubt, it is
From your own simple innocence; which makes
Your wrong more monstrous and abhorr'd. But, sir,
I now will tell you more. This very minute,

36 **mining** undermining
66 **piety** filial loyalty

It is, or will be doing; and if you
Shall be but pleas'd to go with me, I'll bring you,
I dare not say where you shall see, but where
Your ear shall be a witness of the deed;
Hear yourself written bastard, and profess'd
The common issue of the earth.

BONARIO. I'm maz'd!

MOSCA. Sir, if I do it not, draw your just sword,
And score your vengeance on my front and face;
Mark me your villain. You have too much wrong,
And I do suffer for you, sir. My heart
Weeps blood in anguish—

BONARIO. Lead. I follow thee. [*Exeunt.*]

SCENE III. *A room in Volpone's house.*

[*Enter* VOLPONE, NANO, ANDROGYNO, *and* CASTRONE.]

VOLPONE. Mosca stays long, methinks.—Bring forth your sports,
And help to make the wretched time more sweet.

NANO. Dwarf, fool, and eunuch, well met here we be.
A question it were now, whether of us three,
Being all the known delicates of a rich man,
In pleasing him, claim the precedency can?

CASTRONE. I claim for myself.

ANDROGYNO. And so doth the fool.

NANO. 'Tis foolish indeed; let me set you both to school.
First for your dwarf, he's little and witty,
And everything, as it is little, is pretty;
Else why do men say to a creature of my shape,
So soon as they see him, "It's a pretty little ape"?
And why a pretty ape, but for pleasing imitation
Of greater men's action, in a ridiculous fashion?
Beside, this feat body of mine doth not crave
Half the meat, drink, and cloth, one of your bulks will have.
Admit your fool's face be the mother of laughter,

78 **front** brow

Yet, for his brain, it must always come after;
And though that do feed him, it's a pitiful case,
His body is beholding to such a bad face.
[*One knocks.*]
VOLPONE. Who's there? My couch; away! Look, Nano, see.—
[*Exeunt* ANDROGYNO *and* CASTRONE.]
Give me my caps first—go, inquire. [*Exit* NANO.] Now, Cupid
Send it be Mosca, and with fair return.
[*Re-enter* NANO.]
NANO. It is the beauteous Madam—
VOLPONE. Would-be—is it?
NANO. The same.
VOLPONE. Now torment on me! Squire her in;
For she will enter, or dwell here for ever.
Nay, quickly. [*Exit* NANO; VOLPONE *retires to his couch.*]—That my fit were past! I fear
A second hell too, that my loathing this
Will quite expel my appetite to the other.
Would she were taking now her tedious leave.
Lord, how it threats me what I am to suffer!

SCENE IV

[*Enter* NANO *and* LADY POLITIC WOULD-BE]
LADY. I thank you, good sir. Pray you signify
Unto your patron I am here.—This band
Shows not my neck enough.—I trouble you, sir;
Let me request you bid one of my women
Come hither to me. [*Exit* NANO.]—In good faith, I am dress'd
Most favorably today; it is no matter;
'Tis well enough.
[*Re-enter* NANO *with a* WAITING WOMAN.]
Look, see, these petulant things!
How they have done this!
VOLPONE [*aside*]. I do feel the fever
Ent'ring in at mine ears; oh, for a charm
To fright it hence.

LADY. Come nearer. Is this curl
In his right place? or this? Why is this higher
Than all the rest? You ha' not wash'd your eyes yet?
Or do they not stand even i' your head?
Where's your fellow? call her. [*Exit* WOMAN.]
NANO [*aside*]. Now, St. Mark
Deliver us! anon she'll beat her women,
Because her nose is red.
[*Re-enter* WOMAN *with another.*]
LADY. I pray you view
This tire, forsooth. Are all things apt, or no?
WOMAN. One hair a little here sticks out, forsooth.
LADY. Does 't so, forsooth! and where was your dear sight,
When it did so, forsooth? What now! bird-ey'd?
And you, too? 'Pray you, both approach and mend it.
Now, by that light I muse you're not asham'd!
I, that have preach'd these things so oft unto you,
Read you the principles, argu'd all the grounds,
Disputed every fitness, every grace,
Call'd you to counsel of so frequent dressings—
NANO [*aside*]. More carefully than of your fame or honor.
LADY. Made you acquainted what an ample dowry
The knowledge of these things would be unto you,
Able alone to get you noble husbands
At your return; and you thus to neglect it!
Besides, you seeing what a curious nation
Th' Italians are, what will they say of me?
"The English lady cannot dress herself."
Here's a fine imputation to our country!
Well, go your ways, and stay i' the next room.
This fucus was too coarse too; it's no matter.—
Good sir, you'll give 'em entertainment?
[*Exeunt* NANO *and* WAITING WOMAN.]
VOLPONE [*aside*]. The storm comes toward me.
LADY [*going to the couch*]. How does my Volpone?
VOLPONE. Troubled with noise; I cannot sleep. I dreamt

41 **curious** fastidious
46 **fucus** rouge

That a strange Fury ent'red now my house,
And, with the dreadful tempest of her breath,
Did cleave my roof asunder.
LADY. Believe me, and I
Had the most fearful dream, could I remember 't—
VOLPONE [*aside*]. Out on my fate! I ha' giv'n her the occasion
How to torment me: she will tell me hers.
LADY. Methought the golden mediocrity,
Polite, and delicate—
VOLPONE. O, if you do love me,
No more; I sweat, and suffer, at the mention
Of any dream. Feel how I tremble yet.
LADY. Alas, good soul! the passion of the heart.
Seed-pearl were good now, boil'd with syrup of apples,
Tincture of gold, and coral, citron-pills,
Your elecampane root, myrobalans—
VOLPONE. Ay me, I have ta'en a grasshopper by the wing!
LADY. Burnt silk and amber. You have muscadel
Good i' the house—
VOLPONE. You will not drink, and part?
LADY. No, fear not that. I doubt we shall not get
Some English saffron—half a dram would serve;
Your sixteen cloves, a little musk, dried mints,
Bugloss, and barley meal—
VOLPONE [*aside*]. She's in again;
Before I feign'd diseases—now I have one.
LADY. And these appli'd with a right scarlet cloth—
VOLPONE [*aside*]. Another flood of words! a very torrent!
LADY. Shall I, sir, make you a poultice?
VOLPONE. No, no, no.
I am very well; you need prescribe no more.
LADY. I have a little studied physic; but now
I'm all for music, save i' the forenoons,
An hour or two for painting. I would have
A lady, indeed, t' have all letters and arts,

59 **the . . . mediocrity** a personification of the Golden Mean
64 **passion . . . heart** a symptom of love-melancholy. A catalogue of supposed remedies follows

Be able to discourse, to write, to paint;
But principal, as Plato holds, your music
(And so does wise Pythagoras, I take it)
Is your true rapture, when there is consent
In face, in voice, and clothes, and is, indeed,
Our sex's chiefest ornament.

VOLPONE. The poet
As old in time as Plato, and as knowing,
Says that your highest female grace is silence.

LADY. Which o' your poets? Petrarch, or Tasso, or Dante?
Guarini? Ariosto? Aretine?
Cieco di Hadria? I have read them all.

VOLPONE [*aside*]. Is everything a cause to my destruction?

LADY. I think I ha' two or three of 'em about me.

VOLPONE [*aside*]. The sun, the sea, will sooner both stand still
Than her eternal tongue! Nothing can 'scape it.

LADY. Here's *Pastor Fido*—

VOLPONE [*aside*]. Profess obstinate silence;
That's now my safest.

LADY. All our English writers,
I mean such as are happy in th' Italian,
Will deign to steal out of this author, mainly;
Almost as much as from Montagnié:
He has so modern and facile a vein,
Fitting the time, and catching the court-ear.
Your Petrarch is more passionate, yet he,
In days of sonneting, trusted 'em with much.
Dante is hard, and few can understand him.
But for a desperate wit, there's Aretine!
Only, his pictures are a little obscene—
You mark me not!

90 **consent** harmony
103 **Pastor Fido** Guarini's *Faithful Shepherd,* a pastoral tragi-comedy then much in vogue as a model of elegant style and sentiment
109 **Montagnié** Montaigne
113 **trusted 'em with much** was much copied by English sonnet writers
115 **desperate** extraordinary **Aretine** Pietro Aretino, author of sonnets based on obscene drawings by Giulio Romano

VOLPONE. Alas, my mind's perturb'd.
LADY. Why, in such cases, we must cure ourselves,
Make use of our philosophy—
VOLPONE. Oh, ay me!
LADY. And as we find our passions do rebel,
Encounter 'em with reason, or divert 'em,
By giving scope unto some other humor
Of lesser danger; as, in politic bodies,
There's nothing more doth overwhelm the judgment,
And clouds the understanding, than too much
Settling and fixing, and, as 'twere, subsiding
Upon one object. For the incorporating
Of these same outward things into that part
Which we call mental, leaves some certain faeces
That stop the organs, and, as Plato says,
Assassinates our knowledge.
VOLPONE [*aside*]. Now, the spirit
Of patience help me.
LADY. Come, in faith, I must
Visit you more, a'days, and make you well—
Laugh and be lusty.
VOLPONE [*aside*]. My good angel save me!
LADY. There was but one sole man in all the world
With whom I e'er could sympathise; and he
Would lie you, often, three, four hours together
To hear me speak; and be sometimes so rapt,
As he would answer me quite from the purpose,
Like you, and you are like him, just. I'll discourse,
An 't be but only, sir, to bring you asleep,
How we did spend our time and loves together,
For some six years.
VOLPONE. Oh, oh, oh, oh, oh, oh!
LADY. For we were coaetanei, and brought up—
VOLPONE [*aside*]. Some power, some fate, some fortune rescue me!

150 **coaetanei** of the same age

SCENE V

[*Enter* MOSCA.]

MOSCA. God save you, madam.

LADY. Good sir.

VOLPONE. Mosca! welcome—
[*aside*]. Welcome to my redemption.

MOSCA [*aside*]. Why, sir?

VOLPONE [*aside*]. Oh,
Rid me of this my torture, quickly, there;
My madam with the everlasting voice.
The bells, in time of pestilence, ne'er made
Like noise, or were in that perpetual motion—
The cockpit comes not near it. All my house,
But now, steam'd like a bath with her thick breath,
A lawyer could not have been heard; nor scarce
Another woman, such a hail of words
She has let fall. For hell's sake, rid her hence.

MOSCA. Has she presented?

VOLPONE. Oh, I do not care:
I'll take her absence upon any price,
With any loss.

MOSCA. Madam—

LADY. I ha' brought your patron
A toy, a cap here, of mine own work—

MOSCA. 'Tis well.
I had forgot to tell you I saw your knight
Where you'd little think it—

LADY. Where?

MOSCA. Marry,
Where yet, if you make haste, you may apprehend him,
Rowing upon the water in a gondola,
With the most cunning courtesan of Venice.

11 **bells** which, in time of plague, were tolled almost continuously for the dead and dying

18 **presented** given a present

29 **Marry** indeed

LADY. Is 't true?
MOSCA. Pursue 'em, and believe your eyes;
Leave me to make your gift. [*Exit* LADY.]—I knew 'twould take;
For, lightly, they that use themselves most license,
Are still most jealous.
VOLPONE. Mosca, hearty thanks
For thy quick fiction, and delivery of me.
Now to my hopes, what say'st thou?
[*Re-enter* LADY.]
LADY. But do you hear, sir?—
VOLPONE [*aside*]. Again! I fear a paroxysm.
LADY. Which way
Row'd they together?
MOSCA. Toward the Rialto.
LADY. I pray you lend me your dwarf.
MOSCA. I pray you take him.
[*Exit* LADY.]
Your hopes, sir, are like happy blossoms, fair,
And promise timely fruit, if you will stay
But the maturing. Keep you at your couch;
Corbaccio will arrive straight, with the will;
When he is gone, I'll tell you more. [*Exit.*]
VOLPONE. My blood,
My spirits are return'd; I am alive;
And, like your wanton gamester at primero,
Whose thought had whisper'd to him, not go less,
Methinks I lie, and draw—for an encounter.

SCENE VI

[*Enter* MOSCA *and* BONARIO.]

MOSCA. Sir, here conceal'd [*opening a door*] you may hear all. But, pray you,
Have patience, sir; [*One knocks.*] the same 's your father knocks.

36 **lightly . . . license** generally, those who allow themselves most leeway
57 **primero** a kind of poker, on the terms of which Volpone puns as he draws the curtain of his bed

I am compell'd to leave you. [*Exit.*]
BONARIO. Do so.—Yet
Cannot my thought imagine this a truth. [*Goes in.*]

SCENE VII

[*Enter* MOSCA, CORVINO, *and* CELIA.]

MOSCA. Death on me! You are come too soon. What meant you?
Did not I say I would send?
CORVINO. Yes, but I fear'd
You might forget it, and then they prevent us.
MOSCA. Prevent!—[*aside*] Did e'er man haste so for his horns?
A courtier would not ply it so for a place.—
Well, now there is no helping it, stay here;
I'll presently return. [*Exit.*]
CORVINO. Where are you, Celia?
You know not wherefore I have brought you hither?
CELIA. Not well, except you told me.
CORVINO. Now I will.
Hark hither. [*They retire to one side.*]

[*Re-enter* MOSCA.]

MOSCA [*to* BONARIO]. Sir, your father hath sent word
It will be half an hour ere he come;
And therefore, if you please to walk the while
Into the gallery—at the upper end,
There are some books to entertain the time;
And I'll take care no man shall come unto you, sir.
BONARIO. Yes, I will stay there.—[*aside*] I do doubt this fellow. [*Exit.*]
MOSCA [*looking after him*]. There; he is far enough; he can hear nothing.
And for his father, I can keep him off.
CORVINO [*advancing with* CELIA]. Nay, now, there is no starting back, and therefore,
Resolve upon it; I have so decreed.

8 **ply . . . place** try so hard to wangle an official position

It must be done. Nor would I move 't afore,
Because I would avoid all shifts and tricks,
That might deny me.

CELIA. Sir, let me beseech you,
Affect not these strange trials; if you doubt
My chastity, why, lock me up for ever;
Make me the heir of darkness. Let me live
Where I may please your fears, if not your trust.

CORVINO. Believe it, I have no such humor, I.
All that I speak I mean; yet I am not mad;
Not horn-mad, see you? Go to, show yourself
Obedient, and a wife.

CELIA. O Heaven!

CORVINO. I say it,
Do so.

CELIA. Was this the train?

CORVINO. I have told you reasons;
What the physicians have set down; how much
It may concern me; what my engagements are;
My means, and the necessity of those means
For my recovery. Wherefore, if you be
Loyal, and mine, be won; respect my venture.

CELIA. Before your honor?

CORVINO. Honor! tut, a breath.
There's no such thing in nature; a mere term
Invented to awe fools. What is my gold
The worse for touching, clothes for being look'd on?
Why, this 's no more. An old decrepit wretch,
That has no sense, no sinew; takes his meat
With others' fingers; only knows to gape
When you do scald his gums; a voice, a shadow;
And what can this man hurt you?

CELIA [*aside*]. Lord! what spirit
Is this hath ent'red him?

CORVINO. And for your fame,

31 **move 't afore** propose it before now
46 **train** trick
65 **fame** reputation

That's such a jig; as if I would go tell it,
Cry it on the Piazza! Who shall know it
But he that cannot speak it, and this fellow,
Whose lips are i' my pocket? Save yourself—
If you'll proclaim 't, you may,—I know no other
Should come to know it.

CELIA. Are Heaven and saints then nothing?
Will they be blind or stupid?

CORVINO. How?

CELIA. Good sir,
Be jealous still, emulate them; and think
What hate they burn with toward every sin.

CORVINO. I grant you; if I thought it were a sin
I would not urge you. Should I offer this
To some young Frenchman, or hot Tuscan blood
That had read Aretine, conn'd all his prints,
Knew every quirk within lust's labyrinth,
And were profess'd critic in lechery;
And I would look upon him, and applaud him;
This were a sin: but here, 'tis contrary,
A pious work, mere charity, for physic,
And honest polity, to assure mine own.

CELIA. O Heaven! canst thou suffer such a change?

VOLPONE [*aside*]. Thou art mine honor, Mosca, and my pride,
My joy, my tickling, my delight! Go bring 'em.

MOSCA. Please you draw near, sir.

CORVINO. Come on, what—
You will not be rebellious? By that light—

MOSCA. Sir, Signior Corvino, here, is come to see you.

VOLPONE. Oh.

MOSCA. And hearing of the consultation had,
So lately, for your health, is come to offer,
Or rather, sir, to prostitute—

CORVINO. Thanks, sweet Mosca.

MOSCA. Freely, unask'd, or unentreated—

CORVINO. Well.

MOSCA. As the true fervent instance of his love,

66 **jig** jest

His own most fair and proper wife, the beauty
Only of price in Venice—

CORVINO. 'Tis well urg'd.

MOSCA. To be your comfortress, and to preserve you.

VOLPONE. Alas, I am past, already! 'Pray you, thank him
For his good care and promptness; but for that,
'Tis a vain labor e'en to fight 'gainst Heaven;
Applying fire to a stone—uh, uh, uh, uh!—
Making a dead leaf grow again. I take
His wishes gently, though; and you may tell him
What I have done for him; marry, my state is hopeless!
Will him to pray for me; and t' use his fortune
With reverence when he comes to 't.

MOSCA. Do you hear, sir?
Go to him with your wife.

CORVINO. Heart of my father!
Wilt thou persist thus? Come, I pray thee, come.
Thou seest 'tis nothing, Celia. By this hand,
I shall grow violent. Come, do 't, I say.

CELIA. Sir, kill me, rather. I will take down poison,
Eat burning coals, do anything—

CORVINO. Be damn'd!
Heart, I will drag thee hence home by the hair;
Cry thee a strumpet through the streets; rip up
Thy mouth unto thine ears; and slit thy nose,
Like a raw rochet—Do not tempt me, come;
Yield; I am loth—Death! I will buy some slave
Whom I will kill, and bind thee to him alive,
And at my window hang you forth, devising
Some monstrous crime, which I, in capital letters,
Will eat into thy flesh with aqua fortis,
And burning cor'sives, on this stubborn breast.
Now, by the blood thou hast incens'd, I'll do it!

CELIA. Sir, what you please, you may; I am your martyr.

CORVINO. Be not thus obstinate; I ha' not deserv'd it.

104 **Only of price** peerless
128 **rochet** large-headed fish
134 **cor'sives** corrosives

Think who it is entreats you. 'Pray thee, sweet;
Good faith, thou shalt have jewels, gowns, attires,
What thou wilt think, and ask. Do but go kiss him.
Or touch him but. For my sake. At my suit.
This once. No? not? I shall remember this.
Will you disgrace me thus? Do you thirst my undoing?

MOSCA. Nay, gentle lady, be advis'd.

CORVINO. No, no.
She has watch'd her time. God's precious, this is scurvy,
'Tis very scurvy; and you are—

MOSCA. Nay, good sir.

CORVINO. An errant locust—by heaven, a locust!—Whore,
Crocodile, that hast thy tears prepar'd,
Expecting how thou'lt bid 'em flow.

MOSCA. Nay, 'pray you, sir!
She will consider.

CELIA. Would my life would serve
To satisfy—

CORVINO. 'Sdeath! if she would but speak to him,
And save my reputation, 'twere somewhat;
But spitefully to affect my utter ruin!

MOSCA [*aside to* CORVINO]. Ay, now you have put your fortune in her hands.
Why, i' faith, it is her modesty, I must quit her.
If you were absent, she would be more coming;
I know it, and dare undertake for her.
What woman can before her husband? 'Pray you,
Let us depart and leave her here.

CORVINO. Sweet Celia,
Thou mayst redeem all yet; I'll say no more.
If not, esteem yourself as lost.—Nay, stay there.

[*Exit with* MOSCA.]

CELIA. O God, and his good angels! whither, whither,
Is shame fled human breasts? that with such ease,
Men dare put off your honors, and their own?

141 **suit** plea
156 **'Sdeath** by God's death (the Crucifixion)
161 **quit** acquit

Is that which ever was a cause of life
Now plac'd beneath the basest circumstance,
And modesty an exile made, for money?

VOLPONE. Ay, in Corvino, and such earth-fed minds,
[*He leaps off from his couch.*]
That never tasted the true heav'n of love.
Assure thee, Celia, he that would sell thee,
Only for hope of gain, and that uncertain,
He would have sold his part of Paradise
For ready money, had he met a copeman.
Why art thou maz'd to see me thus reviv'd?
Rather applaud thy beauty's miracle;
'Tis thy great work, that hath, not now alone,
But sundry times, rais'd me, in several shapes,
And, but this morning, like a mountebank,
To see thee at thy window; ay, before
I would have left my practice for thy love,
In varying figures I would have contended
With the blue Proteus, or the horned flood.
Now art thou welcome.

CELIA. Sir!

VOLPONE. Nay, fly me not,
Nor let thy false imagination
That I was bedrid, make thee think I am so—
Thou shalt not find it. I am now as fresh,
As hot, as high, and in as jovial plight
As when, in that so celebrated scene,
At recitation of our comedy,
For entertainment of the great Valois,
I acted young Antinoüs, and attracted
The eyes and ears of all the ladies present,
T' admire each graceful gesture, note, and footing. [*Sings.*]

173 **cause of life** principle to be defended with life itself
182 **copeman** dealer
189 **left . . . practice** left off my stratagems
190–91 **contended . . . flood** rivaled the Old Man of the Sea or even Achelous, Greek legendary figures adept at transforming themselves
201 **Valois** Henry III of France, who visited Venice in 1574
202 **Antinoüs** a handsome boy beloved by the Roman emperor Hadrian

Come, my Celia, let us prove,
While we can, the sports of love.
Time will not be ours for ever,
He, at length, our good will sever.
Spend not then his gifts in vain.
Suns that set may rise again;
But if once we lose this light,
'Tis with us perpetual night.
Why should we defer our joys?
Fame and rumor are but toys.
Cannot we delude the eyes
Of a few poor household spies?
Or his easier ears beguile,
Thus removed by our wile?
'Tis no sin love's fruits to steal,
But the sweet thefts to reveal;
To be taken, to be seen,
These have crimes accounted been.

CELIA. Some serene blast me, or dire lightning strike
This my offending face.

VOLPONE. Why droops my Celia?
Thou hast, in place of a base husband, found
A worthy lover; use thy fortune well,
With secrecy and pleasure. See, behold,
What thou art queen of; not in expectation,
As I feed others, but possess'd and crown'd.
See, here, a rope of pearl; and each more orient
Than that the brave Egyptian queen carous'd.
Dissolve and drink 'em. See, a carbuncle,
May put out both the eyes of our St. Mark;
A diamond would have bought Lollia Paulina,

223 **serene** baneful night mist

232 **that . . . carous'd** the pearl which Cleopatra drank in a cup of wine (an example of great luxury)

234 **put . . . Mark** outshine the jewels in the treasury of St. Mark's cathedral

235 **Lollia Paulina** a notorious Roman beauty whom the emperor Caligula married and divorced

When she came in like starlight, hid with jewels
That were the spoils of provinces; take these,
And wear and lose 'em; yet remains an earring
To purchase them again, and this whole state.
A gem but worth a private patrimony
Is nothing; we will eat such at a meal.
The heads of parrots, tongues of nightingales,
The brains of peacocks and of estriches,
Shall be our food; and, could we get the phoenix,
Though nature lost her kind, she were our dish.

CELIA. Good sir, these things might move a mind affected
With such delights; but I, whose innocence
Is all I can think wealthy, or worth th' enjoying,
And which, once lost, I have naught to lose beyond it,
Cannot be taken with these sensual baits.
If you have conscience—

VOLPONE. 'Tis the beggar's virtue;
If thou hast wisdom, hear me, Celia.
Thy baths shall be the juice of July-flowers,
Spirit of roses and of violets,
The milk of unicorns, and panthers' breath
Gather'd in bags and mix'd with Cretan wines.
Our drink shall be prepared gold and amber,
Which we will take until my roof whirl round
With the vertigo; and my dwarf shall dance,
My eunuch sing, my fool make up the antic,
Whilst we, in changed shapes, act Ovid's tales:
Thou like Europa now, and I like Jove;
Then I like Mars, and thou like Erycine;
So of the rest, till we have quite run through
And wearied all the fables of the gods.
Then will I have thee in more modern forms,
Attired like some sprightly dame of France,
Brave Tuscan lady, or proud Spanish beauty;

254 **July-flowers** gillyflowers

262 **Ovid's tales** his *Metamorphoses* ("Transformations") relating such stories as that of Europa, a maiden abducted by Jove in the shape of a bull, and the love-affair of Venus (**Erycine**) and Mars

Sometimes unto the Persian sophy's wife,
Or the Grand Signior's mistress; and, for change,
To one of our most artful courtesans,
Or some quick Negro, or cold Russian;
And I will meet thee in as many shapes,
Where we may so transfuse our wand'ring souls
Out at our lips, and score up sums of pleasures,

That the curious shall not know
How to tell them as they flow;
And the envious, when they find
What their number is, be pin'd.

CELIA. If you have ears that will be pierc'd—or eyes
That can be open'd—a heart, may be touch'd—
Or any part that yet sounds man about you—
If you have touch of holy saints, or Heaven,
Do me the grace to let me 'scape. If not,
Be bountiful and kill me. You do know
I am a creature hither ill betray'd
By one whose shame I would forget it were;
If you will deign me neither of these graces,
Yet feed your wrath, sir, rather than your lust,
(It is a vice comes nearer manliness)
And punish that unhappy crime of nature,
Which you miscall my beauty; flay my face,
Or poison it with ointments for seducing
Your blood to this rebellion. Rub these hands
With what may cause an eating leprosy,
E'en to my bones and marrow, anything
That may disfavor me, save in my honor.
And I will kneel to you, pray for you, pay down
A thousand hourly vows, sir, for your health;
Report, and think you virtuous—

VOLPONE. Think me cold,
Frozen, and impotent, and so report me!

270 sophy's king's
271 Grand Signior's Sultan of Turkey's

That I had Nestor's hernia, thou wouldst think.
I do degenerate, and abuse my nation,
To play with opportunity thus long;
I should have done the act, and then have parley'd.
Yield, or I'll force thee.

CELIA. O! just God!

VOLPONE. In vain—

BONARIO [*leaps out from where* MOSCA *had plac'd him*]. Forbear, foul ravisher, libidinous swine;
Free the forc'd lady, or thou di'st, impostor.
But that I am loth to snatch thy punishment
Out of the hand of justice, thou shouldst yet
Be made the timely sacrifice of vengeance,
Before this altar and this dross, thy idol.—
Lady, let's quit the place; it is the den
Of villainy; fear naught: you have a guard;
And he ere long shall meet his just reward.

[*Exeunt* BONARIO *and* CELIA.]

VOLPONE. Fall on me, roof, and bury me in ruin;
Become my grave, that wert my shelter. Oh!
I am unmask'd, unspirited, undone,
Betray'd to beggary, to infamy—

SCENE VIII

[*Enter* MOSCA.]

MOSCA. Where shall I run, most wretched shame of men,
To beat out my unlucky brains?

VOLPONE. Here, here.
What! dost thou bleed?

MOSCA. O, that his well-driv'n sword
Had been so courteous to have cleft me down
Unto the navel, ere I liv'd to see
My life, my hopes, my spirits, my patron, all
Thus desperately engaged, by my error.

304 **Nestor's** the aged Homeric hero's

VOLPONE. Woe on thy fortune.
MOSCA. And my follies, sir.
VOLPONE. Th' hast made me miserable.
MOSCA. And myself, sir.
Who would have thought he would have hearken'd so?
VOLPONE. What shall we do?
MOSCA. I know not; if my heart
Could expiate the mischance, I'd pluck it out.
Will you be pleas'd to hang me, or cut my throat?
And I'll requite you, sir. Let's die like Romans,
Since we have liv'd like Grecians. [*They knock without.*]
VOLPONE. Hark! who's there?
I hear some footing; officers, the saffi,
Come to apprehend us! I do feel the brand
Hissing already at my forehead; now
Mine ears are boring.
MOSCA. To your couch, sir, you;
Make that place good, however. [VOLPONE *lies down as before.*]
—[*aside*] Guilty men
Suspect what they deserve still.—Signior Corbaccio!

SCENE IX

[*Enter* CORBACCIO.]

CORBACCIO. Why, how now, Mosca?
MOSCA. O, undone, amaz'd, sir.
Your son, I know not by what accident,
Acquainted with your purpose to my patron,
Touching your will and making him your heir,
Ent'red our house with violence, his sword drawn,
Sought for you, call'd you wretch, unnatural,
Vow'd he would kill you.
CORBACCIO. Me?

21 **like Romans** by suicide, as if honorably
22 **like Grecians** for pleasure
24 **saffi** police
27 **boring** being pierced (as punishment)

MOSCA. Yes, and my patron.

CORBACCIO. This act shall disinherit him indeed.
Here is the will.

MOSCA. 'Tis well, sir.

CORBACCIO. Right and well:
Be you as careful now for me.

[*Enter* VOLTORE *behind*.]

MOSCA. My life, sir,
Is not more tender'd; I am only yours.

CORBACCIO. How does he? Will he die shortly, think'st thou?

MOSCA. I fear
He'll outlast May.

CORBACCIO. Today?

MOSCA. No, last out May, sir.

CORBACCIO. Couldst thou not gi' him a dram?

MOSCA. Oh, by no means, sir.

CORBACCIO. Nay, I'll not bid you.

VOLTORE [*coming forward*]. This is a knave, I see.

MOSCA [*aside*]. How! Signior Voltore! did he hear me?

VOLTORE. Parasite!

MOSCA. Who's that?—Oh, sir, most timely welcome—

VOLTORE. Scarce,
To the discovery of your tricks, I fear.
You are his, only? and mine also, are you not?

MOSCA. Who? I, sir!

VOLTORE. You, sir. What device is this
About a will?

MOSCA. A plot for you, sir.

VOLTORE. Come,
Put not your foists upon me; I shall scent 'em.

MOSCA. Did you not hear it?

VOLTORE. Yes, I hear Corbaccio
Hath made your patron there his heir.

MOSCA. 'Tis true,
By my device, drawn to it by my plot,
With hope—

20 **tender'd** cared for
41 **Put . . . foists** Do not try your deceits

VOLTORE. Your patron should reciprocate?
And you have promis'd?
MOSCA. For your good I did, sir.
Nay, more, I told his son, brought, hid him here,
Where he might hear his father pass the deed;
Being persuaded to it by this thought, sir,
That the unnaturalness, first, of the act,
And then his father's oft disclaiming in him
(Which I did mean t' help on), would sure enrage him
To do some violence upon his parent,
On which the law should take sufficient hold,
And you be stated in a double hope.
Truth be my comfort, and my conscience,
My only aim was to dig you a fortune
Out of these two rotten sepulchres—
VOLTORE. I cry thee mercy, Mosca.
MOSCA. Worth your patience,
And your great merit, sir. And see the change!
VOLTORE. Why, what success?
MOSCA. Most hapless! You must help, sir.
Whilst we expected th' old raven, in comes
Corvino's wife, sent hither by her husband—
VOLTORE. What, with a present?
MOSCA. No, sir, on visitation
(I'll tell you how anon); and, staying long,
The youth he grows impatient, rushes forth,
Seizeth the lady, wounds me, makes her swear
(Or he would murder her—that was his vow)
T' affirm my patron to have done her rape;
Which how unlike it is, you see! and hence,
With that pretext he's gone, t' accuse his father,
Defame my patron, defeat you—
VOLTORE. Where's her husband?
Let him be sent for straight.
MOSCA. Sir, I'll go fetch him.
VOLTORE. Bring him to the Scrutineo.
MOSCA. Sir, I will.

83 **Scrutineo** Senate House

VOLTORE. This must be stopp'd.
MOSCA. Oh, you do nobly, sir.
Alas, 'twas labor'd all, sir, for your good;
Nor was there want of counsel in the plot.
But Fortune can, at any time, o'erthrow
The projects of a hundred learned clerks, sir.
CORBACCIO [*listening*]. What's that?
VOLTORE. Wilt please you, sir, to go along?
[*Exit* CORBACCIO, *followed by* VOLTORE.]
MOSCA. Patron, go in, and pray for our success.
VOLPONE. Need makes devotion; Heaven your labor bless! [*Exeunt.*]

ACT IV

SCENE I. A street.

[*Enter* SIR POLITIC WOULD-BE *and* PEREGRINE.]

POLITIC. I told you, sir, it was a plot; you see
What observation is. You mention'd me
For some instructions; I will tell you, sir,
(Since we are met here in this height of Venice)
Some few particulars I have set down,
Only for this meridian, fit to be known
Of your crude traveller; and they are these.
I will not touch, sir, at your phrase, or clothes,
For they are old.
PEREGRINE. Sir, I have better.
POLITIC. Pardon,
I meant, as they are themes.
PEREGRINE. Oh, sir, proceed;

2 **mention'd** applied to
12 **old** trite

I'll slander you no more of wit, good sir.
POLITIC. First, for your garb, it must be grave and serious,
Very reserv'd and lock'd; not tell a secret
On any terms, not to your father; scarce
A fable, but with caution; make sure choice
Both of your company and discourse; beware
You never speak a truth—
PEREGRINE. How!
POLITIC. Not to strangers,
For those be they you must converse with most;
Others I would not know, sir, but at distance
So as I still might be a saver in 'em—
You shall have tricks else pass'd upon you, hourly.
And then, for your religion, profess none,
But wonder at the diversity of all;
And, for your part, protest, were there no other
But simply the laws o' th' land, you could content you.
Nic. Machiavel and Monsieur Bodin, both
Were of this mind. Then must you learn the use
And handling of your silver fork at meals,
The metal of your glass (these are main matters
With your Italian); and to know the hour
When you must eat your melons and your figs.
PEREGRINE. Is that a point of state too?
POLITIC. Here, it is;
For your Venetian, if he see a man
Preposterous in the least, he has him straight;
He has; he strips him. I'll acquaint you, sir,
I now have liv'd here, 'tis some fourteen months.
Within the first week of my landing here,
All took me for a citizen of Venice,
I knew the forms so well—
PEREGRINE [*aside*]. And nothing else.
POLITIC. I had read Contarene, took me a house,

18 **garb** demeanor
28 **be . . . in** play it safe with
34 **Bodin** a writer on statecraft, like **Contarini** (l. 50)
37 **metal . . . glass** fine distinctions in glassware

Dealt with my Jews to furnish it with movables—
Well, if I could but find one man, one man,
To mine own heart, whom I durst trust, I would—

PEREGRINE. What? what, sir?

POLITIC. Make him rich; make him a fortune:
He should not think again. I would command it.

PEREGRINE. As how?

POLITIC. With certain projects that I have,
Which I may not discover.

PEREGRINE [*aside*]. If I had
But one to wager with, I would lay odds now,
He tells me instantly.

POLITIC. One is (and that
I care not greatly who knows) to serve the state
Of Venice with red herrings for three years,
And at a certain rate, from Rotterdam,
Where I have correspondence. There's a letter,
Sent me from one o' th' states, and to that purpose;
He cannot write his name, but that's his mark.

PEREGRINE. He is a chandler?

POLITIC. No, a cheesemonger.
There are some other too with whom I treat
About the same negotiation;
And I will undertake it; for 'tis thus:
I'll do 't with ease; I have cast it all. Your hoy
Carries but three men in her, and a boy;
And she shall make me three returns a year:
So if there come but one of three, I save;
If two, I can defalk. But this is now,
If my main project fail.

PEREGRINE. Then you have others?

POLITIC. I should be loth to draw the subtle air

51 **movables** household goods
68 **states** Dutchmen of high rank
70 **chandler** candlemaker (the paper being so greasy)
75 **hoy** small coastal vessel
77 **returns** round trips
78 **I save** I'm safe
79 **defalk** make a profit

Of such a place without my thousand aims.
I'll not dissemble, sir: where'er I come,
I love to be considerative; and 'tis true,
I have at my free hours thought upon
Some certain goods unto the state of Venice,
Which I do call my cautions; and, sir, which
I mean, in hope of pension, to propound
To the Great Council, then unto the Forty,
So to the Ten. My means are made already—

PEREGRINE. By whom?

POLITIC. Sir, one that though his place b' obscure,
Yet he can sway, and they will hear him. He's
A *commandadore*.

PEREGRINE. What, a common serjeant?

POLITIC. Sir, such as they are, put it in their mouths,
What they should say, sometimes; as well as greater.
I think I have my notes to show you—[*searching his pockets*]

PEREGRINE. Good, sir.

POLITIC. But you shall swear unto me, on your gentry,
Not to anticipate—

PEREGRINE. I, sir?

POLITIC. Nor reveal
A circumstance—my paper is not with me.

PEREGRINE. O, but you can remember, sir.

POLITIC. My first is
Concerning tinder boxes. You must know,
No family is here without its box.
Now, sir, it being so portable a thing,
Put case that you or I were ill affected
Unto the state, sir; with it in our pockets,
Might not I go into the Arsenal,
Or you come out again, and none the wiser?

PEREGRINE. Except yourself, sir.

POLITIC. Go to, then. I therefore
Advertise to the state, how fit it were

90–91 **Great . . . Ten** governing bodies of the Venetian Republic
95 **commandadore** sergeant-at-arms, a minor officer of the law courts
101 **gentry** honor as a gentleman

That none but such as were known patriots,
Sound lovers of their country, should be suffer'd
T' enjoy them in their houses; and even those
Seal'd at some office, and at such a bigness
As might not lurk in pockets.

PEREGRINE. Admirable!

POLITIC. My next is, how t' inquire, and be resolv'd
By present demonstration, whether a ship,
Newly arriv'd from Syria, or from
Any suspected part of all the Levant,
Be guilty of the plague; and where they use
To lie out forty, fifty days, sometimes,
About the Lazaretto, for their trial,
I'll save that charge and loss unto the merchant,
And in an hour clear the doubt.

PEREGRINE. Indeed, sir?

POLITIC. Or—I will lose my labor.

PEREGRINE. 'My faith, that's much.

POLITIC. Nay, sir, conceive me. 'Twill cost me in onions,
Some thirty livres—

PEREGRINE. Which is one pound sterling.

POLITIC. Beside my waterworks. For this I do, sir:
First, I bring in your ship 'twixt two brick walls—
But those the state shall venture. On the one
I strain me a fair tarpaulin, and in that
I stick my onions, cut in halves; the other
Is full of loopholes, out at which I thrust
The noses of my bellows; and those bellows
I keep, with waterworks, in perpetual motion
(Which is the easi'st matter of a hundred).
Now, sir, your onion, which doth naturally
Attract th' infection, and your bellows blowing
The air upon him, will show, instantly,
By his chang'd color, if there be contagion;
Or else remain as fair as at the first.

121 **seal'd** registered
130 **About . . . Lazaretto** in quarantine
141 **venture** invest in

Now 'tis known, 'tis nothing.
PEREGRINE. You are right, sir.
POLITIC. I would I had my note.
PEREGRINE. 'Faith, so would I;
But you ha' done well for once, sir.
POLITIC. Were I false,
Or would be made so, I could show you reasons
How I could sell this state now to the Turk,
Spite of their galleys, or their—[*examining his papers*]
PEREGRINE. Pray you, Sir Pol.
POLITIC. I have 'em not about me.
PEREGRINE. That I fear'd.
They are there, sir?
POLITIC. No, this is my diary,
Wherein I note my actions of the day.
PEREGRINE. 'Pray you let's see, sir.—What is here? "*Notandum*,
A rat had gnawn my spur-leathers; notwithstanding,
I put on new, and did go forth; but first
I threw three beans over the threshold. *Item*,
I went and bought two toothpicks, whereof one
I burst immediately, in a discourse
With a Dutch merchant, 'bout *ragion' del stato*.
From him I went and paid a *moccinigo*
For piecing my silk stockings; by the way
I cheapen'd sprats; and at St. Mark's I urin'd."—
'Faith these are politic notes!
POLITIC. Sir, I do slip
No action of my life, thus but I quote it.
PEREGRINE. Believe me, it is wise!
POLITIC. Nay, sir, read forth.

161 **their** the Venetians'
168 **Notandum** for the record
174 **ragion' del stato** matters of state
177 **cheapen'd** priced

SCENE II

[*Enter, at a distance,* LADY POLITIC WOULD-BE, NANO, *and the two* WAITING WOMEN.]

LADY. Where should this loose knight be, trow? Sure h' is hous'd.
NANO. Why, then he's fast.
LADY. Ay, he plays both with me.
I pray you stay. This heat will do more harm
To my complexion than his heart is worth.
(I do not care to hinder, but to take him.)
How it comes off! [*Rubs her cheeks.*]
WOMAN. My master's yonder.
LADY. Where?
WOMAN. With a young gentleman.
LADY. That same's the party!
In man's apparel.—'Pray you, sir, jog my knight.
I will be tender to his reputation,
However he demerit.
POLITIC. My lady!
PEREGRINE. Where?
POLITIC. 'Tis she indeed, sir; you shall know her. She is,
Were she not mine, a lady of that merit,
For fashion and behavior, and for beauty,
I durst compare—
PEREGRINE. It seems you are not jealous,
That dare commend her.
POLITIC. Nay, and for discourse—
PEREGRINE. Being your wife, she cannot miss that.
POLITIC. Madam,
Here is a gentleman, 'pray you use him fairly;
He seems a youth, but he is—
LADY. None?
POLITIC. Yes, one
Has put his face as soon into the world—

15 jog nudge

LADY. You mean, as early? But today?
POLITIC. How's this!
LADY. Why, in this habit, sir; you apprehend me.
Well, Master Would-be, this doth not become you;
I had thought the odor, sir, of your good name
Had been more precious to you; that you would not
Have done this dire massacre on your honor;
One of your gravity, and rank besides!
But knights, I see, care little for the oath
They make to ladies—chiefly their own ladies.
POLITIC. Now, by my spurs, the symbol of my knighthood—
PEREGRINE [*aside*]. Lord, how his brain is humbled for an oath.
POLITIC. I reach you not.
LADY. Right, sir: your polity
May bear it through thus.—[*to* PEREGRINE] Sir, a word with you.
I would be loth to contest publicly
With any gentlewoman, or to seem
Froward, or violent, as the courtier says;
It comes too near rusticity in a lady,
Which I would shun by all means; and however
I may deserve from Master Would-be, yet
'T have one fair gentlewoman thus be made
Th' unkind instrument to wrong another,
And one she knows not, ay, and to persever;
In my poor judgment, is not warranted
From being a solecism in our sex,
If not in manners.
PEREGRINE. How is this!
POLITIC. Sweet madam,
Come nearer to your aim.
LADY. Marry, and will, sir.
Since you provoke me with your impudence,
And laughter of your light land-siren here,

34 **But** only
36 **this habit** male attire
45 **humbled** brought low, i.e., to his heels
60 **solecism** impropriety

Your Sporus, your hermaphrodite—

PEREGRINE. What's here?
Poetic fury and historic storms!

POLITIC. The gentleman, believe it, is of worth
And of our nation.

LADY. Ay, your Whitefriars nation?
Come, I blush for you, Master Would-be, I;
And am asham'd you should ha' no more forehead
Than thus to be the patron, or St. George,
To a lewd harlot, a base fricatrice,
A female devil, in a male outside.

POLITIC. Nay,
An you be such a one! I must bid adieu
To your delights. The case appears too liquid. [*Exit.*]

LADY. Ay, you may carry 't clear, with your state-face!—
But for your carnival concupiscence,
Who here is fled for liberty of conscience,
From furious persecution of the marshal,
Her will I disc'ple.

PEREGRINE. This is fine, i' faith!
And do you use this often? Is this part
Of your wit's exercise, 'gainst you have occasion?
Madam—

LADY. Go to, sir.

PEREGRINE. Do you hear me, lady?
Why, if your knight have set you to beg shirts,
Or to invite me home, you might have done it
A nearer way by far.

LADY. This cannot work you
Out of my snare.

68 **Sporus** Roman eunuch, a notorious victim of the emperor Nero's perversions
73 **Whitefriars nation** criminals (Whitefriars being a district in London where lawbreakers were safe from arrest)
75 **forehead** self-respect
76 **St. George** the patron saint of England
77 **fricatrice** prostitute
81 **liquid** transparent
86 **disc'ple** punish
88 **use** do

PEREGRINE. Why, am I in it, then?
Indeed your husband told me you were fair,
And so you are; only your nose inclines,
That side that's next the sun, to the queen-apple.
LADY. This cannot be endur'd by any patience.

SCENE III

[*Enter* MOSCA.]

MOSCA. What's the matter, madam?
LADY. If the Senate
Right not my quest in this, I will protest 'em
To all the world no aristocracy.
MOSCA. What is the injury, lady?
LADY. Why, the callet
You told me of, here I have ta'en disguis'd.
MOSCA. Who? this? what means your Ladyship? The creature
I mention'd to you is apprehended now,
Before the Senate; you shall see her—
LADY. Where?
MOSCA. I'll bring you to her. This young gentleman,
I saw him land this morning at the port.
LADY. Is 't possible? How has my judgment wander'd!
Sir, I must, blushing, say to you, I have err'd;
And plead your pardon.
PEREGRINE. What! more changes yet?
LADY. I hope you've not the malice to remember
A gentlewoman's passion. If you stay
In Venice here, please you to use me, sir—
MOSCA. Will you go, madam?
LADY. 'Pray you, sir, use me; in faith,
The more you see me the more I shall conceive
You have forgot our quarrel.
[*Exeunt* LADY WOULD-BE, MOSCA, NANO, *and* WAITING WOMEN.]
PEREGRINE. This is rare!

101 **queen-apple** red-cheeked apple
8 **callet** wench

Sir Politic Would-be? No, Sir Politic Bawd!
To bring me thus acquainted with his wife!
Well, wise Sir Pol, since you have practis'd thus
Upon my freshmanship, I'll try your salthead,
What proof it is against a counterplot. [*Exit.*]

SCENE IV. *The Senate House.*

[*Enter* VOLTORE, CORBACCIO, CORVINO, *and* MOSCA.]

VOLTORE. Well, now you know the carriage of the business,
Your constancy is all that is requir'd
Unto the safety of it. [*He stands aside.*]
MOSCA. Is the lie
Safely convey'd amongst us? Is that sure?
Knows every man his burden?
CORVINO. Yes.
MOSCA. Then shrink not.
CORVINO. But knows the advocate the truth?
MOSCA. Oh, sir,
By no means; I devis'd a formal tale,
That salv'd your reputation. But be valiant, sir.
CORVINO. I fear no one but him, that this his pleading
Should make him stand for a co-heir—
MOSCA. Co-halter!
Hang him; we will but use his tongue, his noise,
As we do croaker's here.
CORVINO. Ay, what shall he do?
MOSCA. When we ha' done, you mean?
CORVINO. Yes.
MOSCA. Why, we'll think;
Sell him for mummia: he's half dust already.—

32 **salthead** seniority or "seasoned" experience, also connoting lechery
1 **carriage** setup
8 **burden** part
11 **the advocate** Voltore
19 **croaker's** Corbaccio's
24 **mummia** a drug made from mummies

[*to* VOLTORE] Do you not smile, to see this buffalo,
How he doth sport it with his head?—[*aside*] I should,
If all were well and past.—[*to* CORBACCIO] Sir, only you
Are he that shall enjoy the crop of all,
And these not know for whom they toil.

CORBACCIO. Ay, peace.

MOSCA [*to* CORVINO]. But you shall eat it.—[*aside*] Much!—[*then to* VOLTORE *again*] Worshipful sir,
Mercury sit upon your thund'ring tongue,
Or the French Hercules, and make your language
As conquering as his club, to beat along,
As with a tempest, flat, our adversaries;
But much more yours, sir.

VOLTORE. Here they come; ha' done.

MOSCA. I have another witness, if you need, sir,
I can produce.

VOLTORE. Who is it?

MOSCA. Sir, I have her.

SCENE V

[*Enter four* AVOCATORI, BONARIO, CELIA, NOTARIO, COMMANDADORI, SAFFI, *and other* OFFICERS OF JUSTICE.]

1 AVOCATORE. The like of this the Senate never heard of.

2 AVOCATORE. 'Twill come most strange to them when we report it.

4 AVOCATORE. The gentlewoman has been ever held
Of unreproved name.

3 AVOCATORE. So, the young man.

4 AVOCATORE. The more unnatural part that of his father.

2 AVOCATORE. More of the husband.

1 AVOCATORE. I not know to give
His act a name, it is so monstrous!

4 AVOCATORE. But the impostor, he is a thing created
T' exceed example!

25 **buffalo** cuckold (Corvino)
33 **Mercury** god of eloquence, perjury, and commerce
34 **French Hercules** Ogmius, a legendary spellbinder

1 AVOCATORE. And all after-times!
2 AVOCATORE. I never heard a true voluptuary
Describ'd but him.
3 AVOCATORE. Appear yet those were cited?
NOTARIO. All but the old magnifico, Volpone.
1 AVOCATORE. Why is not he here?
MOSCA. Please your Fatherhoods.
Here is his advocate. Himself's so weak,
So feeble—
4 AVOCATORE. What are you?
BONARIO. His parasite,
His knave, his pander. I beseech the court
He may be forc'd to come, that your grave eyes
May bear strong witness of his strange impostures.
VOLTORE. Upon my faith and credit with your Virtues,
He is not able to endure the air.
2 AVOCATORE. Bring him, however.
3 AVOCATORE. We will see him.
4 AVOCATORE. Fetch him.
VOLTORE. Your Fatherhoods' fit pleasures be obey'd;
[*Exeunt* OFFICERS.]
But sure, the sight will rather move your pities
Than indignation. May it please the court,
In the meantime, he may be heard in me.
I know this place most void of prejudice,
And therefore crave it, since we have no reason
To fear our truth should hurt our cause.
3 AVOCATORE. Speak free.
VOLTORE. Then know, most honor'd fathers, I must now
Discover to your strangely abused ears,
The most prodigious and most frontless piece
Of solid impudence and treachery
That ever vicious nature yet brought forth
To shame the state of Venice. This lewd woman,
That wants no artificial looks or tears
To help the visor she has now put on,
Hath long been known a close adulteress

45 **frontless** shameless
51 **close** secret

To that lascivious youth there; not suspected,
I say, but known, and taken in the act
With him; and by this man, the easy husband,
Pardon'd; whose timeless bounty makes him now
Stand here, the most unhappy, innocent person
That ever man's own goodness made accus'd.
For these, not knowing how to owe a gift
Of that dear grace, but with their shame, being plac'd
So above all powers of their gratitude,
Began to hate the benefit, and, in place
Of thanks, devise t' extirp the memory
Of such an act. Wherein I pray your Fatherhoods
To observe the malice, yea, the rage of creatures
Discover'd in their evils; and what heart
Such take, ev'n from their crimes. But that anon
Will more appear. This gentleman, the father,
Hearing of this foul fact, with many others,
Which daily struck at his too tender ears,
And griev'd in nothing more than that he could not
Preserve himself a parent (his son's ills
Growing to that strange flood), at last decreed
To disinherit him.

1 AVOCATORE. These be strange turns!

2 AVOCATORE. The young man's fame was ever fair and honest.

VOLTORE. So much more full of danger is his vice,
That can beguile so, under shade of virtue.
But, as I said, my honor'd sires, his father
Having this settled purpose, by what means
To him betray'd, we know not, and this day
Appointed for the deed; that parricide
I cannot style him better, by confederacy
Preparing this his paramour to be there,
Ent'red Volpone's house (who was the man,
Your Fatherhoods must understand, design'd
For the inheritance), there sought his father:—
But with what purpose sought he him, my Lords?

55 **timeless** untimely
62 **extirp** extirpate

I tremble to pronounce it, that a son
Unto a father, and to such a father,
Should have so foul, felonious intent–
It was to murder him; when, being prevented
By his more happy absence, what then did he?
Not check his wicked thoughts; no, now new deeds
(Mischief doth ever end where it begins)–
An act of horror, fathers! He dragg'd forth
The aged gentleman that had there lain bedrid
Three years and more, out off his innocent couch,
Naked upon the floor; there left him; wounded
His servant in the face; and with this strumpet,
The stale to his forg'd practice, who was glad
To be so active,–I shall here desire
Your Fatherhoods to note but my collections,
As most remarkable,–thought at once to stop
His father's ends, discredit his free choice
In the old gentleman, redeem themselves,
By laying infamy upon this man,
To whom, with blushing, they should owe their lives.

1 AVOCATORE. What proofs have you of this?

BONARIO. Most honor'd fathers,
I humbly crave there be no credit given
To this man's mercenary tongue.

2 AVOCATORE. Forbear.

BONARIO. His soul moves in his fee.

3 AVOCATORE. O, sir.

BONARIO. This fellow,
For six sols more would plead against his Maker.

1 AVOCATORE. You do forget yourself.

VOLTORE. Nay, nay, grave fathers,
Let him have scope! Can any man imagine
That he will spare his accuser, that would not
Have spar'd his parent?

100 **stale** decoy
102 **collections** conclusions, summary
105 **gentleman** Volpone
106 **this man** Corvino

1 AVOCATORE. Well, produce your proofs.
CELIA. I would I could forget I were a creature.
VOLTORE. Signior Corbaccio.
4 AVOCATORE. What is he?
VOLTORE. The father.
2 AVOCATORE. Has he had an oath?
NOTARIO. Yes.
CORBACCIO. What must I do now?
NOTARIO. Your testimony's crav'd.
CORBACCIO. Speak to the knave?
I'll ha' my mouth first stopp'd with earth; my heart
Abhors his knowledge: I disclaim in him.
1 AVOCATORE. But for what cause?
CORBACCIO. The mere portent of nature.
He is an utter stranger to my loins.
BONARIO. Have they made you to this!
CORBACCIO. I will not hear thee,
Monster of men, swine, goat, wolf, parricide;
Speak not, thou viper.
BONARIO. Sir, I will sit down,
And rather wish my innocence should suffer
Than I resist the authority of a father.
VOLTORE. Signior Corvino.
2 AVOCATORE. This is strange!
1 AVOCATORE. Who's this?
NOTARIO. The husband.
4 AVOCATORE. Is he sworn?
NOTARIO. He is.
3 AVOCATORE. Speak then.
CORVINO. This woman, please your Fatherhoods, is a whore,
Of most hot exercise, more than a partridge,
Upon record—
1 AVOCATORE. No more.
CORVINO. Neighs like a jennet.
NOTARIO. Preserve the honor of the court.
CORVINO. I shall,

135 **The . . . nature** the direct evidence of his unnatural behavior
137 **made** brought

And modesty of your most reverend ears.
And yet I hope that I may say these eyes
Have seen her glu'd unto that piece of cedar,
That fine well-timber'd gallant; and that here
The letters may be read, thorough the horn,
That make the story perfect.

MOSCA [*aside to* CORVINO]. Excellent, sir!

CORVINO [*aside to* MOSCA]. There is no shame in this now, is there?

MOSCA [*aside to* CORVINO]. None.

CORVINO. Or if I said, I hop'd that she were onward
To her damnation, if there be a hell
Greater than whore and woman, a good Catholic
May make the doubt.

3 AVOCATORE. His grief hath made him frantic.

1 AVOCATORE. Remove him hence.

2 AVOCATORE. Look to the woman. [*She swoons.*]

CORVINO. Rare!
Prettily feign'd! again!

4 AVOCATORE. Stand from about her.

1 AVOCATORE. Give her the air.

3 AVOCATORE [*to* MOSCA]. What can you say?

MOSCA. My wound,
May 't please your Wisdoms, speaks for me, receiv'd
In aid of my good patron, when he miss'd
His sought-for father, when that well-taught dame
Had her cue giv'n her to cry out, "A rape!"

BONARIO. O most laid impudence! Fathers—

3 AVOCATORE. Sir, be silent;
You had your hearing free, so must they theirs.

2 AVOCATORE. I do begin to doubt th' imposture here.

4 AVOCATORE. This woman has too many moods.

VOLTORE. Grave fathers,

161 **here** on my forehead

162 **horn** of a cuckold; also the sheet of transparent horn used to protect the page of a child's reader

167–70 **Or . . . doubt** Or if I were to say I hoped that she were going to hell, an orthodox Catholic might still doubt whether there is a hell worse than being a whore and woman

184 **laid** contrived

She is a creature of a most profess'd
And prostituted lewdness.

CORVINO. Most impetuous!
Unsatisfied, grave fathers!

VOLTORE. May her feignings
Not take your wisdoms. But this day she baited
A stranger, a grave knight, with her loose eyes
And more lascivious kisses. This man saw 'em
Together on the water, in a gondola.

MOSCA. Here is the lady herself, that saw 'em too,
Without; who then had in the open streets
Pursu'd them, but for saving her knight's honor.

1 AVOCATORE. Produce that lady.

2 AVOCATORE. Let her come. [*Exit* MOSCA.]

4 AVOCATORE. These things,
They strike with wonder!

3 AVOCATORE. I am turn'd a stone!

SCENE VI

[*Re-enter* MOSCA *with* LADY WOULD-BE.]

MOSCA. Be resolute, madam.

LADY. Ay, this same is she.—
Out, thou chameleon harlot! now thine eyes
Vie tears with the hyena. Dar'st thou look
Upon my wronged face?—I cry your pardons.
I fear I have forgettingly transgress'd
Against the dignity of the court—

2 AVOCATORE. No, madam.

LADY. And been exorbitant—

2 AVOCATORE. You have not, lady.

4 AVOCATORE. These proofs are strong.

LADY. Surely, I had no purpose
To scandalize your honors, or my sex's.

3 AVOCATORE. We do believe it.

LADY. Surely you may believe it.

2 AVOCATORE. Madam, we do.

LADY. Indeed you may; my breeding
Is not so coarse—
4 AVOCATORE. We know it.
LADY. To offend
With pertinacy—
3 AVOCATORE. Lady—
LADY. Such a presence;
No, surely.
1 AVOCATORE. We will think it.
LADY. You may think it.
1 AVOCATORE. Let her o'ercome.—What witnesses have you,
To make good your report?
BONARIO. Our consciences.
CELIA. And Heaven, that never fails the innocent.
1 AVOCATORE. These are no testimonies.
BONARIO. Not in your courts,
Where multitude and clamor overcomes.
1 AVOCATORE. Nay, then you do wax insolent.
[VOLPONE *is brought in, as impotent.*]
VOLTORE. Here, here,
The testimony comes that will convince,
And put to utter dumbness their bold tongues.
See here, grave fathers, here's the ravisher,
The rider on men's wives, the great impostor,
The grand voluptuary! Do you not think
These limbs should affect venery? or these eyes
Covet a concubine? Pray you mark these hands.
Are they not fit to stroke a lady's breasts?
Perhaps he doth dissemble!
BONARIO. So he does.
VOLTORE. Would you ha' him tortur'd?
BONARIO. I would have him prov'd.
VOLTORE. Best try him then with goads, or burning irons;
Put him to the strappado; I have heard
The rack hath cur'd the gout; faith, give it him,
And help him of a malady; be courteous.
I'll undertake, before these honor'd fathers,
He shall have yet as many left diseases,

As she has known adulterers, or thou strumpets.
O, my most equal hearers, if these deeds,
Acts of this bold and most exorbitant strain,
May pass with sufferance, what one citizen
But owes the forfeit of his life, yea, fame,
To him that dares traduce him? Which of you
Are safe, my honor'd fathers? I would ask,
With leave of your grave Fatherhoods, if their plot
Have any face or color like to truth?
Or if, unto the dullest nostril here,
It smell not rank, and most abhorred slander?
I crave your care of this good gentleman,
Whose life is much endanger'd by their fable;
And as for them, I will conclude with this:
That vicious persons, when they are hot, and flesh'd
In impious acts, their constancy abounds:
Damn'd deeds are done with greatest confidence.

1 AVOCATORE. Take 'em to custody, and sever them.

2 AVOCATORE. 'Tis pity two such prodigies should live.

1 AVOCATORE. Let the old gentleman be return'd with care.

[*Exeunt* OFFICERS *with* VOLPONE.]

I am sorry our credulity wrong'd him.

4 AVOCATORE. These are two creatures!

3 AVOCATORE. I have an earthquake in me!

2 AVOCATORE. Their shame, even in their cradles, fled their faces.

4 AVOCATORE. You have done a worthy service to the state, sir,
In their discovery.

1 AVOCATORE. You shall hear, ere night,
What punishment the court decrees upon 'em.

[*Exeunt* AVOCATORI, NOTARIO, *and* OFFICERS *with* BONARIO *and* CELIA.]

VOLTORE. We thank your Fatherhoods.—How like you it?

MOSCA. Rare.
I'd ha' your tongue, sir, tipp'd with gold for this;
I'd ha' you be the heir to the whole city;
The earth I'd have want men ere you want living:

58 **equal** equitable
71 **flesh'd** plunged

They are bound to erect your statue in St. Mark's.—
Signior Corvino, I would have you go
And show yourself that you have conquer'd.
CORVINO. Yes.
MOSCA. It was much better that you should profess
Yourself a cuckold thus, than that the other
Should have been prov'd.
CORVINO. Nay, I consider'd that;
Now it is her fault.
MOSCA. Then, it had been yours.
CORVINO. True.—[*aside to* MOSCA] I do doubt this advocate still.
MOSCA [*aside*]. I' faith,
You need not; I dare ease you of that care.
CORVINO [*aside*]. I trust thee, Mosca.
MOSCA [*aside*]. As your own soul, sir.
[*Exit* CORVINO.]
CORBACCIO. Mosca!
MOSCA. Now for your business, sir.
CORBACCIO. How? ha' you business?
MOSCA. Yes, yours, sir.
CORBACCIO. O, none else?
MOSCA. None else, not I.
CORBACCIO. Be careful then.
MOSCA. Rest you with both your eyes, sir.
CORBACCIO. Dispatch it.
MOSCA. Instantly.
CORBACCIO. And look that all,
Whatever, be put in, jewels, plate, monies,
Household stuff, bedding, curtains.
MOSCA. Curtain-rings, sir;
Only, the advocate's fee must be deducted.
CORBACCIO. I'll pay him now; you'll be too prodigal.
MOSCA. Sir, I must tender it.
CORBACCIO. Two *cecchines* is well.
MOSCA. No, six, sir.
CORBACCIO. 'Tis too much.
MOSCA. He talk'd a great while;

116 **Rest . . . eyes** Don't lose a wink of sleep

You must consider that, sir.
CORBACCIO. Well, there's three—
MOSCA. I'll give it him.
CORBACCIO. Do so, and there's for thee. [*Exit.*]
MOSCA [*aside*]. Bountiful bones! What horrid strange offence
Did he commit 'gainst nature, in his youth,
Worthy this age?—[*aside to* VOLTORE] You see, sir, how I work
Unto your ends; take you no notice.
VOLTORE. No,
I'll leave you.
MOSCA [*aside*]. All is yours, the devil and all,
Good advocate.—Madam, I'll bring you home.
LADY. No, I'll go see your patron.
MOSCA. That you shall not;
I'll tell you why. My purpose is to urge
My patron to reform his will, and for
The zeal you have shown today, whereas before
You were but third or fourth, you shall be now
Put in the first; which would appear as begg'd
If you were present. Therefore—
LADY. You shall sway me.
[*Exeunt.*]

ACT V

SCENE I. A room in Volpone's house.

[*Enter* VOLPONE.]

VOLPONE. Well, I am here, and all this brunt is past.
I ne'er was in dislike with my disguise
Till this fled moment: here 'twas good, in private;
But in your public, *cave,* whilst I breathe.

4 **cave** beware

'Fore God, my left leg 'gan to have the cramp.
And I apprehended straight some power had struck me
With a dead palsy. Well, I must be merry,
And shake it off. A many of these fears
Would put me into some villainous disease,
Should they come thick upon me. I'll prevent 'em.
Give me a bowl of lusty wine, to fright
This humor from my heart.—[*He drinks.*] Hum, hum, hum!—
'Tis almost gone already; I shall conquer.
Any device now of rare ingenious knavery,
That would possess me with a violent laughter,
Would make me up again!—[*Drinks again.*] So, so, so, so!—
This heat is life; 'tis blood by this time.—Mosca!

SCENE II

[*Enter* MOSCA.]

MOSCA. How now, sir? Does the day look clear again?
Are we recover'd, and wrought out of error,
Into our way, to see our path before us?
Is our trade free once more?

VOLPONE. Exquisite Mosca!

MOSCA. Was it not carri'd learnedly?

VOLPONE. And stoutly:
Good wits are greatest in extremities.

MOSCA. It were folly beyond thought to trust
Any grand act unto a cowardly spirit.
You are not taken with it enough, methinks.

VOLPONE. Oh, more than if I had enjoy'd the wench;
The pleasure of all womankind's not like it.

MOSCA. Why, now you speak, sir. We must here be fix'd;
Here we must rest; this is our masterpiece;
We cannot think to go beyond this.

VOLPONE. True,
Thou hast play'd thy prize, my precious Mosca.

17 **rest** stop

MOSCA. Nay, sir,
To gull the court—
VOLPONE. And quite divert the torrent
Upon the innocent.
MOSCA. Yes, and to make
So rare a music out of discords—
VOLPONE. Right.
That yet to me's the strangest! how th' hast borne it!
That these, being so divided 'mongst themselves,
Should not scent somewhat, or in me or thee,
Or doubt their own side.
MOSCA. True, they will not see 't.
Too much light blinds 'em, I think. Each of 'em
Is so possess'd and stuff'd with his own hopes
That anything unto the contrary,
Never so true, or never so apparent,
Never so palpable, they will resist it—
VOLPONE. Like a temptation of the Devil.
MOSCA. Right, sir.
Merchants may talk of trade, and your great signiors
Of land that yields well; but if Italy
Have any glebe more fruitful than these fellows,
I am deceiv'd. Did not your advocate rare?
VOLPONE. Oh—"My most honor'd fathers, my grave fathers,
Under correction of your Fatherhoods,
What face of truth is here? If these strange deeds
May pass, most honor'd fathers"—I had much ado
To forbear laughing.
MOSCA. 'T seem'd to me you sweat, sir.
VOLPONE. In troth, I did a little.
MOSCA. But confess, sir,
Were you not daunted?
VOLPONE. In good faith, I was
A little in a mist, but not dejected;
Never, but still myself.
MOSCA. I think it, sir.
Now, so truth help me, I must needs say this, sir,

43 **rare** excellently

And out of conscience for your advocate,
He has taken pains, in faith, sir, and deserv'd,
In my poor judgment, I speak it under favor,
Not to contrary you, sir, very richly—
Well—to be cozen'd.

VOLPONE. Troth, and I think so too,
By that I heard him in the latter end.

MOSCA. O, but before, sir: had you heard him first
Draw it to certain heads, then aggravate,
Then use his vehement figures—I look'd still
When he would shift a shirt; and doing this
Out of pure love, no hope of gain—

VOLPONE. 'Tis right.
I cannot answer him, Mosca, as I would,
Not yet; but for thy sake, at thy entreaty,
I will begin, ev'n now—to vex 'em all,
This very instant.

MOSCA. Good, sir.

VOLPONE. Call the dwarf
And eunuch forth.

MOSCA. Castrone, Nano!

[*Enter* CASTRONE *and* NANO.]

NANO. Here.

VOLPONE. Shall we have a jig now?

MOSCA. What you please, sir.

VOLPONE. Go,
Straight give out about the streets, you two,
That I am dead; do it with constancy,
Sadly, do you hear? Impute it to the grief
Of this late slander. [*Exeunt* CASTRONE *and* NANO.]

MOSCA. What do you mean, sir?

VOLPONE. Oh,
I shall have instantly my Vulture, Crow,
Raven, come flying hither, on the news,
To peck for carrion, my she-wolf, and all,

62 **cozen'd** cheated
67 **figures** of speech and gesture
68 **shift** change (because of his violent exertions)

Greedy, and full of expectation—
MOSCA. And then to have it ravish'd from their mouths?
VOLPONE. 'Tis true. I will ha' thee put on a gown,
And take upon thee, as thou wert mine heir;
Show 'em a will. Open that chest, and reach
Forth one of those that has the blanks. I'll straight
Put in thy name.
MOSCA. It will be rare, sir.
VOLPONE. Ay,
When they e'en gape, and find themselves deluded—
MOSCA. Yes.
VOLPONE. And thou use them scurvily. Dispatch;
Get on thy gown.
MOSCA. But what, sir, if they ask
After the body?
VOLPONE. Say, it was corrupted.
MOSCA. I'll say it stunk, sir; and was fain t' have it
Coffin'd up instantly, and sent away.
VOLPONE. Anything; what thou wilt.—Hold, here's my will.
Get thee a cap, a count-book, pen and ink,
Papers afore thee; sit as thou wert taking
An inventory of parcels. I'll get up
Behind the curtain, on a stool, and hearken;
Sometime peep over, see how they do look,
With what degrees their blood doth leave their faces!
O, 'twill afford me a rare meal of laughter.
MOSCA. Your advocate will turn stark dull upon it.
VOLPONE. It will take off his oratory's edge.
MOSCA. But your clarissimo, old roundback, he
Will crump you like a hog-louse, with the touch.
VOLPONE. And what Corvino?
MOSCA. O, sir, look for him,
Tomorrow morning, with a rope and a dagger,
To visit all the streets; he must run mad.
My Lady too, that came into the court,

95 **gown** a gentleman's attire
121 **clarissimo** grandee (Corbaccio)
122 **crump you** crumple up

To bear false witness for your Worship—
VOLPONE. Yes.
And kiss'd me 'fore the fathers, when my face
Flow'd all with oils—
MOSCA. And sweat, sir. Why, your gold
Is such another med'cine, it dries up
All those offensive savors. It transforms
The most deformed, and restores 'em lovely,
As 'twere the strange poetical girdle. Jove
Could not invent t' himself a shroud more subtle
To pass Acrisius' guards. It is the thing
Makes all the world her grace, her youth, her beauty.
VOLPONE. I think she loves me.
MOSCA. Who? the lady, sir?
She's jealous of you.
VOLPONE. Dost thou say so?
[*Knocking within.*]
MOSCA. Hark.
There's some already.
VOLPONE. Look.
MOSCA. It is the Vulture;
He has the quickest scent.
VOLPONE. I'll to my place,
Thou to thy posture. [*Goes behind the curtain.*]
MOSCA. I am set.
VOLPONE. But, Mosca,
Play the artificer now: torture 'em rarely.

SCENE III

[*Enter* VOLTORE.]

VOLTORE. How now, my Mosca?
MOSCA [*writing*]. Turkey carpets, nine—
VOLTORE. Taking an inventory! that is well.

136 **girdle** of Venus
138 **Acrisius** whose daughter, Danae, was seduced by Jove disguised in a shower of gold

MOSCA. Two suits of bedding, tissue—

VOLTORE. Where's the will?
Let me read that the while.

[*Enter* SERVANTS *with* CORBACCIO *in a chair.*]

CORBACCIO. So, set me down,
And get you home. [*Exeunt* SERVANTS.]

VOLTORE. Is he come now, to trouble us?

MOSCA. Of cloth of gold, two more—

CORBACCIO. Is it done, Mosca?

MOSCA. Of several velvets, eight—

VOLTORE. I like his care.

CORBACCIO. Dost thou not hear?

[*Enter* CORVINO.]

CORVINO. Ha! is the hour come, Mosca?

VOLPONE [*aside*]. Ay, now they muster. [*Peeps from behind a traverse.*]

CORVINO. What does the advocate here?
Or this Corbaccio?

CORBACCIO. What do these here?

[*Enter* LADY WOULD-BE.]

LADY. Mosca!
Is his thread spun?

MOSCA. Eight chests of linen—

VOLPONE [*aside*]. Oh,
My fine Dame Would-be, too!

CORVINO. Mosca, the will,
That I may show it these, and rid 'em hence.

MOSCA. Six chests of diaper, four of damask—there. [*Gives the will.*]

CORBACCIO. Is that the will?

MOSCA [*writing*]. Down-beds, and bolsters—

VOLPONE [*aside*]. Rare!
Be busy still. Now they begin to flutter;
They never think of me. Look, see, see, see!
How their swift eyes run over the long deed,
Unto the name, and to the legacies,
What is bequeath'd them there—

21 **traverse** curtain
27 **thread** of life

MOSCA. Ten suits of hangings—
VOLPONE [*aside*]. Ay, in their garters, Mosca. Now their hopes
Are at the gasp.
VOLTORE. Mosca the heir!
CORBACCIO. What's that?
VOLPONE [*aside*]. My advocate is dumb; look to my merchant—
He has heard of some strange storm; a ship is lost—
He faints. My Lady will swoon. Old glazen-eyes,
He hath not reach'd his despair yet.
CORBACCIO. All these
Are out of hope; I am, sure, the man. [*Takes the will.*]
CORVINO. But, Mosca—
MOSCA. Two cabinets—
CORVINO. Is this in earnest?
MOSCA. One
Of ebony—
CORVINO. Or do you but delude me?
MOSCA. The other, mother-of-pearl—I am very busy.
Good faith, it is a fortune thrown upon me—
Item, one salt of agate—not my seeking.
LADY. Do you hear, sir?
MOSCA. A perfum'd box—'pray you forbear;
You see I am troubled—made of an onyx—
LADY. How!
MOSCA. Tomorrow or next day, I shall be at leisure
To talk with you all.
CORVINO. Is this my large hope's issue?
LADY. Sir, I must have a fairer answer.
MOSCA. Madam!
Marry, and shall: 'pray you, fairly quit my house.
Nay, raise no tempest with your looks; but hark you,
Remember what your Ladyship off'red me
To put you in, an heir; go to; think on it.
And what you said e'en your best madams did
For maintenance, and why not you? Enough.
Go home, and use the poor Sir Pol, your knight, well,

47 **merchant** Corvino
61 **salt** salt-dish

For fear I tell some riddles; go, be melancholic.
[*Exit* LADY WOULD-BE.]

VOLPONE [*aside*]. Oh, my fine devil!

CORVINO. Mosca, pray you a word.

MOSCA. Lord! will not you take your dispatch hence yet?
Methinks, of all, you should have been th' example.
Why should you stay here? with what thought, what promise?
Hear you; do not you know, I know you an ass,
And that you would most fain have been a wittol
If fortune would have let you? that you are
A declar'd cuckold, on good terms? This pearl,
You'll say, was yours? right; this diamond?
I'll not deny 't, but thank you. Much here else?
It may be so. Why, think that these good works
May help to hide your bad. I'll not betray you;
Although you be but extraordinary,
And have it only in title, it sufficeth:
Go home; be melancholic too, or mad. [*Exit* CORVINO.]

VOLPONE [*aside*]. Rare Mosca! how his villainy becomes him!

VOLTORE [*aside*]. Certain he doth delude all these for me.

CORBACCIO. Mosca the heir?

VOLPONE [*aside*]. O, his four eyes have found it!

CORBACCIO. I am cozen'd, cheated, by a parasite-slave;
Harlot, th' hast gull'd me.

MOSCA. Yes, sir. Stop your mouth,
Or I shall draw the only tooth is left.
Are not you he, that filthy covetous wretch,
With the three legs, that here, in hope of prey,
Have, any time this three year, snuff'd about,
With your most grov'ling nose, and would have hir'd
Me to the pois'ning of my patron, sir?
Are not you he that have today in court
Profess'd the disinheriting of your son?
Perjur'd yourself? Go home, and die, and stink;
If you but croak a syllable, all comes out:
Away, and call your porters! [*Exit* CORBACCIO.] Go, go, stink.

93 **but extraordinary** a cuckold only in a special sense

VOLPONE [*aside*]. Excellent varlet!

VOLTORE. Now, my faithful Mosca,
I find thy constancy—

MOSCA. Sir!

VOLTORE. Sincere.

MOSCA [*writing*]. A table
Of porphyry—I mar'l you'll be thus troublesome.

VOLTORE. Nay, leave off now, they are gone.

MOSCA. Why, who are you?
What! who did send for you? Oh, cry you mercy,
Reverend sir! Good faith, I am griev'd for you,
That any chance of mine should thus defeat
Your (I must needs say) most deserving travails;
But I protest, sir, it was cast upon me,
And I could almost wish to be without it,
But that the will o' th' dead must be observ'd.
Marry, my joy is that you need it not;
You have a gift, sir, (thank your education)
Will never let you want, while there are men,
And malice, to breed causes. Would I had
But half the like, for all my fortune, sir.
If I have any suits, as I do hope,
Things being so easy and direct, I shall not,
I will make bold with your obstreperous aid
(Conceive me) for your fee, sir. In meantime,
You that have so much law, I know ha' the conscience
Not to be covetous of what is mine.
Good sir, I thank you for my plate; 'twill help
To set up a young man. Good faith, you look
As you were costive; best go home and purge, sir.

[*Exit* VOLTORE.]

VOLPONE [*coming from behind the curtain*]. Bid him eat lettuce well.
My witty mischief,
Let me embrace thee. O that I could now
Transform thee to a Venus!—Mosca, go,

114 **varlet** servant
133 **causes** law cases
137 **obstreperous** clamorous

Straight take my habit of clarissimo,
And walk the streets; be seen, torment 'em more;
We must pursue, as well as plot. Who would
Have lost this feast?

MOSCA. I doubt it will lose them.

VOLPONE. O, my recovery shall recover all.
That I could now but think on some disguise
To meet 'em in, and ask 'em questions.
How I would vex 'em still at every turn!

MOSCA. Sir, I can fit you.

VOLPONE. Canst thou?

MOSCA. Yes, I know
One o' the commandadori, sir; so like you,
Him will I straight make drunk, and bring you his habit.

VOLPONE. A rare disguise, and answering thy brain!
O, I will be a sharp disease unto 'em.

MOSCA. Sir, you must look for curses—

VOLPONE. Till they burst;
The Fox fares ever best when he is curs'd. [*Exeunt.*]

SCENE IV. *A hall in Sir Politic's house.*

[*Enter* PEREGRINE *disguised and three* MERCATORI.]

PEREGRINE. Am I enough disguis'd?

1 MERCATORE. I warrant you.

PEREGRINE. All my ambition is to fright him only.

2 MERCATORE. If you could ship him away, 'twere excellent.

3 MERCATORE. To Zant, or to Aleppo!

PEREGRINE. Yes, and ha' his
Adventures put i' th' Book of Voyages,
And his gull'd story regist'red for truth!
Well, gentlemen, when I am in awhile,
And that you think us warm in our discourse,

149 **habit of clarissimo** robes of state
153 **doubt** fear
9 **Book of Voyages** travel narratives, of which Richard Hakluyt's *Principal Navigations, Voyages, and Discoveries* was the type

Know your approaches.
1 MERCATORE. Trust it to our care.
[*Exeunt* MERCATORI.]

[*Enter* WAITING WOMAN.]

PEREGRINE. Save you, fair lady! Is Sir Pol within?
WOMAN. I do not know, sir.
PEREGRINE. 'Pray you say unto him
Here is a merchant, upon earnest business,
Desires to speak with him.
WOMAN. I will see, sir. [*Exit.*]
PEREGRINE. 'Pray you.
I see the family is all female here.

[*Re-enter* WAITING WOMAN.]

WOMAN. He says, sir, he has weighty affairs of state,
That now require him whole; some other time
You may possess him.
PEREGRINE. 'Pray you say again,
If those require him whole, these will exact him,
Whereof I bring him tidings. [*Exit* WOMAN.] What might be
His grave affair of state now! How to make
Bolognian sausages here in Venice, sparing
One o' th' ingredients?

[*Re-enter* WAITING WOMAN.]

WOMAN. Sir, he says he knows
By your word "tidings," that you are no statesman,
And therefore wills you stay.
PEREGRINE. Sweet, 'pray you return him
I have not read so many proclamations,
And studied them for words, as he has done—
But—here he deigns to come. [*Exit* WOMAN.]

[*Enter* SIR POLITIC.]

POLITIC. Sir, I must crave
Your courteous pardon. There hath chanc'd today
Unkind disaster 'twixt my lady and me;
And I was penning my apology,

30 **exact** draw out; as opposed to *require,* which literally means *call back.* Peregrine is matching Sir Politic's Latinisms.
37 **"tidings"** (a plain English word)

To give her satisfaction, as you came now.
PEREGRINE. Sir, I am griev'd I bring you worse disaster.
The gentleman you met at th' port today,
That told you he was newly arriv'd—
POLITIC. Ay, was
A fugitive punk?
PEREGRINE. No, sir, a spy set on you;
And he has made relation to the Senate,
That you profess'd to him to have a plot
To sell the state of Venice to the Turk.
POLITIC. O me!
PEREGRINE. For which warrants are sign'd by this time,
To apprehend you, and to search your study
For papers—
POLITIC. Alas, sir, I have none, but notes
Drawn out of play-books—
PEREGRINE. All the better, sir.
POLITIC. And some essays. What shall I do?
PEREGRINE. Sir, best
Convey yourself into a sugar-chest;
Or, if you could lie round, a frail were rare;
And I could send you aboard.
POLITIC. Sir, I but talk'd so.
For discourse sake merely. [*They knock without.*]
PEREGRINE. Hark! they are there.
POLITIC. I am a wretch, a wretch!
PEREGRINE. What will you do, sir?
Have you ne'er a currant-butt to leap into?
They'll put you to the rack; you must be sudden.
POLITIC. Sir, I have an ingine—
3 MERCATORE [*within*]. Sir Politic Would-be!
2 MERCATORE [*within*]. Where is he?
POLITIC. That I've thought upon, before time.
PEREGRINE. What is it?

53 **punk** prostitute
68 **frail . . . rare** basket would be fine
75 **currant-butt** wine cask
77 **ingine** invention

POLITIC. I shall ne'er endure the torture.—
Marry, it is, sir, of a tortoise shell,
Fitted for these extremities; 'pray you, sir, help me.
Here I have a place, sir, to put back my legs,
Please you to lay it on, sir, [*Lies down while* PEREGRINE *places the shell upon him.*] with this cap,
And my black gloves. I'll lie, sir, like a tortoise,
Till they are gone.

PEREGRINE. And call you this an ingine?

POLITIC. Mine own device.—Good sir, bid my wife's women
To burn my papers. [*Exit* PEREGRINE.]

[*The three* MERCATORI *rush in.*]

1 MERCATORE. Where's he hid?

3 MERCATORE. We must,
And will, sure, find him.

2 MERCATORE. Which is his study?

[*Re-enter* PEREGRINE.]

1 MERCATORE. What
Are you, sir?

PEREGRINE. I am a merchant, that came here
To look upon this tortoise.

3 MERCATORE. How?

1 MERCATORE. St. Mark!
What beast is this?

PEREGRINE. It is a fish.

2 MERCATORE. Come out here!

PEREGRINE. Nay, you may strike him, sir, and tread upon him;
He'll bear a cart.

1 MERCATORE. What, to run over him?

PEREGRINE. Yes, sir.

3 MERCATORE. Let's jump upon him.

2 MERCATORE. Can he not go?

PEREGRINE. He creeps, sir.

1 MERCATORE. Let's see him creep.

PEREGRINE. No, good sir, you will hurt him.

2 MERCATORE. Heart, I'll see him creep, or prick his guts.

3 MERCATORE. Come out here.

PEREGRINE. 'Pray you, sir!—[*aside to* SIR POLITIC] Creep a little.

1 MERCATORE. Forth.
2 MERCATORE. Yet further.
PEREGRINE. Good sir!—[*aside*] Creep!
2 MERCATORE. We'll see his legs.
[*They pull off the shell and discover him.*]
3 MERCATORE. Gods so, he has garters!
1 MERCATORE. Ay, and gloves!
2 MERCATORE. Is this
Your fearful tortoise?
PEREGRINE [*discovering himself*]. Now, Sir Pol, we are even;
For your next project I shall be prepar'd;
I am sorry for the funeral of your notes, sir.
1 MERCATORE. 'Twere a rare motion to be seen in Fleet Street.
2 MERCATORE. Ay, i' the term.
1 MERCATORE. Or Smithfield, in the fair.
3 MERCATORE. Methinks 'tis but a melancholic sight!
PEREGRINE. Farewell, most politic tortoise.
[*Exeunt* PEREGRINE *and* MERCATORI.]
[*Re-enter* WAITING WOMAN.]
POLITIC. Where's my Lady?
Knows she of this?
WOMAN. I know not, sir.
POLITIC. Inquire.—
Oh, I shall be the fable of all feasts,
The freight of the gazetti, ship-boys' tale;
And, which is worst, even talk for ordinaries.
WOMAN. My Lady's come most melancholic home,
And says, sir, she will straight to sea, for physic.
POLITIC. And I, to shun this place and clime for ever,
Creeping with house on back, and think it well
To shrink my poor head in my politic shell. [*Exeunt.*]

132 **motion** show
133 **term** when prisoners from the Fleet prison were led to trial
134 **Smithfield** London market, site of the great annual fair
144 **The . . . gazetti** grist for the gossip-sheets

SCENE V. A room in Volpone's house.

[*Enter* VOLPONE *and* MOSCA, *the first in the habit of a commandadore, the other of a clarissimo.*]

VOLPONE. Am I then like him?
MOSCA. O, sir, you are he;
No man can sever you.
VOLPONE. Good.
MOSCA. But what am I?
VOLPONE. 'Fore Heav'n, a brave clarissimo; thou becom'st it!
Pity thou wert not born one.
MOSCA. If I hold
My made one, 'twill be well.
VOLPONE. I'll go and see
What news first at the court. [*Exit.*]
MOSCA. Do so.—My Fox
Is out on his hole, and ere he shall re-enter,
I'll make him languish in his borrow'd case,
Except he come to composition with me.—
Androgyno, Castrone, Nano!
[*Enter* ANDROGYNO, CASTRONE, *and* NANO.]
ALL. Here.
MOSCA. Go, recreate yourselves abroad; go, sport.—
[*Exeunt all but* MOSCA.]
So, now I have the keys, and am possess'd.
Since he will needs be dead afore his time,
I'll bury him, or gain by him. I am his heir,
And so will keep me, till he share, at least.
To cozen him of all, were but a cheat
Well plac'd; no man would construe it a sin;
Let his sport pay for 't. This is call'd the Fox-trap. [*Exit.*]

17 **case** skin
18 **composition** terms

SCENE VI. A Street.

[*Enter* CORBACCIO *and* CORVINO.]

CORBACCIO. They say the court is set.
CORVINO. We must maintain
Our first tale good, for both our reputations.
CORBACCIO. Why, mine's no tale; my son would there have kill'd me.
CORVINO. That's true; I had forgot;—[*aside*] mine is, I am sure.—
But for your will, sir.
CORBACCIO. Ay, I'll come upon him
For that hereafter, now his patron's dead.

[*Enter* VOLPONE *disguised.*]

VOLPONE. Signior Corvino! and Corbaccio! sir,
Much joy unto you.
CORVINO. Of what?
VOLPONE. The sudden good
Dropp'd down upon you—
CORBACCIO. Where?
VOLPONE. And none knows how—
From old Volpone, sir.
CORBACCIO. Out, errant knave!
VOLPONE. Let not your too much wealth, sir, make you furious.
CORBACCIO. Away, thou varlet.
VOLPONE. Why, sir?
CORBACCIO. Dost thou mock me?
VOLPONE. You mock the world, sir; did you not change wills?
CORBACCIO. Out, harlot.
VOLPONE. O! belike you are the man,
Signior Corvino? Faith, you carry it well;
You grow not mad withal; I love your spirit.
You are not overleaven'd with your fortune.
You should ha' some would swell now like a wine-vat,
With such an autumn.—Did he gi' you all, sir?
CORVINO. Avoid, you rascal.
VOLPONE. Troth, your wife has shown
Herself a very woman; but you are well,
You need not care, you have a good estate,

To bear it out, sir, better by this chance—
Except Corbaccio have a share.

CORBACCIO. Hence, varlet.

VOLPONE. You will not be acknown, sir; why, 'tis wise.
Thus do all gamesters, at all games, dissemble:
No man will seem to win. [*Exeunt* CORVINO *and* CORBACCIO.]
Here comes my vulture,
Heaving his beak up i' the air, and snuffing.

SCENE VII

[*Enter* VOLTORE.]

VOLTORE. Outstripp'd thus, by a parasite! a slave!
Would run on errands, and make legs for crumbs!
Well, what I'll do—

VOLPONE. The court stays for your Worship.
I e'en rejoice, sir, at your Worship's happiness,
And that it fell into so learned hands,
That understand the fingering—

VOLTORE. What do you mean?

VOLPONE. I mean to be a suitor to your Worship,
For the small tenement, out of reparations,
That at the end of your long row of houses,
By the Piscaria; it was, in Volpone's time,
Your predecessor, ere he grew diseas'd,
A handsome, pretty, custom'd bawdyhouse
As any was in Venice, none disprais'd;
But fell with him: his body and that house
Decay'd together.

VOLTORE. Come, sir, leave your prating.

VOLPONE. Why, if your Worship give me but your hand
That I may ha' the refusal, I have done.
'Tis a mere toy to you, sir, candle-rents;
As your learn'd Worship knows—

14 **Piscaria** fishmarket
16 **custom'd** well patronized
22 **refusal** option
23 **candle-rents** small change

VOLTORE. What do I know?
VOLPONE. Marry, no end of your wealth, sir; God decrease it!
VOLTORE. Mistaking knave! what, mock'st thou my misfortune?
[*Exit.*]
VOLPONE. His blessing on your heart, sir; would 'twere more!—
Now to my first again, at the next corner. [*Exit.*]

SCENE VIII. *Another corner of the street.*

[*Enter* CORBACCIO *and* CORVINO, MOSCA *passant.*]
CORBACCIO. See, in our habit! see the impudent varlet!
CORVINO. That I could shoot mine eyes at him, like gun-stones.
[*Enter* VOLPONE.]
VOLPONE. But is this true, sir, of the parasite?
CORBACCIO. Again, t' afflict us? monster!
VOLPONE. In good faith, sir,
I am heartily griev'd, a beard of your grave length
Should be so overreach'd. I never brook'd
That parasite's hair; methought his nose should cozen:
There still was somewhat in his look, did promise
The bane of a clarissimo.
CORBACCIO. Knave—
VOLPONE. Methinks
Yet you, that are so traded i' the world,
A witty merchant, the fine bird, Corvino,
That have such moral emblems on your name,
Should not have sung your shame, and dropp'd your cheese,
To let the Fox laugh at your emptiness.
CORVINO. Sirrah, you think the privilege of the place,
And your red saucy cap, that seems to me
Nail'd to your jolt-head with those two *cecchines*,
Can warrant your abuses; come you hither;
You shall perceive, sir, I dare beat you; approach.

2 **gun-stones** cannon balls
19 **sung** like the crow whom the fox flattered in Aesop's fable
23 **jolt-head** blockhead **cecchines** gold buttons

VOLPONE. No haste, sir, I do know your valor well,
Since you durst publish what you are, sir.

CORVINO. Tarry,
I'd speak with you.

VOLPONE. Sir, sir, another time—

CORVINO. Nay, now.

VOLPONE. O God, sir! I were a wise man,
Would stand the fury of a distracted cuckold.

[MOSCA *walks by 'em.*]

CORBACCIO. What, come again!

VOLPONE. Upon 'em, Mosca; save me.

CORBACCIO. The air's infected where he breathes.

CORVINO. Let's fly him.

[*Exeunt* CORVINO *and* CORBACCIO.]

VOLPONE. Excellent basilisk! turn upon the Vulture.

SCENE IX

[*Enter* VOLTORE.]

VOLTORE. Well, flesh-fly, it is summer with you now;
Your winter will come on.

MOSCA. Good advocate,
'Pray thee not rail, nor threaten out of place thus;
Thou 'lt make a solecism, as Madam says.
Get you a biggin more; your brain breaks loose. [*Exit.*]

VOLTORE. Well, sir.

VOLPONE. Would you ha' me beat the insolent slave?
Throw dirt upon his first good clothes?

VOLTORE. This same
Is doubtless some familiar!

VOLPONE. Sir, the court,
In troth, stays for you. I am mad, a mule
That never read Justinian should get up
And ride an advocate. Had you no quirk

40 **basilisk** mythical serpent whose breath or look could kill
8 **biggin more** larger cap
13 **familiar** demon to tempt me

To avoid gullage, sir, by such a creature?
I hope you do but jest; he has not done 't;
This 's but confederacy to blind the rest.
You are the heir?

VOLTORE. A strange, officious,
Troublesome knave! Thou dost torment me.

VOLPONE. I know—
It cannot be, sir, that you should be cozen'd;
'Tis not within the wit of man to do it;
You are so wise, so prudent; and 'tis fit
That wealth and wisdom still should go together.

[*Exeunt.*]

SCENE X. The Senate House.

[*Enter four* AVOCATORI, NOTARIO, BONARIO, CELIA, CORBACCIO, CORVINO, COMMANDADORI, SAFFI, *etc.*]

1 AVOCATORE. Are all the parties here?

NOTARIO. All but the advocate.

2 AVOCATORE. And here he comes.

[*Enter* VOLTORE *and* VOLPONE.]

1 AVOCATORE. Then bring 'em forth to sentence.

VOLTORE. O, my most honor'd fathers, let your mercy
Once win upon your justice, to forgive—
I am distracted—

VOLPONE [*aside*]. What will he do now?

VOLTORE. Oh,
I know not which t' address myself to first;
Whether your Fatherhoods, or these innocents—

CORVINO [*aside*]. Will he betray himself?

VOLTORE. Whom equally
I have abus'd, out of most covetous ends—

CORVINO. The man is mad!

CORBACCIO. What's that?

CORVINO. He is possess'd.

21 possess'd i.e., by a demon

VOLTORE. For which, now struck in conscience, here I prostrate
Myself at your offended feet, for pardon.
1, 2 AVOCATORI. Arise.
CELIA. O Heav'n, how just thou art!
VOLPONE. I am caught
I' mine own noose—
CORVINO [*to* CORBACCIO]. Be constant, sir; naught now
Can help but impudence.
1 AVOCATORE. Speak forward.
COMMANDADORE. Silence!
VOLTORE. It is not passion in me, reverend fathers,
But only conscience, conscience, my good sires,
That makes me now tell truth. That parasite,
That knave, hath been the instrument of all.
1 AVOCATORE. Where is that knave? Fetch him.
VOLPONE. I go. [*Exit.*]
CORVINO. Grave fathers,
This man's distracted; he confess'd it now:
For, hoping to be old Volpone's heir,
Who now is dead—
3 AVOCATORE. How?
2 AVOCATORE. Is Volpone dead?
CORVINO. Dead since, grave fathers.
BONARIO. O sure vengeance!
1 AVOCATORE. Stay;
Then he was no deceiver?
VOLTORE. Oh, no, none.
This parasite, grave fathers—
CORVINO. He does speak
Out of mere envy, 'cause the servant's made
The thing he gap'd for. Please your Fatherhoods,
This is the truth, though I'll not justify
The other, but he may be somedeal faulty.
VOLTORE. Ay, to your hopes, as well as mine, Corvino;
But I'll use modesty. Pleaseth your Wisdoms

29 **impudence** sheer audacity
53–4 **justify . . . faulty** guarantee that Mosca is not somewhat deceitful
56 **modesty** moderation

To view these certain notes, and but confer them;
As I hope favor, they shall speak clear truth.
CORVINO. The Devil has ent'red him!
BONARIO. Or bides in you.
4 AVOCATORE. We have done ill, by a public officer
To send for him, if he be heir.
2 AVOCATORE. For whom?
4 AVOCATORE. Him that they call the parasite.
3 AVOCATORE. 'Tis true,
He is a man of great estate, now left.
4 AVOCATORE. Go you, and learn his name, and say the court
Entreats his presence here, but to the clearing
Of some few doubts. [*Exit* NOTARIO.]
2 AVOCATORE. This same's a labyrinth!
1 AVOCATORE. Stand you unto your first report?
CORVINO. My state,
My life, my fame—
BONARIO. Where is 't?
CORVINO. Are at the stake.
1 AVOCATORE. Is yours so too?
CORBACCIO. The advocate's a knave,
And has a forked tongue—
2 AVOCATORE. Speak to the point.
CORBACCIO. So is the parasite too.
1 AVOCATORE. This is confusion.
VOLTORE. I do beseech your Fatherhoods, read but those—
[*Giving them papers.*]
CORVINO. And credit nothing the false spirit hath writ:
It cannot be but he's possess'd, grave fathers.
[*The scene closes.*]

SCENE XI. *A street.*

[*Enter* VOLPONE.]

VOLPONE. To make a snare for mine own neck, and run

57 **confer** compare

My head into it, wilfully! with laughter!
When I had newly 'scap'd, was free and clear!
Out of mere wantonness! Oh, the dull devil
Was in this brain of mine when I devis'd it,
And Mosca gave it second; he must now
Help to sear up this vein, or we bleed dead.
[*Enter* NANO, ANDROGYNO, *and* CASTRONE.]
How now! Who let you loose? Whither go you now?
What, to buy gingerbread, or to drown kitlings?

NANO. Sir, Master Mosca call'd us out of doors,
And bid us all go play, and took the keys.

ANDROGYNO. Yes.

VOLPONE. Did Master Mosca take the keys? Why, so!
I'm farther in. These are my fine conceits!
I must be merry, with a mischief to me!
What a vile wretch was I, that could not bear
My fortune soberly? I must ha' my crotchets,
And my conundrums!—Well, go you, and seek him;
His meaning may be truer than my fear.
Bid him he straight come to me to the court;
Thither will I, and, if 't be possible,
Unscrew my advocate, upon new hopes.
When I provok'd him, then I lost myself. [*Exeunt.*]

SCENE XII. *The Senate House.*

[AVOCATORI, *etc., are discovered, as before.*]

1 AVOCATORE. These things can ne'er be reconcil'd. He here
[*Shows the papers.*]
Professeth that the gentleman was wrong'd,
And that the gentlewoman was brought thither,
Forc'd by her husband, and there left.

VOLTORE. Most true.

CELIA. How ready is Heav'n to those that pray!

17 **conceits** fancy devices
18 **must** had to
20 **crotchets** little eccentricities

1 AVOCATORE. But that
Volpone would have ravish'd her, he holds
Utterly false, knowing his impotence.
CORVINO. Grave fathers, he is possess'd; again, I say,
Possess'd; nay, if there be possession,
And obsession, he has both.
3 AVOCATORE. Here comes our officer.

[*Enter* VOLPONE.]

VOLPONE. The parasite will straight be here, grave fathers.
4 AVOCATORE. You might invent some other name, Sir Varlet.
3 AVOCATORE. Did not the notary meet him?
VOLPONE. Not that I know.
4 AVOCATORE. His coming will clear all.
2 AVOCATORE. Yet it is misty.
VOLTORE. May 't please your Fatherhoods—
VOLPONE [*whispers to the* ADVOCATE]. Sir, the parasite
Will'd me to tell you that his master lives;
That you are still the man; your hopes the same;
And this was only a jest—
VOLTORE. How?
VOLPONE. Sir, to try
If you were firm, and how you stood affected.
VOLTORE. Art sure he lives?
VOLPONE. Do I live, sir?
VOLTORE. O me!
I was too violent.
VOLPONE. Sir, you may redeem it.
They said you were possess'd; fall down, and seem so:
I'll help to make it good. [VOLTORE *falls.*] God bless the man!—
[*aside to* VOLTORE] Stop your wind hard, and swell.—See, see, see, see!
He vomits crooked pins! His eyes are set,
Like a dead hare's hung in a poulter's shop!
His mouth's running away! Do you see, signior?
Now it is in his belly.
CORVINO. Ay, the devil!

41 **crooked pins** indicating demonic possession

VOLPONE. Now in his throat.
CORVINO. Ay, I perceive it plain.
VOLPONE. 'Twill out, 'twill out! stand clear. See where it flies!
In shape of a blue toad, with a bat's wings!
Do not you see it, sir?
CORBACCIO. What? I think I do.
CORVINO. 'Tis too manifest.
VOLPONE. Look! he comes t' himself!
VOLTORE. Where am I?
VOLPONE. Take good heart, the worst is past, sir.
You're dispossess'd.
1 AVOCATORE. What accident is this?
2 AVOCATORE. Sudden and full of wonder!
3 AVOCATORE. If he were
Possess'd, as it appears, all this is nothing.
CORVINO. He has been often subject to these fits.
1 AVOCATORE. Show him that writing:—do you know it, sir?
VOLPONE [*aside to* VOLTORE]. Deny it, sir, forswear it; know it not.
VOLTORE. Yes, I do know it well: it is my hand;
But all that it contains is false.
BONARIO. O practice!
2 AVOCATORE. What maze is this!
1 AVOCATORE. Is he not guilty then,
Whom you there name the parasite?
VOLTORE. Grave fathers,
No more than his good patron, old Volpone.
4 AVOCATORE. Why, he is dead.
VOLTORE. O no, my honor'd fathers.
He lives—
1 AVOCATORE. How! lives?
VOLTORE. Lives.
2 AVOCATORE. This is subtler yet!
3 AVOCATORE. You said he was dead!
VOLTORE. Never.
3 AVOCATORE. You said so!
CORVINO. I heard so.
4 AVOCATORE. Here comes the gentleman; make him way.
[*Enter* MOSCA.]

3 AVOCATORE. A stool.
4 AVOCATORE [*aside*]. A proper man! and, were Volpone dead,
A fit match for my daughter.
3 AVOCATORE. Give him way.
VOLPONE [*aside to* MOSCA]. Mosca, I was a'most lost: the advocate
Had betray'd all; but now it is recover'd;
All's on the hinge again—say I am living.
MOSCA. What busy knave is this?—Most reverend fathers,
I sooner had attended your grave pleasures,
But that my order for the funeral
Of my dear patron did require me—
VOLPONE [*aside*]. Mosca!
MOSCA. Whom I intend to bury like a gentleman.
VOLPONE [*aside*]. Ay, quick, and cozen me of all.
2 AVOCATORE. Still stranger!
More intricate!
1 AVOCATORE. And come about again!
4 AVOCATORE [*aside*]. It is a match; my daughter is bestow'd.
MOSCA [*aside to* VOLPONE]. Will you gi' me half?
VOLPONE [*aside*]. First I'll be hang'd.
MOSCA [*aside*]. I know
Your voice is good; cry not so loud.
1 AVOCATORE. Demand
The advocate.—Sir, did not you affirm
Volpone was alive?
VOLPONE. Yes, and he is;
This gent'man told me so.—[*aside to* MOSCA] Thou shalt have half.
MOSCA. Whose drunkard is this same? Speak, some that know him;
I never saw his face.—[*aside to* VOLPONE] I cannot now
Afford it you so cheap.
VOLPONE [*aside*]. No?
1 AVOCATORE. What say you?
VOLTORE. The officer told me.
VOLPONE. I did, grave fathers,
And will maintain he lives, with mine own life,
And that this creature [*pointing to* MOSCA] told me.—[*aside*] I was born

With all good stars my enemies.

MOSCA. Most grave fathers,
If such an insolence as this must pass
Upon me, I am silent; 'twas not this
For which you sent, I hope.

2 AVOCATORE. Take him away.

VOLPONE. Mosca!

3 AVOCATORE. Let him be whipp'd.

VOLPONE [*aside to* MOSCA]. Wilt thou betray me?
Cozen me?

3 AVOCATORE. And taught to bear himself
Toward a person of his rank.

4 AVOCATORE. Away.

MOSCA. I humbly thank your Fatherhoods.

VOLPONE. Soft, soft;—[*aside*] whipp'd!
And lose all that I have! If I confess,
It cannot be much more.

4 AVOCATORE. Sir, are you married?

VOLPONE. They'll be alli'd anon; I must be resolute;
The Fox shall here uncase. [*He puts off his disguise.*]

MOSCA [*aside*]. Patron!

VOLPONE. Nay, now
My ruins shall not come alone; your match
I'll hinder sure; my substance shall not glue you,
Nor screw you into a family.

MOSCA [*aside*]. Why, patron!

VOLPONE. I am Volpone, and this [*pointing to* MOSCA] is my knave;
This [*to* VOLTORE], his own knave; this [*to* CORBACCIO], avarice's
fool;
This [*to* CORVINO], a chimaera of wittol, fool, and knave:
And, reverend fathers, since we all can hope
Naught but a sentence, let's not now despair it.
You hear me brief.

CORVINO. May it please your Fatherhoods—

COMMANDADORE. Silence.

1 AVOCATORE. The knot is now undone, by miracle!

2 AVOCATORE. Nothing can be more clear.

3 AVOCATORE. Or can more prove

These innocent.

1 AVOCATORE. Give 'em their liberty.

BONARIO. Heaven could not long let such gross crimes be hid.

2 AVOCATORE. If this be held the highway to get riches,
May I be poor.

3 AVOCATORE. This 's not the gain, but torment.

1 AVOCATORE. These possess wealth, as sick men possess fevers,
Which trulier may be said to possess them.

2 AVOCATORE. Disrobe that parasite.

CORVINO and MOSCA. Most honor'd fathers—

1 AVOCATORE. Can you plead aught to stay the course of justice?
If you can, speak.

CORVINO and VOLTORE. We beg favor.

CELIA. And mercy.

1 AVOCATORE. You hurt your innocence, suing for the guilty.
Stand forth; and, first, the parasite. You appear
T' have been the chiefest minister, if not plotter,
In all these lewd impostures, and now, lastly,
Have with your impudence abus'd the court,
And habit of a gentleman of Venice,
Being a fellow of no birth or blood;
For which our sentence is, first, thou be whipp'd;
Then live perpetual prisoner in our galleys.

VOLPONE. I thank you for him.

MOSCA. Bane to thy wolfish nature!

1 AVOCATORE. Deliver him to the saffi.—Thou, Volpone,
By blood and rank a gentleman, canst not fall
Under like censure; but our judgment on thee
Is that thy substance all be straight confiscate
To the hospital of the Incurabili.
And since the most was gotten by imposture,
By feigning lame, gout, palsy, and such diseases,
Thou art to lie in prison, cramp'd with irons,
Till thou be'st sick and lame indeed.—Remove him.

VOLPONE. This is called mortifying of a Fox.

1 AVOCATORE. Thou, Voltore, to take away the scandal
Thou hast giv'n all worthy men of thy profession,
Art banish'd from their fellowship, and our state.—
Corbaccio!—Bring him near.—We here possess

Thy son of all thy state, and confine thee
To the monastery of San' Spirito;
Where, since thou knew'st not how to live well here,
Thou shalt be learn'd to die well.

CORBACCIO. Ha! what said he?

COMMANDADORE. You shall know anon, sir.

1 AVOCATORE. Thou, Corvino, shalt
Be straight embark'd from thine own house, and row'd
Round about Venice, through the Grand Canal,
Wearing a cap, with fair long ass's ears,
Instead of horns; and so to mount, a paper
Pinn'd on thy breast, to the Berlina.

CORVINO. Yes,
And have mine eyes beat out with stinking fish,
Bruis'd fruit, and rotten eggs—'tis well. I am glad
I shall not see my shame yet.

1 AVOCATORE. And to expiate
Thy wrongs done to thy wife, thou art to send her
Home to her father, with her dowry trebled;
And these are all your judgments.

ALL. Honor'd fathers—

1 AVOCATORE. Which may not be revok'd. Now you begin,
When crimes are done and past, and to be punish'd,
To think what your crimes are.—Away with them!
Let all that see these vices thus rewarded,
Take heart, and love to study 'em. Mischiefs feed
Like beasts, till they be fat, and then they bleed. [*Exeunt.*]

VOLPONE

The seasoning of a play is the applause.
Now, though the Fox be punish'd by the laws,
He yet doth hope, there is no suff'ring due,
For any fact which he hath done 'gainst you;
If there be, censure him; here he doubtful stands.
If not, fare jovially, and clap your hands. [*Exit.*]

210 **Berlina** pillory
218 **judgments** sentences

MOLIÈRE
1622–1673

THE MISER
1668

Perhaps the most novel aspect of *The Miser,* if one compares it to either *Volpone* or Shakespeare's play treating of avarice, *The Merchant of Venice,* is its unruffled joy. The great Elizabethan plays show avarice corrupting its possessor and fearfully threatening the lives of his victims. There is a certain somberness, a quality of the deepest moral earnestness, underlying these plays, however gay they may appear in many scenes. In *The Miser,* however, vice creates no agonies and folly has no lasting sting. Harpagon, moreover, undergoes no morally revealing change. He is at the end as splendidly stupid, pinchpenny, and self-centered as he was at the beginning.

Such a difference reflects no difference in the judgment rendered. Molière, like Jonson and Shakespeare, sees avarice as dehumanizing. It translates spirit into thing so that Volpone can lust for Celia somewhat as he lusts for Corvino's pearl, Shylock can put his daughter and his ducats into the same scale, and Harpagon can balance the treasure of filial happiness against the contents of his moneybox. Molière, however, is content to laugh at the avaricious as one might laugh at a monkey in the zoo. What a ludicrously unreasonable thing this miser is, he seems to say; how like a man, and yet how infinitely beneath him. And he invites the sensible members of his audience to share in his detached amusement.

It is this appeal to good sense that gives *The Miser* its distinctive qualities of plot, characterization, and device. The plot is elementary, a tissue of theatrical devices terminated by the miraculous reunion, in the nick of time, of a long separated family. Such a plot, conventional in its beginning and absurd in its ending, asks for no earnest contemplation. It is the staple of comic literature everywhere, asking for delectation rather than for a deep comprehension of the moral laws underlying the flux of human experience. The characters are similarly unreal. They are, in fact, stock types: the conventional lovers sententious in dialogue; the two-dimensional miser as flat in delineation as his beloved coins; the clownish servant forever avoiding, forever getting a well-merited beating; and the busybody matchmaker contriving an endless series of engagements. They are as old-new as the props in the theater's basement and are hardly to be taken as flesh and blood. So also are the devices, which for all their multiplicity reduce to a kind of geometrical design—purpose against cross purpose, the characters moving and speaking in the exaggerated and jerky style we associate now with vaudeville humor and early animated cartoons.

Molière develops his play in this manner because he assumes and invites us to assume a stable world with stable values. Such a world is secure in its virtue—vice cannot threaten it; secure in its wisdom—folly cannot subvert it. In its security, it can confront the absurdities of flesh and the aberrations of spirit with the humane enjoyment that comes from having mastered them. It can laugh at La Flèche's patching things up between Harpagon and Cleanth—without changing anything at all—or at Harpagon's seizing his own arm in the panic he experiences when the moneybox is stolen. It can smile at and with the absurd conclusion, for though it knows that true love does not always find a way and that separated families are not always reunited, it recognizes in the miracle a myth of its own aspirations and in the wise, tolerant, and humane Anselm, not only a foil to Harpagon, but the gentle embodiment of its own world of values.

THE MISER / *MOLIÈRE*

TRANSLATED BY LLOYD PARKS

Characters

HARPAGON	*father of Cleanth and Elise, and in love with Marianne*
CLEANTH	*Harpagon's son, and in love with Marianne*
ELISE	*Harpagon's daughter, and in love with Valère*
VALÈRE	*Anselm's son, and in love with Elise*
MARIANNE	*Anselm's daughter, and in love with Cleanth*
ANSELM	*father of Valère and Marianne*
FROSINE	*a woman of intrigue*
MASTER SIMON	*a broker*
MASTER JACQUES	*Harpagon's coachman and cook*
LA FLÈCHE	*Cleanth's valet*
DAME CLAUDE	*Harpagon's maid*
BRINDAVOINE	*Harpagon's lackey*
LA MERLUCHE	*Harpagon's lackey*
A COMMISSARY AND HIS CLERK	

SCENE. *Paris, Harpagon's house.*

ACT I

[*Enter* VALÈRE *and* ELISE.]

VALÈRE. What is it, charming Elise? Are you melancholy? After all the obliging assurances you so kindly gave of faith in me? Alas! I see you sighing in the midst of my joy! Tell me, do you regret our engagement—to which my ardor has perhaps constrained you?

ELISE. No, Valère, I could not regret what I have done for you. I feel myself drawn by powers far too sweet, and I lack strength to wish that things were not as they are. But to tell the truth, I fear to think of the consequences. I am much afraid that I love you a little more than I ought.

VALÈRE. Ah! Elise, what can you have to fear from the kindness you have shown me?

ELISE. Alas! a hundred things: my father's wrath, reproaches from my family, the censure of the world—but most of all, Valère, a change in your heart and that criminal coldness with which those of your sex most often repay the over-ardent testimonies of innocent love.

VALÈRE. Oh! do not do me the wrong of judging me by others. Suspect me of anything, Elise, but not that I should fail in my duty to you. I love you too much for that, and I will love you as long as I live.

ELISE. Ah! that is the way you all talk. All men are alike in their speech; their actions alone reveal their differences.

VALÈRE. If our actions alone reveal what we are, then at least wait and judge my heart by mine; and do not invent crimes for me simply because unhappy apprehension has bred unjust fear. I beg you, do not kill me with mortal blows of outrageous suspicion. Give me time to convince you, by a thousand and one proofs, that my intentions are honorable.

ELISE. Alas! how easily we are persuaded by those we love! Yes, Valère, I think you have no room in your heart for deceit. I am convinced that you love me truly, and will always be faithful to me. I have no wish to doubt you; I am sad only because I fear I may be blamed by others.

VALÈRE. What is it that worries you?

ELISE. I would have nothing to fear if everyone saw you as I do. For in your very person I see enough to justify what I have done. My heart has all your merit for its defense, reinforced by that gratitude which Heaven has bade me owe you. Not an hour passes but I picture to myself the terrible catastrophe which brought us into one another's sight; your amazing generosity, which made you risk your life to preserve mine from the fury of the waves; the great pains you took, how tenderly you cared for me after lifting me from the water; and the assiduous homage of your ardent love, which neither time nor difficulty has discouraged; which causes you to neglect both family and fatherland; which detains you in this place, and makes you hide your rank for my sake; and which has reduced you to wearing my father's livery. All of this has certainly made a wonderful impression on me, and in my eyes is justification enough for the engagement I have consented to. But perhaps that is not enough to justify it to the world, nor am I sure that every one feels as I do.

VALÈRE. For all that you have said, it is only through my love that I pretend to merit your esteem, and as for your scruples, a father like yours is justification enough for anything you might do. His excessive avarice and the austere manner in which he lives with his children might well authorize far stranger things than this. Pardon me, charming Elise, for talking this way in front of you, but you know there is no good to be said on that score. But, if, as I hope, I can finally find my parents again, it will not be hard to win him over. I am waiting impatiently for news of them, and I will go and inquire if it is much longer in coming.

ELISE. Oh! Valère, do not go away, I beg you. Think only of winning my father's confidence.

VALÈRE. You have seen how I go about it; you saw how artfully compliant I was obliged to be in order to introduce myself into his service—under what mask of sympathy and agreement I disguise my feelings to please him—what role I play to gain his affection. And I am making admirable progress. I have discovered that, to win men over, there is no better way than to trick yourself out in their inclinations, fall in with their maxims, burn incense to their faults, and applaud everything they do. One need have no fear of overdoing complaisance. No matter how obviously you play on their feelings, the shrewdest men are always the greatest dupes when it comes to flattery. There is nothing so impertinent or so ridiculous that you can't make them swallow it—if you season it well with praise. Sincerity, of course, suffers a little by this trade. But if you need certain men, you must adapt yourself to them. And, since there is no other way of winning them over, it is not the flatterers who are at fault, but those who wish to be flattered.

ELISE. Why don't you try to gain my brother's support too—in the event my maid should decide to tell our secret?

VALÈRE. I cannot manage both of them at the same time. The father's temperament and the son's are so opposed, it would be hard to accommodate the confidings of both at once. But you, for your part, could approach your brother, and avail yourself of his friendship to get him to act on our behalf. There he comes now. I'll withdraw. Use the occasion to sound him out, but don't disclose our affair unless you think the time is ripe. [*Exit.*]

ELISE. I don't know if I will have the courage to confide in him.

[*Enter* CLEANTH.]

CLEANTH. I am very happy to find you alone, Elise. I have been burning to unburden a secret to you.

ELISE. Here I am, ready to listen, Cleanth. What do you wish to tell me?

CLEANTH. A thousand things, Elise—all bound up in three words: I'm in love.

ELISE. You are in love?

CLEANTH. I am in love. But before I say more, I know I am dependent on my father; that the name of son subjects me to his wishes; that we should not commit ourselves without the consent of those who brought us into the world; that Heaven has made them the masters of our troth; that we are enjoined not to pledge it except by their direction; that having never been affected by foolish passions, they are in a condition to be deceived much less often than we are, and can see more clearly what is best for us. I know that we ought to trust the light of their prudence rather than the blindness of our passion and that the extravagance of youth most often lures us toward the precipice of sorrow. I am telling all this to you, Elise, so that you won't take the trouble to tell it to *me*. For, to tell the truth, my love will not listen. So, please do not make objections.

ELISE. Are you engaged, Cleanth, to her whom you love?

CLEANTH. No, but I am resolved to be. And again I beg you not to offer any reasons to dissuade me.

ELISE. Am I such a stranger, Cleanth?

CLEANTH. No, Elise; but you are not in love. You do not know the violence that tender love does to our hearts. I mistrust your prudence.

ELISE. Alas! Cleanth, let us not talk of my prudence. There is no one who is not deficient in that at least once in a lifetime; and if I opened my heart to you, perhaps in your eyes I should seem far less prudent than you are.

CLEANTH. Ah! I wish to Heaven, that your heart, like mine . . .

ELISE. First of all, let us finish with your affair. Tell me, who is she. . . .

CLEANTH. A young lady who has lived but a short time in this neighborhood, and who seems to have been made to inspire love in all who see her. Nature never shaped anything more lovable. I felt transported the moment I saw her. Her name is Marianne and she lives under the protection of her mother—a good woman who is almost always ill, and whom her daughter holds in such loving regard, it is unbelievable. She waits on her, takes pity on her, and consoles her so tenderly that it touches your heart. She has the most charming way in the world of going about her business. A thousand graces shine through her every action. Such alluring sweetness, such engaging goodness, such adorable civility! such . . . Oh! Elise, if you could only see her!

ELISE. I see a great deal of her, Cleanth, through what you have told me. And to understand her, it is enough for me that you love her.

CLEANTH. I have discovered, in a roundabout way, that they are not very well provided for, and that even with frugal management, they can hardly stretch their income far enough to cover all their needs. Imagine, Elise, what a pleasure it would be to be able to raise the fortunes of the person one loves, adroitly to supply a little help for the modest needs of a virtuous family. And think how unpleasant it must be for me to be powerless to taste that pleasure because of my father's stinginess, to be powerless to surprise this beautiful girl with some proof of my love for her.

ELISE. Oh! Cleanth, I can easily conceive how exasperated you must feel.

CLEANTH. Ah! Elise, much more so than you can imagine. Really, have you ever seen anything more cruel than the rigorous economy he imposes on us, than this queer stinginess under which we languish? What good will wealth do us, if it comes only when we are past the age when we can most enjoy it, if even to maintain myself I am now obliged to go into debt on every side, and if I am reduced with you to seeking help from tradesmen to find the means to wear decent clothes? I really wanted to ask you to help me find out father's attitude toward my present feelings. If I find him contrary, I am resolved to go away, in the company of that wonderful creature, to enjoy whatever fortune Providence may offer us. I am having somebody look everywhere for money to borrow for this purpose; and, if your affairs are in the same state as mine, if father insists on opposing our desires, we will both leave him, and free ourselves of this tyranny, to which his insupportable avarice has so long subjected us.

ELISE. It is only too true that he gives us more reason every day to regret our mother's death, and that . . .

CLEANTH. I can hear his voice. Let us go somewhere else to conclude our confidences. Later we will join forces and assault his hard heart together.

[*Exeunt.*]

[*Enter* HARPAGON *and* LA FLÈCHE.]

HARPAGON. Get out of here at once, and don't answer back! Go on, leave my house! You master-mind of crime! You born gallows bait!

FLÈCHE [*aside*]. I have never seen anything so wicked as this cursèd old man, and I believe, begging your pardon, he has a devil in his flesh.

HARPAGON. Are you muttering between your teeth?

FLÈCHE. Why chase me out of the house?

HARPAGON. As though you didn't know why! Scoundrel! Go quickly before I beat you!

FLÈCHE. What have I done?

HARPAGON. You have done enough to make me want you to leave.

FLÈCHE. My master your son gave me orders to wait for him.

HARPAGON. Go and wait for him in the street, not here in my house, standing there as stiff and straight as a post to watch what goes on and profit from everything. . . . I will not have someone continually spying on my business, a traitor whose cursèd eyes besiege all my actions, devour all I possess, and ferret about in every corner for something to steal.

FLÈCHE. How the deuce do you expect anyone to steal from you? Can you rob a man when he keeps everything under lock and key, and stands guard day and night?

HARPAGON. I will lock up whatever I think should be locked up, and I will stand guard as I please. [*to audience*] There, isn't that the talk of a spy who watches everything you do? I tremble lest he suspect something about my money. [*to* LA FLÈCHE] Are you the kind of man who would go about spreading the story that I have money hidden away?

FLÈCHE. *Do* you have money hidden away?

HARPAGON. No, you rascal, I didn't say that. [*aside*] I'm losing my temper. [*to* LA FLÈCHE] I mean, would you go around spreading the story that I do have some—out of malice?

FLÈCHE. Hoho! what difference does it make to us, if you have or have not? Things are always the same for us anyway.

HARPAGON. Ha! you play the reasoner! I'll teach you how to reason with your ears. [*lifting his hand to give* LA FLÈCHE *a box on the ear*] One last time—get out of here!

FLÈCHE. All right, I'm going.

HARPAGON. Wait. You're not taking anything of mine with you?

FLÈCHE. What could I take of yours?

HARPAGON. Come here, so I can see. Show me your hands.

FLÈCHE. There they are.

HARPAGON [*sarcastically*]. Your other hands.

FLÈCHE. My other hands?

HARPAGON. Yes.

FLÈCHE [*good-humoredly*]. There they are.

HARPAGON [*pointing to* LA FLÈCHE's *breeches*]. Have you put anything inside there?

FLÈCHE. See for yourself.

HARPAGON [*feeling the knees of* LA FLÈCHE's *breeches*]. These breeches are just right for hiding stolen goods, and I wish somebody had been hanged for it. . . .

FLÈCHE. Ah! how well a man like that deserves what he fears, and what pleasure it would give me to steal from him.

HARPAGON. Eh?

FLÈCHE. What?

HARPAGON. What did you say about stealing?

FLÈCHE. I said that you are poking everywhere to see if I have stolen anything from you.

HARPAGON. That's what I intend to do.

FLÈCHE [*aside*]. A pox on avarice and the avaricious!

HARPAGON. How's that? What did you say?

FLÈCHE. What did I say?

HARPAGON. Yes. What did you say about avarice and the avaricious?

FLÈCHE. I said, a pox on avarice and the avaricious.

HARPAGON. Who are you talking about?

FLÈCHE. About avaricious men.

HARPAGON. And who are they, these avaricious men?

FLÈCHE. They are misers and villains.

HARPAGON. But who do you mean by that?

FLÈCHE. What are you so upset about?

HARPAGON. I am upset about what I ought to be upset about.

FLÈCHE. Do you think I mean you?

HARPAGON. I think what I think. But I want you to tell me who you were speaking to when you said that.

FLÈCHE. I . . . I was speaking to my beret.

HARPAGON. And I might well knock it off.

FLÈCHE. Would you stop me from cursing avaricious men?

HARPAGON. No, but I'll stop you from chattering and being insolent. Keep quiet.

FLÈCHE. I haven't named anybody.

HARPAGON. I'll thrash you if you talk.

FLÈCHE. If your nose feels snotty, blow it.

HARPAGON. Will you be quiet?

FLÈCHE. Yes, in spite of myself.

HARPAGON. Ah! ah!

FLÈCHE [*showing him one of his waist-coat pockets*]. Look, here's another pocket. Are you satisfied?

HARPAGON. Come now, give it back to me without any more searching.

FLÈCHE. What?

HARPAGON. What you took from me.

FLÈCHE. I took nothing from you.

HARPAGON. Are you sure?

FLÈCHE. Positive.

HARPAGON. Goodbye! Go to the devil!

FLÈCHE. Well, I must say, I have been very handsomely dismissed!

HARPAGON. At least I have laid something to your conscience.

[*Exit* LA FLÈCHE.]

That rascal of a valet makes me uneasy, and I don't care to see the limping cur around here. [*alone*] It's certainly no small worry having a large sum of money in this house, and it's a lucky man who has his fortune well invested, and can carry what he needs for expenses on his own person. It's no little problem to find, in an entire house, a safe hiding place for it. Because, to my way of thinking, your strong-boxes are suspect; I'd never trust my money to one. In my opinion they are nothing but bait for thieves, they are what a thief always goes after first.

[*Enter* CLEANTH *and* ELISE *unnoticed*.]

Still, I don't know if it was wise to bury the ten thousand écus I was paid yesterday in the garden. Ten thousand gold écus is a rather large sum to have about the house. [*noticing* CLEANTH *and* ELISE] Oh! Heavens! I must have given myself away! I must have been carried away by anxiety—and I think I spoke out loud while I was reasoning with myself all alone here. . . . What's the matter?

CLEANTH. Nothing, father.

HARPAGON. Have you been there very long?

ELISE. We have just come.

HARPAGON. You heard . . .

CLEANTH. What, father?

HARPAGON. There . . .

ELISE. What?

HARPAGON. What I just said.

CLEANTH. No.

HARPAGON. Yes, you did, you did.

ELISE. I beg your pardon, but we didn't.

HARPAGON. I can plainly see you heard something. I was talking to myself about how hard it is to find money these days, and I said that anyone who happens to have ten thousand écus about the house is a very lucky man.

281 **écus** The monetary units mentioned in the play had the following values: twelve **deniers** = one **sol**; twenty sols = one **franc**; three francs = one **écu**; ten francs = one **pistole**; twenty francs = one **gold louis.**

CLEANTH. We held back for fear of interrupting you.

HARPAGON. I am only too glad to let you know what I said. So you won't get it all wrong and think it is I who have the ten thousand écus.

CLEANTH. We don't concern ourselves with your affairs.

HARPAGON. Would to God I had that much money, ten thousand écus!

CLEANTH. I don't believe it.

HARPAGON. It would be a fine thing for me.

ELISE. These are matters . . .

HARPAGON. I could certainly use it.

CLEANTH. I think that . . .

HARPAGON. It would set me up very comfortably.

ELISE. You are . . .

HARPAGON. I wouldn't complain then, as I do now, about how hard the times are!

CLEANTH. My God, father, you have no room to complain: everyone knows you are well-off.

HARPAGON. What! I am well-off? Those who say so are liars. Nothing could be more untrue. And those who go around spreading such a story are all villains.

ELISE. Don't be angry.

HARPAGON. It is very strange that my own children should betray me and become my enemies.

CLEANTH. Am I your enemy because I say you are well-off?

HARPAGON. Yes. That kind of talk and your extravagant spending will one day cause somebody to come here and to cut my throat, under the impression that my clothes are lined with money.

CLEANTH. What extravagant spending have I done?

HARPAGON. What? Is there anything more scandalous than the sumptuous clothes that you parade all over the city? Yesterday I was criticizing your sister, but this is far worse. This cries out to Heaven for vengeance; and, taking you from head to foot, there is enough on you to buy a good piece of property. I have told you twenty times, son, that your ways displease me very much. You are breaking your neck to look like a marquis, and in order to go about dressed as you are, I am sure you must be stealing from me.

CLEANTH. Ha! how could I steal from you?

HARPAGON. How should I know? Then where do you get the

means to keep up your fashionable appearance?

CLEANTH. I, father? Why, I gamble, and, since I am very lucky, I put all the money I win on my back.

HARPAGON. That is very ill-advised. If you are lucky at cards you ought to profit by it, and invest your money at an honest interest, so that one day you will find it has . . . I should like very much to know, not to mention the rest, what good are all those ribbons you are garnished with from head to foot, as if half a dozen laces would not be enough to hold up your breeches? Is it really necessary to spend your money on wigs, when you can wear the hair that grows on your head, which doesn't cost a sou? I'll wager your wigs and ribbons alone are worth at least twenty pistoles. And twenty pistoles bring in eight francs, six sols, and eight deniers a year, even at eight per cent interest.

CLEANTH. You are quite right.

HARPAGON. Enough of that; let us talk about something else. Eh? [*aside, seeing* CLEANTH *and* ELISE *making signs to one another*] I think they are signalling one another to pick my pockets. [*to* CLEANTH *and* ELISE] What do those signs mean?

ELISE. We were bargaining as to who should speak first, my brother or myself. Both of us have something to tell you.

HARPAGON. And I, too, have something to tell both of you.

CLEANTH. It is about marriage, father, that we wish to speak with you.

HARPAGON. And it is marriage also that I want to discuss with you.

ELISE. Oh! father!

HARPAGON. Why "Oh! father!"? Is it the word, daughter, or the thing that frightens you?

CLEANTH. Marriage could be frightening in both respects, depending on how you mean it. And we are afraid that our inclinations might not agree with your choice.

HARPAGON. Have a little patience. Don't get alarmed. I know what is best for you both, and neither one of you will have reason to complain of anything I intend to do. Now, to begin at the beginning, tell me, have you ever seen a girl named Marianne, who lives not far from here?

CLEANTH. Yes, father.

348 laces ties lacing the breeches to the doublet. Men of fashion often ornamented their laces with ribbons.

HARPAGON [*to* ELISE]. And you?

ELISE. I have heard of her.

HARPAGON. What do you think of this girl, Cleanth?

CLEANTH. An extremely charming person.

HARPAGON. Her physiognomy?

CLEANTH. Very honest and intelligent.

HARPAGON. Her air and manner?

CLEANTH. Exquisite, to be sure.

HARPAGON. Don't you think a girl like that is worth some consideration?

CLEANTH. Yes, father.

HARPAGON. That she might be a very desirable match?

CLEANTH. Very desirable.

HARPAGON. That she looks very much as though she would make a good housewife?

CLEANTH. No doubt.

HARPAGON. And that a husband would be completely satisfied with her?

CLEANTH. Surely.

HARPAGON. There is one slight obstacle. I am afraid she may not have as much money as one might reasonably expect.

CLEANTH. Ah! father, money is no consideration when it is a question of marrying an honest woman.

HARPAGON. Pardon me, if I disagree! But there is always this to be said: if a fortune does not measure up to one's expectations, one can always try to make it up some other way.

CLEANTH. Of course.

HARPAGON. Well—I am happy to find that you agree with me, because her maidenly conduct and sweet disposition have won my heart, and I am resolved to marry her. Provided she has some kind of property.

CLEANTH. Eh?

HARPAGON. What?

CLEANTH. You say you have resolved . . .

HARPAGON. To marry Marianne.

CLEANTH. Who? you, you?

HARPAGON. Yes. I, I, I! What do you mean by that?

CLEANTH. I feel dizzy all of a sudden. I think I'll go. [*Exit* CLEANTH.]

HARPAGON. It will pass. Quick, go into the kitchen and drink a large glass of plain water. [*to* ELISE] There's one of your lily-livered dandies—no more constitution than a chicken! Well, daughter, that's what I have decided for myself. As for your brother, I have a certain widow in mind that someone spoke to me about this very morning. And as for you, I am going to give you to Signor Anselm.

ELISE. To Signor Anselm?

HARPAGON. Yes. A man who is mature, prudent and wise, who is not over fifty, and who is famous for his great wealth.

ELISE. I would rather not get married at all, father, if you please.

HARPAGON. And I, my little girl, my pet, would rather you did get married, if you please.

ELISE. I beg your pardon, father.

HARPAGON. I beg your pardon, daughter.

ELISE. I am Signor Anselm's most humble servant, but, with your permission, I will not marry him.

HARPAGON. I am your very humble valet, but, with your permission, you shall marry him—this very evening.

ELISE. This very evening?

HARPAGON. This very evening.

ELISE. That shall never be, father.

HARPAGON. That shall be, daughter.

ELISE. No.

HARPAGON. Yes.

ELISE. I tell you, no.

HARPAGON. I tell you, yes.

ELISE. You shall never force me to do such a thing.

HARPAGON. I shall force you to do such a thing.

ELISE. I would kill myself sooner than marry such a husband.

HARPAGON. You will not kill yourself, and you shall marry him. Such audacity! Did you ever hear of a daughter talking to her father that way?

ELISE. Did you ever hear of a father marrying off his daughter that way?

HARPAGON. It is a match which will admit of no objection. And I will wager that everyone will approve my choice.

ELISE. And I will wager that no reasonable person could possibly approve it.

HARPAGON. Here is Valère. Would you be willing to let him be the judge of this matter for both of us?

ELISE. I'll consent to that.

HARPAGON. Will you abide by his decision?

ELISE. Yes. I will stand by whatever he says.

HARPAGON. It's settled then.

[*Enter* VALÈRE.]

Here, Valère. We have elected you to decide who is in the right, my daughter or myself.

VALÈRE. You, sir, there's no contradicting that.

HARPAGON. You know, of course, what we are talking about.

VALÈRE. No, but you couldn't be wrong; you are reason itself.

HARPAGON. Tonight I want to give her a husband who is as rich as he is wise, and the hussy tells me to my face she will have no part of him. What do you say to that?

VALÈRE. What do I say to that?

HARPAGON. Yes.

VALÈRE. Hoho!

HARPAGON. What?

VALÈRE. I say that fundamentally I am of your opinion; and that you couldn't possibly be wrong; but on the other hand, she is not absolutely in the wrong either, and . . .

HARPAGON. How so! Signior Anselm is a considerable match. He is a gentleman: noble, cultured, poised, intelligent and very rich; and he has no children left from his first marriage. Could she do better?

VALÈRE. True, but she might tell you that you are hurrying things somewhat, and that she ought to have a little time at least to find out whether she can adapt her temperament to . . .

HARPAGON. This is an opportunity that must be grasped by the forelock. This match offers me an advantage which I would find in no other. He has agreed to take her without a dowry and . . .

VALÈRE. Without a dowry?

HARPAGON. Yes.

VALÈRE. Ah! I have nothing more to say. You see, here is a reason that is entirely convincing; one can only defer to it. . . .

HARPAGON. To me it represents a considerable saving.

VALÈRE. Certainly. There's no denying it. It's true your daughter may suggest to you that marriage is a more important step than you are inclined to think; that it is a question of being happy or unhappy for the rest of one's life; and that a partnership which will last till death should never be entered on without great precaution.

HARPAGON. Without a dowry!

VALÈRE. You are right. That decides everything, naturally. Though there are those who might tell you that in such matters you certainly ought to have some regard for your daughter's inclinations, and that the great difference in age, in temperament, and in sensibility would render such a marriage liable to very unhappy accidents.

HARPAGON. Without a dowry!

VALÈRE. Oh! there's no gainsaying that, as everyone knows. Who the deuce would argue the point? Not that there aren't many fathers who are more interested in their daughters' happiness than in the money they give with them; who would never sacrifice them to their own interest; and who seek, above all else, to insure that sweet conformity in marriage which is a continuous source of honor, tranquillity and joy, and which . . .

HARPAGON. Without a dowry!

VALÈRE. Very true. That closes every mouth. Without a dowry! An irrefutable argument!

HARPAGON. Wait! I think I hear a dog barking. [*aside*] Is someone trying to get at my money? [*to* VALÈRE] Don't move; I'll be back in a minute. [*Exit* HARPAGON.]

ELISE. Are you joking, Valère, talking to him this way?

VALÈRE. I don't want to sour him. This way I can better accomplish my own ends. Opposing his ideas to his face is a sure way to spoil everything. There are certain minds you have to take by the bias. Some temperaments are inimical to any kind of resistance: they stiffen themselves against the truth, and always balk when they confront the straight road of reason. You can guide them where you want to take them only by leading them in a roundabout way. Pretend that you consent to what he wants; you will be more certain to get your way in the end. . . .

ELISE. But this marriage, Valère?

VALÈRE. We'll break it on the bias.

ELISE. What can we contrive if it is to be concluded tonight?

VALÈRE. You must ask them to delay it. Feign a sickness.

518–19 **by the bias** by indirection

ELISE. But they will discover the pretense—if they call in the doctor.

VALÈRE. Are you joking? Do doctors know anything about sickness? Come now, with doctors you can have any sickness you please, and they will find reasons for your having it, and tell you where it comes from.

[*Enter* HARPAGON.]

HARPAGON [*aside*]. It was nothing, thank God!

VALÈRE. As a last resort we could run away and leave all this behind. And if your love, Elise, is capable of firmness . . . [*seeing* HARPAGON] Yes, a daughter should obey her father. She should have no concern for what her husband is like; and, when such a powerful argument as *without a dowry* intervenes, she should be ready to accept whatever is given her.

HARPAGON. Good! That was well said, that!

VALÈRE. Sir, I beg pardon if I have been too forward, and for having made so bold as to talk to her this way.

HARPAGON. What do you mean? I am delighted. And I want to give you absolute power over her. [*to* ELISE] There's no good running away. [ELISE *moves to the end of the stage.*] I give him the same authority over you that God gave me, and I expect you to do everything he tells you.

VALÈRE [*to* ELISE]. After that how can you resist my remonstrances! Sir, I will follow her and continue the lessons I have been giving her.

HARPAGON. Yes, you will oblige me. Truly . . .

VALÈRE. I think it is good to pull in the reins with her.

HARPAGON. That's right, you should. . . .

VALÈRE. Don't worry about a thing; I am sure I can manage this.

HARPAGON. Do, do as you like. I am going to take a little walk through the city. I'll be back shortly.

VALÈRE. Yes, money is the most precious thing in the world, and you ought to thank God for the honest father He has given you. He knows what it takes to live. When someone offers to take a girl without a dowry, she ought not to look any further. Everything is included in *without a dowry;* it takes the place of beauty, youth, birth, honor, intelligence and probity. [*Exeunt* VALÈRE *and* ELISE.]

HARPAGON. Ah! bravo, bravo! Spoken like an oracle. Lucky the man with such a servant!

ACT II

[CLEANTH *is on stage. Enter* LA FLÈCHE.]

CLEANTH. Ah! you traitor! What new mischief have you been getting into? Didn't I give you orders? . . .

FLÈCHE. Yes sir! I came here with every intention of waiting for you, but your father, the most ungracious man in the world, chased me out of the house, in spite of myself, and I came close to getting a beating.

CLEANTH. How goes our business? Things are more pressing now than ever. Since I last saw you, I have discovered that my own father is my rival.

FLÈCHE. Your father is in love?

CLEANTH. Yes; and I had all the trouble in the world to keep him from seeing how much this news distressed me.

FLÈCHE. Him, dabbling in love? What the devil can he be thinking of? Does public opinion mean nothing to him? Was love made for men built like that?

CLEANTH. It must be for my sins that he has got this idea into his head.

FLÈCHE. For what reason do you keep your love a secret from him?

CLEANTH. So that he will be less suspicious. So that he won't suspect my actions should it become necessary to try and prevent his marriage. What answer did they give you?

FLÈCHE. By Heaven, sir, those that have to borrow are in a very bad way! A man has to put up with strange things when he is reduced, as you are, to putting himself into the hands of sharks.

CLEANTH. You couldn't get the money?

FLÈCHE. Not exactly. Our Master Simon, the broker, who was recommended to us as an energetic, determined man, assures me he has left no stone unturned to serve you—and that your face alone has won his heart.

CLEANTH. Will I get the fifteen thousand francs I asked for?

FLÈCHE. Yes, but there are some trifling conditions attached—which you must accept, if you expect anything to be done.

CLEANTH. Did he let you speak to the man who is supposed to lend the money?

FLÈCHE. Oh, really, it is not so simple as all that. He took more pains to hide himself than you do yourself; it is all much more mysterious than you might think. They will by no means tell his name, and they are going to bring you together today in a private house, so that he can learn from your own lips who your family is and what your expectations are. But I don't have the slightest doubt that your father's name alone will make things easy for you.

CLEANTH. And especially the fact that our mother is dead, whose property no one can take from me.

FLÈCHE. Here are a few articles which he himself dictated to our go-between, to be shown to you before any action will be taken.

"Supposing that the lender is satisfied with the collateral offered, and that the borrower has reached his majority and is from a family whose estate is large, solid, assured and free from all encumbrance, a valid and precise contract will be drawn up in the presence of a notary, the most honest man available, who, for that reason, must be chosen by the lender, to whom it is of the utmost importance that the contract be properly drawn up."

CLEANTH. I have no objection to that.

FLÈCHE. "The lender, in order not to burden his conscience with any scruples, intends to charge no more than six per cent interest."

CLEANTH. Six per cent interest? By Jove, an honest fellow indeed! There is no reason to complain about that.

FLÈCHE. Indeed not!

"But, since the said lender does not have the sum required in his own house, and because, in order to oblige the borrower, he is forced to borrow himself at the rate of twenty per cent, it is only fair that the said, first borrower should pay this interest without prejudice to the other, considering that it is only to oblige him that the said lender will borrow the sum requested."

CLEANTH. What the devil! What Jew, what Arab am I dealing with? That's more than twenty-five per cent interest!

FLÈCHE. That's right. That's what I told him. You had better look into it yourself.

CLEANTH. What is there to look into? I need money. I will have to agree to anything.

FLÈCHE. That's what I told him.

CLEANTH. Is there something else?

FLÈCHE. Only a small item.

"Of the fifteen thousand francs that are requested, the lender can count on only twelve thousand francs in cash. As for the remaining thousand écus, the borrower must take them in furniture, clothing, and jewelry, a list of which follows this note, and which the said lender has, in all good faith, priced as moderately as he possibly can."

CLEANTH. What does he mean by that?

FLÈCHE. Listen to the list.

"First: one four-poster bed, with Hungarian point lace handsomely sewn on olive-colored cloth, with six chairs, and a counterpane of the same material; all in good condition and lined with changeable red and blue taffeta.

"In addition: one bedstead canopy of good, dry rose-colored serge, with silk fringes."

CLEANTH. What does he expect me to do with that?

FLÈCHE. Hold on.

"In addition: a set of tapestries; the subject of which is *The Amours of Gombaut and Macaea.*

"In addition: one large walnut table, with twelve columns, or turned pillars, pulling out at either end, and fitted with half-a-dozen joint stools under it."

CLEANTH. My God! What good will that do me?

FLÈCHE. Be patient.

"In addition: three large muskets inlaid with mother-of-pearl, with three matching tripods.

"In addition: one brick furnace with two retorts and three recipients, very useful for anyone interested in distilling.

"In addition: a Bologna lute with all its strings, or few lacking.

"In addition: a troll-madam table and a chess board, with a goose game restored from the Greeks; all very fine to pass away the time when one has nothing to do.

"In addition: a lizard skin, three feet long, and half-filled with straw—a very agreeable curiosity to hang from a bedroom ceiling.

92 ***The Amours . . . Macaea*** a popular rustic romance of the time
103 **troll-madam** game played with ivory balls rolled into numbered holes or compartments

"The total mentioned above, easily worth more than four thousand, five hundred francs, is reduced in price to one thousand écus by the moderation of the lender."

CLEANTH. May the plague choke him and his moderation, the traitor! Cut-throat that he is! Have you ever heard of such usury? Can't he be satisfied with the furious interest he demands, without making me take all the junk he has heaped up, for three thousand francs? I won't get more than two hundred écus for the lot! And yet I must resign myself and consent to whatever he wants. He is in a position to make me accept anything. The dog has me by the throat.

FLÈCHE. Sir, I see you taking the very same road, no offense intended, that Panurge followed to his ruin: taking money in advance, buying dear and selling cheap, and eating your wheat in the blade.

CLEANTH. What would you have me do? You see what young men are reduced to by the cursèd avarice of their fathers! Is it any wonder, after this, that the sons should wish their fathers' death?

FLÈCHE. I must confess, the stinginess of yours would infuriate the calmest man in the world. I am not strongly inclined toward the gallows, thank God, and when I am with my colleagues, seeing them taking big chances for small gains, I always know when to pull my iron out of the fire, and when it is prudent to drop out of any adventure that smells ever so little of the gallows. But, to tell the truth, the way your father acts tempts me very much to steal from him. And I think, if I did rob him, I would be doing a good deed.

CLEANTH. Give me the note; I want to look it over again.

[*Enter* MASTER SIMON *and* HARPAGON.]

SIMON. Yes sir, he is a young man in need of money. The state of his affairs obliges him to find some, and he will agree to anything you prescribe.

HARPAGON. But are you convinced, Master Simon, that I will run no risk? Are you acquainted with the name, the fortune and the family of the party for whom you are speaking?

SIMON. No, I cannot give you any definite information about him; and it was only by chance that he was directed to me; but he himself will enlighten you about everything. And his man assures me that you will be satisfied when you meet him. All I can tell you is that

119 **Panurge** the improvident rascal in Rabelais' *Gargantua and Pantagruel*

his family is very rich, that his mother is already dead, and that he will guarantee, if you wish it, that his father will die before eight months are out.

HARPAGON. That is something, indeed. Charity, Master Simon, obliges us to make others happy when it is in our power to do so.

SIMON. To be sure.

FLÈCHE [*low to* CLEANTH]. What does this mean? Our Master Simon talking to your father!

CLEANTH [*low to* LA FLÈCHE]. Could they have told him who I am? or have you betrayed me?

SIMON [*noticing* CLEANTH *and* LA FLÈCHE]. Aha! you are in a hurry! Who told you this was the house? [*to* HARPAGON] In any event, sir, it was not I who revealed your name and lodgings. But, in my opinion, no great harm has been done: they are discreet fellows, and now you can discuss your business together.

HARPAGON. What?

SIMON. This is the gentleman who wants to borrow the fifteen thousand francs, the one I was telling you about.

HARPAGON. What! you rascal! It is you who abandon yourself to such culpable extremities!

CLEANTH. What! father, it is you who carry on this shameful business! [*Exit* MASTER SIMON *and* LA FLÈCHE.]

HARPAGON. It is you who want to ruin yourself by such deplorable borrowing!

CLEANTH. It is you who seek to enrich yourself by this criminal usury!

HARPAGON. Do you dare, after that, to show your face to me?

CLEANTH. Do you dare, after that, to show your face to the world?

HARPAGON. Tell me, aren't you ashamed to descend to such debauchery, to hurl yourself into horrible expenditure, and shamefully to squander the wealth that your ancestors have amassed for you by the sweat of their brows?

CLEANTH. How can you help but blush for disgracing your class this way with this trade you practise, sacrificing your honor and reputation to your insatiable desire to pile écu on écu and outdoing, in point of interest, the most infamous subtleties ever invented by the most notorious usurers?

HARPAGON. Get out of my sight, scoundrel, get out of my sight!

CLEANTH. Who is the greater criminal in your opinion: the man who buys money because he needs it, or the man who steals money but has no use for it?

HARPAGON. Leave the room I tell you, and stop chafing my ears. [*Exit* CLEANTH.] I am not a bit sorry that this has happened; it is a warning to me to watch everything he does more closely than ever.

[*Enter* FROSINE.]

FROSINE. Sir . . .

HARPAGON. Wait a moment. I'll be back to talk with you. [*aside*] It's about time I take a peek at my money. [*Exit.*]

[*Enter* LA FLÈCHE.]

FLÈCHE. The whole thing is very amusing. He must surely have a large store of supplies somewhere in the house, because we couldn't find a thing that's listed in the inventory he gave us.

FROSINE. Ah! it's you, my poor La Flèche! To what do we owe this meeting?

FLÈCHE. Aha! it's you, Frosine! What are *you* doing here?

FROSINE. What I do everywhere else: play the go-between in negotiations, make myself useful to others, and profit as much as I possibly can by whatever slight talent I may have. You know that in this world one is obliged to live by one's wits. And for women like myself Heaven has provided no other source of income than intrigue and persistency.

FLÈCHE. Do you have some business with the master of the house?

FROSINE. Yes, I am transacting some small business for him—for which I hope to be compensated.

FLÈCHE. By him? Ah! in faith, you'll have to be pretty sharp to get anything out of *him;* I warn you, money costs very dearly in this house.

FROSINE. There are certain services that are wonderfully effective.

FLÈCHE. I am your humble servant. But you don't know Signor Harpagon, yet. Signor Harpagon is of all humans the least human, the hardest and tightest mortal of all mortals. No service can push his gratitude far enough to make him unclench his fists. Of praise, esteem, benevolent words and friendship as much as you like, but money?—nothing doing. There is nothing more dry and withered than his favors and caresses, and "give" is a word for which he has such an aversion that he never says "I give," but "I lend, you good-day."

FROSINE. Mercy me! I know the art of milking a man. I have the secret for bringing out his tenderness, for tickling his heart, for finding his soft spot.

FLÈCHE. Useless here! If money is involved, I defy you to touch the man in question. On that score he is a Turk; and his turkery is the despair of all who know him; you could be dying, and he wouldn't turn a hair. In a word, he loves money more than reputation, honor or virtue, and the sight of anyone who expects to be paid throws him into convulsions. It wounds him mortally. It pierces his heart. It tears out his entrails. And if . . . He's coming back; I must be going. [*Exit.*]

[*Enter* HARPAGON.]

HARPAGON [*aside*]. All is as it should be. [*to* FROSINE] How now! What is it, Frosine?

FROSINE. Ah! Mercy me, how well you are looking! You are the very picture of health!

HARPAGON. Who? I?

FROSINE. Never have I seen your color so fresh and jovial.

HARPAGON. Really?

FROSINE. Never in your life were you as young as you are now; I see men of twenty-five who are older than you.

HARPAGON. Nevertheless, Frosine, I'm a good sixty years old.

FROSINE. Well, what is that, sixty years old? A worry indeed! It's the bloom of life, that is. And now you are entering on a man's prime season.

HARPAGON. That's true. However, twenty years less wouldn't do me any harm, as I see it.

FROSINE. Are you joking? You have no need of them. You bid fair to live to be a hundred.

HARPAGON. Do you think so?

FROSINE. Of course. You show every indication. Hold still a bit. Oh, there it is! There it is! Between your two eyes!—a sign of long life!

HARPAGON. Do you know something about these things?

FROSINE. Certainly. Show me your hand. Ah! Mercy me, what a life line!

HARPAGON. How's that?

FROSINE. Don't you see how far that line goes?

HARPAGON. Well, yes. What does it mean?

FROSINE. By my faith, I said a hundred years, but you will pass the one hundred and twenty mark.

HARPAGON. Is it possible?

FROSINE. You deserve a beating. I tell you, you will bury your children and your children's children.

HARPAGON. So much the better! How goes our little transaction?

FROSINE. Need you ask? Did anyone ever see me start anything I couldn't finish? I have an especially wonderful talent for marriages. There aren't two people in the world that I couldn't find a way to couple in no time at all. If I had the notion, I believe I could marry the Grand Turk to the Republic of Venice. But, to be sure, there wasn't any such great difficulty involved in this affair. Since I have business at their house, I have already discussed you at length with both of them; and I told the mother what plans you had conceived for Marianne, on seeing her pass through the street and take the air at her window.

HARPAGON. She answered . . .

FROSINE. She received the proposition with joy! And when I informed her that you are very desirous her daughter should be present tonight at the signing of the marriage contract which is to take place here, she readily consented. And she has entrusted her daughter to me for the evening.

HARPAGON. I am obliged, Frosine, to give a supper for Signor Anselm, and I would like her to attend this feast.

FROSINE. A good idea. After dinner, she is to pay your daughter a visit; from here she plans to go and see the fair; and afterwards she can come back for supper.

HARPAGON. Fine! They can go together in my carriage. Which I will lend them.

FROSINE. That will suit her perfectly.

HARPAGON. But, Frosine, have you talked to the mother about the money she can give her daughter? Did you tell her she ought to help a little, herself? That she should make some special effort? That she should bleed herself for an occasion like this? For, I tell you again, no one marries a girl unless she brings something in.

270 **Grand Turk** the Sultan. Turkey and Venice were conventional instances of irreconcilable hostility.

FROSINE. What! This is a girl who will bring you twelve thousand francs a year.

HARPAGON. Twelve thousand francs a year?

FROSINE. Yes. First of all: those who raised and nurtured her were very sparing on food. She is a girl used to living on salad, milk, cheese, and apples, and consequently doesn't require a richly set table, or fancy jellies or barley syrup all the time, or all the other delicacies that most women must have. And this is no trifling matter. It will make a difference of at least three thousand francs a year. Besides, she feels that true elegance lies in simplicity, and she doesn't care for magnificent clothes, or rich jewelry, or sumptuous furniture —things which young ladies are usually so passionately addicted to. And that little item is worth more than four thousand francs a year. What's more, she has a tremendous aversion to cards—a thing not common in women nowadays. I know of one in our neighborhood who, at thirties and forties, mind you, lost twenty thousand francs this year! But suppose we take only a quarter of that. Five thousand francs a year for cards, and four thousand francs for clothes and jewelry, make nine thousand francs. And we will figure one thousand écus for food. Isn't that your twelve thousand francs a year —every sou of it?

HARPAGON. Yes, not bad: but this account has nothing real in it.

FROSINE. I beg your pardon. Is the great sobriety that she will bring to your marriage nothing real? Or her inheritance of a great love for simplicity in dress? Or the acquisition of a great fund of hatred for cards?

HARPAGON. It is a mockery to try and make up a dowry out of the expenses that she won't put me to. I won't give a receipt for something I don't receive. I must be able to touch something.

FROSINE. Mercy me! you will touch enough. They spoke to me about a certain country where they have some property. You shall be the master of it.

HARPAGON. That remains to be seen. But Frosine, there is something else that bothers me. The girl is young, as you can see, and young people usually like only their own kind, and seek only their company. I am afraid that a man of my age might not be to her

310 **thirties and forties** the card game *trente et quarante* or *rouge et noir,* distantly related to blackjack

taste, and that this might cause some little disorder in my house, which would not suit me at all!

FROSINE. Ah! how little you know her! This is another thing about her that I was going to mention. She has a frightful aversion to all young men, and feels no love except for the old.

HARPAGON. Her?

FROSINE. Yes, her. I wish you could hear her on that subject. She can't so much as stand the sight of a young fellow; but she is in ecstasy, she tells me, when she can look at a handsome old man with a majestic beard. For her, the oldest are the most charming. And I warn you not to go and make yourself look younger than you are. She likes a man to be sixty at the very least. It wasn't four months ago, that, all set to be married, she broke off the marriage on the spot because her lover let it be known he was only fifty-six years old—and didn't use spectacles to sign the contract.

HARPAGON. Just for that?

FROSINE. Yes. She says she simply couldn't be satisfied with a man of fifty-six, and above all, she is for the nose that wears spectacles.

HARPAGON. Really, this is something altogether new!

FROSINE. It goes much deeper than most people know. Like most young girls she has a few paintings and a few prints in her room, but what do you think the subjects are? Adonises? Cephaluses? Parises? or Apollos? No. They are handsome portraits of Saturn, of King Priam, of old Nestor, and good father Anchises on his son's shoulders!

HARPAGON. That is admirable! I should never have suspected it. And I am very happy to learn she has that kind of disposition. In fact, had *I* been a woman, I wouldn't have liked young men at all.

FROSINE. I can well believe you. What are they but fancy drugs? And to love them, ha! They are nothing but handsome idiots, good-looking fops that make you envy their complexions. I'd really like to know what there is to them!

HARPAGON. As for me, I can't understand it. I don't know why some women are so fond of them.

FROSINE. They must be stark mad. To find youth amiable! Is there any common sense in it? Are they men, these young dandies? Can you become attached to one of those animals?

353–55 **Adonises . . . Anchises** types of youthful beauty contrasted with types of elderly worth

HARPAGON. That's what I have always said—with their effeminate, milk-fed voices, and their three little wisps of beard turned up like cat's whiskers, with their mouse-colored wigs, and their sloppy breeches, and their puffed-out stomachs!

FROSINE. They are well-built, indeed, compared with a person like you! [*to the audience*] There's a man for you! There is someone who is a pleasure to look at! This is how a man should be made and dressed to inspire love.

HARPAGON. You like the way I look?

FROSINE. I should say! You are ravishing, you ought to have your portrait painted. Turn round a bit, if you please. You couldn't be better. Let me see you walk. [*to the audience*] Here is a body that is trim, supple and tall as it ought to be. And not marked by any infirmity.

HARPAGON. None to speak of, thank God! [*coughs*] Except my catarrh that bothers me from time to time.

FROSINE. That is nothing. Your catarrh is not unbecoming to you. You cough gracefully.

HARPAGON. But tell me, hasn't Marianne seen me yet? Hasn't she noticed me at all, passing by her house?

FROSINE. No. But we have talked about you a great deal. I sketched a portrait of your person for her. And I did not fail to boast of your merits and the advantage it would be for her to have a husband like you.

HARPAGON. You have done well. And I thank you.

FROSINE. I would like, sir, to ask a small favor of you. I have a lawsuit that I am on the point of losing for want of a little money; and you could easily assure my winning this suit if you would show me some little kindness. [HARPAGON *frowns.*] Ah! how well you will please her! What a marvellous impression your old-fashioned ruff will make! But she will be especially charmed by your breeches, attached to your doublet with laces; they'll make her go wild over you. A laced-up lover will seem to her a wonderful treat.

HARPAGON. Really, it delights me to hear you say it.

FROSINE. To tell the truth, sir, this suit is of the utmost importance to me. I am ruined if I lose it, and the least bit of help would set everything right for me. [HARPAGON *frowns.*] I wish you could have seen the rapture in her face when she heard me speak of you. Her eyes sparkled with joy as I recited your qualities. In short, I left her in a state of extreme impatience to see this marriage entirely concluded.

HARPAGON. You have given me great pleasure, Frosine. And I must confess, I am under all the obligation in the world to you.

FROSINE. I beg you, sir, to give me the slight help I need. It will put me on my feet again. And I will be eternally indebted to you.

HARPAGON. Goodbye! I must get my mail ready.

FROSINE. I assure you, sir, you couldn't relieve me in a greater need.

HARPAGON. I will leave orders, so my coach will be ready to take you to the fair.

FROSINE. I would not importune you, were I not forced to do so—out of necessity.

HARPAGON. And I'll see to it that supper is ready early so that you won't get sick.

FROSINE. Do not refuse me this favor, I beg of you.

HARPAGON. I am going. There, someone is calling me. I'll see you by and by. [*Exit* HARPAGON.]

FROSINE. May the fever rack you! Cur! Villain! The devil take you! The miser was deaf to all my attacks. Nevertheless I must not drop his suit: for in any case, there is the other party. I am sure of a good reward from them!

ACT III

[*On stage:* HARPAGON, CLEANTH, ELISE, VALÈRE, DAME CLAUDE, MASTER JACQUES, BRINDAVOINE *and* LA MERLUCHE.]

HARPAGON. Here, all of you come here. I want to give you orders for this evening, and assign everyone a job. Step forward, Dame Claude. Let's begin with you. Good, I see you are already armed. I consign to you the task of cleaning up the house; but be especially careful not to rub the furniture too hard, or you'll wear it out. Furthermore, I assign you to see to the bottles during supper. And if any of them are carried off, or if anything is broken, you will be responsible, and I'll deduct it from your wages.

JACQUES [*aside*]. A convenient punishment.

HARPAGON [*to* DAME CLAUDE]. Go. . . . [*Exit* DAME CLAUDE.] You, Brindavoine, and you, La Merluche, are appointed to rinse the glasses, and to serve the wine—but only when someone is thirsty. And don't follow the example of those impudent lackies who go and *incite* people to drink and put the notion in their heads when they aren't even thinking about it. Wait until they have asked you more than once, and remember always to bring a lot of water.

JACQUES [*aside*]. Yes, pure wine goes to the head.

MERLUCHE. Shall we take our canvas smocks off, sir?

HARPAGON. Yes, when you see the guests coming, and be careful not to spoil your clothes.

BRINDAVOINE. You know very well, sir, that one side of my doublet is covered with a big spot of lamp-oil.

MERLUCHE. And I, sir, have a big hole in the back of my breeches, and I can be seen, begging your pardon . . .

HARPAGON. Peace! Keep that side discreetly turned toward the wall, and always show your front side to the world. And you, always hold your hat like this [*holds his hat over his chest*] when you serve.

[*Exeunt* LA MERLUCHE *and* BRINDAVOINE.]

And as for you, my daughter, keep an eye open when they clear away the table, and see to it that nothing goes to waste. That's a proper job for a young girl. But meanwhile, prepare yourself to receive my fiancée, who is coming to pay you a visit, and take you to the fair with her. Did you hear what I said?

ELISE. Yes, father.

HARPAGON. And you, my son, the dandy whose latest escapade I was so good as to forgive, don't you go getting any ideas either and make sour faces at her.

CLEANTH. I, father? Sour faces? And for what reason?

HARPAGON. By God, we know the drift of children whose fathers remarry, and how they feel toward what is called a stepmother. But, if you would like me to forget your last prank, I especially recommend that you treat this person to some of your most cheerful looks and give her the best reception you possibly can.

CLEANTH. To tell you the truth, father, I cannot promise you to be very glad she is to become my stepmother. I should be lying if I told you I would. But as for receiving her well and showing her a pleasant face, I promise to obey you punctually on that score.

HARPAGON. At least take care you do.

CLEANTH. You will see you will have no reason to complain.

HARPAGON. You will do wisely. [*Exeunt* CLEANTH *and* ELISE.] Valère, help me with this. Oh, there you are, Master Jacques! Come here. I have saved you for the last.

JACQUES. Is it to your coachman, sir, or is it to your cook you wish to speak? For I am one and the other.

HARPAGON. To the two of you.

JACQUES. But to which of us first?

HARPAGON. To the cook.

JACQUES. One moment then if you please. [*Takes off his coachman's coat and appears dressed as a cook.*]

HARPAGON. What the deuce kind of ceremony is this?

JACQUES. You have only to speak.

HARPAGON. I have committed myself, Master Jacques, to give a supper tonight.

JACQUES [*aside*]. This is miraculous!

HARPAGON. Tell me now, will you give us a fine feast?

JACQUES. Yes, if you give me a good deal of money.

HARPAGON. What the devil! always money! It seems they have nothing else to say: money, money, money! That's the sword they keep by their bed, money!

VALÈRE. I have never heard a more impertinent answer. How miraculous it is to be able to set out a fine feast when you have a lot of money! It is the easiest thing in the world to do, and there is no man so poor in wit that he couldn't do as much. But it is a clever man who can talk about providing a fine feast for little money!

JACQUES. A fine feast for little money?

VALÈRE. Yes.

JACQUES. By my faith, Mr. Steward, you would oblige us if you would let us in on your secret—and if you will take my place as cook! You meddle so much in this house already, you might as well be the factotum.

HARPAGON. Be quiet. What will we need?

JACQUES. There is your steward who will provide a fine feast at small cost.

HARPAGON. Ha! I want you to answer me.

JACQUES. How many will you be at table?

HARPAGON. We will be eight or ten. When there is enough for eight, there is plenty for ten.

VALÈRE. Naturally.

JACQUES. Very well, we will need four kinds of soup and five other dishes. Soups, entrées . . .

HARPAGON. What the devil! That's enough to feed a whole city.

JACQUES. Roast . . .

HARPAGON [*putting his hand over* MASTER JACQUES' *mouth*]. Ah! traitor, you are eating up all my money!

JACQUES. Side dishes . . .

HARPAGON [*putting his hand over* MASTER JACQUES' *mouth again*]. More?

VALÈRE. Do you want to make everybody split open? Do you think our master invites people in order to *murder* them with food? Go and read the rules of health a while—and ask the doctors if there is anything more prejudicial to man than excessive eating.

HARPAGON. He is right.

VALÈRE. Learn, Master Jacques, you and the like of you, that a table overloaded with food is a cut-throat; that if you want to prove yourself a friend to those you invite, frugality should reign at the meals you serve; and that, according to the saying of the ancients, we should eat to live, and not live to eat.

HARPAGON. Oh! but that was well said! Come here, I want to embrace you for that saying. It is the most beautiful sentence I have ever heard in my life. We should live to eat, and not eat to li . . . No, that isn't it. How was it you said it?

VALÈRE. We should eat to live, and not live to eat.

HARPAGON. Yes, do you hear that? Who was the great man who said it?

VALÈRE. At the moment I can't recall his name.

HARPAGON. Remember to write it down for me. I want to have it carved in gold letters above the mantelpiece in my dining room.

VALÈRE. I won't forget. And as for your supper, you have only to leave it to me. I will order things to be done as they should be.

HARPAGON. Take care of it then.

JACQUES. So much the better; it will mean less trouble for me.

HARPAGON. We should have those things that people don't eat much of, that satisfy the appetite quickly: a nice mutton stew, rather fat, with some kind of a meat-pie well garnished and chestnuts to go with it. Yes, that! And let there be a lot of it.

VALÈRE. Leave everything to me.

HARPAGON. Now, Master Jacques, my coach must be cleaned up.

JACQUES. One moment. That was addressed to the coachman. [*Exit, and reappears in his coachman's coat.*] You said . . . ?

HARPAGON. That you should clean up my coach, and have my horses ready to drive to the fair.

JACQUES. Your horses, sir? Faith, they are in no condition to walk. I won't say they are down on their litters. The poor beasts don't have any, so I'd be speaking very improperly. But you make them observe such strict fasts that they are now no more than ideas or ghosts or appearances of horses.

HARPAGON. No wonder they are sick; they do nothing.

JACQUES. And because they do nothing, sir, must they eat nothing? It would be much better for them, poor animals, to work a lot, and to eat accordingly. It breaks my heart to see them so weak, because, to tell the truth, I have so much affection for my horses, that when I see them suffer, it's just as though it were myself. Every day I take food out of my own mouth to feed them; it is a very hard nature, sir, that feels no pity for the next one.

HARPAGON. It won't be much work for them to go as far as the fair.

JACQUES. No, sir, I haven't the courage to drive them, and it would lie on my conscience if I hit them with the whip, in the condition they're in. How do you expect them to pull a carriage?—they can't even pull themselves.

VALÈRE. Sir, I will ask our neighbor Picard if he will be good enough to drive them. Besides, we shall need him here to help prepare the supper.

JACQUES. Very well! I'd still rather they died under someone else's hands and not mine.

VALÈRE. Master Jacques is intent on cavilling.

JACQUES. Mister Steward is intent on seeming indispensable.

HARPAGON. Peace!

JACQUES. Sir, I can't stand flatterers, and I can see what he is doing. He continually restricts the bread, the wine, the wood, the salt, and the candles just to scratch your ear, to win your favor. It makes me angry. And it grieves me to hear what people say about you every day. Because I feel a real affection for you, in spite of myself; and after my horses, you are the person I like most.

HARPAGON. Could I learn from you, Master Jacques, what people say about me?

JACQUES. Yes, sir, if I could be sure it wouldn't make you angry.

HARPAGON. No, not in the least.

JACQUES. Pardon me, but I know very well you'd fly into a rage.

HARPAGON. Not at all. On the contrary, it will give me great pleasure to learn what is said about me.

JACQUES. Sir, since it is your wish, I tell you frankly: people everywhere are laughing at you. They taunt us with a thousand jokes about you on all sides, and they are never so happy as when tearing you to ribbons or making up countless stories about your stinginess. One says that you have special almanacs printed, in which you have doubled the quarter-days and vigils, so you can take advantage of the fasts you impose on your household. Another says you always have a quarrel ready to pick with your valets when it is time for holiday gifts, or when they are leaving, so you'll have a reason for not giving them anything. This one tells the story that you once tried to bring your neighbor's cat to court for eating up the remainder of a leg of mutton. Somebody else says that you yourself were caught coming to steal your horses' oats, and that in the dark your coachman, the one before me, gave you I don't know how many blows with his stick, which you didn't care to say anything about. Shall I go on? We can't go anywhere without hearing people pull you apart. You are the talk of the town, the laughing-stock of the world. And they never refer to you except by the name of miser, cut-throat, villain, or shark.

HARPAGON. You are a fool, a scoundrel, a rascal, an insolent knave! [*Beats him.*]

JACQUES. There! Didn't I say it would be that way? You wouldn't believe me. I warned you that you would get angry if I told you the truth.

HARPAGON. Then learn how to talk. [*Exit* HARPAGON.]

180 **quarter-days . . . vigils** periods of fasting

VALÈRE. As far as I can see, Master Jacques, you are poorly paid for your frankness.

JACQUES. By God! Mister Upstart, playing the man of importance, it is none of your business. Save your laughs for your own beating when you get it, and don't come laughing at mine.

VALÈRE. Ah! good Master Jacques, please don't be angry.

JACQUES [*aside*]. He's backing down. I'll pretend to be tough, and if he is fool enough to be afraid of me, I'll give him a little thrashing. Did you know, Mister Comedian, that I myself never laugh?—and that if you get my temper up you are likely to be laughing out of the other side of your mouth?

VALÈRE. Gently now!

JACQUES. Why gently? What if I don't feel like being gentle?

VALÈRE. Please!

JACQUES. You are an impertinent fellow.

VALÈRE. Good Master Jacques!

JACQUES. There is no such person as good Master Jacques. If I get a stick, I'll beat the importance out of you.

VALÈRE [*picking up the stick on the table*]. What did you say? a stick?

JACQUES. Oh! I wasn't talking about that one.

VALÈRE. Did you know, Mister Fool, that I am man enough to thrash you?

JACQUES. I don't doubt it.

VALÈRE. That you are, by any standard, nothing but a miserable cook?

JACQUES. I know very well.

VALÈRE. And that you don't know me yet?

JACQUES. I beg your pardon.

VALÈRE. You'll beat me, you say?

JACQUES. I was joking.

VALÈRE. And your joking is not to my taste. This will teach you that you're a scurvy joker. [*Beats him.*]

[*Exit* VALÈRE.]

JACQUES. A pox on sincerity! It's a wretched practice. Here and now I renounce it, and I will never tell the truth again. As for my master, I'll let that go—he has some right to beat me. But, as for this steward, I'll take my revenge if I can.

[*Enter* FROSINE *and* MARIANNE.]

FROSINE. Do you know, Master Jacques, if your master is at home?

JACQUES. Yes, he certainly is. I know it all too well!

FROSINE. Tell him, pray, that we are here. [*Exit* MASTER JACQUES.]

MARIANNE. Ah! Frosine, I am in such a strange state! If I must tell what I feel: I am very much afraid of this interview.

FROSINE. But why? What is it that worries you?

MARIANNE. Alas! Need you ask? Can't you imagine the alarm of a person just about to see the rack she is to be tortured on?

FROSINE. I can plainly see that Harpagon is not the rack you would choose to embrace if you're thinking of an agreeable death. And I know by your expression that the dandy you were telling me about is somewhere in your thoughts.

MARIANNE. Yes, Frosine. That I do not wish to deny. The respectful visits he paid at our house have had, I must confess, some effect on my heart.

FROSINE. But have you learned *who* he is?

MARIANNE. No, I don't in the least know *who* he is, but I do know he is fashioned in a way that inspires love and that, if the choice were left at my disposal, I would take him sooner than any other, and that he contributes not a little to make me find the husband you would give me a horrible torment.

FROSINE. Mercy me! all those dandies are agreeable enough, and they play their parts very well, but most of them are poor as church-mice. You would do much better to take an old husband who will leave you a lot of money. I will admit that the senses will not find full measure on the side which I am speaking for, and there are some slightly distasteful details to be endured with such a husband—but it won't be for long. His death, believe me, will soon put you in a position to pick a more attractive one, who will make up for everything.

MARIANNE. Bless me, Frosine, it seems a very strange business when, to be happy, one must hope or wait for the demise of someone. And death does not always lend itself to the plans we make.

FROSINE. Are you joking? You are marrying him only on the understanding that he will soon leave you a widow. That ought to be one of the articles in the contract. It would be very impertinent in him not to die before three months are out.

[*Enter* HARPAGON.]

Speak of the devil . . .

MARIANNE. Ah! Frosine, what a face!

HARPAGON. Do not be offended, my beauty, if I come to you wearing spectacles. I know that your charms are striking enough—are visible enough by themselves—that there is no need of glasses to perceive them. But after all, it is through glasses we observe the stars, and I maintain and guarantee that you are a star. And what a star! The most beautiful star in the realm of stars. Frosine, she doesn't say a word, and she doesn't show, so it seems to me, that she is at all pleased to see me.

FROSINE. That is because she is still all surprise. And then, the girls nowadays are always shy about showing straightway what is in their hearts.

[*Enter* ELISE.]

HARPAGON. You are right. [*to* MARIANNE] Here, darling beauty, is my daughter, who has come to greet you.

MARIANNE. I acquit myself, madam, much too tardily of this visit.

ELISE. You have done that, madam, which I ought to have done. It was my place to anticipate you.

HARPAGON. You see how tall she is; but weeds grow fast.

MARIANNE [*aside to* FROSINE]. Oh, what an unpleasant man!

HARPAGON. What does the beauty say?

FROSINE. That she thinks you are wonderful.

HARPAGON. You do me too much honor, adorable darling.

MARIANNE [*aside to* FROSINE]. Such an animal!

HARPAGON. I am obliged for your sentiments.

MARIANNE [*aside to* FROSINE]. I can't stand any more of this.

[*Enter* CLEANTH.]

HARPAGON. Here is my son, who also comes to pay you his respects.

MARIANNE [*aside to* FROSINE]. Ah! Frosine, what a coincidence! This is the very person I spoke to you about.

FROSINE. The adventure is fantastic.

HARPAGON. I see you are astonished to find that I have such big children; but I shall soon be rid of them both.

CLEANTH. Madam, to tell the truth, this is an encounter which I by no means expected; and my father surprised me not a little when he told me a while ago of his intentions.

MARIANNE. I can say the same for myself. This is an unforeseen meeting, which has surprised me as much as it has you. I too was not at all prepared for such an encounter.

CLEANTH. It is true that my father, madam, could not make a handsomer choice, and the honor of seeing you is a real joy for me; but for all that, I will not assure you that I rejoice over the design you may have to become my stepmother. That compliment, I confess, is too much for me; it is a title, if you please, that I do not want for you. This speech may seem brutal in the eyes of some, but I am sure you are a person who will take it in the right sense. You can easily imagine, madam, that this is a marriage which is bound to be somewhat repugnant to me; for you know what kind of man I am and how much it clashes with my interests. In short, you will not be offended if I tell you, with my father's permission, that if things depended on me, these nuptials would never take place.

HARPAGON. Your compliment is very impertinent! What a nice confession to make to her!

MARIANNE. And I, in answer to you, have this to say: our feelings are quite mutual. If it is true that you would find it repugnant to have me for a stepmother, it would be no less so for me, I assure you, to have you for a stepson. Do not think, pray, that it is I who seek to be the source of your uneasiness. I should be very sorry to cause you any displeasure; and if I did not see myself forced to it by an absolute power, I give you my word, I would never consent to a marriage that pains you.

HARPAGON. She is right. A stupid compliment like that deserves a stupid answer. I beg pardon, my beauty, for my son's impertinence. He is a young ass who doesn't yet know the weight of his own words.

MARIANNE. I assure you that what he said has not offended me in the least. On the contrary, it has been a pleasure to hear him express his true sentiments. I like that kind of confession from him. If he had spoken in any other way, I would have far less esteem for him.

HARPAGON. It is very kind of you to forgive his faults this way. Time will make him wiser, and you will see that he will have a change of heart.

CLEANTH. No, father, it is not capable of change; and I earnestly entreat madam to believe that.

HARPAGON. Just see how extravagant he is! He goes on more rashly than ever.

CLEANTH. Would you have me belie my heart?

HARPAGON. Again! Would you mind changing the subject?

CLEANTH. Very well, since you wish me to speak in a different manner . . . Permit me, madam, to put myself in my father's place, to confess that I have never seen anything in the world as lovely as you; that I can conceive nothing to equal the happiness of pleasing you; and that the title of your husband is a glory, a felicity, that I would prefer to the destiny of the greatest prince on earth. Yes, madam, the happiness of possessing you, is in my estimation, the fairest of all fortunes; it is the goal of my whole ambition. I would do anything to make such a conquest; and the most powerful obstacles . . .

HARPAGON. Moderation, son, if you please.

CLEANTH. This is a compliment I am paying the lady, for you.

HARPAGON. By God! I have a tongue to express myself, and I have no need of a proxy the likes of you. Here, bring chairs.

FROSINE. No. It will be better for us to go directly to the fair. Then we'll be back early and have the whole time afterward to talk with you.

HARPAGON. Then tell them to hitch up the horses to the carriage. I beg you to excuse me, my beauty, for not having thought to give you a little refreshment before you start out.

CLEANTH. I have provided for that, father. I had them bring a few plates of Chinese oranges, some lemons, and some preserves; which I sent for in your name.

HARPAGON [*aside to* VALÈRE]. Valère!

VALÈRE. He's out of his head.

CLEANTH. Do you think, father, that it isn't enough? Madam will please have the kindness to excuse it.

MARIANNE. It was not at all necessary.

CLEANTH. Have you ever, madam, seen more fire in a diamond than in this one you see on my father's finger? [*Takes ring off* HARPAGON's *finger.*]

MARIANNE. It is true that it shines quite brightly.

CLEANTH. You must see it from close up. [*Puts ring on* MARIANNE's *hand.*]

MARIANNE. It is very handsome, I must say, and it sparkles a great deal. [*Begins to take ring off her finger.*]

CLEANTH. No, no, madam; it is on hands much too lovely. My father makes you a present of it.

HARPAGON. I?

CLEANTH. Isn't it true, father, that you want the lady to keep it for love of you?

HARPAGON [*aside to* CLEANTH]. What is this?

CLEANTH. Foolish question. He makes a sign to me that I should make you accept it.

MARIANNE. I don't at all want . . .

CLEANTH. Are you joking? He has no intention of taking it back.

HARPAGON [*aside*]. I'm losing my temper.

MARIANNE. It would be . . .

CLEANTH. No, I tell you, you will offend him.

MARIANNE. Please . . .

CLEANTH. Out of the question.

HARPAGON [*aside*]. A pox . . .

CLEANTH. Your refusal is making him angry.

HARPAGON [*aside to* CLEANTH]. Ah! you traitor!

CLEANTH. You see he's getting desperate.

HARPAGON [*aside to* CLEANTH]. You murderer, you!

CLEANTH. Father, it's not my fault. I am doing what I can to oblige her to keep it, but she is determined.

HARPAGON [*aside to* CLEANTH]. Scoundrel!

CLEANTH. You are the cause, madam, of my father's quarreling with me.

HARPAGON [*aside to* CLEANTH]. Knave!

CLEANTH. You will make him ill. Please, madam, do not resist any longer.

FROSINE. Mercy me! what a fuss! Keep the ring if the gentleman wants you to have it.

MARIANNE. So that you won't fly into a rage, I will keep it for the time being; and I will find another opportunity to return it.

[*Enter* BRINDAVOINE.]

BRINDAVOINE. Sir, there's a man here who wants to talk to you.

HARPAGON. Tell him I am busy, and to come back some other time.

BRINDAVOINE. He says he has money for you.

HARPAGON [*to* MARIANNE]. Please excuse me. I'll be back presently.

[*Enter* LA MERLUCHE *running; collides with* HARPAGON *and knocks him down.*]

MERLUCHE. Sir . . .

HARPAGON. Ah! I am dying!

CLEANTH. What is it, father, are you hurt?

HARPAGON. The traitor must surely have been paid by my debtors to make me break my neck.

VALÈRE [*to* HARPAGON]. There's no harm done.

MERLUCHE. I beg your pardon, sir, I thought I did right to come running.

HARPAGON. What are you here for, murderer?

MERLUCHE. To tell you that neither of your horses has any shoes.

HARPAGON. Take them to the blacksmith, right away.

CLEANTH. While waiting for the horses to be shod, father, I will do the honors of the house for you, and conduct madam into the garden, where I shall have the refreshments served.

[*Exeunt* FROSINE, ELISE, MARIANNE *and* CLEANTH.]

HARPAGON. Valère, keep an eye on all that; and take care, pray, to save me as much as you can, so that we can send it back to the dealer.

VALÈRE. Rest assured. [*Exit* VALÈRE.]

HARPAGON. Oh, impertinent son! You are trying to ruin me!

ACT IV

[*Enter* CLEANTH, MARIANNE, ELISE *and* FROSINE.]

CLEANTH. Let us go in again; we shall be much better off in here. There is no longer anyone suspect around, and we can speak freely.

ELISE. Yes, madam, my brother has confided to me the love he bears you. I know what pain and frustration such obstacles can cause; and it is a most kindly sympathy, I assure you, that provokes my interest in your adventure.

MARIANNE. It is a sweet consolation to see a person like you interested in oneself, and I implore you, madam, always to cherish your generous friendship for me—so capable of softening the cruel blows of misfortune.

FROSINE. By my faith, you are unlucky people, both of you, for not having told me about your affair before all this happened. I could, no doubt, have warded off these troubles. I wouldn't have brought matters to such a pass as this.

CLEANTH. What can you expect? It is my evil destiny has willed it so. But, dear Marianne, what have you resolved to do?

MARIANNE. Alas! am I in a position to resolve anything? Dependent as I am, can I do more than hope?

CLEANTH. Is there nothing in your heart to encourage me but barren hope? No benevolent pity? No helpful kindness? No lively affection at all?

MARIANNE. What can I tell you? Put yourself in my place, and see what I can do. Advise me. Order me. I put myself in your hands. And I believe you are too reasonable to demand more of me than is allowed by honor and decorum.

CLEANTH. Alas! to what am I reduced if you limit me to the pallid sentiments that rigorous honor and scrupulous decorum will allow?

MARIANNE. But what would you have me do? Even though I could ignore many of the niceties which our sex is obliged to observe, I have too much consideration for my mother. She has reared me with extreme tenderness. I could never resolve to do anything that would cause her displeasure. Go and speak to her. Do everything in your power to win her over. You may do and say whatever you please; I give you my permission. And if it is only a question of declaring in your favor, I readily consent to make a confession to her of all that I feel for you.

CLEANTH. Frosine, my poor Frosine, would you help us?

FROSINE. By my faith, is there any need to ask? I will with all my heart. You know that by nature I am human enough. Heaven didn't give me a heart of bronze, and I am only too eager to do little services for people when I see they love one another sincerely and honorably. What can we do about this?

CLEANTH. Think a little, I beg you.

MARIANNE. Show us a way.

ELISE. Invent something that will undo what you have done.

FROSINE. That is rather difficult. [*to* MARIANNE] As to your mother, she is not altogether unreasonable: perhaps you could win her over, and make her decide to transfer the gift she intends for the father to the son. [*to* CLEANTH] But the worst part of this is that your father is—your father.

CLEANTH. That's understood.

FROSINE. I mean he will bear a grudge if she refuses him openly, and he will be in no humor afterward to give his consent to your marriage. It will be necessary, to do it well, that the refusal come from himself. We must try by some means to make her distasteful to him.

CLEANTH. You are right.

FROSINE. Yes, I am right. I know it very well. That is what has to be done. But the deuce of it is to find a way. Wait; if we had a woman, getting on in years, with my talent, and who could act well enough to counterfeit a lady of quality, with the help of a train made up in a hurry and some bizarre name of marchioness or viscountess, who we could pretend comes from Brittany, I could be clever enough to convince him that she was a rich person who, besides her houses, had a hundred thousand écus in solid silver, that she was hopelessly in love with him, and wanted to be his wife so badly that she would sign over all her property to him in a marriage contract. I don't in the least doubt that he would lend an ear to the proposition. For, in short, although he loves you very much, he loves money a little more. And, once blinded by this illusion, once he has consented to what concerns you most, it will matter little afterward if he is undeceived when he looks more closely into the estate of our marchioness.

CLEANTH. This is all very well thought out.

FROSINE. Leave it to me. I just thought of a friend of mine who is the very woman we want.

CLEANTH. Rest assured, Frosine, of my gratitude if you succeed in this. But dear Marianne, let us begin by persuading your mother; there is still much to be done to break off this marriage. For your part, I beseech you, make every effort you possibly can. Use all the power that her love for you gives you over her. Unfold your eloquent graces without reserve—those all-powerful charms that Heaven has located in your eyes and lips. And forget none, please, of those tender expressions, or those soft entreaties, or those touching caresses to which, I am persuaded, no one could refuse anything.

[*Enter* HARPAGON.]

MARIANNE. I will do all in my power, and I won't forget a thing.

HARPAGON [*aside*]. Hey! what's this? My son kisses the hand of his future stepmother; and his future stepmother does not offer much resistance. Could there be more to this than meets the eye?

ELISE. Here is my father.

HARPAGON. The carriage is ready. You can leave when you please.

CLEANTH. Since you are not going, father, I will drive them myself.

HARPAGON. No, stay. They can go just as well by themselves. I need you here. [*Exeunt* FROSINE, ELISE *and* MARIANNE.]

HARPAGON. Oh! by the way, apart from the question of her becoming your stepmother, what do you think of this person?

CLEANTH. What do I think of her?

HARPAGON. Yes—of her manner, her figure, her beauty, and her wit?

CLEANTH. So so.

HARPAGON. What do you mean?

CLEANTH. To tell you frankly, I did not find her what I thought her to be. She has the manner of an out-and-out coquette, her figure is rather awkward, her beauty is mediocre, and she has a very common kind of wit. But don't think, father, that I am trying to set you against her. Because, stepmother for stepmother, I like this one as much as I would any other.

HARPAGON. Nevertheless you were telling her a while ago . . .

CLEANTH. I did say a few nice things to her in your name—but that was to please you.

HARPAGON. So then, you don't feel the slightest inclination for her?

CLEANTH. I? None at all.

HARPAGON. That's too bad, for it puts an end to an idea that came into my head. Seeing her here made me reflect on my age, and I thought to myself that people might find fault with me for marrying such a young girl. This consideration made me abandon my plans; but, since I have already asked her to marry and am bound by my word, I would have given her to you—if you had not shown such an aversion.

CLEANTH. To me?

HARPAGON. To you.

CLEANTH. In marriage?

HARPAGON. In marriage.

CLEANTH. Listen. It is true she is not much to my taste. But to make you happy, father, I will resign myself to marrying her—since it is your wish.

HARPAGON. Mine? I am more reasonable than you think. I would not force your inclination.

CLEANTH. Pardon me, I will do myself this violence out of love for you.

HARPAGON. No, no. A marriage can never be happy where there is no affection.

CLEANTH. Affection is something, father, that will come afterwards, perhaps. They say that love is often the fruit of marriage.

HARPAGON. No, the venture ought not to be risked on the man's side. There may be painful consequences to which I would not care to expose myself. If you had felt some inclination for her earlier, I would have had you marry her in my place. But since that is not the case, I will carry out my first plan, and marry her myself.

CLEANTH. Very well, father, since this is the way things are, I am obliged to bare my heart to you: I must reveal our secret. The truth is that I have loved her since the first time I saw her out walking, that my intention up to a while ago was to ask you if I could have her for my wife, and that nothing has held me back but your declaration of your own sentiments and fear of displeasing you.

HARPAGON. Have you visited her?

CLEANTH. Yes, father.

HARPAGON. Very often?

CLEANTH. Often enough—for the time I had.

HARPAGON. Were you well received?

CLEANTH. Very well. But they did not know who I was. That is why Marianne was so surprised a while ago.

HARPAGON. Did you declare your passion to her, and your intention of marrying her?

CLEANTH. Certainly, and I have even broached the subject a little to her mother.

HARPAGON. Did she give your proposal a hearing?

CLEANTH. Yes, a very civil one.

HARPAGON. And does her daughter return your love appreciably?

CLEANTH. If appearances are to be trusted, I am persuaded, father, that she feels some affection for me.

HARPAGON. I am happy to learn such a secret. It is exactly what I wanted to know. And now, son, do you know what you will have to do? You will have to think, if you please, about getting over your love, about giving up your pursuit of this person whom I intend for myself, and about marrying, in a short time, the woman I have chosen for you!

CLEANTH. So, father, you have tricked me! Very well! Since things have come to this pass, I declare to you that I will never cease loving Marianne, that I will go to any limit to dispute the conquest with you, and though you have the mother's consent on your side, I will perhaps find others who will fight for me.

HARPAGON. What? You scoundrel! You have the audacity to stalk my game?

CLEANTH. It is you who are stalking mine: I knew her first.

HARPAGON. Am I not your father? Don't you owe me your respect?

CLEANTH. These are not matters in which the children are obliged to defer to their fathers. Love knows no master.

HARPAGON. I'll teach you to know me—by the mastery of a good stick.

CLEANTH. All your threats will do no good.

HARPAGON. Will you renounce Marianne?

CLEANTH. On no account.

HARPAGON. Bring me a stick, quickly.

[*Enter* MASTER JACQUES.]

JACQUES. Now, now, now! gentlemen, what is this? What can you be thinking of?

CLEANTH. I laugh at it all.

JACQUES. Ah! gently, sir.

HARPAGON. To talk with such impudence!

JACQUES. Oh! sir, please.

CLEANTH. I won't yield an inch.

JACQUES. Eh, what? to your father?

HARPAGON. Leave him to me. [*Menaces* CLEANTH *with his stick.*]

JACQUES. Eh, what? to your son? Once more, leave off, for my sake.

HARPAGON. I want to make *you,* Master Jacques, judge of this affair—to prove I am right.

JACQUES. I am willing. [*to* CLEANTH] Go a little farther off.

HARPAGON. I am in love with a girl I want to marry, and that scoundrel has the impudence to be in love with the same girl at the same time, and intends, despite my orders, to marry her.

JACQUES. Ah! he is in the wrong.

HARPAGON. Isn't it a shocking thing for a son to enter into competition with his father? Shouldn't he, out of respect, refrain from meddling where my affections are involved?

JACQUES. You are right. Let me talk to him. Stay here.

[*Goes to* CLEANTH.]

CLEANTH. Yes, of course, since he has chosen you for judge, I'll not back out. It isn't important to me who it is, and I too am willing to refer myself to you, Master Jacques, in this matter of our difference.

JACQUES. You do me great honor.

CLEANTH. I am very much taken with a young lady who returns all my interest, and who has tenderly received the offer of my heart; and my father has taken it into his head to trouble our love by making her an offer of marriage.

JACQUES. He is in the wrong, surely.

CLEANTH. Isn't he ashamed, at his age, to dream of marrying? Is it becoming in him to be amorous? Wouldn't he do better to leave that business to young fellows?

JACQUES. You are right; he is making a fool of himself. Let me say a few words to him. [*Returns to* HARPAGON.] Well, your son is not so strange as you make him out to be; he has submitted to reason. He says he knows that he owes you respect, that he was carried away by the heat of the argument, and that he will not refuse to submit to anything that pleases you, provided you intend to treat him better than you have done, and that you give him someone in marriage with whom he will have reason to be satisfied.

HARPAGON. Ah, tell him, Master Jacques, that with this provision, he may expect anything he *wants* from me; and that, Marianne excepted, he is at liberty to choose any girl he pleases.

JACQUES. Leave it to me. [*to* CLEANTH] Well, your father is not as unreasonable as you make him out to be, and he admitted to me that it was only your rage that roused his temper, that he is angry only about the way you conducted yourself, and that he will be very much disposed to grant all your wishes provided you will go about it gently, and show him the deference, respect, and submission that a son owes his father.

CLEANTH. Ah! Master Jacques, you can assure him that if he grants me Marianne, he will see that I will always be the most submissive man in the world, and that I will never do anything except by his wish.

JACQUES [*going to* HARPAGON]. It's done. He consents to what you ask.

HARPAGON. It's the happiest conclusion in the world.

JACQUES [*going to* CLEANTH]. It's all decided. He is satisfied with your promises.

CLEANTH. Heaven be praised!

JACQUES [*in the middle of the stage*]. Gentlemen, you have only to talk together. Here you are in agreement now, and you were about to fall out because of a misunderstanding!

CLEANTH. My poor Master Jacques, I will be obliged to you for life.

JACQUES. It was nothing, sir.

HARPAGON. You have made me happy, Master Jacques, and you deserve a reward. [MASTER JACQUES *put out his hand.*] Go—I shall remember it, I assure you.

JACQUES. I kiss your hand. [*Exit* MASTER JACQUES.]

CLEANTH. I beg your pardon, father, for showing my temper in that way.

HARPAGON. It was nothing.

CLEANTH. I assure you, it gives me all the concern in the world.

HARPAGON. As for myself, it gives me all the joy in the world to see you reasonable.

CLEANTH. How good of you to forget my fault so quickly!

HARPAGON. One easily forgets his child's faults when one sees him return to the path of duty.

CLEANTH. What! you harbor no resentment for all my extravagance?

HARPAGON. You oblige me not to by the submission and respect you show.

CLEANTH. And I, I promise you, father, will bear the memory of your kindness to the grave.

HARPAGON. And I, I promise you that there is nothing you shall not have from me.

CLEANTH. Ah! father, I have nothing more to ask: you gave me all when you gave me Marianne.

HARPAGON. What?

CLEANTH. I say, father, that you have made me too happy. You gave me all when you agreed to give me Marianne.

HARPAGON. Who said anything about giving you Marianne?

CLEANTH. You, father.

HARPAGON. I?

CLEANTH. Certainly.

HARPAGON. What! You are the one who promised to renounce her.

CLEANTH. I renounce her?

HARPAGON. Yes.

CLEANTH. Not in the least.

HARPAGON. You haven't abandoned your pretensions to her?

CLEANTH. On the contrary, I am more determined than ever.

HARPAGON. What! you rascal, again?

CLEANTH. Nothing can change my mind.

HARPAGON. Let me at you, traitor!

CLEANTH. Do whatever you please.

HARPAGON. I forbid you ever to see me again.

CLEANTH. It's all the same to me.

HARPAGON. I abandon you.

CLEANTH. Abandon me.

HARPAGON. I disown you as my son.

CLEANTH. So be it.

HARPAGON. I disinherit you.

CLEANTH. Anything you like.

HARPAGON. And I give you my curse.

CLEANTH. I have no need of your gifts. [*Exit* HARPAGON.]

[*Enter* LA FLÈCHE.]

FLÈCHE. Ah! sir! I have found you just in time! Follow me quickly.

CLEANTH. What's the matter?

FLÈCHE. Follow me, I tell you—our troubles are over.

CLEANTH. What?

FLÈCHE [*shows him the chest*]. Here's your way out.

CLEANTH. How?

FLÈCHE. Your father's treasure. I dug it up!

CLEANTH. Where was it?

FLÈCHE. You shall know everything. Run. I hear him screaming.

[*Exeunt* LA FLÈCHE *and* CLEANTH.]

[*Enter* HARPAGON.]

HARPAGON. Stop thief! Stop thief! Stop assassin! Stop murderer! Justice, Divine Justice! I am ruined! I've been murdered! He cut my throat, he stole my money! Who can it be? What's become of him?

Where is he? Where is he hiding? What shall I do to find him? Where shall I run? Where shan't I run? Isn't that he there? Isn't this he here? Who's this? [*Sees his own shadow and grabs his own arm.*] Stop! Give me back my money, you rogue. . . . Ah! it is myself. My mind is unhinged, and I don't know where I am, who I am, or what I am doing. [*Falls to his knees.*] Alas! my poor money, my poor money, my dear friend, they have taken you from me. And since they carried you off, I've lost my support, my consolation, my joy. Everything is at an end for me; I have no more to do in this world! I cannot live without you! It's finished. I can no more. [*Lies down.*] I am dying. I am dead. I am buried! Isn't there anybody who would like to bring me back to life by returning my dear money or by telling me who took it? [*rising to his knees*] What did you say? It was nobody. [*Stands.*] Whoever did the job must have watched very closely for his chance; for he chose exactly the time when I was talking to my treacherous son. [*Takes his hat and cane.*] I'll go out. I'll go and demand justice. I'll order them to torture everyone in my house for a confession: the maids, the valets, my son, my daughter—and myself too! What a crowd of people! Everybody I cast my eyes on arouses my suspicion, and everything seems to be my thief. Eh! what are you talking about there? About the man that robbed me? Why are you making that noise up there? Is my thief there? [*Kneels and addresses the audience.*] Please, if anyone has any information about my thief, I beg you to tell me. Are you sure he isn't hidden there among you? They all look at me and laugh. [*Rises.*] You will probably see that they all had a part in this robbery. Here, quick, commissaries, archers, provosts, judges, tortures, scaffolds, and executioners! I want to have everybody hanged. And if I don't recover my money, I'll hang myself afterward!

ACT V

[*On stage:* HARPAGON, *the* COMMISSARY *and his clerk.*]

COMMISSARY. Leave me alone. I know my business, thank God! I didn't start investigating robberies yesterday. I wish I had a sack of francs for every man I've sent to the gallows!

HARPAGON. All the magistrates are interested in taking this case in hand. What's more, if no one sees to it that I recover my money, I shall demand justice from Justice herself!

COMMISSARY. We must follow the prescribed procedure. How much was it you said was in this moneybox?

HARPAGON. Ten thousand écus, to the sou.

COMMISSARY. Ten thousand écus?

HARPAGON. Ten thousand écus.

COMMISSARY. It was a considerable theft.

HARPAGON. No penalty would be too great for the enormity of the crime. If it goes unpunished, nothing is too sacred to be safe.

COMMISSARY. In what coin was the sum?

HARPAGON. In good gold louis and solid pistoles.

COMMISSARY. Whom do you suspect of this theft?

HARPAGON. Everybody! I want you to arrest the whole city and the suburbs!

COMMISSARY. We musn't frighten anyone, take my word for it. We must try and obtain some evidence quietly. Then afterward we can proceed more rigorously in recovering the deniers that were taken from you.

[*Enter* MASTER JACQUES *from the kitchen.*]

JACQUES. I'll be back in a little while. First I want you to cut his throat. Then I want you to singe his feet. Then I want you to put him in boiling water. Then I want you to hang him from the ceiling.

HARPAGON. Who? The man who robbed me?

JACQUES. I was talking about the suckling pig your steward just sent me. I want to dress him for you according to my fancy.

HARPAGON. That is not the question. You must talk to this gentleman about something else.

COMMISSARY. Don't be frightened. I am not a man who would cause you scandal. Everything will be done quietly.

JACQUES. Is the gentleman one of your supper guests?

COMMISSARY. Now, my dear friend, you must hide nothing from your master.

JACQUES. Faith, sir, I will show you all I know: I will treat you the best I possibly can.

HARPAGON. We aren't talking about that.

JACQUES. If I can't give you as fine a feast as I want to, it's the fault of a certain gentleman, a certain steward, who has clipped my wings with the scissors of his economy.

HARPAGON. Traitor! We are investigating something more important than supper. I want you to give me information about the money that was stolen from me.

JACQUES. Did someone steal your money?

HARPAGON. Yes, you rascal! And I'll have you hanged if you don't give it back.

COMMISSARY. For Heaven's sake, don't bully him! I can see by his face he's an honest man. Without making us send him to jail, he will tell you everything you want to know. Yes, my friend, if you tell us what you know, no harm will come to you. You will be rewarded by your master, as you deserve to be. Just this morning someone took his money. Is it possible you don't have some information about this matter?

JACQUES [*aside*]. Exactly what I need to get my revenge on our steward! Ever since he came into this house he has been the favorite —only *his* advice is listened to. Then, too, the beating he gave me sticks in my craw.

HARPAGON. What are you mumbling about?

COMMISSARY. Leave him alone. He is preparing to give you satisfaction. I told you he is an honest man.

JACQUES. Sir, since you want me to tell you something about this business, I think it was a certain gentleman, a certain steward, who did the job.

HARPAGON. Valère?

JACQUES. Yes.

HARPAGON. He? Who seemed to be so trustworthy?

JACQUES. Himself. I think he is the one who robbed you.

HARPAGON. On what grounds do you think so?

JACQUES. On what grounds?

HARPAGON. Yes.

JACQUES. I think so . . . on the grounds that . . . I think so.

COMMISSARY. But it is necessary that you tell us what proof you have.

HARPAGON. Did you see him sneaking around the place where I

kept my money?

JACQUES. Yes, certainly. Where did you keep your money?

HARPAGON. In the garden.

JACQUES. Exactly. I saw him sneaking through the garden. What was this money in?

HARPAGON. A moneybox.

JACQUES. That's it. I saw him with a moneybox.

HARPAGON. This moneybox . . . What did it look like? I'll soon see if it was mine.

JACQUES. What did it look like?

HARPAGON. Yes.

JACQUES. It looked like . . . it looked like a moneybox.

COMMISSARY. Of course. But describe it a little, so we can see . . .

JACQUES. It was a large moneybox.

HARPAGON. The one that was stolen from me was small.

JACQUES. Oh, yes—it was small if you want to look at it that way. I call it large on account of what it contained.

COMMISSARY. What color was it?

JACQUES. What color?

COMMISSARY. Yes.

JACQUES. It was the color of . . . yes, the color of it was . . . Can't you help me out a bit?

HARPAGON. Eh!

JACQUES. Wasn't it red?

HARPAGON. No, gray.

JACQUES. Oh! yes, grayish-red. That's what I meant to say.

HARPAGON. There isn't the slightest doubt. That is definitely it. Write, sir, write down his testimony. Heavens! who's to be trusted nowadays? You can't put your faith in anything! After this, I fear I am a man who might rob himself.

JACQUES. Sir, he is coming back. At least don't go and tell him it was I who told you this.

[*Enter* VALÈRE.]

HARPAGON. Advance. Come. Confess the darkest deed, the most horrible atrocity ever committed.

VALÈRE. What do you mean, sir?

HARPAGON. What! traitor, you do not even blush for your crime?

VALÈRE. What crime can you be talking of?

HARPAGON. What crime am I talking of? Infamous! As though you didn't know what I mean! It is useless for you to try and cover up. The deed has been discovered. Someone has just told me all. Really! How could you abuse my kindness that way—insinuate yourself into my house to betray me—to play a trick of that kind on me!

VALÈRE. Sir, since someone has told you all, I shall not try to find a way out. I deny nothing.

JACQUES [*aside*]. Hoho! Could I have guessed right without thinking?

VALÈRE. It was my intention to speak to you about it, and I wanted to wait for more favorable conditions to do so. But since things are the way they are, I beg you not to be angry. Be good enough to hear my reasons.

HARPAGON. And what wonderful reasons can you give me, infamous thief?

VALÈRE. Ah! sir, I have not deserved those names. It is true I am guilty of an offense against you. But, after all, my fault is pardonable.

HARPAGON. How, pardonable? A premeditated crime? An assassination of this sort?

VALÈRE. Please don't lose your temper. When you have heard me, you will see that the evil done is not so great as you make it out.

HARPAGON. The evil is not so great as I make it out! What? My blood! My entrails!—You scoundrel!

VALÈRE. Your blood, sir, has not fallen into evil hands. I belong to a class which is not beneath it, and there is nothing in all this for which I cannot make full reparation.

HARPAGON. That is my intention precisely—that you shall make full restitution of what you have ravished from me.

VALÈRE. Your honor, sir, shall be fully satisfied.

HARPAGON. It has nothing to do with honor. But, tell me, what ever possessed you to do it?

VALÈRE. Alas! You are asking me?

HARPAGON. Yes I really am.

VALÈRE. A god who is his own excuse for everything he does: Love.

HARPAGON. Love?

VALÈRE. Yes.

HARPAGON. A beautiful love, a beautiful love indeed! Love of my gold louis.

VALÈRE. No, sir, it was not in the least your wealth that tempted me. That wasn't what dazzled me. And I swear I will make no claims whatsoever on your property, provided you let me keep what I have.

HARPAGON. I will do no such thing, by God! See how insolent he is! He wants to keep the proceeds of his theft.

VALÈRE. Do you call it a theft?

HARPAGON. Do I call it a theft! A treasure like that!

VALÈRE. A treasure indeed! The most precious you have, without a doubt! But your giving me such a treasure would be no real loss to you. I ask you on bended knee to give me this enchanting treasure. If you want to do right you will grant my request.

HARPAGON. I will do nothing of the kind. What is he saying?

VALÈRE. We have promised to be faithful to one another. We have vowed never to separate.

HARPAGON. Your vow is admirable. Your promise is amusing.

VALÈRE. We are engaged to an eternal union.

HARPAGON. I shall forbid the banns, I assure you.

VALÈRE. Naught but death can part us.

HARPAGON. You are certainly bewitched by my money.

VALÈRE. I have told you, sir, it was not selfish interest that drove me to do what I have done. My heart was not impelled by the motives you suspect. A nobler idea was my inspiration.

HARPAGON. You'll see: it is out of Christian charity he wants to keep my money! But I'll set all to rights. The law, you brazen scoundrel, will make me amends for everything!

VALÈRE. You may proceed as you like in the matter. I am ready to suffer any violence that will please you. But at least believe, I beg, that if any harm is done, I am the only one to accuse. Your daughter is in no way to blame for any of this.

HARPAGON. Certainly I believe that. It would be very strange, indeed, if my daughter had a part in this crime. But I want to get my treasure back. I want you to confess where you have carried it off to!

VALÈRE. I? Your treasure has not been carried off at all, but is here —at home.

HARPAGON [*aside*]. Oh, my dear moneybox! [*to* VALÈRE] My treasure has not left the house?

VALÈRE. No, sir.

HARPAGON. Well. Tell me now, haven't you even . . . tampered a bit?

VALÈRE. I, tamper? Ah! you do us both a great wrong. The love that consumes me is wholly pure and respectful.

HARPAGON [*aside*]. He's consumed with love for my moneybox?

VALÈRE. I would have died rather than reveal to your treasure a single offensive thought. It would have been an insult to so much honor and virtue.

HARPAGON [*aside*]. My moneybox honorable and virtuous?

VALÈRE. I limited my desires to the pleasure of merely seeing. No criminal act has profaned the passion that is inspired by those lovely eyes.

HARPAGON [*aside*]. My moneybox's lovely eyes? He talks like a lover discussing his mistress.

VALÈRE. Dame Claude, sir, knows the truth of this adventure. She can bear witness . . .

HARPAGON. What! my maid is an accomplice in this business?

VALÈRE. Yes, sir, she stood as a witness at our engagement. But it was not until she had learned how honorable were my intentions that she helped me to persuade your daughter to pledge her fidelity to me and accept my pledge in return.

HARPAGON [*aside*]. Ha? Is his fear of the law making his mind wander? [*to* VALÈRE] Why confuse us by bringing my daughter into this?

VALÈRE. I tell you, sir, I had all the trouble in the world to persuade modesty to grant what love desired.

HARPAGON. Whose modesty?

VALÈRE. Your daughter's. And it wasn't until yesterday that she was able to make up her mind and sign a mutual promise of marriage with me.

HARPAGON. My daughter signed a promise of marriage with you?

VALÈRE. Just as I, on my part, signed one with her.

HARPAGON. O Heavens! Another disgrace!

JACQUES [*to the* COMMISSARY]. Write, sir, write.

HARPAGON. Aggravation of misfortune! Excess of despair! Come, sir, do the duty of your office. Draw me up an indictment against him as a thief and an instigator.

VALÈRE. Those are names which do not belong to me. When it is known who I am . . .

[*Enter* ELISE, MARIANNE *and* FROSINE.]

HARPAGON. Ah! profligate daughter! Unworthy of a father like me! This is how you put into practice the lessons I gave you! You let yourself become infatuated with an infamous thief! You promise him your hand without my consent! But you will be undone, both of you. [*to* ELISE] Four good, strong walls will answer for your conduct. [*to* VALÈRE] A good, tall gallows will give me satisfaction for your audacity.

VALÈRE. It is not your passion that will judge the matter. I will at least be heard before I am condemned.

HARPAGON. I was mistaken to say the gallows. You will be broken alive on the wheel.

ELISE. Ah! father, be a little more human in your sentiments, I beseech you. Do not push things to the violent extreme of paternal power. Do not let yourself be carried away by the first impulse of passion. Give yourself time. Consider what you wish to do. Take pains. Look more closely at the person who has roused your wrath. He is not what your eyes have judged him to be. You will find it far less strange that I should have given myself to him when you learn that, were it not for him, you would have lost me long ago, and forever. Yes, father, he is the man who saved me from the great peril, the peril you know I was so close to in the water—the man to whom you owe the life of the same daughter who . . .

HARPAGON. All that is nothing. It would have been better for me had he let you drown and not do what he has done.

ELISE. Father, out of paternal love for me . . .

HARPAGON. No, no! I won't hear another word. The law must do its duty.

JACQUES [*aside*]. You'll pay for the beating you gave me.

FROSINE [*aside*]. This is a queer mix-up.

[*Enter* ANSELM.]

ANSELM. What is it, Signor Harpagon? I see you are very much disturbed.

HARPAGON. Ah! Signor Anselm, you now behold the most unfortunate of men. Here is I don't know how much trouble and disorder to complicate the contract you came to sign! My money has been attacked! My honor has been attacked! And there stands a traitor, a profligate who has violated all that is most sacred to man—who has insinuated himself into my house under the name of servant in order to steal my money and seduce my daughter!

VALÈRE. Who cares about this money that you make so much noise about?

HARPAGON. Yes, they have made each other a promise of marriage. This outrage is your concern, Signor Anselm. You are the man who ought to take action against him. Have him prosecuted by the law! Revenge yourself for his insolence!

ANSELM. I have no intention of forcing myself on anybody or of making any claims to a heart that has already given itself to another. But of course I am ready to fight for your interests. As if the cause were my own.

HARPAGON. This gentleman here is an honest commissary, who assures me that he will neglect no part of his official duty. [*to the* COMMISSARY] Indict him, sir, in due form! And make everything sound very criminal!

VALÈRE. I don't see what sort of crime you can make out of my passion for your daughter or what punishment you think I can be condemned to for our engagement. When it is known who I am . . .

HARPAGON. I don't give a damn for all those tales. Nowadays the world is only too full of thieves of nobility, of impostors who take advantage of their insignificance and impudently bedeck themselves with the first illustrious name they take a fancy to.

VALÈRE. I'll have you know I am too honest to adorn myself with aught that is not mine. All Naples can testify to my birth.

ANSELM. Careful. Watch what you say. You run a greater risk here than you think. You have before you a man to whom all Naples is known and who can easily see through a trumped-up story.

VALÈRE. I am a man with nothing to fear. If you know Naples, you know who Don Thomas d'Alburcy was.

ANSELM. Of course I know who he was. Few people were better acquainted with him than I.

HARPAGON. I don't give a damn for Don Thomas or Don Smith.

ANSELM. Please, let him talk. We will see what he has to say about him.

VALÈRE. I have this to say: it was he who brought me into the world.

ANSELM. He?

VALÈRE. Yes.

ANSELM. Come now. You deceive yourself. Try some other story that might be more successful. Don't expect to save yourself by this imposture.

VALÈRE. Watch what you say. This is no imposture. I advance no claim that I cannot easily justify.

ANSELM. What! You dare to call yourself the son of Thomas d'Alburcy?

VALÈRE. I dare. And I am ready to defend that truth against no matter whom.

ANSELM. Fantastic audacity! Learn to your confusion that it was sixteen years ago, at the very least, that the man you speak of perished at sea with his wife and children while trying to save their lives from the cruel persecutions that accompanied the disorder at Naples and which precipitated the exile of more than one noble family.

VALÈRE. Yes, but learn to your own confusion, that his seven-year-old son, with a single servant, was saved from the shipwreck by a Spanish vessel—and that the son then saved now speaks to you. Learn that the captain of that vessel, touched by my misfortune, took a liking to me and brought me up as his own son—that arms have been my occupation since the time I was able to hold them—that I learned a short time ago that my father is not dead, as I had always thought—that while passing through this city in search of him an adventure planned by Heaven gave me a glimpse of charming Elise—that the sight of her made me a slave to her beauty—and that the violence of my love and her father's severity made me resolve to enter into his house and send another in search of my parents.

ANSELM. What proof do you have beyond your bare word that this is not a fable you have constructed on a foundation of truth?

VALÈRE. The Spanish captain, a ruby signet that belonged to my father, an agate bracelet that my mother placed upon my arm, and old Pedro, the servant who with me was saved from the shipwreck.

MARIANNE. Alas! I myself can answer for what you have said. You are not deceiving us. Your account has made clear to me that you are my brother!

VALÈRE. You, my sister?

MARIANNE. Yes. My heart was moved the moment you opened your mouth. Our mother, whom you will see again, has diverted me a thousand times with the misfortunes of our family. Heaven did not suffer us either to perish in that unhappy shipwreck—but our lives were saved only at the expense of our liberty. They were pirates who took us, my mother and me, off the wreckage of our vessel. After ten years of slavery, we regained our liberty through a happy accident, and returned to Naples. There we found that all our property had been sold and were not able to uncover any news of my father. We sailed for Genoa, where my mother went to gather up the sad remains of our dissipated family fortune. From there, fleeing the barbarous injustice of her kinsmen, she came to these parts, where she has lived scarcely more than a languishing life.

ANSELM. O Heaven—such are the signs of Thy power! How clearly Thou hast shown us that Thou alone canst work miracles! Embrace me, children both! Mingle your joy with that of your father!

VALÈRE. You are our father?

MARIANNE. Is it for you my mother has shed so many tears?

ANSELM. Yes, my daughter, yes, my son, I am Don Thomas d'Alburcy, whom Heaven saved from the waves with all the money he had with him—and who, believing for more than sixteen years you all were dead, was preparing, after long voyages, to seek the consolation of a new family through marriage with a good and gentle young lady. When I saw how much my life would be in danger should I return to Naples, I abandoned the idea forever. Having found a way to sell what I had there, I established my residence here. Under the name of Anselm I sought to leave behind the sorrows of the name which has caused me so many reverses.

HARPAGON. Is that your son?

ANSELM. Yes.

HARPAGON. I hold you responsible for the ten thousand écus he stole from me.

ANSELM. He? He stole from you?

HARPAGON. He himself.

VALÈRE. Who told you?

HARPAGON. Master Jacques.

VALÈRE. It is you that say so?

JACQUES. Look, I'm not saying a thing.

HARPAGON. Yes. This gentleman is the commissary who took down his testimony.

VALÈRE. Can you believe me capable of such a villainous deed?

HARPAGON. Capable or not capable, I want my money back.

[*Enter* CLEANTH *and* LA FLÈCHE.]

CLEANTH. Torment yourself no longer, father. Accuse no one. I have uncovered some information about your affair, and I have come to tell you that, if you will resign yourself to letting me marry Marianne, your money will be returned to you.

HARPAGON. Where is it?

CLEANTH. Don't worry. It's in a place that I will answer for. Everything depends on me. It only remains for you to tell me your decision. You can choose whether to give me Marianne or lose your money-box.

HARPAGON. Nothing has been removed from it?

CLEANTH. Nothing. Let us see if it is your intention to subscribe to this marriage and join your consent to that of her mother—who has given her the liberty to choose between us two.

MARIANNE. But you do not realize that his consent is not enough, or that Heaven, along with my brother, whom you now behold [*Points to* VALÈRE.] has restored my father to me. You must win me from *him*.

ANSELM. Heaven, my children, did not restore me to you in order that I should oppose your desires. Signor Harpagon, you very well know that the choice of a young lady falls to the son and not to the father. Come now, don't make people say what is too obvious to need expression. Give your consent to this double ceremony as I have.

HARPAGON. Before I can make up my mind, I must see my money-box.

CLEANTH. You shall see it safe and sound.

HARPAGON. I have no money to give my children for their marriages.

ANSELM. Oh well, I have some for both of them. Don't let that bother you.

HARPAGON. You will commit yourself to stand the cost of both these marriages?

ANSELM. Yes, I will commit myself. Are you satisfied?

HARPAGON. Yes, provided that you have me a suit made for the wedding.

ANSELM. Agreed. Come, let us indulge the happiness which this joyous day bestows upon us.

COMMISSARY. Hold, gentlemen! Hold on, one moment, if you please! Who is going to pay for all the writing I've done?

HARPAGON. We have no need of your writing.

COMMISSARY. No? But I, on the other hand, can't pretend to have done it for nothing.

HARPAGON [*points to* MASTER JACQUES]. As payment I give you this man. Take him and hang him.

JACQUES. Alas! what is a man supposed to do? They beat me before for telling the truth. Now they want to hang me for lying.

ANSELM. Signor Harpagon, you ought to pardon him his trickery.

HARPAGON. You'll pay the commissary then.

ANSELM. So be it. Let us go at once and share our joy with your mother.

HARPAGON. And I, to see my dear, dear moneybox.

RICHARD BRINSLEY SHERIDAN
1751–1816

THE RIVALS
1775

The author of *The Rivals* was an ebullient young man of twenty-four, and one can argue that the only really apt comment on his play is pure and exuberant laughter. Unless there is laughter, at least, all comment is fruitless. When Mrs. Malaprop, with her customary misapplication of a word, writes, "Female punctuation forbids me to say more," or when Bob Acres' valet, to express admiration for his master's new clothes, says, "There a'nt a dog in the house but would bark," one is first of all amused; if he is not amused, there is no basis for discussing things further. But laughter is not likely to fail *The Rivals* now. It has brought merriment in both theater and study throughout its long history.

Sheridan's humor is of several kinds, and often of several kinds at once. The play can be sheerly witty; some of its quips—those of Captain Absolute's man Fag, for instance—could stand alone in collections of clever sayings. Sometimes it comments on prevailing mores and so moves toward "comedy of manners"; Lydia Languish and Faulkland, though differing from each other, are both parodies of fashionable sentimentality. And sometimes it puts personal eccentricities on display and so moves toward "comedy of humours"—a type which the present text has already exemplified in parts of *Volpone* and *The Miser*. Inasmuch as Mrs. Malaprop has proved the most memorable person in the play, and inasmuch as she and her fellow eccentrics tend to upstage the hero and heroine in theatrical performances, humours comedy is perhaps the most vital of the three strains. But the real genius of the play lies in its simultaneous realization of more than one comic possibility. Sir Lucius O'Trigger, for example, intent on a duel, says to his puzzled adversary, "Pray, Sir, be easy: the quarrel is a very pretty quarrel as it stands—we should only spoil it by trying to explain it." The expression is at once so deft, and the penchant for bloodshed so extreme, that one cannot separate the wit from Sir Lucius's quarrelsome "humour."

Such a classification of things laughed at, however, if allowed to stand alone, would suggest fallaciously that comedy has no other task than to find matter for mirth. Comedy becomes disorderly and raucous unless it also satisfies our minds and consciences that it is laughing at things which deserve ridicule. *The Rivals* is good comedy not only because it is lavish of humor but because its sense of the absurd is both reasonable and moral. It quite frankly evaluates human relationships, especially relationships between men and women, and postulates an ideal relationship based on a combination of good sense and genuine feeling. In their departures from this ideal, Sheridan's characters form that arabesque of follies at which we laugh.

Among the characters who err in their romantic relationships, Lydia Languish is deficient in both sense and feeling; until the last act she is more enamored of her own role as romantic lover than she is in love with Absolute. Faulkland, too, is more concerned with himself than with his affianced. Sir Lucius is fantastically willing to fight for a mistress; Bob Acres, ludicrously unwilling. And Mrs. Malaprop's weakness for Sir Lucius is mere wishful thinking, empty alike of both reason and true passion.

In the midst of this company, Captain Absolute, though falling far short of personal perfection, represents the ideal, the "absolute" man. He is really in love. For the meltingly lovely Lydia he is willing to make extreme sacrifices. Yet he has not sacrificed his good sense to his sentiment. He does not love Lydia's faults. And he knows, as she does not, that, other things being equal, it is better to be young and in love on a substantial income than on a pitifully small one. It is this concept of the passionate yet reasonable man which gives the play its ethical center.

Without such an ethical center, *The Rivals* would fragment into a gallery of fantastics. Without its humor, it might embody the most admirable of lessons, but no audience would remain to admire.

THE RIVALS : *SHERIDAN*

Characters

CAPTAIN ABSOLUTE	
LYDIA LANGUISH	
SIR ANTHONY ABSOLUTE	*father of Captain Absolute*
MRS. MALAPROP	*aunt of Lydia Languish*
FAULKLAND	
JULIA MELVILLE	*cousin of Lydia Languish*
BOB ACRES	
SIR LUCIUS O'TRIGGER	
FAG	*valet of Captain Absolute*
LUCY	*lady's maid of Lydia Languish*
DAVID	*valet of Bob Acres*
COACHMAN	
MAID	
BOY	
SERVANTS	

SCENE. *Bath.*
TIME OF ACTION. *Within one day.*

SCENE **Bath** a fashionable health and pleasure resort in southwest England. Places in Bath which are referred to include the **Pump Room**, where the fashionable assembled to drink the mineral waters; **Gyde's Porch**, an entranceway to some older ballrooms (?); the **North** and **South Parades** or promenades; the **New Room**(s), ballroom(s) opened in 1771; **King's-Mead-Fields** in the outskirts of town; and **Spring Gardens**, a riverside picnic ground.

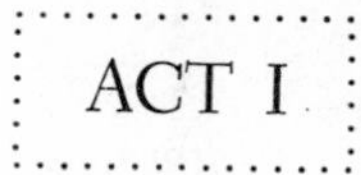

SCENE I

SCENE. *A street in Bath.*

[*Coachman crosses the stage.—Enter* FAG, *looking after him.*]

FAG. What!—Thomas!—Sure, 'tis he?—What!—Thomas!—Thomas!

COACHMAN. Hey!—Odd's life!—Mr. Fag!—give us your hand, my old fellow-servant.

FAG. Excuse my glove, Thomas:—I'm dev'lish glad to see you, my lad: why, my prince of charioteers, you look as hearty!—but who the deuce thought of seeing you in Bath!

COACHMAN. Sure, Master, Madam Julia, Harry, Mrs. Kate, and the postilion be all come!

FAG. Indeed!

COACHMAN. Aye! Master thought another fit of the gout was coming to make him a visit: so he'd a mind to gi't the slip, and whip! we were all off at an hour's warning.

FAG. Aye, aye! hasty in everything, or it would not be Sir Anthony Absolute!

COACHMAN. But tell us, Mr. Fag, how does young master? Odd! Sir Anthony will stare to see the Captain here!

4 **Odd's life** The first of a number of minced oaths. These are profane expressions which have been mispronounced at some time in the past, either euphemistically or in the natural course of repetition, and which, as their origins have been forgotten, have passed into general slang. Modern examples are "Gosh!" "Darn!" "Goldern it!" "Golly Ned!" The less familiar minced oaths in *The Rivals,* together with the words they mince, include **Lud** Lord; **Odd** God; **Odd's life** God's life; **Odd rabbit it** (variant of "Odd rat it") God rot it; **Odd so** God's oath; **Oons** (variant of "Zounds") God's wounds, an oath on the wounds of Christ; **'Sdeath** God's death, an oath on the death of Christ; **Zooks** (variant of "Gadzooks") God's hooks, an oath on the nails of the cross; and **Zounds** God's wounds (see "Oons" above). Bob Acres' "referential oaths" put together the form "Odds" with terms from the context of his thought.

FAG. I do not serve Captain Absolute now.

COACHMAN. Why sure!

FAG. At present I am employed by Ensign Beverley.

COACHMAN. I doubt, Mr. Fag, you ha'n't changed for the better.

FAG. I have not changed, Thomas.

COACHMAN. No! why, didn't you say you had left young master?

FAG. No.——Well, honest Thomas, I must puzzle you no farther: briefly then—Captain Absolute and Ensign Beverley are one and the same person.

COACHMAN. The devil they are!

FAG. So it is indeed, Thomas; and the *Ensign*-half of my master being on guard at present—the *Captain* has nothing to do with me.

COACHMAN. So, so!—What, this is some freak, I warrant!——Do tell us, Mr. Fag, the meaning o't—you know I ha' trusted you.

FAG. You'll be secret, Thomas?

COACHMAN. As a coach-horse.

FAG. Why then the cause of all this is—LOVE—Love, Thomas, who (as you may get read to you) has been a masquerader ever since the days of Jupiter.

COACHMAN. Aye, aye;—I guessed there was a lady in the case: but pray, why does your master pass only for *Ensign*? Now if he had shammed *General*, indeed——

FAG. Ah! Thomas, there lies the mystery o' the matter. Hark'ee, Thomas, my master is in love with a lady of a very singular taste: a lady who likes him better as a *half-pay Ensign* than if she knew he was son and heir to Sir Anthony Absolute, a baronet of three thousand a year!

COACHMAN. That is an odd taste indeed!—but has she got the stuff, Mr. Fag? is she rich, hey?

FAG. Rich!—why, I believe she owns half the stocks—Z——ds! Thomas, she could pay the national debt as easily as I could my washerwoman! She has a lap-dog that eats out of gold—she feeds her parrot with small pearls—and all her thread-papers are made of bank-notes!

COACHMAN. Bravo!—Faith!—Odd! I warrant she has a set of thousands at least. But does she draw kindly with the Captain?

53 **thread-papers** papers on which thread is wound
55–56 **set of thousands** six-horse team worth thousands of pounds

FAG. As fond as pigeons.

COACHMAN. May one hear her name?

FAG. Miss Lydia Languish. But there is an old tough aunt in the way; though, by the bye, she has never seen my master, for he got acquainted with Miss while on a visit in Gloucestershire.

COACHMAN. Well—I wish they were once harnessed together in matrimony.——But pray, Mr. Fag, what kind of a place is this Bath? I ha' heard a deal of it—here's a mort o' merry-making, hey?

FAG. Pretty well, Thomas, pretty well—'tis a good lounge. In the morning we go to the Pump-room (though neither my master nor I drink the waters); after breakfast we saunter on the Parades, or play a game at billiards; at night we dance: but d——n the place, I'm tired of it: their regular hours stupefy me—not a fiddle nor a card after eleven! However, Mr Faulkland's gentleman and I keep it up a little in private parties—I'll introduce you there, Thomas: you'll like him much.

COACHMAN. Sure I know Mr. Du-Peigne—you know his master is to marry Madam Julia.

FAG. I had forgot.——But Thomas, you must polish a little—indeed you must. Here now—this wig! what the devil do you do with a *wig*, Thomas?—none of the London whips of any degree of *ton* wear *wigs* now.

COACHMAN. More's the pity! more's the pity, I say—Odd's life! when I heard how the lawyers and doctors had took to their own hair, I thought how 'twould go next:—Odd rabbit it! when the fashion had got foot on the Bar, I guessed 'twould mount to the Box! But 'tis all out of character, believe me, Mr. Fag: and look'ee, I'll never gi' up mine—the lawyers and doctors may do as they will.

FAG. Well, Thomas, we'll not quarrel about that.

COACHMAN. Why, bless you, the gentlemen of they professions ben't all of a mind—for in our village now, tho'ff *Jack Gauge*, the *exciseman*, has ta'en to his carrots, there's little Dick, the farrier,

65 **lounge** place to spend leisure time

82 **had got foot . . . Box** i.e., had caught on among lawyers, I guessed it would then catch on among coachmen

88–90 **has ta'en . . . heads** has begun to wear his natural red hair, there's little Dick, the farrier, swears he'll never forsake his wig, though all his professional associates should appear wearing their own hair

swears he'll never forsake his *bob,* tho' all the college should appear with their own heads!

FAG. Indeed! well said, Dick! But hold—mark! mark! Thomas.

COACHMAN. Zooks! 'tis the Captain!—Is that the lady with him?

FAG. No! no! that is Madam Lucy—my master's mistress's maid. They lodge at that house—but I must after him to tell him the news.

COACHMAN. Odd! he's giving her money!——Well, Mr. Fag——

FAG. Good-bye, Thomas.—I have an appointment in Gyde's Porch this evening at eight; meet me there, and we'll make a little party.

[*Exeunt severally.*]

SCENE II

SCENE. *A dressing-room in* MRS. MALAPROP'S *lodgings.*

[LYDIA *sitting on a sofa, with a book in her hand.* LUCY, *as just returned from a message.*]

LUCY. Indeed, Ma'am, I traversed half the town in search of it: I don't believe there's a circulating library in Bath I ha'n't been at.

LYDIA. And could not you get *The Reward of Constancy*?

LUCY. No, indeed, Ma'am.

LYDIA. Nor *The Fatal Connection*?

LUCY. No, indeed, Ma'am.

LYDIA. Nor *The Mistakes of the Heart*?

LUCY. Ma'am, as ill-luck would have it, Mr. Bull said Miss Sukey Saunter had just fetched it away.

LYDIA. Heigh-ho! Did you inquire for *The Delicate Distress*?

LUCY. Or *The Memoirs of Lady Woodford*? Yes, indeed, Ma'am. I asked everywhere for it; and I might have brought it from Mr. Frederick's, but Lady Slattern Lounger, who had just sent it home, had so soiled and dog's-eared it, it wa'n't fit for a Christian to read.

LYDIA. Heigh-ho!—Yes, I always know when Lady Slattern has been before me. She has a most observing thumb; and I believe cherishes her nails for the convenience of making marginal notes.——Well, child, what *have* you brought me?

LUCY. Oh! here, Ma'am. [*taking books from under her cloak, and from her pockets*] This is *The Gordian Knot,* and this *Peregrine Pickle.* Here are *The Tears of Sensibility* and *Humphry Clinker.* This is *The Memoirs of a Lady of Quality, written by herself,* and here the second volume of *The Sentimental Journey.*

LYDIA. Heigh-ho!—What are those books by the glass?

LUCY. The great one is only *The Whole Duty of Man*—where I press a few blonds, Ma'am.

LYDIA. Very well—give me the *sal volatile.*

LUCY. Is it in a blue cover, Ma'am?

LYDIA. My smelling bottle, you simpleton!

LUCY. Oh, the drops!—Here, Ma'am.

LYDIA. Hold!—here's some one coming——quick! see who it is. [*Exit* LUCY.]

Surely I heard my cousin Julia's voice!

[*Re-enter* LUCY.]

LUCY. Lud! Ma'am, here is Miss Melville.

LYDIA. Is it possible!——

[*Enter* JULIA.]

My dearest Julia, how delighted am I!—[*Embrace.*] How unexpected was this happiness!

JULIA. True, Lydia—and our pleasure is the greater; but what has been the matter?—you were denied to me at first!

LYDIA. Ah! Julia, I have a thousand things to tell you! But first inform me what has conjured you to Bath? Is Sir Anthony here?

JULIA. He is—we are arrived within this hour, and I suppose he will be here to wait on Mrs. Malaprop as soon as he is dressed.

LYDIA. Then, before we are interrupted, let me impart to you some of my distress! I know your gentle nature will sympathize with me, though your prudence may condemn me! My letters have informed you of my whole connexion with Beverley—but I have lost him, Julia! My aunt has discovered our intercourse by a note she intercepted, and has confined me ever since! Yet, would you believe it? she has fallen absolutely in love with a tall Irish baronet she met one night since we have been here, at Lady Macshuffle's rout.

JULIA. You jest, Lydia!

LYDIA. No, upon my word. She really carries on a kind of cor-

31 **blonds** silk laces
58 **rout** evening party

respondence with him, under a feigned name though, till she chooses to be known to him; but it is a *Delia* or a *Celia,* I assure you.

JULIA. Then surely she is now more indulgent to her niece.

LYDIA. Quite the contrary. Since she has discovered her own frailty she is become more suspicious of mine. Then I must inform you of another plague! That odious Acres is to be in Bath to-day; so that I protest I shall be teased out of all spirits!

JULIA. Come, come, Lydia, hope the best. Sir Anthony shall use his interest with Mrs. Malaprop.

LYDIA. But you have not heard the worst. Unfortunately I had quarreled with my poor Beverley just before my aunt made the discovery, and I have not seen him since to make it up.

JULIA. What was his offence?

LYDIA. Nothing at all! But, I don't know how it was, as often as we had been together we had never had a quarrel! And, somehow, I was afraid he would never give me an opportunity. So last Thursday I wrote a letter to myself to inform myself that Beverley was at that time paying his addresses to another woman. I signed it *your friend unknown,* showed it to Beverley, charged him with his falsehood, put myself in a violent passion, and vowed I'd never see him more.

JULIA. And you let him depart so, and have not seen him since?

LYDIA. 'Twas the next day my aunt found the matter out. I intended only to have teased him three days and a half, and now I've lost him forever!

JULIA. If he is as deserving and sincere as you have represented him to me, he will never give you up so. Yet consider, Lydia, you tell me he is but an ensign, and you have thirty thousand pounds!

LYDIA. But you know I lose most of my fortune if I marry without my aunt's consent, till of age; and that is what I have determined to do ever since I knew the penalty. Nor could I love the man who would wish to wait a day for the alternative.

JULIA. Nay, this is caprice!

LYDIA. What, does Julia tax me with caprice? I thought her lover Faulkland had enured her to it.

JULIA. I do not love even *his* faults.

LYDIA. But a-propos—you have sent to him, I suppose?

JULIA. Not yet, upon my word, nor has he the least idea of my being in Bath. Sir Anthony's resolution was so sudden I could not inform him of it.

LYDIA. Well, Julia, you are your own mistress (though under the protection of Sir Anthony), yet have you for this long year been a slave to the caprice, the whim, the jealousy of this ungrateful Faulkland, who will ever delay assuming the right of a husband, while you suffer him to be equally imperious as a lover.

JULIA. Nay, you are wrong entirely. We were contracted before my father's death. That, and some consequent embarrassments, have delayed what I know to be my Faulkland's most ardent wish. He is too generous to trifle on such a point. And for his character, you wrong him there too. No, Lydia, he is too proud, too noble to be jealous: if he is captious, 'tis without dissembling; if fretful, without rudeness. Unused to the fopperies of love, he is negligent of the little duties expected from a lover—but being unhackneyed in the passion, his affection is ardent and sincere; and as it engrosses his whole soul, he expects every thought and emotion of his mistress to move in unison with his. Yet, though his pride calls for this full return, his humility makes him undervalue those qualities in him which would entitle him to it; and not feeling why he should be loved to the degree he wishes, he still suspects that he is not loved enough. This temper, I must own, has cost me many unhappy hours; but I have learned to think myself his debtor for those imperfections which arise from the ardour of his attachment.

LYDIA. Well, I cannot blame you for defending him. But tell me candidly, Julia, had he never saved your life, do you think you should have been attached to him as you are? Believe me, the rude blast that overset your boat was a prosperous gale of love to him.

JULIA. Gratitude may have strengthened my attachment to Mr. Faulkland, but I loved him before he had preserved me; yet surely that alone were an obligation sufficient——

LYDIA. Obligation! Why, a water-spaniel would have done as much! Well, I should never think of giving my heart to a man because he could swim!

JULIA. Come, Lydia, you are too inconsiderate.

LYDIA. Nay, I do but jest.—— What's here?

[*Enter* LUCY *in a hurry.*]

LUCY. O Ma'am, here is Sir Anthony Absolute just come home with your aunt.

LYDIA. They'll not come here.—— Lucy, do you watch.

[*Exit* LUCY.]

JULIA. Yet I must go. Sir Anthony does not know I am here, and if we meet, he'll detain me, to show me the town. I'll take another opportunity of paying my respects to Mrs. Malaprop, when she shall treat me, as long as she chooses, with her select words so ingeniously *misapplied,* without being *mispronounced.*

[*Re-enter* LUCY.]

LUCY. O lud! Ma'am, they are both coming upstairs.

LYDIA. Well, I'll not detain you, coz. Adieu, my dear Julia. I'm sure you are in haste to send to Faulkland. There—through my room you'll find another stair-case.

JULIA. Adieu.—— [*Embrace.*] [*Exit* JULIA.]

LYDIA. Here, my dear Lucy, hide these books. Quick, quick! Fling *Peregrine Pickle* under the toilet—throw *Roderick Random* into the closet—put *The Innocent Adultery* into *The Whole Duty of Man* —thrust *Lord Aimworth* under the sofa—cram *Ovid* behind the bolster —there—put *The Man of Feeling* into your pocket—so, so,—now lay *Mrs. Chapone* in sight, and leave *Fordyce's Sermons* open on the table.

LUCY. Oh burn it, Ma'am! the hair-dresser has torn away as far as *Proper Pride.*

LYDIA. Never mind—open at *Sobriety.*—Fling me *Lord Chesterfield's Letters.*—Now for 'em.

[*Enter* MRS. MALAPROP, *and* SIR ANTHONY ABSOLUTE.]

MRS. MALAPROP. There, Sir Anthony, there sits the deliberate simpleton who wants to disgrace her family, and lavish herself on a fellow not worth a shilling!

LYDIA. Madam, I thought you once——

MRS. MALAPROP. You thought, Miss! I don't know any business you have to think at all. Thought does not become a young woman. But the point we would request of you is, that you will promise to forget this fellow—to illiterate him, I say, quite from your memory.

LYDIA. Ah! Madam! our memories are independent of our wills. It is not so easy to forget.

MRS. MALAPROP. But I say it is, Miss; there is nothing on earth so easy as to *forget,* if a person chooses to set about it. I'm sure I have as much forgot your poor dear uncle as if he had never existed—and I thought it my duty so to do; and let me tell you, Lydia, these violent memories don't become a young woman.

SIR ANTHONY. Why sure she won't pretend to remember what she's ordered not!—aye, this comes of her reading!

LYDIA. What crime, Madam, have I committed to be treated thus?

MRS. MALAPROP. Now don't attempt to extirpate yourself from the matter; you know I have proof controvertible of it. But tell me, will you promise to do as you're bid? Will you take a husband of your friend's choosing?

LYDIA. Madam, I must tell you plainly, that had I no preference for anyone else, the choice you have made would be my aversion.

MRS. MALAPROP. What business have you, Miss, with *preference* and *aversion*? They don't become a young woman; and you ought to know, that as both always wear off, 'tis safest in matrimony to begin with a little *aversion.* I am sure I hated your poor dear uncle before marriage as if he'd been a blackamoor—and yet, Miss, you are sensible what a wife I made!—and when it pleased heaven to release me from him, 'tis unknown what tears I shed! But suppose we were going to give you another choice, will you promise us to give up this Beverley?

LYDIA. Could I belie my thoughts so far as to give that promise, my actions would certainly as far belie my words.

MRS. MALAPROP. Take yourself to your room. You are fit company for nothing but your own ill-humours.

LYDIA. Willingly, Ma'am—I cannot change for the worse.

[*Exit* LYDIA.]

MRS. MALAPROP. There's a little intricate hussy for you!

SIR ANTHONY. It is not to be wondered at, Ma'am—all this is the natural consequence of teaching girls to read. Had I a thousand daughters, by heaven! I'd as soon have them taught the black art as their alphabet!

MRS. MALAPROP. Nay, nay, Sir Anthony, you are an absolute misanthropy.

SIR ANTHONY. In my way hither, Mrs. Malaprop, I observed your niece's maid coming forth from a circulating library! She had a book in each hand—they were half-bound volumes, with marble covers! From that moment I guessed how full of duty I should see her mistress!

MRS. MALAPROP. Those are vile places, indeed!

SIR ANTHONY. Madam, a circulating library in a town is as an evergreen tree of diabolical knowledge! It blossoms through the year! And depend on it, Mrs. Malaprop, that they who are so fond of handling the leaves, will long for the fruit at last.

MRS. MALAPROP. Fie, fie, Sir Anthony, you surely speak laconically!

SIR ANTHONY. Why, Mrs. Malaprop, in moderation, now, what would you have a woman know?

MRS. MALAPROP. Observe me, Sir Anthony. I would by no means wish a daughter of mine to be a progeny of learning; I don't think so much learning becomes a young woman; for instance—I would never let her meddle with Greek, or Hebrew, or Algebra, or Simony, or Fluxions, or Paradoxes, or such inflammatory branches of learning—neither would it be necessary for her to handle any of your mathematical, astronomical, diabolical instruments;—but, Sir Anthony, I would send her, at nine years old, to a boarding-school, in order to learn a little ingenuity and artifice. Then, Sir, she should have a supercilious knowledge in accounts—and as she grew up, I would have her instructed in geometry, that she might know something of the contagious countries—but above all, Sir Anthony, she should be mistress of orthodoxy, that she might not misspell, and mispronounce words so shamefully as girls usually do; and likewise that she might reprehend the true meaning of what she is saying. This, Sir Anthony, is what I would have a woman know—and I don't think there is a superstitious article in it.

SIR ANTHONY. Well, well, Mrs. Malaprop, I will dispute the point no further with you; though I must confess that you are a truly moderate and polite arguer, for almost every third word you say is on my side of the question. But, Mrs. Malaprop, to the more important point in debate—you say you have no objection to my proposal.

MRS. MALAPROP. None, I assure you. I am under no positive engagement with Mr. Acres, and as Lydia is so obstinate against him, perhaps your son may have better success.

SIR ANTHONY. Well, Madam, I will write for the boy directly.

He knows not a syllable of this yet, though I have for some time had the proposal in my head. He is at present with his regiment.

MRS. MALAPROP. We have never seen your son, Sir Anthony; but I hope no objection on his side.

SIR ANTHONY. Objection!—let him object if he dare! No, no, Mrs. Malaprop, Jack knows that the least demur puts me in a frenzy directly. My process was always very simple—in their young days, 'twas "Jack do this";—if he demurred—I knocked him down—and if he grumbled at that—I always sent him out of the room.

MRS. MALAPROP. Aye, and the properest way, o' my conscience! —nothing is so conciliating to young people as severity. Well, Sir Anthony, I shall give Mr. Acres his discharge, and prepare Lydia to receive your son's invocations; and I hope you will represent *her* to the Captain as an object not altogether illegible.

SIR ANTHONY. Madam, I will handle the subject prudently. Well, I must leave you—and let me beg you, Mrs. Malaprop, to enforce this matter roundly to the girl; take my advice—keep a tight hand; if she rejects this proposal—clap her under lock and key—and if you were just to let the servants forget to bring her dinner for three or four days, you can't conceive how she'd come about!

[*Exit* SIR ANTHONY.]

MRS. MALAPROP. Well, at any rate I shall be glad to get her from under my intuition. She has somehow discovered my partiality for Sir Lucius O'Trigger—sure, Lucy can't have betrayed me! No, the girl is such a simpleton, I should have made her confess it.—— [*calls*] Lucy!—Lucy—Had she been one of your artificial ones, I should never have trusted her.

[*Enter* LUCY.]

LUCY. Did you call, Ma'am?

MRS. MALAPROP. Yes, girl. Did you see Sir Lucius while you was out?

LUCY. No, indeed, Ma'am, not a glimpse of him.

MRS. MALAPROP. You are sure, Lucy, that you never mentioned——

LUCY. O Gemini! I'd sooner cut my tongue out.

MRS. MALAPROP. Well, don't let your simplicity be imposed on.

LUCY. No, Ma'am.

MRS. MALAPROP. So, come to me presently, and I'll give you another letter to Sir Lucius; but mind, Lucy—if ever you betray what you are intrusted with (unless it be other people's secret to me) you forfeit my malevolence forever, and your being a simpleton shall be no excuse for your locality. [*Exit* MRS. MALAPROP.]

LUCY. Ha! ha! ha!—So, my dear *simplicity,* let me give you a little respite—[*altering her manner*]—let girls in my station be as fond as they please of appearing expert, and knowing in their trusts—commend me to a mask of *silliness,* and a pair of sharp eyes for my own interest under it! Let me see to what account have I turned my *simplicity* lately—[*Looks at a paper.*] For *abetting Miss Lydia Languish in a design of running away with an Ensign!—in money—sundry times—twelve pound twelve—gowns, five—hats, ruffles, caps, &c., &c.—numberless! From the said Ensign, within this last month, six guineas and a half.*—About a quarter's pay!—Item, *from Mrs. Malaprop, for betraying the young people to her*—when I found matters were likely to be discovered—*two guineas, and a black paduasoy.*—Item, *from Mr. Acres, for carrying divers letters*—which I never delivered—*two guineas, and a pair of buckles.*—Item, *from Sir Lucius O'Trigger—three crowns—two gold pocket-pieces—and a silver snuff-box!*—Well done, *simplicity!*—Yet I was forced to make my Hibernian believe that he was corresponding, not with the *aunt,* but with the *niece:* for, though not overrich, I found he had too much pride and delicacy to sacrifice the feelings of a gentleman to the necessities of his fortune. [*Exit.*]

ACT II

SCENE I

SCENE. CAPTAIN ABSOLUTE'S *lodgings.*

[CAPTAIN ABSOLUTE *and* FAG.]

FAG. Sir, while I was there Sir Anthony came in: I told him you had sent me to inquire after his health, and to know if he was at leisure to see you.

ABSOLUTE. And what did he say on hearing I was at Bath?

FAG. Sir, in my life I never saw an elderly gentleman more astonished! He started back two or three paces, rapped out a dozen interjectoral oaths, and asked what the devil had brought you here!

ABSOLUTE. Well, Sir, and what did you say?

FAG. Oh, I lied, Sir—I forget the precise lie; but you may depend on't, he got no truth from me. Yet, with submission, for fear of blunders in future, I should be glad to fix what *has* brought us to Bath, in order that we may lie a little consistently. Sir Anthony's servants were curious, Sir, very curious indeed.

ABSOLUTE. You have said nothing to them?

FAG. Oh, not a word, Sir—not a word. Mr. Thomas, indeed, the coachman (whom I take to be the discreetest of whips)——

ABSOLUTE. 'Sdeath!—you rascal! you have not trusted him!

FAG. Oh, *no,* Sir!—no—no—not a syllable, upon my veracity! He was, indeed, a little inquisitive; but I was sly, Sir—devilish sly!—My master (said I), honest Thomas (you know, Sir, one says *honest* to one's inferiors), is come to Bath to *recruit*—yes, Sir—I said, *to recruit*—and whether for men, money, or constitution, you know, Sir, is nothing to him, nor anyone else.

ABSOLUTE. Well—*recruit* will do—let it be so——

FAG. Oh, Sir, recruit will do surprisingly—indeed, to give the thing an air, I told Thomas that your Honour had already enlisted five disbanded chairmen, seven minority waiters, and thirteen billiard markers.

ABSOLUTE. You blockhead, never say more than is necessary.

FAG. I beg pardon, Sir—I beg pardon—— But with submission, a lie is nothing unless one supports it. Sir, whenever I draw on my invention for a good current lie, I always forge indorsements, as well as the bill.

ABSOLUTE. Well, take care you don't hurt your credit by offering too much security. Is Mr. Faulkland returned?

FAG. He is above, Sir, changing his dress.

ABSOLUTE. Can you tell whether he has been informed of Sir Anthony's and Miss Melville's arrival?

FAG. I fancy not, Sir; he has seen no one since he came in but

30–32 **five . . . markers** five sedan chair bearers who have been dismissed, seven unemployed waiters, and thirteen men who chalk up scores in billiard rooms.

his gentleman, who was with him at Bristol.——I think, Sir, I hear Mr. Faulkland coming down——

ABSOLUTE. Go tell him I am here.

FAG. Yes, Sir [*going*]. I beg pardon, Sir, but should Sir Anthony call, you will do me the favour to remember that we are *recruiting,* if you please.

ABSOLUTE. Well, well.

FAG. And in tenderness to my character, if your Honour could bring in the chairmen and waiters, I shall esteem it as an obligation; for though I never scruple a lie to serve my master, yet it hurts one's conscience to be found out. [*Exit.*]

ABSOLUTE. Now for my whimsical friend—if he does not know that his mistress is here, I'll tease him a little before I tell him——

[*Enter* FAULKLAND.]

Faulkland, you're welcome to Bath again; you are punctual in your return.

FAULKLAND. Yes; I had nothing to detain me when I had finished the business I went on. Well, what news since I left you? How stand matters between you and Lydia?

ABSOLUTE. Faith, much as they were; I have not seen her since our quarrel; however, I expect to be recalled every hour.

FAULKLAND. Why don't you persuade her to go off with you at once?

ABSOLUTE. What, and lose two-thirds of her fortune? You forget that, my friend. No, no, I could have brought her to that long ago.

FAULKLAND. Nay then, you trifle too long—if you are sure of *her,* propose to the aunt *in your own character,* and write to Sir Anthony for his consent.

ABSOLUTE. Softly, softly, for though I am convinced my little Lydia would elope with me as Ensign Beverley, yet am I by no means certain that she would take me with the impediment of our friend's consent, a regular humdrum wedding, and the reversion of a good fortune on my side; no, no, I must prepare her gradually for the discovery, and make myself necessary to her, before I risk it.——Well, but Faulkland, you'll dine with us to-day at the hotel?

FAULKLAND. Indeed, I cannot: I am not in spirits to be of such a party.

ABSOLUTE. By heavens! I shall forswear your company. You are

74 **reversion of** prospect of inheriting

the most teasing, captious, incorrigible lover! Do love like a man!

FAULKLAND. I own I am unfit for company.

ABSOLUTE. Am not *I* a lover; aye, and a romantic one too? Yet do I carry everywhere with me such a confounded farrago of doubts, fears, hopes, wishes, and all the flimsy furniture of a country miss's brain!

FAULKLAND. Ah! Jack, your heart and soul are not, like mine, fixed immutably on one only object. You throw for a large stake, but losing—you could stake, and throw again. But I have set my sum of happiness on this cast, and not to succeed were to be stripped of all.

ABSOLUTE. But, for heaven's sake! what grounds for apprehension can your whimsical brain conjure up at present?

FAULKLAND. What grounds for apprehension did you say? Heavens! are there not a thousand! I fear for her spirits—her health —her life. My absence may fret her; her anxiety for my return, her fears for me, may oppress her gentle temper. And for her health— does not every hour bring me cause to be alarmed? If it rains, some shower may even then have chilled her delicate frame! If the wind be keen, some rude blast may have affected her! The heat of noon, the dews of the evening, may endanger the life of her, for whom only I value mine. O! Jack, when delicate and feeling souls are separated, there is not a feature in the sky, not a movement of the elements, not an aspiration of the breeze, but hints some cause for a lover's apprehension!

ABSOLUTE. Aye, but we may choose whether we will take the hint or not. So then, Faulkland, if you were convinced that Julia were well and in spirits, you would be entirely content?

FAULKLAND. I should be happy beyond measure—I am anxious only for that.

ABSOLUTE. Then to cure your anxiety at once—Miss Melville is in perfect health, and is at this moment in Bath!

FAULKLAND. Nay, Jack—don't trifle with me.

ABSOLUTE. She is arrived here with my father within this hour.

FAULKLAND. Can you be serious?

ABSOLUTE. I thought you knew Sir Anthony better than to be surprised at a sudden whim of this kind. Seriously then, it is as I tell you—upon my honour.

FAULKLAND. My dear friend!—Hollo, Du-Peigne! my hat—my dear Jack—now nothing on earth can give me a moment's uneasiness.

[*Enter* FAG.]

FAG. Sir, Mr. Acres just arrived is below.

ABSOLUTE. Stay, Faulkland, this Acres lives within a mile of Sir Anthony, and he shall tell you how your mistress has been ever since you left her.—— Fag, show the gentleman up. [*Exit* FAG.]

FAULKLAND. What, is he much acquainted in the family?

ABSOLUTE. Oh, very intimate. I insist on your not going: besides, his character will divert you.

FAULKLAND. Well, I should like to ask him a few questions.

ABSOLUTE. He is likewise a rival of mine—that is of my *other self's,* for he does not think his friend Captain Absolute ever saw the lady in question; and it is ridiculous enough to hear him complain to me of *one Beverley,* a concealed skulking rival, who——

FAULKLAND. Hush! He's here.

[*Enter* ACRES.]

ACRES. Hah! my dear friend, noble captain, and honest Jack, how dost thou? Just arrived, faith, as you see. Sir, your humble servant. Warm work on the roads, Jack!—Odds whips and wheels! I've travelled like a comet, with a tail of dust all the way as long as the Mall.

ABSOLUTE. Ah! Bob, you are indeed an eccentric planet, but we know your attraction hither. Give me leave to introduce Mr. Faulkland to you; Mr. Faulkland, Mr. Acres.

ACRES. Sir, I am most heartily glad to see you: Sir, I solicit your connexions.——Hey, Jack—what—this is Mr. Faulkland, who——?

ABSOLUTE. Aye, Bob, Miss Melville's Mr. Faulkland.

ACRES. Odd so! she and your father can be but just arrived before me—I suppose you have seen them. Ah! Mr. Faulkland, you are indeed a happy man.

FAULKLAND. I have not seen Miss Melville yet, Sir. I hope she enjoyed full health and spirits in Devonshire?

ACRES. Never knew her better in my life, Sir—never better. Odds blushes and blooms! she has been as healthy as the German Spa.

139 **the Mall** the promenade in St. James's Park in London

152–53 **the German Spa** the original health resort itself. Reference is to a long-established watering place in Belgium.

FAULKLAND. Indeed! I did hear that she had been a little indisposed.

ACRES. False, false, Sir—only said to vex you: quite the reverse, I assure you.

FAULKLAND. There, Jack, you see she has the advantage of me; I had almost fretted myself ill.

ABSOLUTE. Now are you angry with your mistress for not having been sick.

FAULKLAND. No, no, you misunderstand me: yet surely a little trifling indisposition is not an unnatural consequence of absence from those we love. Now confess—isn't there something unkind in this violent, robust, unfeeling health?

ABSOLUTE. Oh, it was very unkind of her to be well in your absence, to be sure!

ACRES. Good apartments, Jack.

FAULKLAND. Well, Sir, but you were saying that Miss Melville has been so *exceedingly* well—what, then she has been merry and gay, I suppose? Always in spirits—hey?

ACRES. Merry! Odds crickets! she has been the belle and spirit of the company wherever she has been—so lively and entertaining! so full of wit and humour!

FAULKLAND. There, Jack, there! Oh, by my soul! there is an innate levity in woman, that nothing can overcome. What! happy, and I away!

ABSOLUTE. Have done—how foolish this is! Just now you were only apprehensive for your mistress's *spirits*.

FAULKLAND. Why, Jack, have I been the joy and spirit of the company?

ABSOLUTE. No, indeed, you have not.

FAULKLAND. Have I been lively and entertaining?

ABSOLUTE. Oh, upon my word, I acquit you.

FAULKLAND. Have I been full of wit and humour?

ABSOLUTE. No, faith; to do you justice, you have been confoundedly stupid indeed.

ACRES. What's the matter with the gentleman?

ABSOLUTE. He is only expressing his great satisfaction at hearing that Julia has been so well and happy—that's all—hey, Faulkland?

FAULKLAND. Oh! I am rejoiced to hear it—yes, yes, she has a *happy* disposition!

ACRES. That she has indeed. Then she is so accomplished—so sweet a voice—so expert at her harpsichord—such a mistress of flat and sharp, squallante, rumblante, and quiverante! There was this time month—Odds minims and crotchets! how she did chirrup at Mrs. Piano's concert!

FAULKLAND. There again, what say you to this? You see she has been all mirth and song—not a thought of me!

ABSOLUTE. Pho! man, is not music the food of love?

FAULKLAND. Well, well, it may be so.—— Pray, Mr.—— what's his d——d name? Do you remember what songs Miss Melville sung?

ACRES. Not I, indeed.

ABSOLUTE. Stay now, they were some pretty, melancholy, purling-stream airs, I warrant; perhaps you may recollect; did she sing *"When absent from my soul's delight"*?

ACRES. No, that wa'n't it.

ABSOLUTE. Or *"Go, gentle gales"*?—*"Go, gentle gales!"* [*Sings.*]

ACRES. Oh no! nothing like it. Odds! now I recollect one of them—*"My heart's my own, my will is free."* [*Sings.*]

FAULKLAND. Fool! fool that I am! to fix all my happiness on such a trifler! 'Sdeath! to make herself the pipe and ballad-monger of a circle! to soothe her light heart with catches and glees! What can you say to this, Sir?

ABSOLUTE. Why, that I should be glad to hear my mistress had been so merry, *Sir*.

FAULKLAND. Nay, nay, nay—I am not sorry that she has been happy—no, no, I am glad of that—I would not have had her sad or sick—yet surely a sympathetic heart would have shown itself even in the choice of a song: she might have been temperately healthy, and, somehow, plaintively gay; but she has been dancing too, I doubt not!

ACRES. What does the gentleman say about dancing?

ABSOLUTE. He says the lady we speak of dances as well as she sings.

ACRES. Aye, truly, does she—there was at our last race-ball——

FAULKLAND. Hell and the devil! There! there!—I told you so! I

195 **squallante . . . quiverante** fictitious musical terms
196 **minims and crotchets** half-notes and quarter-notes
212 **pipe** piper
213 **catches and glees** humorous rounds and other part-songs

told you so! Oh! she thrives in my absence! Dancing! But her whole feelings have been in opposition with mine! I have been anxious, silent, pensive, sedentary—my days have been hours of care, my nights of watchfulness. She has been all Health! Spirit! Laugh! Song! Dance! Oh! d——n'd, d——n'd levity!

ABSOLUTE. For heaven's sake! Faulkland, don't expose yourself so. Suppose she has danced, what then? Does not the ceremony of society often oblige——

FAULKLAND. Well, well, I'll contain myself. Perhaps, as you say, for form sake. What, Mr. Acres, you were praising Miss Melville's manner of dancing a *minuet*—hey?

ACRES. Oh I dare insure her for that—but what I was going to speak of was her *country dancing*. Odds swimmings! she has such an air with her!

FAULKLAND. Now disappointment on her! Defend this, Absolute, why don't you defend this? Country-dances! jigs, and reels! Am I to blame now? A minuet I could have forgiven—I should not have minded that—I say I should not have regarded a minuet—but *country-dances!* Z——ds! had she made one in a cotillion—I believe I could have forgiven even that—but to be monkey-led for a night! to run the gauntlet through a string of amorous palming puppies! to show paces like a managed filly! O Jack, there never can be but *one* man in the world whom a truly modest and delicate woman ought to pair with in a *country-dance;* and even then, the rest of the couples should be her great uncles and aunts!

ABSOLUTE. Aye, to be sure!—grandfathers and grandmothers!

FAULKLAND. If there be but one vicious mind in the Set, 'twill spread like a contagion—the action of their pulse beats to the lascivious movement of the jig—their quivering, warm-breathed sighs impregnate the very air—the atmosphere becomes electrical to love, and each amorous spark darts through every link of the chain! I must leave you—I own I am somewhat flurried—and that confounded looby has perceived it. [*going*]

ABSOLUTE. Nay, but stay, Faulkland, and thank Mr. Acres for his good news.

FAULKLAND. D——n his news! [*Exit* FAULKLAND.]

259 **looby** oaf

ABSOLUTE. Ha! ha! ha! Poor Faulkland! Five minutes since—"nothing on earth could give him a moment's uneasiness!"

ACRES. The gentleman wa'n't angry at my praising his mistress, was he?

ABSOLUTE. A little jealous, I believe, Bob.

ACRES. You don't say so? Ha! ha! jealous of me?—that's a good joke.

ABSOLUTE. There's nothing strange in that, Bob: let me tell you, that sprightly grace and insinuating manner of yours will do some mischief among the girls here.

ACRES. Ah! you joke—ha! ha!—mischief—ha! ha! But you know I am not my own property; my dear Lydia has forestalled me. She could never abide me in the country, because I used to dress so badly—but odds frogs and tambours! I shan't take matters so here—now ancient madam has no voice in it. I'll make my old clothes know who's master. I shall straightway cashier the hunting-frock, and render my leather breeches incapable. My hair has been in training some time.

ABSOLUTE. Indeed!

ACRES. Aye—and tho'ff the side-curls are a little restive, my hind-part takes to it very kindly.

ABSOLUTE. O, you'll polish, I doubt not.

ACRES. Absolutely I propose so. Then if I can find out this Ensign Beverley, odds triggers and flints! I'll make him know the difference o't.

ABSOLUTE. Spoke like a man—but pray, Bob, I observe you have got an odd kind of a new method of swearing——

ACRES. Ha! ha! you've taken notice of it? 'Tis genteel, isn't it? I didn't invent it myself, though; but a commander in our militia—a great scholar, I assure you—says that there is no meaning in the common oaths, and that nothing but their antiquity makes them respectable, because, he says, the ancients would never stick to an oath or two, but would say, by Jove! or by Bacchus! or by Mars! or by Venus! or by Pallas! according to the sentiment; so that to swear with propriety, says my little major, the "oath should be an echo to

277 **frogs and tambours** ornamental loop fastenings and the embroidery on them

the sense"; and this we call the *oath referential,* or *sentimental swearing*—ha! ha! ha! 'tis genteel, isn't it?

ABSOLUTE. Very genteel, and very new, indeed—and I dare say will supplant all other figures of imprecation.

ACRES. Aye, aye, the best terms will grow obsolete. Damns have had their day.

[*Enter* FAG.]

FAG. Sir, there is a gentleman below desires to see you. Shall I show him into the parlour?

ABSOLUTE. Aye—you may.

ACRES. Well, I must be gone——

ABSOLUTE. Stay; who is it, Fag?

FAG. Your father, Sir.

ABSOLUTE. You puppy, why didn't you show him up directly? [*Exit* FAG.]

ACRES. You have business with Sir Anthony. I expect a message from Mrs. Malaprop at my lodgings. I have sent also to my dear friend, Sir Lucius O'Trigger. Adieu, Jack! We must meet at night, when you shall give me a dozen bumpers to little Lydia.

ABSOLUTE. That I will, with all my heart. [*Exit* ACRES.] Now for a parental lecture. I hope he has heard nothing of the business that has brought me here. I wish the gout had held him fast in Devonshire, with all my soul!

[*Enter* SIR ANTHONY.]

Sir, I am delighted to see you here; and looking so well! Your sudden arrival at Bath made me apprehensive for your health.

SIR ANTHONY. Very apprehensive, I dare say, Jack. What, you are recruiting here, hey?

ABSOLUTE. Yes, Sir, I am on duty.

SIR ANTHONY. Well, Jack, I am glad to see you, though I did not expect it, for I was going to write to you on a little matter of business. Jack, I have been considering that I grow old and infirm, and shall probably not trouble you long.

ABSOLUTE. Pardon me, Sir, I never saw you look more strong and hearty; and I pray frequently that you may continue so.

SIR ANTHONY. I hope your prayers may be heard with all my heart. Well then, Jack, I have been considering that I am so strong and hearty, I may continue to plague you a long time. Now, Jack, I am sensible that the income of your commission, and what I have hitherto allowed you, is but a small pittance for a lad of your spirit.

ABSOLUTE. Sir, you are very good.

SIR ANTHONY. And it is my wish, while yet I live, to have my boy make some figure in the world. I have resolved, therefore, to fix you at once in a noble independence.

ABSOLUTE. Sir, your kindness overpowers me—such generosity makes the gratitude of reason more lively than the sensations even of filial affection.

SIR ANTHONY. I am glad you are so sensible of my attention—and you shall be master of a large estate in a few weeks.

ABSOLUTE. Let my future life, Sir, speak my gratitude: I cannot express the sense I have of your munificence. Yet, Sir, I presume you would not wish me to quit the army?

SIR ANTHONY. Oh, that shall be as your wife chooses.

ABSOLUTE. My wife, Sir!

SIR ANTHONY. Aye, aye—settle that between you—settle that between you.

ABSOLUTE. A *wife,* Sir, did you say?

SIR ANTHONY. Aye, a wife—why; did not I mention her before?

ABSOLUTE. Not a word of her, Sir.

SIR ANTHONY. Odd so!—I mus'n't forget *her,* though. Yes, Jack, the independence I was talking of is by a marriage—the fortune is saddled with a wife—but I suppose that makes no difference.

ABSOLUTE. Sir! Sir!—you amaze me!

SIR ANTHONY. Why, what the devil's the matter with the fool? Just now you were all gratitude and duty.

ABSOLUTE. I was, Sir—you talked to me of independence and a fortune, but not a word of a wife.

SIR ANTHONY. Why—what difference does that make? Odd's life, Sir! if you have the estate, you must take it with the live stock on it, as it stands.

ABSOLUTE. If my happiness is to be the price, I must beg leave to decline the purchase. Pray, Sir, who is the lady?

SIR ANTHONY. What's that to you, Sir? Come, give me your promise to love, and to marry her directly.

ABSOLUTE. Sure, Sir, this is not very reasonable, to summon my affections for a lady I know nothing of!

SIR ANTHONY. I am sure, Sir, 'tis more unreasonable in you to *object* to a lady you know nothing of.

ABSOLUTE. Then, Sir, I must tell you plainly that my inclinations are fixed on another—my heart is engaged to an angel.

SIR ANTHONY. Then pray let it send an excuse. It is very sorry—but *business* prevents its waiting on her.

ABSOLUTE. But my vows are pledged to her.

SIR ANTHONY. Let her foreclose, Jack; let her foreclose; they are not worth redeeming: besides, you have the angel's vows in exchange, I suppose; so there can be no loss there.

ABSOLUTE. You must excuse me, Sir, if I tell you, once for all, that in this point I cannot obey you.

SIR ANTHONY. Hark'ee, Jack: I have heard you for some time with patience—I have been cool—quite cool; but take care—you know I am compliance itself when I am not thwarted—no one more easily led when I have my own way; but don't put me in a frenzy.

ABSOLUTE. Sir, I must repeat it—in this I cannot obey you.

SIR ANTHONY. Now, d——n me! if ever I call you *Jack* again while I live!

ABSOLUTE. Nay, Sir, but hear me.

SIR ANTHONY. Sir, I won't hear a word—not a word! not one word! so give me your promise by a nod—and I'll tell you what, Jack—I mean, you dog—if you don't, by——

ABSOLUTE. What, Sir, promise to link myself to some mass of ugliness! to——

SIR ANTHONY. Z——ds! Sirrah! the lady shall be as ugly as I choose: she shall have a hump on each shoulder; she shall be as crooked as the Crescent; her one eye shall roll like the Bull's in Cox's Museum—she shall have a skin like a mummy, and the beard of a Jew—she shall be all this, Sirrah!—yet I'll make you ogle her all day, and sit up all night to write sonnets on her beauty.

ABSOLUTE. This is reason and moderation indeed!

403–04 **the Bull's . . . Museum** a toy bull, a mechanical marvel of the time

SIR ANTHONY. None of your sneering, puppy! no grinning, jackanapes!

ABSOLUTE. Indeed, Sir, I never was in a worse humour for mirth in my life.

SIR ANTHONY. 'Tis false, Sir! I know you are laughing in your sleeve; I know you'll grin when I am gone, Sirrah!

ABSOLUTE. Sir, I hope I know my duty better.

SIR ANTHONY. None of your passion, Sir! none of your violence! if you please. It won't do with me, I promise you.

ABSOLUTE. Indeed, Sir, I never was cooler in my life.

SIR ANTHONY. 'Tis a confounded lie!—I know you are in a passion in your heart; I know you are, you hypocritical young dog! But it won't do.

ABSOLUTE. Nay, Sir, upon my word.

SIR ANTHONY. So you will fly out! Can't you be cool, like me? What the devil good can *passion* do! *Passion* is of no service, you impudent, insolent, overbearing reprobate!—There you sneer again! don't provoke me! But you rely upon the mildness of my temper—you do, you dog! you play upon the meekness of my disposition! Yet take care—the patience of a saint may be overcome at last!—but mark! I give you six hours and a half to consider of this: if you then agree, without any condition, to do everything on earth that I choose, why—confound you! I may in time forgive you. If not, z——ds! don't enter the same hemisphere with me! don't dare to breathe the same air, or use the same light with me; but get an atmosphere and a sun of your own! I'll strip you of your commission; I'll lodge a five-and-threepence in the hands of trustees, and you shall live on the interest. I'll disown you, I'll disinherit you, I'll unget you! and—d——n me, if ever I call you Jack again! [*Exit* SIR ANTHONY.]

[ABSOLUTE *solus.*]

ABSOLUTE. Mild, gentle, considerate Father—I kiss your hands. What a tender method of giving his opinion in these matters Sir Anthony has! I dare not trust him with the truth. I wonder what old wealthy hag it is that he wants to bestow on me! Yet he married himself for love! and was in his youth a bold intriguer, and a gay companion!

433–34 **lodge . . . trustees** deposit five shillings and threepence (a quarter-guinea) in the hands of executors

[*Enter* FAG.]

FAG. Assuredly, Sir, our father is wrath to a degree; he comes downstairs eight or ten steps at a time—muttering, growling, and thumping the bannisters all the way: I, and the cook's dog, stand bowing at the door—rap! he gives me a stroke on the head with his cane; bids me carry that to my master; then kicking the poor turnspit into the area, d——ns us all for a puppy triumvirate! Upon my credit, Sir, were I in your place, and found my father such very bad company, I should certainly drop his acquaintance.

ABSOLUTE. Cease your impertinence, Sir, at present. Did you come in for nothing more? Stand out of the way!

[*Pushes him aside, and exit.*]

[FAG *solus.*]

FAG. Soh! Sir Anthony trims my master. He is afraid to reply to his father—then vents his spleen on poor Fag! When one is vexed by one person, to revenge one's self on another who happens to come in the way is the vilest injustice. Ah! it shows the worst temper—the basest——

[*Enter Errand-Boy.*]

BOY. Mr. Fag! Mr. Fag! your master calls you.

FAG. Well, you little dirty puppy, you need not bawl so!——The meanest disposition! the——

BOY. Quick, quick, Mr. Fag!

FAG. *Quick, quick,* you impudent jackanapes! am I to be commanded by you too? you little, impertinent, insolent, kitchen-bred——

[*Exit, kicking and beating him.*]

SCENE II

SCENE. *The North Parade.*

[*Enter* LUCY.]

LUCY. So—I shall have another rival to add to my mistress's list—Captain Absolute. However, I shall not enter his name till my purse

450 **area** sunken space before the basement door
457 **trims** abuses

has received notice in form. Poor Acres is dismissed! Well, I have done him a last friendly office in letting him know that Beverley was here before him. Sir Lucius is generally more punctual when he expects to hear from his *dear Dalia,* as he calls her: I wonder he's not here! I have a little scruple of conscience from this deceit; though I should not be paid so well, if my hero knew that *Delia* was near fifty, and her own mistress.

[*Enter* SIR LUCIUS O'TRIGGER.]

SIR LUCIUS. Hah! my little embassadress—upon my conscience, I have been looking for you; I have been on the South Parade this half-hour.

LUCY [*speaking simply*]. O Gemini! and I have been waiting for your worship here on the North.

SIR LUCIUS. Faith!—maybe that was the reason we did not meet; and it is very comical, too, how you could go out and I not see you—for I was only taking a nap at the Parade Coffee-house, and I chose the *window* on purpose that I might not miss you.

LUCY. My stars! Now I'd wager a sixpence I went by while you were asleep.

SIR LUCIUS. Sure enough it must have been so—and I never dreamt it was so late, till I waked. Well, but my little girl, have you got nothing for me?

LUCY. Yes, but I have: I've got a letter for you in my pocket.

SIR LUCIUS. Oh faith! I guessed you weren't come empty-handed—well—let me see what the dear creature says.

LUCY. There, Sir Lucius. [*Gives him a letter.*]

SIR LUCIUS [*reads*]. *Sir—there is often a sudden incentive impulse in love, that has a greater induction than years of domestic combination: such was the commotion I felt at the first superfluous view of Sir Lucius O'Trigger.*—Very pretty, upon my word.—*Female punctuation forbids me to say more; yet let me add, that it will give me joy infallible to find Sir Lucius worthy the last criterion of my affections.* DELIA. Upon my conscience! Lucy, your lady is a great mistress of language. Faith, she's quite the queen of the dictionary!—for the devil a word dare refuse coming at her call—though one would think it was quite out of hearing.

LUCY. Aye, Sir, a lady of her experience——

SIR LUCIUS. Experience! what, at seventeen?

LUCY. O true, Sir—but then she reads so—my stars! how she will read off-hand!

SIR LUCIUS. Faith, she must be very deep read to write this way—though she is rather an arbitrary writer too—for here are a great many poor words pressed into the service of this note, that would get their *habeas corpus* from any court in Christendom.

LUCY. Ah! Sir Lucius, if you were to hear how she talks of you!

SIR LUCIUS. Oh tell her I'll make her the best husband in the world, and Lady O'Trigger into the bargain! But we must get the old gentlewoman's consent—and do everything fairly.

LUCY. Nay, Sir Lucius, I thought you wa'n't rich enough to be so nice!

SIR LUCIUS. Upon my word, young woman, you have hit it: I am so poor that I can't afford to do a dirty action. If I did not want money I'd steal your mistress and her fortune with a great deal of pleasure. However, my pretty girl [*Gives her money.*], here's a little something to buy you a ribband; and meet me in the evening, and I'll give you an answer to this. So, hussy, take a kiss beforehand to put you in mind. [*Kisses her.*]

LUCY. O lud! Sir Lucius—I never seed such a gemman! My lady won't like you if you're so impudent.

SIR LUCUIS. Faith she will, Lucy—— That same—pho! what's the name of it?—*Modesty!*—is a quality in a lover more praised by the women than liked; so, if your mistress asks you whether Sir Lucius ever gave you a kiss, tell her *fifty*—my dear.

LUCY. What, would you have me tell her a lie?

SIR LUCIUS. Ah, then, you baggage! I'll make it a truth presently.

LUCY. For shame now; here is someone coming.

SIR LUCIUS. Oh faith, I'll quiet your conscience.

[*Sees* FAG.—*Exit, humming a tune.*]

[*Enter* FAG.]

FAG. So, so, Ma'am. I humbly beg pardon.

LUCY. O lud!—now, Mr. Fag, you flurry one so.

FAG. Come, come, Lucy, here's no one by—so a little less simplicity, with a grain or two more sincerity, if you please. You play false with us, Madam. I saw you give the baronet a letter. My master shall know this, and if he don't call him out—I will.

55 **nice** scrupulous

LUCY. Ha! ha! ha! you gentlemen's gentlemen are so hasty. That letter was from Mrs. Malaprop, simpleton. She is taken with Sir Lucius's address.

FAG. How! what tastes some people have! Why, I suppose I have walked by her window an hundred times. But what says our young lady? Any message to my master?

LUCY. Sad news, Mr. Fag! A worse rival than Acres! Sir Anthony Absolute has proposed his son.

FAG. What, Captain Absolute?

LUCY. Even so. I overheard it all.

FAG. Ha! ha! ha!—very good, faith. Good-bye, Lucy, I must away with this news.

LUCY. Well—you may laugh, but it is true, I assure you. [*going*] But—Mr. Fag—tell your master not to be cast down by this.

FAG. Oh, he'll be so disconsolate!

LUCY. And charge him not to think of quarrelling with young Absolute.

FAG. Never fear!—never fear!

LUCY. Be sure—bid him keep up his spirits.

FAG. We will—we will. [*Exeunt severally.*]

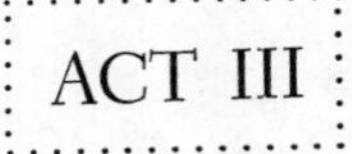

ACT III

SCENE I

SCENE. *The North Parade.*

[*Enter* ABSOLUTE.]

ABSOLUTE. 'Tis just as Fag told me, indeed. Whimsical enough, faith! My father wants to *force* me to marry the very girl I am plotting to run away with! He must not know of my connexion with her yet awhile. He has too summary a method of proceeding in these matters. However, I'll read my recantation instantly. My conversion is something sudden, indeed, but I can assure him it is very *sincere*.

——So, so—here he comes. He looks plaguy gruff. [*Steps aside.*]

[*Enter* SIR ANTHONY.]

SIR ANTHONY. No—I'll die sooner than forgive him. *Die,* did I say? I'll live these fifty years to plague him. At our last meeting, his impudence had almost put me out of temper. An obstinate, passionate, self-willed boy! Who can he take after? This is my return for getting him before all his brothers and sisters!—for putting him, at twelve years old, into a marching regiment, and allowing him fifty pounds a year, beside his pay ever since! But I have done with him; he's anybody's son for me. I never will see him more—never—never—never—never!

ABSOLUTE. Now for a penitential face.

SIR ANTHONY. Fellow, get out of my way.

ABSOLUTE. Sir, you see a penitent before you.

SIR ANTHONY. I see an impudent scoundrel before me.

ABSOLUTE. A sincere penitent. I am come, Sir, to acknowledge my error, and to submit entirely to your will.

SIR ANTHONY. What's that?

ABSOLUTE. I have been revolving, and reflecting, and considering on your past goodness, and kindness, and condescension to me.

SIR ANTHONY. Well, Sir?

ABSOLUTE. I have been likewise weighing and balancing what you were pleased to mention concerning duty, and obedience, and authority.

SIR ANTHONY. Well, puppy?

ABSOLUTE. Why, then, Sir, the result of my reflections is—a resolution to sacrifice every inclination of my own to your satisfaction.

SIR ANTHONY. Why, now you talk sense—absolute sense—I never heard anything more sensible in my life. Confound you, you shall be *Jack* again!

ABSOLUTE. I am happy in the appellation.

SIR ANTHONY. Why then, Jack, my dear Jack, I will now inform you who the lady really is. Nothing but your passion and violence, you silly fellow, prevented my telling you at first. Prepare, Jack, for wonder and rapture! prepare!—— What think you of Miss Lydia Languish?

ABSOLUTE. Languish! What, the Languishes of Worcestershire?

SIR ANTHONY. Worcestershire! No. Did you never meet Mrs.

Malaprop and her niece, Miss Languish, who came into our country just before you were last ordered to your regiment?

ABSOLUTE. Malaprop! Languish! I don't remember ever to have heard the names before. Yet, stay–I think I do recollect something. ––*Languish! Languish!* She squints, don't she? A little, red-haired girl?

SIR ANTHONY. Squints? A red-haired girl! Z––ds, no!

ABSOLUTE. Then I must have forgot; it can't be the same person.

SIR ANTHONY. Jack! Jack! what think you of blooming, love-breathing seventeen?

ABSOLUTE. As to that, Sir, I am quite indifferent. If I can please you in the matter, 'tis all I desire.

SIR ANTHONY. Nay, but Jack, such eyes! such eyes! so innocently wild! so bashfully irresolute! Not a glance but speaks and kindles some thought of love! Then, Jack, her cheeks! her cheeks, Jack! so deeply blushing at the insinuations of her tell-tale eyes! Then, Jack, her lips!–O Jack, lips smiling at their own discretion; and if not smiling, more sweetly pouting, more lovely in sullenness!

ABSOLUTE [*aside*]. That's she, indeed. Well done, old gentleman!

SIR ANTHONY. Then, Jack, her neck!–O Jack! Jack!

ABSOLUTE. And which is to be mine, Sir, the niece or the aunt?

SIR ANTHONY. Why, you unfeeling, insensible puppy, I despise you! When I was of your age, such a description would have made me fly like a rocket! The *aunt*, indeed! Odd's life! when I ran away with your mother, I would not have touched anything old or ugly to gain an empire.

ABSOLUTE. Not to please your father, Sir?

SIR ANTHONY. To please my father! Z––ds! not to please–– Oh, my father!–Odd so!–yes–yes!–if my father, indeed, had desired–that's quite another matter. Though he wa'n't the indulgent father that I am, Jack.

ABSOLUTE. I dare say not, Sir.

SIR ANTHONY. But, Jack, you are not sorry to find your mistress is so beautiful?

ABSOLUTE. Sir, I repeat it; if I please you in this affair, 'tis all I desire. Not that I think a woman the worse for being handsome; but, Sir, if you please to recollect, you before hinted something about a hump or two, one eye, and a few more graces of that kind. Now, without being very nice, I own I should rather choose a wife of mine to have the usual number of limbs, and a limited quantity of back: and though *one* eye may be very agreeable, yet as the prejudice has always run in favour of *two,* I would not wish to affect a singularity in that article.

SIR ANTHONY. What a phlegmatic sot it is! Why, Sirrah, you're an anchorite! a vile, insensible stock. You a soldier! you're a walking block, fit only to dust the company's regimentals on! Odd's life! I've a great mind to marry the girl myself!

ABSOLUTE. I am entirely at your disposal, Sir; if you should think of addressing Miss Languish yourself, I suppose you would have me marry the *aunt;* or if you should change your mind, and take the old lady—'tis the same to me—I'll marry the *niece.*

SIR ANTHONY. Upon my word, Jack, thou'rt either a very great hypocrite, or——But come, I know your indifference on such a subject must be all a lie—I'm sure it must—come, now—damn your demure face!—come, confess, Jack—you have been lying—ha'n't you? you have been playing the hypocrite, hey?—I'll never forgive you if you ha'n't been lying and playing the hypocrite.

ABSOLUTE. I'm sorry, Sir, that the respect and duty which I bear to you should be so mistaken.

SIR ANTHONY. Hang your respect and duty! But come along with me, I'll write a note to Mrs. Malaprop, and you shall visit the lady directly. Her eyes shall be the Promethean torch to you—come along. I'll never forgive you if you don't come back stark mad with rapture and impatience. If you don't, egad, I'll marry the girl myself!

[*Exeunt.*]

SCENE II

SCENE. JULIA's *dressing-room.*

[FAULKLAND *solus.*]

FAULKLAND. They told me Julia would return directly; I wonder she is not yet come! How mean does this captious, unsatisfied temper

111 **be . . . you** kindle a fire in you as Prometheus' torch, lit on Olympus, first kindled fires on earth

of mine appear to my cooler judgment! Yet I know not that I indulge it in any other point: but on this one subject, and to this one subject, whom I think I love beyond my life, I am ever ungenerously fretful, and madly capricious! I am conscious of it—yet I cannot correct myself! What tender, honest joy sparkled in her eyes when we met! How delicate was the warmth of her expressions! I was ashamed to appear less happy, though I had come resolved to wear a face of coolness and upbraiding. Sir Anthony's presence prevented my proposed expostulations, yet I must be satisfied that she has not been so *very* happy in my absence. She is coming! Yes! I know the nimbleness of her tread when she thinks her impatient Faulkland counts the moments of her stay.

[*Enter* JULIA.]

JULIA. I had not hoped to see you again so soon.

FAULKLAND. Could I, Julia, be contented with my first welcome—restrained as we were by the presence of a third person?

JULIA. O Faulkland, when your kindness can make me thus happy, let me not think that I discovered something of coldness in your first salutation.

FAULKLAND. 'Twas but your fancy, Julia. I *was* rejoiced to see you—to see you in such health. Sure I had no cause for coldness?

JULIA. Nay then, I see you have taken something ill. You must not conceal from me what it is.

FAULKLAND. Well then—shall I own to you—that my joy at hearing of your health and arrival here, by your neighbour Acres, was somewhat damped by his dwelling much on the high spirits you had enjoyed in Devonshire—on your mirth, your singing, dancing, and I know not what! For such is my temper, Julia, that I should regard every mirthful moment in your absence as a treason to constancy. The mutual tear that steals down the cheek of parting lovers is a compact that no smile shall live there till they meet again.

JULIA. Must I never cease to tax my Faulkland with this teasing minute caprice? Can the idle reports of a silly boor weigh in your breast against my tried affection?

FAULKLAND. They have no weight with me, Julia: no, no—I am happy if you have been so—yet only say that you did not sing with *mirth*—say that you *thought* of Faulkland in the dance.

JULIA. I never can be happy in your absence. If I wear a countenance of content, it is to show that my mind holds no doubt of my

Faulkland's truth. If I seemed sad, it were to make malice triumph, and say that I had fixed my heart on one who left me to lament his roving, and my own credulity. Believe me, Faulkland, I mean not to upbraid you when I say that I have often dressed sorrow in smiles, lest my friends should guess whose unkindness had caused my tears.

FAULKLAND. You were ever all goodness to me. Oh, I am a brute when I but admit a doubt of your true constancy!

JULIA. If ever, without such cause from you, as I will not suppose possible, you find my affections veering but a point, may I become a proverbial scoff for levity and base ingratitude.

FAULKLAND. Ah! Julia, that last word is grating to me. I would I had no title to your *gratitude!* Search your heart, Julia; perhaps what you have mistaken for love, is but the warm effusion of a too thankful heart!

JULIA. For what quality must I love you?

FAULKLAND. For no quality! To regard me for any quality of mind or understanding were only to *esteem* me. And for person—I have often wished myself deformed, to be convinced that I owed no obligation *there* for any part of your affection.

JULIA. Where Nature has bestowed a show of nice attention in the features of a man, he should laugh at it as misplaced. I have seen men who in *this* vain article perhaps might rank above you; but my heart has never asked my eyes if it were so or not.

FAULKLAND. Now this is not well from *you,* Julia. I despise person in a man. Yet if you loved me as I wish, though I were an Æthiop, you'd think none so fair.

JULIA. I see you are determined to be unkind. The *contract* which my poor father bound us in gives you more than a lover's privilege.

FAULKLAND. Again, Julia, you raise ideas that feed and justify my doubts. I would not have been more free—no—I am proud of my restraint. Yet—yet—perhaps your high respect alone for this solemn compact has fettered your inclinations, which else had made a worthier choice. How shall I be sure, had you remained unbound in thought and promise, that I should still have been the object of your persevering love?

JULIA. Then try me now. Let us be free as strangers as to what is past: *my* heart will not feel more liberty!

FAULKLAND. There now! so hasty, Julia! so anxious to be free! If your love for me were fixed and ardent, you would not loose your hold, even though I wished it!

JULIA. Oh, you torture me to the heart! I cannot bear it.

FAULKLAND. I do not mean to distress you. If I loved you less I should never give you an uneasy moment. But hear me. All my fretful doubts arise from this: women are not used to weigh, and separate the motives of their affections; the cold dictates of prudence, gratitude, or filial duty, may sometimes be mistaken for the pleadings of the heart. I would not boast—yet let me say that I have neither age, person, or character to found dislike on; my fortune such as few ladies could be charged with *indiscretion* in the match. O Julia! when *Love* receives such countenance from *Prudence,* nice minds will be suspicious of its birth.

JULIA. I know not whither your insinuations would tend, but as they seem pressing to insult me, I will spare you the regret of having done so. I have given you no cause for this! [*Exit in tears.*]

FAULKLAND. In tears! Stay, Julia: stay but for a moment.—— The door is fastened! Julia!—my soul—but for one moment. I hear her sobbing! 'Sdeath! what a brute am I to use her thus! Yet stay!—— Aye—she is coming now. How little resolution there is in woman! How a few soft words can turn them!——No, faith!—she is *not* coming either! Why, Julia—my love—say but that you forgive me—come but to tell me that. Now, this is being *too* resentful.——Stay! she *is* coming too—I thought she would—no *steadiness* in anything! her going away must have been a mere trick then. She sha'n't see that I was hurt by it. I'll affect indifference. [*Hums a tune: then listens.*]—— No—Z——ds! she's *not* coming!—nor don't intend it, I suppose. This is not *steadiness,* but *obstinacy!* Yet I deserve it. What, after so long an absence to quarrel with her tenderness!—'twas barbarous and unmanly! I should be ashamed to see her now. I'll wait till her just resentment is abated—and when I distress her so again, may I lose her forever, and be linked instead to some antique virago, whose gnawing passions, and long-hoarded spleen shall make me curse my folly half the day, and all the night! [*Exit.*]

SCENE III

SCENE. MRS. MALAPROP'S *lodgings.*

[MRS. MALAPROP, *with a letter in her hand, and* CAPTAIN ABSOLUTE.]

MRS. MALAPROP. Your being Sir Anthony's son, Captain, would itself be a sufficient accommodation; but from the ingenuity of your appearance, I am convinced you deserve the character here given of you.

ABSOLUTE. Permit me to say, Madam, that as I never yet have had the pleasure of seeing Miss Languish, my principal inducement in this affair at present is the honour of being allied to Mrs. Malaprop; of whose intellectual accomplishments, elegant manners, and unaffected learning, no tongue is silent.

MRS. MALAPROP. Sir, you do me infinite honour! I beg, Captain, you'll be seated. [*Sit.*] Ah! few gentlemen now-a-days know how to value the ineffectual qualities in a woman! few think how a little knowledge becomes a gentlewoman! Men have no sense now but for the worthless flower of beauty!

ABSOLUTE. It is but too true, indeed, Ma'am. Yet I fear our ladies should share the blame—they think our admiration of *beauty* so great, that *knowledge* in *them* would be superfluous. Thus, like garden-trees, they seldom show fruit till time has robbed them of the more specious blossom. Few, like Mrs. Malaprop and the orange-tree, are rich in both at once!

MRS. MALAPROP. Sir—you overpower me with good-breeding. [*aside*] He is the very pineapple of politeness!—— You are not ignorant, Captain, that this giddy girl has somehow contrived to fix her affections on a beggarly, strolling, eaves-dropping Ensign, whom none of us have seen, and nobody knows anything of.

ABSOLUTE. Oh, I have heard the silly affair before. I'm not at all prejudiced against her on *that* account.

MRS. MALAPROP. You are very good, and very considerate, Captain. I am sure I have done everything in my power since I exploded the affair! Long ago I laid my positive conjunctions on her never to think on the fellow again; I have since laid Sir Anthony's preposition before her; but, I'm sorry to say, she seems resolved to decline every particle that I enjoin her.

ABSOLUTE. It must be very distressing, indeed, Ma'am.

MRS. MALAPROP. Oh! it gives me the hydrostatics to such a degree! I thought she had persisted from corresponding with him; but behold this very day I have interceded another letter from the fellow! I believe I have it in my pocket.

ABSOLUTE [*aside*]. Oh the devil! my last note.

MRS. MALAPROP. Aye, here it is.

ABSOLUTE [*aside*]. Aye, my note, indeed! Oh the little traitress Lucy!

MRS. MALAPROP. There, perhaps you may know the writing. [*Gives him the letter.*]

ABSOLUTE. I think I have seen the hand before—yes, I certainly must have seen this hand before——

MRS. MALAPROP. Nay, but read it, Captain.

ABSOLUTE [*reads*]. "*My soul's idol, my adored Lydia!*"——Very tender, indeed!

MRS. MALAPROP. Tender! aye, and profane, too, o' my conscience!

ABSOLUTE. "*I am excessively alarmed at the intelligence you send me, the more so as my new rival*"——

MRS. MALAPROP. That's *you*, Sir.

ABSOLUTE. "*Has universally the character of being an accomplished gentleman, and a man of honour.*"—— Well, that's handsome enough.

MRS. MALAPROP. Oh, the fellow had some design in writing so.

ABSOLUTE. That he had, I'll answer for him, Ma'am.

MRS. MALAPROP. But go on, Sir—you'll see presently.

ABSOLUTE. "*As for the old weather-beaten she-dragon who guards you*"——Who can he mean by that?

MRS. MALAPROP. Me! Sir—*me!*—he means *me!* There—what do you think now? But go on a little further.

ABSOLUTE. Impudent scoundrel!—"*it shall go hard but I will elude her vigilance, as I am told that the same ridiculous vanity which makes her dress up her coarse features, and deck her dull chat with hard words which she don't understand*"——

MRS. MALAPROP. There, Sir! an attack upon my language! What do you think of that?—an aspersion upon my parts of speech! Was ever such a brute! Sure if I reprehend anything in this world, it is the use of my oracular tongue, and a nice derangement of epitaphs!

ABSOLUTE. He deserves to be hanged and quartered! Let me see—"*same ridiculous vanity*"——

MRS. MALAPROP. You need not read it again, Sir.

ABSOLUTE. I beg pardon, Ma'am—"*does also lay her open to the grossest deceptions from flattery and pretended admiration*"—an impudent coxcomb!—"*so that I have a scheme to see you shortly with the old harridan's consent, and even to make her a go-between in our interviews.*"—Was ever such assurance!

MRS. MALAPROP. Did you ever hear anything like it? He'll elude my vigilance, will he? Yes, yes! ha! ha! He's very likely to enter these doors! We'll try who can plot best!

ABSOLUTE. So we will, Ma'am—so we will. Ha! ha! ha! A conceited puppy, ha! ha! ha! Well, but Mrs. Malaprop, as the girl seems so infatuated by this fellow, suppose you were to wink at her corresponding with him for a little time—let her even plot an elopement with him—then do you connive at her escape—while *I*, just in the nick, will have the fellow laid by the heels, and fairly contrive to carry her off in his stead.

MRS. MALAPROP. I am delighted with the scheme; never was anything better perpetrated!

ABSOLUTE. But, pray, could not I see the lady for a few minutes now? I should like to try her temper a little.

MRS. MALAPROP. Why, I don't know—I doubt she is not prepared for a visit of this kind. There is a decorum in these matters.

ABSOLUTE. O Lord! she won't mind *me*—only tell her Beverley——

MRS. MALAPROP. Sir!——

ABSOLUTE [*aside*]. Gently, good tongue.

MRS. MALAPROP. What did you say of Beverley?

ABSOLUTE. Oh, I was going to propose that you should tell her, by way of jest, that it was Beverley who was below—she'd come down fast enough then—ha! ha! ha!

MRS. MALAPROP. 'Twould be a trick she well deserves. Besides, you know the fellow tells her he'll get my consent to see her—ha! ha! Let him if he can, I say again. [*calling*] Lydia, come down here!——He'll make me a *go-between in their interviews!*—ha! ha! ha!

97 **doubt** fear

—Come down, I say, Lydia!—I don't wonder at your laughing, ha! ha! ha!—his impudence is truly ridiculous.

ABSOLUTE. 'Tis very ridiculous, upon my soul, Ma'am, ha! ha! ha!

MRS. MALAPROP. The little hussy won't hear. Well, I'll go and tell her at once who it is. She shall know that Captain Absolute is come to wait on her. And I'll make her behave as becomes a young woman.

ABSOLUTE. As you please, Ma'am.

MRS. MALAPROP. For the present, Captain, your servant. Ah! you've not done laughing yet, I see—*elude my vigilance!*—yes, yes, ha! ha! ha! [*Exit.*]

ABSOLUTE. Ha! ha! ha! one would think now that I might throw off all disguise at once, and seize my prize with security—but such is Lydia's caprice that to undeceive were probably to lose her. I'll see whether she knows me. [*Walks aside, and seems engaged in looking at the pictures.*]

[*Enter* LYDIA.]

LYDIA. What a scene am I now to go through! Surely nothing can be more dreadful than to be obliged to listen to the loathsome addresses of a stranger to one's heart. I have heard of girls persecuted as I am, who have appealed in behalf of their favoured lover to the generosity of his rival: suppose I were to try it. There stands the hated rival—an officer, too!—but oh, how unlike my Beverley! I wonder he don't begin. Truly he seems a very negligent wooer! Quite at his ease, upon my word! I'll speak first. [*aloud*] Mr. Absolute.

ABSOLUTE. Madam. [*Turns around.*]

LYDIA. O heavens! Beverley!

ABSOLUTE. Hush!—hush, my life! Softly! Be not surprised.

LYDIA. I am so astonished! and so terrified! and so overjoyed! For heaven's sake! how came you here?

ABSOLUTE. Briefly—I have deceived your aunt. I was informed that my new rival was to visit here this evening, and contriving to have him kept away, have passed myself on *her* for Captain Absolute.

LYDIA. Oh, charming! And she really takes you for young Absolute?

ABSOLUTE. Oh, she's convinced of it.

LYDIA. Ha! ha! ha! I can't forbear laughing to think how her sagacity is overreached!

ABSOLUTE. But we trifle with our precious moments. Such another opportunity may not occur. Then let me now conjure my kind, my condescending angel, to fix the time when I may rescue her from undeserved persecution, and with a licensed warmth plead for my reward.

LYDIA. Will you then, Beverley, consent to forfeit that portion of my paltry wealth? that burden on the wings of love?

ABSOLUTE. Oh, come to me—rich only thus—in loveliness. Bring no portion to me but thy love—'twill be generous in you, Lydia—for well you know, it is the only dower your poor Beverley can repay.

LYDIA. How persuasive are his words! How charming will poverty be with him!

ABSOLUTE. Ah! my soul, what a life will we then live! Love shall be our idol and support! We will worship him with a monastic strictness; abjuring all worldly toys, to center every thought and action there. Proud of calamity, we will enjoy the wreck of wealth; while the surrounding gloom of adversity shall make the flame of our pure love show doubly bright. By heavens! I would fling all goods of fortune from me with a prodigal hand to enjoy the scene where I might clasp my Lydia to my bosom, and say, the world affords no smile to me—but here. [*embracing her*]——[*aside*] If she holds out now the devil is in it!

LYDIA [*aside*]. Now could I fly with him to the Antipodes! but my persecution is not yet come to a crisis.

[*Enter* MRS. MALAPROP, *listening*.]

MRS. MALAPROP [*aside*]. I am impatient to know how the little hussy deports herself.

ABSOLUTE. So pensive, Lydia!—is then your warmth abated?

MRS. MALAPROP [*aside*]. *Warmth abated!* So! she has been in a passion, I suppose.

LYDIA. No—nor ever can while I have life.

MRS MALAPROP [*aside*]. An ill-tempered little devil! She'll be *in a passion all her life*—will she?

LYDIA. Think not the idle threats of my ridiculous aunt can ever have any weight with me.

MRS. MALAPROP [*aside*]. Very dutiful, upon my word!

LYDIA. Let her choice be Captain Absolute, but Beverley is mine.

MRS. MALAPROP [*aside*]. I am astonished at her assurance!—to his face—this is to his face!

ABSOLUTE. Thus then let me enforce my suit. [*kneeling*]

MRS. MALAPROP [*aside*]. Aye—poor young man! down on his knees entreating for pity! I can contain no longer.—[*aloud*] Why, thou vixen! I have overheard you.

ABSOLUTE [*aside*]. Oh, confound her vigilance!

MRS. MALAPROP. Captain Absolute—I know not how to apologize for her shocking rudeness.

ABSOLUTE [*aside*]. So—all's safe, I find.—[*aloud*] I have hopes, Madam, that time will bring the young lady——

MRS. MALAPROP. Oh, there's nothing to be hoped for from her! She's as headstrong as an allegory on the banks of Nile.

LYDIA. Nay, Madam, what do you charge me with now?

MRS. MALAPROP. Why, thou unblushing rebel—didn't you tell this gentleman to his face that you loved another better?—didn't you say you never would be his?

LYDIA. No, Madam—I did not.

MRS. MALAPROP. Good heavens! what assurance! Lydia, Lydia, you ought to know that lying don't become a young woman! Didn't you boast that Beverley—that stroller Beverley—possessed your heart? Tell me that, I say.

LYDIA. 'Tis true, Ma'am, and none but Beverley——

MRS. MALAPROP. Hold—hold, Assurance! you shall not be so rude.

ABSOLUTE. Nay, pray Mrs. Malaprop, don't stop the young lady's speech: she's very welcome to talk thus—it does not hurt *me* in the least, I assure you.

MRS. MALAPROP. You are *too* good, Captain—*too* amiably patient—but come with me, Miss. Let us see you again soon, Captain. Remember what we have fixed.

ABSOLUTE. I shall, Ma'am.

MRS. MALAPROP. Come, take a graceful leave of the gentleman.

LYDIA. May every blessing wait on my Beverley, my loved Bev——

MRS. MALAPROP. Hussy! I'll choke the word in your throat!—come along—come along.

[*Exeunt severally,* ABSOLUTE *kissing his hand to* LYDIA—MRS. MALAPROP *stopping her from speaking.*]

SCENE IV

SCENE. ACRES's *lodgings.*

[ACRES *and* DAVID, ACRES *as just dressed.*]

ACRES. Indeed, David—do you think I become it so?

DAVID. You are quite another creature, believe me, master, by the Mass! an' we've any luck we shall see the Devon monkeyrony in all the print-shops in Bath!

ACRES. Dress *does* make a difference, David.

DAVID. 'Tis all in all, I think. Difference! why, an' you were to go now to Clod-Hall, I am certain the old lady wouldn't know you: Master Butler wouldn't believe his own eyes, and Mrs. Pickle would cry, "Lard presarve me!"—our dairy-maid would come giggling to the door, and I warrant Dolly Tester, your Honour's favourite, would blush like my waistcoat. Oons! I'll hold a gallon, there a'n't a dog in the house but would bark, and I question whether *Phillis* would wag a hair of her tail!

ACRES. Aye, David, there's nothing like polishing.

DAVID. So I says of your Honour's boots; but the boy never heeds me!

ACRES. But, David, has Mr. De-la-Grace been here? I must rub up my balancing, and chasing, and boring.

DAVID. I'll call again, Sir.

ACRES. Do—and see if there are any letters for me at the post office.

DAVID. I will. By the Mass, I can't help looking at your head! If I hadn't been by at the cooking, I wish I may die if I should have known the dish again myself! [*Exit.*]

[ACRES *comes forward, practising a dancing step.*]

ACRES. Sink, slide—coupee! Confound the first inventors of cotillions! say I—they are as bad as algebra to us country gentlemen. I

4–5 **an' . . . print-shops** if we've any luck, we shall see pictures of you, the Devonshire dandy, in all the print-shops

21 **balancing . . . boring** anglicized French dancing terms. Acres continues to use such terms and to corrupt some of them

can walk a minuet easy enough when I'm forced! and I have been accounted a good stick in a country-dance. Odds jigs and tabours! I never valued your cross-over to couple—figure in—right and left—and I'd foot it with e'er a captain in the county! But these outlandish heathen allemandes and cotillions are quite beyond me! I shall never prosper at 'em, that's sure. Mine are true-born English legs—they don't understand their curst French lingo! their *pas* this, and *pas* that, and *pas* t'other! D——n me! my feet don't like to be called paws! No, 'tis certain I have most anti-Gallican toes!

[*Enter* SERVANT.]

SERVANT. Here is Sir Lucius O'Trigger to wait on you, Sir.

ACRES. Show him in.

[*Enter* SIR LUCIUS.]

SIR LUCIUS. Mr. Acres, I am delighted to embrace you.

ACRES. My dear Sir Lucius, I kiss your hands.

SIR LUCIUS. Pray, my friend, what has brought you so suddenly to Bath?

ACRES. Faith! I have followed Cupid's Jack-a-Lantern, and find myself in a quagmire at last. In short, I have been very ill-used, Sir Lucius. I don't choose to mention names, but look on me as on a very ill-used gentleman.

SIR LUCIUS. Pray, what is the case? I ask no names.

ACRES. Mark me, Sir Lucius, I fall as deep as need be in love with a young lady—her friends take my part—I follow her to Bath—send word of my arrival, and receive answer that the lady is to be otherwise disposed of. This, Sir Lucius, I call being ill-used.

SIR LUCIUS. Very ill, upon my conscience. Pray, can you divine the cause of it?

ACRES. Why, there's the matter: she has another lover, one Beverley, who, I am told, is now in Bath. Odds slanders and lies! he must be at the bottom of it.

SIR LUCIUS. A rival in the case, is there? And you think he has supplanted you unfairly?

ACRES. Unfairly!—to be sure he has. He never could have done it fairly.

SIR LUCIUS. Then sure you know what is to be done!

ACRES. Not I, upon my soul!

SIR LUCIUS. We wear no swords here, but you understand me.

ACRES. What! fight him?

SIR LUCIUS. Aye, to be sure: what can I mean else?

ACRES. But he has given me no provocation.

SIR LUCIUS. Now, I think he has given you the greatest provocation in the world. Can a man commit a more heinous offence against another than to fall in love with the same woman? Oh, by my soul, it is the most unpardonable breach of friendship!

ACRES. Breach of friendship! Aye, aye; but I have no acquaintance with this man. I never saw him in my life.

SIR LUCIUS. That's no argument at all—he has the less right then to take such a liberty.

ACRES. 'Gad, that's true. I grow full of anger, Sir Lucius! I fire apace! Odds hilts and blades! I find a man may have a deal of valour in him and not know it! But couldn't I contrive to have a little right of my side?

SIR LUCIUS. What the devil signifies *right* when your *honour* is concerned? Do you think Achilles, or my little Alexander the Great ever inquired where the right lay? No, by my soul, they drew their broadswords, and left the lazy sons of peace to settle the justice of it.

ACRES. Your words are a grenadier's march to my heart! I believe courage must be catching! I certainly do feel a kind of valour rising, as it were—a kind of courage, as I may say. Odds flints, pans, and triggers! I'll challenge him directly.

SIR LUCIUS. Ah, my little friend! if we had Blunderbuss-Hall here—I could show you a range of ancestry, in the O'Trigger line, that would furnish the New Room, every one of whom had killed his man! For though the mansion-house and dirty acres have slipped through my fingers, I thank heaven our honour, and the family-pictures, are as fresh as ever.

ACRES. O Sir Lucius! I have had ancestors too! every man of 'em colonel or captain in the militia! Odds balls and barrels! say no more—I'm braced for it. The thunder of your words has soured the milk of human kindness in my breast! Z——ds! as the man in the play says, "I could do such deeds!"

SIR LUCIUS. Come, come, there must be no passion at all in the case—these things should always be done civilly.

ACRES. I must be in a passion, Sir Lucius—I must be in a rage.

Dear Sir Lucius, let me be in a rage, if you love me. Come, here's pen and paper. [*Sits down to write.*] I would the ink were red! Indite, I say, indite! How shall I begin? Odds bullets and blades! I'll write a good bold hand, however.

SIR LUCIUS. Pray compose yourself.

ACRES. Come now, shall I begin with an oath? Do, Sir Lucius, let me begin with a damme.

SIR LUCIUS. Pho! pho! do the thing decently and like a Christian. Begin now—"*Sir*"——

ACRES. That's too civil by half.

SIR LUCIUS. "*To prevent the confusion that might arise*"——

ACRES. Well——

SIR LUCIUS. "*From our both addressing the same lady*"——

ACRES. Aye—there's the reason—"*same lady*"—Well——

SIR LUCIUS. "*I shall expect the honour of your company*"——

ACRES. Z——ds! I'm not asking him to dinner.

SIR LUCIUS. Pray be easy.

ACRES. Well then—"*honour of your company*"——

SIR LUCIUS. "*To settle our pretensions*"——

ACRES. Well——

SIR LUCIUS. Let me see—aye, King's-Mead-Fields will do—"*In King's-Mead-Fields.*"

ACRES. So that's done.——Well, I'll fold it up presently; my own crest—a hand and dagger shall be the seal.

SIR LUCIUS. You see now, this little explanation will put a stop at once to all confusion or misunderstanding that might arise between you.

ACRES. Aye, we fight to prevent any misunderstanding.

SIR LUCIUS. Now, I'll leave you to fix your own time. Take my advice, and you'll decide it this evening if you can; then let the worst come of it, 'twill be off your mind to-morrow.

ACRES. Very true.

SIR LUCIUS. So I shall see nothing more of you, unless it be by letter, till the evening. I would do myself the honour to carry your message; but, to tell you a secret, I believe I shall have just such another affair on my own hands. There is a gay captain here who put a jest on me lately at the expense of my country, and I only want to fall in with the gentleman to call him out.

ACRES. By my valour, I should like to see you fight first! Odd's life! I should like to see you kill him, if it was only to get a little lesson.

SIR LUCIUS. I shall be very proud of instructing you. Well for the present—but remember now, when you meet your antagonist, do everything in a mild and agreeable manner. Let your courage be as keen, but at the same time as polished, as your sword.

[*Exeunt severally.*]

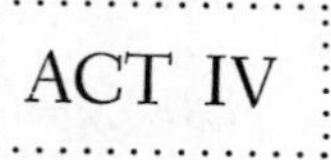

ACT IV

SCENE I

SCENE. ACRES's *lodgings.*

[ACRES *and* DAVID.]

DAVID. Then, by the Mass, Sir! I would do no such thing—ne'er a Sir Lucius O'Trigger in the kingdom should make me fight, when I wa'n't so minded. Oons! what will the old lady say when she hears o't!

ACRES. Ah! David, if you had heard Sir Lucius! Odds sparks and flames! he would have roused your valour.

DAVID. Not he, indeed. I hates such bloodthirsty cormorants. Look'ee, master, if you'd wanted a bout at boxing, quarterstaff, or shortstaff, I should never be the man to bid you cry off: but for your curst sharps and snaps, I never knew any good come of 'em.

ACRES. But my honour, David, my honour! I must be very careful of my honour.

DAVID. Aye, by the Mass! and I would be very careful of it; and I think in return my *honour* couldn't do less than to be very careful of *me.*

ACRES. Odds blades! David, no gentleman will ever risk the loss of his honour!

14 **sharps and snaps** swords and pistols

DAVID. I say then, it would be but civil in *honour* never to risk the loss of a *gentleman*. Look'ee, master, this *honour* seems to me to be a marvellous false friend; aye, truly, a very courtier-like servant. Put the case, I was a gentleman (which, thank God, no one can say of me); well—my honour makes me quarrel with another gentleman of my acquaintance. So—we fight. (Pleasant enough that.) Boh!—I kill him (the more's my luck). Now, pray who gets the profit of it? Why, my *honour*. But put the case that he kills me!—by the Mass! I go to the worms, and my honour whips over to my enemy!

ACRES. No, David—in that case—odds crowns and laurels!—your honour follows you to the grave.

DAVID. Now, that's just the place where I could make a shift to do without it.

ACRES. Z——ds, David, you're a coward! It doesn't become my valour to listen to you. What, shall I disgrace my ancestors? Think of that, David—think what it would be to disgrace my ancestors!

DAVID. Under favour, the surest way of not disgracing them is to keep as long as you can out of their company. Look'ee now, master, to go to them in such haste—with an ounce of lead in your brains—I should think might as well be let alone. Our ancestors are very good kind of folks; but they are the last people I should choose to have a visiting acquaintance with.

ACRES. But David, now, you don't think there is such very, very, *very* great danger, hey? Odd's life! people often fight without any mischief done!

DAVID. By the Mass, I think 'tis ten to one against you! Oons! here to meet some lion-headed fellow, I warrant, with his d——n'd double-barrelled swords, and cut-and-thrust pistols! Lord bless us! it makes me tremble to think o't. Those be such desperate bloody-minded weapons! Well, I never could abide 'em! from a child I never could fancy 'em! I suppose there a'n't so merciless a beast in the world as your loaded pistol!

ACRES. Z——ds! I *won't* be afraid! Odds fire and fury! you sha'n't make me afraid! Here is the challenge, and I have sent for my dear friend Jack Absolute to carry it for me.

DAVID. Aye, i' the name of mischief, let *him* be the messenger. For my part, I wouldn't lend a hand to it for the best horse in your stable. By the Mass! it don't look like another letter! It is, as I may say, a designing and malicious-looking letter! and I warrant smells of gunpowder, like a soldier's pouch! Oons! I wouldn't swear it mayn't go off!

ACRES. Out, you poltroon! You ha'n't the valour of a grasshopper.

DAVID. Well, I say no more—'twill be sad news, to be sure, at Clod-Hall!—but I ha' done. How Phillis will howl when she hears of it! Aye, poor bitch, she little thinks what shooting her master's going after! And I warrant old Crop, who has carried your Honour, field and road, these ten years, will curse the hour he was born. [*whimpering*]

ACRES. It won't do, David—I am determined to fight—so get along, you coward, while I'm in the mind.

[*Enter* SERVANT.]

SERVANT. Captain Absolute, Sir.

ACRES. Oh! show him up. [*Exit* SERVANT.]

DAVID. Well, heaven send we be all alive this time to-morrow.

ACRES. What's that! Don't provoke me, David!

DAVID. Good-bye, master. [*whimpering*]

ACRES. Get along, you cowardly, dastardly, croaking raven.

[*Exit* DAVID.]

[*Enter* ABSOLUTE.]

ABSOLUTE. What's the matter, Bob?

ACRES. A vile, sheep-hearted blockhead! If I hadn't the valour of St. George and the dragon to boot——

ABSOLUTE. But what did you want with me, Bob?

ACRES. Oh! There——[*Gives him the challenge.*]

ABSOLUTE. *"To Ensign Beverley."* [*aside*] So—what's going on now? [*aloud*] Well, what's this?

ACRES. A challenge!

ABSOLUTE. Indeed! Why, you won't fight him, will you, Bob?

ACRES. 'Egad, but I will, Jack. Sir Lucius has wrought me to it. He has left me full of rage, and I'll fight this evening, that so much good passion mayn't be wasted.

ABSOLUTE. But what have I to do with this?

ACRES. Why, as I think you know something of this fellow, I want you to find him out for me, and give him this mortal defiance.

ABSOLUTE. Well, give it to me, and trust me he gets it.

ACRES. Thank you, my dear friend, my dear Jack; but it is giving you a great deal of trouble.

ABSOLUTE. Not in the least—I beg you won't mention it. No trouble in the world, I assure you.

ACRES. You are very kind. What it is to have a friend! You couldn't be my second—could you, Jack?

ABSOLUTE. Why no, Bob—not in *this* affair. It would not be quite so proper.

ACRES. Well then, I must get my friend Sir Lucius. I shall have your good wishes, however, Jack.

ABSOLUTE. Whenever he meets you, believe me.

[*Enter* SERVANT.]

SERVANT. Sir Anthony Absolute is below, inquiring for the Captain.

ABSOLUTE. I'll come instantly. Well, my little hero, success attend you. [*going*]

ACRES. Stay—stay, Jack. If Beverley should ask you what kind of a man your friend Acres is, do tell him I am a devil of a fellow—will you, Jack?

ABSOLUTE. To be sure I shall. I'll say you are a determined dog—hey, Bob?

ACRES. Aye, do, do—and if that frightens him, 'egad, perhaps he mayn't come. So tell him I generally kill a man a week—will you, Jack?

ABSOLUTE. I will, I will; I'll say you are called in the country *"Fighting Bob!"*

ACRES. Right, right—'tis all to prevent mischief; for I don't want to take his life if I clear my honour.

ABSOLUTE. No!—that's very kind of you.

ACRES. Why, you don't wish me to kill him—do you, Jack?

ABSOLUTE. No, upon my soul, I do not. But a devil of a fellow, hey? [*going*]

ACRES. True, true—but stay—stay, Jack. You may add that you never saw me in such a rage before—a most devouring rage!

ABSOLUTE. I will, I will.

ACRES. Remember, Jack—a determined dog!

ABSOLUTE. Aye, aye, *"Fighting Bob!"* [*Exeunt severally.*]

SCENE II

SCENE. MRS. MALAPROP's *lodgings.*

[MRS. MALAPROP *and* LYDIA.]

MRS. MALAPROP. Why, thou perverse one! tell me what you can object to him? Isn't he a handsome man? tell me that. A genteel man? a pretty figure of a man?

LYDIA [*aside*]. She little thinks whom she is praising!—[*aloud*] So is Beverley, Ma'am.

MRS. MALAPROP. No caparisons, Miss, if you please! Caparisons don't become a young woman. No! Captain Absolute is indeed a fine gentleman!

LYDIA [*aside*]. Aye, the Captain Absolute *you* have seen.

MRS. MALAPROP. Then he's *so* well bred; *so* full of alacrity, and adulation! and has *so much* to say for himself—in such good language, too! His physiognomy so grammatical! Then his presence is so noble! I protest, when I saw him, I thought of what Hamlet says in the play: "Hesperian curls!—the front of *Job* himself! An eye, like *March*, to threaten at command—a station, like Harry Mercury, new"—something about kissing on a hill—however, the similitude struck me directly.

LYDIA [*aside*]. How enraged she'll be presently when she discovers her mistake!

[*Enter* SERVANT.]

SERVANT. Sir Anthony and Captain Absolute are below, Ma'am.

MRS. MALAPROP. Show them up here. [*Exit* SERVANT.] Now, Lydia, I insist on your behaving as becomes a young woman. Show your good breeding at least, though you have forgot your duty.

LYDIA. Madam, I have told you my resolution; I shall not only give him no encouragement, but I won't even speak to, or look at him. [*Flings herself into a chair with her face from the door.*]

[*Enter* SIR ANTHONY *and* ABSOLUTE.]

16 **what Hamlet says** *cf.* HAMLET, III, iv, 56–59: "Hyperion's curls, the front of Jove himself,/ An eye like Mars, to threaten and command;/ A station like the herald Mercury/ New-lighted on a heaven-kissing hill."

SIR ANTHONY. Here we are, Mrs. Malaprop, come to mitigate the frowns of unrelenting beauty—and difficulty enough I had to bring this fellow. I don't know what's the matter; but if I hadn't held him by force, he'd have given me the slip.

MRS. MALAPROP. You have infinite trouble, Sir Anthony, in the affair. I am ashamed for the cause!—[*aside to her*] Lydia, Lydia, rise, I beseech you!—pay your respects!

SIR ANTHONY. I hope, Madam, that Miss Languish has reflected on the worth of this gentleman, and the regard due to her aunt's choice, and *my* alliance.—[*aside to him*] Now, Jack, speak to her!

ABSOLUTE [*aside*]. What the devil shall I do!—[*aloud*] You see, Sir, she won't even look at me whilst you are here. I knew she wouldn't! I told you so. Let me entreat you, Sir, to leave us together!

[ABSOLUTE *seems to expostulate with his father.*]

LYDIA [*aside*]. I wonder I ha'n't heard my aunt exclaim yet! Sure she can't have looked at him! Perhaps their regimentals are alike, and she is something blind.

SIR ANTHONY. I say, Sir, I won't stir a foot yet!

MRS. MALAPROP. I am sorry to say, Sir Anthony, that my affluence over my niece is very small.—[*aside to her*] Turn round, Lydia; I blush for you!

SIR ANTHONY. May I not flatter myself that Miss Languish will assign what cause of dislike she can have to my son! Why don't you begin, Jack?—[*aside to him*] Speak, you puppy—speak!

MRS. MALAPROP. It is impossible, Sir Anthony, she can have any. She will not *say* she has.—[*aside to her*] Answer, hussy! why don't you answer?

SIR ANTHONY. Then, Madam, I trust that a childish and hasty predilection will be no bar to Jack's happiness.—[*aside to him*] Z——ds! Sirrah! why don't you speak?

LYDIA [*aside*]. I think my lover seems as little inclined to conversation as myself. How strangely blind my aunt must be!

ABSOLUTE. Hem! hem!—Madam—hem!—[ABSOLUTE *attempts to speak, then returns to* SIR ANTHONY.]—Faith! Sir, I am so confounded! and so—so—confused! I told you I should be so, Sir, I knew it. The —the—tremor of my passion entirely takes away my presence of mind.

SIR ANTHONY. But it don't take away your voice, fool, does it? Go up, and speak to her directly!

[ABSOLUTE *makes signs to* MRS. MALAPROP *to leave them together.*]

MRS. MALAPROP. Sir Anthony, shall we leave them together?—[*aside to her*] Ah! you stubborn little vixen!

SIR ANTHONY. Not yet, Ma'am, not yet!—[*aside to him*] What the devil are you at? Unlock your jaws, Sirrah, or——

[ABSOLUTE *draws near* LYDIA.]

ABSOLUTE [*aside*]. Now heaven send she may be too sullen to look round! I must disguise my voice.—[*Speaks in a low hoarse tone.*] Will not Miss Languish lend an ear to the mild accents of true love? Will not——

SIR ANTHONY. What the devil ails the fellow? Why don't you speak out?—not stand croaking like a frog in a quinsy!

ABSOLUTE. The—the—excess of my awe, and my—my—my modesty quite choke me!

SIR ANTHONY. Ah! your *modesty* again! I'll tell you what, Jack, if you don't speak out directly, and glibly, too, I shall be in such a rage! Mrs. Malaprop, I wish the lady would favour us with something more than a side-front!

[MRS. MALAPROP *seems to chide* LYDIA.]

ABSOLUTE. So! All will out I see! [*Goes up to* LYDIA, *speaks softly.*] Be not surprised, my Lydia; suppress all surprise at present.

LYDIA [*aside*]. Heavens! 'tis Beverley's voice! Sure he can't have imposed on Sir Anthony, too!—[*Looks round by degrees, then starts up*]. Is this possible—my Beverley!—how can this be?—my Beverley?

ABSOLUTE [*aside*]. Ah! 'tis all over.

SIR ANTHONY. Beverley!—the devil!—Beverley! What can the girl mean? This is my son, Jack Absolute!

MRS. MALAPROP. For shame, hussy! for shame! your head runs so on that fellow that you have him always in your eyes! Beg Captain Absolute's pardon directly.

LYDIA. I see no Captain Absolute, but my loved Beverley!

SIR ANTHONY. Z——ds! the girl's mad!—her brain's turned by reading!

MRS. MALAPROP. O' my conscience, I believe so! What do you mean by Beverley, hussy? You saw Captain Absolute before to-day; there he is—your husband that shall be.

LYDIA. With all my soul, Ma'am. When I refuse my Beverley——

SIR ANTHONY. Oh! she's as mad as Bedlam! Or has this fellow been playing us a rogue's trick! Come here, Sirrah!—who the devil are you?

ABSOLUTE. Faith, Sir, I am not quite clear myself, but I'll endeavour to recollect.

SIR ANTHONY. Are you my son, or not? Answer for your mother, you dog, if you won't for me.

MRS. MALAPROP. Aye, Sir, who are you? Oh mercy! I begin to suspect!——

ABSOLUTE [*aside*]. Ye Powers of Impudence befriend me!—[*aloud*] Sir Anthony, most assuredly I am your wife's son; and that I sincerely believe myself to be *yours* also, I hope my duty has always shown.——Mrs. Malaprop, I am your most respectful admirer—and shall be proud to add *affectionate nephew*.——I need not tell my Lydia, that she sees her faithful Beverley, who, knowing the singular generosity of her temper, assumed that name, and a station which has proved a test of the most disinterested love, which he now hopes to enjoy in a more elevated character.

LYDIA [*sullenly*]. So!—there will be no elopement after all!

SIR ANTHONY. Upon my soul, Jack, thou art a very impudent fellow! to do you justice, I think I never saw a piece of more consummate assurance!

ABSOLUTE. Oh you flatter me, Sir—you compliment—'tis my *modesty* you know, Sir—my *modesty* that has stood in my way.

SIR ANTHONY. Well, I am glad you are not the dull, insensible varlet you pretended to be, however! I'm glad you have made a fool of your father, you dog—I am. So this was your *penitence*, your *duty*, and *obedience!* I thought it was d——d sudden! You *never heard their names before*, not you! *What!* The *Languishes of Worcestershire*, hey?—*if you could please me in the affair, 'twas all you desired!*—Ah! you dissembling villain! What!—[*pointing to* LYDIA] *she squints, don't she?—a little red-haired girl!*—hey? Why, you hypocritical young rascal! I wonder you a'n't ashamed to hold up your head!

ABSOLUTE. 'Tis with difficulty, Sir. I *am* confused—very much confused, as you must perceive.

MRS. MALAPROP. O lud! Sir Anthony!—a new light breaks in upon me! Hey! how! what! Captain, did *you* write the letters then? What! —am I to thank *you* for the elegant compilation of *"an old weather-beaten she-dragon"*—hey? O mercy! was it *you* that reflected on my parts of speech?

ABSOLUTE. Dear Sir! my modesty will be overpowered at last, if you don't assist me. I shall certainly not be able to stand it!

SIR ANTHONY. Come, come, Mrs. Malaprop, we must forget and forgive. Odd's life! matters have taken so clever a turn all of a sudden, that I could find in my heart to be so good-humoured! and so gallant!—hey! Mrs. Malaprop!

MRS. MALAPROP. Well, Sir Anthony, since *you* desire it, we will not anticipate the past; so mind, young people: our retrospection will now be all to the future.

SIR ANTHONY. Come, we must leave them together; Mrs. Malaprop, they long to fly into each other's arms. I warrant!—[*aside*] Jack —isn't the cheek as I said, hey?—and the eye, you rogue!—and the lip—hey? Come, Mrs. Malaprop, we'll not disturb their tenderness—theirs is the time of life for happiness!—[*Sings.*] *"Youth's the season made for joy"*—hey! Odd's life! I'm in such spirits, I don't know what I couldn't do! Permit me, Ma'am—[*Gives his hand to* MRS. MALAPROP. *Sings.*] Tol-de-rol!—'gad, I should like a little fooling myself. Tol-de-rol! de-rol! [*Exit singing, and handing* MRS. MALAPROP.]

[LYDIA *sits sullenly in her chair.*]

ABSOLUTE [*aside*]. So much thought bodes me no good.——[*aloud*] So grave, Lydia!

LYDIA. Sir!

ABSOLUTE [*aside*]. So!—egad! I thought as much! That d——d monosyllable has froze me!——[*aloud*] What, Lydia, now that we are as happy in our friends' consent, as in our mutual vows——

LYDIA [*peevishly*]. *Friends' consent,* indeed!

ABSOLUTE. Come, come, we must lay aside some of our romance —a little *wealth* and *comfort* may be endured after all. And for your fortune, the lawyers shall make such settlements as——

LYDIA. *Lawyers!* I *hate* lawyers!

ABSOLUTE. Nay then, we will not wait for their lingering forms but instantly procure the license, and——

LYDIA. The *license*! I *hate* license!

ABSOLUTE. O my love! be not so unkind! Thus let me intreat—— [*kneeling*]

LYDIA. Pshaw! what signifies kneeling when you know I *must* have you?

ABSOLUTE [*rising*]. Nay, Madam, there shall be no constraint upon your inclinations, I promise you. If I have lost your heart, I resign the rest.—[*aside*] 'Gad, I must try what a little *spirit* will do.

LYDIA [*rising*]. Then, Sir, let me tell you, the interest you had there was acquired by a mean, unmanly imposition, and deserves the punishment of fraud. What, you have been treating *me* like a child! —humouring my romance! and laughing, I suppose, at your success!

ABSOLUTE. You wrong me, Lydia, you wrong me. Only hear——

LYDIA. So, while *I* fondly imagined we were deceiving my relations, and flattered myself that I should outwit and incense them all —behold! my hopes are to be crushed at once, by my aunt's consent and approbation!—and *I* am myself the only dupe at last! [*walking about in heat*] But here, Sir, here is the picture—Beverley's picture! [*taking a miniature from her bosom*] which I have worn, night and day, in spite of threats and entreaties! There, Sir [*Flings it to him.*]— and be assured I throw the original from my heart as easily.

ABSOLUTE. Nay, nay, Ma'am, we will not differ as to that. Here [*talking out a picture*], here is Miss Lydia Languish. What a difference! Aye, *there* is the heavenly assenting smile that first gave soul and spirit to my hopes!—those are the lips which sealed a vow, as yet scarce dry in Cupid's calendar!—and *there,* the half resentful blush that *would* have checked the ardour of my thanks. Well, all that's past—all over indeed! There, Madam, in beauty, that copy is not equal to you, but in my mind its merit over the original, in being still the same, is such—that—I cannot find in my heart to part with it. [*Puts it up again.*]

LYDIA [*softening*]. 'Tis *your own* doing, Sir. I—I—I suppose you are perfectly satisfied.

ABSOLUTE. Oh, most certainly. Sure now this is much better than being in love! Ha! ha! ha!—there's some spirit in *this!* What signifies breaking some scores of solemn promises, half an hundred vows, under one's hand, with the marks of a dozen or two angels to witness!—all that's of no consequence, you know. To be sure, people will say that Miss didn't know her own mind—but never mind that: or perhaps they may be ill-natured enough to hint that the gentleman grew tired of the lady and forsook her—but don't let that fret you.

LYDIA. There's no bearing his insolence. [*Bursts into tears.*]

[*Enter* MRS. MALAPROP *and* SIR ANTHONY.]

MRS. MALAPROP [*entering*]. Come, we must interrupt your billing and cooing a while.

LYDIA. This is worse than your treachery and deceit, you base ingrate! [*sobbing*]

SIR ANTHONY. What the devil's the matter now! Z——ds! Mrs. Malaprop, this is the *oddest billing* and *cooing* I ever heard! But what the deuce is the meaning of it? I'm quite astonished!

ABSOLUTE. Ask the lady, Sir.

MRS. MALAPROP. Oh mercy! I'm quite analysed, for my part! Why, Lydia, what is the reason of this?

LYDIA. Ask the *gentleman,* Ma'am.

SIR ANTHONY. Z——ds! I shall be in a frenzy!—— Why, Jack, you are not come out to be anyone else, are you?

MRS. MALAPROP. Aye, Sir, there's no more *trick,* is there? You are not like Cerberus, *three* gentlemen at once, are you?

ABSOLUTE. You'll not let me speak. I say the lady can account for this much better than I can.

LYDIA. Ma'am, you once commanded me never to think of Beverley again. There is the man—I now obey you:—for, from this moment, I renounce him forever. [*Exit* LYDIA.]

MRS. MALAPROP. Oh mercy! and miracles! what a turn here is! Why, sure, Captain, you haven't behaved disrespectfully to my niece?

SIR ANTHONY. Ha! ha! ha!—ha! ha! ha!—now I see it—ha! ha! ha! —now I see it—you have been too lively, Jack.

ABSOLUTE. Nay, Sir, upon my word——

SIR ANTHONY. Come, no lying, Jack—I'm sure *'twas* so.

MRS. MALAPROP. O lud! Sir Anthony! Oh fie, Captain!

ABSOLUTE. Upon my soul, Ma'am——

SIR ANTHONY. Come, no excuses, Jack; why, your father, you rogue, was so before you: the blood of the Absolutes was always impatient. Ha! ha! ha! poor little Lydia!—why, you've frightened her, you dog, you have.

ABSOLUTE. By all that's good, Sir——

SIR ANTHONY. Z——ds! say no more, I tell you. Mrs. Malaprop shall make your peace.—— You must make his peace, Mrs. Malaprop; you must tell her 'tis Jack's way—tell her 'tis all our ways—it runs in the blood of our family! Come, away, Jack—ha! ha! ha! Mrs. Malaprop—a young villain! [*Pushes him out.*]

MRS. MALAPROP. Oh, Sir Anthony! Oh fie, Captain!

[*Exeunt severally.*]

SCENE III

SCENE. *The North Parade.*

[*Enter* SIR LUCIUS O'TRIGGER.]

SIR LUCIUS. I wonder where this Captain Absolute hides himself. Upon my conscience! these officers are always in one's way in love-affairs. I remember I might have married Lady Dorothy Carmine, if it had not been for a little rogue of a major, who ran away with her before she could get a sight of me! And I wonder too what it is the ladies can see in them to be so fond of them—unless it be a touch of the old serpent in 'em, that makes the little creatures be caught, like vipers, with a bit of red cloth.—— Hah!—isn't this the Captain coming?—faith it is! There is a probability of succeeding about that fellow that is mighty provoking! Who the devil is he talking to? [*Steps aside.*]

[*Enter* CAPTAIN ABSOLUTE.]

ABSOLUTE. To what fine purpose I have been plotting! A noble reward for all my schemes, upon my soul! A little gypsy! I did not think her romance could have made her so d——d absurd either. 'Sdeath, I never was in a worse humour in my life! I could cut my own throat, or any other person's, with the greatest pleasure in the world!

SIR LUCIUS. Oh, faith! I'm in the luck of it—I never could have found him in a sweeter temper for my purpose—to be sure I'm just come in the nick! Now to enter into conversation with him, and so quarrel genteelly. [SIR LUCIUS *goes up to* ABSOLUTE.]—With regard to that matter, Captain, I must beg leave to differ in opinion with you.

ABSOLUTE. Upon my word then, you must be a very subtle disputant, because, Sir, I happened just then to be giving no opinion at all.

SIR LUCIUS. That's no reason. For give me leave to tell you, a man may *think* an untruth as well as *speak* one.

ABSOLUTE. Very true, Sir, but if a man never utters his thoughts I should think they might stand a chance of escaping controversy.

SIR LUCIUS. Then, Sir, you differ in opinion with me, which amounts to the same thing.

ABSOLUTE. Hark'ee, Sir Lucius—if I had not before known you to be a gentleman, upon my soul, I should not have discovered it at this interview, for what you can drive at, unless you mean to quarrel with me, I cannot conceive!

SIR LUCIUS. I humbly thank you, Sir, for the quickness of your apprehension. [*bowing*] You have named the very thing I would be at.

ABSOLUTE. Very well, Sir—I shall certainly not balk your inclinations—but I should be glad you would please to explain your motives.

SIR LUCIUS. Pray, Sir, be easy: the quarrel is a very pretty quarrel as it stands—we should only spoil it by trying to explain it. However, your memory is very short or you could not have forgot an affront you passed on me within this week. So no more, but name your time and place.

ABSOLUTE. Well, Sir, since you are so bent on it, the sooner the better; let it be this evening—here, by the Spring-Gardens. We shall scarcely be interrupted.

SIR LUCIUS. Faith! that same interruption in affairs of this nature shows very great ill-breeding. I don't know what's the reason, but in England, if a thing of this kind gets wind, people make such a pother that a gentleman can never fight in peace and quietness. However, if it's the same to you, Captain, I should take it as a particular kindness if you'd let us meet in King's-Mead-Fields, as a little business will call me there about six o'clock, and I may dispatch both matters at once.

ABSOLUTE. 'Tis the same to me exactly. A little after six, then, we will discuss this matter more seriously.

SIR LUCIUS. If you please, Sir, there will be very pretty small-sword light, though it won't do for a long shot. So that matter's settled! and my mind's at ease! [*Exit* SIR LUCIUS.]

[*Enter* FAULKLAND, *meeting* ABSOLUTE.]

ABSOLUTE. Well met. I was going to look for you. O Faulkland! all the dæmons of spite and disappointment have conspired against me! I'm so vexed that if I had not the prospect of a resource in being knocked o' the head by and by, I should scarce have spirits to tell you the cause.

FAULKLAND. What can you mean? Has Lydia changed her mind? I should have thought her duty and inclination would now have pointed to the same object.

ABSOLUTE. Aye, just as the eyes do of a person who squints: when her love-eye was fixed on me—t'other—her eye of duty, was finely obliqued:—but when duty bid her point that the same way—off t'other turned on a swivel, and secured its retreat with a frown!

FAULKLAND. But what's the resource you——

ABSOLUTE. Oh, to wind up the whole, a good-natured Irishman here has [*mimicking* SIR LUCIUS] begged leave to have the pleasure of cutting my throat, and I mean to indulge him—that's all.

FAULKLAND. Prithee, be serious.

ABSOLUTE. 'Tis fact, upon my soul. Sir Lucius O'Trigger—you know him by sight—for some affront, which I am sure I never intended, has obliged me to meet him this evening at six o'clock: 'tis on that account I wished to see you—you must go with me.

FAULKLAND. Nay, there must be some mistake, sure. Sir Lucius shall explain himself—and I dare say matters may be accommodated. But this evening, did you say? I wish it had been any other time.

ABSOLUTE. Why? there will be light enough. There will (as Sir Lucius says) "be very pretty small-sword light, though it won't do for a long shot." Confound his long shots!

FAULKLAND. But I am myself a good deal ruffled by a difference I have had with Julia. My vile tormenting temper has made me treat her so cruelly that I shall not be myself till we are reconciled.

ABSOLUTE. By heavens, Faulkland, you don't deserve her.

[*Enter* SERVANT, *gives* FAULKLAND *a letter*.]

FAULKLAND. O Jack! this is from Julia. I dread to open it. I fear it may be to take a last leave—perhaps to bid me return her letters and restore—— Oh! how I suffer for my folly!

ABSOLUTE. Here—let me see. [*Takes the letter and opens it.*] Aye, a final sentence indeed!—'tis all over with you, faith!

FAULKLAND. Nay, Jack—don't keep me in suspense.

ABSOLUTE. Hear then.—"*As I am convinced that my dear* FAULK-

LAND's *own reflections have already upbraided him for his last unkindness to me, I will not add a word on the subject. I wish to speak with you as soon as possible.—Yours ever and truly,* JULIA."—There's stubbornness and resentment for you! [*Gives him the letter.*] Why, man, you don't seem one whit happier at this.

FAULKLAND. Oh, yes, I am—but—but——

ABSOLUTE. Confound your *buts.* You never hear anything that would make another man bless himself, but you immediately d——n it with a *but.*

FAULKLAND. Now, Jack, as you are my friend, own honestly—don't you think there is something forward, something indelicate, in this haste to forgive? Women should never sue for reconciliation: that should always come from us. They should retain their coldness till *wooed* to kindness—and their *pardon,* like their *love,* should "not unsought be won."

ABSOLUTE. I have not patience to listen to you—thou'rt incorrigible! —so say no more on the subject. I must go to settle a few matters. Let me see you before six—remember—at my lodgings. A poor industrious devil like me, who have toiled, and drudged, and plotted to gain my ends, and am at last disappointed by other people's folly, may in pity be allowed to swear and grumble a little; but a captious sceptic in love, a slave to fretfulness and whim, who has no difficulties but of his own creating, is a subject more fit for ridicule than compassion!

[*Exit* ABSOLUTE.]

FAULKLAND. I feel his reproaches, yet I would not change this too exquisite nicety for the gross content with which *he* tramples on the thorns of love. His engaging me in this duel has started an idea in my head, which I will instantly pursue. I'll use it as the touchstone of Julia's sincerity and disinterestedness. If her love prove pure and sterling ore, my name will rest on it with honour!—and once I've stamped it there, I lay aside my doubts forever—; but if the dross of selfishness, the alloy of pride predominate, 'twill be best to leave her as a toy for some less cautious fool to sigh for. [*Exit* FAULKLAND.]

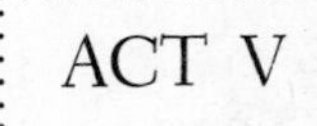

ACT V

SCENE I

SCENE. JULIA'S *dressing-room.*

[JULIA *sola.*]

JULIA. How this message has alarmed me! What dreadful accident can he mean? why such charge to be alone? O Faulkland! how many unhappy moments, how many tears, have you cost me!

[*Enter* FAULKLAND.]

JULIA. What means this?—why this caution, Faulkland?

FAULKLAND. Alas! Julia, I am come to take a long farewell.

JULIA. Heavens! what do you mean?

FAULKLAND. You see before you a wretch whose life is forfeited. Nay, start not! the infirmity of my temper has drawn all this misery on me. I left you fretful and passionate—an untoward accident drew me into a quarrel—the event is that I must fly this kingdom instantly. O Julia, had I been so fortunate as to have called you mine entirely before this mischance had fallen on me, I should not so deeply dread my banishment!

JULIA. My soul is oppressed with sorrow at the nature of your misfortune: had these adverse circumstances arisen from a less fatal cause, I should have felt strong comfort in the thought that I could now chase from your bosom every doubt of the warm sincerity of my love. My heart has long known no other guardian. I now entrust my person to your honour—we will fly together. When safe from pursuit, my father's will may be fulfilled, and I receive a legal claim to be the partner of your sorrows, and tenderest comforter. Then on the bosom of your wedded Julia, you may lull your keen regret to slumbering; while virtuous love, with a cherub's hand, shall smooth the brow of upbraiding thought, and pluck the thorn from compunction.

FAULKLAND. O Julia! I am bankrupt in gratitude! But the time is so pressing, it calls on you for so hasty a resolution—would you not wish some hours to weigh the advantages you forego, and what little compensation poor Faulkland can make you beside his solitary love?

JULIA. I ask not a moment. No, Faulkland, I have loved you for yourself: and if I now, more than ever, prize the solemn engagement which so long has pledged us to each other, it is because it leaves no room for hard aspersions on my fame, and puts the seal of duty to an act of love.—— But let us not linger. Perhaps this delay——

FAULKLAND. 'Twill be better I should not venture out again till dark. Yet am I grieved to think what numberless distresses will press heavy on your gentle disposition!

JULIA. Perhaps your fortune may be forfeited by this unhappy act. I know not whether 'tis so, but sure that alone can never make us unhappy. The little I have will be sufficient to support us; and exile never should be splendid.

FAULKLAND. Aye, but in such an abject state of life, my wounded pride perhaps may increase the natural fretfulness of my temper, till I become a rude, morose companion, beyond your patience to endure. Perhaps the recollection of a deed my conscience cannot justify may haunt me in such gloomy and unsocial fits that I shall hate the tenderness that would relieve me, break from your arms, and quarrel with your fondness!

JULIA. If your thoughts should assume so unhappy a bent, you will the more want some mild and affectionate spirit to watch over and console you, one who, by bearing *your* infirmities with gentleness and resignation, may teach you *so* to bear the evils of your fortune.

FAULKLAND. Julia, I have proved you to the quick! and with this useless device I throw away all my doubts. How shall I plead to be forgiven this last unworthy effect of my restless, unsatisfied disposition?

JULIA. Has no such disaster happened as you related?

FAULKLAND. I am ashamed to own that it was all pretended; yet in pity, Julia, do not kill me with resenting a fault which never can be repeated, but sealing, this once, my pardon, let me to-morrow, in the face of heaven, receive my future guide and monitress, and expiate my past folly by years of tender adoration.

JULIA. Hold, Faulkland! That you are free from a crime which I before feared to name, heaven knows how sincerely I rejoice! These are tears of thankfulness for that! But that your cruel doubts should have urged you to an imposition that has wrung my heart, gives me now a pang more keen than I can express!

FAULKLAND. By heavens! Julia——

JULIA. Yet hear me. My father loved you, Faulkland! and you preserved the life that tender parent gave me; in his presence I pledged my hand—joyfully pledged it—where before I had given my heart. When, soon after, I lost that parent, it seemed to me that Providence had, in Faulkland, shown me whither to transfer without a pause my grateful duty, as well as my affection: hence I have been content to bear from you what pride and delicacy would have forbid me from another. I will not upbraid you by repeating how you have trifled with my sincerity.

FAULKLAND. I confess it all! yet hear——

JULIA. After such a year of trial, I might have flattered myself that I should not have been insulted with a new probation of my sincerity, as cruel as unnecessary! I now see it is not in your nature to be content or confident in love. With this conviction, I never will be yours. While I had hopes that my persevering attention and unreproaching kindness might in time reform your temper, I should have been happy to have gained a dearer influence over you; but I will not furnish you with a licensed power to keep alive an incorrigible fault, at the expense of one who never would contend with you.

FAULKLAND. Nay, but Julia, by my soul and honour, if after this——

JULIA. But one word more. As my faith has once been given to you, I never will barter it with another. I shall pray for your happiness with the truest sincerity; and the dearest blessing I can ask of heaven to send you will be to charm you from that unhappy temper which alone has prevented the performance of our solemn engagement. All I request of *you* is that you will yourself reflect upon this infirmity, and when you number up the many true delights it has deprived you of, let it not be your *least* regret that it lost you the love of one, who would have followed you in beggary through the world!
[*Exit.*]

FAULKLAND. She's gone!—forever! There was an awful resolution in her manner, that riveted me to my place. O fool!—dolt!—barbarian! Curst as I am with more imperfections than my fellow-wretches, kind Fortune sent a heaven-gifted cherub to my aid, and, like a ruffian, I have driven her from my side! I must now haste to my appointment. Well, my mind is tuned for such a scene. I shall wish only to become a principal in it, and reverse the tale my cursed folly put me upon forging here. O love!—tormentor!—fiend! whose influence, like the moon's, acting on men of dull souls, makes idiots of them, but meeting subtler spirits, betrays their course, and urges sensibility to madness! [*Exit.*]

[*Enter* MAID *and* LYDIA.]

MAID. My mistress, Ma'am, I know, was here just now—perhaps she is only in the next room. [*Exit* MAID.]

LYDIA. Heigh-ho! Though he has used me so, this fellow runs strangely in my head. I believe one lecture from my grave cousin will make me recall him.

[*Enter* JULIA.]

LYDIA. O Julia, I am come to you with such an appetite for consolation.—Lud! child, what's the matter with you? You have been crying! I'll be hanged if that Faulkland has not been tormenting you!

JULIA. You mistake the cause of my uneasiness. Something *has* flurried me a little. Nothing that you can guess at.—[*aside*] I would not accuse Faulkland to a sister!

LYDIA. Ah! whatever vexations you may have, I can assure you mine surpass them.—— You know who Beverley proves to be?

JULIA. I will now own to you, Lydia, that Mr. Faulkland had before informed me of the whole affair. Had young Absolute been the person you took him for, I should not have accepted your confidence on the subject without a serious endeavour to counteract your caprice.

LYDIA. So, then, I see I have been deceived by everyone! But I don't care—I'll never have him.

JULIA. Nay, Lydia——

LYDIA. Why, is it not provoking? when I thought we were coming to the prettiest distress imaginable, to find myself made a mere Smithfield bargain of at last! There had I projected one of the most sentimental elopements! so becoming a disguise! so amiable a ladder of ropes! Conscious moon—four horses—Scotch parson—with such sur-

142 **Smithfield bargain** article of trade. Smithfield was a London market

prise to Mrs. Malaprop, and such paragraphs in the newspapers! Oh, I shall die with disappointment!

JULIA. I don't wonder at it!

LYDIA. Now—sad reverse!—what have I to expect, but, after a deal of flimsy preparation, with a bishop's license, and my aunt's blessing, to go simpering up to the altar; or perhaps be cried three times in a country-church, and have an unmannerly fat clerk ask the consent of every butcher in the parish to join John Absolute and Lydia Languish, Spinster! Oh, that I should live to hear myself called Spinster!

JULIA. Melancholy, indeed!

LYDIA. How mortifying to remember the dear delicious shifts I used to be put to, to gain half a minute's conversation with this fellow! How often have I stole forth in the coldest night in January, and found him in the garden, stuck like a dripping statue! There would he kneel to me in the snow, and sneeze and cough so pathetically! he shivering with cold, and I with apprehension! and while the freezing blast numbed our joints, how warmly would he press me to pity his flame, and glow with mutual ardour! Ah, Julia, that was something like being in love!

JULIA. If I were in spirits, Lydia, I should chide you only by laughing heartily at you: but it suits more the situation of my mind, at present, earnestly to entreat you not to let a man, who loves you with sincerity, suffer that unhappiness from your caprice, which I know too well caprice can inflict.

LYDIA. O lud! what has brought my aunt here?

[*Enter* MRS. MALAPROP, FAG, *and* DAVID.]

MRS. MALAPROP. So! so! here's fine work!—here's fine suicide, parricide, and simulation going on in the fields! and Sir Anthony not to be found to prevent the antistrophe!

JULIA. For heaven's sake, Madam, what's the meaning of this?

MRS. MALAPROP. That gentleman can tell you—'twas he enveloped the affair to me.

LYDIA [*to* FAG]. Do, Sir, will you, inform us.

FAG. Ma'am, I should hold myself very deficient in every requisite that forms the man of breeding if I delayed a moment to give all the information in my power to a lady so deeply interested in the affair as you are.

LYDIA. But quick! quick, Sir!

FAG. True, Ma'am, as you say, one should be quick in divulging matters of this nature; for should we be tedious, perhaps while we are flourishing on the subject, two or three lives may be lost!

LYDIA. O patience! Do, Ma'am, for heaven's sake! tell us what is the matter!

MRS. MALAPROP. Why, murder's the matter! slaughter's the matter! killing's the matter! But he can tell you the perpendiculars.

LYDIA. Then, prithee, Sir, be brief.

FAG. Why then, Ma'am—as to murder, I cannot take upon me to say—and as to slaughter, or manslaughter, that will be as the jury finds it.

LYDIA. But who, Sir—who are engaged in this?

FAG. Faith, Ma'am, one is a young gentleman whom I should be very sorry anything was to happen to—a very pretty behaved gentleman! We have lived much together, and always on terms.

LYDIA. But who is this? who! who! who!

FAG. My master, Ma'am, my master—I speak of my master.

LYDIA. Heavens! What, Captain Absolute!

MRS. MALAPROP. Oh, to be sure, you are frightened now!

JULIA. But who are with him, Sir?

FAG. As to the rest, Ma'am, this gentleman can inform you better than I.

JULIA [*to* DAVID]. Do speak, friend.

DAVID. Look'ee, my lady—by the Mass! there's mischief going on. Folks don't use to meet for amusement with fire-arms, fire-locks, fire-engines, fire-screens, fire-office, and the devil knows what other crackers beside! This, my lady, I say, has an angry favour.

JULIA. But who is there beside Captain Absolute, friend?

DAVID. My poor master—under favour, for mentioning him first. You know me, my lady—I am David, and my master, of course, is, or *was,* Squire Acres. Then comes Squire Faulkland.

JULIA. Do, Ma'am, let us instantly endeavour to prevent mischief.

MRS. MALAPROP. Oh fie—it would be very inelegant in us: we should only participate things.

209 **fire-office** office of a fire-insurance company
210 **crackers** explosives

DAVID. Ah! do, Mrs. Aunt, save a few lives. They are desperately given, believe me. Above all, there is that bloodthirsty Philistine, Sir Lucius O'Trigger.

MRS. MALAPROP. Sir Lucius O'Trigger! O mercy! have they drawn poor little dear Sir Lucius into the scrape? Why, how you stand, girl! you have no more feeling than one of the Derbyshire putrefactions!

LYDIA. What are we to do, Madam?

MRS. MALAPROP. Why, fly with the utmost felicity, to be sure, to prevent mischief. Here, friend—you can show us the place?

FAG. If you please, Ma'am, I will conduct you.—— David, do you look for Sir Anthony. [*Exit* DAVID.]

MRS. MALAPROP. Come, girls!—this gentleman will exhort us.—— Come, Sir, you're our envoy—lead the way, and we'll precede.

FAG. Not a step before the ladies for the world!

MRS. MALAPROP. You're sure you know the spot?

FAG. I think I can find it, Ma'am; and one good thing is we shall hear the report of the pistols as we draw near, so we can't well miss them; never fear, Ma'am, never fear. [*Exeunt, he talking.*]

SCENE II

SCENE. *South Parade.*

[*Enter* ABSOLUTE, *putting his sword under his greatcoat.*]

ABSOLUTE. A sword seen in the streets of Bath would raise as great an alarm as a mad dog. How provoking this is in Faulkland! never punctual! I shall be obliged to go without him at last. Oh, the devil! here's Sir Anthony! How shall I escape him? [*Muffles up his face, and takes a circle to go off.*]

[*Enter* SIR ANTHONY.]

SIR ANTHONY. How one may be deceived at a little distance! Only that I see he don't know me, I could have sworn that was Jack!—— Hey! 'Gad's life! it is. Why, Jack!—what are you afraid of, hey!—

223 **putrefactions** petrifactions, the rock formations for which Derbyshire is well known

Sure I'm right.—Why, Jack!—Jack Absolute! [*Goes up to him.*]

ABSOLUTE. Really, Sir, you have the advantage of me: I don't remember ever to have had the honour. My name is Saunderson, at your service.

SIR ANTHONY. Sir, I beg your pardon—I took you—hey!—why, z——ds! it is—stay—[*Looks up to his face.*] So, so—your humble servant, Mr. Saunderson! Why, you scoundrel, what tricks are you after now?

ABSOLUTE. Oh! a joke, Sir, a joke! I came here on purpose to look for you, Sir.

SIR ANTHONY. You did! Well, I am glad you were so lucky. But what are you muffled up so for? What's this for?—hey?

ABSOLUTE. 'Tis cool, Sir; isn't it?—rather chilly, somehow. But I shall be late—I have a particular engagement.

SIR ANTHONY. Stay. Why, I thought you were looking for me? Pray, Jack, where is't you are going?

ABSOLUTE. Going, Sir!

SIR ANTHONY. Aye—where are you going?

ABSOLUTE. Where am I going?

SIR ANTHONY. You unmannerly puppy!

ABSOLUTE. I was going, Sir, to—to—to—to Lydia—Sir, to Lydia, to make matters up if I could; and I was looking for you, Sir, to—to——

SIR ANTHONY. To go with you, I suppose. Well, come along.

ABSOLUTE. Oh! z——ds! no, Sir, not for the world! I wished to meet with you, Sir—to—to—to—— You find it cool, I'm sure, Sir—you'd better not stay out.

SIR ANTHONY. Cool!—not at all. Well, Jack—and what will you say to Lydia?

ABSOLUTE. O, Sir, beg her pardon, humour her, promise and vow. But I detain you, Sir—consider the cold air on your gout.

SIR ANTHONY. Oh, not at all!—not at all! I'm in no hurry. Ah! Jack, you youngsters, when once you are wounded here—[*putting his hand to* ABSOLUTE's *breast*] Hey! what the deuce have you got here?

ABSOLUTE. Nothing, Sir—nothing.

SIR ANTHONY. What's this? here's something d——d hard!

ABSOLUTE. Oh, trinkets, Sir! trinkets—a bauble for Lydia!

SIR ANTHONY. Nay, let me see your taste. [*Pulls his coat open, the sword falls.*] Trinkets!—a bauble for Lydia! Z——ds! Sirrah, you are not going to cut her throat, are you?

ABSOLUTE. Ha! ha! ha! I thought it would divert you, Sir; though I didn't mean to tell you till afterwards.

SIR ANTHONY. You didn't? Yes, this is a very diverting trinket, truly!

ABSOLUTE. Sir, I'll explain to you. You know, Sir, Lydia is romantic, dev'lish romantic, and very absurd of course. Now, Sir, I intend, if she refuses to forgive me, to unsheathe this sword and swear I'll fall upon its point, and expire at her feet!

SIR ANTHONY. Fall upon a fiddle-stick's end! Why, I suppose it is the very thing that would please her. Get along, you fool.

ABSOLUTE. Well, Sir, you shall hear of my success—you shall hear. "O Lydia!—forgive me, or this pointed steel"—says I.

SIR ANTHONY. "O, booby! stab away and welcome"—says she. Get along!—and d——n your trinkets! [*Exit* ABSOLUTE.]

[*Enter* DAVID, *running.*]

DAVID. Stop him! Stop him! Murder! Thief! Fire! Stop fire! Stop fire! O! Sir Anthony—call! call! bid 'em stop! Murder! Fire!

SIR ANTHONY. Fire! Murder! Where?

DAVID. Oons! he's out of sight! and I'm out of breath, for my part! O, Sir Anthony, why didn't you stop him? why didn't you stop him?

SIR ANTHONY. Z——ds! the fellow's mad! Stop whom? Stop Jack?

DAVID. Aye, the Captain, Sir! there's murder and slaughter——

SIR ANTHONY. Murder!

DAVID. Aye, please you, Sir Anthony, there's all kinds of murder, all sorts of slaughter to be seen in the fields: there's fighting going on, Sir—bloody sword-and-gun fighting!

SIR ANTHONY. Who are going to fight, dunce?

DAVID. Everybody that I know of, Sir Anthony—everybody is going to fight; my poor master, Sir Lucius O'Trigger, your son, the Captain——

SIR ANTHONY. Oh, the dog! I see his tricks.—— Do you know the place?

DAVID. King's-Mead-Fields.

SIR ANTHONY. You know the way?

DAVID. Not an inch; but I'll call the mayor—aldermen—constables —church-wardens—and beadles—we can't be too many to part them.

SIR ANTHONY. Come along—give me your shoulder! we'll get assistance as we go. The lying villain! Well, I shall be in such a frenzy! So—this was the history of his trinkets! I'll bauble him! [*Exeunt.*]

SCENE III

SCENE. *King's-Mead-Fields.*

[SIR LUCIUS *and* ACRES, *with pistols.*]

ACRES. By my valour! then, Sir Lucius, forty yards is a good distance. Odds levels and aims! I say it is a good distance.

SIR LUCIUS. Is it for muskets or small field-pieces? Upon my conscience, Mr. Acres, you must leave those things to me. Stay now—I'll show you. [*Measures paces along the stage.*] There now, that is a very pretty distance—a pretty gentleman's distance.

ACRES. Z——ds! we might as well fight in a sentry-box! I tell you, Sir Lucius, the farther he is off, the cooler I shall take my aim.

SIR LUCIUS. Faith! then I suppose you would aim at him best of all if he was out of sight!

ACRES. No, Sir Lucius, but I should think forty, or eight and thirty yards——

SIR LUCIUS. Pho! pho! nonsense! Three or four feet between the mouths of your pistols is as good as a mile.

ACRES. Odds bullets, no! By my valour! there is no merit in killing him so near: do, my dear Sir Lucius, let me bring him down at a long shot—a long shot, Sir Lucius, if you love me!

SIR LUCIUS. Well—the gentleman's friend and I must settle that. But tell me now, Mr. Acres, in case of an accident, is there any little will or commission I could execute for you?

ACRES. I am much obliged to you, Sir Lucius, but I don't understand——

SIR LUCIUS. Why, you may think there's no being shot at without a little risk, and if an unlucky bullet should carry a *quietus* with it—I say it will be no time then to be bothering you about family matters.

ACRES. A *quietus!*

SIR LUCIUS. For instance, now—if that should be the case—would you choose to be pickled and sent home? or would it be the same to you to lie here in the Abbey? I'm told there is very snug lying in the Abbey.

ACRES. Pickled! Snug lying in the Abbey! Odds tremors! Sir Lucius, don't talk so!

SIR LUCIUS. I suppose, Mr. Acres, you never were engaged in an affair of this kind before?

ACRES. No, Sir Lucius, never before.

SIR LUCIUS. Ah! that's a pity! there's nothing like being used to a thing. Pray now, how would you receive the gentleman's shot?

ACRES. Odds files! I've practised that. There, Sir Lucius—there [*Puts himself in an attitude.*]—a side-front, hey? Odd! I'll make myself small enough: I'll stand edge-ways.

SIR LUCIUS. Now—you're quite out, for if you stand so when I take my aim—— [*levelling at him*]

ACRES. Z——ds! Sir Lucius—are you sure it is not cocked?

SIR LUCIUS. Never fear.

ACRES. But—but—you don't know—it may go off of its own head!

SIR LUCIUS. Pho! be easy. Well, now if I hit you in the body, my bullet has a double chance, for if it misses a vital part on your right side, 'twill be very hard if it don't succeed on the left!

ACRES. A vital part!

SIR LUCIUS. But, there—fix yourself so. [*placing him*] Let him see the broad side of your full front—there—now a ball or two may pass clean through your body, and never do any harm at all.

ACRES. Clean through me! a ball or two clean through me!

SIR LUCIUS. Aye, may they; and it is much the genteelest attitude into the bargain.

ACRES. Look'ee! Sir Lucius—I'd just as lieve be shot in an awkward posture as a genteel one—so, by my valour! I will stand edge-ways.

SIR LUCIUS [*looking at his watch*]. Sure they don't mean to disappoint us. Hah? No, faith—I think I see them coming.

ACRES. Hey! what!—coming!——

SIR LUCIUS. Aye. Who are those yonder getting over the stile?

ACRES. There are two of them indeed! Well—let them come—hey, Sir Lucius? We—we—we—we—won't run.

SIR LUCIUS. Run!

ACRES. No—I say—we *won't* run, by my valour!

SIR LUCIUS. What the devil's the matter with you?

ACRES. Nothing—nothing—my dear friend—my dear Sir Lucius—but—I—I—I don't feel quite so bold, somehow—as I did.

SIR LUCIUS. Oh fie! consider your honour.

ACRES. Aye—true—my honour. Do, Sir Lucius, edge in a word or two every now and then about my honour.

SIR LUCIUS [*looking*]. Well, here they're coming.

ACRES. Sir Lucius—if I wa'n't with you, I should almost think I was afraid. If my valour should leave me! Valour will come and go.

SIR LUCIUS. Then, pray, keep it fast while you have it.

ACRES. Sir Lucius—I doubt it is going—yes—my valour is certainly going! it is sneaking off! I feel it oozing out as it were at the palms of my hands!

SIR LUCIUS. Your honour—your honour. Here they are.

ACRES. Oh mercy! now that I were safe at Clod-Hall! or could be shot before I was aware!

[*Enter* FAULKLAND *and* ABSOLUTE.]

SIR LUCIUS. Gentlemen, your most obedient—hah!—what—Captain Absolute! So, I suppose, Sir, you are come here, just like myself—to do a kind office, first for your friend—then to proceed to business on your own account.

ACRES. What, Jack! my dear Jack! my dear friend!

ABSOLUTE. Hark'ee, Bob, Beverley's at hand.

SIR LUCIUS. Well, Mr. Acres, I don't blame your saluting the gentleman civilly. So, Mr. Beverley [*to* FAULKLAND], if you'll choose your weapons, the Captain and I will measure the ground.

FAULKLAND. *My* weapons, Sir!

ACRES. Odd's life! Sir Lucius, I'm not going to fight Mr. Faulkland; these are my particular friends.

SIR LUCIUS. What, Sir, did not you come here to fight Mr. Acres?

FAULKLAND. Not I, upon my word, Sir.

SIR LUCIUS. Well, now, that's mighty provoking! But I hope, Mr. Faulkland, as there are three of us come on purpose for the game, you won't be so cantankerous as to spoil the party by sitting out.

ABSOLUTE. Oh pray, Faulkland, fight to oblige Sir Lucius.

FAULKLAND. Nay, if Mr. Acres is so bent on the matter——

ACRES. No, no, Mr. Faulkland—I'll bear my disappointment like a Christian. Look'ee, Sir Lucius, there's no occasion at all for me to fight; and if it is the same to you, I'd as lieve let it alone.

SIR LUCIUS. Observe me, Mr. Acres—I must not be trifled with. You have certainly challenged somebody, and you came here to fight him. Now, if that gentleman is willing to represent him, I can't see, for my soul, why it isn't just the same thing.

ACRES. Why no, Sir Lucius—I tell you, 'tis one Beverley I've challenged—a fellow you see, that dare not show his face! If *he* were here, I'd make him give up his pretensions directly!

ABSOLUTE. Hold, Bob—let me set you right. There is no such man as Beverley in the case. The person who assumed that name is before you; and as his pretensions are the same in both characters, he is ready to support them in whatever way you please.

SIR LUCIUS. Well, this is lucky! Now you have an opportunity——

ACRES. What, quarrel with my dear friend Jack Absolute? Not if he were fifty Beverleys! Z——ds! Sir Lucius, you would not have me be so unnatural.

SIR LUCIUS. Upon my conscience, Mr. Acres, your valour has *oozed* away with a vengeance!

ACRES. Not in the least! Odds backs and abettors! I'll be your second with all my heart, and if you should get a *quietus*, you may command me entirely. I'll get you *snug lying* in the *Abbey here;* or *pickle* you, and send you over to Blunderbuss-Hall, or anything of the kind, with the greatest pleasure.

SIR LUCIUS. Pho! pho! you are little better than a coward.

ACRES. Mind, gentlemen, he calls me a *coward;* coward was the word, by my valour!

SIR LUCIUS. Well, Sir?

ACRES. Look'ee, Sir Lucius, 'tisn't that I mind the word coward—*coward* may be said in joke. But if you had called me a *poltroon,* odds daggers and balls!——

SIR LUCIUS. Well, Sir?

ACRES. ——I should have thought you a very ill-bred man.

SIR LUCIUS. Pho! you are beneath my notice.

ABSOLUTE. Nay, Sir Lucius, you can't have a better second than my friend Acres. He is a most *determined dog,* called in the country, *Fighting Bob*. He generally *kills a man a week;* don't you, Bob?

ACRES. Aye—at home!

SIR LUCIUS. Well then, Captain, 'tis we must begin. So come out, my little counsellor, [*Draws his sword.*] and ask the gentleman whether he will resign the lady without forcing you to proceed against him.

ABSOLUTE. Come on then, Sir; [*Draws.*] since you won't let it be an amicable suit, here's my reply.

[*Enter* SIR ANTHONY, DAVID, *and the Women.*]

DAVID. Knock 'em all down, sweet Sir Anthony; knock down my master in particular, and bind his hands over to their good behaviour!

SIR ANTHONY. Put up, Jack, put up, or I shall be in a frenzy. How came you in a duel, Sir?

ABSOLUTE. Faith, Sir, that gentleman can tell you better than I; 'twas he called on me, and you know, Sir, I serve his Majesty.

SIR ANTHONY. Here's a pretty fellow! I catch him going to cut a man's throat, and he tells me he serves his Majesty! Z——ds! Sirrah, then how durst you draw the King's sword against one of his subjects?

ABSOLUTE. Sir, I tell you! That gentleman called me out, without explaining his reasons.

SIR ANTHONY. Gad! Sir, how came you to call my son out, without explaining your reasons?

SIR LUCIUS. Your son, Sir, insulted me in a manner which my honour could not brook.

SIR ANTHONY. Z——ds! Jack, how durst you insult the gentleman in a manner which his honour could not brook?

MRS. MALAPROP. Come, come, let's have no honour before ladies. Captain Absolute, come here. How could you intimidate us so? Here's Lydia has been terrified to death for you.

ABSOLUTE. For fear I should be killed, or escape, Ma'am?

MRS. MALAPROP. Nay, no delusions to the past. Lydia is convinced; speak, child.

SIR LUCIUS. With your leave, Ma'am, I must put in a word here. I believe I could interpret the young lady's silence. Now mark——

LYDIA. What is it you mean, Sir?

SIR LUCIUS. Come, come, Delia, we must be serious now—this is no time for trifling.

LYDIA. 'Tis true, Sir; and your reproof bids me offer this gentleman my hand, and solicit the return of his affections.

ABSOLUTE. O! my little angel, say you so? Sir Lucius, I perceive there must be some mistake here. With regard to the affront which you affirm I have given you, I can only say that it could not have been intentional. And as you must be convinced that I should not fear to support a real injury, you shall now see that I am not ashamed to atone for an inadvertency. I ask your pardon. But for this lady, while honoured with her approbation, I will support my claim against any man whatever.

SIR ANTHONY. Well said, Jack! and I'll stand by you, my boy.

ACRES. Mind, I give up all my claim—I make no pretensions to anything in the world—and if I can't get a wife without fighting for her, by my valour! I'll live a bachelor.

SIR LUCIUS. Captain, give me your hand—an affront handsomely acknowledged becomes an obligation—and as for the lady, if she chooses to deny her own handwriting here—— [*Takes out letters.*]

MRS. MALAPROP. Oh, he will dissolve my mystery! Sir Lucius, perhaps there's some mistake—perhaps, I can illuminate——

SIR LUCIUS. Pray, old gentlewoman, don't interfere where you have no business. Miss Languish, are you my Delia, or not?

LYDIA. Indeed, Sir Lucius, I am not.

[LYDIA *and* ABSOLUTE *walk aside.*]

MRS. MALAPROP. Sir Lucius O'Trigger, ungrateful as you are, I own the soft impeachment—pardon my blushes, I am Delia.

SIR LUCIUS. You Delia!—pho! pho! be easy.

MRS. MALAPROP. Why, thou barbarous Vandyke!—those letters are mine. When you are more sensible of my benignity, perhaps I may be brought to encourage your addresses.

SIR LUCIUS. Mrs. Malaprop, I am extremely sensible of your condescension; and whether you or Lucy have put this trick upon me, I am equally beholden to you. And to show you I'm not ungrateful —— Captain Absolute! since you have taken that lady from me, I'll give you my Delia into the bargain.

ABSOLUTE. I am much obliged to you, Sir Lucius; but here's our friend, Fighting Bob, unprovided for.

SIR LUCIUS. Hah! little Valour—here, will you make your fortune?

ACRES. Odds wrinkles! No. But give me your hand, Sir Lucius; forget and forgive; but if ever I give you a chance of *pickling* me again, say Bob Acres is a dunce, that's all.

SIR ANTHONY. Come, Mrs. Malaprop, don't be cast down—you are in your bloom yet.

MRS. MALAPROP. O Sir Anthony!—men are all barbarians——

[*All retire but* JULIA *and* FAULKLAND.]

JULIA [*aside*]. He seems dejected and unhappy—not sullen. There was some foundation, however, for the tale he told me. O woman! how true should be your judgment, when your resolution is so weak!

FAULKLAND. Julia! how can I sue for what I so little deserve? I dare not presume—yet Hope is the child of Penitence.

JULIA. Oh! Faulkland, you have not been more faulty in your unkind treatment of me than I am now in wanting inclination to resent it. As my heart honestly bids me place my weakness to the account of love, I should be ungenerous not to admit the same plea for yours.

FAULKLAND. Now I shall be blest indeed!

[SIR ANTHONY *comes forward.*]

SIR ANTHONY. What's going on here? So you have been quarrelling too, I warrant. Come, Julia, I never interfered before; but let me have a hand in the matter at last. All the faults I have ever seen in my friend Faulkland seemed to proceed from what he calls the *delicacy* and *warmth* of his affection for you. There, marry him directly, Julia; you'll find he'll mend surprisingly!

[*The rest come forward.*]

SIR LUCIUS. Come now, I hope there is no dissatisfied person but what is content; for as I have been disappointed myself, it will be very hard if I have not the satisfaction of seeing other people succeed better——

ACRES. You are right, Sir Lucius. So, Jack, I wish you joy—Mr. Faulkland the same.—— Ladies,—come now, to show you I'm neither vexed nor angry, odds tabours and pipes! I'll order the fiddles in half an hour to the New Rooms, and I insist on your all meeting me there.

SIR ANTHONY. Gad! Sir, I like your spirit; and at night we single lads will drink a health to the young couples, and a husband to Mrs. Malaprop.

FAULKLAND. Our partners are stolen from us, Jack—I hope to be congratulated by each other—*yours* for having checked in time the errors of an ill-directed imagination, which might have betrayed an innocent heart; and *mine,* for having, by her gentleness and candour, reformed the unhappy temper of one who by it made wretched whom he loved most, and tortured the heart he ought to have adored.

ABSOLUTE. Well, Faulkland, we have both tasted the bitters, as well as the sweets, of love—with this difference only, that *you* always prepared the bitter cup for yourself, while *I*——

LYDIA. Was always obliged to *me* for it, hey! Mr. Modesty?—— But come, no more of that: our happiness is now as unalloyed as general.

JULIA. Then let us study to preserve it so; and while Hope pictures to us a flattering scene of future Bliss, let us deny its pencil those colours which are too bright to be lasting. When Hearts deserving Happiness would unite their fortunes, Virtue would crown them with an unfading garland of modest, hurtless flowers; but ill-judging Passion will force the gaudier Rose into the wreath, whose thorn offends them, when its leaves are dropt! [*Exeunt omnes.*]

HENRIK IBSEN
1828–1906

HEDDA GABLER
1890

IBSEN HAS LONG been regarded as a special critic of Norwegian society in the Eighteen-Seventies and Eighties, and hence as somewhat exclusively of his own time. Perhaps, however, the view of Ibsen as passé is now itself passé. He never was primarily a social critic; he was primarily dramatic craftsman and moralist. And his mature plays are still virtually unique in the firmness of their dramaturgy and of their moral conviction.

Hedda Gabler, the fruit of forty years of theatrical experience, represents his craftsmanship at its most assured. It is an almost perfectly artistic play—concentrated, coherent, symmetrical; and its structure is an almost perfect reflection of the nature of its leading character.

The central motive in the play is Hedda's desire to mold a human destiny. She conceives this destiny as a triumph of the Dionysian spirit, for she would know vicariously an abandon which she cannot know in her own person; and she selects a man as her deputy because, having rejected her own womanhood, she identifies herself with the dominant male role. The play rises naturally to crisis when she sends Lövborg out, as she imagines, to an evening of exultant revel. But the collapse of her venture is inherent in the spirit in which she conceived it. What she calls her "craving for life" is not a natural appetite; her will to dominate men incorporates also her will to destroy them; she has inevitably selected a weakling to do her living for her. When the third-act curtain rises on the gray weariness of the morning after, the play has turned as inevitably toward her catastrophe as before this it turned toward her illusory triumph. Her own character is a fate as unrelenting as any which the Delphic Oracle could have pronounced. Hence the spare and classic structure of the play.

If *Hedda Gabler* is like the classic drama in its deft ordering of plot, it resembles it too in its multitude of ironies. But as its plot is spun not by divine agency but by human character, so also its ironies are derived not from a metaphysical perspective but from an ethical one.

Enough of these ironies tend toward comedy to lighten the whole with a genuine if sometimes grim humor. There is, for example, Aunt Julia's utterly devoted, utterly damning admiration for a nephew whom "no one can beat" at "collecting and arranging things." There is Tesman's own perfectly daft accession of wonder when Hedda burns the manuscript ("I wonder, now, whether this sort of thing is usual in young wives? Eh?"). There is the descent from Hedda's breathless memory of "something beautiful, something fascinating—something daring" to the bathos of the thing remembered: the prurient girl, hiding behind an illustrated paper and listening to her young man talk about sex.

As these instances make clear, however, the disparities which such irony calls attention to are ethically revealing as well as sometimes amusing. Ibsen often invites a double perspective of this sort when he is most deeply earnest. When he wants to emphasize the difference between a superficial social view of people and a profoundly ethical view, he so orders his play that characters who are in sharp ethical contrast are placed in ironic juxtaposition.

Hedda herself is high fashion. She has style and wit, and a kind of verve. But from a moral perspective, the attributes for which she is so generally admired are inconsequential. To contrast with her, Ibsen introduces good people and right actions through the back and side doors, so to speak, in humble and almost ridiculous guise. Lovingkindness enters in the person of a garrulous maiden aunt bearing an old pair of embroidered morning slippers. Rectitude glimmers, goes out, then glimmers again in her dull and pedantic nephew. But the most exact foil to Hedda is the fragile young woman from the provinces, "dressed not quite in the latest fashion," who reveals by little and little the fullness of womanly courage and passion. Through these lesser characters, Ibsen would show us that human goodness is no respecter of persons, and that it characteristically reveals itself in those whom complacency would overlook and pride disdain.

HEDDA GABLER : *IBSEN*

TRANSLATED BY

WILLIAM ARCHER AND SIR EDMUND GOSSE

Characters

GEORGE TESMAN
HEDDA TESMAN : *his wife*
MISS JULIANA TESMAN : *his aunt*
MRS. ELVSTED
JUDGE BRACK
EILERT LÖVBORG
BERTA : *servant at the Tesman's*

SCENE. *Tesman's villa, in the west end of Christiania.*

Characters: Judge Brack In Norway during the 1880's official position was a general determinant of social standing, and official titles were in frequent use. The titles which may prove obscure or misleading in this translation are those of "Judge" Brack, an assessor, or associate judge; "Secretary" Falk, a cabinet minister; and "Sheriff" Elvsted, a district magistrate. Tesman, as holder of a scholarship in his field, has an officially conferred status though he is called by no title

ACT I

A spacious, handsome and tastefully furnished drawing-room, decorated in dark colors. In the back, a wide doorway with curtains drawn back, leading into a smaller room decorated in the same style as the drawing-room. In the right-hand wall of the front room, a folding door leading out to the hall. In the opposite wall, on the left, a glass door, also with curtains drawn back. Through the panes can be seen part of a verandah outside, and trees covered with autumn foliage. An oval table, with a cover on it, and surrounded by chairs, stands well forward. In front, by the wall on the right, a wide stove of dark porcelain, a high-backed arm-chair, a cushioned foot-rest, and two foot-stools. A settee, with a small round table in front of it, fills the upper right-hand corner. In front, on the left, a little way from the wall, a sofa. Farther back than the glass door, a piano. On either side of the doorway at the back a whatnot with terra-cotta and majolica ornaments.—Against the back wall of the inner room a sofa, with a table, and one or two chairs. Over the sofa hangs the portrait of a handsome elderly man in a General's uniform. Over the table a hanging lamp, with an opal glass shade.—A number of bouquets are arranged about the drawing-room, in vases and glasses. Others lie upon the tables. The floors in both rooms are covered with thick carpets.—Morning light. The sun shines in through the glass door.

[MISS JULIANA TESMAN, *with her bonnet on and carrying a parasol, comes in from the hall, followed by* BERTA, *who carries a bouquet wrapped in paper.* MISS TESMAN *is a comely and pleasant-looking lady of about sixty-five. She is nicely but simply dressed in a gray walking-costume.* BERTA *is a middle-aged woman of plain and rather countrified appearance.*]

MISS TESMAN [*stops close to the door, listens, and says softly*]. Upon my word, I don't believe they are stirring yet!

BERTA [*also softly*]. I told you so, Miss. Remember how late the steamboat got in last night. And then, when they got home!—good

Lord, what a lot the young mistress had to unpack before she could get to bed.

MISS TESMAN. Well, well—let them have their sleep out. But let us see that they get a good breath of the fresh morning air when they do appear. [*She goes to the glass door and throws it open.*]

BERTA [*beside the table, at a loss what to do with the bouquet in her hand*]. I declare there isn't a bit of room left. I think I'll put it down here, Miss. [*She places it on the piano.*]

MISS TESMAN. So you've got a new mistress now, my dear Berta. Heaven knows it was a wrench to me to part with you.

BERTA [*on the point of weeping*]. And do you think it wasn't hard for me too, Miss? After all the blessed years I've been with you and Miss Rina.

MISS TESMAN. We must make the best of it, Berta. There was nothing else to be done. George can't do without you, you see—he absolutely can't. He has had you to look after him ever since he was a little boy.

BERTA. Ah, but, Miss Julia, I can't help thinking of Miss Rina lying helpless at home there, poor thing. And with only that new girl, too! She'll never learn to take proper care of an invalid.

MISS TESMAN. Oh, I shall manage to train her. And of course, you know, I shall take most of it upon myself. You needn't be uneasy about my poor sister, my dear Berta.

BERTA. Well, but there's another thing, Miss. I'm so mortally afraid I shan't be able to suit the young mistress.

MISS TESMAN. Oh, well—just at first there may be one or two things——

BERTA. Most like she'll be terrible grand in her ways.

MISS TESMAN. Well, you can't wonder at that—General Gabler's daughter! Think of the sort of life she was accustomed to in her father's time. Don't you remember how we used to see her riding down the road along with the General? In that long black habit—and with feathers in her hat?

BERTA. Yes, indeed—I remember well enough—! But good Lord, I should never have dreamt in those days that she and Master George would make a match of it.

MISS TESMAN. Nor I.—But, by-the-bye, Berta—while I think of it: in future you mustn't say Master George. You must say Dr. Tesman.

BERTA. Yes, the young mistress spoke of that too—last night—the moment they set foot in the house. Is it true, then, Miss?

MISS TESMAN. Yes, indeed it is. Only think, Berta—some foreign university has made him a doctor—while he has been abroad, you understand. I hadn't heard a word about it, until he told me himself upon the pier.

BERTA. Well, well, he's clever enough for anything, he is. But I didn't think he'd have gone in for doctoring people too.

MISS TESMAN. No, no, it's not that sort of doctor he is. [*Nods significantly.*] But let me tell you, we may have to call him something still grander before long.

BERTA. You don't say so! What can that be, Miss?

MISS TESMAN [*smiling*]. H'm—wouldn't you like to know! [*with emotion*] Ah, dear, dear—if my poor brother could only look up from his grave now, and see what his little boy has grown into! [*Looks around.*] But bless me, Berta—why have you done this? Taken the chintz covers off all the furniture?

BERTA. The mistress told me to. She can't abide covers on the chairs, she says.

MISS TESMAN. Are they going to make this their everyday sitting-room then?

BERTA. Yes, that's what I understood—from the mistress. Master George—the doctor—he said nothing.

[GEORGE TESMAN *comes from the right into the inner room, humming to himself, and carrying an unstrapped empty portmanteau. He is a middle-sized, young-looking man of thirty-three, rather stout, with a round, open, cheerful face, fair hair and beard. He wears spectacles, and is somewhat carelessly dressed in comfortable indoor clothes.*]

MISS TESMAN. Good morning, good morning, George.

TESMAN [*in the doorway between the rooms*]. Aunt Julia! Dear Aunt Julia! [*Goes up to her and shakes hands warmly.*] Come all this way—so early! Eh?

MISS TESMAN. Why of course I had to come and see how you were getting on.

TESMAN. In spite of your having had no proper night's rest?

MISS TESMAN. Oh, that makes no difference to me.

TESMAN. Well, I suppose you got home all right from the pier? Eh?

MISS TESMAN. Yes, quite safely, thank goodness. Judge Brack was good enough to see me right to my door.

TESMAN. We were so sorry we couldn't give you a seat in the carriage. But you saw what a pile of boxes Hedda had to bring with her.

MISS TESMAN. Yes, she had certainly plenty of boxes.

BERTA [*to* TESMAN]. Shall I go in and see if there's anything I can do for the mistress?

TESMAN. No thank you, Berta—you needn't. She said she would ring if she wanted anything.

BERTA [*going towards the right*]. Very well.

TESMAN. But look here—take this portmanteau with you.

BERTA [*taking it*]. I'll put it in the attic.

[*She goes out by the hall door.*]

TESMAN. Fancy, Auntie—I had the whole of that portmanteau chock full of copies of documents. You wouldn't believe how much I have picked up from all the archives I have been examining—curious old details that no one has had any idea of——

MISS TESMAN. Yes, you don't seem to have wasted your time on your wedding trip, George.

TESMAN. No, that I haven't. But do take off your bonnet, Auntie. Look here! Let me untie the strings—eh?

MISS TESMAN [*while he does so*]. Well, well—this is just as if you were still at home with us.

TESMAN [*with the bonnet in his hand, looks at it from all sides*]. Why, what a gorgeous bonnet you've been investing in!

MISS TESMAN. I bought it on Hedda's account.

TESMAN. On Hedda's account? Eh?

MISS TESMAN. Yes, so that Hedda needn't be ashamed of me if we happened to go out together.

TESMAN [*patting her cheek*]. You always think of everything, Aunt Julia. [*Lays the bonnet on a chair beside the table.*] And now, look here—suppose we sit comfortably on the sofa and have a little chat, till Hedda comes.

[*They seat themselves. She places her parasol in the corner of the sofa.*]

MISS TESMAN [*takes both his hands and looks at him*]. What a delight it is to have you again, as large as life, before my very eyes, George! My George—my poor brother's own boy!

TESMAN. And it's a delight for me, too, to see you again, Aunt Julia! You, who have been father and mother in one to me.

MISS TESMAN. Oh, yes, I know you will always keep a place in your heart for your old aunts.

TESMAN. And what about Aunt Rina? No improvement—eh!

MISS TESMAN. Oh, no—we can scarcely look for any improvement in her case, poor thing. There she lies, helpless, as she has lain for all these years. But heaven grant I may not lose her yet awhile! For if I did, I don't know what I should make of my life, George—especially now that I haven't you to look after any more.

TESMAN [*patting her back*]. There, there, there——!

MISS TESMAN [*suddenly changing her tone*]. And to think that here you are a married man, George!—And that you should be the one to carry off Hedda Gabler, the beautiful Hedda Gabler! Only think of it—she, that was so beset with admirers!

TESMAN [*hums a little and smiles complacently*]. Yes, I fancy I have several good friends about town who would like to stand in my shoes—eh?

MISS TESMAN. And then this fine long wedding-tour you have had! More than five—nearly six months——

TESMAN. Well, for me it has been a sort of tour of research as well. I have had to do so much grubbing among old records—and to read no end of books too, Auntie.

MISS TESMAN. Oh, yes, I suppose so. [*more confidentially, and lowering her voice a little*] But listen now, George—have you nothing —nothing special to tell me?

TESMAN. As to our journey?

MISS TESMAN. Yes.

TESMAN. No, I don't know of anything except what I have told you in my letters. I had a doctor's degree conferred on me—but that I told you yesterday.

MISS TESMAN. Yes, yes, you did. But what I mean is—haven't you any—any—expectations——?

TESMAN. Expectations?

MISS TESMAN. Why, you know, George—I'm your old auntie!

TESMAN. Why, of course I have expectations.

MISS TESMAN. Ah!

TESMAN. I have every expectation of being a professor one of these days.

MISS TESMAN. Oh, yes, a professor——

TESMAN. Indeed, I may say I am certain of it. But my dear Auntie—you know all about that already!

MISS TESMAN [*laughing to herself*]. Yes, of course I do. You are quite right there. [*changing the subject*] But we were talking about your journey. It must have cost a great deal of money, George?

TESMAN. Well, you see—my handsome traveling-scholarship went a good way.

MISS TESMAN. But I can't understand how you can have made it go far enough for two.

TESMAN. No, that's not so easy to understand—eh?

MISS TESMAN. And especially traveling with a lady—they tell me that makes it ever so much more expensive.

TESMAN. Yes, of course—it makes it a little more expensive. But Hedda had to have this trip, Auntie! She really had to. Nothing else would have done.

MISS TESMAN. No, no, I suppose not. A wedding-tour seems to be quite indispensable nowadays.—But tell me now—have you gone thoroughly over the house yet?

TESMAN. Yes, you may be sure I have. I have been afoot ever since daylight.

MISS TESMAN. And what do you think of it all?

TESMAN. I'm delighted! Quite delighted! Only I can't think what we are to do with the two empty rooms between this inner parlor and Hedda's bedroom.

MISS TESMAN [*laughing*]. Oh, my dear George, I dare say you may find some use for them—in the course of time.

TESMAN. Why of course you are quite right, Aunt Julia! You mean as my library increases—eh?

MISS TESMAN. Yes, quite so, my dear boy. It was your library I was thinking of.

TESMAN. I am specially pleased on Hedda's account. Often and often, before we were engaged, she said that she would never care to live anywhere but in Secretary Falk's villa.

MISS TESMAN. Yes, it was lucky that this very house should come into the market, just after you had started.

TESMAN. Yes, Aunt Julia, the luck was on our side, wasn't it—eh?

MISS TESMAN. But the expense, my dear George! You will find it very expensive, all this.

TESMAN [*looks at her, a little cast down*]. Yes, I suppose I shall, Aunt!

MISS TESMAN. Oh, frightfully!

TESMAN. How much do you think? In round numbers?—Eh?

MISS TESMAN. Oh, I can't even guess until all the accounts come in.

TESMAN. Well, fortunately, Judge Brack has secured the most favorable terms for me,—so he said in a letter to Hedda.

MISS TESMAN. Yes, don't be uneasy, my dear boy.—Besides, I have given security for the furniture and all the carpets.

TESMAN. Security? You? My dear Aunt Julia—what sort of security could you give?

MISS TESMAN. I have given a mortgage on our annuity.

TESMAN [*jumps up*]. What! On your—and Aunt Rina's annuity!

MISS TESMAN. Yes, I knew of no other plan, you see.

TESMAN [*placing himself before her*]. Have you gone out of your senses, Auntie! Your annuity—it's all that you and Aunt Rina have to live upon.

MISS TESMAN. Well, well, don't get so excited about it. It's only a matter of form you know—Judge Brack assured me of that. It was he that was kind enough to arrange the whole affair for me. A mere matter of form, he said.

TESMAN. Yes, that may be all very well. But nevertheless——

MISS TESMAN. You will have your own salary to depend upon now. And, good heavens, even if we did have to pay up a little——! To eke things out a bit at the start——! Why, it would be nothing but a pleasure to us.

TESMAN. Oh, Auntie—will you never be tired of making sacrifices for me!

MISS TESMAN [*rises and lays her hands on his shoulders*]. Have I had any other happiness in this world except to smooth your way for you, my dear boy? You, who have had neither father nor mother to depend on. And now we have reached the goal, George! Things have looked black enough for us, sometimes; but, thank heaven, now you have nothing to fear.

TESMAN. Yes, it is really marvelous how everything has turned out for the best.

MISS TESMAN. And the people who opposed you—who wanted to

bar the way for you—now you have them at your feet. They have fallen, George. Your most dangerous rival—his fall was the worst.—And now he has to lie on the bed he has made for himself—poor misguided creature.

TESMAN. Have you heard anything of Eilert? Since I went away, I mean.

MISS TESMAN. Only that he is said to have published a new book.

TESMAN. What! Eilert Lövborg! Recently—eh?

MISS TESMAN. Yes, so they say. Heaven knows whether it can be worth anything! Ah, when your new book appears—that will be another story, George! What is it to be about?

TESMAN. It will deal with the domestic industries of Brabant during the Middle Ages.

MISS TESMAN. Fancy—to be able to write on such a subject as that!

TESMAN. However, it may be some time before the book is ready. I have all these collections to arrange first, you see.

MISS TESMAN. Yes, collecting and arranging—no one can beat you at that. There you are my poor brother's own son.

TESMAN. I am looking forward eagerly to setting to work at it; especially now that I have my own delightful home to work in.

MISS TESMAN. And, most of all, now that you have got the wife of your heart, my dear George.

TESMAN [*embracing her*]. Oh, yes, yes, Aunt Julia. Hedda—she is the best part of all! [*Looks towards the doorway.*] I believe I hear her coming—eh?

[HEDDA *enters from the left through the inner room. She is a woman of nine-and-twenty. Her face and figure show refinement and distinction. Her complexion is pale and opaque. Her steel-gray eyes express a cold, unruffled repose. Her hair is of an agreeable medium brown, but not particularly abundant. She is dressed in a tasteful, somewhat loose-fitting morning-gown.*]

MISS TESMAN [*going to meet* HEDDA]. Good morning, my dear Hedda! Good morning, and a hearty welcome.

HEDDA [*holds out her hand*]. Good morning, dear Miss Tesman! So early a call! That is kind of you.

MISS TESMAN [*with some embarrassment*]. Well—has the bride slept well in her new home?

HEDDA. Oh yes, thanks. Passably.

TESMAN [*laughing*]. Passably! Come, that's good, Hedda! You were sleeping like a stone when I got up.

HEDDA. Fortunately. Of course one has always to accustom one's self to new surroundings, Miss Tesman—little by little. [*looking towards the left*] Oh—there the servant has gone and opened the verandah door, and let in a whole flood of sunshine.

MISS TESMAN [*going towards the door*]. Well, then, we will shut it.

HEDDA. No, no, not that! Tesman, please draw the curtains. That will give a softer light.

TESMAN [*at the door*]. All right—all right. There now, Hedda, now you have both shade and fresh air.

HEDDA. Yes, fresh air we certainly must have, with all these stacks of flowers—— But—won't you sit down, Miss Tesman?

MISS TESMAN. No, thank you. Now that I have seen that everything is all right here—thank heaven!—I must be getting home again. My sister is lying longing for me, poor thing.

TESMAN. Give her my very best love, Auntie; and say I shall look in and see her later in the day.

MISS TESMAN. Yes, yes, I'll be sure to tell her. But by-the-bye, George—[*feeling in her dress pocket*]—I have almost forgotten—I have something for you here.

TESMAN. What is it, Auntie? Eh?

MISS TESMAN [*produces a flat parcel wrapped in newspaper and hands it to him*]. Look here, my dear boy.

TESMAN [*opening the parcel*]. Well, I declare!—Have you really saved them for me, Aunt Julia! Hedda, isn't this touching—eh?

HEDDA [*beside the whatnot on the right*]. Well, what is it?

TESMAN. My old morning-shoes! My slippers.

HEDDA. Indeed. I remember you often spoke of them while we were abroad.

TESMAN. Yes, I missed them terribly. [*Goes up to her.*] Now you shall see them, Hedda!

HEDDA [*going towards the stove*]. Thanks, I really don't care about it.

TESMAN [*following her*]. Only think—ill as she was, Aunt Rina embroidered these for me. Oh you can't think how many associations cling to them.

HEDDA [*at the table*]. Scarcely for me.

MISS TESMAN. Of course not for Hedda, George.

TESMAN. Well, but now that she belongs to the family, I thought——

HEDDA [*interrupting*]. We shall never get on with this servant, Tesman.

MISS TESMAN. Not get on with Berta?

TESMAN. Why, dear, what puts that in your head? Eh?

HEDDA [*pointing*]. Look there! She has left her old bonnet lying about on a chair.

TESMAN [*in consternation, drops the slippers on the floor*]. Why, Hedda——

HEDDA. Just fancy, if any one should come in and see it.

TESMAN. But Hedda—that's Aunt Julia's bonnet.

HEDDA. Is it!

MISS TESMAN [*taking up the bonnet*]. Yes, indeed it's mine. And what's more, it's not old, Madame Hedda.

HEDDA. I really did not look closely at it, Miss Tesman.

MISS TESMAN [*trying on the bonnet*]. Let me tell you it's the first time I have worn it—the very first time.

TESMAN. And a very nice bonnet it is too—quite a beauty!

MISS TESMAN. Oh, it's no such great thing, George. [*Looks around her.*] My parasol——? Ah, here. [*Takes it.*] For this is mine too—[*mutters*]—not Berta's.

TESMAN. A new bonnet and a new parasol! Only think, Hedda!

HEDDA. Very handsome indeed.

TESMAN. Yes, isn't it? But Auntie, take a good look at Hedda before you go! See how handsome she is!

MISS TESMAN. Oh, my dear boy, there's nothing new in that. Hedda was always lovely. [*She nods and goes towards the right.*]

TESMAN [*following*]. Yes, but have you noticed what splendid condition she is in? How she has filled out on the journey?

HEDDA [*crossing the room*]. Oh, do be quiet——!

MISS TESMAN [*who has stopped and turned*]. Filled out?

TESMAN. Of course you don't notice it so much now that she has that dress on. But I, who can see——

HEDDA [*at the glass door, impatiently*]. Oh, you can't see anything.

TESMAN. It must be the mountain air in the Tyrol——

HEDDA [*curtly, interrupting*]. I am exactly as I was when I started.

TESMAN. So you insist; but I'm quite certain you are not. Don't you agree with me, Auntie?

MISS TESMAN [*who has been gazing at her with folded hands*]. Hedda is lovely—lovely—lovely. [*Goes up to her, takes her head between both hands, draws it downwards, and kisses her hair*]. God bless and preserve Hedda Tesman—for George's sake.

HEDDA [*gently freeing herself*]. Oh—! Let me go.

MISS TESMAN [*in quiet emotion*]. I shall not let a day pass without coming to see you.

TESMAN. No you won't, will you, Auntie? Eh?

MISS TESMAN. Good-bye—good-bye!

[*She goes out by the hall door.* TESMAN *accompanies her. The door remains half open.* TESMAN *can be heard repeating his message to Aunt Rina and his thanks for the slippers.*]

[*In the meantime,* HEDDA *walks about the room raising her arms and clenching her hands as if in desperation. Then she flings back the curtains from the glass door, and stands there looking out.*]

[*Presently* TESMAN *returns and closes the door behind him.*]

TESMAN [*picks up the slippers from the floor*]. What are you looking at, Hedda?

HEDDA [*once more calm and mistress of herself*]. I am only looking at the leaves. They are so yellow—so withered.

TESMAN [*wraps up the slippers and lays them on the table*]. Well you see, we are well into September now.

HEDDA [*again restless*]. Yes, to think of it!—Already in—in September.

TESMAN. Don't you think Aunt Julia's manner was strange, dear? Almost solemn? Can you imagine what was the matter with her? Eh?

HEDDA. I scarcely know her, you see. Is she often like that?

TESMAN. No, not as she was to-day.

HEDDA [*leaving the glass door*]. Do you think she was annoyed about the bonnet?

TESMAN. Oh, scarcely at all. Perhaps a little, just at the moment——

HEDDA. But what an idea, to pitch her bonnet about in the drawing-room! No one does that sort of thing.

TESMAN. Well you may be sure Aunt Julia won't do it again.

HEDDA. In any case, I shall manage to make my peace with her.

TESMAN. Yes, my dear, good Hedda, if you only would.

HEDDA. When you call this afternoon, you might invite her to spend the evening here.

TESMAN. Yes, that I will. And there's one thing more you could do that would delight her heart.

HEDDA. What is it?

TESMAN. If you could only prevail on yourself to say *du* to her. For my sake, Hedda? Eh?

HEDDA. No, no, Tesman—you really mustn't ask that of me. I have told you so already. I shall try to call her "Aunt"; and you must be satisfied with that.

TESMAN. Well, well. Only I think now that you belong to the family, you——

HEDDA. H'm—I can't in the least see why——

[*She goes up towards the middle doorway.*]

TESMAN [*after a pause*]. Is there anything the matter with you, Hedda? Eh?

HEDDA. I'm only looking at my old piano. It doesn't go at all well with all the other things.

TESMAN. The first time I draw my salary, we'll see about exchanging it.

HEDDA. No, no—no exchanging. I don't want to part with it. Suppose we put it there in the inner room, and then get another here in its place. When it's convenient, I mean.

TESMAN [*a little taken aback*]. Yes—of course we could do that.

HEDDA [*takes up the bouquet from the piano*]. These flowers were not here last night when we arrived.

TESMAN. Aunt Julia must have brought them for you.

HEDDA [*examining the bouquet*]. A visiting-card. [*Takes it out and reads.*] "Shall return later in the day." Can you guess whose card it is?

TESMAN. No. Whose? Eh?

HEDDA. The name is "Mrs. Elvsted."

TESMAN. Is it really? Sheriff Elvsted's wife? Miss Rysing that was.

HEDDA. Exactly. The girl with the irritating hair, that she was always showing off. An old flame of yours, I've been told.

TESMAN [*laughing*]. Oh, that didn't last long; and it was before I knew you, Hedda. But fancy her being in town!

HEDDA. It's odd that she should call upon us. I have scarcely seen her since we left school.

TESMAN. I haven't seen her either for—heaven knows how long. I wonder how she can endure to live in such an out-of-the-way hole—eh?

HEDDA [*after a moment's thought says suddenly*]. Tell me, Tesman—isn't it somewhere near there that he—that—Eilert Lövborg is living?

TESMAN. Yes, he is somewhere in that part of the country.

[BERTA *enters by the hall door.*]

BERTA. That lady, ma'am, that brought some flowers a little while ago, is here again. [*pointing*] The flowers you have in your hand, ma'am.

HEDDA. Ah, is she? Well, please show her in.

[BERTA *opens the door for* MRS. ELVSTED, *and goes out herself.—* MRS. ELVSTED *is a woman of fragile figure, with pretty, soft features. Her eyes are light blue, large, round, and somewhat prominent, with a startled, inquiring expression. Her hair is remarkably light, almost flaxen, and unusually abundant and wavy. She is a couple of years younger than* HEDDA. *She wears a dark visiting dress, tasteful, but not quite in the latest fashion.*]

HEDDA [*receives her warmly*]. How do you do, my dear Mrs. Elvsted? It's delightful to see you again.

MRS. ELVSTED [*nervously, struggling for self-control*]. Yes, it's a very long time since we met.

TESMAN [*gives her his hand*]. And we too—eh?

HEDDA. Thanks for your lovely flowers——

MRS. ELVSTED. Oh, not at all—— I would have come straight here yesterday afternoon; but I heard that you were away——

TESMAN. Have you just come to town? Eh?

MRS. ELVSTED. I arrived yesterday, about midday. Oh, I was quite in despair when I heard that you were not at home.

HEDDA. In despair! How so?

TESMAN. Why, my dear Mrs. Rysing—I mean Mrs. Elvsted——

HEDDA. I hope that you are not in any trouble?

MRS. ELVSTED. Yes, I am. And I don't know another living creature here that I can turn to.

HEDDA [*laying the bouquet on the table*]. Come—let us sit here on the sofa——

MRS. ELVSTED. Oh, I am too restless to sit down.

HEDDA. Oh no, you're not. Come here.

[*She draws* MRS. ELVSTED *down upon the sofa and sits at her side.*]

TESMAN. Well? What is it, Mrs. Elvsted?

HEDDA. Has anything particular happened to you at home?

MRS. ELVSTED. Yes—and no. Oh—I am so anxious you should not misunderstand me——

HEDDA. Then your best plan is to tell us the whole story, Mrs. Elvsted.

TESMAN. I suppose that's what you have come for—eh?

MRS. ELVSTED. Yes, yes—of course it is. Well then, I must tell you—if you don't already know—that Eilert Lövborg is in town, too.

HEDDA. Lövborg——!

TESMAN. What! Has Eilert Lövborg come back? Fancy that, Hedda!

HEDDA. Well, well—I hear it.

MRS. ELVSTED. He has been here a week already. Just fancy—a whole week! In this terrible town, alone! With so many temptations on all sides.

HEDDA. But my dear Mrs. Elvsted—how does he concern you so much?

MRS. ELVSTED [*looks at her with a startled air, and says rapidly*]. He was the children's tutor.

HEDDA. Your children's?

MRS. ELVSTED. My husband's. I have none.

HEDDA. Your step-children's, then?

MRS. ELVSTED. Yes.

TESMAN [*somewhat hesitatingly*]. Then was he—I don't know how to express it—was he—regular enough in his habits to be fit for the post? Eh?

MRS. ELVSTED. For the last two years his conduct has been irreproachable.

TESMAN. Has it indeed? Fancy that, Hedda!

HEDDA. I hear it.

MRS. ELVSTED. Perfectly irreproachable, I assure you! In every respect. But all the same—now that I know he is here—in this great town—and with a large sum of money in his hands—I can't help being in mortal fear for him.

TESMAN. Why did he not remain where he was? With you and your husband? Eh?

MRS. ELVSTED. After his book was published he was too restless and unsettled to remain with us.

TESMAN. Yes, by-the-bye, Aunt Julia told me he had published a new book.

MRS. ELVSTED. Yes, a big book, dealing with the march of civilization—in broad outline, as it were. It came out about a fortnight ago. And since it has sold so well, and been so much read—and made such a sensation——

TESMAN. Has it indeed? It must be something he has had lying by since his better days.

MRS. ELVSTED. Long ago, you mean?

TESMAN. Yes.

MRS. ELVSTED. No, he has written it all since he has been with us—within the last year.

TESMAN. Isn't that good news, Hedda? Think of that.

MRS. ELVSTED. Ah, yes, if only it would last!

HEDDA. Have you seen him here in town?

MRS. ELVSTED. No, not yet. I have had the greatest difficulty in finding out his address. But this morning I discovered it at last.

HEDDA [*looks searchingly at her*]. Do you know, it seems to me a little odd of your husband—h'm——

MRS. ELVSTED [*starting nervously*]. Of my husband! What?

HEDDA. That he should send you to town on such an errand—that he does not come himself and look after his friend.

MRS. ELVSTED. Oh, no, no—my husband has no time. And besides, I—I had some shopping to do.

HEDDA [*with a slight smile*]. Ah, that is a different matter.

MRS. ELVSTED [*rising quickly and uneasily*]. And now I beg and implore you, Mr. Tesman—receive Eilert Lövborg kindly if he comes to you! And that he is sure to do. You see you were such great friends in the old days. And then you are interested in the same studies—the same branch of science—so far as I can understand.

TESMAN. We used to be, at any rate.

MRS. ELVSTED. That is why I beg so earnestly that you—you too—

will keep a sharp eye upon him. Oh, you will promise me that, Mr. Tesman—won't you?

TESMAN. With the greatest of pleasure, Mrs. Rysing——

HEDDA. Elvsted.

TESMAN. I assure you I shall do all I possibly can for Eilert. You may rely upon me.

MRS. ELVSTED. Oh, how very, very kind of you! [*Presses his hands.*] Thanks, thanks, thanks! [*frightened*] You see, my husband is very fond of him!

HEDDA [*rising*]. You ought to write to him, Tesman. Perhaps he may not care to come to you of his own accord.

TESMAN. Well, perhaps it would be the right thing to do, Hedda? Eh?

HEDDA. And the sooner the better. Why not at once?

MRS. ELVSTED [*imploringly*]. Oh, if you only would!

TESMAN. I'll write this moment. Have you his address, Mrs.—Mrs. Elvsted?

MRS. ELVSTED. Yes. [*Takes a slip of paper from her pocket, and hands it to him.*] Here it is.

TESMAN. Good, good. Then I'll go in—— [*Looks about him.*] By-the-bye,—my slippers? Oh, here. [*Takes the packet, and is about to go.*]

HEDDA. Be sure you write him a cordial, friendly letter. And a good long one too.

TESMAN. Yes, I will.

MRS. ELVSTED. But please, please don't say a word to show that I have suggested it.

TESMAN. No, how could you think I would? Eh?

[*He goes out to the right, through the inner room.*]

HEDDA [*goes up to* MRS. ELVSTED, *smiles, and says in a low voice*]. There. We have killed two birds with one stone.

MRS. ELVSTED. What do you mean?

HEDDA. Could you not see that I wanted him to go?

MRS. ELVSTED. Yes, to write the letter——

HEDDA. And that I might speak to you alone.

MRS. ELVSTED [*confused*]. About the same thing?

HEDDA. Precisely.

MRS. ELVSTED [*apprehensively*]. But there is nothing more, Mrs. Tesman! Absolutely nothing!

HEDDA. Oh, yes, but there is. There is a great deal more—I can see that. Sit here—and we'll have a cosy, confidential chat. [*She forces* MRS. ELVSTED *to sit in the easy-chair beside the stove, and seats herself on one of the footstools.*]

MRS. ELVSTED [*anxiously, looking at her watch*]. But, my dear Mrs. Tesman—I was really on the point of going.

HEDDA. Oh, you can't be in such a hurry.—Well? Now tell me something about your life at home.

MRS. ELVSTED. Oh, that is just what I care least to speak about.

HEDDA. But to me, dear——? Why, weren't we school-fellows?

MRS. ELVSTED. Yes, but you were in the class above me. Oh, how dreadfully afraid of you I was then!

HEDDA. Afraid of me?

MRS. ELVSTED. *Yes,* dreadfully. For when we met on the stairs you used always to pull my hair.

HEDDA. Did I, really?

MRS. ELVSTED. Yes, and once you said you would burn it off my head.

HEDDA. Oh, that was all nonsense, of course.

MRS. ELVSTED. Yes, but I was so silly in those days.—And since then, too—we have drifted so far—far apart from each other. Our circles have been so entirely different.

HEDDA. Well then, we must try to drift together again. Now listen! At school we said *du* to each other; and we called each other by our Christian names——

MRS. ELVSTED. No, I am sure you must be mistaken.

HEDDA. No, not at all! I can remember quite distinctly. So now we are going to renew our old friendship. [*Draws the footstool closer to* MRS. ELVSTED.] There now! [*Kisses her cheek.*] You must say *du* to me and call me Hedda.

MRS. ELVSTED [*presses and pats her hands*]. Oh, how good and kind you are! I am not used to such kindness.

HEDDA. There, there, there! And I shall say *du* to you, as in the old days, and call you my dear Thora.

MRS. ELVSTED. My name is Thea.

628 **du** thou. Norwegian, like French and German, has a familiar second-person pronoun *du* ("thou") which is sharply distinguished from the formal or neutral *de* ("you"). The most significant occurrences of both pronouns are called attention to in footnotes

HEDDA. Why, of course! I meant Thea. [*Looks at her compassionately.*] So you are not accustomed to goodness and kindness, Thea? Not in your own home?

MRS. ELVSTED. Oh, if I only had a home! But I haven't any; I have never had a home.

HEDDA [*looks at her for a moment*]. I almost suspected as much.

MRS. ELVSTED [*gazingly helplessly before her*]. Yes—yes—yes.

HEDDA. I don't quite remember—was it not as housekeeper that you first went to Mr. Elvsted's?

MRS. ELVSTED. I really went as governess. But his wife—his late wife—was an invalid,—and rarely left her room. So I had to look after the housekeeping as well.

HEDDA. And then—at last—you became mistress of the house.

MRS. ELVSTED [*sadly*]. Yes, I did.

HEDDA. Let me see—about how long ago was that?

MRS. ELVSTED. My marriage?

HEDDA. Yes.

MRS. ELVSTED. Five years ago.

HEDDA. To be sure; it must be that.

MRS. ELVSTED. Oh, those five years——! Or at all events the last two or three of them! Oh, if you could only imagine——

HEDDA [*giving her a little slap on the hand*]. *De?* Fie, Thea!

MRS. ELVSTED. Yes, yes, I will try—— Well if—you could only imagine and understand——

HEDDA [*lightly*]. Eilert Lövborg has been in your neighborhood about three years, hasn't he?

MRS. ELVSTED [*looks at her doubtfully*]. Eilert Lövborg? Yes—he has.

HEDDA. Had you known him before, in town here?

MRS. ELVSTED. Scarcely at all. I mean—I knew him by name of course.

HEDDA. But you saw a good deal of him in the country?

MRS. ELVSTED. Yes, he came to us every day. You see, he gave the children lessons; for in the long run I couldn't manage it all myself.

HEDDA. No, that's clear.—And your husband——? I suppose he is often away from home?

MRS. ELVSTED. Yes. Being Sheriff, you know, he has to travel about a good deal in his district.

HEDDA [*leaning against the arm of the chair*]. Thea—my poor, sweet Thea—now you must tell me everything—exactly as it stands.

MRS. ELVSTED. Well then, you must question me.

HEDDA. What sort of a man is your husband, Thea? I mean—you know—in everyday life. Is he kind to you?

MRS. ELVSTED [*evasively*]. I am sure he means well in everything.

HEDDA. I should think he must be altogether too old for you. There is at least twenty years' difference between you, is there not?

MRS. ELVSTED [*irritably*]. Yes, that is true, too. Everything about him is repellent to me! We have not a thought in common. We have no single point of sympathy—he and I.

HEDDA. But is he not fond of you all the same? In his own way?

MRS. ELVSTED. Oh, I really don't know. I think he regards me simply as a useful property. And then it doesn't cost much to keep me. I am not expensive.

HEDDA. That is stupid of you.

MRS. ELVSTED [*shakes her head*]. It cannot be otherwise—not with him. I don't think he really cares for any one but himself—and perhaps a little for the children.

HEDDA. And for Eilert Lövborg, Thea.

MRS. ELVSTED [*looking at her*]. For Eilert Lövborg? What puts that into your head?

HEDDA. Well, my dear—I should say, when he sends you after him all the way to town—— [*smiling almost imperceptibly*] And besides, you said so yourself, to Tesman.

MRS. ELVSTED [*with a little nervous twitch*]. Did I? Yes, I suppose I did. [*vehemently, but not loudly*] No—I may just as well make a clean breast of it at once! For it must all come out in any case.

HEDDA. Why, my dear Thea——?

MRS. ELVSTED. Well, to make a long story short: My husband did not know that I was coming.

HEDDA. What! Your husband didn't know it!

MRS. ELVSTED. No, of course not. For that matter, he was away from home himself—he was traveling. Oh, I could bear it no longer, Hedda! I couldn't indeed—so utterly alone as I should have been in future.

HEDDA. Well? And then?

MRS. ELVSTED. So I put together some of my things—what I needed most—as quietly as possible. And then I left the house.

HEDDA. Without a word?

MRS. ELVSTED. Yes—and took the train straight to town.

HEDDA. Why, my dear, good Thea—to think of you daring to do it!

MRS. ELVSTED [*rises and moves about the room*]. What else could I possibly do?

HEDDA. But what do you think your husband will say when you go home again?

MRS. ELVSTED [*at the table, looks at her*]. Back to him?

HEDDA. Of course.

MRS. ELVSTED. I shall never go back to him again.

HEDDA [*rising and going towards her*]. Then you have left your home—for good and all?

MRS. ELVSTED. Yes. There was nothing else to be done.

HEDDA. But then—to take flight so openly.

MRS. ELVSTED. Oh, it's impossible to keep things of that sort secret.

HEDDA. But what do you think people will say of you, Thea?

MRS. ELVSTED. They may say what they like for aught *I* care. [*Seats herself wearily and sadly on the sofa.*] I have done nothing but what I had to do.

HEDDA [*after a short silence*]. And what are your plans now? What do you think of doing?

MRS. ELVSTED. I don't know yet. I only know this, that I must live here, where Eilert Lövborg is—if I am to live at all.

HEDDA [*takes a chair from the table, seats herself beside her, and strokes her hands*]. My dear Thea—how did this—this friendship—between you and Eilert Lövborg come about?

MRS. ELVSTED. Oh, it grew up gradually. I gained a sort of influence over him.

HEDDA. Indeed?

MRS. ELVSTED. He gave up his old habits. Not because I asked him to, for I never dared do that. But of course he saw how repulsive they were to me; and so he dropped them.

HEDDA [*concealing an involuntary smile of scorn*]. Then you have reclaimed him—as the saying goes—my little Thea.

MRS. ELVSTED. So he says himself, at any rate. And he, on his side, has made a real human being of me—taught me to think, and to understand so many things.

HEDDA. Did he give you lessons too, then?

MRS. ELVSTED. No, not exactly lessons. But he talked to me—talked about such an infinity of things. And then came the lovely, happy time when I began to share in his work—when he allowed me to help him!

HEDDA. Oh, he did, did he?

MRS. ELVSTED. Yes! He never wrote anything without my assistance.

HEDDA. You were two good comrades, in fact?

MRS. ELVSTED [*eagerly*]. Comrades! Yes, fancy, Hedda—that is the very word he used!—Oh, I ought to feel perfectly happy; and yet I cannot; for I don't know how long it will last.

HEDDA. Are you no surer of him than that?

MRS. ELVSTED [*gloomily*]. A woman's shadow stands between Eilert Lövborg and me.

HEDDA [*looks at her anxiously*]. Who can that be?

MRS. ELVSTED. I don't know. Some one he knew in his—in his past. Some one he has never been able wholly to forget.

HEDDA. What has he told you—about this?

MRS. ELVSTED. He has only once—quite vaguely—alluded to it.

HEDDA. Well! And what did he say?

MRS. ELVSTED. He said that when they parted, she threatened to shoot him with a pistol.

HEDDA [*with cold composure*]. Oh, nonsense! No one does that sort of thing here.

MRS. ELVSTED. No. And that is why I think it must have been that red-haired singing woman whom he once——

HEDDA. Yes, very likely.

MRS. ELVSTED. For I remember they used to say of her that she carried loaded firearms.

HEDDA. Oh—then of course it must have been she.

MRS. ELVSTED [*wringing her hands*]. And now just fancy, Hedda —I hear that this singing-woman—that she is in town again! Oh, I don't know what to do——

HEDDA [*glancing towards the inner room*]. Hush! Here comes Tesman. [*Rises and whispers.*] Thea—all this must remain between you and me.

MRS. ELVSTED [*springing up*]. Oh, yes, yes! for heaven's sake——!

[GEORGE TESMAN, *with a letter in his hand, comes from the right through the inner room.*]

TESMAN. There now—the epistle is finished.

HEDDA. That's right. And now Mrs. Elvsted is just going. Wait a moment—I'll go with you to the garden gate.

TESMAN. Do you think Berta could post the letter, Hedda dear?

HEDDA [*takes it*]. I will tell her to.

[BERTA *enters from the hall.*]

BERTA. Judge Brack wishes to know if Mrs. Tesman will receive him.

HEDDA. Yes, ask Judge Brack to come in. And look here—put this letter in the post.

BERTA [*taking the letter*]. Yes, ma'am.

[*She opens the door for* JUDGE BRACK *and goes out herself.* BRACK *is a man of forty-five; thick-set, but well-built and elastic in his movements. His face is roundish with an aristocratic profile. His hair is short, still almost black, and carefully dressed. His eyes are lively and sparkling. His eyebrows thick. His moustaches are also thick, with short-cut ends. He wears a well-cut walking-suit, a little too youthful for his age. He uses an eye-glass, which he now and then lets drop.*]

JUDGE BRACK [*with his hat in his hand, bowing*]. May one venture to call so early in the day?

HEDDA. Of course one may.

TESMAN [*presses his hand*]. You are welcome at any time. [*Introducing him*]. Judge Brack—Miss Rysing——

HEDDA. Oh——!

BRACK [*bowing*]. Ah—delighted——

HEDDA [*looks at him and laughs*]. It's nice to have a look at you by daylight, Judge!

BRACK. Do you find me—altered?

HEDDA. A little younger, I think.

BRACK. Thank you so much.

TESMAN. But what do you think of Hedda—eh? Doesn't she look flourishing? She has actually——

HEDDA. Oh, do leave me alone. You haven't thanked Judge Brack for all the trouble he has taken——

BRACK. Oh, nonsense—it was a pleasure to me——

HEDDA. Yes, you are a friend indeed. But here stands Thea all impatience to be off—so *au revoir,* Judge. I shall be back again presently. [*Mutual salutations.* MRS. ELVSTED *and* HEDDA *go out by the hall door.*]

BRACK. Well,—is your wife tolerably satisfied——

TESMAN. Yes, we can't thank you sufficiently. Of course she talks of a little re-arrangement here and there; and one or two things are still wanting. We shall have to buy some additional trifles.

BRACK. Indeed!

TESMAN. But we won't trouble you about these things. Hedda says she herself will look after what is wanting.—— Shan't we sit down? Eh?

BRACK. Thanks, for a moment. [*Seats himself beside the table.*] There is something I wanted to speak to you about, my dear Tesman.

TESMAN. Indeed? Ah, I understand! [*seating himself*] I suppose it's the serious part of the frolic that is coming now. Eh?

BRACK. Oh, the money question is not so very pressing; though, for that matter, I wish we had gone a little more economically to work.

TESMAN. But that would never have done, you know! Think of Hedda, my dear fellow! You, who know her so well——. I couldn't possibly ask her to put up with a shabby style of living!

BRACK. No, no—that is just the difficulty.

TESMAN. And then—fortunately—it can't be long before I receive my appointment.

BRACK. Well, you see—such things are often apt to hang fire for a time.

TESMAN. Have you heard anything definite? Eh?

BRACK. Nothing exactly definite—— [*interrupting himself*] But, by-the-bye—I have one piece of news for you.

TESMAN. Well?

BRACK. Your old friend, Eilert Lövborg, has returned to town.

TESMAN. I know that already.

BRACK. Indeed! How did you learn it?

TESMAN. From that lady who went out with Hedda.

BRACK. Really? What was her name? I didn't quite catch it.

TESMAN. Mrs. Elvsted.

BRACK. Aha—Sheriff Elvsted's wife? Of course—he has been living up in their regions.

TESMAN. And fancy—I'm delighted to hear that he is quite a reformed character!

BRACK. So they say.

TESMAN. And then he has published a new book—eh?

BRACK. Yes, indeed he has.

TESMAN. And I hear it has made some sensation!

BRACK. Quite an unusual sensation.

TESMAN. Fancy—isn't that good news! A man of such extraordinary talents—— I felt so grieved to think that he had gone irretrievably to ruin.

BRACK. That was what everybody thought.

TESMAN. But I cannot imagine what he will take to now! How in the world will he be able to make his living? Eh?

[*During the last words,* HEDDA *has entered by the hall door.*]

HEDDA [*to* BRACK, *laughing with a touch of scorn*]. Tesman is forever worrying about how people are to make their living.

TESMAN. Well, you see, dear—we were talking about poor Eilert Lövborg.

HEDDA [*glancing at him rapidly*]. Oh, indeed? [*Seats herself in the arm-chair beside the stove and asks indifferently.*] What is the matter with him?

TESMAN. Well—no doubt he has run through all his property long ago; and he can scarcely write a new book every year—eh? So I really can't see what is to become of him.

BRACK. Perhaps I can give you some information on that point.

TESMAN. Indeed!

BRACK. You must remember that his relations have a good deal of influence.

TESMAN. Oh, his relations, unfortunately have entirely washed their hands of him.

BRACK. At one time they called him the hope of the family.

TESMAN. At one time, yes! But he has put an end to all that.

HEDDA. Who knows? [*with a slight smile*] I hear they have reclaimed him up at Sheriff Elvsted's——

BRACK. And then this book that he has published——

TESMAN. Well, well, I hope to goodness they may find something for him to do. I have just written to him. I asked him to come and see us this evening, Hedda dear.

BRACK. But, my dear fellow, you are booked for my bachelors' party this evening. You promised on the pier last night.

HEDDA. Had you forgotten, Tesman?

TESMAN. Yes, I had utterly forgotten.

BRACK. But it doesn't matter, for you may be sure he won't come.

TESMAN. What makes you think that? Eh?

BRACK [*with a little hesitation, rising and resting his hands on the back of his chair*]. My dear Tesman—and you too, Mrs. Tesman—I think I ought not to keep you in the dark about something that—that——

TESMAN. That concerns Eilert——?

BRACK. Both you and him.

TESMAN. Well, my dear Judge, out with it.

BRACK. You must be prepared to find your appointment deferred longer than you desired or expected.

TESMAN [*jumping up uneasily*]. Is there some hitch about it? Eh?

BRACK. The nomination may perhaps be made conditional on the result of a competition——

TESMAN. Competition! Think of that, Hedda!

HEDDA [*learns farther back in the chair*]. Aha—aha!

TESMAN. But who can my competitor be? Surely not——?

BRACK. Yes, precisely—Eilert Lövborg.

TESMAN [*clasping his hands*]. No, no—it's quite inconceivable! Quite impossible! Eh?

BRACK. H'm—that is what it may come to, all the same.

TESMAN. Well but, Judge Brack—it would show the most incredible lack of consideration for me. [*Gesticulates with his arms.*] For—just think—I'm a married man. We have been married on the strength of these prospects, Hedda and I; and run deep into debt; and borrowed money from Aunt Julia too. Good heavens, they had as good as promised me the appointment. Eh?

BRACK. Well, well, well—no doubt you will get it in the end; only after a contest.

HEDDA [*immovable in her arm-chair*]. Fancy, Tesman, there will be a sort of sporting interest in that.

TESMAN. Why, my dearest Hedda, how can you be so indifferent about it?

HEDDA [*as before*]. I am not at all indifferent. I am most eager to see who wins.

BRACK. In any case, Mrs. Tesman, it is best that you should know how matters stand. I mean—before you set about the little purchases I hear you are threatening.

HEDDA. This can make no difference.

BRACK. Indeed! Then I have no more to say. Good-bye! [*to* TESMAN] I shall look in on my way back from my afternoon walk, and take you home with me.

TESMAN. Oh yes, yes—your news has quite upset me.

HEDDA [*reclining, holds out her hand*]. Good-bye, Judge; and be sure you call in the afternoon.

BRACK. Many thanks. Good-bye, good-bye!

TESMAN [*accompanying him to the door*]. Good-bye, my dear Judge! You must really excuse me——

[JUDGE BRACK *goes out by the hall door.*]

TESMAN [*crosses the room*]. Oh, Hedda—one should never rush into adventures. Eh?

HEDDA [*looks at him, smiling*]. Do you do that?

TESMAN. Yes, dear—there is no denying—it was adventurous to go and marry and set up house upon mere expectations.

HEDDA. Perhaps you are right there.

TESMAN. Well—at all events, we have our delightful home, Hedda! Fancy, the home we both dreamed of—the home we were in love with, I may almost say. Eh?

HEDDA [*rising slowly and wearily*]. It was part of our compact that we were to go into society—to keep open house.

TESMAN. Yes, if you only knew how I had been looking forward to it! Fancy—to see you as hostess—in a select circle? Eh? Well, well, well—for the present we shall have to get on without society, Hedda—only to invite Aunt Julia now and then.—Oh, I intended you to lead such an utterly different life, dear——!

HEDDA. Of course I cannot have my man in livery just yet.

TESMAN. Oh no, unfortunately. It would be out of the question for us to keep a footman, you know.

HEDDA. And the saddle-horse I was to have had——

TESMAN [*aghast*]. The saddle-horse!

HEDDA. ——I suppose I must not think of that now.

TESMAN. Good heavens, no!—that's as clear as daylight.

HEDDA [*goes up the room*]. Well, I shall have one thing at least to kill time with in the meanwhile.

TESMAN [*beaming*]. Oh, thank heaven for that! What is it, Hedda? Eh?

HEDDA [*in the middle doorway, looks at him with covert scorn*]. My pistols, George.

TESMAN [*in alarm*]. Your pistols!

HEDDA [*with cold eyes*]. General Gabler's pistols.

[*She goes out through the inner room, to the left.*]

TESMAN [*rushes up to the middle doorway and calls after her*]. No, for heaven's sake, Hedda darling—don't touch those dangerous things! For my sake, Hedda! Eh?

ACT II

The room at the TESMANS' *as in the first act, except that the piano has been removed, and an elegant little writing-table with book-shelves put in its place. A smaller table stands near the sofa at the left. Most of the bouquets have been taken away.* MRS. ELVSTED'S *bouquet is upon the large table in front.—It is afternoon.*

[HEDDA, *dressed to receive callers, is alone in the room. She stands by the open glass door, loading a revolver. The fellow to it lies in an open pistol-case on the writing-table.*]

HEDDA [*looks down the garden, and calls*]. So you are here again, Judge!

BRACK [*is heard calling from a distance*]. As you see, Mrs. Tesman!

HEDDA [*raises the pistol and points*]. Now I'll shoot you, Judge Brack!

BRACK [*calling unseen*]. No, no, no! Don't stand aiming at me!

HEDDA. This is what comes of sneaking in by the back way. [*She fires.*]

BRACK [*nearer*]. Are you out of your senses——!

HEDDA. Dear me—did I happen to hit you?

BRACK [*still outside*]. I wish you would let these pranks alone!

HEDDA. Come in then, Judge.

[JUDGE BRACK, *dressed as though for a men's party, enters by the glass door. He carries a light overcoat over his arm.*]

BRACK. What the deuce—haven't you tired of that sport, yet? What are you shooting at?

HEDDA. Oh, I am only firing in the air.

BRACK [*gently takes the pistol out of her hand*]. Allow me, madam! [*Looks at it.*] Ah—I know this pistol well! [*Looks around.*] Where is the case? Ah, here it is. [*Lays the pistol in it, and shuts it.*] Now we won't play at that game any more to-day.

HEDDA. Then what in heaven's name would you have me do with myself?

BRACK. Have you had no visitors?

HEDDA [*closing the glass door*]. Not one. I suppose all our set are still out of town.

BRACK. And is Tesman not at home either?

HEDDA [*at the writing-table, putting the pistol-case in a drawer which she shuts*]. No. He rushed off to his aunt's directly after lunch; he didn't expect you so early.

BRACK. H'm—how stupid of me not to have thought of that!

HEDDA [*turning her head to look at him*]. Why stupid?

BRACK. Because if I had thought of it I should have come a little—earlier.

HEDDA [*crossing the room*]. Then you would have found no one to receive you; for I have been in my room changing my dress ever since lunch.

BRACK. And is there no sort of little chink that we could hold a parley through?

HEDDA. You have forgotten to arrange one.

BRACK. That was another piece of stupidity.

HEDDA. Well, we must just settle down here—and wait. Tesman is not likely to be back for some time yet.

BRACK. Never mind; I shall not be impatient.

[HEDDA *seats herself in the corner of the sofa.* BRACK *lays his overcoat over the back of the nearest chair, and sits down, but keeps his hat in his hand. A short silence. They look at each other.*]

HEDDA. Well?

BRACK [*in the same tone*]. Well?

HEDDA. I spoke first.

BRACK [*bending a little forward*]. Come, let us have a cosy little chat, Mrs. Hedda.

HEDDA [*leaning further back in the sofa*]. Does it not seem like a whole eternity since our last talk? Of course I don't count those few words yesterday evening and this morning.

BRACK. You mean since our last confidential talk? Our last *tête-à-tête?*

HEDDA. Well, yes—since you put it so.

BRACK. Not a day has passed but I have wished that you were home again.

HEDDA. And I have done nothing but wish the same thing.

BRACK. You? Really, Mrs. Hedda? And I thought you had been enjoying your tour so much!

HEDDA. Oh, yes, you may be sure of that!

BRACK. But Tesman's letters spoke of nothing but happiness.

HEDDA. Oh, Tesman! You see, he thinks nothing so delightful as grubbing in libraries and making copies of old parchments, or whatever you call them.

BRACK [*with a spice of malice*]. Well, that is his vocation in life—or part of it at any rate.

HEDDA. Yes, of course; and no doubt when it's your vocation—— But *I!* Oh, my dear Mr. Brack, how mortally bored I have been.

BRACK [*sympathetically*]. Do you really say so? In downright earnest?

HEDDA. Yes, you can surely understand it——! To go for six whole months without meeting a soul that knew anything of our circle, or could talk about the things we are interested in.

BRACK. Yes, yes—I too should feel that a deprivation.

HEDDA. And then, what I found most intolerable of all——

BRACK. Well?

HEDDA. ——was being everlastingly in the company of—one and the same person——

BRACK [*with a nod of assent*]. Morning, noon, and night, yes—at all possible times and seasons.

HEDDA. I said "everlastingly."

BRACK. Just so. But I should have thought, with our excellent Tesman, one could——

HEDDA. Tesman is—a specialist, my dear Judge.

BRACK. Undeniably.

HEDDA. And specialists are not at all amusing to travel with. Not in the long run at any rate.

BRACK. Not even—the specialist one happens to love?

HEDDA. Faugh—don't use that sickening word!

BRACK [*taken aback*]. What do you say, Mrs. Hedda?

HEDDA [*half laughing, half irritated*]. You should just try it! To hear of nothing but the history of civilization, morning, noon, and night——

BRACK. Everlastingly.

HEDDA. Yes, yes, yes! And then all this about the domestic industry of the middle ages——! That's the most disgusting part of it!

BRACK [*looks searchingly at her*]. But tell me—in that case, how am I to understand your——? H'm——

HEDDA. My accepting George Tesman, you mean?

BRACK. Well, let us put it so.

HEDDA. Good heavens, do you see anything so wonderful in that?

BRACK. Yes and no—Mrs. Hedda.

HEDDA. I had positively danced myself tired, my dear Judge. My day was done—— [*with a slight shudder*] Oh no—I won't say that; nor think it either!

BRACK. You have assuredly no reason to.

HEDDA. Oh, reasons—— [*watching him closely*] And George Tesman—after all, you must admit that he is correctness itself.

BRACK. His correctness and respectability are beyond all question.

HEDDA. And I don't see anything absolutely ridiculous about him.—Do you?

BRACK. Ridiculous? N—no—I shouldn't exactly say so——

HEDDA. Well—and his powers of research, at all events, are untiring.—I see no reason why he should not one day come to the front, after all.

BRACK [*looks at her hesitatingly*]. I thought that you, like every one else, expected him to attain the highest distinction.

HEDDA [*with an expression of fatigue*]. Yes, so I did.—And then, since he was bent, at all hazards, on being allowed to provide for me—I really don't know why I should not have accepted his offer?

BRACK. No—if you look at it in that light——

HEDDA. It was more than my other adorers were prepared to do for me, my dear Judge.

BRACK [*laughing*]. Well, I can't answer for all the rest; but as for myself, you know quite well that I have always entertained a —a certain respect for the marriage tie—for marriage as an institution, Mrs. Hedda.

HEDDA [*jestingly*]. Oh, I assure you I have never cherished any hopes with respect to you.

BRACK. All I require is a pleasant and intimate interior, where I can make myself useful in every way, and am free to come and go as—as a trusted friend——

HEDDA. Of the master of the house, do you mean?

BRACK [*bowing*]. Frankly—of the mistress first of all; but of course of the master, too, in the second place. Such a triangular friendship —if I may call it so—is really a great convenience for all parties, let me tell you.

HEDDA. Yes, I have many a time longed for some one to make a third on our travels. Oh—those railway-carriage *tête-à-têtes*——!

BRACK. Fortunately your wedding journey is over now.

HEDDA [*shaking her head*]. Not by a long—long way. I have only arrived at a station on the line.

BRACK. Well, then the passengers jump out and move about a little, Mrs. Hedda.

HEDDA. I never jump out.

BRACK. Really?

HEDDA. No—because there is always some one standing by to——

BRACK [*laughing*]. To look at your ankles, do you mean?

HEDDA. Precisely.

BRACK. Well but, dear me——

HEDDA [*with a gesture of repulsion*]. I won't have it. I would rather keep my seat where I happen to be—and continue the *tête-à-tête*.

BRACK. But suppose a third person were to jump in and join the couple.

HEDDA. Ah—that is quite another matter!

BRACK. A trusted, sympathetic friend——

HEDDA. ——with a fund of conversation on all sorts of lively topics——

BRACK. ——and not the least bit of a specialist!

HEDDA [*with an audible sigh*]. Yes, that would be a relief indeed.

BRACK [*hears the front door open, and glances in that direction*]. The triangle is completed.

HEDDA [*half aloud*]. And on goes the train.

[GEORGE TESMAN, *in a gray walking-suit, with a soft felt hat, enters from the hall. He has a number of unbound books under his arm and in his pockets.*]

TESMAN [*goes up to the table beside the corner settee*]. Ouf—what a load for a warm day—all these books. [*Lays them on the table.*] I'm positively perspiring, Hedda. Hallo—are you there already, my dear Judge? Eh? Berta didn't tell me.

BRACK [*rising*]. I came in through the garden.

HEDDA. What books have you got there?

TESMAN [*stands looking them through*]. Some new books on my special subjects—quite indispensable to me.

HEDDA. Your special subjects?

BRACK. Yes, books on his special subjects, Mrs. Tesman. [BRACK *and* HEDDA *exchange a confidential smile.*]

HEDDA. Do you need still more books on your special subjects?

TESMAN. Yes, my dear Hedda, one can never have too many of them. Of course one must keep up with all that is written and published.

HEDDA. Yes, I suppose one must.

TESMAN [*searching among his books*]. And look here—I have got hold of Eilert Lövborg's new book too. [*offering it to her*] Perhaps you would like to glance through it, Hedda? Eh?

HEDDA. No, thank you. Or rather—afterwards perhaps.

TESMAN. I looked into it a little on the way home.

BRACK. Well, what do you think of it—as a specialist?

TESMAN. I think it shows quite remarkable soundness of judgment. He never wrote like that before. [*putting the books together*] Now I shall take all these into my study. I'm longing to cut the leaves——! And then I must change my clothes. [*to* BRACK] I suppose we needn't start just yet? Eh?

BRACK. Oh, dear no—there is not the slightest hurry.

TESMAN. Well then, I will take my time. [*Is going with his books, but stops in the doorway and turns.*] By-the-bye, Hedda—Aunt Julia is not coming this evening.

HEDDA. Not coming? Is it that affair of the bonnet that keeps her away?

TESMAN. Oh, not at all. How could you think such a thing of Aunt Julia? Just fancy——! The fact is, Aunt Rina is very ill.

HEDDA. She always is.

TESMAN. Yes, but to-day she is much worse than usual, poor dear.

HEDDA. Oh, then it's only natural that her sister should remain with her. I must bear my disappointment.

TESMAN. And you can't imagine, dear, how delighted Aunt Julia seemed to be—because you had come home looking so flourishing!

HEDDA [*half aloud, rising*]. Oh, those everlasting aunts!

TESMAN. What?

HEDDA [*going to the glass door*]. Nothing.

TESMAN. Oh, all right.

[*He goes through the inner room, out to the right.*]

BRACK. What bonnet were you talking about?

HEDDA. Oh, it was a little episode with Miss Tesman this morning. She had laid down her bonnet on the chair there—[*Looks at him and smiles.*]—And I pretended to think it was the servant's.

BRACK [*shaking his head*]. Now my dear Mrs. Hedda, how could you do such a thing? To that excellent old lady, too!

HEDDA [*nervously crossing the room*]. Well, you see—these impulses come over me all of a sudden; and I cannot resist them. [*Throws herself down in the easy-chair by the stove.*] Oh, I don't know how to explain it.

BRACK [*behind the easy-chair*]. You are not really happy—that is at the bottom of it.

HEDDA [*looking straight before her*]. I know of no reason why I should be—happy. Perhaps you can give me one?

BRACK. Well—amongst other things, because you have got exactly the home you had set your heart on.

HEDDA [*looks up at him and laughs*]. Do you too believe in that legend?

BRACK. Is there nothing in it, then?

HEDDA. Oh, yes, there is something in it.

BRACK. Well?

HEDDA. There is this in it, that I made use of Tesman to see me home from evening parties last summer——

BRACK. I, unfortunately, had to go quite a different way.

HEDDA. That's true. I know you were going a different way last summer.

BRACK [*laughing*]. Oh fie, Mrs. Hedda! Well, then—you and Tesman——?

HEDDA. Well, we happened to pass here one evening; Tesman, poor fellow, was writhing in the agony of having to find conversation; so I took pity on the learned man——

BRACK [*smiles doubtfully*]. You took pity? H'm——

HEDDA. Yes, I really did. And so—to help him out of his torment—I happened to say, in pure thoughtlessness, that I should like to live in this villa.

BRACK. No more than that?

HEDDA. Not that evening.

BRACK. But afterwards?

HEDDA. Yes, my thoughtlessness had consequences, my dear Judge.

BRACK. Unfortunately that too often happens, Mrs. Hedda.

HEDDA. Thanks! So you see it was this enthusiasm for Secretary Falk's villa that first constituted a bond of sympathy between George Tesman and me. From that came our engagement and our marriage, and our wedding journey, and all the rest of it. Well, well, my dear Judge—as you make your bed so you must lie, I could almost say.

BRACK. This is exquisite! And you really cared not a rap about it all the time?

HEDDA. No, heaven knows I didn't.

BRACK. But now? Now that we have made it so homelike for you?

HEDDA. Uh—the rooms all seem to smell of lavender and dried rose-leaves.—But perhaps it's Aunt Julia that has brought that scent with her.

BRACK [*laughing*]. No, I think it must be a legacy from the late Mrs. Secretary Falk.

HEDDA. Yes, there is an odor of mortality about it. It reminds me of a bouquet—the day after the ball. [*Clasps her hands behind her head, leans back in her chair and looks at him.*] Oh, my dear Judge—you cannot imagine how horribly I shall bore myself here.

BRACK. Why should not you, too, find some sort of vocation in life, Mrs. Hedda?

HEDDA. A vocation—that should attract me?

BRACK. If possible, of course.

HEDDA. Heaven knows what sort of a vocation that could be. I often wonder whether—— [*breaking off*] But that would never do either.

BRACK. Who can tell? Let me hear what it is.

HEDDA. Whether I might not get Tesman to go into politics, I mean.

BRACK [*laughing*]. Tesman? No, really now, political life is not the thing for him—not at all in his line.

HEDDA. No, I daresay not.—But if I could get him into it all the same?

BRACK. Why—what satisfaction could you find in that? If he is not fitted for that sort of thing, why should you want to drive him into it?

HEDDA. Because I am bored, I tell you! [*after a pause*] So you think it quite out of the question that Tesman should ever get into the ministry?

BRACK. H'm—you see, my dear Mrs. Hedda—to get into the ministry, he would have to be a tolerably rich man.

HEDDA [*rising impatiently*]. Yes, there we have it! It is this genteel poverty I have managed to drop into——! [*Crosses the room.*] That is what makes life so pitiable! So utterly ludicrous!—For that's what it is.

BRACK. Now *I* should say the fault lay elsewhere.

HEDDA. Where, then?

BRACK. You have never gone through any really stimulating experience.

HEDDA. Anything serious, you mean?

BRACK. Yes, you may call it so. But now you may perhaps have one in store.

HEDDA [*tossing her head*]. Oh, you're thinking of the annoyances about this wretched professorship! But that must be Tesman's own affair. I assure you I shall not waste a thought upon it.

BRACK. No, no, I daresay not. But suppose now that what people call—in elegant language—a solemn responsibility were to come upon you? [*smiling*] A new responsibility, Mrs. Hedda?

HEDDA [*angrily*]. Be quiet! Nothing of that sort will ever happen!

BRACK [*warily*]. We will speak of this again a year hence—at the very outside.

HEDDA [*curtly*]. I have no turn for anything of the sort, Judge Brack. No responsibilities for me!

BRACK. Are you so unlike the generality of women as to have no turn for duties which——?

HEDDA [*beside the glass door*]. Oh, be quiet, I tell you!—I often think there is only one thing in the world I have any turn for.

BRACK [*drawing near to her*]. And what is that, if I may ask?

HEDDA [*stands looking out*]. Boring myself to death. Now you know it. [*Turns, looks towards the inner room, and laughs.*] Yes, as I thought! Here comes the Professor.

BRACK [*softly, in a tone of warning*]. Come, come, come, Mrs. Hedda!

[GEORGE TESMAN, *dressed for the party, with his gloves and hat in his hand, enters from the right through the inner room.*]

TESMAN. Hedda, has no message come from Eilert Lövborg? Eh?

HEDDA. No.

TESMAN. Then you'll see he'll be here presently.

BRACK. Do you really think he will come?

TESMAN. Yes, I am almost sure of it. For what you were telling us this morning must have been a mere floating rumor.

BRACK. You think so?

TESMAN. At any rate, Aunt Julia said she did not believe for a moment that he would ever stand in my way again. Fancy that!

BRACK. Well then, that's all right.

TESMAN [*placing his hat and gloves on a chair on the right*]. Yes, but you must really let me wait for him as long as possible.

BRACK. We have plenty of time yet. None of my guests will arrive before seven or half-past.

TESMAN. Then meanwhile we can keep Hedda company, and see what happens. Eh?

HEDDA [*placing* BRACK's *hat and overcoat upon the corner settee*]. And at the worst Mr. Lövborg can remain here with me.

BRACK [*offering to take his things*]. Oh, allow me, Mrs. Tesman! —What do you mean by "At the worst"?

HEDDA. If he won't go with you and Tesman.

TESMAN [*looks dubiously at her*]. But, Hedda dear—do you think it would quite do for him to remain with you? Eh? Remember, Aunt Julia can't come.

HEDDA. No, but Mrs. Elvsted is coming. We three can have a cup of tea together.

TESMAN. Oh, yes, that will be all right.

BRACK [*smiling*]. And that would perhaps be the safest plan for him.

HEDDA. Why so?

BRACK. Well, you know, Mrs. Tesman, how you used to gird at my little bachelor parties. You declared they were adapted only for men of the strictest principles.

HEDDA. But no doubt Mr. Lövborg's principles are strict enough now. A converted sinner——

[BERTA *appears at the hall door.*]

BERTA. There's a gentleman asking if you are at home, ma'am——

HEDDA. Well, show him in.

TESMAN [*softly*]. I'm sure it is he! Fancy that!

[EILERT LÖVBORG *enters from the hall. He is slim and lean; of the same age as* TESMAN, *but looks older and somewhat worn-out. His hair and beard are of a blackish brown, his face long and pale, but with patches of color on the cheek-bones. He is dressed in a well-cut black visiting suit, quite new. He has dark gloves and a silk hat. He stops near the door, and makes a rapid bow, seeming somewhat embarrassed.*]

TESMAN [*goes up to him and shakes him warmly by the hand*]. Well, my dear Eilert—so at last we meet again!

EILERT LÖVBORG [*speaks in a subdued voice*]. Thanks for your letter, Tesman. [*approaching* HEDDA] Will you too shake hands with me, Mrs. Tesman?

HEDDA [*taking his hand*]. I am glad to see you, Mr. Lövborg. [*with a motion of her hand*] I don't know whether you two gentlemen——?

LÖVBORG [*bowing slightly*]. Judge Brack, I think.

BRACK [*doing likewise*]. Oh, yes,—in the old days——

TESMAN [*to* LÖVBORG, *with his hands on his shoulders*]. And now you must make yourself entirely at home, Eilert! Mustn't he, Hedda? —For I hear you are going to settle in town again? Eh?

LÖVBORG. Yes, I am.

TESMAN. Quite right, quite right. Let me tell you, I have got hold of your new book; but I haven't had time to read it yet.

LÖVBORG. You may spare yourself the trouble.

TESMAN. Why so?

LÖVBORG. Because there is very little in it.

TESMAN. Just fancy—how can you say so?

BRACK. But it has been very much praised, I hear.

LÖVBORG. That was what I wanted; so I put nothing into the book but what every one would agree with.

BRACK. Very wise of you.

TESMAN. Well but, my dear Eilert——!

LÖVBORG. For now I mean to win myself a position again—to make a fresh start.

TESMAN [*a little embarrassed*]. Ah, that is what you wish to do? Eh?

LÖVBORG [*smiling, lays down his hat, and draws a packet, wrapped in paper, from his coat pocket*]. But when this one appears, George Tesman, you will have to read it. For this is the real book—the book I have put my true self into.

TESMAN. Indeed? And what is it?

LÖVBORG. It is the continuation.

TESMAN. The continuation? Of what?

LÖVBORG. Of the book.

TESMAN. Of the new book?

LÖVBORG. Of course.

TESMAN. Why, my dear Eilert—does it not come down to our own days?

LÖVBORG. Yes, it does; and this one deals with the future.

TESMAN. With the future! But, good heavens, we know nothing of the future!

LÖVBORG. No; but there is a thing or two to be said about it all the same. [*Opens the packet.*] Look here——

TESMAN. Why, that's not your handwriting.

LÖVBORG. I dictated it. [*turning over the pages*] It falls into two sections. The first deals with the civilizing forces of the future. And here is the second—[*running through the pages towards the end*]—forecasting the probable line of development.

TESMAN. How odd now! I should never have thought of writing anything of that sort.

HEDDA [*at the glass door, drumming on the pane*]. H'm—I daresay not.

LÖVBORG [*replacing the manuscript in its paper and laying the packet on the table*]. I brought it, thinking I might read you a little of it this evening.

TESMAN. That was very good of you, Eilert. But this evening——? [*looking at* BRACK] I don't quite see how we can manage it——

LÖVBORG. Well then, some other time. There is no hurry.

BRACK. I must tell you, Mr. Lövborg—there is a little gathering at my house this evening—mainly in honor of Tesman, you know——

LÖVBORG [*looking for his hat*]. Oh—then I won't detain you——

BRACK. No, but listen—will you not do me the favor of joining us?

LÖVBORG [*curtly and decidedly*]. No, I can't—thank you very much.

BRACK. Oh, nonsense—do! We shall be quite a select little circle. And I assure you we shall have a "lively time," as Mrs. Hed—as Mrs. Tesman says.

LÖVBORG. I have no doubt of it. But nevertheless——

BRACK. And then you might bring your manuscript with you, and read it to Tesman at my house. I could give you a room to yourselves.

TESMAN. Yes, think of that, Eilert,—why shouldn't you? Eh?

HEDDA [*interposing*]. But, Tesman, if Mr. Lövborg would really rather not! I am sure Mr. Lövborg is much more inclined to remain here and have supper with me.

LÖVBORG [*looking at her*]. With you, Mrs. Tesman?

HEDDA. And with Mrs. Elvsted.

LÖVBORG. Ah—— [*lightly*] I saw her for a moment this morning.

HEDDA. Did you? Well, she is coming this evening. So you see you are almost bound to remain, Mr. Lövborg, or she will have no one to see her home.

LÖVBORG. That's true. Many thanks, Mrs. Tesman—in that case I will remain.

HEDDA. Then I have one or two orders to give the servant——

[*She goes to the hall door and rings.* BERTA *enters.* HEDDA *talks to her in a whisper, and points towards the inner room.* BERTA *nods and goes out again.*]

TESMAN [*at the same time, to* LÖVBORG]. Tell me, Eilert—is it this new subject—the future—that you are going to lecture about?

LÖVBORG. Yes.

TESMAN. They told me at the bookseller's, that you are going to deliver a course of lectures this autumn.

LÖVBORG. That is my intention. I hope you won't take it ill, Tesman.

TESMAN. Oh no, not in the least! But——?

LÖVBORG. I can quite understand that it must be disagreeable to you.

TESMAN [*cast down*]. Oh, I can't expect you, out of consideration for me, to——

LÖVBORG. But I shall wait till you have received your appointment.

TESMAN. Will you wait? Yes, but—yes, but—are you not going to compete with me? Eh?

LÖVBORG. No; it is only the moral victory I care for.

TESMAN. Why, bless me—then Aunt Julia was right after all! Oh yes—I knew it! Hedda! Just fancy—Eilert Lövborg is not going to stand in our way!

HEDDA [*curtly*]. Our way? Pray leave me out of the question.

[*She goes up towards the inner room, where* BERTA *is placing a tray with decanters and glasses on the table.* HEDDA *nods approval, and comes forward again.* BERTA *goes out.*]

TESMAN [*at the same time*]. And you, Judge Brack—what do you say to this? Eh?

BRACK. Well, I say that a moral victory—h'm—may be all very fine——

TESMAN. Yes, certainly. But all the same——

HEDDA [*looking at* TESMAN *with a cold smile*]. You stand there looking as if you were thunderstruck——

TESMAN. Yes—so I am—I almost think——

BRACK. Don't you see, Mrs. Tesman, a thunderstorm has just passed over?

HEDDA [*pointing towards the inner room*]. Will you not take a glass of cold punch, gentlemen?

BRACK [*looking at his watch*]. A stirrup-cup? Yes, it wouldn't come amiss.

TESMAN. A capital idea, Hedda! Just the thing! Now that the weight has been taken off my mind——

HEDDA. Will you not join them, Mr. Lövborg?

LÖVBORG [*with a gesture of refusal*]. No, thank you. Nothing for me.

BRACK. Why, bless me—cold punch is surely not poison.

LÖVBORG. Perhaps not for every one.

HEDDA. I will keep Mr. Lövborg company in the meantime.

TESMAN. Yes, yes, Hedda dear, do.

[*He and* BRACK *go into the inner room, seat themselves, drink punch, smoke cigarettes, and carry on a lively conversation during what follows.* EILERT LÖVBORG *remains beside the stove.* HEDDA *goes to the writing-table.*]

HEDDA [*raising her voice a little*]. Do you care to look at some photographs, Mr. Lövborg? You know Tesman and I made a tour in the Tyrol on our way home?

[*She takes up an album, and places it on the table beside the sofa, in the further corner of which she seats herself.* EILERT LÖVBORG *approaches, stops, and looks at her. Then he takes a chair and seats himself at her left, with his back towards the inner room.*]

HEDDA [*opening the album*]. Do you see this range of mountains, Mr. Lövborg? It's the Ortler group. Tesman has written the name underneath. Here it is: "The Ortler group near Meran."

LÖVBORG [*who has never taken his eyes off her, says softly and slowly*]. Hedda—Gabler!

HEDDA [*glancing hastily at him*]. Ah! Hush!

LÖVBORG [*repeats softly*]. Hedda Gabler!

HEDDA [*looking at the album*]. That was my name in the old days—when we two knew each other.

LÖVBORG. And I must teach myself never to say Hedda Gabler again—never, as long as I live.

HEDDA [*still turning over the pages*]. Yes, you must. And I think you ought to practice in time. The sooner the better, I should say.

LÖVBORG [*in a tone of indignation*]. Hedda Gabler married? And married to—George Tesman!

HEDDA. Yes—so the world goes.

LÖVBORG. Oh, Hedda, Hedda—how could you throw yourself away!

HEDDA [*looks sharply at him*]. What? I can't allow this!

LÖVBORG. What do you mean? [TESMAN *comes into the room and goes towards the sofa.*]

HEDDA [*hears him coming and says in an indifferent tone*]. And this is a view from the Val d'Ampezzo, Mr. Lövborg. Just look at these peaks! [*Looks affectionately up at* TESMAN.] What's the name of these curious peaks, dear?

TESMAN. Let me see? Oh, those are the Dolomites.

HEDDA. Yes, that's it!—Those are the Dolomites, Mr. Lövborg.

TESMAN. Hedda dear,—I only wanted to ask whether I shouldn't bring you a little punch after all? For yourself at any rate—eh?

HEDDA. Yes, do, please; and perhaps a few biscuits.

TESMAN. No cigarettes?

HEDDA. No.

TESMAN. Very well.

[*He goes into the inner room and out to the right.* BRACK *sits in the inner room, and keeps an eye from time to time on* HEDDA *and* LÖVBORG.]

LÖVBORG [*softly, as before*]. Answer me, Hedda—how could you go and do this?

HEDDA [*apparently absorbed in the album*]. If you continue to say *du* to me I won't talk to you.

LÖVBORG. May I not say *du* when we are alone?

HEDDA. No. You may think it; but you mustn't say it.

LÖVBORG. Ah, I understand. It is an offense against George Tesman, whom you—love.

560 you *du*
587 you *de*. After this Lövborg reverts to the formal pronoun, which Hedda uses throughout

HEDDA [*glances at him and smiles*]. Love? What an idea!

LÖVBORG. You don't love him then!

HEDDA. But I won't hear of any sort of unfaithfulness! Remember that.

LÖVBORG. Hedda—answer me one thing——

HEDDA. Hush!

[TESMAN *enters with a small tray from the inner room.*]

TESMAN. Here you are! Isn't this tempting? [*He puts the tray on the table.*]

HEDDA. Why do you bring it yourself?

TESMAN [*filling the glasses*]. Because I think it's such fun to wait upon you, Hedda.

HEDDA. But you have poured out two glasses. Mr. Lövborg said he wouldn't have any——

TESMAN. No, but Mrs. Elvsted will soon be here, won't she?

HEDDA. Yes, by-the-bye—Mrs. Elvsted——

TESMAN. Had you forgotten her? Eh?

HEDDA. We were so absorbed in these photographs. [*Shows him a picture.*] Do you remember this little village?

TESMAN. Oh, it's that one just below the Brenner Pass. It was there we passed the night——

HEDDA. ——and met that lively party of tourists.

TESMAN. Yes, that was the place. Fancy—if we could only have had you with us, Eilert! Eh? [*He returns to the inner room and sits beside* BRACK.]

LÖVBORG. Answer me this one thing, Hedda——

HEDDA. Well?

LÖVBORG. Was there no love in your friendship for me either? Not a spark—not a tinge of love in it?

HEDDA. I wonder if there was? To me it seems as though we were two good comrades—two thoroughly intimate friends. [*smilingly*] You especially were frankness itself.

LÖVBORG. It was you that made me so.

HEDDA. As I look back upon it all, I think there was really something beautiful, something fascinating—something daring—in—in that secret intimacy—that comradeship which no living creature so much as dreamed of.

LÖVBORG. Yes, yes, Hedda! Was there not?—When I used to come to your father's in the afternoon—and the General sat over at the window reading his papers—with his back towards us——

HEDDA. And we two on the corner sofa——

LÖVBORG. Always with the same illustrated paper before us——

HEDDA. For want of an album, yes.

LÖVBORG. Yes, Hedda, and when I made my confessions to you—told you about myself, things that at that time no one else knew! There I would sit and tell you of my escapades—my days and nights of devilment. Oh, Hedda—what was the power in you that forced me to confess these things?

HEDDA. Do you think it was any power in me?

LÖVBORG. How else can I explain it? And all those—those roundabout questions you used to put to me——

HEDDA. Which you understood so particularly well——

LÖVBORG. How could you sit and question me like that? Question me quite frankly——

HEDDA. In roundabout terms, please observe.

LÖVBORG. Yes, but frankly nevertheless. Cross-question me about—all that sort of thing?

HEDDA. And how could you answer, Mr. Lövborg?

LÖVBORG. Yes, that is just what I can't understand—in looking back upon it. But tell me now, Hedda—was there not love at the bottom of our friendship? On your side, did you not feel as though you might purge my stains away if I made you my confessor? Was it not so?

HEDDA. No, not quite.

LÖVBORG. What was your motive, then?

HEDDA. Do you think it quite incomprehensible that a young girl—when it can be done—without any one knowing——

LÖVBORG. Well?

HEDDA. ——should be glad to have a peep, now and then, into a world which——

LÖVBORG. Which——?

HEDDA. ——which she is forbidden to know anything about?

LÖVBORG. So that was it?

HEDDA. Partly. Partly—I almost think.

LÖVBORG. Comradeship in the thirst for life. But why should not that, at any rate, have continued?

HEDDA. The fault was yours.

LÖVBORG. It was you that broke with me.

HEDDA. Yes, when our friendship threatened to develop into something more serious. Shame upon you, Eilert Lövborg! How could you think of wronging your—your frank comrade?

LÖVBORG [*clenching his hands*]. Oh, why did you not carry out your threat? Why did you not shoot me down?

HEDDA. Because I have such a dread of scandal.

LÖVBORG. Yes, Hedda, you are a coward at heart.

HEDDA. A terrible coward. [*changing her tone*] But it was a lucky thing for you. And now you have found ample consolation at the Elvsteds'.

LÖVBORG. I know what Thea has confided to you.

HEDDA. And perhaps you have confided to her something about us?

LÖVBORG. Not a word. She is too stupid to understand anything of that sort.

HEDDA. Stupid?

LÖVBORG. She is stupid about matters of that sort.

HEDDA. And I am cowardly. [*Bends over towards him, without looking him in the face, and says more softly*—] But now I will confide something to you.

LÖVBORG [*eagerly*]. Well?

HEDDA. The fact that I dared not shoot you down——

LÖVBORG. Yes!

HEDDA. ——that was not my most arrant cowardice—that evening.

LÖVBORG [*looks at her a moment, understands, and whispers passionately*]. Oh, Hedda! Hedda Gabler! Now I begin to see a hidden reason beneath our comradeship! You and I——! After all, then, it was your craving for life——

HEDDA [*softly, with a sharp glance*]. Take care! Believe nothing of the sort!

[*Twilight has begun to fall. The hall door is opened from without by* BERTA.]

HEDDA [*closes the album with a bang and calls smilingly*]. Ah, at last! My darling Thea,—come along!

693 **you** *du*

[MRS. ELVSTED *enters from the hall. She is in evening dress. The door is closed behind her.*]

HEDDA [*on the sofa, stretches out her arms towards her*]. My sweet Thea—you can't think how I have been longing for you!

[MRS. ELVSTED, *in passing, exchanges slight salutations with the gentlemen in the inner room, then goes up to the table and gives* HEDDA *her hands.* EILERT LÖVBORG *has risen. He and* MRS. ELVSTED *greet each other with a silent nod.*]

MRS. ELVSTED. Ought I to go in and talk to your husband for a moment?

HEDDA. Oh, not at all. Leave those two alone. They will soon be going.

MRS. ELVSTED. Are they going out?

HEDDA. Yes, to a supper-party.

MRS. ELVSTED [*quickly, to* LÖVBORG]. Not you?

LÖVBORG. No.

HEDDA. Mr. Lövborg remains with us.

MRS. ELVSTED [*takes a chair and is about to seat herself at his side*]. Oh, how nice it is here!

HEDDA. No, thank you, my little Thea! Not there! You'll be good enough to come over here to me. I will sit between you.

MRS. ELVSTED. Yes, just as you please.

[*She goes round the table and seats herself on the sofa on* HEDDA'S *right.* LÖVBORG *re-seats himself on his chair.*]

LÖVBORG [*after a short pause, to* HEDDA]. Is not she lovely to look at?

HEDDA [*lightly stroking her hair*]. Only to look at?

LÖVBORG. Yes. For we two—she and I—we are two real comrades. We have absolute faith in each other; so we can sit and talk with perfect frankness——

HEDDA. Not round about, Mr. Lövborg?

LÖVBORG. Well——

MRS. ELVSTED [*softly, clinging close to* HEDDA]. Oh, how happy I am, Hedda; for, only think, he says I have inspired him too.

HEDDA [*looks at her with a smile*]. Ah! Does he say that, dear?

LÖVBORG. And then she is so brave, Mrs. Tesman!

MRS. ELVSTED. Good heavens—am I brave?

LÖVBORG. Exceedingly—where your comrade is concerned.

HEDDA. Ah, yes—courage! If one only had that!

LÖVBORG. What then? What do you mean?

HEDDA. Then life would perhaps be liveable, after all. [*with a sudden change of tone*] But now, my dearest Thea, you really must have a glass of cold punch.

MRS. ELVSTED. No, thanks—I never take anything of that kind.

HEDDA. Well then, you, Mr. Lövborg.

LÖVBORG. Nor I, thank you.

MRS. ELVSTED. No, he doesn't either.

HEDDA [*looks fixedly at him*]. But if I say you shall?

LÖVBORG. It would be no use.

HEDDA [*laughing*]. Then I, poor creature, have no sort of power over you?

LÖVBORG. Not in that respect.

HEDDA. But seriously, I think you ought to—for your own sake.

MRS. ELVSTED. Why, Hedda——!

LÖVBORG. How so?

HEDDA. Or rather on account of other people.

LÖVBORG. Indeed?

HEDDA. Otherwise people might be apt to suspect that—in your heart of hearts—you did not feel quite secure—quite confident of yourself.

MRS. ELVSTED [*softly*]. Oh please, Hedda——

LÖVBORG. People may suspect what they like—for the present.

MRS. ELVSTED [*joyfully*]. Yes, let them!

HEDDA. I saw it plainly in Judge Brack's face a moment ago.

LÖVBORG. What did you see?

HEDDA. His contemptuous smile, when you dared not go with them into the inner room.

LÖVBORG. Dared not? Of course I preferred to stop here and talk to you.

MRS. ELVSTED. What could be more natural, Hedda?

HEDDA. But the Judge could not guess that. And I saw, too, the way he smiled and glanced at Tesman when you dared not accept his invitation to this wretched little supper-party of his.

LÖVBORG. Dared not! Do you say I dared not?

HEDDA. *I* don't say so. But that was how Judge Brack understood it.

LÖVBORG. Well, let him.

HEDDA. Then you are not going with them?

LÖVBORG. I will stay here with you and Thea.

MRS. ELVSTED. Yes, Hedda—how can you doubt that?

HEDDA [*smiles and nods approvingly to* LÖVBORG]. Firm as a rock! Faithful to your principles, now and forever! Ah, that is how a man should be! [*Turns to* MRS. ELVSTED *and caresses her.*] Well now, what did I tell you, when you came to us this morning in such a state of distraction——

LÖVBORG [*surprised*]. Distraction!

MRS. ELVSTED [*terrified*]. Hedda—oh Hedda——!

HEDDA. You can see for yourself; you haven't the slightest reason to be in such mortal terror—— [*interrupting herself*] There! Now we can all three enjoy ourselves!

LÖVBORG [*who has given a start*]. Ah—what is all this, Mrs. Tesman?

MRS. ELVSTED. Oh my God, Hedda! What are you saying? What are you doing?

HEDDA. Don't get excited! That horrid Judge Brack is sitting watching you.

LÖVBORG. So she was in mortal terror! On my account!

MRS. ELVSTED [*softly and piteously*]. Oh, Hedda—now you have ruined everything!

LÖVBORG [*looks fixedly at her for a moment. His face is distorted*]. So that was my comrade's frank confidence in me?

MRS. ELVSTED [*imploringly*]. Oh, my dearest friend—only let me tell you——

LÖVBORG [*takes one of the glasses of punch, raises it to his lips, and says in a low, husky voice*]. Your health, Thea!

[*He empties the glass, puts it down, and takes the second.*]

MRS. ELVSTED [*softly*]. Oh, Hedda, Hedda—how could you do this?

HEDDA. *I* do it? *I*? Are you crazy?

LÖVBORG. Here's to your health too, Mrs. Tesman. Thanks for the truth. Hurrah for the truth!

[*He empties the glass and is about to re-fill it.*]

HEDDA [*lays her hand on his arm*]. Come, come—no more for the present. Remember you are going out to supper.

MRS. ELVSTED. No, no, no!

HEDDA. Hush! They are sitting watching you.

LÖVBORG [*putting down the glass*]. Now, Thea—tell me the truth——

MRS. ELVSTED. Yes.

LÖVBORG. Did your husband know that you had come after me?

MRS. ELVSTED [*wringing her hands*]. Oh, Hedda—do you hear what he is asking?

LÖVBORG. Was it arranged between you and him that you were to come to town and look after me? Perhaps it was the Sheriff himself that urged you to come? Aha, my dear—no doubt he wanted my help in his office! Or was it at the card-table that he missed me?

MRS. ELVSTED [*softly, in agony*]. Oh, Lövborg, Lövborg——!

LÖVBORG [*seizes a glass and is on the point of filling it*]. Here's a glass for the old Sheriff too!

HEDDA [*preventing him*]. No more just now. Remember, you have to read your manuscript to Tesman.

LÖVBORG [*calmly, putting down the glass*]. It was stupid of me all this, Thea—to take it in this way, I mean. Don't be angry with me, my dear, dear comrade. You shall see—both you and the others—that if I was fallen once—now I have risen again! Thanks to you, Thea.

MRS. ELVSTED [*radiant with joy*]. Oh, heaven be praised——!

[BRACK *has in the meantime looked at his watch. He and* TESMAN *rise and come into the drawing-room.*]

BRACK [*takes his hat and overcoat*]. Well, Mrs. Tesman, our time has come.

HEDDA. I suppose it has.

LÖVBORG [*rising*]. Mine too, Judge Brack.

MRS. ELVSTED [*softly and imploringly*]. Oh, Lövborg, don't do it!

HEDDA [*pinching her arm*]. They can hear you!

MRS. ELVSTED [*with a suppressed shriek*]. Ow!

LÖVBORG [*to* BRACK]. You were good enough to invite me.

BRACK. Well, are you coming after all?

LÖVBORG. Yes, many thanks.

BRACK. I'm delighted——

LÖVBORG [*to* TESMAN, *putting the parcel of MS. in his pocket*].

I should like to show you one or two things before I send it to the printer's.

TESMAN. Fancy—that will be delightful. But, Hedda dear, how is Mrs. Elvsted to get home? Eh?

HEDDA. Oh, that can be managed somehow.

LÖVBORG [*looking towards the ladies*]. Mrs. Elvsted? Of course, I'll come again and fetch her. [*approaching*] At ten or thereabouts, Mrs. Tesman? Will that do?

HEDDA. Certainly. That will do capitally.

TESMAN. Well, then, that's all right. But you must not expect me so early, Hedda.

HEDDA. Oh, you may stop as long—as long as ever you please.

MRS. ELVSTED [*trying to conceal her anxiety*]. Well then, Mr. Lövborg—I shall remain here until you come.

LÖVBORG [*with his hat in his hand*]. Pray do, Mrs. Elvsted.

BRACK. And now off goes the excursion train, gentlemen! I hope we shall have a lively time, as a certain fair lady puts it.

HEDDA. Ah, if only the fair lady could be present unseen——!

BRACK. Why unseen?

HEDDA. In order to hear a little of your liveliness at first hand, Judge Brack.

BRACK [*laughing*]. I should not advise the fair lady to try it.

TESMAN [*also laughing*]. Come, you're a nice one, Hedda! Fancy that!

BRACK. Well, good-bye, good-bye, ladies.

LÖVBORG [*bowing*]. About ten o'clock, then.

[BRACK, LÖVBORG, *and* TESMAN *go out by the hall door. At the same time* BERTA *enters from the inner room with a lighted lamp, which she places on the dining-room table; she goes out by the way she came.*]

MRS. ELVSTED [*who has risen and is wandering restlessly about the room*]. Hedda—Hedda—what will come of all this?

HEDDA. At ten o'clock—he will be here. I can see him already—with vine-leaves in his hair—flushed and fearless——

MRS. ELVSTED. Oh, I hope he may.

HEDDA. And then, you see—then he will have regained control over himself. Then he will be a free man for all his days.

886 **vine-leaves** the garland of Dionysus, symbol of divine intoxication

MRS. ELVSTED. Oh God!—if he would only come as you see him now!

HEDDA. He will come as I see him—so, and not otherwise! [*Rises and approaches* THEA.] You may doubt him as long as you please; I believe in him. And now we will try——

MRS. ELVSTED. You have some hidden motive in this, Hedda!

HEDDA. Yes, I have. I want for once in my life to have power to mold a human destiny.

MRS. ELVSTED. Have you not the power?

HEDDA. I have not—and have never had it.

MRS. ELVSTED. Not your husband's?

HEDDA. Do you think that is worth the trouble? Oh, if you could only understand how poor I am. And fate has made you so rich! [*Clasps her passionately in her arms.*] I think I must burn your hair off, after all.

MRS. ELVSTED. Let me go! Let me go! I am afraid of you, Hedda!

BERTA [*in the middle doorway*]. Tea is laid in the dining-room, ma'am.

HEDDA. Very well. We are coming.

MRS. ELVSTED. No, no, no! I would rather go home alone! At once!

HEDDA. Nonsense! First you shall have a cup of tea, you little stupid. And then—at ten o'clock—Eilert Lövborg will be here—with vine-leaves in his hair. [*She drags* MRS. ELVSTED *almost by force towards the middle doorway.*]

ACT III

The room at the TESMANS'. *The curtains are drawn over the middle doorway, and also over the glass door. The lamp, half turned down, and with a shade over it, is burning on the table. In the stove, the door of which stands open, there has been a fire, which is now nearly burnt out.*

[MRS. ELVSTED, *wrapped in a large shawl, and with her feet upon a foot-rest, sits close to the stove, sunk back in the arm-chair.* HEDDA, *fully dressed, lies sleeping upon the sofa, with a sofa-blanket over her.*]

MRS. ELVSTED [*after a pause, suddenly sits up in her chair, and listens eagerly. Then she sinks back again wearily, moaning to herself*]. Not yet!—Oh God—oh God—not yet!

[BERTA *slips in by the hall door. She has a letter in her hand.*]

MRS. ELVSTED [*turns and whispers eagerly*]. Well—has any one come?

BERTA [*softly*]. Yes, a girl has brought this letter.

MRS. ELVSTED [*quickly, holding out her hand*]. A letter! Give it to me!

BERTA. No, it's for Dr. Tesman, ma'am.

MRS. ELVSTED. Oh, indeed.

BERTA. It was Miss Tesman's servant that brought it. I'll lay it here on the table.

MRS. ELVSTED. Yes, do.

BERTA [*laying down the letter*]. I think I had better put out the lamp. It's smoking.

MRS. ELVSTED. Yes, put it out. It must soon be daylight now.

BERTA [*putting out the lamp*]. It is daylight already, ma'am.

MRS. ELVSTED. Yes, broad day! And no one come back yet——!

BERTA. Lord bless you, ma'am! I guessed how it would be.

MRS. ELVSTED. You guessed?

BERTA. Yes, when I saw that a certain person had come back to town—and that he went off with them. For we've heard enough about that gentleman before now.

MRS. ELVSTED. Don't speak so loud. You will waken Mrs. Tesman.

BERTA [*looks towards the sofa and sighs*]. No, no—let her sleep, poor thing. Shan't I put some wood on the fire?

MRS. ELVSTED. Thanks, not for me.

BERTA. Oh, very well. [*She goes softly out by the hall door.*]

HEDDA [*is awakened by the shutting of the door, and looks up*]. What's that——?

MRS. ELVSTED. It was only the servant——

HEDDA [*looking about her*]. Oh, we're here——! Yes, now I remember. [*Sits erect upon the sofa, stretches herself, and rubs her eyes.*] What o'clock is it, Thea?

MRS. ELVSTED [*looks at her watch*]. It's past seven.

HEDDA. When did Tesman come home?

MRS. ELVSTED. He has not come.

HEDDA. Not come home yet?

MRS. ELVSTED [*rising*]. No one has come.

HEDDA. Think of our watching and waiting here till four in the morning——

MRS. ELVSTED [*wringing her hands*]. And how I watched and waited for him!

HEDDA [*yawns, and says with her hand before her mouth*]. Well, well—we might have spared ourselves the trouble.

MRS. ELVSTED. Did you get a little sleep?

HEDDA. Oh yes; I believe I have slept pretty well. Have you not?

MRS. ELVSTED. Not for a moment. I couldn't, Hedda!—not to save my life.

HEDDA [*rises and goes towards her*]. There, there, there! There's nothing to be so alarmed about. I understand quite well what has happened.

MRS. ELVSTED. Well, what do you think? Won't you tell me?

HEDDA. Why, of course it has been a very late affair at Judge Brack's——

MRS. ELVSTED. Yes, yes, that is clear enough. But all the same——

HEDDA. And then, you see, Tesman hasn't cared to come home and ring us up in the middle of the night. [*laughing*] Perhaps he wasn't inclined to show himself either—immediately after a jollification.

MRS. ELVSTED. But in that case—where can he have gone?

HEDDA. Of course he has gone to his aunts' and slept there. They have his old room ready for him.

MRS. ELVSTED. No, he can't be with them; for a letter has just come for him from Miss Tesman. There it lies.

HEDDA. Indeed? [*Looks at the address.*] Why yes, it's addressed in Aunt Julia's own hand. Well then, he has remained at Judge Brack's. And as for Eilert Lövborg—he is sitting, with vine-leaves in his hair, reading his manuscript.

MRS. ELVSTED. Oh Hedda, you are just saying things you don't believe a bit.

HEDDA. You really are a little blockhead, Thea.

MRS. ELVSTED. Oh yes, I suppose I am.

HEDDA. And how mortally tired you look.

MRS. ELVSTED. Yes, I am mortally tired.

HEDDA. Well then, you must do as I tell you. You must go into my room and lie down for a little while.

MRS. ELVSTED. Oh no, no—I shouldn't be able to sleep.

HEDDA. I am sure you would.

MRS. ELVSTED. Well, but your husband is certain to come soon now; and then I want to know at once——

HEDDA. I shall take care to let you know when he comes.

MRS. ELVSTED. Do you promise me, Hedda?

HEDDA. Yes, rely upon me. Just you go in and have a sleep in the meantime.

MRS. ELVSTED. Thanks; then I'll try to.

[*She goes off through the inner room.*]

[HEDDA *goes up to the glass door and draws back the curtains. The broad daylight streams into the room. Then she takes a little hand-glass from the writing-table, looks at herself in it, and arranges her hair. Next she goes to the hall door and presses the bell-button.* BERTA *presently appears at the hall door.*]

BERTA. Did you want anything, ma'am?

HEDDA. Yes; you must put some more wood in the stove. I am shivering.

BERTA. Bless me—I'll make up the fire at once. [*She rakes the embers together and lays a piece of wood upon them; then stops and listens.*] That was a ring at the front door, ma'am.

HEDDA. Then go to the door. I will look after the fire.

BERTA. It'll soon burn up. [*She goes out by the hall door.*]

[HEDDA *kneels on the foot-rest and lays some more pieces of wood in the stove. After a short pause,* GEORGE TESMAN *enters from the hall. He looks tired and rather serious. He steals on tiptoe towards the middle doorway and is about to slip through the curtains.*]

HEDDA [*at the stove, without looking up*]. Good morning.

TESMAN [*turns*]. Hedda! [*approaching her*] Good heavens—are you up so early? Eh?

HEDDA. Yes, I am up very early this morning.

TESMAN. And I never doubted you were still sound asleep! Fancy that, Hedda!

HEDDA. Don't speak so loud. Mrs. Elvsted is resting in my room.

TESMAN. Has Mrs. Elvsted been here all night?

HEDDA. Yes, since no one came to fetch her.

TESMAN. Ah, to be sure.

HEDDA [*closes the door of the stove and rises*]. Well, did you enjoy yourself at Judge Brack's?

TESMAN. Have you been anxious about me? Eh?

HEDDA. No, I should never think of being anxious. But I asked if you had enjoyed yourself.

TESMAN. Oh yes,—for once in a way. Especially the beginning of the evening; for then Eilert read me part of his book. We arrived more than an hour too early—fancy that! And Brack had all sorts of arrangements to make—so Eilert read to me.

HEDDA [*seating herself by the table on the right*]. Well? Tell me, then——

TESMAN [*sitting on a footstool near the stove*]. Oh Hedda, you can't conceive what a book that is going to be! I believe it is one of the most remarkable things that have ever been written. Fancy that!

HEDDA. Yes, yes; I don't care about that——

TESMAN. I must make a confession to you, Hedda. When he had finished reading—a horrid feeling came over me.

HEDDA. A horrid feeling?

TESMAN. I felt jealous of Eilert for having had it in him to write such a book. Only think, Hedda!

HEDDA. Yes, yes, I am thinking!

TESMAN. And then how pitiful to think that he—with all his gifts—should be irreclaimable after all.

HEDDA. I suppose you mean that he has more courage than the rest?

TESMAN. No, not at all—I mean that he is incapable of taking his pleasures in moderation.

HEDDA. And what came of it all—in the end?

TESMAN. Well, to tell the truth, I think it might best be described as an orgy, Hedda.

HEDDA. Had he vine-leaves in his hair?

TESMAN. Vine-leaves? No, I saw nothing of the sort. But he made a long, rambling speech in honor of the woman who had inspired him in his work—that was the phrase he used.

HEDDA. Did he name her?

TESMAN. No, he didn't; but I can't help thinking he meant Mrs. Elvsted. You may be sure he did.

HEDDA. Well—where did you part from him?

TESMAN. On the way to town. We broke up—the last of us at any rate—all together; and Brack came with us to get a breath of fresh air. And then, you see, we agreed to take Eilert home; for he had had far more than was good for him.

HEDDA. I daresay.

TESMAN. But now comes the strange part of it, Hedda; or, I should rather say, the melancholy part of it. I declare I am almost ashamed—on Eilert's account—to tell you——

HEDDA. Oh, go on——!

TESMAN. Well, as we were getting near town, you see, I happened to drop a little behind the others. Only for a minute or two—fancy that!

HEDDA. Yes, yes, yes, but——?

TESMAN. And then, as I hurried after them—what do you think I found by the wayside? Eh?

HEDDA. Oh, how should I know!

TESMAN. You mustn't speak of it to a soul, Hedda! Do you hear! Promise me, for Eilert's sake. [*Draws a parcel, wrapped in paper, from his coat pocket.*] Fancy, dear—I found this.

HEDDA. Is not that the parcel he had with him yesterday?

TESMAN. Yes, it is the whole of his precious, irreplaceable manuscript! And he had gone and lost it, and knew nothing about it. Only fancy, Hedda! So deplorably——

HEDDA. But why did you not give him back the parcel at once?

TESMAN. I didn't dare to—in the state he was then in——

HEDDA. Did you not tell any of the others that you had found it?

TESMAN. Oh, far from it! You can surely understand that, for Eilert's sake, I wouldn't do that.

HEDDA. So no one knows that Eilert Lövborg's manuscript is in your possession?

TESMAN. No. And no one must know it.

HEDDA. Then what did you say to him afterwards?

TESMAN. I didn't talk to him again at all; for when we got in among the streets, he and two or three of the others gave us the slip and disappeared. Fancy that!

HEDDA. Indeed! They must have taken him home then.

TESMAN. Yes, so it would appear. And Brack, too, left us.

HEDDA. And what have you been doing with yourself since?

TESMAN. Well, I and some of the others went home with one of the party, a jolly fellow, and took our morning coffee with him; or perhaps I should rather call it our night coffee—eh? But now, when I have rested a little, and given Eilert, poor fellow, time to have his sleep out, I must take this back to him.

HEDDA [*holds out her hand for the packet*]. No—don't give it to him! Not in such a hurry, I mean. Let me read it first.

TESMAN. No, my dearest Hedda, I mustn't, I really mustn't.

HEDDA. You must not?

TESMAN. No—for you can imagine what a state of despair he will be in when he awakens and misses the manuscript. He has no copy of it, you must know! He told me so.

HEDDA [*looking searchingly at him*]. Can such a thing not be reproduced? Written over again?

TESMAN. No, I don't think that would be possible. For the inspiration, you see——

HEDDA. Yes, yes—I suppose it depends on that. [*lightly*] But, by-the-bye—here is a letter for you.

TESMAN. Fancy——!

HEDDA [*handing it to him*]. It came early this morning.

TESMAN. It's from Aunt Julia! What can it be? [*He lays the packet on the other footstool, opens the letter, runs his eye through it, and jumps up.*] Oh, Hedda—she says that poor Aunt Rina is dying!

HEDDA. Well, we were prepared for that.

TESMAN. And that if I want to see her again, I must make haste. I'll run in to them at once.

HEDDA [*suppressing a smile*]. Will you run?

TESMAN. Oh, dearest Hedda—if you could only make up your mind to come with me! Just think!

HEDDA [*rises and says wearily, repelling the idea*]. No, no, don't ask me. I will not look upon sickness and death. I loathe all sorts of ugliness.

TESMAN. Well, well, then——! [*bustling around*] My hat—My overcoat——? Oh, in the hall—I do hope I mayn't come too late, Hedda! Eh?

HEDDA. Oh, if you run——

[BERTA *appears at the hall door.*]

BERTA. Judge Brack is at the door, and wishes to know if he may come in.

TESMAN. At this time! No, I can't possibly see him.

HEDDA. But I can. [*to* BERTA] Ask Judge Brack to come in.

[BERTA *goes out.*]

HEDDA [*quickly whispering*]. The parcel, Tesman! [*She snatches it up from the stool.*]

TESMAN. Yes, give it to me!

HEDDA. No, no, I will keep it till you come back.

[*She goes to the writing-table and places it in the book-case.* TESMAN *stands in a flurry of haste, and cannot get his gloves on.* JUDGE BRACK *enters from the hall.*]

HEDDA [*nodding to him*]. You are an early bird, I must say.

BRACK. Yes, don't you think so? [*to* TESMAN] Are you on the move, too?

TESMAN. Yes, I must rush off to my aunts'. Fancy—the invalid one is lying at death's door, poor creature.

BRACK. Dear me, is she indeed? Then on no account let me detain you. At such a critical moment——

TESMAN. Yes, I must really rush—Good-bye! Good-bye!

[*He hastens out by the hall door.*]

HEDDA [*approaching*]. You seem to have made a particularly lively night of it at your rooms, Judge Brack.

BRACK. I assure you I have not had my clothes off, Mrs. Hedda.

HEDDA. Not you, either?

BRACK. No, as you may see. But what has Tesman been telling you of the night's adventures?

HEDDA. Oh, some tiresome story. Only that they went and had coffee somewhere or other.

BRACK. I have heard about that coffee-party already. Eilert Lövborg was not with them, I fancy?

HEDDA. No, they had taken him home before that.

BRACK. Tesman, too?

HEDDA. No, but some of the others, he said.

BRACK [*smiling*]. George Tesman is really an ingenuous creature, Mrs. Hedda.

HEDDA. Yes, heaven knows he is. Then is there something behind all this?

BRACK. Yes, perhaps there may be.

HEDDA. Well then, sit down, my dear Judge, and tell your story in comfort.

[*She seats herself to the left of the table.* BRACK *sits near her, at the long side of the table.*]

HEDDA. Now then?

BRACK. I had special reasons for keeping track of my guests—or rather of some of my guests—last night.

HEDDA. Of Eilert Lövborg among the rest, perhaps?

BRACK. Frankly, yes.

HEDDA. Now you make me really curious——

BRACK. Do you know where he and one or two of the others finished the night, Mrs. Hedda?

HEDDA. If it is not quite unmentionable, tell me.

BRACK. Oh no, it's not at all unmentionable. Well, they put in an appearance at a particularly animated soirée.

HEDDA. Of the lively kind?

BRACK. Of the very liveliest——

HEDDA. Tell me more of this, Judge Brack——

BRACK. Lövborg, as well as the others, had been invited in advance. I knew all about it. But he had declined the invitation; for now, as you know, he has become a new man.

HEDDA. Up at the Elvsteds', yes. But he went after all, then?

BRACK. Well, you see, Mrs. Hedda—unhappily the spirit moved him at my rooms last evening——

HEDDA. Yes, I hear he found inspiration.

BRACK. Pretty violent inspiration. Well, I fancy that altered his purpose; for we men folk are unfortunately not always so firm in our principles as we ought to be.

HEDDA. Oh, I am sure you are an exception, Judge Brack. But as to Lövborg——?

BRACK. To make a long story short—he landed at last in Mademoiselle Diana's rooms.

HEDDA. Mademoiselle Diana's?

BRACK. It was Mademoiselle Diana that was giving the soirée, to a select circle of her admirers and her lady friends.

HEDDA. Is she a red-haired woman?

BRACK. Precisely.

HEDDA. A sort of a—singer?

BRACK. Oh yes—in her leisure moments. And moreover a mighty huntress—of men—Mrs. Hedda. You have no doubt heard of her. Eilert Lövborg was one of her most enthusiastic protectors—in the days of his glory.

HEDDA. And how did all this end?

BRACK. Far from amicably, it appears. After a most tender meeting, they seem to have come to blows——

HEDDA. Lövborg and she?

BRACK. Yes. He accused her or her friends of having robbed him. He declared that his pocket-book had disappeared—and other things as well. In short, he seems to have made a furious disturbance.

HEDDA. And what came of it all?

BRACK. It came to a general scrimmage, in which the ladies as well as the gentlemen took part. Fortunately the police at last appeared on the scene.

HEDDA. The police too?

BRACK. Yes. I fancy it will prove a costly frolic for Eilert Lövborg, crazy being that he is.

HEDDA. How so?

BRACK. He seems to have made a violent resistance—to have hit one of the constables on the head and torn the coat off his back. So they had to march him off to the police-station with the rest.

HEDDA. How have you learnt all this?

BRACK. From the police themselves.

HEDDA [*gazing straight before her*]. So that is what happened. Then he had no vine-leaves in his hair.

BRACK. Vine-leaves, Mrs. Hedda?

HEDDA [*changing her tone*]. But tell me now, Judge—what is your real reason for tracking out Eilert Lövborg's movements so carefully?

BRACK. In the first place, it could not be entirely indifferent to me if it should appear in the police-court that he came straight from my house.

HEDDA. Will the matter come into court, then?

BRACK. Of course. However, I should scarcely have troubled so much about that. But I thought that, as a friend of the family, it was my duty to supply you and Tesman with a full account of his nocturnal exploits.

HEDDA. Why so, Judge Brack?

BRACK. Why, because I have a shrewd suspicion that he intends to use you as a sort of blind.

HEDDA. Oh, how can you think such a thing!

BRACK. Good heavens, Mrs. Hedda—we have eyes in our head. Mark my words! This Mrs. Elvsted will be in no hurry to leave town again.

HEDDA. Well, even if there should be anything between them, I suppose there are plenty of other places where they could meet.

BRACK. Not a single home. Henceforth, as before, every respectable house will be closed against Eilert Lövborg.

HEDDA. And so ought mine to be, you mean?

BRACK. Yes. I confess it would be more than painful to me if this personage were to be made free of your house. How superfluous, how intrusive, he would be, if he were to force his way into——

HEDDA. ——into the triangle?

BRACK. Precisely. It would simply mean that I should find myself homeless.

HEDDA [*looks at him with a smile*]. So you want to be the one cock in the basket—that is your aim.

BRACK [*nods slowly and lowers his voice*]. Yes, that is my aim. And for that I will fight—with every weapon I can command.

HEDDA [*her smile vanishing*]. I see you are a dangerous person—when it comes to the point.

BRACK. Do you think so?

HEDDA. I am beginning to think so. And I am exceedingly glad to think—that you have no sort of hold over me.

BRACK [*laughing equivocally*]. Well, well, Mrs. Hedda—perhaps you are right there. If I had, who knows what I might be capable of?

HEDDA. Come, come now, Judge Brack. That sounds almost like a threat.

BRACK [*rising*]. Oh, not at all! The triangle, you know, ought, if possible, to be spontaneously constructed.

HEDDA. There I agree with you.

BRACK. Well, now I have said all I had to say; and I had better be getting back to town. Good-bye, Mrs. Hedda. [*He goes towards the glass door.*]

HEDDA [*rising*]. Are you going through the garden?

BRACK. Yes, it's a short cut for me.

HEDDA. And then it is the back way, too.

BRACK. Quite so. I have no objection to back ways. They may be piquant enough at times.

HEDDA. When there is ball practice going on, you mean?

BRACK [*in the doorway, laughing to her*]. Oh, people don't shoot their tame poultry, I fancy.

HEDDA [*also laughing*]. Oh no, when there is only one cock in the basket——

[*They exchange laughing nods of farewell. He goes. She closes the door behind him.* HEDDA, *who has become quite serious, stands for a moment looking out. Presently she goes and peeps through the curtain over the middle doorway. Then she goes to the writing-table, takes* LÖVBORG'S *packet out of the book case, and is on the point of looking through its contents.* BERTA *is heard speaking loudly in the hall.* HEDDA *turns and listens. Then she hastily locks up the packet in the drawer, and lays the key on the inkstand.* EILERT LÖVBORG, *with his great coat on and his hat in his hand, tears open the hall door. He looks somewhat confused and irritated.*]

LÖVBORG [*looking towards the hall*]. And I tell you I must and will come in! There!

[*He closes the door, turns and sees* HEDDA, *at once regains his self-control, and bows.*]

HEDDA [*at the writing-table*]. Well, Mr. Lövborg, this is rather a late hour to call for Thea.

LÖVBORG. You mean rather an early hour to call on you. Pray pardon me.

HEDDA. How do you know that she is still here?

LÖVBORG. They told me at her lodgings that she had been out all night.

HEDDA [*going to the oval table*]. Did you notice anything about the people of the house when they said that?

LÖVBORG [*looks inquiringly at her*]. Notice anything about them?

HEDDA. I mean, did they seem to think it odd?

LÖVBORG [*suddenly understanding*]. Oh yes, of course! I am dragging her down with me! However, I didn't notice anything.—I suppose Tesman is not up yet?

HEDDA. No—I think not——

LÖVBORG. When did he come home?

HEDDA. Very late.

LÖVBORG. Did he tell you anything?

HEDDA. Yes, I gathered that you had had an exceedingly jolly evening at Judge Brack's.

LÖVBORG. Nothing more?

HEDDA. I don't think so. However, I was so dreadfully sleepy—— [MRS. ELVSTED *enters through the curtains of the middle doorway.*]

MRS. ELVSTED [*going towards him*]. Ah, Lövborg! At last——!

LÖVBORG. Yes, at last. And too late!

MRS. ELVSTED [*looks anxiously at him*]. What is too late?

LÖVBORG. Everything is too late now. It is all over with me.

MRS. ELVSTED. Oh no, no—don't say that!

LÖVBORG. You will say the same when you hear——

MRS. ELVSTED. I won't hear anything!

HEDDA. Perhaps you would prefer to talk to her alone! If so, I will leave you.

LÖVBORG. No, stay—you too. I beg you to stay.

MRS. ELVSTED. Yes, but I won't hear anything, I tell you.

LÖVBORG. It is not last night's adventures that I want to talk about.

MRS. ELVSTED. What is it then——?

LÖVBORG. I want to say that now our ways must part.

MRS. ELVSTED. Part!

HEDDA [*involuntarily*]. I knew it!

LÖVBORG. You can be of no more service to me, Thea.

MRS. ELVSTED. How can you stand there and say that! No more service to you! Am I not to help you now, as before? Are we not to go on working together?

LÖVBORG. Henceforward I shall do no work.

MRS. ELVSTED [*despairingly*]. Then what am I to do with my life?

LÖVBORG. You must try to live your life as if you had never known me.

MRS. ELVSTED. But you know I cannot do that!

LÖVBORG. Try if you cannot, Thea. You must go home again——

MRS. ELVSTED [*in vehement protest*]. Never in this world! Where you are, there will I be also! I will not let myself be driven away like this! I will remain here! I will be with you when the book appears.

HEDDA [*half aloud, in suspense*]. Ah yes—the book!

LÖVBORG [*looks at her*]. My book and Thea's; for that is what it is.

MRS. ELVSTED. Yes, I feel that it is. And that is why I have a right to be with you when it appears! I will see with my own eyes how respect and honor pour in upon you afresh. And the happiness—the happiness—oh, I must share it with you!

LÖVBORG. Thea—our book will never appear.

HEDDA. Ah!

MRS. ELVSTED. Never appear!

LÖVBORG. Can never appear.

MRS. ELVSTED [*in agonized foreboding*]. Lövborg—what have you done with the manuscript?

HEDDA [*looks anxiously at him*]. Yes, the manuscript——?

MRS. ELVSTED. Where is it?

LÖVBORG. Oh Thea—don't ask me about it!

MRS. ELVSTED. Yes, yes, I will know. I demand to be told at once.

LÖVBORG. The manuscript—Well then—I have torn the manuscript into a thousand pieces.

MRS. ELVSTED [*shrieks*]. Oh no, no——!

HEDDA [*involuntarily*]. But that's not——

LÖVBORG [*looks at her*]. Not true, you think?

HEDDA [*collecting herself*]. Oh well, of course—since you say so. But it sounded so improbable——

LÖVBORG. It is true, all the same.

MRS. ELVSTED [*wringing her hands*]. Oh God—oh God, Hedda—torn his own work to pieces!

LÖVBORG. I have torn my own life to pieces. So why should I not tear my life-work too——?

MRS. ELVSTED. And you did this last night?

LÖVBORG. Yes, I tell you! Tore it into a thousand pieces and scattered them on the fiord—far out. There there is cool sea-water at any rate—let them drift upon it—drift with the current and the wind. And then presently they will sink—deeper and deeper—as I shall, Thea.

MRS. ELVSTED. Do you know, Lövborg, that what you have done with the book—I shall think of it to my dying day as though you had killed a little child.

LÖVBORG. Yes, you are right. It is a sort of child-murder.

MRS. ELVSTED. How could you, then——! Did not the child belong to me too?

HEDDA [*almost inaudibly*]. Ah, the child——

MRS. ELVSTED [*breathing heavily*]. It is all over then. Well, well, now I will go, Hedda.

HEDDA. But you are not going away from town?

MRS. ELVSTED. Oh, I don't know what I shall do. I see nothing but darkness before me. [*She goes out by the hall door.*]

HEDDA [*stands waiting for a moment*]. So you are not going to see her home, Mr. Lövborg?

LÖVBORG. I? Through the streets? Would you have people see her walking with me?

HEDDA. Of course I don't know what else may have happened last night. But is it so utterly irretrievable?

LÖVBORG. It will not end with last night—I know that perfectly well. And the thing is that now I have no taste for that sort of life either. I won't begin it anew. She has broken my courage and my power of braving life out.

HEDDA [*looking straight before her*]. So that pretty little fool has had her fingers in a man's destiny. [*Looks at him.*] But all the same, how could you treat her so heartlessly?

LÖVBORG. Oh, don't say that it was heartless!

HEDDA. To go and destroy what has filled her whole soul for months and years! You do not call that heartless!

LÖVBORG. To you I can tell the truth, Hedda.

HEDDA. The truth?

LÖVBORG. First promise me—give me your word—that what I now confide to you Thea shall never know.

HEDDA. I give you my word.

LÖVBORG. Good. Then let me tell you that what I said just now was untrue.

HEDDA. About the manuscript?

LÖVBORG. Yes. I have not torn it to pieces—nor thrown it into the fiord.

HEDDA. No, no— But—where is it then?

LÖVBORG. I have destroyed it none the less—utterly destroyed it, Hedda!

HEDDA. I don't understand.

LÖVBORG. Thea said that what I had done seemed to her like a child-murder.

HEDDA. Yes, so she said.

LÖVBORG. But to kill his child—that is not the worst thing a father can do to it.

HEDDA. Not the worst?

LÖVBORG. No. I wanted to spare Thea from hearing the worst.

HEDDA. Then what is the worst?

LÖVBORG. Suppose now, Hedda, that a man—in the small hours of the morning—came home to his child's mother after a night of riot and debauchery, and said: "Listen—I have been here and there—in this place and in that. And I have taken our child with me—to this place and to that. And I have lost the child—utterly lost it. The devil knows into what hands it may have fallen—who may have had their clutches on it."

HEDDA. Well—but when all is said and done, you know—that was only a book——

LÖVBORG. Thea's pure soul was in that book.

HEDDA. Yes, so I understand.

LÖVBORG. And you can understand, too, that for her and me together no future is possible.

HEDDA. What path do you mean to take then?

LÖVBORG. None. I will only try to make an end of it all—the sooner the better.

HEDDA [*a step nearer to him*]. Eilert Lövborg—listen to me. Will you not try to—to do it beautifully?

LÖVBORG. Beautifully? [*smiling*] With vine-leaves in my hair, as you used to dream in the old days——?

HEDDA. No, no. I have lost my faith in the vine-leaves. But beautifully, nevertheless! For once in a way!—Good-bye! You must go now—and do not come here any more.

LÖVBORG. Good-bye, Mrs. Tesman. And give George Tesman my love. [*He is on the point of going.*]

HEDDA. No, wait! I must give you a memento to take with you.

[*She goes to the writing-table and opens the drawer and the pistol-case; then returns to* LÖVBORG *with one of the pistols.*]

LÖVBORG [*looks at her*]. This? Is this the memento?

HEDDA [*nodding slowly*]. Do you recognize it? It was aimed at you once.

LÖVBORG. You should have used it then.

HEDDA. Take it—and do you use it now.

LÖVBORG [*puts the pistol in his breast pocket*]. Thanks!

HEDDA. And beautifully, Eilert Lövborg. Promise me that!

LÖVBORG. Good-bye, Hedda Gabler.

[*He goes out by the hall door.*]

[HEDDA *listens for a moment at the door. Then she goes up to the writing-table, takes out the packet of manuscript, peeps under the cover, draws a few of the sheets half out, and looks at them. Next she goes over and seats herself in the arm-chair beside the stove, with the packet in her lap. Presently she opens the stove door, and then the packet.*]

HEDDA [*throws one of the quires into the fire and whispers to herself*]. Now I am burning your child, Thea!—Burning it, curly-locks! [*throwing one or two more quires into the stove*] Your child and Eilert Lövborg's. [*Throws the rest in.*] I am burning—I am burning your child.

ACT IV

The same rooms at the TESMANS'. *It is evening. The drawing-room is in darkness. The back room is lighted by the hanging lamp over the table. The curtains over the glass door are drawn close.*

[HEDDA, *dressed in black, walks to and fro in the dark room. Then she goes into the back room and disappears for a moment to the left. She is heard to strike a few chords on the piano. Presently she comes in sight again, and returns to the drawing-room.* BERTA *enters from the right, through the inner room, with a lighted lamp, which she places on the table in front of the corner settee in the drawing-room. Her eyes are red with weeping, and she has black ribbons in her cap. She goes quietly and circumspectly out to the right.* HEDDA, *goes up to the glass door, lifts the curtain a little aside, and looks out into the darkness. Shortly afterwards,* MISS TESMAN, *in mourning, with a bonnet and veil on, comes in from the hall.* HEDDA *goes towards her and holds out her hand.*]

MISS TESMAN. Yes, Hedda, here I am, in mourning and forlorn; for now my poor sister has at last found peace.

HEDDA. I have heard the news already, as you see. Tesman sent me a card.

MISS TESMAN. Yes, he promised me he would. But nevertheless I thought that to Hedda—here in the house of life—I ought myself to bring the tidings of death.

HEDDA. That was very kind of you.

MISS TESMAN. Ah, Rina ought not to have left us just now. This is not the time for Hedda's house to be a house of mourning.

HEDDA [*changing the subject*]. She died quite peacefully, did she not, Miss Tesman?

MISS TESMAN. Oh, her end was so calm, so beautiful. And then she had the unspeakable happiness of seeing George once more—and bidding him good-bye.—Has he come home yet?

HEDDA. No. He wrote that he might be detained. But won't you sit down?

MISS TESMAN. No thank you, my dear, dear Hedda. I should like to, but I have so much to do. I must prepare my dear one for her rest as well as I can. She shall go to her grave looking her best.

HEDDA. Can I not help you in any way?

MISS TESMAN. Oh, you must not think of it! Hedda Tesman must have no hand in such mournful work. Nor let her thoughts dwell on it either—not at this time.

HEDDA. One is not always mistress of one's thoughts——

MISS TESMAN [*continuing*]. Ah yes, it is the way of the world. At home we shall be sewing a shroud; and here there will soon be sewing too, I suppose—but of another sort, thank God!

[GEORGE TESMAN *enters by the hall door.*]

HEDDA. Ah, you have come at last!

TESMAN. You here, Aunt Julia? With Hedda? Fancy that!

MISS TESMAN. I was just going, my dear boy. Well, have you done all you promised?

TESMAN. No; I'm really afraid I have forgotten half of it. I must come to you again to-morrow. To-day my brain is all in a whirl. I can't keep my thoughts together.

MISS TESMAN. Why, my dear George, you mustn't take it in this way.

TESMAN. Mustn't——? How do you mean?

MISS TESMAN. Even in your sorrow you must rejoice, as I do—rejoice that she is at rest.

TESMAN. Oh yes, yes—you are thinking of Aunt Rina.

HEDDA. You will feel lonely now, Miss Tesman.

MISS TESMAN. Just at first, yes. But that will not last very long, I hope. I daresay I shall soon find an occupant for poor Rina's little room.

TESMAN. Indeed? Who do you think will take it? Eh?

MISS TESMAN. Oh, there's always some poor invalid or other in want of nursing, unfortunately.

HEDDA. Would you really take such a burden upon you again?

MISS TESMAN. A burden! Heaven forgive you, child—it has been no burden to me.

HEDDA. But suppose you had a total stranger on your hands——

MISS TESMAN. Oh, one soon makes friends with sick folk; and it's such an absolute necessity for me to have some one to live for. Well, heaven be praised, there may soon be something in this house, too, to keep an old aunt busy.

HEDDA. Oh, don't trouble about anything here.

TESMAN. Yes, just fancy what a nice time we three might have together, if——?

HEDDA. If——?

TESMAN [*uneasily*]. Oh, nothing. It will all come right. Let us hope so—eh?

MISS TESMAN. Well, well, I daresay you two want to talk to each other. [*smiling*] And perhaps Hedda may have something to tell you too, George. Good-bye! I must go home to Rina. [*turning at the door*] How strange it is to think that now Rina is with me and with my poor brother as well!

TESMAN. Yes, fancy that, Aunt Julia! Eh?

[MISS TESMAN *goes out by the hall door.*]

HEDDA [*follows* TESMAN *coldly and searchingly with her eyes*]. I almost believe your Aunt Rina's death affects you more than it does your Aunt Julia.

TESMAN. Oh, it's not that alone. It's Eilert I am so terribly uneasy about.

HEDDA [*quickly*]. Is there anything new about him?

TESMAN. I looked in at his rooms this afternoon, intending to tell him the manuscript was in safe keeping.

HEDDA. Well, did you not find him?

TESMAN. No. He wasn't at home. But afterwards I met Mrs. Elvsted, and she told me that he had been here early this morning.

HEDDA. Yes, directly after you had gone.

TESMAN. And he said that he had torn his manuscript to pieces—eh?

HEDDA. Yes, so he declared.

TESMAN. Why, good heavens, he must have been completely out of his mind! And I suppose you thought it best not to give it back to him, Hedda?

HEDDA. No, he did not get it.

TESMAN. But of course you told him that we had it?

HEDDA. No. [*quickly*] Did you tell Mrs. Elvsted?

TESMAN. No; I thought I had better not. But you ought to have told him. Fancy, if, in desperation, he should go and do himself some injury! Let me have the manuscript, Hedda! I will take it to him at once. Where is it?

HEDDA [*cold and immovable, leaning on the arm-chair*]. I have not got it.

TESMAN. Have not got it? What in the world do you mean?

HEDDA. I have burnt it—every line of it.

TESMAN [*with a violent movement of terror*]. Burnt! Burnt Eilert's manuscript!

HEDDA. Don't scream so. The servant might hear you.

TESMAN. Burnt! Why, good God——! No, no, no! It's impossible!

HEDDA. It is so, nevertheless.

TESMAN. Do you know what you have done, Hedda? It's unlawful appropriation of lost property. Fancy that! Just ask Judge Brack, and he'll tell you what it is.

HEDDA. I advise you not to speak of it—either to Judge Brack, or to any one else.

TESMAN. But how could you do anything so unheard-of? What put it into your head? What possessed you? Answer me that—eh?

HEDDA [*suppressing an almost imperceptible smile*]. I did it for your sake, George.

TESMAN. For my sake!

HEDDA. This morning, when you told me about what he had read to you——

TESMAN. Yes, yes—what then?

HEDDA. You acknowledged that you envied him his work.

TESMAN. Oh, of course I didn't mean that literally.

HEDDA. No matter—I could not bear the idea that any one should throw you into the shade.

TESMAN [*in an outburst of mingled doubt and joy*]. Hedda! Oh, is this true? But—but—I never knew you to show your love like that before. Fancy that!

HEDDA. Well, I may as well tell you that—just at this time—— [*impatiently, breaking off*] No, no; you can ask Aunt Julia. She will tell you, fast enough.

TESMAN. Oh, I almost think I understand you, Hedda! [*Clasps his hands together.*] Great heavens! do you really mean it! Eh?

HEDDA. Don't shout so. The servant might hear.

TESMAN [*laughing in irrepressible glee*]. The servant! Why, how absurd you are, Hedda. It's only my old Berta! Why, I'll tell Berta myself.

HEDDA [*clenching her hands together in desperation*]. Oh, it is killing me,—it is killing me, all this!

TESMAN. What is, Hedda? Eh?

HEDDA [*coldly, controlling herself*]. All this—absurdity—George.

TESMAN. Absurdity! Do you see anything absurd in my being overjoyed at the news! But after all perhaps I had better not say anything to Berta.

HEDDA. Oh—why not that too?

TESMAN. No, no, not yet! But I must certainly tell Aunt Julia. And then that you have begun to call me George too! Fancy that! Oh, Aunt Julia will be so happy—so happy.

HEDDA. When she hears that I have burnt Eilert Lövborg's manuscript—for your sake?

TESMAN. No, by-the-bye—that affair of the manuscript—of course nobody must know about that. But that you love me so much, Hedda —Aunt Julia must really share my joy in that! I wonder, now, whether this sort of thing is usual in young wives? Eh?

HEDDA. I think you had better ask Aunt Julia that question too.

TESMAN. I will indeed, some time or other. [*Looks uneasy and downcast again.*] And yet the manuscript—the manuscript! Good God! it is terrible to think what will become of poor Eilert now.

[MRS. ELVSTED, *dressed as in the first act, with hat and cloak, enters by the hall door.*]

MRS. ELVSTED [*greets them hurriedly, and says in evident agitation*]. Oh, dear Hedda, forgive my coming again.

HEDDA. What is the matter with you, Thea?

TESMAN. Something about Eilert Lövborg again—eh?

MRS. ELVSTED. Yes! I am dreadfully afraid some misfortune has happened to him.

HEDDA [*seizes her arm*]. Ah,—do you think so?

TESMAN. Why, good Lord—what makes you think that, Mrs. Elvsted?

MRS. ELVSTED. I heard them talking of him at my boarding-house —just as I came in. Oh, the most incredible rumors are afloat about him to-day.

166 **love me** "burn for me" in the Norwegian

TESMAN. Yes, fancy, so I heard too! And I can bear witness that he went straight home to bed last night. Fancy that!

HEDDA. Well, what did they say at the boarding-house?

MRS. ELVSTED. Oh, I couldn't make out anything clearly. Either they knew nothing definite, or else—— They stopped talking when they saw me; and I did not dare to ask.

TESMAN [*moving about uneasily*]. We must hope—we must hope that you misunderstood them, Mrs. Elvsted.

MRS. ELVSTED. No, no; I am sure it was of him they were talking. And I heard something about the hospital or——

TESMAN. The hospital?

HEDDA. No—surely that cannot be!

MRS. ELVSTED. Oh, I was in such mortal terror! I went to his lodgings and asked for him there.

HEDDA. You could make up your mind to that, Thea!

MRS. ELVSTED. What else could I do? I really could bear the suspense no longer.

TESMAN. But you didn't find him either—eh?

MRS. ELVSTED. No. And the people knew nothing about him. He hadn't been home since yesterday afternoon, they said.

TESMAN. Yesterday! Fancy, how could they say that?

MRS. ELVSTED. Oh, I am sure somehing terrible must have happened to him.

TESMAN. Hedda dear—how would it be if I were to go and make inquiries——?

HEDDA. No, no—don't you mix yourself up in this affair.

[JUDGE BRACK, *with his hat in his hand, enters by the hall door, which* BERTA *opens, and closes behind him. He looks grave and bows in silence.*]

TESMAN. Oh, is that you, my dear Judge? Eh?

BRACK. Yes. It was imperative I should see you this evening.

TESMAN. I can see you have heard the news about Aunt Rina.

BRACK. Yes, that among other things.

TESMAN. Isn't it sad—eh?

BRACK. Well, my dear Tesman, that depends on how you look at it.

TESMAN [*looks doubtfully at him*]. Has anything else happened?

BRACK. Yes.

HEDDA [*in suspense*]. Anything sad, Judge Brack?

BRACK. That, too, depends on how you look at it, Mrs. Tesman.

MRS. ELVSTED [*unable to restrain her anxiety*]. Oh! it is something about Eilert Lövborg!

BRACK [*with a glance at her*]. What makes you think that, Madam? Perhaps you have already heard something——?

MRS. ELVSTED [*in confusion*]. No, nothing at all, but——

TESMAN. Oh, for heaven's sake, tell us!

BRACK [*shrugging his shoulders*]. Well, I regret to say Eilert Lövborg has been taken to the hospital. He is lying at the point of death.

MRS. ELVSTED [*shrieks*]. Oh God! Oh God——

TESMAN. To the hospital! And at the point of death.

HEDDA [*involuntarily*]. So soon then——

MRS. ELVSTED [*wailing*]. And we parted in anger, Hedda!

HEDDA [*whispers*]. Thea—Thea—be careful!

MRS. ELVSTED [*not heeding her*]. I must go to him! I must see him alive!

BRACK. It is useless, Madam. No one will be admitted.

MRS. ELVSTED. Oh, at least tell me what has happened to him? What is it?

TESMAN. You don't mean to say that he has himself—— Eh?

HEDDA. Yes, I am sure he has.

TESMAN. Hedda, how can you——?

BRACK [*keeping his eyes fixed upon her*]. Unfortunately you have guessed quite correctly, Mrs. Tesman.

MRS. ELVSTED. Oh, how horrible!

TESMAN. Himself, then! Fancy that!

HEDDA. Shot himself!

BRACK. Rightly guessed again, Mrs. Tesman.

MRS. ELVSTED [*with an effort at self-control*]. When did it happen, Mr. Brack?

BRACK. This afternoon—between three and four.

TESMAN. But, good Lord, where did he do it? Eh?

BRACK [*with some hesitation*]. Where? Well—I suppose at his lodgings.

MRS. ELVSTED. No, that cannot be; for I was there between six and seven.

BRACK. Well, then, somewhere else. I don't know exactly. I only know that he was found——. He had shot himself—in the breast.

MRS. ELVSTED. Oh, how terrible! That he should die like that!

HEDDA [*to* BRACK]. Was it in the breast?

BRACK. Yes—as I told you.

HEDDA. Not in the temple?

BRACK. In the breast, Mrs. Tesman.

HEDDA. Well, well—the breast is a good place, too.

BRACK. How do you mean, Mrs. Tesman?

HEDDA [*evasively*]. Oh, nothing—nothing.

TESMAN. And the wound is dangerous, you say—eh?

BRACK. Absolutely mortal. The end has probably come by this time.

MRS. ELVSTED. Yes, yes, I feel it. The end! The end! Oh, Hedda——!

TESMAN. But tell me, how have you learnt all this?

BRACK [*curtly*]. Through one of the police. A man I had some business with.

HEDDA [*in a clear voice*]. At last a deed worth doing!

TESMAN [*terrified*]. Good heavens, Hedda! what are you saying?

HEDDA. I say there is beauty in this.

BRACK. H'm, Mrs. Tesman——

TESMAN. Beauty! Fancy that!

MRS. ELVSTED. Oh, Hedda, how can you talk of beauty in such an act!

HEDDA. Eilert Lövborg has himself made up his account with life. He has had the courage to do—the one right thing.

MRS. ELVSTED. No, you must never think that was how it happened! It must have been in delirium that he did it.

TESMAN. In despair!

HEDDA. That he did not. I am certain of that.

MRS. ELVSTED. Yes, yes! In delirium! Just as when he tore up our manuscript.

BRACK [*starting*]. The manuscript? Has he torn that up?

MRS. ELVSTED. Yes, last night.

TESMAN [*whispers softly*]. Oh, Hedda, we shall never get over this.

BRACK. H'm, very extraordinary.

TESMAN [*moving about the room*]. To think of Eilert going out of the world in this way! And not leaving behind him the book that would have immortalized his name——

MRS. ELVSTED. Oh, if only it could be put together again!

TESMAN. Yes, if it only could! I don't know what I would not give——

MRS. ELVSTED. Perhaps it can, Mr. Tesman.

TESMAN. What do you mean?

MRS. ELVSTED [*searches in the pocket of her dress*]. Look here. I have kept all the loose notes he used to dictate from.

HEDDA [*a step forward*]. Ah——!

TESMAN. You have kept them, Mrs. Elvsted! Eh?

MRS. ELVSTED. Yes, I have them here. I put them in my pocket when I left home. Here they still are——

TESMAN. Oh, do let me see them!

MRS. ELVSTED [*hands him a bundle of papers*]. But they are in such disorder—all mixed up.

TESMAN. Fancy, if we could make something out of them, after all! Perhaps if we two put our heads together——

MRS. ELVSTED. Oh, yes, at least let us try——

TESMAN. We will manage it! We must! I will dedicate my life to this task.

HEDDA. You, George? Your life?

TESMAN. Yes, or rather all the time I can spare. My own collections must wait in the meantime. Hedda—you understand, eh? I owe this to Eilert's memory.

HEDDA. Perhaps.

TESMAN. And so, my dear Mrs. Elvsted, we will give our whole minds to it. There is no use in brooding over what can't be undone—eh? We must try to control our grief as much as possible, and——

MRS. ELVSTED. Yes, yes, Mr. Tesman, I will do the best I can.

TESMAN. Well then, come here. I can't rest until we have looked through the notes. Where shall we sit? Here? No, in there, in the back room. Excuse me, my dear Judge. Come with me, Mrs. Elvsted.

MRS. ELVSTED. Oh, if only it were possible!

[TESMAN *and* MRS. ELVSTED *go into the back room. She takes off her hat and cloak. They both sit at the table under the hanging lamp, and are soon deep in an eager examination of the papers.* HEDDA *crosses to the stove and sits in the arm-chair. Presently* BRACK *goes up to her.*]

HEDDA [*in a low voice*]. Oh, what a sense of freedom it gives one, this act of Eilert Lövborg's.

BRACK. Freedom, Mrs. Hedda? Well, of course, it is a release for him——

HEDDA. I mean for me. It gives me a sense of freedom to know that a deed of deliberate courage is still possible in this world,—a deed of spontaneous beauty.

BRACK [*smiling*]. H'm—my dear Mrs. Hedda——

HEDDA. Oh, I know what you are going to say. For you are a kind of a specialist too, like—you know!

BRACK [*looking hard at her*]. Eilert Lövborg was more to you than perhaps you are willing to admit to yourself. Am I wrong?

HEDDA. I don't answer such questions. I only know Eilert Lövborg has had the courage to live his life after his own fashion. And then—the last great act, with its beauty! Ah! that he should have the will and the strength to turn away from the banquet of life—so early.

BRACK. I am sorry, Mrs. Hedda,—but I fear I must dispel an amiable illusion.

HEDDA. Illusion?

BRACK. Which could not have lasted long in any case.

HEDDA. What do you mean?

BRACK. Eilert Lövborg did not shoot himself voluntarily.

HEDDA. Not voluntarily?

BRACK. No. The thing did not happen exactly as I told it.

HEDDA [*in suspense*]. Have you concealed something? What is it?

BRACK. For poor Mrs. Elvsted's sake I idealized the facts a little.

HEDDA. What are the facts?

BRACK. First, that he is already dead.

HEDDA. At the hospital?

BRACK. Yes—without regaining consciousness.

HEDDA. What more have you concealed?

BRACK. This—the event did not happen at his lodgings.

HEDDA. Oh, that can make no difference.

BRACK. Perhaps it may. For I must tell you—Eilert Lövborg was found shot in—in Mademoiselle Diana's boudoir.

HEDDA [*makes a motion as if to rise, but sinks back again*]. That is impossible, Judge Brack! He cannot have been there again to-day.

BRACK. He was there this afternoon. He went there, he said, to demand the return of something which they had taken from him. Talked wildly about a lost child——

HEDDA. Ah—so that was why——

BRACK. I thought probably he meant his manuscript; but now I hear he destroyed that himself. So I suppose it must have been his pocket-book.

HEDDA. Yes, no doubt. And there—there he was found?

BRACK. Yes, there. With a pistol in his breast-pocket, discharged. The ball had lodged in a vital part.

HEDDA. In the breast—yes.

BRACK. No—in the bowels.

HEDDA [*looks up at him with an expression of loathing*]. That too! Oh, what curse is it that makes everything I touch turn ludicrous and mean?

BRACK. There is one point more, Mrs. Hedda—another disagreeable feature in the affair.

HEDDA. And what is that?

BRACK. The pistol he carried——

HEDDA [*breathless*]. Well? What of it?

BRACK. He must have stolen it.

HEDDA [*leaps up*]. Stolen it! That is not true! He did not steal it!

BRACK. No other explanation is possible. He must have stolen it—— Hush!

[TESMAN *and* MRS. ELVSTED *have risen from the table in the back room, and come into the drawing-room.*]

TESMAN [*with the papers in both his hands*]. Hedda dear, it is almost impossible to see under that lamp. Think of that!

HEDDA. Yes, I am thinking.

TESMAN. Would you mind our sitting at your writing-table—eh?

HEDDA. If you like. [*quickly*] No, wait! Let me clear it first!

TESMAN. Oh, you needn't trouble, Hedda. There is plenty of room.

HEDDA. No, no; let me clear it, I say! I will take these things in and put them on the piano. There! [*She has drawn out an object, covered with sheet music, from under the book-case, places several other pieces of music upon it, and carries the whole into the inner room, to the left.* TESMAN *lays the scraps of paper on the writing-table, and moves the lamp there from the corner table.* HEDDA *returns.*]

HEDDA [*behind* MRS. ELVSTED'S *chair, gently ruffling her hair*]. Well, my sweet Thea,—how goes it with Eilert Lövborg's monument?

MRS. ELVSTED [*looks dispiritedly up at her*]. Oh, it will be terribly hard to put in order.

TESMAN. We must manage it. I am determined. And arranging other people's papers is just the work for me.

[HEDDA *goes over to the stove, and seats herself on one of the foot-stools.* BRACK *stands over her, leaning on the arm-chair.*]

HEDDA [*whispers*]. What did you say about the pistol?

BRACK [*softly*]. That he must have stolen it.

HEDDA. Why stolen it?

BRACK. Because every other explanation ought to be impossible, Mrs. Hedda.

HEDDA. Indeed?

BRACK [*glances at her*]. Of course Eilert Lövborg was here this morning. Was he not?

HEDDA. Yes.

BRACK. Were you alone with him?

HEDDA. Part of the time.

BRACK. Did you not leave the room whilst he was here?

HEDDA. No.

BRACK. Try to recollect. Were you not out of the room a moment?

HEDDA. Yes, perhaps just a moment—out in the hall.

BRACK. And where was your pistol-case during that time?

HEDDA. I had it locked up in——

BRACK. Well, Mrs. Hedda?

HEDDA. The case stood there on the writing-table.

BRACK. Have you looked since, to see whether both the pistols are there?

HEDDA. No.

BRACK. Well, you need not. I saw the pistol found in Lövborg's pocket, and I knew it at once as the one I had seen yesterday—and before, too.

HEDDA. Have you it with you?

BRACK. No; the police have it.

HEDDA. What will the police do with it?

BRACK. Search till they find the owner.

HEDDA. Do you think they will succeed?

BRACK [*bends over her and whispers*]. No, Hedda Gabler—not so long as I say nothing.

HEDDA [*looks frightened at him*]. And if you do not say nothing, —what then?

BRACK [*shrugs his shoulders*]. There is always the possibility that the pistol was stolen.

HEDDA [*firmly*]. Death rather than that.

BRACK [*smiling*]. People say such things—but they don't do them.

HEDDA [*without replying*]. And supposing the pistol was stolen, and the owner is discovered? What then?

BRACK. Well, Hedda—then comes the scandal.

HEDDA. The scandal!

BRACK. Yes, the scandal—of which you are mortally afraid. You will, of course, be brought before the court—both you and Mademoiselle Diana. She will have to explain how the thing happened—whether it was an accidental shot or murder. Did the pistol go off as he was trying to take it out of his pocket, to threaten her with? Or did she tear the pistol out of his hand, shoot him, and push it back into his pocket? That would be quite like her; for she is an able-bodied young person, this same Mademoiselle Diana.

HEDDA. But *I* have nothing to do with all this repulsive business.

BRACK. No. But you will have to answer the question: Why did you give Eilert Lövborg the pistol? And what conclusions will people draw from the fact that you did give it to him?

HEDDA [*lets her head sink*]. That is true. I did not think of that.

BRACK. Well, fortunately, there is no danger, so long as I say nothing.

HEDDA [*looks up at him*]. So I am in your power, Judge Brack.

You have me at your beck and call, from this time forward.

BRACK [*whispers softly*]. Dearest Hedda—believe me—I shall not abuse my advantage.

HEDDA. I am in your power none the less. Subject to your will and your demands. A slave, a slave then! [*Rises impetuously.*] No, I cannot endure the thought of that! Never!

BRACK [*looks half-mockingly at her*]. People generally get used to the inevitable.

HEDDA [*returns his look*]. Yes, perhaps. [*She crosses to the writing-table. Suppressing an involuntary smile, she imitates* TESMAN'S *intonations.*] Well? Are you getting on, George? Eh?

TESMAN. Heaven knows, dear. In any case it will be the work of months.

HEDDA [*as before*]. Fancy that! [*Passes her hands softly through* MRS. ELVSTED'S *hair.*] Doesn't it seem strange to you, Thea? Here are you sitting with Tesman—just as you used to sit with Eilert Lövborg?

MRS. ELVSTED. Ah, if I could only inspire your husband in the same way.

HEDDA. Oh, that will come too—in time.

TESMAN. Yes, do you know, Hedda—I really think I begin to feel something of the sort. But won't you go and sit with Brack again?

HEDDA. Is there nothing I can do to help you two?

TESMAN. No, nothing in the world. [*turning his head*] I trust to you to keep Hedda company, my dear Brack.

BRACK [*with a glance at* HEDDA]. With the very greatest of pleasure.

HEDDA. Thanks. But I am tired this evening. I will go in and lie down a little on the sofa.

TESMAN. Yes, do dear—eh?

[HEDDA *goes into the back room and draws the curtains. A short pause. Suddenly she is heard playing a wild dance on the piano.*]

MRS. ELVSTED [*starts from her chair*]. Oh—what is that?

TESMAN [*runs to the doorway*]. Why, my dearest Hedda—don't play dance music to-night! Just think of Aunt Rina! And of Eilert too!

HEDDA [*puts her head out between the curtains*]. And of Aunt

Julia. And of all the rest of them.—After this, I will be quiet. [*Closes the curtains again.*]

TESMAN [*at the writing-table*]. It's not good for her to see us at this distressing work. I'll tell you what, Mrs. Elvsted,—you shall take the empty room at Aunt Julia's, and then I will come over in the evenings, and we can sit and work there—eh?

HEDDA [*in the inner room*]. I hear what you are saying, Tesman. But how am *I* to get through the evenings out here?

TESMAN [*turning over the papers*]. Oh, I daresay Judge Brack will be so kind as to look in now and then, even though I am out.

BRACK [*in the arm-chair, calls out gaily*]. Every blessed evening, with all the pleasure in life, Mrs. Tesman! We shall get on capitally together, we two!

HEDDA [*speaking loud and clear*]. Yes, don't you flatter yourself we will, Judge Brack? Now that you are the one cock in the basket——

[*A shot is heard within.* TESMAN, MRS. ELVSTED, *and* BRACK *leap to their feet.*]

TESMAN. Oh, now she is playing with those pistols again.

[*He throws back the curtains and runs in, followed by* MRS. ELVSTED. HEDDA *lies stretched on the sofa, lifeless. Confusion and cries.* BERTA *enters in alarm from the right.*]

TESMAN [*shrieks to* BRACK]. Shot herself! Shot herself in the temple! Fancy that!

BRACK [*half-fainting in the arm-chair*]. Good God!—people don't do such things.

ANTON CHEKHOV
1860–1904

THE CHERRY ORCHARD
a comedy in four acts
1904

THERE ARE RANGES of significance in almost every detail of *The Cherry Orchard,* which give the playgoer a sense, sometimes rather mysterious, that a great many meaningful things are going on all the while and which make the play delightful to read and reread closely. The work may remind us of a sequence in an athletic event—a march downfield in a football game, let us say—during which the spectator is continuously aware of more constituent happenings than he can quite keep track of, and which he can later watch with fuller understanding on slow-motion film.

In Lyubov's first-act entrance, for example, the spectator at once takes in a number of significant impressions, which, when dwelt on, he finds to comprise all the major components of the play. In this scene Lyubov is preceded by the hobbling figure of the old house-servant Firs and followed by a chaotic assembly of family, friends, and servants. "Joyfully through her tears," she greets the room as her one-time nursery. "And here I am," she adds, "like a little child." But the other characters interrupt at once, one with an idle complaint about the trains' not running on time, and another with a comment on the appetite of her pet dog. The audience sees immediately that Lyubov's entrance is anticipated by a discordant happening and is shortly swallowed up in confusion. And if one dwells upon the source of these impressions—Firs crossing the stage, Lyubov's reaction to the nursery, the idle interruptions—he sees also a fuller metaphoric meaning: the order of things to which she would return is moribund now, though her feeling for it remains; and misrule or the absence of any intelligible rule has succeeded it.

In making every detail tell in this way, Chekhov inevitably states his major ideas over and over again. Their recurrence is not obtrusive, since they receive a different coloration every time they appear: as they are embodied in particular speeches they take on both those hues of emotion and attitude with which the speaker endows them and those with which we endow the speaker. But we recognize them as recurring, though with a difference, and we find them interacting with one another from the beginning of the play to the end. We recognize them, that is, as formal elements. Chekhov has used ideas somewhat as a composer uses melodic phrases. His play is a quasi-musical interweaving of memories of a past order of things with the fact of present chaos.

The cherry orchard itself, a relic of the past order of things, is the most significant embodiment of idea in the work to which it gives its name, and a simple catalogue of references to the orchard illustrates Chekhov's manner of developing and varying his themes. The first stage direction mentions the orchard: "The cherry trees are in flower." In Act I Lopahin says, "The cherry orchard must be cut down." And later in the act Lyubov exclaims, "Oh, my childhood, my innocence! . . . Oh, my orchard! . . . you are young again and full of happiness." Trofimov says in Act II that "Your orchard is a fearful thing . . . dreaming of centuries gone by and tortured by fearful visions . . . We must first expiate our past." When Lopahin gains the estate in Act III he shouts, "Come, all of you, and look how Yermolay Lopahin will take his axe to the cherry orchard!" In Act IV Lyubov again addresses the orchard: "Oh, my orchard, my sweet beautiful orchard! my life, my youth, my happiness, good-bye!" And the last stage direction reads: "All is still again, and there is nothing heard but the strokes of the axe far away in the orchard."

Such is the form of *The Cherry Orchard* and such, in part, its meaning. It perhaps should be added that any discussion of the play, including this one, tends to take its tone too largely from the play's general import, which is sad and dark. Chekhov understands very well the over-all haplessness of the scene upon which he looks. But seeing the people in this scene clearly and steadily, he finds them in equal parts pitiful and absurd, and bodies them forth in a work which holds humor and compassion in delicate balance—a work aptly subtitled *A Comedy in Four Acts.*

THE CHERRY ORCHARD / CHEKHOV

A COMEDY IN FOUR ACTS

TRANSLATED BY CONSTANCE GARNETT

Characters

MADAME RANEVSKY (LYUBOV ANDREYEVNA)	*the owner of the Cherry Orchard*
ANYA	*her daughter, aged 17*
VARYA	*her adopted daughter, aged 24*
GAEV (LEONID ANDREYEVITCH)	*brother of Madame Ranevsky*
LOPAHIN (YERMOLAY ALEXEYEVITCH)	*a merchant*
TROFIMOV (PYOTR SERGEYEVITCH)	*a student*
SEMYONOV-PISHTCHIK	*a landowner*
CHARLOTTA IVANOVNA	*a governess*
EPIHODOV (SEMYON PANTALEYEVITCH)	*a clerk*
DUNYASHA	*a maid*
FIRS	*an old valet, aged 87*
YASHA	*a young valet*
A VAGRANT	
THE STATION MASTER	
A POST-OFFICE CLERK	
VISITORS, SERVANTS	

SCENE. *The estate of* MADAME RANEVSKY.

Characters: Russians have three names: a given name (Lyubov), a patronymic (Andreyevna = daughter of Andrey), and a surname (Ranevsky). In the Russia of Chekhov's day, decorum prescribed title and surname (Madame Ranevsky) for formal relationships; given name and patronymic (Lyubov Andreyevna) for relationships somewhat less formal; given name alone for familiarity; and a diminutive of the given name (Lyuba for Lyubov) to indicate affection or condescension.

ACT I

A room, which has always been called the nursery. One of the doors leads into ANYA'S *room. Dawn, sun rises during the scene. May, the cherry trees in flower, but it is cold in the garden with the frost of early morning. Windows closed.*

[*Enter* DUNYASHA *with a candle and* LOPAHIN *with a book in his hand.*]

LOPAHIN. The train's in, thank God. What time is it?

DUNYASHA. Nearly two o'clock. [*Puts out the candle.*] It's daylight already.

LOPAHIN. The train's late! Two hours, at least. [*Yawns and stretches.*] I'm a pretty one; what a fool I've been. Came here on purpose to meet them at the station and dropped asleep. . . . Dozed off as I sat in the chair. It's annoying. . . . You might have waked me.

DUNYASHA. I thought you had gone. [*Listens.*] There, I do believe they're coming!

LOPAHIN [*listens*]. No, what with the luggage and one thing and another. [*a pause*] Lyubov Andreyevna has been abroad five years; I don't know what she is like now. . . . She's a splendid woman. A good-natured, kind-hearted woman. I remember when I was a lad of fifteen, my poor father—he used to keep a little shop here in the village in those days—gave me a punch in the face with his fist and made my nose bleed. We were in the yard here, I forget what we'd come about—he had had a drop. Lyubov Andreyevna—I can see her now—she was a slim young girl then—took me to wash my face, and then brought me into this very room, into the nursery. "Don't cry, little peasant," says she, "it will be well in time for your wedding day." . . . [*a pause*] Little peasant. . . . My father was a peasant, it's true, but here am I in a white waistcoat and brown shoes, like a pig in a bun shop. Yes, I'm a rich man, but for all my money, come to think, a peasant I was, and a peasant I am. [*Turns*

3 **garden** orchard. The Russian word *sad,* which appears here and in the title, means both garden and orchard.

over the pages of the book.] I've been reading this book and I can't make head or tail of it. I fell asleep over it [*a pause*].

DUNYASHA. The dogs have been awake all night, they feel that the mistress is coming.

LOPAHIN. Why, what's the matter with you, Dunyasha?

DUNYASHA. My hands are all of a tremble. I feel as though I should faint.

LOPAHIN. You're a spoilt soft creature, Dunyasha. And dressed like a lady too, and your hair done up. That's not the thing. One must know one's place.

[*Enter* EPIHODOV *with a nosegay; he wears a pea-jacket and highly polished creaking topboots; he drops the nosegay as he comes in.*]

EPIHODOV [*picking up the nosegay*]. Here! the gardener's sent this, says you're to put it in the dining-room. [*Gives* DUNYASHA *the nosegay.*]

LOPAHIN. And bring me some kvass.

DUNYASHA. I will. [*Goes out.*]

EPIHODOV. It's chilly this morning, three degrees of frost, though the cherries are all in flower. I can't say much for our climate [*sighs*]. I can't. Our climate is not often propitious to the occasion. Yermolay Alexeyevitch, permit me to call your attention to the fact that I purchased myself a pair of boots the day before yesterday, and they creak, I venture to assure you, so that there's no tolerating them. What ought I to grease them with?

LOPAHIN. Oh, shut up! Don't bother me.

EPIHODOV. Every day some misfortune befalls me. I don't complain, I'm used to it, and I wear a smiling face.

[DUNYASHA *comes in, hands* LOPAHIN *the kvass.*]

EPIHODOV. I am going. [*Stumbles against a chair, which falls over.*] There! [*as though triumphant*] There you see now, excuse the expression, an accident like that among others . . . It's positively remarkable. [*Goes out.*]

DUNYASHA. Do you know, Yermolay Alexeyevitch, I must confess, Epihodov has made me a proposal.

LOPAHIN. Ah!

DUNYASHA. I'm sure I don't know. . . . He's a harmless fellow, but sometimes when he begins talking, there's no making anything of it. It's all very fine and expressive, only there's no understanding it. I've a sort of liking for him too. He loves me to distraction. He's an unfortunate man; every day there's something. They tease him about it—two and twenty misfortunes they call him.

LOPAHIN [*listening*]. There! I do believe they're coming.

DUNYASHA. They are coming! What's the matter with me? . . . I'm cold all over.

LOPAHIN. They really are coming. Let's go and meet them. Will she know me? It's five years since I saw her.

DUNYASHA [*in a flutter*]. I shall drop this very minute. . . . Ah, I shall drop.

[*There is a sound of two carriages driving up to the house.* LOPAHIN *and* DUNYASHA *go out quickly. The stage is left empty. A noise is heard in the adjoining rooms.* FIRS, *who has driven to meet* MADAME RANEVSKY, *crosses the stage hurriedly leaning on a stick. He is wearing old-fashioned livery and a high hat. He says something to himself, but not a word can be distinguished. The noise behind the scenes goes on increasing. A voice: "Come, let's go in here." Enter* LYUBOV ANDREYEVNA, ANYA, *and* CHARLOTTA IVANOVNA *with a pet dog on a chain, all in travelling dresses.* VARYA *in an out-door coat with a kerchief over her head,* GAEV, SEMYONOV-PISHTCHIK, LOPAHIN, DUNYASHA *with bag and parasol, servants with other articles. All walk across the room.*]

ANYA. Let's come in here. Do you remember what room this is, mamma?

LYUBOV [*joyfully, through her tears*]. The nursery!

VARYA. How cold it is, my hands are numb. [*to* LYUBOV ANDREYEVNA] Your rooms, the white room and the lavender one, are just the same as ever, mamma.

LYUBOV. My nursery, dear delightful room. . . . I used to sleep here when I was little. . . . [*Cries.*] And here I am, like a little child. . . . [*Kisses her brother and* VARYA, *and then her brother again.*] Varya's just the same as ever, like a nun. And I knew Dunyasha. [*Kisses* DUNYASHA.]

GAEV. The train was two hours late. What do you think of that? Is that the way to do things?

CHARLOTTA [*to* PISHTCHIK]. My dog eats nuts, too.

PISHTCHIK [*wonderingly*]. Fancy that!

[*They all go out except* ANYA *and* DUNYASHA.]

DUNYASHA. We've been expecting you so long. [*Takes* ANYA's *hat and coat.*]

ANYA. I haven't slept for four nights on the journey. I feel dreadfully cold.

DUNYASHA. You set out in Lent, there was snow and frost, and now? My darling! [*Laughs and kisses her.*] I *have* missed you, my precious, my joy. I must tell you . . . I can't put it off a minute. . . .

ANYA [*wearily*]. What now?

DUNYASHA. Epihodov, the clerk, made me a proposal just after Easter.

ANYA. It's always the same thing with you. . . . [*straightening her hair*] I've lost all my hairpins. . . . [*She is staggering from exhaustion.*]

DUNYASHA. I don't know what to think, really. He does love me, he does love me so!

ANYA [*looking towards her door, tenderly*]. My own room, my windows just as though I had never gone away. I'm home! Tomorrow morning I shall get up and run into the garden. . . . Oh, if I could get to sleep! I haven't slept all the journey, I was so anxious and worried.

DUNYASHA. Pyotr Sergeyevitch came the day before yesterday.

ANYA [*joyfully*]. Petya!

DUNYASHA. He's asleep in the bath house, he has settled in there. I'm afraid of being in their way, says he. [*glancing at her watch*] I was to have waked him, but Varvara Mihalovna told me not to. Don't you wake him, says she.

[*Enter* VARYA *with a bunch of keys at her waist.*]

VARYA. Dunyasha, coffee and make haste. . . . Mamma's asking for coffee.

DUNYASHA. This very minute. [*Goes out.*]

VARYA. Well, thank God, you've come. You're home again. [*petting her*] My little darling has come back! My precious beauty has come back again!

ANYA. I have had a time of it!

VARYA. I can fancy.

ANYA. We set off in Holy Week—it was so cold then, and all the way Charlotta would talk and show off her tricks. What did you want to burden me with Charlotta for?

VARYA. You couldn't have travelled all alone, darling. At seventeen!

ANYA. We got to Paris at last, it was cold there—snow. I speak French shockingly. Mamma lives on the fifth floor, I went up to her and there were a lot of French people, ladies, an old priest with a book. The place smelt of tobacco and so comfortless. I felt sorry, oh! so sorry for mamma all at once, I put my arms round her neck, and hugged her and wouldn't let her go. Mamma was as kind as she could be, and she cried. . . .

VARYA [*through her tears*]. Don't speak of it, don't speak of it!

ANYA. She had sold her villa at Mentone, she had nothing left, nothing. I hadn't a farthing left either, we only just had enough to get here. And mamma doesn't understand! When we had dinner at the stations, she always ordered the most expensive things and gave the waiters a whole rouble. Charlotta's just the same. Yasha too must have the same as we do; it's simply awful. You know Yasha is mamma's valet now, we brought him here with us.

VARYA. Yes, I've seen the young rascal.

ANYA. Well, tell me—have you paid the arrears on the mortgage?

VARYA. How could we get the money?

ANYA. Oh, dear! Oh, dear!

VARYA. In August the place will be sold.

ANYA. My goodness!

LOPAHIN [*peeps in at the door and moos like a cow*]. Moo! [*Disappears.*]

VARYA [*weeping*]. There, that's what I could do to him. [*Shakes her fist.*]

ANYA [*embracing* VARYA, *softly*]. Varya, has he made you an offer? [VARYA *shakes her head.*] Why, but he loves you. Why is it you don't come to an understanding? What are you waiting for?

VARYA. I believe that there never will be anything between us. He has a lot to do, he has no time for me . . . and takes no notice of me. Bless the man, it makes me miserable to see him. . . . Everyone's talking of our being married, everyone's congratulating me, and all the while there's really nothing in it; it's all like a dream! [*in another tone*] You have a new brooch like a bee.

ANYA [*mournfully*]. Mamma bought it. [*Goes into her own room and in a light-hearted childish tone:*] And you know, in Paris I went up in a balloon!

VARYA. My darling's home again! My pretty is home again!

[DUNYASHA *returns with the coffee-pot and is making the coffee.*]

VARYA [*standing at the door*]. All day long, darling, as I go about looking after the house, I keep dreaming all the time. If only we could marry you to a rich man, then I should feel more at rest. Then I would go off by myself on a pilgrimage to Kiev, to Moscow . . . and so I would spend my life going from one place to another. . . . I would go on and on. . . . What bliss!

ANYA. The birds are singing in the garden. What time is it?

VARYA. It must be nearly three. It's time you were asleep, darling. [*going into* ANYA's *room*] What bliss!

[YASHA *enters with a rug and a travelling bag.*]

YASHA [*crosses the stage, mincingly*]. May one come in here, pray?

DUNYASHA. I shouldn't have known you, Yasha. How you have changed abroad.

YASHA. H'm! . . . And who are you?

DUNYASHA. When you went away, I was that high. [*Shows distance from floor.*] Dunyasha, Fyodor's daughter. . . . You don't remember me!

YASHA. H'm! . . . You're a peach! [*Looks round and embraces her: she shrieks and drops a saucer.* YASHA *goes out hastily.*]

VARYA [*in the doorway, in a tone of vexation*]. What now?

DUNYASHA [*through her tears*]. I have broken a saucer.

VARYA. Well, that brings good luck.

ANYA [*coming out of her room*]. We ought to prepare mamma: Petya is here.

VARYA. I told them not to wake him.

ANYA [*dreamily*]. It's six years since father died. Then only a month later little brother Grisha was drowned in the river, such a pretty boy he was, only seven. It was more than mamma could bear, so she went away, went away without looking back. [*shuddering*] . . . How well I understand her, if only she knew! [*a pause*] And

Petya Trofimov was Grisha's tutor, he may remind her.

[*Enter* FIRS: *he is wearing a pea-jacket and a white waistcoat.*]

FIRS [*goes up to the coffee-pot, anxiously*]. The mistress will be served here. [*Puts on white gloves.*] Is the coffee ready? [*sternly to* DUNYASHA] Girl! Where's the cream?

DUNYASHA Ah, mercy on us! [*Goes out quickly.*]

FIRS [*fussing round the coffee-pot*]. Ech! you good-for-nothing! [*muttering to himself*] Come back from Paris. And the old master used to go to Paris too . . . horses all the way. [*Laughs.*]

VARYA. What is it, Firs?

FIRS. What is your pleasure? [*gleefully*] My lady has come home! I have lived to see her again! Now I can die. [*Weeps with joy.*]

[*Enter* LYUBOV ANDREYEVNA, GAEV *and* SEMYONOV-PISHTCHIK; *the latter is in a short-waisted full coat of fine cloth, and full trousers.* GAEV, *as he comes in, makes a gesture with his arms and his whole body, as though he were playing billiards.*]

LYUBOV. How does it go? Let me remember. Cannon off the red!

GAEV. That's it—in off the white! Why, once, sister, we used to sleep together in this very room, and now I'm fifty-one, strange as it seems.

LOPAHIN. Yes, time flies.

GAEV. What do you say?

LOPAHIN. Time, I say, flies.

GAEV. What a smell of patchouli!

ANYA. I'm going to bed. Good-night, mamma. [*Kisses her mother.*]

LYUBOV. My precious darling. [*Kisses her hands.*] Are you glad to be home? I can't believe it.

ANYA. Good-night, uncle.

GAEV [*kissing her face and hands*]. God bless you! How like you are to your mother! [*to his sister*] At her age you were just the same, Lyuba.

[ANYA *shakes hands with* LOPAHIN *and* PISHTCHIK, *then goes out, shutting the door after her.*]

LYUBOV. She's quite worn out.

PISHTCHIK. Aye, it's a long journey, to be sure.

VARYA [*to* LOPAHIN *and* PISHTCHIK]. Well, gentlemen? It's three o'clock and time to say good-bye.

LYUBOV [*laughs*]. You're just the same as ever, Varya. [*Draws her to her and kisses her.*] I'll just drink my coffee and then we will all go and rest. [FIRS *puts a cushion under her feet.*] Thanks, friend. I am so fond of coffee, I drink it day and night. Thanks, dear old man. [*Kisses* FIRS.]

VARYA. I'll just see whether all the things have been brought in. [*Goes out.*]

LYUBOV. Can it really be me sitting here? [*Laughs.*] I want to dance about and clap my hands. [*Covers her face with her hands.*] And I could drop asleep in a moment! God knows I love my country, I love it tenderly; I couldn't look out of the window in the train, I kept crying so. [*through her tears*] But I must drink my coffee, though. Thank you, Firs, thanks, dear old man. I'm so glad to find you still alive.

FIRS. The day before yesterday.

GAEV. He's rather deaf.

LOPAHIN. I have to set off for Harkov directly, at five o'clock. . . . It is annoying! I wanted to have a look at you, and a little talk. . . . You are just as splendid as ever.

PISHTCHIK [*breathing heavily*]. Handsomer, indeed. . . . Dressed in Parisian style . . . completely bowled me over.

LOPAHIN. Your brother, Leonid Andreyevitch here, is always saying that I'm a low-born knave, that I'm a money-grubber, but I don't care one straw for that. Let him talk. Only I do want you to believe in me as you used to. I do want your wonderful tender eyes to look at me as they used to in the old days. Merciful God! My father was a serf of your father and of your grandfather, but you—you—did so much for me once, that I've forgotten all that; I love you as though you were my kin . . . more than my kin.

LYUBOV. I can't sit still, I simply can't. . . . [*Jumps up and walks about in violent agitation.*] This happiness is too much for me. . . . You may laugh at me, I know I'm silly. . . . My own bookcase. [*Kisses the bookcase.*] My little table.

GAEV. Nurse died while you were away.

LYUBOV [*sits down and drinks coffee*]. Yes, the Kingdom of Heaven be hers! You wrote me of her death.

GAEV. And Anastasy is dead. Squinting Petruchka has left me and is in service now with the police captain in the town. [*Takes a box of caramels out of his pocket and sucks one.*]

PISHTCHIK. My daughter, Dashenka, wishes to be remembered to you.

LOPAHIN. I want to tell you something very pleasant and cheering. [*glancing at his watch*] I'm going directly . . . there's no time to say much . . . well, I can say it in a couple of words. I needn't tell you your cherry orchard is to be sold to pay your debts; the 22nd of August is the date fixed for the sale; but don't you worry, dearest lady, you may sleep in peace, there is a way of saving it. . . . This is what I propose. I beg your attention! Your estate is not twenty miles from the town, the railway runs close by it, and if the cherry orchard and the land along the river bank were cut up into building plots and then let on lease for summer villas, you would make an income of at least 25,000 roubles a year out of it.

GAEV. That's all rot, if you'll excuse me.

LYUBOV. I don't quite understand you, Yermolay Alexeyevitch.

LOPAHIN. You will get a rent of at least 25 roubles a year for a three-acre plot from summer visitors, and if you say the word now, I'll bet you what you like there won't be one square foot of ground vacant by the autumn, all the plots will be taken up. I congratulate you; in fact, you are saved. It's a perfect situation with that deep river. Only, of course, it must be cleared—all the old buildings, for example, must be removed, this house too, which is really good for nothing, and the old cherry orchard must be cut down.

LYUBOV. Cut down? My dear fellow, forgive me, but you don't know what you are talking about. If there is one thing interesting—remarkable indeed—in the whole province, it's just our cherry orchard.

LOPAHIN. The only thing remarkable about the orchard is that it's a very large one. There's a crop of cherries every alternate year, and then there's nothing to be done with them, no one buys them.

GAEV. This orchard is mentioned in the "Encyclopædia."

LOPAHIN [*glancing at his watch*]. If we don't decide on something and don't take some steps, on the 22nd of August the cherry orchard and the whole estate too will be sold by auction. Make up your minds! There is no other way of saving it, I'll take my oath on that. No, No!

FIRS. In the old days, forty or fifty years ago, they used to dry the cherries, soak them, pickle them, make jam too, and they used . . .

GAEV. Be quiet, Firs.

FIRS. And they used to send the preserved cherries to Moscow and to Harkov by the wagon-load. That brought the money in! And the preserved cherries in those days were soft and juicy, sweet and fragrant. . . . They knew the way to do them then. . . .

LYUBOV. And where is the recipe now?

FIRS. It's forgotten. Nobody remembers it.

PISHTCHIK [*to* LYUBOV ANDREYEVNA]. What's it like in Paris? Did you eat frogs there?

LYUBOV. Oh, I ate crocodiles.

PISHTCHIK. Fancy that now!

LOPAHIN. There used to be only the gentlefolks and the peasants in the country, but now there are these summer visitors. All the towns, even the small ones, are surrounded nowadays by these summer villas. And one may say for sure, that in another twenty years there'll be many more of these people and that they'll be everywhere. At present the summer visitor only drinks tea in his verandah, but maybe he'll take to working his bit of land too, and then your cherry orchard would become happy, rich and prosperous. . . .

GAEV [*indignant*]. What rot!

[*Enter* VARYA *and* YASHA.]

VARYA. There are two telegrams for you, mamma. [*Takes out keys and opens an old-fashioned bookcase with a loud crack.*] Here they are.

LYUBOV. From Paris. [*Tears the telegrams, without reading them.*] I have done with Paris.

GAEV. Do you know, Lyuba, how old that bookcase is? Last week I pulled out the bottom drawer and there I found the date branded on it. The bookcase was made just a hundred years ago. What do you say to that? We might have celebrated its jubilee. Though it's an inanimate object, still it is a *book* case.

PISHTCHIK [*amazed*]. A hundred years! Fancy that now.

GAEV. Yes. . . . It is a thing . . . [*feeling the bookcase*] Dear, honoured bookcase! Hail to thee who for more than a hundred years hast served the pure ideals of good and justice; thy silent call to fruitful labour has never flagged in those hundred years, maintaining [*in tears*] in the generations of man, courage and faith in a brighter future and fostering in us ideals of good and social consciousness [*a pause*].

LOPAHIN. Yes. . . .

LYUBOV. You are just the same as ever, Leonid.

GAEV [*a little embarrassed*]. Cannon off the right into the pocket!

LOPAHIN [*looking at his watch*]. Well, it's time I was off.

YASHA [*handing* LYUBOV ANDREYEVNA *medicine*]. Perhaps you will take your pills now.

PISHTCHIK. You shouldn't take medicines, my dear madam . . . they do no harm and no good. Give them here . . . honoured lady. [*Takes the pill-box, pours the pills into the hollow of his hand, blows on them, puts them in his mouth and drinks off some kvass.*] There!

LYUBOV [*in alarm*]. Why, you must be out of your mind!

PISHTCHIK. I have taken all the pills.

LOPAHIN. What a glutton! [*All laugh.*]

FIRS. His honour stayed with us in Easter week, ate a gallon and a half of cucumbers . . . [*Mutters.*]

LYUBOV. What is he saying?

VARYA. He has taken to muttering like that for the last three years. We are used to it.

YASHA. His declining years!

[CHARLOTTA IVANOVNA, *a very thin, lanky figure in a white dress with a lorgnette in her belt, walks across the stage.*]

LOPAHIN. I beg your pardon, Charlotta Ivanovna, I have not had time to greet you. [*Tries to kiss her hand.*]

CHARLOTTA [*pulling away her hand*]. If I let you kiss my hand, you'll be wanting to kiss my elbow, and then my shoulder.

LOPAHIN. I've no luck today! [*All laugh.*] Charlotta Ivanovna, show us some tricks!

LYUBOV. Charlotta, do show us some tricks!

CHARLOTTA. I don't want to. I'm sleepy. [*Goes out.*]

LOPAHIN. In three weeks' time we shall meet again. [*Kisses* LYUBOV ANDREYEVNA'S *hand.*] Good-bye till then—I must go. [*to* GAEV] Good-bye. [*Kisses* PISHTCHIK.] Good-bye. [*Gives his hand to* VARYA, *then to* FIRS *and* YASHA.] I don't want to go. [*to* LYUBOV ANDREYEVNA] If you think over my plan for the villas and make up your mind, then let me know; I will lend you 50,000 roubles. Think of it seriously.

VARYA [*angrily*]. Well, do go, for goodness' sake.

LOPAHIN. I'm going, I'm going. [*Goes out.*]

GAEV. Low-born knave! I beg pardon, though . . . Varya is going to marry him, he's Varya's fiancé.

VARYA. Don't talk nonsense, uncle.

LYUBOV. Well, Varya, I shall be delighted. He's a good man.

PISHTCHIK. He is, one must acknowledge, a most worthy man. And my Dashenka . . . says too that . . . she says . . . various things. [*Snores, but at once wakes up.*] But all the same, honoured lady, could you oblige me . . . with a loan of 240 roubles . . . to pay the interest on my mortgage tomorrow?

VARYA [*dismayed*]. No, no.

LYUBOV. I really haven't any money.

PISHTCHIK. It will turn up. [*Laughs.*] I never lose hope. I thought everything was over, I was a ruined man, and lo and behold—the railway passed through my land and . . . they paid me for it. And something else will turn up again, if not today, then tomorrow . . . Dashenka'll win two hundred thousand . . . she's got a lottery ticket.

LYUBOV. Well, we've finished our coffee, we can go to bed.

FIRS [*brushes* GAEV, *reprovingly*]. You have got on the wrong trousers again! What am I to do with you?

VARYA [*softly*]. Anya's asleep. [*Softly opens the window.*] Now the sun's risen, it's not a bit cold. Look, mamma, what exquisite trees! My goodness! And the air! The starlings are singing!

GAEV [*opens another window*]. The orchard is all white. You've not forgotten it, Lyuba? That long avenue that runs straight, straight as an arrow, how it shines on a moonlight night. You remember? You've not forgotten?

LYUBOV [*looking out of the window into the garden*]. Oh, my childhood, my innocence! It was in this nursery I used to sleep, from here I looked out into the orchard, happiness waked with me every morning and in those days the orchard was just the same, nothing has changed. [*Laughs with delight.*] All, all white! Oh, my orchard! After the dark gloomy autumn, and the cold winter; you are young again, and full of happiness, the heavenly angels have never left you. . . . If I could cast off the burden that weighs on my heart, if I could forget the past!

GAEV. H'm! and the orchard will be sold to pay our debts; it seems strange. . . .

LYUBOV. See, our mother walking . . . all in white, down the avenue! [*Laughs with delight.*] It is she!

GAEV. Where?

VARYA. Oh, don't, mamma!

LYUBOV. There is no one. It was my fancy. On the right there, by the path to the arbour, there is a white tree bending like a woman. . . .

[*Enter* TROFIMOV *wearing a shabby student's uniform and spectacles.*]

LYUBOV. What a ravishing orchard! White masses of blossoms, blue sky. . . .

TROFIMOV. Lyubov Andreyevna! [*She looks round at him.*] I will just pay my respects to you and then leave you at once. [*Kisses her hand warmly.*] I was told to wait until morning, but I hadn't the patience to wait any longer. . . .

[LYUBOV ANDREYEVNA *looks at him in perplexity.*]

VARYA [*through her tears*]. This is Petya Trofimov.

TROFIMOV. Petya Trofimov, who was your Grisha's tutor. . . . Can I have changed so much?

[LYUBOV ANDREYEVNA *embraces him and weeps quietly.*]

GAEV [*in confusion*]. There, there, Lyuba.

VARYA [*crying*]. I told you, Petya, to wait till tomorrow.

LYUBOV. My Grisha . . . my boy . . . Grisha . . . my son!

VARYA. We can't help it, mamma, it is God's will.

TROFIMOV [*softly through his tears*]. There . . . there.

LYUBOV [*weeping quietly*]. My boy was lost . . . drowned. Why? Oh, why, dear Petya? [*more quietly*] Anya is asleep in there, and I'm talking loudly . . . making this noise. . . . But, Petya? Why have you grown so ugly? Why do you look so old?

TROFIMOV. A peasant-woman in the train called me a mangy-looking gentleman.

LYUBOV. You were quite a boy then, a pretty little student, and now your hair's thin—and spectacles. Are you really a student still? [*Goes towards the door.*]

TROFIMOV. I seem likely to be a perpetual student.

LYUBOV [*kisses her brother, then* VARYA]. Well, go to bed. . . . You are older too, Leonid.

PISHTCHIK [*follows her*]. I suppose it's time we were asleep. . . . Ugh! my gout. I'm staying the night! Lyubov Andreyevna, my dear soul, if you could . . . tomorrow morning . . . 240 roubles.

GAEV. That's always his story.

PISHTCHIK. 240 roubles . . . to pay the interest on my mortgage.

LYUBOV. My dear man, I have no money.

PISHTCHIK. I'll pay it back, my dear . . . a trifling sum.

LYUBOV. Oh, well, Leonid will give it you . . . You give him the money, Leonid.

GAEV. Me give it him! Let him wait till he gets it!

LYUBOV. It can't be helped, give it him. He needs it. He'll pay it back.

[LYUBOV ANDREYEVNA, TROFIMOV, PISHTCHIK *and* FIRS *go out.* GAEV, VARYA *and* YASHA *remain.*]

GAEV. Sister hasn't got out of the habit of flinging away her money. [*to* YASHA] Get away, my good fellow, you smell of the hen-house.

YASHA [*with a grin*]. And you, Leonid Andreyevitch, are just the same as ever.

GAEV. What's that? [*to* VARYA] What did he say?

VARYA [*to* YASHA]. Your mother has come from the village; she has been sitting in the servants' room since yesterday, waiting to see you.

YASHA. Oh, bother her!

VARYA. For shame!

YASHA. What's the hurry? She might just as well have come tomorrow. [*Goes out.*]

VARYA. Mamma's just the same as ever, she hasn't changed a bit. If she had her own way, she'd give away everything.

GAEV. Yes. [*a pause*] If a great many remedies are suggested for some disease, it means that the disease is incurable. I keep thinking and racking my brains; I have many schemes, a great many, and that really means none. If we could only come in for a legacy from somebody, or marry our Anya to a very rich man, or we might go to Yaroslavl and try our luck with our old aunt, the Countess. She's very, very rich, you know.

VARYA [*weeps*]. If God would help us.

GAEV. Don't blubber. Aunt's very rich, but she doesn't like us. First, sister married a lawyer instead of a nobleman. . . .

[ANYA *appears in the doorway.*]

GAEV. And then her conduct, one can't call it virtuous. She is good, and kind, and nice, and I love her, but, however one allows for extenuating circumstances, there's no denying that she's an immoral woman. One feels it in her slightest gesture.

VARYA [*in a whisper*]. Anya's in the doorway.

GAEV. What do you say? [*a pause*] It's queer, there seems to be something wrong with my right eye. I don't see as well as I did. And on Thursday when I was in the district Court . . .

[*Enter* ANYA.]

VARYA. Why aren't you asleep, Anya?

ANYA. I can't get to sleep.

GAEV. My pet. [*Kisses* ANYA'S *face and hands.*] My child. [*Weeps.*] You are not my niece, you are my angel, you are everything to me. Believe me, believe . . .

ANYA. I believe you, uncle. Everyone loves you and respects you . . . but, uncle dear, you must be silent . . . simply be silent. What were you saying just now about my mother, about your own sister? What made you say that?

GAEV. Yes, yes . . . [*Puts his hand over his face.*] Really, that was awful! My God, save me! And today I made a speech to the bookcase . . . so stupid! And only when I had finished, I saw how stupid it was.

VARYA. It's true, uncle, you ought to keep quiet. Don't talk, that's all.

ANYA. If you could keep from talking, it would make things easier for you, too.

GAEV. I won't speak. [*Kisses* ANYA'S *and* VARYA'S *hands.*] I'll be silent. Only this is about business. On Thursday I was in the district Court; well, there was a large party of us there and we began talking of one thing and another, and this and that, and do you know, I believe that it will be possible to raise a loan on an I.O.U. to pay the arrears on the mortgage.

VARYA. If the Lord would help us!

GAEV. I'm going on Tuesday; I'll talk of it again. [*to* VARYA] Don't blubber. [*to* ANYA] Your mamma will talk to Lopahin; of course, he won't refuse her. And as soon as you're rested you shall go to Yaroslavl to the Countess, your great-aunt. So we shall all set to work in three directions at once, and the business is done. We shall pay off arrears, I'm convinced of it. [*Puts a caramel in his mouth.*] I swear on my honour, I swear by anything you like, the estate shan't be sold. [*excitedly*] By my own happiness, I swear it! Here's my hand on it, call me the basest, vilest of men, if I let it come to an auction! Upon my soul I swear it!

ANYA [*her equanimity has returned, she is quite happy*]. How good you are, uncle, and how clever! [*Embraces her uncle.*] I'm at peace now! Quite at peace! I'm happy!

[*Enter* FIRS.]

FIRS [*reproachfully*]. Leonid Andreyevitch, have you no fear of God? When are you going to bed?

GAEV. Directly, directly. You can go, Firs. I'll . . . yes, I will undress myself. Come, children, bye-bye. We'll go into details tomorrow, but now go to bed. [*Kisses* ANYA *and* VARYA.] I'm a man of the 'eighties. They run down that period, but still I can say I have had to suffer not a little for my convictions in my life. It's not for nothing that the peasant loves me. One must know the peasant! One must know how . . .

ANYA. At it again, uncle!

VARYA. Uncle dear, you'd better be quiet!

FIRS [*angrily*]. Leonid Andreyevitch!

GAEV. I'm coming. I'm coming. Go to bed. Potted the shot—there's a shot for you! A beauty! [*Goes out,* FIRS *hobbling after him.*]

ANYA. My mind's at rest now. I don't want to go to Yaroslavl, I don't like my great-aunt, but still my mind's at rest. Thanks to uncle. [*Sits down.*]

VARYA. We must go to bed. I'm going. Something unpleasant happened while you were away. In the old servants' quarters there are only the old servants, as you know—Efimyushka, Polya and Yevstigney—and Karp too. They began letting stray people in to spend the night—I said nothing. But all at once I heard they had been spreading a report that I gave them nothing but pease pudding to eat. Out of stinginess, you know. . . . And it was all Yevstigney's doing. . . . Very well, I said to myself. . . . If that's how it is, I thought, wait

577 **'eighties** a period of political reaction in Russia. The 'sixties saw major political and social reforms; the **'seventies** (II. 117) saw those reforms undermined; the **'eighties** saw a return to repressive oligarchy. Gaev thinks of his reactionary leanings as devotion to old-fashioned ideals.

a bit. I sent for Yevstigney. . . . [*Yawns.*] He comes. . . . "How's this, Yevstigney," I said, "you could be such a fool as to? . . . " [*looking at* ANYA] Anitchka! [*a pause*] She's asleep. [*Puts her arm round* ANYA.] Come to bed . . . come along! [*Leads her.*] My darling has fallen asleep! Come . . . [*They go.*]

[*Far away beyond the orchard a shepherd plays on a pipe.* TROFIMOV *crosses the stage and, seeing* VARYA *and* ANYA, *stands still.*]

VARYA. Sh! asleep, asleep. Come, my own.

ANYA [*softly, half asleep*]. I'm so tired. Still those bells. Uncle . . . dear . . . mamma and uncle. . . .

VARYA. Come, my own, come along. [*They go into* ANYA'S *room.*]

TROFIMOV [*tenderly*]. My sunshine! My spring.

THE CURTAIN FALLS

ACT II

The open country. An old shrine, long abandoned and fallen out of the perpendicular; near it a well, large stones that have apparently once been tombstones, and an old garden seat. The road to GAEV'S *house is seen. On one side rise dark poplars; and there the cherry orchard begins. In the distance a row of telegraph poles and far, far away on the horizon there is faintly outlined a great town, only visible in very fine clear weather. It is near sunset.* CHARLOTTA, YASHA *and* DUNYASHA *are sitting on the seat.* EPIHODOV *is standing near, playing something mournful on a guitar. All sit plunged in thought.* CHARLOTTA *wears an old forage cap; she has taken a gun from her shoulder and is tightening the buckle on the strap.*

CHARLOTTA [*musingly*]. I haven't a real passport of my own, and I don't know how old I am, and I always feel that I'm a young thing. When I was a little girl, my father and mother used to travel about to fairs and give performances—very good ones. And I used to dance *salto-mortale* and all sorts of things. And when papa and

17 **salto-mortale** the "leap of death," a standing somersault in which only the feet touch the ground

mamma died, a German lady took me and had me educated. And so I grew up and became a governess. But where I came from, and who I am, I don't know. . . . Who my parents were, very likely they weren't married . . . I don't know. [*Takes a cucumber out of her pocket and eats.*] I know nothing at all. [*a pause*] One wants to talk and has no one to talk to . . . I have nobody.

EPIHODOV [*plays on the guitar and sings*]. "What care I for the noisy world! What care I for friends or foes!" How agreeable it is to play on the mandolin!

DUNYASHA. That's a guitar, not a mandolin. [*Looks in a hand-mirror and powders herself.*]

EPIHODOV. To a man mad with love, it's a mandolin. [*Sings.*] "Were her heart but aglow with love's mutual flame." [YASHA *joins in.*]

CHARLOTTA. How shockingly these people sing! Foo! Like jackals!

DUNYASHA [*to* YASHA]. What happiness, though, to visit foreign lands.

YASHA. Ah, yes! I rather agree with you there. [*Yawns, then lights a cigar.*]

EPIHODOV. That's comprehensible. In foreign lands everything has long since reached full complexion.

YASHA. That's so, of course.

EPIHODOV. I'm a cultivated man, I read remarkable books of all sorts, but I can never make out the tendency I am myself precisely inclined for, whether to live or to shoot myself, speaking precisely, but nevertheless I always carry a revolver. Here it is . . . [*Shows revolver.*]

CHARLOTTA. I've had enough, and now I'm going. [*Puts on the gun.*] Epihodov, you're a very clever fellow, and a very terrible one too, all the women must be wild about you. Br-r-r! [*Goes.*] These clever fellows are all so stupid; there's not a creature for me to speak to. . . . Always alone, alone, nobody belonging to me . . . and who I am, and why I'm on earth, I don't know.

[*Walks away slowly.*]

EPIHODOV. Speaking precisely, not touching upon other subjects, I'm bound to admit about myself, that destiny behaves mercilessly to me, as a storm to a little boat. If, let us suppose, I am mistaken, then why did I wake up this morning, to quote an example, and look round, and there on my chest was a spider of fearful magnitude . . . like this. [*Shows with both hands.*] And then I take up a jug of kvass, to quench my thirst, and in it there is something in the highest degree unseemly of the nature of a cockroach. [*a pause*] Have you read Buckle? [*a pause*] I am desirous of troubling you, Dunyasha, with a couple of words.

DUNYASHA. Well, speak.

EPIHODOV. I should be desirous to speak with you alone. [*Sighs.*]

DUNYASHA [*embarrassed*]. Well—only bring me my mantle first. It's by the cupboard. It's rather damp here.

EPIHODOV. Certainly. I will fetch it. Now I know what I must do with my revolver. [*Takes guitar and goes off playing on it.*]

YASHA. Two and twenty misfortunes! Between ourselves, he's a fool. [*Yawns.*]

DUNYASHA. God grant he doesn't shoot himself! [*a pause*] I am so nervous, I'm always in a flutter. I was a little girl when I was taken into our lady's house, and now I have quite grown out of peasant ways, and my hands are white, as white as a lady's. I'm such a delicate, sensitive creature, I'm afraid of everything. I'm so frightened. And if you deceive me, Yasha, I don't know what will become of my nerves.

YASHA [*kisses her*]. You're a peach! Of course a girl must never forget herself; what I dislike more than anything is a girl being flighty in her behaviour.

DUNYASHA. I'm passionately in love with you, Yasha; you are a man of culture—you can give your opinion about anything. [*a pause*]

YASHA [*yawns*]. Yes, that's so. My opinion is this: if a girl loves anyone, that means that she has no principles. [*a pause*] It's pleasant smoking a cigar in the open air. [*Listens.*] Someone's coming this way . . . it's the gentlefolk. [DUNYASHA *embraces him impulsively.*] Go home, as though you had been to the river to bathe; go by that path, or else they'll meet you and suppose I have made an appointment with you here. That I can't endure.

DUNYASHA [*coughing softly*]. The cigar has made my head ache. . . . [*Goes off.*]

[YASHA *remains sitting near the shrine. Enter* LYUBOV ANDREYEVNA, GAEV *and* LOPAHIN.]

60 **Buckle** nineteenth century English historian, highly regarded in Russia as an advanced thinker

LOPAHIN. You must make up your mind once for all—there's no time to lose. It's quite a simple question, you know. Will you consent to letting the land for building or not? One word in answer: Yes or no? Only one word!

LYUBOV. Who is smoking such horrible cigars here? [*Sits down.*]

GAEV. Now the railway line has been brought near, it's made things very convenient. [*Sits down.*] Here we have been over and lunched in town. Cannon off the white! I should like to go home and have a game.

LYUBOV. You have plenty of time.

LOPAHIN. Only one word! [*beseechingly*] Give me an answer!

GAEV [*yawning*]. What do you say?

LYUBOV [*looks in her purse*]. I had quite a lot of money here yesterday, and there's scarcely any left today. My poor Varya feeds us all on milk soup for the sake of economy; the old folks in the kitchen get nothing but pease pudding, while I waste my money in a senseless way. [*Drops purse, scattering gold pieces.*] There, they have all fallen out! [*Annoyed.*]

YASHA. Allow me, I'll soon pick them up. [*Collects the coins.*]

LYUBOV. Pray do, Yasha. And what did I go off to the town to lunch for? Your restaurant's a wretched place with its music and the tablecloth smelling of soap. . . . Why drink so much, Leonid? And eat so much? And talk so much? Today you talked a great deal again in the restaurant, and all so inappropriately. About the era of the 'seventies, about the decadents. And to whom? Talking to waiters about decadents!

LOPAHIN. Yes.

GAEV [*waving his hand*]. I'm incorrigible; that's evident. [*irritably to* YASHA] Why is it you keep fidgeting about in front of us!

YASHA [*laughs*]. I can't help laughing when I hear your voice.

GAEV [*to his sister*]. Either I or he . . .

LYUBOV. Get along! Go away, Yasha.

YASHA [*gives* LYUBOV ANDREYEVNA *her purse*]. Directly. [*hardly able to suppress his laughter*] This minute . . . [*Goes off.*]

LOPAHIN. Deriganov, the millionaire, means to buy your estate. They say he is coming to the sale himself.

117 **decadents** artists and thinkers of the 1890's whose pursuit of novelty in art and politics was widely stigmatized as corrupt

LYUBOV. Where did you hear that?

LOPAHIN. That's what they say in town.

GAEV. Our aunt in Yaroslavl has promised to send help; but when, and how much she will send, we don't know.

LOPAHIN. How much will she send? A hundred thousand? Two hundred?

LYUBOV. Oh, well! . . . Ten or fifteen thousand, and we must be thankful to get that.

LOPAHIN. Forgive me, but such reckless people as you are—such queer, unbusiness-like people—I never met in my life. One tells you in plain Russian your estate is going to be sold, and you seem not to understand it.

LYUBOV. What are we to do? Tell us what to do.

LOPAHIN. I do tell you every day. Every day I say the same thing. You absolutely must let the cherry orchard and the land on building leases; and do it at once, as quick as may be—the auction's close upon us! Do understand! Once make up your mind to build villas, and you can raise as much money as you like, and then you are saved.

LYUBOV. Villas and summer visitors—forgive me saying so—it's so vulgar.

GAEV. There I perfectly agree with you.

LOPAHIN. I shall sob, or scream, or fall into a fit. I can't stand it! You drive me mad! [*to* GAEV] You're an old woman!

GAEV. What do you say?

LOPAHIN. An old woman! [*Gets up to go.*]

LYUBOV [*in dismay*]. No, don't go! Do stay, my dear friend! Perhaps we shall think of something.

LOPAHIN. What is there to think of?

LYUBOV. Don't go, I entreat you! With you here it's more cheerful, anyway. [*a pause*] I keep expecting something, as though the house were going to fall about our ears.

GAEV [*in profound dejection*]. Potted the white! It fails—a kiss.

LYUBOV. We have been great sinners. . . .

LOPAHIN. You have no sins to repent of.

GAEV [*puts a caramel in his mouth*]. They say I've eaten up my property in caramels. [*Laughs.*]

LYUBOV. Oh, my sins! I've always thrown my money away recklessly like a lunatic. I married a man who made nothing but debts. My husband died of champagne—he drank dreadfully. To my misery I loved another man, and immediately—it was my first punishment —the blow fell upon me, here, in the river . . . my boy was drowned and I went abroad—went away for ever, never to return, not to see that river again . . . I shut my eyes, and fled, distracted, and *he* after me . . . pitilessly, brutally. I bought a villa at Mentone, for *he* fell ill there, and for three years I had no rest day or night. His illness wore me out, my soul was dried up. And last year, when my villa was sold to pay my debts, I went to Paris and there he robbed me of everything and abandoned me for another woman; and I tried to poison myself. . . . So stupid, so shameful! . . . And suddenly I felt a yearning for Russia, for my country, for my little girl . . . [*Dries her tears.*] Lord, Lord, be merciful! Forgive my sins! Do not chastise me more! [*Takes a telegram out of her pocket.*] I got this today from Paris. He implores forgiveness, entreats me to return. [*Tears up the telegram.*] I fancy there is music somewhere. [*Listens.*]

GAEV. That's our famous Jewish orchestra. You remember, four violins, a flute and a double bass.

LYUBOV. That still in existence? We ought to send for them one evening, and give a dance.

LOPAHIN [*listens*]. I can't hear. . . . [*Hums softly.*] "For money the Germans will turn a Russian into a Frenchman." [*Laughs.*] I did see such a piece at the theatre yesterday! It was funny!

LYUBOV. And most likely there was nothing funny in it. You shouldn't look at plays, you should look at yourselves a little oftener. How grey your lives are! How much nonsense you talk.

LOPAHIN. That's true. One may say honestly, we live a fool's life. [*pause*] My father was a peasant, an idiot; he knew nothing and taught me nothing, only beat me when he was drunk, and always with his stick. In reality I am just such another blockhead and idiot. I've learnt nothing properly. I write a wretched hand. I write so that I feel ashamed before folks, like a pig.

LYUBOV. You ought to get married, my dear fellow.

189–90 **"For money the Germans . . . Frenchman"** i.e. for money the Germans (numbers of whom had settled in Russia as "experts" in various fields) will turn the barbarian into a model of elegance

LOPAHIN. Yes . . . that's true.

LYUBOV. You should marry our Varya, she's a good girl.

LOPAHIN. Yes.

LYUBOV. She's a good-natured girl, she's busy all day long, and what's more, she loves you. And you have liked her for ever so long.

LOPAHIN. Well? I'm not against it. . . . She's a good girl. [*pause*]

GAEV. I've been offered a place in the bank: 6,000 roubles a year. Did you know?

LYUBOV. You would never do for that! You must stay as you are.

[*Enter* FIRS *with overcoat.*]

FIRS. Put it on, sir, it's damp.

GAEV [*putting it on*]. You bother me, old fellow.

FIRS. You can't go on like this. You went away in the morning without leaving word. [*Looks him over.*]

LYUBOV. You look older, Firs!

FIRS. What is your pleasure?

LOPAHIN. You look older, she said.

FIRS. I've had a long life. They were arranging my wedding before your papa was born. . . . [*Laughs.*] I was the head footman before the emancipation came. I wouldn't consent to be set free then; I stayed on with the old master. . . . [*a pause*] I remember what rejoicings they made and didn't know themselves what they were rejoicing over.

LOPAHIN. Those were fine old times. There was flogging anyway.

FIRS [*not hearing*]. To be sure! The peasants knew their place, and the masters knew theirs; but now they're all at sixes and sevens, there's no making it out.

GAEV. Hold your tongue, Firs. I must go to town tomorrow. I have been promised an introduction to a general, who might let us have a loan.

LOPAHIN. You won't bring that off. And you won't pay your arrears, you may rest assured of that.

LYUBOV. That's all his nonsense. There is no such general.

[*Enter* TROFIMOV, ANYA *and* VARYA.]

GAEV. Here come our girls.

223 **the emancipation** of the serfs in 1861

ANYA. There's mamma on the seat.

LYUBOV [*tenderly*]. Come here, come along. My darlings! [*Embraces* ANYA *and* VARYA.] If you only knew how I love you both. Sit beside me, there, like that. [*All sit down.*]

LOPAHIN. Our perpetual student is always with the young ladies.

TROFIMOV. That's not your business.

LOPAHIN. He'll soon be fifty, and he's still a student.

TROFIMOV. Drop your idiotic jokes.

LOPAHIN. Why are you so cross, you queer fish?

TROFIMOV. Oh, don't persist!

LOPAHIN [*laughs*]. Allow me to ask you what's your idea of me?

TROFIMOV. I'll tell you my idea of you, Yermolay Alexeyevitch: you are a rich man, you'll soon be a millionaire. Well, just as in the economy of nature a wild beast is of use, who devours everything that comes in his way, so you too have your use. [*All laugh.*]

VARYA. Better tell us something about the planets, Petya.

LYUBOV. No, let us go on with the conversation we had yesterday.

TROFIMOV. What was it about?

GAEV. About pride.

TROFIMOV. We had a long conversation yesterday, but we came to no conclusion. In pride, in your sense of it, there is something mystical. Perhaps you are right from your point of view; but if one looks at it simply, without subtlety, what sort of pride can there be, what sense is there in it, if man in his physiological formation is very imperfect, if in the immense majority of cases he is coarse, dull-witted, profoundly unhappy? One must give up glorification of self. One should work, and nothing else.

GAEV. One must die in any case.

TROFIMOV. Who knows? And what does it mean—dying? Perhaps man has a hundred senses, and only the five we know are lost at death, while the other ninety-five remain alive.

LYUBOV. How clever you are, Petya!

LOPAHIN [*ironically*]. Fearfully clever!

TROFIMOV. Humanity progresses, perfecting its powers. Everything that is beyond its ken now will one day become familiar and comprehensible; only we must work, we must with all our powers aid the seeker after truth. Here among us in Russia the workers are few in number as yet. The vast majority of the intellectual people I know, seek nothing, do nothing, are not fit as yet for work of any kind. They call themselves intellectual, but they treat their servants as inferiors, behave to the peasants as though they were animals, learn little, read nothing seriously, do practically nothing, only talk about science and know very little about art. They are all serious people, they all have severe faces, they all talk of weighty matters and air their theories, and yet the vast majority of us—ninety-nine per cent.—live like savages, at the least thing fly to blows and abuse, eat piggishly, sleep in filth and stuffiness, bugs everywhere, stench and damp and moral impurity. And it's clear all our fine talk is only to divert our attention and other people's. Show me where to find the crèches there's so much talk about, and the reading-rooms? They only exist in novels: in real life there are none of them. There is nothing but filth and vulgarity and Asiatic apathy. I fear and dislike very serious faces. I'm afraid of serious conversations. We should do better to be silent.

LOPAHIN. You know, I get up at five o'clock in the morning, and I work from morning to night; and I've money, my own and other people's, always passing through my hands, and I see what people are made of all round me. One has only to begin to do anything to see how few honest, decent people there are. Sometimes when I lie awake at night, I think: "Oh! Lord, thou hast given us immense forests, boundless plains, the widest horizons, and living here we ourselves ought really to be giants."

LYUBOV. You ask for giants! They are no good except in story-books; in real life they frighten us.

[EPIHODOV *advances in the background, playing on the guitar.*]

LYUBOV [*dreamily*]. There goes Epihodov.

ANYA [*dreamily*]. There goes Epihodov.

GAEV. The sun has set, my friends.

TROFIMOV. Yes.

GAEV [*not loudly, but, as it were, declaiming*]. O nature, divine nature, thou art bright with eternal lustre, beautiful and indifferent! Thou, whom we call mother, thou dost unite within thee life and death! Thou dost give life and dost destroy!

VARYA [*in a tone of supplication*]. Uncle!

289 **crèches** day nurseries

ANYA. Uncle, you are at it again!

TROFIMOV. You'd much better be cannoning off the red!

GAEV. I'll hold my tongue, I will.

[*All sit plunged in thought. Perfect stillness. The only thing audible is the muttering of* FIRS. *Suddenly there is a sound in the distance, as it were from the sky—the sound of a breaking harp-string, mournfully dying away.*]

LYUBOV. What is that?

LOPAHIN. I don't know. Somewhere far away a bucket fallen and broken in the pits. But somewhere very far away.

GAEV. It might be a bird of some sort—such as a heron.

TROFIMOV. Or an owl.

LYUBOV [*shudders*]. I don't know why, but it's horrid. [*a pause*]

FIRS. It was the same before the calamity—the owl hooted and the samovar hissed all the time.

GAEV. Before what calamity?

FIRS. Before the emancipation. [*a pause*]

LYUBOV. Come, my friends, let us be going; evening is falling. [*to* ANYA] There are tears in your eyes. What is it, darling? [*Embraces her.*]

ANYA. Nothing, mamma; it's nothing.

TROFIMOV. There is somebody coming.

[THE WAYFARER *appears in a shabby white forage cap and an overcoat; he is slightly drunk.*]

WAYFARER. Allow me to inquire, can I get to the station this way?

GAEV. Yes. Go along that road.

WAYFARER. I thank you most feelingly. [*coughing*] The weather is superb. [*Declaims.*] My brother, my suffering brother! . . . Come out to the Volga! Whose groan do you hear? . . . [*to* VARYA] Mademoiselle, vouchsafe a hungry Russian thirty kopeks.

[VARYA *utters a shriek of alarm.*]

LOPAHIN [*angrily*]. There's a right and a wrong way of doing everything!

LYUBOV [*hurriedly*]. Here, take this. [*Looks in her purse.*] I've no silver. No matter—here's gold for you.

WAYFARER. I thank you most feelingly! [*Goes off.*]

[*Laughter.*]

VARYA [*frightened*]. I'm going home—I'm going . . . Oh, mamma, the servants have nothing to eat, and you gave him gold!

LYUBOV. There's no doing anything with me. I'm so silly! When we get home, I'll give you all I possess. Yermolay Alexeyevitch, you will lend me some more . . . !

LOPAHIN. I will.

LYUBOV. Come, friends, it's time to be going. And Varya, we have made a match of it for you. I congratulate you.

VARYA [*through her tears*]. Mamma, that's not a joking matter.

LOPAHIN. "Ophelia, get thee to a nunnery!"

GAEV. My hands are trembling; it's a long while since I had a game of billiards.

LOPAHIN. "Ophelia! Nymph, in thy orisons be all my sins remember'd."

LYUBOV. Come, it will soon be supper-time.

VARYA. How he frightened me! My heart's simply throbbing.

LOPAHIN. Let me remind you, ladies and gentlemen: on the 22nd of August the cherry orchard will be sold. Think about that! Think about it! [*All go off, except* TROFIMOV *and* ANYA.]

ANYA [*laughing*]. I'm grateful to the wayfarer! He frightened Varya and we are left alone.

TROFIMOV. Varya's afraid we shall fall in love with each other, and for days together she won't leave us. With her narrow brain she can't grasp that we are above love. To eliminate the petty and transitory which hinders us from being free and happy—that is the aim and meaning of our life. Forward! We go forward irresistibly towards the bright star that shines yonder in the distance. Forward! Do not lag behind, friends.

ANYA [*claps her hands*]. How well you speak! [*a pause*] It is divine here today.

TROFIMOV. Yes, it's glorious weather.

ANYA. Somehow, Petya, you've made me so that I don't love the cherry orchard as I used to. I used to love it so dearly. I used to think that there was no spot on earth like our garden.

TROFIMOV. All Russia is our garden. The earth is great and beautiful—there are many beautiful places in it. [*a pause*] Think only, Anya, your grandfather, and great-grandfather, and all your ancestors were slave-owners—the owners of living souls—and from every cherry in the orchard, from every leaf, from every trunk there are human creatures looking at you. Cannot you hear their voices? Oh, it is awful! Your orchard is a fearful thing, and when in the evening or at night one walks about the orchard, the old bark on the trees glimmers dimly in the dusk, and the old cherry trees seem to be dreaming of centuries gone by and tortured by fearful visions. Yes! We are at least two hundred years behind, we have really gained nothing yet, we have no definite attitude to the past, we do nothing but theorise or complain of depression or drink vodka. It is clear that to begin to live in the present we must first expiate our past, we must break with it; and we can expiate it only by suffering, by extraordinary unceasing labour. Understand that, Anya.

ANYA. The house we live in has long ceased to be our own, and I shall leave it, I give you my word.

TROFIMOV. If you have the house keys, fling them into the well and go away. Be free as the wind.

ANYA [*in ecstasy*]. How beautifully you said that!

TROFIMOV. Believe me, Anya, believe me! I am not thirty yet, I am young, I am still a student, but I have gone through so much already! As soon as winter comes I am hungry, sick, careworn, poor as a beggar, and what ups and downs of fortune have I not known! And my soul was always, every minute, day and night, full of inexplicable forebodings. I have a foreboding of happiness, Anya. I see glimpses of it already.

ANYA [*pensively*]. The moon is rising.

[EPIHODOV *is heard playing still the same mournful song on the guitar. The moon rises. Somewhere near the poplars* VARYA *is looking for* ANYA *and calling* "Anya! Where are you?"]

TROFIMOV. Yes, the moon is rising. [*a pause*] Here is happiness—here it comes! It is coming nearer and nearer; already I can hear its footsteps. And if we never see it—if we may never know it—what does it matter? Others will see it after us.

VARYA'S VOICE. Anya! Where are you?

TROFIMOV. That Varya again! [*angrily*] It's revolting!

ANYA. Well, let's go down to the river. It's lovely there.

TROFIMOV. Yes, let's go. [*They go.*]

VARYA'S VOICE. Anya! Anya!

THE CURTAIN FALLS

ACT III

A drawing-room divided by an arch from a larger drawing-room. A chandelier burning. The Jewish orchestra, the same that was mentioned in Act II, is heard playing in the ante-room. It is evening. In the larger drawing-room they are dancing the grand chain. The voice of SEMYONOV-PISHTCHIK: "Promenade à une paire!" *Then enter the drawing-room in couples first* PISHTCHIK *and* CHARLOTTA IVANOVNA, *then* TROFIMOV *and* LYUBOV ANDREYEVNA, *thirdly* ANYA *with* the POST-OFFICE CLERK, *fourthly* VARYA *with the* STATION MASTER, *and other guests.* VARYA *is quietly weeping and wiping away her tears as she dances. In the last couple is* DUNYASHA. *They move across the drawing-room.* PISHTCHIK *shouts*: "Grand rond, balancez!" *and* "Les Cavaliers à genou et remerciez vos dames." FIRS *in a swallow-tail coat brings in seltzer water on a tray.* PISHTCHIK *and* TROFIMOV *enter the drawing-room.*

PISHTCHIK. I am a full-blooded man; I have already had two strokes. Dancing's hard work for me, but as they say, if you're in the pack, you must bark with the rest. I'm as strong, I may say, as a horse. My parent, who would have his joke—may the Kingdom of Heaven be his!—used to say about our origin that the ancient stock of the Semyonov-Pishtchiks was derived from the very horse that Caligula made a member of the senate. [*Sits down.*] But I've no money, that's where the mischief is. A hungry dog believes in nothing but meat. . . . [*Snores, but at once wakes up.*] That's like me . . . I can think of nothing but money.

TROFIMOV. There really is something horsy about your appearance.

PISHTCHIK. Well . . . a horse is a fine beast . . . a horse can be sold.

[*There is the sound of billiards being played in an adjoining room.* VARYA *appears in the arch leading to the larger drawing-room.*]

TROFIMOV [*teasing*]. Madame Lopahin! Madame Lopahin!

VARYA [*angrily*]. Mangy-looking gentleman!

TROFIMOV. Yes, I am a mangy-looking gentleman, and I'm proud of it!

VARYA [*pondering bitterly*]. Here we have hired musicians and nothing to pay them! [*Goes out.*]

TROFIMOV [*to* PISHTCHIK]. If the energy you have wasted during your lifetime in trying to find the money to pay your interest, had gone to something else, you might in the end have turned the world upside down.

PISHTCHIK. Nietzsche, the philosopher, a very great and celebrated man . . . of enormous intellect . . . says in his works, that one can make forged bank-notes.

TROFIMOV. Why, have you read Nietzsche?

PISHTCHIK. What next . . . Dashenka told me. . . . And now I am in such a position, I might just as well forge bank-notes. The day after tomorrow I must pay 310 roubles—130 I have procured. [*Feels in his pockets, in alarm.*] The money's gone! I have lost my money! [*through his tears*] Where's the money? [*gleefully*] Why, here it is behind the lining. . . . It has made me hot all over.

[*Enter* LYUBOV ANDREYEVNA *and* CHARLOTTA IVANOVNA.]

LYUBOV [*hums the Lezginka*]. Why is Leonid so long? What can he be doing in town? [*to* DUNYASHA] Offer the musicians some tea.

TROFIMOV. The sale hasn't taken place, most likely.

LYUBOV. It's the wrong time to have the orchestra, and the wrong time to give a dance. Well, never mind. [*Sits down and hums softly.*]

CHARLOTTA [*gives* PISHTCHIK *a pack of cards*]. Here's a pack of cards. Think of any card you like.

PISHTCHIK. I've thought of one.

CHARLOTTA. Shuffle the pack now. That's right. Give it here, my dear Mr. Pishtchik. Ein, zwei, drei—now look, it's in your breast pocket.

PISHTCHIK [*taking a card out of his breast pocket*]. The eight of spades! Perfectly right! [*wonderingly*] Fancy that now!

CHARLOTTA [*holding pack of cards in her hands, to* TROFIMOV]. Tell me quickly which is the top card.

TROFIMOV. Well, the queen of spades.

CHARLOTTA. It is! [*to* PISHTCHIK] Well, which card is uppermost?

PISHTCHIK. The ace of hearts.

CHARLOTTA. It is! [*Claps her hands, pack of cards disappears.*]

42–43 **one can make** it is ethical to make
52 **the Lezginka** a sprightly Caucasian dance tune

Ah! what lovely weather it is today!

[*A mysterious feminine voice which seems coming out of the floor answers her.* "Oh, yes, it's magnificent weather, madam."]

CHARLOTTA. You are my perfect ideal.

VOICE. And I greatly admire you too, madam.

STATION MASTER [*applauding*]. The lady ventriloquist—bravo!

PISHTCHIK [*wonderingly*]. Fancy that now! Most enchanting Charlotta Ivanovna. I'm simply in love with you.

CHARLOTTA. In love? [*shrugging shoulders*] What do you know of love, guter Mensch, aber schlechter Musikant.

TROFIMOV [*pats* PISHTCHIK *on the shoulder*]. You dear old horse. . . .

CHARLOTTA. Attention, please! Another trick! [*Takes a travelling rug from the chair.*] Here's a very good rug; I want to sell it. [*shaking it out*] Doesn't anyone want to buy it?

PISHTCHIK [*wonderingly*]. Fancy that!

CHARLOTTA. Ein, zwei, drei! [*Quickly picks up rug she has dropped; behind the rug stands* ANYA; *she makes a curtsey, runs to her mother, embraces her and runs back into the larger drawing-room amidst general enthusiasm.*]

LYUBOV [*applauds*]. Bravo! Bravo!

CHARLOTTA. Now again! Ein, zwei, drei! [*Lifts up the rug; behind the rugs stands* VARYA, *bowing.*]

PISHTCHIK [*wonderingly*]. Fancy that now!

CHARLOTTA. That's the end. [*Throws the rug at* PISHTCHIK, *makes a curtsey, runs into the larger drawing-room.*]

PISHTCHIK [*hurries after her*]. Mischievous creature! Fancy! [*Goes out.*]

LYUBOV. And still Leonid doesn't come. I can't understand what he's doing in the town so long! Why, everything must be over by now. The estate is sold, or the sale has not taken place. Why keep us so long in suspense?

VARYA [*trying to console her*]. Uncle's bought it. I feel sure of that.

TROFIMOV [*ironically*]. Oh, yes!

VARYA. Great-aunt sent him an authorisation to buy it in her name, and transfer the debt. She's doing it for Anya's sake, and I'm sure God will be merciful. Uncle will buy it.

80 **guter Mensch . . . Musikant** "a good man but a bad musician"

LYUBOV. My aunt in Yaroslavl sent fifteen thousand to buy the estate in her name, she doesn't trust us—but that's not enough even to pay the arrears. [*Hides her face in her hands.*] My fate is being sealed today, my fate . . .

TROFIMOV [*teasing* VARYA]. Madame Lopahin.

VARYA [*angrily*]. Perpetual student! Twice already you've been sent down from the University.

LYUBOV. Why are you angry, Varya? He's teasing you about Lopahin. Well, what of that? Marry Lopahin if you like, he's a good man, and interesting; if you don't want to, don't! Nobody compels you, darling.

VARYA. I must tell you plainly, mamma, I look at the matter seriously; he's a good man, I like him.

LYUBOV. Well, marry him. I can't see what you're waiting for.

VARYA. Mamma, I can't make him an offer myself. For the last two years, everyone's been talking to me about him. Everyone talks; but he says nothing or else makes a joke. I see what it means. He's growing rich, he's absorbed in business, he has no thoughts for me. If I had money, were it ever so little, if I had only a hundred roubles, I'd throw everything up and go far away. I would go into a nunnery.

TROFIMOV. What bliss!

VARYA [*to* TROFIMOV]. A student ought to have sense! [*in a soft tone with tears*] How ugly you've grown, Petya! How old you look! [*to* LYUBOV ANDREYEVNA, *no longer crying*] But I can't do without work, mamma; I must have something to do every minute.

[*Enter* YASHA.]

YASHA [*hardly restraining his laughter*]. Epihodov has broken a billiard cue! [*Goes out.*]

VARYA. What is Epihodov doing here? Who gave him leave to play billiards? I can't make these people out. [*Goes out.*]

LYUBOV. Don't tease her, Petya. You see she has grief enough without that.

TROFIMOV. She is so very officious, meddling in what's not her business. All the summer she's given Anya and me no peace. She's afraid of a love affair between us. What's it to do with her? Besides, I have given no grounds for it. Such triviality is not in my line. We are above love!

115 **sent down** expelled

LYUBOV. And I suppose I am beneath love. [*very uneasily*] Why is it Leonid's not here? If only I could know whether the estate is sold or not! It seems such an incredible calamity that I really don't know what to think. I am distracted . . . I shall scream in a minute . . . I shall do something stupid. Save me, Petya, tell me something, talk to me!

TROFIMOV. What does it matter whether the estate is sold today or not? That's all done with long ago. There's no turning back, the path is overgrown. Don't worry yourself, dear Lyubov Andreyevna. You mustn't deceive yourself; for once in your life you must face the truth!

LYUBOV. What truth? You see where the truth lies, but I seem to have lost my sight, I see nothing. You settle every great problem so boldly, but tell me, my dear boy, isn't it because you're young—because you haven't yet understood one of your problems through suffering? You look forward boldly, and isn't it that you don't see and don't expect anything dreadful because life is still hidden from your young eyes? You're bolder, more honest, deeper than we are, but think, be just a little magnanimous, have pity on me. I was born here, you know, my father and mother lived here, my grandfather lived here, I love this house. I can't conceive of life without the cherry orchard, and if it really must be sold, then sell me with the orchard. [*Embraces* TROFIMOV, *kisses him on the forehead.*] My boy was drowned here. [*Weeps.*] Pity me, my dear kind fellow.

TROFIMOV. You know I feel for you with all my heart.

LYUBOV. But that should have been said differently, so differently. [*Takes out her handkerchief, telegram falls on the floor.*] My heart is so heavy today. It's so noisy here, my soul is quivering at every sound, I'm shuddering all over, but I can't go away; I'm afraid to be quiet and alone. Don't be hard on me, Petya . . . I love you as though you were one of ourselves. I would gladly let you marry Anya—I swear I would—only, my dear boy, you must take your degree, you do nothing—you're simply tossed by fate from place to place. That's so strange. It is, isn't it? And you must do something with your beard to make it grow somehow. [*Laughs.*] You look so funny!

TROFIMOV [*picks up the telegram*]. I've no wish to be a beauty.

LYUBOV. That's a telegram from Paris. I get one every day. One yesterday and one today. That savage creature is ill again, he's in trouble again. He begs forgiveness, beseeches me to go, and really I ought to go to Paris to see him. You look shocked, Petya. What am I to do, my dear boy, what am I to do? He is ill, he is alone and unhappy, and who'll look after him, who'll keep him from doing the wrong thing, who'll give him his medicine at the right time? And why hide it or be silent? I love him, that's clear. I love him! I love him! He's a millstone about my neck, I'm going to the bottom with him, but I love that stone and can't live without it. [*Presses* TROFIMOV's *hand.*] Don't think ill of me, Petya, don't tell me anything, don't tell me . . .

TROFIMOV [*through his tears*]. For God's sake forgive my frankness: why, he robbed you!

LYUBOV. No! No! No! You mustn't speak like that. [*Covers her ears.*]

TROFIMOV. He is a wretch! You're the only person that doesn't know it! He's a worthless creature! A despicable wretch!

LYUBOV [*getting angry, but speaking with restraint*]. You're twenty-six or twenty-seven years old, but you're still a schoolboy.

TROFIMOV. Possibly.

LYUBOV. You should be a man at your age! You should understand what love means! And you ought to be in love yourself. You ought to fall in love! [*angrily*] Yes, yes, and it's not purity in you, you're simply a prude, a comic fool, a freak.

TROFIMOV [*in horror*]. The things she's saying!

LYUBOV. I am above love! You're not above love, but simply as our Firs here says, "You are a good-for-nothing." At your age not to have a mistress!

TROFIMOV [*in horror*]. This is awful! The things she is saying! [*Goes rapidly into the larger drawing-room clutching his head.*] This is awful! I can't stand it! I'm going. [*Goes off, but at once returns.*] All is over between us! [*Goes off into the ante-room.*]

LYUBOV [*shouts after him*]. Petya! Wait a minute! You funny creature! I was joking! Petya! [*There is a sound of somebody running quickly downstairs and suddenly falling with a crash.* ANYA *and* VARYA *scream, but there is a sound of laughter at once.*]

LYUBOV. What has happened?

[ANYA *runs in.*]

ANYA [*laughing*]. Petya's fallen downstairs! [*Runs out.*]

LYUBOV. What a queer fellow that Petya is!

[*The* STATION MASTER *stands in the middle of the larger room and reads "The Magdalene," by Alexey Tolstoy. They listen to him, but before he has recited many lines strains of a waltz are heard from the ante-room and the reading is broken off. All dance.* TROFIMOV, ANYA, VARYA *and* LYUBOV ANDREYEVNA *come in from the ante-room.*]

LYUBOV. Come, Petya—come, pure heart! I beg your pardon. Let's have a dance! [*Dances with* PETYA.]

[ANYA *and* VARYA *dance.* FIRS *comes in, puts his stick down near the side door.* YASHA *also comes into the drawing-room and looks on at the dancing.*]

YASHA. What is it, old man?

FIRS. I don't feel well. In old days we used to have generals, barons and admirals dancing at our balls, and now we send for the post-office clerk and the station master and even they're not over-anxious to come. I am getting feeble. The old master, the grandfather, used to give sealing-wax for all complaints. I have been taking sealing-wax for twenty years or more. Perhaps that's what's kept me alive.

YASHA. You bore me, old man! [*Yawns.*] It's time you were done with.

FIRS. Ach, you're a good-for-nothing! [*Mutters.*]

[TROFIMOV *and* LYUBOV ANDREYEVNA *dance in larger room and then on to the stage.*]

226 **The Magdalene** a poem which celebrates Christ's sudden appearance at a banquet of dazzling magnificence. Its opening lines follow:

> The crowd seethes—merrymaking, laughter,
> The sound of lutes and clash of cymbals;
> All around are greenness, flowers,
> And between the columns at the entrance of the house
> Sections of heavy brocade
> Are raised in patterned ribbons.
> The chambers are richly furnished,
> Crystal and gold burn everywhere;
> The courtyard is filled with drivers and horses.
> Crowding at the huge banquet table
> The noisy chorus of guests celebrates;
> Their criss-cross conversation
> Goes on, fusing with the music.

(Trans. Horace W. Dewey)

LYUBOV. Merci. I'll sit down a little. [*Sits down.*] I'm tired.

[*Enter* ANYA.]

ANYA [*excitedly*]. There's a man in the kitchen has been saying that the cherry orchard's been sold today.

LYUBOV. Sold to whom?

ANYA. He didn't say to whom. He's gone away.

[*She dances with* TROFIMOV, *and they go off into the larger room.*]

YASHA. There was an old man gossiping there, a stranger.

FIRS. Leonid Andreyevitch isn't here yet, he hasn't come back. He has his light overcoat on, *demi-saison,* he'll catch cold for sure. Ach! Foolish young things!

LYUBOV. I feel as though I should die. Go, Yasha, find out to whom it has been sold.

YASHA. But he went away long ago, the old chap. [*Laughs.*]

LYUBOV [*with slight vexation*]. What are you laughing at? What are you pleased at?

YASHA. Epihodov is so funny. He's a silly fellow, two and twenty misfortunes.

LYUBOV. Firs, if the estate is sold, where will you go?

FIRS. Where you bid me, there I'll go.

LYUBOV. Why do you look like that? Are you ill? You ought to be in bed.

FIRS. Yes. [*ironically*] Me go to bed and who's to wait here? Who's to see to things without me? I'm the only one in all the house.

YASHA [*to* LYUBOV ANDREYEVNA]. Lyubov Andreyevna, permit me to make a request of you; if you go back to Paris again, be so kind as to take me with you. It's positively impossible for me to stay here. [*looking about him; in an undertone*] There's no need to say it, you see for yourself—an uncivilised country, the people have no morals, and then the dullness! The food in the kitchen's abominable, and then Firs runs after one muttering all sorts of unsuitable words. Take me with you, please do!

[*Enter* PISHTCHIK.]

PISHTCHIK. Allow me to ask you for a waltz, my dear lady. [LYUBOV ANDREYEVNA *goes with him.*] Enchanting lady, I really must borrow of you just 180 roubles [*dances*], only 180 roubles. [*They pass into the larger room.*]

YASHA [*hums softly*]. "Knowest thou my soul's emotion."

[*In the larger drawing-room, a figure in a gray top hat and in check trousers is gesticulating and jumping about. Shouts of* "Bravo, Charlotta Ivanovna."]

DUNYASHA [*she has stopped to powder herself*]. My young lady tells me to dance. There are plenty of gentlemen, and too few ladies, but dancing makes me giddy and makes my heart beat. Firs, the post-office clerk said something to me just now that quite took my breath away.

[*Music becomes more subdued.*]

FIRS. What did he say to you?

DUNYASHA. He said I was like a flower.

YASHA [*yawns*]. What ignorance! [*Goes out.*]

DUNYASHA. Like a flower. I am a girl of such delicate feelings, I am awfully fond of soft speeches.

FIRS. Your head's being turned.

[*Enter* EPIHODOV.]

EPIHODOV. You have no desire to see me, Dunyasha. I must be an insect. [*Sighs.*] Ah! life!

DUNYASHA. What is it you want?

EPIHODOV. Undoubtedly you may be right. [*Sighs.*] But of course, if one looks at it from that point of view, if I may so express myself, you have, excuse my plain speaking, reduced me to a complete state of mind. I know my destiny. Every day some misfortune befalls me and I have long ago grown accustomed to it, so that I look upon my fate with a smile. You gave me your word, and though I . . .

DUNYASHA. Let us have a talk later, I entreat you, but now leave me in peace, for I am lost in reverie. [*Plays with her fan.*]

EPIHODOV. I have a misfortune every day, and if I may venture to express myself, I merely smile at it, I even laugh.

[VARYA *enters from the larger drawing-room.*]

VARYA. You still have not gone, Epihodov. What a disrespectful creature you are, really! [*to* DUNYASHA] Go along, Dunyasha! [*to* EPIHODOV] First you play billiards and break the cue, then you go wandering about the drawing-room like a visitor!

EPIHODOV. You really cannot, if I may so express myself, call me to account like this.

VARYA. I'm not calling you to account, I'm speaking to you: You do nothing but wander from place to place and don't do your work. We keep you as a counting-house clerk, but what use you are I can't say.

EPIHODOV [*offended*]. Whether I work or whether I walk, whether I eat or whether I play billiards, is a matter to be judged by persons of understanding and my elders.

VARYA. You dare to tell me that! [*firing up*] You dare! You mean to say I've no understanding. Begone from here! This minute!

EPIHODOV [*intimidated*]. I beg you to express yourself with delicacy.

VARYA [*beside herself with anger*]. This moment! get out! away! [*He goes towards the door, she following him.*] Two and twenty misfortunes! Takes yourself off! Don't let me set eyes on you! [EPIHODOV *has gone out, behind the door his voice,* "I shall lodge a complaint against you."] What! You're coming back? [*Snatches up the stick* FIRS *has put down near the door.*] Come! Come! Come! I'll show you! What! you're coming? Then take that! [*She swings the stick, at the very moment that* LOPAHIN *comes in.*]

LOPAHIN. Very much obliged to you!

VARYA [*angrily and ironically*]. I beg your pardon!

LOPAHIN. Not at all! I humbly thank you for your kind reception!

VARYA. No need of thanks for it. [*Moves away, then looks round and asks softly.*] I haven't hurt you?

LOPAHIN. Oh, no! Not at all! There's an immense bump coming up, though!

VOICES FROM LARGER ROOM. Lopahin has come! Yermolay Alexeyevitch!

PISHTCHIK. What do I see and hear? [*Kisses* LOPAHIN.] There's a whiff of cognac about you, my dear soul, and we're making merry here too!

[*Enter* LYUBOV ANDREYEVNA.]

LYUBOV. Is it you, Yermolay Alexeyevitch? Why have you been so long? Where's Leonid?

LOPAHIN. Leonid Andreyevitch arrived with me. He is coming.

LYUBOV [*in agitation*]. Well! Well! Was there a sale? Speak!

LOPAHIN [*embarrassed, afraid of betraying his joy*]. The sale was over at four o'clock. We missed our train—had to wait till half-past nine. [*sighing heavily*] Ugh! I feel a little giddy.

[*Enter* GAEV. *In his right hand he has purchases, with his left hand he is wiping away his tears.*]

LYUBOV. Well, Leonid? What news? [*impatiently, with tears*] Make haste, for God's sake!

GAEV [*makes her no answer, simply waves his hand. To* FIRS, *weeping*]. Here, take them; there's anchovies, Kertch herrings. I have eaten nothing all day. What I have been through! [*Door into the billiard room is open. There is heard a knocking of balls and the voice of* YASHA *saying* "Eighty-seven." GAEV'S *expression changes, he leaves off weeping.*] I am fearfully tired. Firs, come and help me change my things. [*Goes to his own room across the larger drawing-room.*]

PISHTCHIK. How about the sale? Tell us, do!

LYUBOV. Is the cherry orchard sold?

LOPAHIN. It is sold.

LYUBOV. Who has bought it?

LOPAHIN. I have bought it.

[*A pause.* LYUBOV *is crushed; she would fall down if she were not standing near a chair and table.* VARYA *takes keys from her waistband, flings them on the floor in middle of drawing-room and goes out.*]

LOPAHIN. I have bought it! Wait a bit, ladies and gentlemen, pray. My head's a bit muddled, I can't speak. [*Laughs.*] We came to the auction. Deriganov was there already. Leonid Andreyevitch only had 15,000 and Deriganov bid 30,000, besides the arrears, straight off. I saw how the land lay. I bid against him. I bid 40,000, he bid 45,000, I said 55, and so he went on, adding 5 thousands and I adding 10. Well . . . So it ended. I bid 90, and it was knocked down to me. Now the cherry orchard's mine! Mine! [*Chuckles.*] My God, the cherry orchard's mine! Tell me that I'm drunk, that I'm out of my mind, that it's all a dream. [*Stamps with his feet.*] Don't laugh at me! If my father and my grandfather could rise from their graves and see all that has happened! How their Yermolay, ignorant, beaten Yermolay, who used to run about barefoot in winter, how that very Yermolay has bought the finest estate in the world! I have bought the estate where my father and grandfather were slaves, where they weren't even admitted into the kitchen. I am asleep, I am dreaming! It is all fancy, it is the work of your imagination plunged in the darkness of ignorance. [*Picks up keys, smiling fondly.*] She threw away the keys; she means to show she's not the housewife now. [*Jingles the keys.*] Well, no matter. [*The orchestra is heard tuning up.*] Hey, musicians! Play! I want to hear you. Come, all of you, and look how Yermolay Lopahin will take the axe to the cherry orchard, how the trees will fall to the ground! We will build houses on it and our grandsons and great-grandsons will see a new life springing up there. Music! Play up!

[*Music begins to play.* LYUBOV ANDREYEVNA *has sunk into a chair and is weeping bitterly.*]

LOPAHIN [*reproachfully*]. Why, why didn't you listen to me? My poor friend! Dear lady, there's no turning back now. [*with tears*] Oh, if all this could be over, oh, if our miserable disjointed life could somehow soon be changed!

PISHTCHIK [*takes him by the arm; in an undertone*]. She's weeping, let us go and leave her alone. Come. [*Takes him by the arm and leads him into the larger drawing-room.*]

LOPAHIN. What's that? Musicians, play up! All must be as I wish it. [*with irony*] Here comes the new master, the owner of the cherry orchard! [*Accidentally tips over a little table, almost upsetting the candelabra.*] I can pay for everything! [*Goes out with* PISHTCHIK. *No one remains on the stage or in the larger drawing-room except* LYUBOV, *who sits huddled up, weeping bitterly. The music plays softly.* ANYA *and* TROFIMOV *come in quickly.* ANYA *goes up to her mother and falls on her knees before her.* TROFIMOV *stands at the entrance to the larger drawing-room.*]

ANYA. Mamma! Mamma, you're crying, dear, kind, good mamma! My precious! I love you! I bless you! The cherry orchard is sold, it is gone, that's true, that's true! But don't weep, mamma! Life is still before you, you have still your good, pure heart! Let us go, let us go, darling, away from here! We will make a new garden, more splendid than this one; you will see it, you will understand. And joy, quiet, deep joy, will sink into your soul like the sun at evening! And you will smile, mamma! Come, darling, let us go!

THE CURTAIN FALLS

ACT IV

SCENE: *Same as in First Act. There are neither curtains on the windows nor pictures on the walls: only a little furniture remains piled up in a corner as if for sale. There is a sense of desolation; near the outer door and in the background of the scene are packed trunks, travelling bags, etc. On the left the door is open, and from here the voices of* VARYA *and* ANYA *are audible.* LOPAHIN *is standing waiting.* YASHA *is holding a tray with glasses full of champagne. In front of the stage* EPIHODOV *is tying up a box. In the background behind the scene a hum of talk from the peasants who have come to say good-bye. The voice of* GAEV: "Thanks, brothers, thanks!"

YASHA. The peasants have come to say good-bye. In my opinion, Yermolay Alexeyevitch, the peasants are good-natured, but they don't know much about things.

[*The hum of talk dies away. Enter across front of stage* LYUBOV ANDREYEVNA *and* GAEV. *She is not weeping, but is pale; her face is quivering—she cannot speak.*]

GAEV. You gave them your purse, Lyuba. That won't do—that won't do!

LYUBOV. I couldn't help it! I couldn't help it! [*Both go out.*]

LOPAHIN [*in the doorway, calls after them*]. You will take a glass at parting? Please do. I didn't think to bring any from the town, and at the station I could only get one bottle. Please take a glass. [*a pause*] What? You don't care for any? [*Comes away from the door.*] If I'd known, I wouldn't have bought it. Well, and I'm not going to drink it. [YASHA *carefully sets the tray down on a chair.*] You have a glass, Yasha, anyway.

YASHA. Good luck to the travellers, and luck to those that stay behind! [*Drinks.*] This champagne isn't the real thing, I can assure you.

LOPAHIN. It cost eight roubles the bottle. [*a pause*] It's devilish cold here.

YASHA. They haven't heated the stove today—it's all the same since we're going. [*Laughs.*]

LOPAHIN. What are you laughing for?

YASHA. For pleasure.

LOPAHIN. Though it's October, it's as still and sunny as though it were summer. It's just right for building! [*Looks at his watch; says in doorway:*] Take note, ladies and gentlemen, the train goes in forty-seven minutes; so you ought to start for the station in twenty minutes. You must hurry up!

[TROFIMOV *comes in from out of doors wearing a great-coat.*]

TROFIMOV. I think it must be time to start, the horses are ready. The devil only knows what's become of my goloshes; they're lost. [*in the doorway*] Anya! My goloshes aren't here. I can't find them.

LOPAHIN. And I'm getting off to Harkov. I am going in the same train with you. I'm spending all the winter at Harkov. I've been wasting all my time gossiping with you and fretting with no work to do. I can't get on without work. I don't know what to do with my hands, they flap about so queerly, as if they didn't belong to me.

TROFIMOV. Well, we're just going away, and you will take up your profitable labours again.

LOPAHIN. Do take a glass.

TROFIMOV. No, thanks.

LOPAHIN. Then you're going to Moscow now?

TROFIMOV. Yes. I shall see them as far as the town, and tomorrow I shall go on to Moscow.

LOPAHIN. Yes, I daresay, the professors aren't giving any lectures, they're waiting for your arrival.

TROFIMOV. That's not your business.

LOPAHIN. How many years have you been at the University?

TROFIMOV. Do think of something newer than that—that's stale and flat. [*Hunts for goloshes.*] You know we shall most likely never see each other again, so let me give you one piece of advice at parting: don't wave your arms about—get out of the habit. And another thing, building villas, reckoning up that the summer visitors will in time become independent farmers—reckoning like that, that's not the thing to do either. After all, I am fond of you: you have fine delicate fingers like an artist, you've a fine delicate soul.

LOPAHIN [*embraces him*]. Good-bye, my dear fellow. Thanks for everything. Let me give you money for the journey, if you need it.

TROFIMOV. What for? I don't need it.

LOPAHIN. Why, you haven't got a halfpenny.

TROFIMOV. Yes, I have, thank you. I got some money for a translation. Here it is in my pocket, [*anxiously*] but where can my goloshes be!

VARYA [*from the next room*]. Take the nasty things! [*Flings a pair of goloshes onto the stage.*]

TROFIMOV. Why are you so cross, Varya? h'm! . . . but those aren't my goloshes.

LOPAHIN. I sowed three thousand acres with poppies in the spring, and now I have cleared forty thousand profit. And when my poppies were in flower, wasn't it a picture! So here, as I say, I made forty thousand, and I'm offering you a loan because I can afford to. Why turn up your nose? I am a peasant—I speak bluntly.

TROFIMOV. Your father was a peasant, mine was a chemist—and that proves absolutely nothing whatever. [LOPAHIN *takes out his pocketbook.*] Stop that—stop that. If you were to offer me two hundred thousand I wouldn't take it. I am an independent man, and everything that all of you, rich and poor alike, prize so highly and hold so dear, hasn't the slightest power over me—it's like so much fluff fluttering in the air. I can get on without you. I can pass by you. I am strong and proud. Humanity is advancing towards the highest truth, the highest happiness which is possible on earth, and I am in the front ranks.

LOPAHIN. Will you get there?

TROFIMOV. I shall get there. [*a pause*] I shall get there, or I shall show others the way to get there.

[*In the distance is heard the stroke of an axe on a tree.*]

LOPAHIN. Good-bye, my dear fellow; it's time to be off. We turn up our noses at one another, but life is passing all the while. When I am working hard without resting, then my mind is more at ease, and it seems to me as though I too know what I exist for; but how many people there are in Russia, my dear boy, who exist, one doesn't know what for. Well, it doesn't matter. That's not what keeps things spinning. They tell me Leonid Andreyevitch has taken a situation. He is going to be a clerk at the bank—6,000 roubles a year. Only, of course, he won't stick to it—he's too lazy.

ANYA [*in doorway*]. Mamma begs you not to let them chop down the orchard until she's gone.

TROFIMOV. Yes, really, you might have the tact.

[*Walks out across the front of the stage.*]

LOPAHIN. I'll see to it! I'll see to it! Stupid fellows!

[*Goes out after him.*]

ANYA. Has Firs been taken to the hospital?

YASHA. I told them this morning. No doubt they have taken him.

ANYA [*to* EPIHODOV, *who passes across the drawing-room*]. Semyon Pantaleyevitch, inquire, please, if Firs has been taken to the hospital.

YASHA [*in a tone of offense*]. I told Yegor this morning—why ask a dozen times?

EPIHODOV. Firs is advanced in years. It's my conclusive opinion no treatment would do him good; it's time he was gathered to his fathers. And I can only envy him. [*Puts a trunk down on a cardboard hat-box and crushes it.*] There now, of course—I knew it would be so.

YASHA [*jeeringly*]. Two and twenty misfortunes!

VARYA [*through the door*]. Has Firs been taken to the hospital?

ANYA. Yes.

VARYA. Why wasn't the note for the doctor taken too?

ANYA. Oh, then, we must send it after them. [*Goes out.*]

VARYA [*from the adjoining room*]. Where's Yasha? Tell him his mother's come to say good-bye to him.

YASHA [*waves his hand*]. They put me out of all patience!

[DUNYASHA *has all this time been busy about the luggage. Now, when* YASHA *is left alone, she goes up to him.*]

DUNYASHA. You might just give me one look, Yasha. You're going away. You're leaving me. [*Weeps and throws herself on his neck.*]

YASHA. What are you crying for? [*Drinks the champagne.*] In six days I shall be in Paris again. Tomorrow we shall get into the express train and roll away in a flash. I can scarcely believe it! *Vive la France!* It doesn't suit me here—it's not the life for me; there's no doing anything. I have seen enough of the ignorance here. I have had enough of it. [*Drinks champagne.*] What are you crying for? Behave yourself properly, and then you won't cry.

DUNYASHA [*powders her face, looking in a pocket-mirror*]. Do send me a letter from Paris. You know how I loved you, Yasha—how I loved you! I am a tender creature, Yasha.

YASHA. Here they are coming! [*Busies himself about the trunks, humming softly. Enter* LYUBOV ANDREYEVNA, GAEV, ANYA *and* CHARLOTTA IVANOVNA.]

GAEV. We ought to be off. There's not much time now. [*looking at* YASHA] What a smell of herrings!

LYUBOV. In ten minutes we must get into the carriage. [*Casts a look about the room.*] Farewell, dear house, dear old home of our fathers! Winter will pass and spring will come, and then you will be no more; they will tear you down! How much those walls have seen! [*Kisses her daughter passionately.*] My treasure, how bright you look! Your eyes are sparkling like diamonds! Are you glad? Very glad?

ANYA. Very glad! A new life is beginning, mamma.

GAEV. Yes, really, everything is all right now. Before the cherry orchard was sold, we were all worried and wretched, but afterwards, when once the question was settled conclusively, irrevocably, we all felt calm and even cheerful. I am a bank clerk now—I am a financier—cannon off the red. And you, Lyuba, after all, you are looking better; there's no question of that.

LYUBOV. Yes. My nerves are better, that's true. [*Her hat and coat are handed to her.*] I'm sleeping well. Carry out my things, Yasha. It's time. [*to* ANYA] My darling, we shall soon see each other again. I am going to Paris. I can live there on the money your Yaroslavl auntie sent us to buy the estate with—hurrah for auntie!—but that money won't last long.

ANYA. You'll come back soon, mamma, won't you? I'll be working up for my examination in the high school, and when I have passed that, I shall set to work and be a help to you. We will read all sorts of things together, mamma, won't we? [*Kisses her mother's hands.*] We will read in the autumn evenings. We'll read lots of books, and a new wonderful world will open out before us. [*dreamily*] Mamma, come soon.

LYUBOV. I shall come, my precious treasure. [*Embraces her.*]

[*Enter* LOPAHIN. CHARLOTTA *softly hums a song.*]

GAEV. Charlotta's happy; she's singing!

CHARLOTTA [*picks up a bundle like a swaddled baby*]. Bye, bye, my baby. [*A baby is heard crying: "Ooah! ooah!"*] Hush, hush, my pretty boy! [*Ooah! ooah!*] Poor little thing! [*Throws the bundle back.*] You must please find me a situation. I can't go on like this.

LOPAHIN. We'll find you one, Charlotta Ivanovna. Don't you worry yourself.

GAEV. Everyone's leaving us. Varya's going away. We have become of no use all at once.

CHARLOTTA. There's nowhere for me to be in the town. I must go away. [*Hums.*] What care I . . .

[*Enter* PISHTCHIK.]

LOPAHIN. The freak of nature!

PISHTCHIK [*gasping*]. Oh! . . . let me get my breath. . . . I'm worn out . . . my most honoured . . . Give me some water.

GAEV. Want some money, I suppose? Your humble servant! I'll go out of the way of temptation. [*Goes out.*]

PISHTCHIK. It's a long while since I have been to see you . . . dearest lady. [*to* LOPAHIN] You are here . . . glad to see you . . . a man of immense intellect . . . take . . . here [*gives* LOPAHIN] 400 roubles. That leaves me owing 840.

LOPAHIN [*shrugging his shoulders in amazement*]. It's like a dream. Where did you get it?

PISHTCHIK. Wait a bit . . . I'm hot . . . a most extraordinary occurrence! Some Englishmen came along and found in my land some sort of white clay. [*to* LYUBOV ANDREYEVNA] And 400 for you . . . most lovely . . . wonderful. [*Gives money.*] The rest later. [*Sips water.*] A young man in the train was telling me just now that a great philosopher advises jumping off a house-top. "Jump!" says he; "the whole gist of the problem lies in that." [*wonderingly*] Fancy that, now! Water, please!

LOPAHIN. What Englishmen?

PISHTCHIK. I have made over to them the rights to dig the clay for twenty-four years . . . and now, excuse me . . . I can't stay . . . I must be trotting on. I'm going to Znoikovo . . . to Kardamanovo. . . . I'm in debt all round. [*Sips.*] . . . To your very good health! . . . I'll come in on Thursday.

LYUBOV. We are just off to the town, and tomorrow I start for abroad.

PISHTCHIK. What! [*in agitation*] Why to the town? Oh, I see the furniture . . . the boxes. No matter . . . [*through his tears*] . . . no matter . . . men of enormous intellect . . . these Englishmen. . . . Never mind . . . be happy. God will succour you . . . no matter . . . everything in this world must have an end. [*Kisses* LYUBOV ANDREYEVNA'S *hand.*] If the rumour reaches you that my end has come, think of this . . . old horse, and say: "There once was such a man in the world . . . Semyonov-Pishtchik . . . the Kingdom of Heaven be his!" . . . most extraordinary weather . . . yes. [*Goes out in violent agitation, but at once returns and says in the doorway:*] Dashenka wishes to be remembered to you. [*Goes out.*]

LYUBOV. Now we can start. I leave with two cares in my heart. The first is leaving Firs ill. [*looking at her watch*] We still have five minutes.

ANYA. Mamma, Firs has been taken to the hospital. Yasha sent him off this morning.

LYUBOV. My other anxiety is Varya. She is used to getting up early and working; and now, without work, she's like a fish out of water. She is thin and pale, and she's crying, poor dear! [*a pause*] You are well aware, Yermolay Alexeyevitch, I dreamed of marrying her to you, and everything seemed to show that you would get married. [*Whispers to* ANYA *and motions to* CHARLOTTA *and both go out.*] She loves you—she suits you. And I don't know—I don't know why it is you seem, as it were, to avoid each other. I can't understand it!

LOPAHIN. I don't understand it myself, I confess. It's queer somehow, altogether. If there's still time, I'm ready now at once. Let's settle it straight off, and go ahead; but without you, I feel I shan't make her an offer.

LYUBOV. That's excellent. Why, a single moment's all that's necessary. I'll call her at once.

LOPAHIN. And there's champagne all ready too. [*looking into the glasses*] Empty! Someone's emptied them already. [YASHA *coughs.*] I call that greedy.

LYUBOV [*eagerly*]. Capital! We will go out. Yasha, *allez!* I'll call her in. [*at the door*] Varya, leave all that; come here. Come along! [*Goes out with* YASHA.]

LOPAHIN [*looking at his watch*]. Yes.

[*A pause. Behind the door, smothered laughter and whispering, and, at last, enter* VARYA.]

VARYA [*looking a long while over the things*]. It is strange, I can't find it anywhere.

LOPAHIN. What are you looking for?

VARYA. I packed it myself, and I can't remember. [*a pause*]

LOPAHIN. Where are you going now, Varvara Mihailova?

VARYA. I? To the Ragulins. I have arranged to go to them to look after the house—as a housekeeper.

LOPAHIN. That's in Yashnovo? It'll be seventy miles away. [*a pause*] So this is the end of life in this house!

VARYA [*looking among the things*]. Where is it? Perhaps I put it in the trunk. Yes, life in this house is over—there will be no more of it.

LOPAHIN. And I'm just off to Harkov—by this next train. I've a lot of business there. I'm leaving Epihodov here, and I've taken him on.

VARYA. Really!

LOPAHIN. This time last year we had snow already, if you remember; but now it's so fine and sunny. Though it's cold, to be sure—three degrees of frost.

VARYA. I haven't looked. [*a pause*] And besides, our thermometer's broken. [*a pause*]

[*Voice at the door from the yard:* "Yermolay Alexeyevitch!"]

LOPAHIN [*as though he had long been expecting this summons*]. This minute!

[LOPAHIN *goes out quickly.* VARYA *sitting on the floor and laying her head on a bag full of clothes, sobs quietly. The door opens.* LYUBOV ANDREYEVNA *comes in cautiously.*]

LYUBOV. Well? [*a pause*] We must be going.

VARYA [*has wiped her eyes and is no longer crying*]. Yes, mamma, it's time to start. I shall have time to get to the Ragulins today, if only you're not late for the train.

LYUBOV [*in the doorway*]. Anya, put your things on.

[*Enter* ANYA, *then* GAEV *and* CHARLOTTA IVANOVNA. GAEV *has on a warm coat with a hood. Servants and cabmen come in.* EPIHODOV *bustles about the luggage.*]

LYUBOV. Now we can start on our travels.

ANYA [*joyfully*]. On our travels!

GAEV. My friends—my dear, my precious friends! Leaving this house for ever, can I be silent? Can I refrain from giving utterance at leave-taking to those emotions which now flood all my being?

ANYA [*supplicatingly*]. Uncle!

VARYA. Uncle, you mustn't!

GAEV [*dejectedly*]. Cannon and into the pocket . . . I'll be quiet. . . .

[*Enter* TROFIMOV *and afterwards* LOPAHIN.]

TROFIMOV. Well, ladies and gentlemen, we must start.

LOPAHIN. Epihodov, my coat!

LYUBOV. I'll stay just one minute. It seems as though I have never seen before what the walls, what the ceilings in this house were like, and now I look at them with greediness, with such tender love.

GAEV. I remember when I was six years old sitting in that window on Trinity Day watching my father going to church.

LYUBOV. Have all the things been taken?

LOPAHIN. I think all. [*putting on overcoat, to* EPIHODOV] You, Epihodov, mind you see everything is right.

EPIHODOV [*in a husky voice*]. Don't you trouble, Yermolay Alexeyevitch.

LOPAHIN. Why, what's wrong with your voice?

EPIHODOV. I've just had a drink of water, and I choked over something.

YASHA [*contemptuously*]. The ignorance!

LYUBOV. We are going—and not a soul will be left here.

LOPAHIN. Not till the spring.

VARYA [*pulls a parasol out of a bundle, as though about to hit someone with it.* LOPAHIN *makes a gesture as though alarmed*]. What is it? I didn't mean anything.

TROFIMOV. Ladies and gentlemen, let us get into the carriage. It's time. The train will be in directly.

VARYA. Petya, here they are, your goloshes, by that box. [*with tears*] And what dirty old things they are!

TROFIMOV [*putting on his goloshes*]. Let us go, friends!

GAEV [*greatly agitated, afraid of weeping*]. The train—the station! Double baulk, ah!

LYUBOV. Let us go!

LOPAHIN. Are we all here? [*Locks the side-door on left.*] The things are all here. We must lock up. Let us go!

ANYA. Good-bye, home! Good-bye to the old life!

TROFIMOV. Welcome to the new life!

[TROFIMOV *goes out with* ANYA. VARYA *looks round the room and goes out slowly.* YASHA *and* CHARLOTTA IVANOVNA, *with her dog, go out.*]

LOPAHIN. Till the spring, then! Come, friends, till we meet! [*Goes out.*]

[LYUBOV ANDREYEVNA *and* GAEV *remain alone. As though they had been waiting for this, they throw themselves on each other's necks, and break into subdued smothered sobbing, afraid of being overheard.*]

GAEV [*in despair*]. Sister, my sister!

LYUBOV. Oh, my orchard!—my sweet, beautiful orchard! My life, my youth, my happiness, good-bye! goodbye!

VOICE OF ANYA [*calling gaily*]. Mamma!

VOICE OF TROFIMOV [*gaily, excitedly*]. Aa—oo!

LYUBOV. One last look at the walls, at the windows. My dear mother loved to walk about this room.

GAEV. Sister, sister!

VOICE OF ANYA. Mamma!

VOICE OF TROFIMOV. Aa—oo!

LYUBOV. We are coming. [*They go out.*]

[*The stage is empty. There is the sound of the doors being locked up, then of the carriages driving away. There is silence. In the stillness there is the dull stroke of an axe in a tree, clanging with a mournful lonely sound. Footsteps are heard.* FIRS *appears in the doorway on the right. He is dressed as always—in a pea-jacket and white waistcoat, with slippers on his feet. He is ill.*]

FIRS [*goes up to the doors, and tries the handles*]. Locked! They have gone. . . . [*Sits down on sofa.*] They have forgotten me. . . . Never mind . . . I'll sit here a bit. . . . I'll be bound Leonid Andreyevitch hasn't put his fur coat on and has gone off in his thin overcoat. [*Sighs anxiously.*] I didn't see after him. . . . These young people . . . [*Mutters something that can't be distinguished.*] Life has slipped by as though I hadn't lived. [*Lies down.*] I'll lie down a bit. . . . There's no strength in you, nothing left you—all gone! Ech! I'm good for nothing. [*Lies motionless.*]

[*A sound is heard that seems to come from the sky, like a breaking harp-string, dying away mournfully. All is still again, and there is heard nothing but the strokes of the axe far away in the orchard.*]

THE CURTAIN FALLS

JOHN SYNGE
1871–1909

RIDERS TO THE SEA
1904

THE STORY OF *Riders to the Sea* is a mere moment in the lives of a few characters, but it holds within it the meaning of what they and millions like them have done and suffered. They have struggled for survival; they have gone down to defeat before the indifferent forces of wind and sea. Out of fatalism touched with faith and out of a supreme weariness, they resign themselves to defeat and in that resignation find release.

Synge captures this moment in the vivid dialect of the islanders. The images are sharp-edged and simple, held in the rise and fall of a speech as naturally cadenced as breathing. The rope is "on a nail by the white boards. I hung it up this morning, for the pig with the black feet was eating it." "There were two men . . . and they rowing round with poteen before the cocks crowed, and the oar of one of them caught the body, and they passing the black cliffs of the north." The images are held, too, in a larger, more complex rhythmic pattern. From start to finish the play is filled with its own echoes. We hear again and again of the pig, the boards, the pony until we begin to realize that such recurrence is itself an image of the lives portrayed—ever changing, ever the same. At the play's end Maurya lives over the deaths of her sons: "I was sitting here with Bartley, and he a baby, lying on my two knees, and I seen two women, and three women, and four women coming in, and they crossing themselves, and not saying a word . . . and there were men coming in after them, and they holding a thing in the half of a red sail." Then comes the stage direction: "She pauses again with her hand stretched out toward the door. It opens softly and old women begin to come in, crossing themselves." And later, "Then men carry in the body of Bartley, laid on a plank, with a bit of a sail over it." Present echoes past, past enters present in a moment which in the perfection of its presentation becomes an image of unchanging human experience.

RIDERS TO THE SEA / *SYNGE*

Characters

MAURYA : *an old woman*
BARTLEY : *her son*
CATHLEEN : *her daughter*
NORA : *a younger daughter*
MEN AND WOMEN

SCENE. *An Island off the West of Ireland.*

Cottage kitchen, with nets, oil-skins, spinning-wheel, some new boards standing by the wall, etc. CATHLEEN, *a girl of about twenty, finishes kneading cake, and puts it down in the pot-oven by the fire; then wipes her hands, and begins to spin at the wheel.* NORA, *a young girl, puts her head in at the door.*

NORA [*in a low voice*]. Where is she?

CATHLEEN. She's lying down, God help her, and may be sleeping, if she's able.

[NORA *comes in softly, and takes a bundle from under her shawl.*]

CATHLEEN [*spinning the wheel rapidly*]. What is it you have?

NORA. The young priest is after bringing them. It's a shirt and a plain stocking were got off a drowned man in Donegal.

[CATHLEEN *stops her wheel with a sudden movement, and leans out to listen.*]

NORA. We're to find out if it's Michael's they are, some time herself will be down looking by the sea.

CATHLEEN. How would they be Michael's, Nora? How would he go the length of that way to the far north?

SCENE pot-oven heated iron plate covered by a pot

NORA. The young priest says he's known the like of it. "If it's Michael's they are," says he, "you can tell herself he's got a clean burial by the grace of God, and if they're not his, let no one say a word about them, for she'll be getting her death," says he, "with crying and lamenting."

[*The door which* NORA *half closed is blown open by a gust of wind.*]

CATHLEEN [*looking out anxiously*]. Did you ask him would he stop Bartley going this day with the horses to the Galway fair?

NORA. "I won't stop him," says he, "but let you not be afraid. Herself does be saying prayers half through the night, and the Almighty God won't leave her destitute," says he, "with no son living."

CATHLEEN. Is the sea bad by the white rocks, Nora?

NORA. Middling bad, God help us. There's a great roaring in the west, and it's worse it'll be getting when the tide's turned to the wind. [*She goes over to the table with the bundle.*] Shall I open it now?

CATHLEEN. Maybe she'd wake up on us, and come in before we'd done. [*coming to the table*] It's a long time we'll be, and the two of us crying.

NORA [*goes to the inner door and listens*]. She's moving about on the bed. She'll be coming in a minute.

CATHLEEN. Give me the ladder, and I'll put them up in the turf-loft, the way she won't know of them at all, and maybe when the tide turns she'll be going down to see would he be floating from the east.

[*They put the ladder against the gable of the chimney;* CATHLEEN *goes up a few steps and hides the bundle in the turf-loft.* MAURYA *comes from the inner room.*]

MAURYA [*looking up at* CATHLEEN *and speaking querulously*]. Isn't it turf enough you have for this day and evening?

CATHLEEN. There's a cake baking at the fire for a short space [*throwing down the turf*] and Bartley will want it when the tide turns if he goes to Connemara.

[NORA *picks up the turf and puts it round the pot-oven.*]

MAURYA [*sitting down on a stool at the fire*]. He won't go this day with the wind rising from the south and west. He won't go this day, for the young priest will stop him surely.

NORA. He'll not stop him, mother, and I heard Eamon Simon and Stephen Pheety and Colum Shawn saying he would go.

MAUYRA. Where is he itself?

NORA. He went down to see would there be another boat sailing in the week, and I'm thinking it won't be long till he's here now, for the tide's turning at the green head, and the hooker's tacking from the east.

CATHLEEN. I hear some one passing the big stones.

NORA [*looking out*]. He's coming now, and he in a hurry.

BARTLEY [*comes in and looks round the room. Speaking sadly and quietly*]. Where is the bit of new rope, Cathleen, was bought in Connemara?

CATHLEEN [*coming down*]. Give it to him, Nora; it's on a nail by the white boards. I hung it up this morning, for the pig with the black feet was eating it.

NORA [*giving him a rope*]. Is that it, Bartley?

MAURYA. You'd do right to leave that rope, Bartley, hanging by the board. [BARTLEY *takes the rope.*] It will be wanting in this place, I'm telling you, if Michael is washed up to-morrow morning, or the next morning, or any morning in the week, for it's a deep grave we'll make him by the grace of God.

BARTLEY [*beginning to work with the rope*]. I've no halter the way I can ride down on the mare, and I must go now quickly. This is the one boat going for two weeks or beyond it, and the fair will be a good fair for horses I heard them saying below.

MAURYA. It's a hard thing they'll be saying below if the body is washed up and there's no man in it to make the coffin, and I after giving a big price for the finest white boards you'd find in Connemara. [*She looks round at the boards.*]

BARTLEY. How would it be washed up, and we after looking each day for nine days, and a strong wind blowing a while back from the west and south?

58 **head** headland, promontory
74–75 **the way** so that
79 **in it** there

MAURYA. If it wasn't found itself, that wind is raising the sea, and there was a star up against the moon, and it rising in the night. If it was a hundred horses, or a thousand horses you had itself, what is the price of a thousand horses against a son where there is one son only?

BARTLEY [*working at the halter, to* CATHLEEN]. Let you go down each day, and see the sheep aren't jumping in on the rye, and if the jobber comes you can sell the pig with the black feet if there is a good price going.

MAURYA. How would the like of her get a good price for a pig?

BARTLEY [*to* CATHLEEN]. If the west wind holds with the last bit of the moon let you and Nora get up weed enough for another cock for the kelp. It's hard set we'll be from this day with no one in it but one man to work.

MAURYA. It's hard set we'll be surely the day you're drownd'd with the rest. What way will I live and the girls with me, and I an old woman looking for the grave?

[BARTLEY *lays down the halter, takes off his old coat, and puts on a newer one of the same flannel.*]

BARTLEY [*to* NORA]. Is she coming to the pier?

NORA [*looking out*]. She's passing the green head and letting fall her sails.

BARTLEY [*getting his purse and tobacco*]. I'll have half an hour to go down, and you'll see me coming again in two days, or in three days, or maybe in four days if the wind is bad.

MAURYA [*turning round to the fire, and putting her shawl over her head*]. Isn't it a hard and cruel man won't hear a word from an old woman, and she holding him from the sea?

CATHLEEN. It's the life of a young man to be going on the sea, and who would listen to an old woman with one thing and she saying it over?

BARTLEY [*taking the halter*]. I must go now quickly. I'll ride down on the red mare, and the gray pony'll run behind me. . . . The blessing of God on you. [*He goes out.*]

MAURYA [*crying out as he is in the door*]. He's gone now, God

97 **kelp** ash of various seaweeds, used as a source for iodine. Bartley's request means: get seaweed enough to make another pile to be burned to ash

99 **set** put to it

spare us, and we'll not see him again. He's gone now, and when the black night is falling I'll have no son left me in the world.

CATHLEEN. Why wouldn't you give him your blessing and he looking round in the door? Isn't it sorrow enough is on every one in this house without your sending him out with an unlucky word behind him, and a hard word in his ear?

[MAURYA *takes up the tongs and begins raking the fire aimlessly without looking round.*]

NORA [*turning towards her*]. You're taking away the turf from the cake.

CATHLEEN [*crying out*]. The Son of God forgive us, Nora, we're after forgetting his bit of bread. [*She comes over to the fire.*]

NORA. And it's destroyed he'll be going till dark night, and he after eating nothing since the sun went up.

CATHLEEN [*turning the cake out of the oven*]. It's destroyed he'll be, surely. There's no sense left on any person in a house where an old woman will be talking for ever.

[MAURYA *sways herself on her stool.*]

CATHLEEN [*cutting off some of the bread and rolling it in a cloth; to* MAURYA]. Let you go down now to the spring well and give him this and he passing. You'll see him then and the dark word will be broken, and you can say "God speed you," the way he'll be easy in his mind.

MAURYA [*taking the bread*]. Will I be in it as soon as himself?

CATHLEEN. If you go now quickly.

MAURYA [*standing up unsteadily*]. It's hard set I am to walk.

CATHLEEN [*looking at her anxiously*]. Give her the stick, Nora, or maybe she'll slip on the big stones.

NORA. What stick?

CATHLEEN. The stick Michael brought from Connemara.

MAURYA [*taking a stick* NORA *gives her*]. In the big world the old people do be leaving things after them for their sons and children, but in this place it is the young men do be leaving things behind for them that do be old. [*She goes out slowly.* NORA *goes over to the ladder.*]

CATHLEEN. Wait, Nora, maybe she'd turn back quickly. She's that sorry, God help her, you wouldn't know the thing she'd do.

156 sorry wretched

NORA. Is she gone round by the bush?

CATHLEEN [*looking out*]. She's gone now. Throw it down quickly, for the Lord knows when she'll be out of it again.

NORA [*getting the bundle from the loft*]. The young priest said he'd be passing to-morrow, and we might go down and speak to him below if it's Michael's they are surely.

CATHLEEN [*taking the bundle*]. Did he say what way they were found?

NORA [*coming down*]. "There were two men," says he, "and they rowing round with poteen before the cocks crowed, and the oar of one of them caught the body, and they passing the black cliffs of the north."

CATHLEEN [*trying to open the bundle*]. Give me a knife, Nora, the string's perished with the salt water, and there's a black knot on it you wouldn't loosen in a week.

NORA [*giving her a knife*]. I've heard tell it was a long way to Donegal.

CATHLEEN [*cutting the string*]. It is surely. There was a man in here a while ago—the man sold us that knife—and he said if you set off walking from the rocks beyond, it would be seven days you'd be in Donegal.

NORA. And what time would a man take, and he floating?

[CATHLEEN *opens the bundle and takes out a bit of a stocking. They look at them eagerly.*]

CATHLEEN [*in a low voice*]. The Lord spare us, Nora! isn't it a queer hard thing to say if it's his they are surely?

NORA. I'll get his shirt off the hook the way we can put the one flannel on the other. [*She looks through some clothes hanging in the corner.*] It's not with them, Cathleen, and where will it be?

CATHLEEN. I'm thinking Bartley put it on him in the morning, for his own shirt was heavy with the salt in it. [*pointing to the corner*] There's a bit of a sleeve was of the same stuff. Give me that and it will do.

[NORA *brings it to her and they compare the flannel.*]

CATHLEEN. It's the same stuff, Nora; but if it is itself aren't there great rolls of it in the shops of Galway, and isn't it many another man may have a shirt of it as well as Michael himself?

170 **perished** stiffened

NORA [*who has taken up the stocking and counted the stitches, crying out*]. It's Michael, Cathleen, it's Michael; God spare his soul, and what will herself say when she hears this story, and Bartley on the sea?

CATHLEEN [*taking the stocking*]. It's a plain stocking.

NORA. It's the second one of the third pair I knitted, and I put up three score stitches, and I dropped four of them.

CATHLEEN [*counts the stitches*]. It's that number is in it. [*crying out*] Ah, Nora, isn't it a bitter thing to think of him floating that way to the far north, and no one to keen him but the black hags that do be flying on the sea?

NORA [*swinging herself round, and throwing out her arms on the clothes*]. And isn't it a pitiful thing when there is nothing left of a man who was a great rower and fisher, but a bit of an old shirt and a plain stocking?

CATHLEEN [*after an instant*]. Tell me is herself coming, Nora? I hear a little sound on the path.

NORA [*looking out*]. She is, Cathleen. She's coming up to the door.

CATHLEEN. Put these things away before she'll come in. Maybe it's easier she'll be after giving her blessing to Bartley, and we won't let on we've heard anything the time he's on the sea.

NORA [*helping* CATHLEEN *to close the bundle*]. We'll put them here in the corner.

[*They put them into a hole in the chimney corner.* CATHLEEN *goes back to the spinning-wheel.*]

NORA. Will she see it was crying I was?

CATHLEEN. Keep your back to the door the way the light'll not be on you.

[NORA *sits down at the chimney corner, with her back to the door.* MAURYA *comes in very slowly, without looking at the girls, and goes over to her stool at the other side of the fire. The cloth with the bread is still in her hand. The girls look at each other, and* NORA *points to the bundle of bread.*]

CATHLEEN [*after spinning for a moment*]. You didn't give him his bit of bread?

[MAURYA *begins to keen softly, without turning round.*]

CATHLEEN. Did you see him riding down?

[MAURYA *goes on keening.*]

CATHLEEN [*a little impatiently*]. God forgive you; isn't it a better thing to raise your voice and tell what you seen, than to be making lamentation for a thing that's done? Did you see Bartley, I'm saying to you.

MAURYA [*with a weak voice*]. My heart's broken from this day.

CATHLEEN [*as before*]. Did you see Bartley?

MAURYA. I seen the fearfulest thing.

CATHLEEN [*leaves her wheel and looks out*]. God forgive you; he's riding the mare now over the green head, and the gray pony behind him.

MAURYA [*starts, so that her shawl falls back from her head and shows her white tossed hair. With a frightened voice*]. The gray pony behind him.

CATHLEEN [*coming to the fire*]. What is it ails you, at all?

MAURYA [*speaking very slowly*]. I've seen the fearfulest thing any person has seen, since the day Bride Dara seen the dead man with the child in his arms.

CATHLEEN and NORA. Uah. [*They crouch down in front of the old woman at the fire.*]

NORA. Tell us what it is you seen.

MAURYA. I went down to the spring well, and I stood there saying a prayer to myself. Then Bartley came along, and he riding on the red mare with the gray pony behind him. [*She puts up her hands, as if to hide something from her eyes.*] The Son of God spare us, Nora!

CATHLEEN. What is it you seen?

MAURYA. I seen Michael himself.

CATHLEEN [*speaking softly*]. You did not, mother; it wasn't Michael you seen, for his body is after being found in the far north, and he's got a clean burial by the grace of God.

MAURYA [*a little defiantly*]. I'm after seeing him this day, and he riding and galloping. Bartley came first on the red mare; and I tried to say "God speed you," but something choked the words in my throat. He went by quickly; and "the blessing of God on you," says he, and I could say nothing. I looked up then, and I crying, at the gray pony, and there was Michael upon it—with fine clothes on him, and new shoes on his feet.

CATHLEEN [*begins to keen*]. It's destroyed we are from this day. It's destroyed, surely.

NORA. Didn't the young priest say the Almighty God wouldn't leave her destitute with no son living?

MAURYA [*in a low voice, but clearly*]. It's little the like of him knows of the sea. . . . Bartley will be lost now, and let you call in Eamon and make me a good coffin out of the white boards, for I won't live after them. I've had a husband, and a husband's father, and six sons in this house—six fine men, though it was a hard birth I had with every one of them and they coming to the world—and some of them were found and some of them were not found, but they're gone now the lot of them. . . . There were Stephen, and Shawn, were lost in the great wind, and found after in the Bay of Gregory of the Golden Mouth, and carried up the two of them on the one plank, and in by that door. [*She pauses for a moment, the girls start as if they heard something through the door that is half open behind them.*]

NORA [*in a whisper*]. Did you hear that, Cathleen? Did you hear a noise in the north-east?

CATHLEEN [*in a whisper*]. There's some one after crying out by the seashore.

MAURYA [*continues without hearing anything*]. There was Sheamus and his father, and his own father again, were lost in a dark night, and not a stick or sign was seen of them when the sun went up. There was Patch after was drowned out of a curragh that turned over. I was sitting here with Bartley, and he a baby, lying on my two knees, and I seen two women, and three women, and four women coming in, and they crossing themselves, and not saying a word. I looked out then, and there were men coming after them, and they holding a thing in the half of a red sail, and water dripping out of it—it was a dry day, Nora—and leaving a track to the door. [*She pauses again with her hand stretched out towards the door. It opens softly and old women begin to come in, crossing themselves on the threshold, and kneeling down in front of the stage with red petticoats over their heads.*]

MAURYA [*half in a dream, to* CATHLEEN]. Is it Patch, or Michael, or what is it at all?

CATHLEEN. Michael is after being found in the far north, and when he is found there how could he be here in this place?

MAURYA. There does be a power of young men floating round in the sea, and what way would they know if it was Michael they had, or another man like him, for when a man is nine days in the sea, and the wind blowing, it's hard set his own mother would be to say what man was it.

CATHLEEN. It's Michael, God spare him, for they're after sending us a bit of his clothes from the far north. [*She reaches out and hands* MAURYA *the clothes that belonged to Michael.* MAURYA *stands up slowly and takes them in her hands.* NORA *looks out.*]

NORA. They're carrying a thing among them and there's water dripping out of it and leaving a track by the big stones.

CATHLEEN [*in a whisper to the women who have come in*]. Is it Bartley it is?

ONE OF THE WOMEN. It is surely, God rest his soul.

[*Two younger women come in and pull out the table. Then men carry in the body of Bartley, laid on a plank, with a bit of a sail over it, and lay it on the table.*]

CATHLEEN [*to the women, as they are doing so*]. What way was he drowned?

ONE OF THE WOMEN. The gray pony knocked him into the sea, and he was washed out where there is a great surf on the white rocks.

[MAURYA *has gone over and knelt down at the head of the table. The women are keening softly and swaying themselves with a slow movement.* CATHLEEN *and* NORA *kneel at the other end of the table. The men kneel near the door.*]

MAURYA [*raising her head and speaking as if she did not see the people around her*]. They're all gone now, and there isn't anything more the sea can do to me. . . . I'll have no call now to be up crying and praying when the wind breaks from the south, and you can hear the surf is in the east, and the surf is in the west, making a great stir with the two noises, and they hitting one on the other. I'll have no call now to be going down and getting Holy Water in the dark nights after Samhain, and I won't care what way the sea is when the other women will be keening. [*to* NORA] Give me the Holy Water, Nora, there's a small sup still on the dresser.

342 **Samhain** November 1, the beginning of the Celtic winter half year

[NORA *gives it to her.*]

MAURYA [*drops Michael's clothes across Bartley's feet, and sprinkles the Holy Water over him*]. It isn't that I haven't prayed for you, Bartley, to the Almighty God. It isn't that I haven't said prayers in the dark night till you wouldn't know what I'd be saying; but it's a great rest I'll have now, and it's time surely. It's a great rest I'll have now, and great sleeping in the long nights after Samhain, if it's only a bit of wet flour we do have to eat, and maybe a fish that would be stinking. [*She kneels down again, crossing herself, and saying prayers under her breath.*]

CATHLEEN [*to an old man*]. Maybe yourself and Eamon would make a coffin when the sun rises. We have fine white boards herself bought, God help her, thinking Michael would be found, and I have a new cake you can eat while you'll be working.

THE OLD MAN [*looking at the boards*]. Are there nails with them?

CATHLEEN. There are not, Colum; we didn't think of the nails.

ANOTHER MAN. It's a great wonder she wouldn't think of the nails, and all the coffins she's seen made already.

CATHLEEN. It's getting old she is, and broken.

[MAURYA *stands up again very slowly and spreads out the pieces of Michael's clothes beside the body, sprinkling them with the last of the Holy Water.*]

NORA [*in a whisper to* CATHLEEN]. She's quiet now and easy; but the day Michael was drowned you could hear her crying out from this to the spring well. It's fonder she was of Michael, and would any one have thought that?

CATHLEEN [*slowly and clearly*]. An old woman will be soon tired with anything she will do, and isn't it nine days herself is after crying and keening, and making great sorrow in the house?

MAURYA [*puts the empty cup mouth downwards on the table, and lays her hands together on Bartley's feet*]. They're all together this time, and the end is come. May the Almighty God have mercy on Bartley's soul, and on Michael's soul, and on the souls of Sheamus and Patch, and Stephen and Shawn; [*bending her head*] and may He have mercy on my soul, Nora, and on the soul of every one is left living in the world. [*She pauses, and the keen rises a little more loudly from the women, then sinks away.*]

MAURYA [*continuing*]. Michael has a clean burial in the far north, by the grace of the Almighty God. Bartley will have a fine coffin out of the white boards, and a deep grave surely. What more can we want than that? No man at all can be living for ever, and we must be satisfied. [*She kneels down again and the curtain falls slowly.*]

SEAN O'CASEY
1884–1964

JUNO AND THE PAYCOCK
1924

TO AN UNUSUAL DEGREE *Juno and the Paycock* draws partly antagonistic dramatic elements together. At any given moment the distinctive focus of the play is located about midway between certain recognizable limits. One of these—and the more obvious—is the matter-of-fact emphasis upon details of Irish tenement life, the catalogue of personal misfortunes, and the swirl of political strife. The other lies in the region of symbolism and is mainly discernible through a sad and often lyric undertone. Sometimes nostalgic, sometimes solemn, it confers on the commonplace a touch of grandeur. Between these limits the play evokes an awareness of potential tragedy.

Rising and subsiding, but always developing, this awareness permits the fusion of otherwise conflicting moods. Thus, in the comic scenes between Joxer, the Captain, and Juno, the audience is led to perceive that these lives are fixed in social and personal misery which they cannot master and can hardly comprehend. This perception links the immediate import of what is said and done to a circumference of meaning that is felt rather than described.

How opposed moods shape the development of a scene and also clarify the focus of the entire play is impressively apparent in the second act. The jollification in honor of Captain Boyle's prospective inheritance contrasts ironically with the tawdry poverty of the setting and the growing foreboding that the prospects are empty. The comic spirit of the party, with its boasts and old songs, has an undertone of longing. It is suddenly broken by Johnny's scream that he has seen the ghost of the murdered Robbie Tancred. For a melodramatic instant the party feels the chill of supernatural fear. The celebrating resumes, to be again suspended by the entrance of Mrs. Tancred on her way to the funeral of her son. A last effort at comfortable cheer droops and perishes in the passing-by of the funeral and the distant murmur of the *Ave Maria*. Each contrasting development has its own integrity; at the same time the alternating moods bracket ever more narrowly the central area of awareness.

As O'Casey interweaves contrasting moods, he also merges different kinds of characterization. The effect is to widen and simultaneously to particularize the tragic significance. Each of the main characters appears to some extent as both theatrical stereotype and distinct individual. Mary in her role of the ruined maiden is a somewhat melodramatic figure, and Joxer is identifiable as a "parasite" out of the old Roman comedy. This element of stereotype firmly sustains the general outline of character. Yet through touches of vigorous realism, as well as the articulate music of the dialogue, each of his persons acquires a measure of individual pathos. Mary has read her Ibsen and reaches after a way of life less mean and ignorant than her environment allows; even Joxer keeps a wisp of dignity and a fleeting awareness of his own suffering.

In Juno, with her queen-goddess name and her cheerless personal destiny, the various modes and the central perception of the play are most fully defined. Under the aspect of comedy she is something of a Xantippe, uselessly harrying her inadequate spouse. Under that of melodrama she is the long-suffering mother, hard-working and indestructible. In the shadowy realm of symbolism, which the play never wholly enters, she is an heroic and pathetic figure, a legendary queen of sorrows. But Juno Boyle is not a Niobe. The symbolic undertone is subdued. Nothing vague is in fact permitted. Yet mere uncompromising realism is lifted above itself, and the well-worn stereotypes and reversals renew their vigor.

The two-pronged ending of the play epitomizes its method and its meaning. First comes the exit of Juno and Mary, without positive hope but without despair: "Sacred heart o' Jesus, take away our hearts o' stone, and give us hearts o' flesh!" As a curtain-line, the sentiment would justly underscore the theme of suffering, but the tone is perhaps too poignant. "There is a pause," says the stage-direction. Then Boyle and Joxer enter, "both of them very drunk." The maudlin stammering of the two castaways, as ignorant of their fate as they are helpless to alter it, sounds a counterpoint to Juno's words. The two endings partly fuse in an image of the old rivalry between creation and chaos.

JUNO AND THE PAYCOCK / O'CASEY

Characters

"CAPTAIN" JACK BOYLE		Residents in the Tenement
JUNO BOYLE	*his wife*	
JOHNNY BOYLE	*their children*	
MARY BOYLE		
"JOXER" DALY		
MRS. MAISIE MADIGAN		
"NEEDLE" NUGENT	*a tailor*	
MRS. TANCRED		
JERRY DEVINE		
CHARLIE BENTHAM	*a school teacher*	
AN IRREGULAR MOBILIZER		
TWO IRREGULARS		
A COAL-BLOCK VENDOR		
A SEWING MACHINE MAN		
TWO FURNITURE REMOVAL MEN		
TWO NEIGHBOURS		

SCENE. The living apartment of a two-room tenancy of the Boyle family, in a tenement house in Dublin.

A few days elapse between ACTS I and II, and two months between ACTS II and III.

During ACT III the curtain is lowered for a few minutes to denote the lapse of one hour.

Period of the play, 1922.

1922 a year in which the newly formed Irish Free State, made up of the southern and chiefly Catholic counties of Ireland, was still torn by bitter dis-

ACT I

The living room of a two-room tenancy occupied by the BOYLE *family in a tenement house in Dublin. Left, a door leading to another part of the house; left of door a window looking into the street; at back a dresser; farther to right at back, a window looking into the back of the house. Between the window and the dresser is a picture of the Virgin; below the picture, on a bracket, is a crimson bowl in which a floating votive light is burning. Farther to the right is a small bed partly concealed by cretonne hangings strung on a twine. To the right is the fireplace; near the fireplace is a door leading to the other room. Beside the fireplace is a box containing coal. On the mantelshelf is an alarm clock lying on its face. In a corner near the window looking into the back is a galvanized bath. A table and some chairs. On the table are breakfast things for one. A teapot is on the hob and a frying-pan stands inside the fender. There are a few books on the dresser and one on the table. Leaning against the dresser is a long-handled shovel—the kind invariably used by labourers when turning concrete or mixing mortar.* JOHNNY BOYLE *is sitting crouched beside the fire.* MARY *with her jumper off—it is lying on the back of a chair—is arranging her hair before a tiny mirror perched on the table. Beside the mirror is stretched out the morning paper, which she looks at when she isn't gazing into the mirror. She is a well-made and good-looking girl of twenty-two. Two forces are working in her mind—one, through the circumstances of her life, pulling her back; the other, through the influence of books she has read, pushing her forward. The opposing forces are apparent in her speech and her manners, both of which are degraded by her environment, and improved by her acquaintance—slight though it be—with literature. The time is early forenoon.*

sension between **Staters,** who would accept the gains already won, and the **Diehards** and **Republicans,** who insisted on full independence and a union including Northern Ireland, even at the price of renewed civil war. Although the Irish Republican Army was being replaced by an unarmed **Civic Guard,** some detachments of **Irregulars** were still agitating by terrorism for independence and union.

MARY [*looking at the paper*]. On a little bye-road, out beyant Finglas, he was found.

[MRS. BOYLE *enters by door on right; she has been shopping and carries a small parcel in her hand. She is forty-five years of age, and twenty years ago she must have been a pretty woman; but her face has now assumed that look which ultimately settles down upon the faces of the women of the working-class; a look of listless monotony and harassed anxiety, blending with an expression of mechanical resistance. Were circumstances favourable, she would probably be a handsome, active and clever woman.*]

MRS. BOYLE. Isn't he come in yet?

MARY. No, mother.

MRS. BOYLE. Oh, he'll come in when he likes; struttin' about the town like a paycock with Joxer, I suppose. I hear all about Mrs. Tancred's son is in this mornin's paper.

MARY. The full details are in it this mornin'; seven wounds he had—one entherin' the neck, with an exit wound beneath the left shoulder-blade; another in the left breast penethratin' the heart, an' . . .

JOHNNY [*springing up from the fire*]. Oh, quit that readin', for God's sake! Are yous losin' all your feelin's? It'll soon be that none of yous'll read anythin' that's not about butcherin'!

[*He goes quickly into the room on left.*]

MARY. He's gettin' very sensitive, all of a sudden!

MRS. BOYLE. I'll read it myself, Mary, by an' by, when I come home. Everybody's sayin' that he was a die-hard—thanks be to God that Johnny had nothin' to do with him this long time. . . . [*opening the parcel and taking out some sausages, which she places on a plate*] Ah, then, if that father o' yours doesn't come in soon for his breakfast, he may go without any; I'll not wait much longer for him.

MARY. Can't you let him get it himself when he comes in?

MRS. BOYLE. Yes, an' let him bring in Joxer Daly along with him? Ay, that's what he'd like, an' that's what he's waitin' for—till he thinks I'm gone to work, an' then sail in with the boul' Joxer, to burn all the coal an' dhrink all the tea in the place, to show them what a good Samaritan he is! But I'll stop here till he comes in, if I have to wait till tomorrow mornin'.

VOICE OF JOHNNY INSIDE. Mother!

64 **boul'** bold

MRS. BOYLE. Yis?

VOICE OF JOHNNY. Bring us in a dhrink o' wather.

MRS. BOYLE. Bring in that fella a dhrink o' wather, for God's sake, Mary.

MARY. Isn't he big an' able enough to come out an' get it himself?

MRS. BOYLE. If you weren't well yourself you'd like somebody to bring you in a dhrink o' wather. [*She brings in drink and returns.*]

MRS. BOYLE. Isn't it terrible to have to be waitin' this way! You'd think he was bringin' twenty poun's a week into the house the way he's goin' on. He wore out the Health Insurance long ago, he's afther wearin' out the unemployment dole, an', now, he's thryin' to wear out me! An' constantly singin', no less, when he ought always to be on his knees offerin' up a Novena for a job!

MARY [*tying a ribbon fillet-wise around her head*]. I don't like this ribbon, ma; I think I'll wear the green—it looks betther than the blue.

MRS. BOYLE. Ah, wear whatever ribbon you like, girl, only don't be botherin' me. I don't know what a girl on strike wants to be wearin' a ribbon round her head for or silk stockin's on her legs either; it's wearin' them things that make the employers think they're givin' yous too much money.

MARY. The hour is past now when we'll ask the employers' permission to wear what we like.

MRS. BOYLE. I don't know why you wanted to walk out for Jennie Claffey; up to this you never had a good word for her.

MARY. What's the use of belongin' to a Trades Union if you won't stand up for your principles? Why did they sack her? It was a clear case of victimization. We couldn't let her walk the streets, could we?

MRS. BOYLE. No, of course yous couldn't—yous wanted to keep her company. Wan victim wasn't enough. When the employers sacrifice wan victim, the Trades Unions go wan betther be sacrificin' a hundred.

MARY. It doesn't matther what you say, ma—a principle's a principle.

MRS. BOYLE. Yis; an' when I go into oul' Murphy's tomorrow, an' he gets to know that, instead o' payin' all, I'm goin' to borry more, what'll he say when I tell him a principle's a principle? What'll we do if he refuses to give us any more on tick?

MARY. He daren't refuse—if he does, can't you tell him he's paid?

MRS. BOYLE. It's lookin' as if he was paid, whether he refuses or no.

[JOHNNY *appears at the door on left. He can be plainly seen now; he is a thin delicate fellow, something younger than* MARY. *He has evidently gone through a rough time. His face is pale and drawn; there is a tremulous look of indefinite fear in his eyes. The left sleeve of his coat is empty, and he walks with a slight halt.*]

JOHNNY. I was lyin' down; I thought yous were gone. Oul' Simon Mackay is thrampin' about like a horse over me head, an' I can't sleep with him—they're like thunder-claps in me brain! The curse o'—God forgive me for goin' to curse!

MRS. BOYLE. There, now; go back an' lie down agan, an' I'll bring you in a nice cup o' tay.

JOHNNY. Tay, tay, tay! You're always thinkin' o' tay. If a man was dyin', you'd thry to make him swally a cup o' tay!

[*He goes back.*]

MRS. BOYLE. I don't know what's goin' to be done with him. The bullet he got in the hip in Easter Week was bad enough, but the bomb that shatthered his arm in the fight in O'Connell Street put the finishin' touch on him. I knew he was makin' a fool of himself. God knows I went down on me bended knees to him not to go agen the Free State.

MARY. He stuck to his principles, an', no matther how you may argue, ma, a principle's a principle.

VOICE OF JOHNNY. Is Mary goin' to stay here?

MARY. No, I'm not goin' to stay here; you can't expect me to be always at your beck an' call, can you?

VOICE OF JOHNNY. I won't stop here be meself!

MRS. BOYLE. Amn't I nicely handicapped with the whole o' yous! I don't know what any o' yous ud do without your ma. [*to* JOHNNY] Your father'll be here in a minute, an' if you want anythin', he'll get it for you.

JOHNNY. I hate assin' him for anythin'. . . . He hates to be assed to stir. . . . Is the light lightin' before the picture o' the Virgin?

MRS. BOYLE. Yis, yis! The wan inside to St. Anthony isn't enough, but he must have another wan to the Virgin here!

[JERRY DEVINE *enters hastily. He is about twenty-five, well set, ac-*

123 **Easter Week** of April 1916, when bloody street-fighting broke out in Dublin

tive and earnest. He is a type, becoming very common now in the Labour Movement, of a mind knowing enough to make the mass of his associates, who know less, a power, and too little to broaden that power for the benefit of all. MARY *seizes her jumper and runs hastily into room left.*]

JERRY [*breathless*]. Where's the Captain, Mrs. Boyle; where's the Captain?

MRS. BOYLE. You may well ass a body that: he's wherever Joxer Daly is—dhrinkin' in something snug or another.

JERRY. Father Farrell is just afther stoppin' to tell me to run up an' get him to go to the new job that's goin' on in Rathmines; his cousin is foreman o' the job, an' Father Farrell was speakin' to him about poor Johnny an' his father bein' idle so long, an' the foreman told Father Farrell to send the Captain up an' he'd give him a start—I wondher where I'd find him?

MRS. BOYLE. You'll find he's ayther in Ryan's or Foley's.

JERRY. I'll run round to Ryan's—I know it's a great house o' Joxer's. [*He rushes out.*]

MRS. BOYLE [*piteously*]. There now, he'll miss that job, or I know for what! If he gets win' o' the word, he'll not come back till evenin', so that it'll be too late. There'll never be any good got out o' him so long as he goes with that shouldher-shruggin' Joxer. I killin' meself workin', an' he sthruttin' about from mornin' till night like a paycock!

[*The steps of two persons are heard coming up a flight of stairs. They are the footsteps of* CAPTAIN BOYLE *and* JOXER. CAPTAIN BOYLE *is singing in a deep, sonorous, self-honouring voice.*]

THE CAPTAIN. Sweet Spirit, hear me prayer! Hear . . . oh . . . hear . . . me prayer . . . hear, oh, hear . . . Oh, he . . . ar . . . oh, he . . . ar . . . me . . . pray . . . er!

JOXER [*outside*]. Ah, that's a darlin' song, a daaarlin' song!

MRS. BOYLE [*viciously*]. Sweet spirit hear his prayer! Oh, then, I'll take me solemn affeydavey, it's not for a job he's prayin'!

[*She sits down on the bed so that the cretonne hangings hide her from the view of those entering.* THE CAPTAIN *comes slowly in. He is a man of about sixty; stout, grey-haired and stocky. His neck is short, and his head looks like a stone ball that one sometimes sees on top of a gate-post. His cheeks, reddish-purple, are puffed out, as if he were always repressing an almost irrepressible ejaculation.*

On his upper lip is a crisp, tightly cropped moustache; he carries himself with the upper part of his body slightly thrown back, and his stomach slightly thrust forward. His walk is a slow, consequential strut. His clothes are dingy, and he wears a faded seaman's cap with a glazed peak.]

BOYLE [*to* JOXER, *who is still outside*]. Come on, come on in, Joxer; she's gone out long ago, man. If there's nothing else to be got, we'll furrage out a cup o' tay, anyway. It's the only bit I get in comfort when she's away. 'Tisn't Juno should be her pet name at all, but Deirdre of the Sorras, for she's always grousin'.

[JOXER *steps cautiously into the room. He may be younger than* THE CAPTAIN *but he looks a lot older. His face is like a bundle of crinkled paper; his eyes have a cunning twinkle; he is spare and loosely built; he has a habit of constantly shrugging his shoulders with a peculiar twitching movement, meant to be ingratiating. His face is invariably ornamented with a grin.*]

JOXER. It's a terrible thing to be tied to a woman that's always grousin'. I don't know how you stick it—it ud put years on me. It's a good job she has to be so often away, for [*with a shrug*] when the cat's away, the mice can play!

BOYLE [*with a commanding and complacent gesture*]. Pull over to the fire, Joxer, an' we'll have a cup o' tay in a minute.

JOXER. Ah, a cup o' tay's a darlin' thing, a daaarlin' thing—the cup that cheers but doesn't . . .

[JOXER'*s rhapsody is cut short by the sight of* JUNO *coming forward and confronting the two cronies. Both are stupefied.*]

MRS. BOYLE [*with sweet irony—poking the fire, and turning her head to glare at* JOXER]. Pull over to the fire, Joxer Daly, an' we'll have a cup o' tay in a minute! Are you sure, now, you wouldn't like an egg?

JOXER. I can't stop, Mrs. Boyle; I'm in a desperate hurry, a desperate hurry.

MRS. BOYLE. Pull over to the fire, Joxer Daly; people is always far more comfortabler here than they are in their own place.

[JOXER *makes hastily for the door.*]

BOYLE [*stirs to follow him; thinks of something to relieve the situation—stops, and says suddenly*]. Joxer!

JOXER [*at door ready to bolt*]. Yis?

191 **Deirdre of the Sorras** a tragic heroine of Irish legend

BOYLE. You know the foreman o' that job that's goin' on down in Killesther, don't you, Joxer?

JOXER [*puzzled*]. Foreman—Killesther?

BOYLE [*with a meaning look*]. He's a butty o' yours, isn't he?

JOXER [*the truth dawning on him*]. The foreman at Killesther—oh, yis, yis. He's an oul' butty o' mine—oh, he's a darlin' man, a daarlin' man.

BOYLE. Oh, then, it's a sure thing. It's a pity we didn't go down at breakfast first thing this mornin'—we might ha' been working now; but you didn't know it then.

JOXER [*with a shrug*]. It's betther late than never.

BOYLE. It's nearly time we got a start, anyhow; I'm fed up knockin' round, doin' nothin'. He promised you—gave you the straight tip?

JOXER. Yis. "Come down on the blow o' dinner," says he, "an' I'll start you, an' any friend you like to brin' with you." Ah, says I, you're a darlin' man, a daaarlin' man.

BOYLE. Well, it couldn't come at a betther time—we're a long time waitin' for it.

JOXER. Indeed we were; but it's a long lane that has no turnin'.

BOYLE. The blow up for dinner is at one—wait till I see what time it 'tis. [*He goes over to the mantelpiece, and gingerly lifts the clock.*]

MRS. BOYLE. Min' now, how you go on fiddlin' with that clock—you know the least little thing sets it asthray.

BOYLE. The job couldn't come at a betther time; I'm feelin' in great fettle, Joxer. I'd hardly believe I ever had a pain in me legs, an' last week I was nearly crippled with them.

JOXER. That's betther and betther; ah, God never shut wan door but he opened another!

BOYLE. It's only eleven o'clock; we've lashins o' time. I'll slip on me oul' moleskins afther breakfast, an' we can saunther down at our ayse. [*putting his hand on the shovel*] I think, Joxer, we'd betther bring our shovels?

JOXER. Yis, Captain, yis; it's betther to go fully prepared an' ready for all eventualities. You bring your long-tailed shovel, an' I'll bring me navvy. We mighten' want them, an', then agen, we might: for

256 **navvy** pick or shovel

want of a nail the shoe was lost, for want of a shoe the horse was lost, an' for want of a horse the man was lost—aw, that's a darlin' proverb, a daarlin' . . .

[*As* JOXER *is finishing his sentence,* MRS. BOYLE *approaches the door and* JOXER *retreats hurriedly. She shuts the door with a bang.*]

BOYLE [*suggestively*]. We won't be long pullin' ourselves together agen when I'm working for a few weeks.

[MRS. BOYLE *takes no notice.*]

BOYLE. The foreman on the job is an oul' butty o' Joxer's; I have an idea that I know him meself. [*silence*] . . . There's a button off the back o' me moleskin trousers. . . . If you leave out a needle an' thread I'll sew it on meself. . . . Thanks be to God, the pains in me legs is gone, anyhow!

MRS. BOYLE [*with a burst*]. Look here, Mr. Jacky Boyle, them yarns won't go down with Juno. I know you an' Joxer Daly of an oul' date, an', if you think you're able to come it over me with them fairy tales, you're in the wrong shop.

BOYLE [*coughing subduedly to relieve the tenseness of the situation*]. U-u-u-ugh.

MRS. BOYLE. Butty o' Joxer's! Oh, you'll do a lot o' good as long as you continue to be a butty o' Joxer's!

BOYLE. U-u-u-ugh.

MRS. BOYLE. Shovel! Ah, then, me boyo, you'd do far more work with a knife an' fork than ever you'll do with a shovel! If there was e'er a genuine job goin' you'd be dh'other way about—not able to lift your arms with the pains in your legs! Your poor wife slavin' to keep the bit in your mouth, an' you gallivantin' about all the day like a paycock!

BOYLE. It ud be betther for a man to be dead, betther for a man to be dead.

MRS. BOYLE [*ignoring the interruption*]. Everybody callin' you "Captain," an' you only wanst on the wather, in an oul' collier from here to Liverpool, when anybody, to listen or look at you, ud take you for a second Christo For Columbus!

BOYLE. Are you never goin' to give us a rest?

MRS. BOYLE. Oh, you're never tired o' lookin' for a rest.

BOYLE. D'ye want to dhrive me out o' the house?

283 **the bit** a bite to eat

MRS. BOYLE. It ud be easier to dhrive you out o' the house than to dhrive you into a job. Here, sit down an' take your breakfast—it may be the last you'll get, for I don't know where the next is goin' to come from.

BOYLE. If I get this job we'll be all right.

MRS. BOYLE. Did ye see Jerry Devine?

BOYLE [*testily*]. No, I didn't see him.

MRS. BOYLE. No, but you seen Joxer. Well, he was here lookin' for you.

BOYLE. Well, let him look!

MRS. BOYLE. Oh, indeed, he may well look, for it ud be hard for him to see you, an' you stuck in Ryan's snug.

BOYLE. I wasn't in Ryan's snug—I don't go into Ryan's.

MRS. BOYLE. Oh, is there a mad dog there? Well, if you weren't in Ryan's you were in Foley's.

BOYLE. I'm telling you for the last three weeks I haven't tasted a dhrop of intoxicatin' liquor. I wasn't in ayther wan snug or dh'other—I could swear that on a prayer-book—I'm as innocent as the child unborn!

MRS. BOYLE. Well, if you'd been in for your breakfast you'd ha' seen him.

BOYLE [*suspiciously*]. What does he want me for?

MRS. BOYLE. He'll be back any minute an' then you'll soon know.

BOYLE. I'll dhrop out an' see if I can meet him.

MRS. BOYLE. You'll sit down an' take your breakfast, an' let me go to me work, for I'm an hour late already waitin' for you.

BOYLE. You needn't ha' waited, for I'll take no breakfast—I've a little spirit left in me still!

MRS. BOYLE. Are you goin' to have your breakfast—yes or no?

BOYLE [*too proud to yield*]. I'll have no breakfast—yous can keep your breakfast. [*plaintively*] I'll knock out a bit somewhere, never fear.

MRS. BOYLE. Nobody's goin' to coax you—don't think that. [*She vigorously replaces the pan and the sausages in the press.*]

BOYLE. I've a little spirit left in me still.

[JERRY DEVINE *enters hastily.*]

JERRY. Oh, here you are at last! I've been searchin' for you everywhere. The foreman in Foley's told me you hadn't left the snug with Joxer ten minutes before I went in.

MRS. BOYLE. An' he swearin' on the holy prayer-book that he wasn't in no snug!

BOYLE [*to* JERRY]. What business is it o' yours whether I was in a snug or no? What do you want to be gallopin' about afther me for? Is a man not to be allowed to leave his house for a minute without havin' a pack o' spies, pimps an' informers cantherin' at his heels?

JERRY. Oh, you're takin' a wrong view of it, Mr. Boyle; I simply was anxious to do you a good turn. I have a message for you from Father Farrell: he says that if you go to the job that's on in Rathmines, an' ask for Foreman Mangan, you'll get a start.

BOYLE. That's all right, but I don't want the motions of me body to be watched the way an asthronomer ud watch a star. If you're folleyin' Mary aself, you've no pereeogative to be folleyin' me. [*suddenly catching his thigh*] U-ugh, I'm afther gettin' a terrible twinge in me right leg!

MRS. BOYLE. Oh, it won't be very long now till it travels into your left wan. It's miraculous that whenever he scents a job in front of him, his legs begin to fail him! Then, me bucko, if you lose this chance, you may go an' furrage for yourself!

JERRY. This job'll last for some time, too, Captain, an' as soon as the foundations are in, it'll be cushy enough.

BOYLE. Won't it be a climbin' job? How d'ye expect me to be able to go up a ladder with these legs? An', if I get up aself, how am I goin' to get down agen?

MRS. BOYLE [*viciously*]. Get wan o' the labourers to carry you down in a hod! You can't climb a laddher, but you can skip like a goat into a snug!

JERRY. I wouldn't let meself be let down that easy, Mr. Boyle; a little exercise, now, might do you all the good in the world.

BOYLE. It's a docthor you should have been, Devine—maybe you know more about the pains in me legs than meself that has them?

JERRY [*irritated*]. Oh, I know nothin' about the pains in your legs; I've brought the message that Father Farrell gave me, an' that's all I can do.

MRS. BOYLE. Here, sit down an' take your breakfast, an' go an' get ready; an' don't be actin' as if you couldn't pull a wing out of a dead bee.

BOYLE. I want no breakfast, I tell you; it ud choke me afther all that's been said. I've a little spirit left in me still.

MRS. BOYLE. Well, let's see your spirit, then, an' go in at wanst an' put on your moleskin trousers!

BOYLE [*moving towards the door on left*]. It ud be betther for a man to be dead! U-ugh! There's another twinge in me other leg! Nobody but meself knows the sufferin' I'm goin' through with the pains in these legs o' mine! [*He goes into the room on left as* MARY *comes out with her hat in her hand.*]

MRS. BOYLE. I'll have to push off now, for I'm terrible late already, but I was determined to stay an' hunt that Joxer this time.

[*She goes off.*]

JERRY. Are you going out, Mary?

MARY. It looks like it when I'm putting on my hat, doesn't it?

JERRY. The bitther word agen, Mary.

MARY. You won't allow me to be friendly with you; if I thry, you deliberately misundherstand it.

JERRY. I didn't always misundherstand it; you were often delighted to have the arms of Jerry around you.

MARY. If you go on talkin' like this, Jerry Devine, you'll make me hate you!

JERRY. Well, let it be either a weddin' or a wake! Listen, Mary, I'm standin' for the Secretaryship of our Union. There's only one opposin' me; I'm popular with all the men, an' a good speaker—all are sayin' that I'll get elected.

MARY. Well?

JERRY. The job's worth three hundred an' fifty pounds a year, Mary. You an' I could live nice an' cosily on that; it would lift you out o' this place an' . . .

MARY. I haven't time to listen to you now—I have to go. [*She is going out when* JERRY *bars the way.*]

JERRY [*appealingly*]. Mary, what's come over you with me for the last few weeks? You hardly speak to me, an' then only a word with a face o' bittherness on it. Have you forgotten, Mary, all the happy evenin's that were as sweet as the scented hawthorn that sheltered the sides o' the road as we sauntered through the country?

MARY. That's all over now. When you get your new job, Jerry, you won't be long findin' a girl far betther than I am for your sweetheart.

JERRY. Never, never, Mary! No matther what happens you'll always be the same to me.

MARY. I must be off; please let me go, Jerry.

JERRY. I'll go a bit o' the way with you.

MARY. You needn't, thanks; I want to be by meself.

JERRY [*catching her arm*]. You're goin' to meet another fella; you've clicked with some one else, me lady!

MARY. That's no concern o' yours, Jerry Devine; let me go!

JERRY. I saw yous comin' out o' the Cornflower Dance Class, an' you hangin' on his arm—a thin, lanky strip of a Micky Dazzler, with a walkin' stick an' gloves!

VOICE OF JOHNNY [*loudly*]. What are you doin' there—pullin' about everything!

VOICE OF BOYLE [*loudly and viciously*]. I'm puttin' on me moleskin trousers!

MARY. You're hurtin' me arm! Let me go, or I'll scream, an' then you'll have the oul' fella out on top of us!

JERRY. Don't be so hard on a fella, Mary, don't be so hard.

BOYLE [*appearing at the door*]. What's the meanin' of all this hillabaloo?

MARY. Let me go, let me go!

BOYLE. D'ye hear me—what's all this hillabaloo about?

JERRY [*plaintively*]. Will you not give us one kind word, one kind word, Mary?

BOYLE. D'ye hear me talkin' to yous? What's all this hillabaloo for?

JERRY. Let me kiss your hand, your little, tiny, white hand!

BOYLE. Your little, tiny, white hand—are you takin' leave o' your senses, man?

[MARY *breaks away and rushes out.*]

BOYLE. This is nice goin's on in front of her father!

JERRY. Ah, dhry up, for God's sake! [*He follows* MARY.]

BOYLE. Chiselurs don't care a damn now about their parents,

442 **Chiselurs** children

they're bringin' their fathers' grey hairs down with sorra to the grave, an' laughin' at it, laughin' at it. Ah, I suppose it's just the same everywhere—the whole worl's in a state o' chassis! [*He sits by the fire.*] Breakfast! Well, they can keep their breakfast for me. Not if they went down on their bended knees would I take it—I'll show them I've a little spirit left in me still! [*He goes over to the press, takes out a plate and looks at it.*] Sassige! Well, let her keep her sassige. [*He returns to the fire, takes up the teapot and gives it a gentle shake.*] The tay's wet right enough. [*A pause; he rises, goes to the press, takes out the sausage, puts it on the pan, and puts both on the fire. He attends the sausage with a fork.*]

BOYLE [*singing*].

When the robins nest agen,
And the flowers are in bloom,
When the Springtime's sunny smile seems to banish all
    sorrow an' gloom;
Then me bonny blue-ey'd lad, if me heart be true till then—
He's promised he'll come back to me,
When the robins nest agen!

[*He lifts his head at the high note, and then drops his eyes to the pan.*]

BOYLE [*singing*].

When the . . .

[*Steps are heard approaching; he whips the pan off the fire and puts it under the bed, then sits down at the fire. The door opens and a bearded man looking in says*]:

You don't happen to want a sewin' machine?

BOYLE [*furiously*]. No, I don't want e'er a sewin' machine! [*He returns the pan to the fire, and commences to sing again.*]

BOYLE [*singing*].

When the robins nest agen,
And the flowers they are in bloom,
He's . . .

[*A thundering knock is heard at the street door.*]

BOYLE. There's a terrible tatheraraa—that's a stranger—that's nobody belongin' to the house. [*Another loud knock.*]

JOXER [*sticking his head in at the door*]. Did ye hear them tatherarahs?

445 chassis Boyle's way of saying *chaos*

BOYLE. Well, Joxer, I'm not deaf.

JOHNNY [*appearing in his shirt and trousers at the door on left; his face is anxious and his voice is tremulous*]. Who's that at the door; who's that at the door? Who gave that knock—d'ye yous hear me—are yous deaf or dhrunk or what?

BOYLE [*to* JOHNNY]. How the hell do I know who 'tis? Joxer, stick your head out o' the window an' see.

JOXER. An' mebbe get a bullet in the kisser? Ah, none o' them thricks for Joxer! It's betther to be a coward than a corpse!

BOYLE [*looking cautiously out of the window*]. It's a fella in a thrench coat.

JOHNNY. Holy Mary, Mother o' God, I . . .

BOYLE. He's goin' away—he must ha' got tired knockin'.

[JOHNNY *returns to the room on left*.]

BOYLE. Sit down an' have a cup o' tay, Joxer.

JOXER. I'm afraid the missus ud pop in on us agen before we'd know where we are. Somethin's tellin' me to go at wanst.

BOYLE. Don't be superstitious, man; we're Dublin men, an' not boyos that's only afther comin' up from the bog o' Allen—though if she did come in, right enough, we'd be caught like rats in a thrap.

JOXER. An' you know the sort she is—she wouldn't listen to reason—an' wanse bitten twice shy.

BOYLE [*going over to the window at back*]. If the worst came to the worst, you could dart out here, Joxer; it's only a dhrop of a few feet to the roof of the return room, an' the first minute she goes into dh'other room, I'll give you the bend, an' you can slip in an' away.

JOXER [*yielding to the temptation*]. Ah, I won't stop very long anyhow. [*picking up a book from the table*] Whose is the buk?

BOYLE. Aw, one o' Mary's; she's always readin' lately—nothin' but thrash, too. There's one I was lookin' at dh'other day: three stories, *The Doll's House, Ghosts,* an' *The Wild Duck*—buks only fit for chiselurs!

JOXER. Didja ever rade *Elizabeth, or Th' Exile o' Sibayria* . . . ah, it's a darlin' story, a daarlin' story!

BOYLE. You eat your sassige, an' never min' *Th' Exile o' Sibayria.*

[*Both sit down;* BOYLE *fills out tea, pours gravy on* JOXER'S *plate, and keeps the sausage for himself.*]

JOXER. What are you wearin' your moleskin trousers for?

BOYLE. I have to go to a job, Joxer. Just afther you'd gone, Devine kem runnin' in to tell us that Father Farrell said if I went down to the job that's goin' on in Rathmines I'd get a start.

JOXER. Be the holy, that's good news!

BOYLE. How is it good news? I wondher if you were in my condition, would you call it good news?

JOXER. I thought . . .

BOYLE. You thought! You think too sudden sometimes, Joxer. D'ye know, I'm hardly able to crawl with the pains in me legs!

JOXER. Yis, yis; I forgot the pains in your legs. I know you can do nothin' while they're at you.

BOYLE. You forgot; I don't think any of yous realize the state I'm in with the pains in me legs. What ud happen if I had to carry a bag o' cement?

JOXER. Ah, any man havin' the like of them pains id be down an' out, down an' out.

BOYLE. I wouldn't mind if he had said it to meself; but, no, oh no, he rushes in an' shouts it out in front o' Juno, an' you know what Juno is, Joxer. We all know Devine knows a little more than the rest of us, but he doesn't act as if he did; he's a good boy, sober, able to talk an' all that, but still . . .

JOXER. Oh, ay; able to argufy, but still . . .

BOYLE. If he's runnin' afther Mary, aself, he's not goin' to be runnin' afther me. Captain Boyle's able to take care of himself. Afther all, I'm not gettin' brought up on Virol. I never heard him usin' a curse; I don't believe he was ever dhrunk in his life—sure he's not like a Christian at all!

JOXER. You're afther takin' the word out o' me mouth—afther all, a Christian's natural, but he's unnatural.

BOYLE. His oul' fella was just the same—a Wicklow man.

JOXER. A Wicklow man! That explains the whole thing. I've met many a Wicklow man in me time, but I never met wan that was any good.

BOYLE. "Father Farrell," says he, "sent me down to tell you." Father Farrell! . . . D'ye know, Joxer, I never like to be beholden to any o' the clergy.

JOXER. It's dangerous, right enough.

BOYLE. If they do anything for you, they'd want you to be livin' in the Chapel. . . . I'm goin' to tell you somethin', Joxer, that I wouldn't tell to anybody else—the clergy always had too much power over the people in this unfortunate country.

JOXER. You could sing that if you had an air to it!

BOYLE [*becoming enthusiastic*]. Didn't they prevent the people in '47 from seizin' the corn, an' they starvin'; didn't they down Parnell; didn't they say that hell wasn't hot enough nor eternity long enough to punish the Fenians? We don't forget, we don't forget them things, Joxer. If they've taken everything else from us, Joxer, they've left us our memory.

JOXER [*emotionally*]. For mem'ry's the only friend that grief can call its own, that grief . . . can . . . call . . . its own!

BOYLE. Father Farrell's beginnin' to take a great intherest in Captain Boyle; because of what Johnny did for his country, says he to me wan day. It's a curious way to reward Johnny be makin' his poor oul' father work. But, that's what the clergy want, Joxer—work, work, work for me an' you; havin' us mulin' from mornin' till night, so that they may be in betther fettle when they come hoppin' round for their dues! Job! Well, let him give his job to wan of his hymn-singin', prayer-spoutin', craw-thumpin' Confraternity men!

[*The voice of a coal-block vendor is heard chanting in the street.*]

VOICE OF COAL VENDOR. Blocks . . . coal-blocks! Blocks . . . coal-blocks!

JOXER. God be with the young days when you were steppin' the deck of a manly ship, with the win' blowin' a hurricane through the masts, an' the only sound you'd hear was, "Port your helm!" an' the only answer, "Port it is, sir!"

BOYLE. Them was days, Joxer, them was days. Nothin' was too hot or too heavy for me then. Sailin' from the Gulf o' Mexico to the Antarctic Ocean. I seen things, I seen things, Joxer, that no mortal

563 '47 1847, a year of the potato famine
564 **Parnell** Charles Stewart Parnell (1847–1891), who led the fight in the British Parliament for Irish home rule. Upon being involved in a divorce scandal, he was opposed by many of his former supporters, including many of the Irish clergy.
565 **Fenians** members of the Sinn Fein, an underground organization that aimed at Irish independence. Some Irishmen regarded them as trouble-makers.
577 **Confraternity men** members of a religious and charitable association

man should speak about that knows his Catechism. Ofen, an' ofen, when I was fixed to the wheel with a marlin-spike, an' the win's blowin' fierce an' the waves lashin' an' lashin', till you'd think every minute was goin' to be your last, an' it blowed, an' blowed—blew is the right word, Joxer, but blowed is what the sailors use. . . .

JOXER. Aw, it's a darlin' word, a daarlin' word.

BOYLE. An', as it blowed an' blowed, I ofen looked up at the sky an' assed meself the question—what is the stars, what is the stars?

VOICE OF COAL VENDOR. Any blocks, coal-blocks; blocks, coal-blocks!

JOXER. Ah, that's the question, that's the question—what is the stars?

BOYLE. An' then, I'd have another look, an' I'd ass meself—what is the moon?

JOXER. Ah, that's the question—what is the moon, what is the moon?

[*Rapid steps are heard coming towards the door.* BOYLE *makes desperate efforts to hide everything;* JOXER *rushes to the window in a frantic effort to get out;* BOYLE *begins to innocently lilt—"Oh, me darlin' Jennie, I will be thrue to thee," when the door is opened, and the black face of the* COAL VENDOR *appears.*]

THE COAL VENDOR. D'yes want any blocks?

BOYLE [*with a roar*]. No, we don't want any blocks!

JOXER [*coming back with a sigh of relief*]. That's afther puttin' the heart across me—I could ha' sworn it was Juno. I'd betther be goin', Captain; you couldn't tell the minute Juno'd hop in on us.

BOYLE. Let her hop in; we may as well have it out first as at last. I've made up me mind—I'm not goin' to do only what she damn well likes.

JOXER. Them sentiments does you credit, Captain; I don't like to say anything as between man an' wife, but I say as a butty, as a butty, Captain, that you've stuck it too long, an' that it's about time you showed a little spunk.

How can a man die betther than facin' fearful odds,
For th' ashes of his fathers an' the temples of his gods.

BOYLE. She has her rights—there's no one denyin' it, but haven't I me rights too?

JOXER. Of course you have—the sacred rights o' man!

BOYLE. Today, Joxer, there's goin' to be issued a proclamation be me, establishin' an independent Republic, an' Juno'll have to take an oath of allegiance.

JOXER. Be firm, be firm, Captain; the first few minutes'll be the worst:—if you gently touch a nettle it'll sting you for your pains; grasp it like a lad of mettle, an's as soft as silk remains!

VOICE OF JUNO OUTSIDE. Can't stop, Mrs. Madigan—I haven't a minute!

JOXER [*flying out of the window*]. Holy God, here she is!

BOYLE [*packing the things away with a rush in the press*]. I knew that fella ud stop till she was in on top of us! [*He sits down by the fire.*]

[JUNO *enters hastily; she is flurried and excited.*]

JUNO. Oh, you're in—you must have been only afther comin' in?

BOYLE. No, I never went out.

JUNO. It's curious, then, you never heard the knockin'. [*She puts her coat and hat on bed.*]

BOYLE. Knockin'? Of course I heard the knockin'.

JUNO. An' why didn't you open the door, then? I suppose you were so busy with Joxer that you hadn't time.

BOYLE. I haven't seen Joxer since I seen him before. Joxer! What ud bring Joxer here?

JUNO. D'ye mean to tell me that the pair of yous wasn't collogin' together here when me back was turned?

BOYLE. What ud we be collogin' together about? I have somethin' else to think of besides collogin' with Joxer. I can swear on all the holy prayer-books . . .

MRS. BOYLE. That you weren't in no snug! Go on in at wanst now, an' take off that moleskin trousers o' yours, an' put on a collar an' tie to smarten yourself up a bit. There's a visitor comin' with Mary in a minute, an' he has great news for you.

BOYLE. A job, I suppose; let us get wan first before we start lookin' for another.

MRS. BOYLE. That's the thing that's able to put the win' up you. Well, it's no job, but news that'll give you the chance o' your life.

BOYLE. What's all the mysthery about?

MRS. BOYLE. G'win an' take off the moleskin trousers when you're told!

[BOYLE *goes into room on left.* MRS. BOYLE *tidies up the room, puts the shovel under the bed, and goes to the press.*]

MRS. BOYLE. Oh, God bless us, looka the way everythin's thrun about! Oh, Joxer was here, Joxer was here!

[MARY *enters with* CHARLIE BENTHAM; *he is a young man of twenty-five, tall, good-looking, with a very high opinion of himself generally. He is dressed in a brown coat, brown knee-breeches, grey stockings, a brown sweater, with a deep blue tie; he carries gloves and a walking-stick.*]

MRS. BOYLE [*fussing round*]. Come in, Mr. Bentham; sit down, Mr. Bentham, in this chair; it's more comfortabler than that, Mr. Bentham. Himself'll be here in a minute; he's just takin' off his trousers.

MARY. Mother!

BENTHAM. Please don't put yourself to any trouble, Mrs. Boyle—I'm quite all right here, thank you.

MRS. BOYLE. An' to think of you knowin' Mary, an' she knowin' the news you had for us, an' wouldn't let on; but it's all the more welcomer now, for we were on our last lap!

VOICE OF JOHNNY INSIDE. What are you kickin' up all the racket for?

BOYLE [*roughly*]. I'm takin' off me moleskin trousers!

JOHNNY. Can't you do it, then, without lettin' th' whole house know you're takin' off your trousers? What d'ye want puttin' them on an' takin' them off again?

BOYLE. Will you let me alone, will you let me alone? Am I never goin' to be done thryin' to please th' whole o' yous?

MRS. BOYLE [*to* BENTHAM]. You must excuse th' state o' th' place, Mr. Bentham; th' minute I turn me back that man o' mine always make a litther o' th' place, a litther o' th' place.

BENTHAM. Don't worry, Mrs. Boyle; it's all right, I assure . . .

BOYLE [*inside*]. Where's me braces; where in th' name o' God did I leave me braces. . . . Ay, did you see where I put me braces?

JOHNNY [*inside, calling out*]. Ma, will you come in here an' take da away ou' o' this or he'll dhrive me mad.

MRS. BOYLE [*going towards door*]. Dear, dear, dear, that man'll be lookin' for somethin' on th' day o' Judgement. [*looking into room and calling to* BOYLE] Look at your braces, man, hangin' round your neck!

BOYLE [*inside*]. Aw, Holy God!

MRS. BOYLE [*calling*]. Johnny, Johnny, come out here for a minute.

JOHNNY. Oh, leave Johnny alone, an' don't be annoyin' him!

MRS. BOYLE. Come on, Johnny, till I inthroduce you to Mr. Bentham. [*to* BENTHAM] Me son, Mr. Bentham; he's afther goin' through the mill. He was only a chiselur of a Boy Scout in Easter Week, when he got hit in the hip; and his arm was blew off in the fight in O'Connell Street. [JOHNNY *comes in.*] Here he is, Mr. Bentham; Mr. Bentham, Johnny. None can deny he done his bit for Irelan', if that's going to do him any good.

JOHNNY [*boastfully*]. I'd do it agen, ma, I'd do it agen; for a principle's a principle.

MRS. BOYLE. Ah, you lost your best principle, me boy, when you lost your arm; them's the only sort o' principles that's any good to a workin' man.

JOHNNY. Ireland only half free'll never be at peace while she has a son left to pull a trigger.

MRS. BOYLE. To be sure, to be sure—no bread's a lot betther than half a loaf. [*calling loudly in to* BOYLE] Will you hurry up there? [BOYLE *enters in his best trousers, which aren't too good, and looks very uncomfortable in his collar and tie.*]

MRS. BOYLE. This is me husband; Mr. Boyle, Mr. Bentham.

BENTHAM. Ah, very glad to know you, Mr. Boyle. How are you?

BOYLE. Ah, I'm not too well at all; I suffer terrible with pains in me legs. Juno can tell you there what . . .

MRS. BOYLE. You won't have many pains in your legs when you hear what Mr. Bentham has to tell you.

BENTHAM. Juno! What an interesting name! It reminds one of Homer's glorious story of ancient gods and heroes.

BOYLE. Yis, doesn't it? You see, Juno was born an' christened in June; I met her in June; we were married in June, an' Johnny was born in June, so wan day I says to her, "You should ha' been called Juno," an' the name stuck to her ever since.

MRS. BOYLE. Here we can talk o' them things agen; let Mr. Bentham say what he has to say now.

BENTHAM. Well, Mr. Boyle, I suppose you'll remember a Mr.

Ellison of Santry—he's a relative of yours, I think.

BOYLE [*viciously*]. Is it that prognosticator an' procrastinator! Of course I remember him.

BENTHAM. Well, he's dead, Mr. Boyle . . .

BOYLE. Sorra many'll go into mournin' for him.

MRS. BOYLE. Wait till you hear what Mr. Bentham has to say, an' then, maybe, you'll change your opinion.

BENTHAM. A week before he died he sent for me to write his will for him. He told me that there were two only that he wished to leave his property to; his second cousin Michael Finnegan of Santry, and John Boyle, his first cousin of Dublin.

BOYLE [*excitedly*]. Me, is it me, me?

BENTHAM. You, Mr. Boyle; I'll read a copy of the will that I have here with me, which has been duly filed in the Court of Probate. [*He takes a paper from his pocket and reads*]:

6th February, 1922.

This is the last Will and Testament of William Ellison, of Santry, in the County of Dublin. I hereby order and wish my property to be sold and divided as follows:—

£20 to the St. Vincent De Paul Society.

£60 for Masses for the repose of my soul (5s. for Each Mass).

The rest of my property to be divided between my first and second cousins.

I hereby appoint Timothy Buckly, of Santry, and Hugh Brierly, of Coolock, to be my Executors.

(*Signed*) WILLIAM ELLISON.
HUGH BRIERLY.
TIMOTHY BUCKLY.
CHARLES BENTHAM, N.T.

BOYLE [*eagerly*]. An' how much'll be comin' out of it, Mr. Bentham?

BENTHAM. The Executors told me that half of the property would be anything between £1500 and £2000.

MARY. A fortune, father, a fortune!

JOHNNY. We'll be able to get out o' this place now, an' go somewhere we're not known.

747 Sorra many very few

MRS. BOYLE. You won't have to trouble about a job for a while, Jack.

BOYLE [*fervently*]. I'll never doubt the goodness o' God agen.

BENTHAM. I congratulate you, Mr. Boyle. [*They shake hands.*]

BOYLE. An' now, Mr. Bentham, you'll have to have a wet.

BENTHAM. A wet?

BOYLE. A wet—a jar—a boul!

MRS. BOYLE. Jack, you're speakin' to Mr. Bentham, an' not to Joxer.

BOYLE [*solemnly*]. Juno . . . Mary . . . Johnny . . . we'll have to go into mournin' at wanst. . . . I never expected that poor Bill ud die so sudden. . . . Well, we all have to die some day . . . you, Juno, today . . . an' me, maybe, tomorrow. . . . It's sad, but it can't be helped. . . . Requiescat in pace . . . or, usin' our oul' tongue like St. Patrick or St. Briget, Guh sayeree jeea ayera!

MARY. Oh, father, that's not Rest in Peace; that's God save Ireland.

BOYLE. U-u-ugh, it's all the same—isn't it a prayer? . . . Juno, I'm done with Joxer; he's nothin' but a prognosticator an' a . . .

JOXER [*climbing angrily through the window and bounding into the room*]. You're done with Joxer, are you? Maybe you thought I'd stop on the roof all the night for you! Joxer out on the roof with the win' blowin' through him was nothin' to you an' your friend with the collar an' tie!

MRS. BOYLE. What in the name o' God brought you out on the roof; what were you doin' there?

JOXER [*ironically*]. I was dhreamin' I was standin' on the bridge of a ship, an' she sailin' the Antarctic Ocean, an' it blowed, an' blowed, an' I lookin' up at the sky an' sayin', what is the stars, what is the stars?

MRS. BOYLE [*opening the door and standing at it*]. Here, get ou' o' this, Joxer Daly; I was always thinkin' you had a slate off.

JOXER [*moving to the door*]. I have to laugh every time I look at the deep sea sailor; an' a row on a river ud make him sea-sick!

BOYLE. Get ou' o' this before I take the law into me own hands!

JOXER [*going out*]. Say aw rewaeawr, but not good-bye. Lookin' for work, an' prayin' to God he won't get it! [*He goes.*]

813 aw rewaeawr *au revoir*

MRS. BOYLE. I'm tired tellin' you what Joxer was; maybe now you see yourself the kind he is.

BOYLE. He'll never blow the froth off a pint o' mine agen, that's a sure thing. Johnny . . . Mary . . . you're to keep yourselves to yourselves for the future. Juno, I'm done with Joxer. . . . I'm a new man from this out. . . . [*clasping* JUNO'S *hand, and singing emotionally*]

Oh, me darlin' Juno, I will be thrue to thee;
Me own, me darlin' Juno, you're all the world to me.

THE CURTAIN FALLS

ACT II

SCENE. *The same, but the furniture is more plentiful, and of a vulgar nature. A glaringly upholstered arm-chair and lounge; cheap pictures and photos everywhere. Every available spot is ornamented with huge vases filled with artificial flowers. Crossed festoons of coloured paper chains stretch from end to end of ceiling. On the table is an old attaché case. It is about six in the evening, and two days after the First Act.* BOYLE, *in his shirt sleeves, is voluptuously stretched on the sofa; he is smoking a clay pipe. He is half asleep. A lamp is lighting on the table. After a few moments' pause the voice of* JOXER *is heard singing softly outside at the door—"Me pipe I'll smoke, as I dhrive me moke—are you there, Mor . . . ee . . . ar . . . i . . . teee!"*

BOYLE [*leaping up, takes a pen in his hand and busies himself with papers*]. Come along, Joxer, me son, come along.

JOXER [*putting his head in*]. Are you be yourself?

BOYLE. Come on, come on; that doesn't matther; I'm masther now, an' I'm goin' to remain masther.

[JOXER *comes in.*]

12 **moke** donkey

JOXER. How d'ye feel now, as a man o' money?

BOYLE [*solemnly*]. It's a responsibility, Joxer, a great responsibility.

JOXER. I suppose 'tis now, though you wouldn't think it.

BOYLE. Joxer, han' me over that attackey case on the table there. [JOXER *hands the case.*] Ever since the Will was passed I've run hundhreds o' dockyments through me han's—I tell you, you have to keep your wits about you. [*He busies himself with papers.*]

JOXER. Well, I won't disturb you; I'll dhrop in when . . .

BOYLE [*hastily*]. It's all right, Joxer, this is the last one to be signed today. [*He signs a paper, puts it into the case, which he shuts with a snap, and sits back pompously in the chair.*] Now, Joxer, you want to see me; I'm at your service—what can I do for you, me man?

JOXER. I've just dhropped in with the £3 : 5s. that Mrs. Madigan riz on the blankets an' table for you, and she says you're to be in no hurry payin' it back.

BOYLE. She won't be long without it; I expect the first cheque for a couple o' hundhred any day. There's the five bob for yourself—go on, take it, man; it'll not be the last you'll get from the Captain. Now an' agen we have our differ, but we're there together all the time.

JOXER. Me for you, an' you for me, like the two Musketeers.

BOYLE. Father Farrell stopped me today an' tole me how glad he was I fell in for the money.

JOXER. He'll be stoppin' you ofen enough now; I suppose it was "Mr." Boyle with him?

BOYLE. He shuk me be the han'. . . .

JOXER [*ironically*]. I met with Napper Tandy, an' he shuk me be the han'!

BOYLE. You're seldom asthray, Joxer, but you're wrong shipped this time. What you're sayin' of Father Farrell is very near to blasfeemey. I don't like any one to talk disrespectful of Father Farrell.

JOXER. You're takin' me up wrong, Captain; I wouldn't let a word be said agen Father Farrell—the heart o' the rowl, that's what he is; I always said he was a darlin' man, a daarlin' man.

BOYLE. Comin' up the stairs who did I meet but that bummer, Nugent. "I seen you talkin' to Father Farrell," says he, with a grin on him. "He'll be folleyin' you," says he, "like a Guardian Angel from this out"—all the time the oul' grin on him, Joxer.

JOXER. I never seen him yet but he had that oul' grin on him!

BOYLE. "Mr. Nugent," says I, "Father Farrell is a man o' the people, an', as far as I know the History of me country, the priests was always in the van of the fight for Irelan's freedom."

JOXER [*fervently*].

Who was it led the van, Soggart Aroon?
Since the fight first began, Soggart Aroon?

BOYLE. "Who are you tellin'?" says he. "Didn't they let down the Fenians, an' didn't they do in Parnell? An' now . . . " "You ought to be ashamed o' yourself," says I, interruptin' him, "not to know the History o' your country." An' I left him gawkin' where he was.

JOXER. Where ignorance 's bliss 'tis folly to be wise; I wondher did he ever read the Story o' Irelan'.

BOYLE. Be J. L. Sullivan? Don't you know he didn't?

JOXER. Ah, it's a darlin' buk, a daarlin' buk!

BOYLE. You'd betther be goin', now, Joxer, his Majesty, Bentham, 'll be here any minute, now.

JOXER. Be the way things is lookin', it'll be a match between him an' Mary. She's thrun over Jerry altogether. Well, I hope it will, for he's a darlin' man.

BOYLE. I'm glad you think so—I don't. [*irritably*] What's darlin' about him?

JOXER [*nonplussed*]. I only seen him twiced; if you want to know me, come an' live with me.

BOYLE. He's too ignified for me—to hear him talk you'd think he knew as much as a Boney's Oraculum. He's given up his job as teacher, an' is goin' to become a solicitor in Dublin—he's been studyin' law. I suppose he thinks I'll set him up, but he's wrong shipped. An' th' other fella—Jerry's as bad. The two o' them ud give you a pain in your face, listenin' to them; Jerry believin' in nothin', an' Bentham believin' in everythin'. One that says all is God an' no man; an' th' other that says all is man an' no God!

65 **Soggart Aroon** Gaelic for "priest beloved," a term referring to one of leaders of an Irish rebellion in the eighteenth century

86 **Boney's Oraculum** apparently one of the books of practical advice for working people, by William ("Boney") Cobbett (1763–1835)

JOXER. Well, I'll be off now.

BOYLE. Don't forget to dhrop down afther a while; we'll have a quiet jar, an' a song or two.

JOXER. Never fear.

BOYLE. An' tell Mrs. Madigan that I hope we'll have the pleasure of her organization at our little enthertainment.

JOXER. Righto; we'll come down together. [*He goes out.*]

[JOHNNY *comes from room on left, and sits down moodily at the fire.* BOYLE *looks at him for a few moments, and shakes his head. He fills his pipe.*]

VOICE OF JUNO AT THE DOOR. Open the door, Jack; this thing has me nearly kilt with the weight.

[BOYLE *opens the door.* JUNO *enters carrying the box of a gramophone, followed by* MARY *carrying the horn, and some parcels.* JUNO *leaves the box on the table and flops into a chair.*]

JUNO. Carryin' that from Henry Street was no joke.

BOYLE. U-u-ugh, that's a grand lookin' insthrument—how much was it?

JUNO. Pound down, an' five to be paid at two shillin's a week.

BOYLE. That's reasonable enough.

JUNO. I'm afraid we're runnin' into too much debt; first the furniture, an' now this.

BOYLE. The whole lot won't be much out of £2000.

MARY. I don't know what you wanted a gramophone for—I know Charlie hates them; he says they're destructive of real music.

BOYLE. Desthructive of music—that fella ud give you a pain in your face. All a gramophone wants is to be properly played; it's thrue wondher is only felt when everythin's quiet—what a gramophone wants is dead silence!

MARY. But, father, Jerry says the same; afther all, you can only appreciate music when your ear is properly trained.

BOYLE. That's another fella ud give you a pain in your face. Properly thrained! I suppose you couldn't appreciate football unless your fut was properly thrained.

MRS. BOYLE [*to* MARY]. Go on in ower that an' dress, or Charlie 'll be in on you, an' tay nor nothin' 'll be ready.

[MARY *goes into room left.*]

127 **ower that** right away

MRS. BOYLE [*arranging table for tea*]. You didn't look at our new gramophone, Johnny?

JOHNNY. 'Tisn't gramophones I'm thinking of.

MRS. BOYLE. An' what is it you're thinkin' of, allana?

JOHNNY. Nothin', nothin', nothin'.

MRS. BOYLE. Sure, you must be thinkin' of somethin'; it's yourself that has yourself the way y'are; sleepin' wan night in me sisther's, an' the nex' in your father's brother's—you'll get no rest goin' on that way.

JOHNNY. I can rest nowhere, nowhere, nowhere.

MRS. BOYLE. Sure, you're not thryin' to rest anywhere.

JOHNNY. Let me alone, let me alone, let me alone, for God's sake.

[*A knock at street door.*]

MRS. BOYLE [*in a flutter*]. Here he is; here's Mr. Bentham!

BOYLE. Well, there's room for him; it's a pity there's not a brass band to play him in.

MRS. BOYLE. We'll han' the tay around, an' not be clusthered round the table, as if we never seen nothin'.

[*Steps are heard approaching, and* JUNO, *opening the door, allows* BENTHAM *to enter.*]

JUNO. Give your hat an' stick to Jack, there . . . sit down, Mr. Bentham . . . no, not there . . . in th' easy chair be the fire . . . there, that's betther. Mary'll be out to you in a minute.

BOYLE [*solemnly*]. I seen be the paper this mornin' that Consols was down half per cent. That's serious, min' you, an' shows the whole counthry's in a state o' chassis.

MRS. BOYLE. What's Consols, Jack?

BOYLE. Consols? Oh, Consols is—oh, there's no use tellin' women what Consols is—th' wouldn't undherstand.

BENTHAM. It's just as you were saying, Mr. Boyle . . .

[MARY *enters charmingly dressed.*]

BENTHAM. Oh, good evening, Mary; how pretty you're looking!

MARY [*archly*]. Am I?

BOYLE. We were just talkin' when you kem in, Mary, I was tellin' Mr. Bentham that the whole counthry's in a state o' chassis.

MARY [*to* BENTHAM]. Would you prefer the green or the blue ribbon round me hair, Charlie?

133 **allana** dear one
153 **Consols** Consolidated Annuities (English government securities)

MRS. BOYLE. Mary, your father's speakin'.

BOYLE [*rapidly*]. I was jus' tellin' Mr. Bentham that the whole counthry's in a state o' chassis.

MARY. I'm sure you're frettin', da, whether it is or no.

MRS. BOYLE. With all our churches an' religions, the worl's not a bit the betther.

BOYLE [*with a commanding gesture*]. Tay!

[MARY *and* MRS. BOYLE *dispense the tea.*]

MRS. BOYLE. An' Irelan's takin' a leaf out o' the worl's buk; when we got the makin' of our own laws I thought we'd never stop to look behind us, but instead of that we never stopped to look before us! If the people ud folly up their religion betther there'd be a betther chance for us—what do you think, Mr. Bentham?

BENTHAM. I'm afraid I can't venture to express an opinion on that point, Mrs. Boyle; dogma has no attraction for me.

MRS. BOYLE. I forgot you didn't hold with us; what's this you said you were?

BENTHAM. A Theosophist, Mrs. Boyle.

MRS. BOYLE. An' what in the name o' God's a Theosophist?

BOYLE. A Theosophist, Juno, 's a—tell her, Mr. Bentham, tell her.

BENTHAM. It's hard to explain in a few words: Theosophy's founded on The Vedas, the religious books of the East. Its central theme is the existence of an all-pervading Spirit—the Life-Breath. Nothing really exists but this one Universal Life-Breath. And whatever even seems to exist separately from this Life-Breath, doesn't really exist at all. It is all vital force in man, in all animals, and in all vegetation. This Life-Breath is called the Prawna.

MRS. BOYLE. The Prawna! What a comical name!

BOYLE. Prawna; yis, the Prawna. [*blowing gently through his lips*] That's the Prawna!

MRS. BOYLE. Whist, whist, Jack.

BENTHAM. The happiness of man depends upon his sympathy with this Spirit. Men who have reached a high state of excellence are called Yogi. Some men become Yogi in a short time, it may take others millions of years.

BOYLE. Yogi! I seen hundhreds of them in the streets o' San Francisco.

BENTHAM. It is said by these Yogi that if we practise certain mental exercises that we would have powers denied to others—for instance, the faculty of seeing things that happen miles and miles away.

MRS. BOYLE. I wouldn't care to meddle with that sort o' belief; it's a very curious religion, altogether.

BOYLE. What's curious about it? Isn't all religions curious? If they weren't, you wouldn't get any one to believe them. But religions is passin' away—they've had their day like everything else. Take the real Dublin people, f'rinstance: they know more about Charlie Chaplin an' Tommy Mix than they do about SS. Peter an' Paul!

MRS. BOYLE. You don't believe in ghosts, Mr. Bentham?

MARY. Don't you know he doesn't, mother?

BENTHAM. I don't know that, Mary. Scientists are beginning to think that what we call ghosts are sometimes seen by persons of a certain nature. They say that sensational actions, such as the killing of a person, demand great energy, and that that energy lingers in the place where the action occurred. People may live in the place and see nothing, when some one may come along whose personality has some peculiar connection with the energy of the place, and, in a flash, the person sees the whole affair.

JOHNNY [*rising swiftly, pale and affected*]. What sort o' talk is this to be goin' on with? Is there nothin' betther to be talkin' about but the killin' o' people? My God, isn't it bad enough for these things to happen without talkin' about them! [*He hurriedly goes into the room on left.*]

BENTHAM. Oh, I'm very sorry, Mrs. Boyle; I never thought . . .

MRS. BOYLE [*apologetically*]. Never mind, Mr. Bentham, he's very touchy. [*A frightened scream is heard from* JOHNNY *inside.*]

MRS. BOYLE. Mother of God! What's that?

[*He rushes out again, his face pale, his lips twitching, his limbs trembling.*]

JOHNNY. Shut the door, shut the door, quick, for God's sake! Great God, have mercy on me! Blessed Mother o' God, shelter me, shelter your son!

MRS. BOYLE [*catching him in her arms*]. What's wrong with you? What ails you? Sit down, sit down, here, on the bed . . . there now . . . there now.

MARY. Johnny, Johnny, what ails you?

JOHNNY. I seen him, I seen him . . . kneelin' in front o' the statue . . . merciful Jesus, have pity on me!

MRS. BOYLE [*to* BOYLE]. Get him a glass o' whisky . . . quick, man, an' don't stand gawkin'.

[BOYLE *gets the whisky.*]

JOHNNY. Sit here, sit here, mother . . . between me an' the door.

MRS. BOYLE. I'll sit beside you as long as you like, only tell me what was it came across you at all?

JOHNNY [*after taking some drink*]. I seen him. . . . I seen Robbie Tancred kneelin' down before the statue . . . an' the red light shinin' on him . . . an' when I went in . . . he turned an' looked at me . . . an' I seen the woun's bleedin' in his breast. . . . Oh, why did he look at me like that . . . it wasn't my fault that he was done in . . . Mother o' God, keep him away from me!

MRS. BOYLE. There, there, child, you've imagined it all. There was nothin' there at all—it was the red light you seen, an' the talk we had put all the rest into your head. Here, dhrink more o' this—it'll do you good. . . . An', now, stretch yourself down on the bed for a little. [*to* BOYLE] Go in, Jack, an' show him it was only in his own head it was.

BOYLE [*making no move*]. E-e-e-eh; it's all nonsense; it was only a shadda he saw.

MARY. Mother o' God, he made me heart lep!

BENTHAM. It was simply due to an overwrought imagination—we all get that way at times.

MRS. BOYLE. There, dear, lie down in the bed, an' I'll put the quilt across you . . . e-e-e-eh, that's it . . . you'll be as right as the mail in a few minutes.

JOHNNY. Mother, go into the room an' see if the light's lightin' before the statue.

MRS. BOYLE [*to* BOYLE]. Jack, run in, an' see if the light's lightin' before the statue.

BOYLE [*to* MARY]. Mary, slip in an' see if the light's lightin' before the statue.

[MARY *hesitates to go in.*]

BENTHAM. It's all right; Mary, I'll go. [*He goes into the room; remains for a few moments, and returns.*]

BENTHAM. Everything's just as it was—the light burning bravely before the statue.

BOYLE. Of course; I knew it was all nonsense.

[*A knock at the door.*]

BOYLE [*going to open the door*]. E-e-e-eh. [*He opens it, and* JOXER, *followed by* MRS. MADIGAN, *enters.* MRS. MADIGAN *is a strong, dapper little woman of about forty-five; her face is almost always a wide-spread smile of complacency. She is a woman who, in a manner at least, can mourn with them that mourn, and rejoice with them that do rejoice. When she is feeling comfortable, she is inclined to be reminiscent; when others say anything, or following a statement made by herself, she has a habit of putting her head a little to one side, and nodding it rapidly several times in succession, like a bird pecking at a hard berry. Indeed, she has a good deal of the bird in her, but the bird instinct is by no means a melodious one. She is ignorant, vulgar and forward, but her heart is generous withal. For instance, she would help a neighbour's sick child; she would probably kill the child, but her intentions would be to cure it; she would be more at home helping a drayman to lift a fallen horse. She is dressed in a rather soiled grey dress and a vivid purple blouse; in her hair is a huge comb, ornamented with huge coloured beads. She enters with a gliding step, beaming smile and nodding head.* BOYLE *receives them effusively.*]

BOYLE. Come on in, Mrs. Madigan; come on in; I was afraid you weren't comin'. . . . [*slyly*] There's some people able to dhress, ay, Joxer?

JOXER. Fair as the blossoms that bloom in the May, an' sweet as the scent of the new mown hay. . . . Ah, well she may wear them.

MRS. MADIGAN [*looking at* MARY]. I know some as are as sweet as the blossoms in the May—oh, no names, no pack dhrill!

BOYLE. An', now, I'll inthroduce the pair o' yous to Mary's intended: Mr. Bentham, this is Mrs. Madigan, an oul' back-parlour neighbour, that, if she could help it at all, ud never see a body shuk!

BENTHAM [*rising, and tentatively shaking the hand of* MRS. MADIGAN]. I'm sure, it's a great pleasure to know you, Mrs. Madigan.

MRS. MADIGAN. An' I'm goin' to tell you, Mr. Bentham, you're goin' to get as nice a bit o' skirt in Mary, there, as ever you seen in your puff. Not like some of the dhressed up dolls that's knockin' about lookin' for men when it's a skelpin' they want. I remember as

308 **pack dhrill** formality
317 **skelpin'** spanking

well as I remember yestherday, the day she was born—of a Tuesday, the 25th o' June, in the year 1901, at thirty-three minutes past wan in the day be Foley's clock, the pub at the corner o' the street. A cowld day it was too, for the season o' the year, an' I remember sayin' to Joxer, there, who I met comin' up th' stairs, that the new arrival in Boyle's ud grow up a hardy chiselur if it lived, an' that she'd be somethin' one o' these days that nobody suspected, an' so signs on it, here she is today, goin' to be married to a young man lookin' as if he'd be fit to commensurate in any position in life it ud please God to call him!

BOYLE [*effusively*]. Sit down, Mrs. Madigan, sit down, me oul' sport. [*to* BENTHAM] This is Joxer Daly, Past Chief Ranger of the Dear Little Shamrock Branch of the Irish National Foresters, an oul' front-top neighbour, that never despaired, even in the darkest days of Ireland's sorra.

JOXER. Nil desperandum, Captain, nil desperandum.

BOYLE. Sit down, Joxer, sit down. The two of us was often in a tight corner.

MRS. BOYLE. Ay, in Foley's snug!

JOXER. An' we kem out of it flyin', we kem out of it flyin', Captain.

BOYLE. An', now, for a dhrink—I know yous won't refuse an oul' friend.

MRS. MADIGAN [*to* JUNO]. Is Johnny not well, Mrs. . . .

MRS. BOYLE [*warningly*]. S-s-s-sh.

MRS. MADIGAN. Oh, the poor darlin'.

BOYLE. Well, Mrs. Madigan, is it tay or what?

MRS. MADIGAN. Well, speakin' for meself, I jus' had me tea a minute ago, an' I'm afraid to dhrink any more—I'm never the same when I dhrink too much tay. Thanks, all the same, Mr. Boyle.

BOYLE. Well, what about a bottle o' stout or a dhrop o' whisky?

MRS. MADIGAN. A bottle o' stout ud be a little too heavy for me stummock afther me tay. . . . A-a-ah, I'll thry the ball o' malt.

[BOYLE *prepares the whisky.*]

MRS. MADIGAN. There's nothin' like a ball o' malt occasional like—too much of it isn't good. [*to* BOYLE, *who is adding water*] Ah, God, Johnny, don't put too much wather on it! [*She drinks.*] I suppose yous'll be lavin' this place.

BOYLE. I'm looking for a place near the sea; I'd like the place that you might say was me cradle, to be me grave as well. The sea is always callin' me.

JOXER. She is callin', callin', callin', in the win, an' on the sea.

BOYLE. Another dhrop o' whisky, Mrs. Madigan?

MRS. MADIGAN. Well, now, it ud be hard to refuse seein' the suspicious times that's in it.

BOYLE [*with a commanding gesture*]. Song! . . . Juno . . . Mary . . . "Home to Our Mount'ins"!

MRS. MADIGAN [*enthusiastically*]. Hear, hear!

JOXER. Oh, tha's a darlin' song, a daarlin' song!

MARY [*bashfully*]. Ah, no, da; I'm not in a singin' humour.

MRS. MADIGAN. Gawn with you, child, an' you only goin' to be marrid; I remember as well as I remember yestherday,—it was on a lovely August evenin', exactly, accordin' to date, fifteen years ago, come the Tuesday folleyin' the nex' that's comin' on, when me own man (the Lord be good to him) an' me was sittin' shy together in a doty little nook on a counthry road, adjacent to The Stiles. "That'll scratch your lovely, little white neck," says he, ketchin' hould of a danglin' bramble branch, holdin' clusters of the loveliest flowers you ever seen, an' breakin' it off, so that his arm fell, accidental like, roun' me waist, an' as I felt it tightenin', an' tightenin', an tightenin', I thought me buzzum was every minute goin' to burst out into a roystherin' song about

> The little green leaves that were shakin' on the threes,
> The gallivantin' butterflies, an' buzzin' o' the bees!

BOYLE. Ordher for the song!

JUNO. Come on, Mary—we'll do our best. [JUNO *and* MARY *stand up, and choosing a suitable position, sing simply "Home to Our Mountains."*]

[*They bow to company, and return to their places.*]

BOYLE [*emotionally, at the end of the song*]. Lull . . . me . . . to . . . rest!

JOXER [*clapping his hands*]. Bravo, bravo! Darlin' girulls, darlin' girulls!

MRS. MADIGAN. Juno, I never seen you in betther form.

BENTHAM. Very nicely rendered indeed.

361 **that's in it** that we live in
372 **doty** cosy

MRS. MADIGAN. A noble call, a noble call!

MRS. BOYLE. What about yourself, Mrs. Madigan? [*After some coaxing,* MRS. MADIGAN *rises, and in a quavering voice sings the following verse.*]

If I were a blackbird I'd whistle and sing;
I'd follow the ship that my thrue love was in;
An' on the top riggin', I'd there build me nest,
An' at night I would sleep on me Willie's white breast!

[*Becoming husky, amid applause, she sits down.*]

MRS. MADIGAN. Ah, me voice is too husky now, Juno; though I remember the time when Maisie Madigan could sing like a nightingale at matin' time. I remember as well as I remember yestherday, at a party given to celebrate the comin' of the first chiselur to Annie an' Benny Jimeson—who was the barber, yous may remember, in Henrietta Street, that, afther Easter Week, hung out a green, white an' orange pole, an', then, when the Tans started their Jazz dancin', whipped it in agen, an' stuck out a red, white an' blue wan instead, givin' as an excuse that a barber's pole was strictly non-political—singin' "An You'll Remember Me," with the top notes quiverin' in a dead hush of pethrified attention, folleyed by a clappin' o' han's that shuk the tumblers on the table, an' capped be Jimeson, the barber, sayin' that it was the best rendherin' of "You'll Remember Me" he ever heard in his natural!

BOYLE [*peremptorily*]. Ordher for Joxer's song!

JOXER. Ah, no, I couldn't; don't ass me, Captain.

BOYLE. Joxer's song, Joxer's song—give us wan of your shut-eyed wans. [JOXER *settles himself in his chair; takes a drink; clears his throat; solemnly closes his eyes, and begins to sing in a very querulous voice.*]

She is far from the lan' where her
young hero sleeps,
An' lovers around her are sighing.
[*He hesitates.*]

406–7 **green, white an' orange** the Irish national colors

407 **Tans** or Black-and-Tans, the English troops that attempted to police Dublin and other parts of Ireland during the civil war. The reprisals with which the English countered Irish terrorism made the 'Tans' both dreaded and detested.

408 **red, white an' blue** the English colors

An' lovers around her are sighin'
. . . sighin' . . . sighin' . . .

[*A pause.*]

BOYLE [*imitating* JOXER].

And lovers around her are sighing!

What's the use of you thryin' to sing the song if you don't know it?

MARY. Thry another one, Mr. Daly—maybe you'd be more fortunate.

MRS. MADIGAN. Gawn, Joxer, thry another wan.

JOXER [*starting again*].

I have heard the mavis singin' his love song to the morn;
I have seen the dew-dhrop clingin' to the rose jus' newly born;
but . . . but . . . [*frantically*] to the rose jus' newly born . . . newly born . . . born.

JOHNNY. Mother, put on the gramophone, for God's sake, an' stop Joxer's bawlin'.

BOYLE [*commandingly*]. Gramophone! . . . I hate to see fellas thryin' to do what they're not able to do. [BOYLE *arranges the gramophone, and is about to start it, when voices are heard of persons descending the stairs.*]

MRS. BOYLE [*warningly*]. Whisht, Jack, don't put it on, don't put it on yet; this must be poor Mrs. Tancred comin' down to go to the hospital—I forgot all about them bringin' the body to the church tonight. Open the door, Mary, an' give them a bit o' light.

[MARY *opens the door, and* MRS. TANCRED—*a very old woman, obviously shaken by the death of her son—appears, accompanied by several neighbours. The first few phrases are spoken before they appear.*]

FIRST NEIGHBOUR. It's a sad journey we're goin' on, but God's good, an' the Republicans won't be always down.

MRS. TANCRED. Ah, what good is that to me now? Whether they're up or down—it won't bring me darlin' boy from the grave.

MRS. BOYLE. Come in an' have a hot cup o' tay, Mrs. Tancred, before you go.

MRS. TANCRED. Ah, I can take nothin' now, Mrs. Boyle—I won't be long afther him.

FIRST NEIGHBOUR. Still an' all, he died a noble death, an' we'll bury him like a king.

MRS. TANCRED. An' I'll go on livin' like a pauper. Ah, what's the pains I suffered bringin' him into the world to carry him to his cradle, to the pains I'm sufferin' now, carryin' him out o' the world to bring him to his grave!

MARY. It would be better for you not to go at all, Mrs. Tancred, but to stay at home beside the fire with some o' the neighbours.

MRS. TANCRED. I seen the first of him, an' I'll see the last of him.

MRS. BOYLE. You'd want a shawl, Mrs. Tancred; it's a cowld night, an' the win's blowin' sharp.

MRS. MADIGAN [*rushing out*]. I've a shawl above.

MRS. TANCRED. Me home is gone, now; he was me only child, an' to think that he was lyin' for a whole night stretched out on the side of a lonely counthry lane, with his head, his darlin' head, that I ofen kissed an' fondled, half hidden in the wather of a runnin' brook. An' I'm told he was the leadher of the ambush where me nex' door neighbour, Mrs. Mannin', lost her Free State soldier son. An' now here's the two of us oul' women, standin' one on each side of a scales o' sorra, balanced be the bodies of our two dead darlin' sons. [MRS. MADIGAN *returns, and wraps a shawl around her.*] God bless you, Mrs. Madigan. . . . [*She moves slowly towards the door.*] Mother o' God, Mother o' God, have pity on the pair of us! . . . O Blessed Virgin, where were you when me darlin' son was riddled with bullets, when me darlin' son was riddled with bullets! . . . Sacred Heart of the Crucified Jesus, take away our hearts o' stone . . . an' give us hearts o' flesh! . . . Take away this murdherin' hate . . . an' give us Thine own eternal love!

[*They pass out of the room.*]

MRS. BOYLE [*explanatorily to* BENTHAM]. That was Mrs. Tancred of the two-pair back; her son was found, e'er yesterday, lyin' out beyant Finglas riddled with bullets. A die-hard he was, be all accounts. He was a nice quiet boy, but lattherly he went to hell, with his Republic first, an' Republic last an' Republic over all. He ofen took tea with us here, in the oul' days, an' Johnny, there, an' him used to be always together.

JOHNNY. Am I always to be havin' to tell you that he was no friend o' mine? I never cared for him, an' he could never stick me. It's not because he was Commandant of the Battalion that I was Quarther-Masther of, that we were friends.

MRS. BOYLE. He's gone, now—the Lord be good to him! God help his poor oul' creature of a mother, for no matther whose friend or enemy he was, he was her poor son.

BENTHAM. The whole thing is terrible, Mrs. Boyle; but the only way to deal with a mad dog is to destroy him.

MRS. BOYLE. An' to think of me forgettin' about him bein' brought to the church tonight, an' we singin' an' all, but it was well we hadn't the gramophone goin', anyhow.

BOYLE. Even if we had aself. We've nothin' to do with these things, one way or t'other. That's the Government's business, an' let them do what we're payin' them for doin'.

MRS. BOYLE. I'd like to know how a body's not to mind these things; look at the way they're afther leavin' the people in this very house. Hasn't the whole house, nearly, been massacreed? There's young Mrs. Dougherty's husband with his leg off; Mrs. Travers that had her son blew up be a mine in Inchegeela, in Co. Cork; Mrs. Mannin' that lost wan of her sons in an ambush a few weeks ago, an' now, poor Mrs. Tancred's only child gone West with his body made a collandher of. Sure, if it's not our business, I don't know whose business it is.

BOYLE. Here, there, that's enough about them things; they don't affect us, an' we needn't give a damn. If they want a wake, well, let them have a wake. When I was a sailor, I was always resigned to meet with a watery grave; an', if they want to be soldiers, well, there's no use o' them squealin' when they meet a soldier's fate.

JOXER. Let me like a soldier fall—me breast expandin' to th' ball!

MRS. BOYLE. In wan way, she deserves all she got; for lately, she let th' die-hards make an open house of th' place; an' for th' last couple of months, either when th' sun was risin', or when th' sun was settin', you had C.I.D. men burstin' into your room, assin' you where were you born, where were you christened, where were you married, an' where would you be buried!

JOHNNY. For God's sake, let us have no more o' this talk.

MRS. MADIGAN. What about Mr. Boyle's song before we start th' gramophone?

527 **C.I.D. men** from the Criminal Investigation Department of Scotland Yard; later, Free State police agents on the trail of the die-hards

MARY [*getting her hat, and putting it on*]. Mother, Charlie and I are goin' out for a little sthroll.

MRS. BOYLE. All right, darlin'.

BENTHAM [*going out with* MARY]. We won't be long away, Mrs. Boyle.

MRS. MADIGAN. Gwan, Captain, gwan.

BOYLE. E-e-e-e-eh, I'd want to have a few more jars in me, before I'd be in fettle for singin'.

JOXER. Give us that poem you writ t'other day. [*to the rest*] Aw, it's a darlin' poem, a daarlin' poem.

MRS. BOYLE. God bless us, is he startin' to write poetry!

BOYLE [*rising to his feet*]. E-e-e-e-eh. [*He recites in an emotional, consequential manner the following verses.*]

Shawn an' I were friends, sir, to me he was all in all.
His work was very heavy and his wages were very small.
None betther on th' beach as Docker, I'll go bail,
'Tis now I'm feelin' lonely, for today he lies in jail.
He was not what some call pious—seldom at church or prayer;
For the greatest scoundrels I know, sir, goes every Sunday there.
Fond of his pint—well, rather, but hated the Boss by creed
But never refused a copper to comfort a pal in need.

E-e-e-e-eh. [*He sits down.*]

MRS. MADIGAN. Grand, grand; you should folley that up, you should folley that up.

JOXER. It's a daarlin' poem!

BOYLE [*delightedly*]. E-e-e-e-eh.

JOHNNY. Are yous goin' to put on th' gramophone tonight, or are yous not?

MRS. BOYLE. Gwan, Jack, put on a record.

MRS. MADIGAN. Gwan, Captain, gwan.

BOYLE. Well, yous'll want to keep a dead silence. [*He sets a record, starts the machine, and it begins to play "If you're Irish, come into the Parlour." As the tune is in full blare, the door is suddenly opened by a brisk, little bald-headed man, dressed circumspectly in a black suit; he glares fiercely at all in the room; he is* "NEEDLE NUGENT," *a tailor. He carries his hat in his hands.*]

NUGENT [*loudly, above the noise of the gramophone*]. Are yous goin' to have that thing bawlin' an' the funeral of Mrs. Tancred's son passin' the house? Have none of yous any respect for the Irish people's National regard for the dead?

[BOYLE *stops the gramophone.*]

MRS. BOYLE. Maybe, Needle Nugent, it's nearly time we had a little less respect for the dead, an' a little more regard for the livin'.

MRS. MADIGAN. We don't want you, Mr. Nugent, to teach us what we learned at our mother's knee. You don't look yourself as if you were dyin' of grief; if y'ass Maisie Madigan anything, I'd call you a real thrue die-hard an' live-soft Republican, attendin' Republican funerals in the day, an' stoppin' up half the night makin' suits for the Civic Guards! [*Persons are heard running down to the street, some saying, "Here it is, here it is."* NUGENT *withdraws, and the rest, except* JOHNNY, *go to the window looking into the street, and look out. Sounds of a crowd coming nearer are heard; a portion are singing.*]

To Jesus' Heart all burning
With fervent love for men,
My heart with fondest yearning
Shall raise its joyful strain.
While ages course along,
Blest be with loudest song,
The Sacred Heart of Jesus
By every heart and tongue.

MRS. BOYLE. Here's the hearse, here's the hearse!

BOYLE. There's t'oul' mother walkin' behin' the coffin.

MRS. MADIGAN. You can hardly see the coffin with the wreaths.

JOXER. Oh, it's a darlin' funeral, a daarlin' funeral!

MRS. MADIGAN. We'd have a betther view from the street.

BOYLE. Yes—this place ud give you a crick in your neck. [*They leave the room, and go down.* JOHNNY *sits moodily by the fire.*]

[*A young man enters; he looks at* JOHNNY *for a moment.*]

THE YOUNG MAN. Quarter-Master Boyle.

JOHNNY [*with a start*]. The Mobilizer!

THE YOUNG MAN. You're not at the funeral?

JOHNNY. I'm not well.

THE YOUNG MAN. I'm glad I've found you; you were stoppin' at your aunt's; I called there but you'd gone. I've to give you an ordher to attend a Battalion Staff meetin' the night afther tomorrow.

JOHNNY. Where?

THE YOUNG MAN. I don't know; you're to meet me at the Pillar at eight o'clock; then we're to go to a place I'll be told of tonight; there we'll meet a mothor that'll bring us to the meeting. They think you might be able to know somethin' about them that gave the bend where Commandant Tancred was shelterin'.

JOHNNY. I'm not goin', then. I know nothing about Tancred.

THE YOUNG MAN [*at the door*]. You'd betther come for your own sake—remember your oath.

JOHNNY [*passionately*]. I won't go! Haven't I done enough for Ireland! I've lost me arm, an' me hip's desthroyed so that I'll never be able to walk right agen! Good God, haven't I done enough for Ireland?

THE YOUNG MAN. Boyle, no man can do enough for Ireland!

[*He goes.*]

[*Faintly in the distance the crowd is heard saying:*]

Hail, Mary, full of grace, the Lord is with Thee;
Blessed art Thou amongst women, and blessed, etc.

THE CURTAIN FALLS

ACT III

SCENE. *The same as Act Two. It is about half-past six on a November evening; a bright fire is burning in the grate;* MARY, *dressed to go out, is sitting on a chair by the fire, leaning forward, her hands under her chin, her elbows on her knees. A look of dejection, mingled with uncertain anxiety, is on her face. A lamp, turned low, is lighting on the table. The votive light under the picture of the Virgin gleams more redly than ever.* MRS. BOYLE *is putting on her hat and coat. It is two months later.*

MRS. BOYLE. An' has Bentham never even written to you since—not one line for the past month?

MARY [*tonelessly*]. Not even a line, mother.

MRS. BOYLE. That's very curious. . . . What came between the two of yous at all? To leave you so sudden, an' yous so great together. . . . To go away t' England, an' not to even leave you his address. . . . The way he was always bringin' you to dances, I thought he was mad afther you. Are you sure you said nothin' to him?

MARY. No, mother—at least nothing that could possibly explain his givin' me up.

MRS. BOYLE. You know you're a bit hasty at times, Mary, an' say things you shouldn't say.

MARY. I never said to him what I shouldn't say, I'm sure of that.

MRS. BOYLE. How are you sure of it?

MARY. Because I love him with all my heart and soul, mother. Why, I don't know; I often thought to myself that he wasn't the man poor Jerry was, but I couldn't help loving him, all the same.

MRS. BOYLE. But you shouldn't be frettin' the way you are; when a woman loses a man, she never knows what she's afther losin', to be sure, but, then, she never knows what she's afther gainin', either. You're not the one girl of a month ago—you look like one pinin' away. It's long ago I had a right to bring you to the doctor, instead of waitin' till tonight.

MARY. There's no necessity, really, mother, to go to the doctor; nothing serious is wrong with me—I'm run down and disappointed, that's all.

MRS. BOYLE. I'll not wait another minute; I don't like the look of you at all. . . . I'm afraid we made a mistake in throwin' over poor Jerry. . . . He'd have been betther for you than that Bentham.

MARY. Mother, the best man for a woman is the one for whom she has the most love, and Charlie had it all.

MRS. BOYLE. Well, there's one thing to be said for him—he couldn't have been thinkin' of the money, or he wouldn't ha' left you. . . . It must ha' been somethin' else.

MARY [*wearily*]. I don't know . . . I don't know, mother . . . only I think . . .

MRS. BOYLE. What d'ye think?

MARY. I imagine . . . he thought . . . we weren't . . . good enough for him.

MRS. BOYLE. An' what was he himself, only a school teacher?

Though I don't blame him for fightin' shy of people like that Joxer fella an' that oul' Madigan wan—nice sort o' people for your father to inthroduce to a man like Mr. Bentham. You might have told me all about this before now, Mary; I don't know why you like to hide everything from your mother; you knew Bentham, an' I'd ha' known nothin' about it if it hadn't bin for the Will; an' it was only today, afther long coaxin', that you let out that he'd left you.

MARY. It would have been useless to tell you—you wouldn't understand.

MRS. BOYLE [*hurt*]. Maybe not. . . . Maybe I wouldn't understand. . . . Well, we'll be off now. [*She goes over to the door left, and speaks to* BOYLE *inside.*]

MRS. BOYLE. We're goin' now to the doctor's. Are you goin' to get up this evenin'?

BOYLE [*from inside*]. The pains in me legs is terrible! It's me should be poppin' off to the doctor instead o' Mary, the way I feel.

MRS. BOYLE. Sorra mend you! A nice way you were in last night—carried in in a frog's march, dead to the world. If that's the way you'll go on when you get the money it'll be the grave for you, an asylum for me and the Poorhouse for Johnny.

BOYLE. I thought you were goin'?

MRS. BOYLE. That's what has you as you are—you can't bear to be spoken to. Knowin' the way we are, up to our ears in debt, it's a wondher you wouldn't ha' got up to go to th' solicitor's an' see if we could ha' gettin' a little o' the money even.

BOYLE [*shouting*]. I can't be goin' up there night, noon an' mornin', can I? He can't give the money till he gets it, can he? I can't get blood out of a turnip, can I?

MRS. BOYLE. It's nearly two months since we heard of the Will, an' the money seems as far off as ever. . . . I suppose you know we owe twenty poun's to oul' Murphy?

BOYLE. I've a faint recollection of you tellin' me that before.

MRS. BOYLE. Well, you'll go over to the shop yourself for the things in future—I'll face him no more.

BOYLE. I thought you said you were goin'?

MRS. BOYLE. I'm goin' now; come on, Mary.

BOYLE. Ey, Juno, ey!

67 **in a frog's march** sprawled prone

MRS. BOYLE. Well, what d'ye want now?

BOYLE. Is there e'er a bottle o' stout left?

MRS. BOYLE. There's two o' them here still.

BOYLE. Show us in one o' them an' leave t'other there till I get up. An' throw us in the paper that's on the table, an' the bottle o' Sloan's Liniment that's in th' drawer.

MRS. BOYLE [*getting the liniment and the stout*]. What paper is it you want—the *Messenger?*

BOYLE. *Messenger! The News o' the World!*

[MRS. BOYLE *brings in the things asked for and comes out again.*]

MRS. BOYLE [*at door*]. Mind the candle, now, an' don't burn the house over our heads. I left t'other bottle o' stout on the table. [*She puts bottle of stout on table. She goes out with* MARY. *A cork is heard popping inside. A pause; then outside the door is heard the voice of* JOXER *lilting softly: "Me pipe I'll smoke, as I dhrive me moke . . . are you . . . there . . . More . . . aar . . . i . . . . tee!" A gentle knock is heard and, after a pause, the door opens, and* JOXER, *followed by* NUGENT, *enters.*]

JOXER. Be God, they must all be out; I was thinkin' there was somethin' up when he didn't answer the signal. We seen Juno an' Mary goin', but I didn't see him, an' it's very seldom he escapes me.

NUGENT. He's not goin' to escape me—he's not goin' to be let go to the fair altogether.

JOXER. Sure, the house couldn't hould them lately; an' he goin' about like a mastherpiece of the Free State counthry; forgettin' their friends; forgettin' God—wouldn't even lift his hat passin' a chapel! Sure they were bound to get a dhrop! An' you really think there's no money comin' to him afther all?

NUGENT. Not as much as a red rex, man; I've been a bit anxious this long time over me money, an' I went up to the solicitor's to find out all I could—ah, man, they were goin' to throw me down the stairs. They toul' me that the oul' cock himself had the stairs worn away comin' up afther it, an' they black in the face tellin' him he'd get nothin'. Some way or another that the Will is writ he won't be entitled to get as much as a make!

116 rex cent
122 make halfpenny

JOXER. Ah, I thought there was somethin' curious about the whole thing; I've bin havin' sthrange dreams for the last couple o' weeks. An' I notice that that Bentham fella doesn't be comin' here now—there must be somethin' on the mat there too. Anyhow, who, in the name o' God, ud leave anythin' to that oul' bummer? Sure it ud be unnatural. An' the way Juno an' him's been throwin' their weight about for the last few months! Ah, him that goes a borrowin' goes a sorrowin'!

NUGENT. Well, he's not goin' to throw his weight about in the suit I made for him much longer. I'm tellin' you seven poun's aren't to be found growin' on the bushes these days.

JOXER. An' there isn't hardly a neighbour in the whole street that hasn't lent him money on the strength of what he was goin' to get, but they're after backing the wrong horse. Wasn't it a mercy o' God that I'd nothin' to give him! The softy I am, you know, I'd ha' lent him me last juice! I must have had somebody's good prayers. Ah, afther all, an honest man's the noblest work o' God! [BOYLE *coughs inside.*] Whisht, damn it, he must be inside in bed.

NUGENT. Inside o' bed or outside of it he's goin' to pay me for that suit, or give it back—he'll not climb up my back as easily as he thinks.

JOXER. Gwan in at wanst, man, an' get it off him, an' don't be a fool.

NUGENT [*going to the door left, opening it and looking in*]. Ah, don't disturb yourself, Mr. Boyle; I hope you're not sick?

BOYLE. Th' oul' legs, Mr. Nugent, the oul' legs.

NUGENT. I just called over to see if you could let me have anything off the suit?

BOYLE. E-e-e-eh, how much is this it is?

NUGENT. It's the same as it was at the start—seven poun's.

BOYLE. I'm glad you kem, Mr. Nugent; I want a good heavy top-coat—Irish frieze, if you have it. How much would a top-coat like that be now?

NUGENT. About six poun's.

BOYLE. Six poun's—six an' seven, six an' seven is thirteen—that'll be thirteen poun's I'll owe you.

[JOXER *slips the bottle of stout that is on the table into his pocket.*

126 **on the mat** the matter

NUGENT *rushes into the room, and returns with the suit on his arm; he pauses at the door.*]

NUGENT. You'll owe me no thirteen poun's. Maybe you think you're betther able to owe it than pay it!

BOYLE [*frantically*]. Here, come back to hell ower that—where're you goin' with them clothes o' mine?

NUGENT. Where am I goin' with them clothes o' yours? Well, I like your damn cheek!

BOYLE. Here, what am I going to dhress meself in when I'm goin' out?

NUGENT. What do I care what you dhress yourself in? You can put yourself in a bolsther cover, if you like. [*He goes towards the other door, followed by* JOXER.]

JOXER. What'll he dhress himself in! Gentleman Jack an' his frieze coat!

[*They go out.*]

BOYLE [*inside*]. Ey, Nugent, ey, Mr. Nugent, Mr. Nugent! [*After a pause* BOYLE *enters hastily, buttoning the braces of his moleskin trousers; his coat and vest are on his arm; he throws these on a chair and hurries to the door on right.*]

BOYLE. Ey, Mr. Nugent, Mr. Nugent!

JOXER [*meeting him at the door*]. What's up, what's wrong, Captain?

BOYLE. Nugent's been here an' took away me suit—the only things I had to go out in!

JOXER. Tuk your suit—for God's sake! An' what were you doin' while he was takin' them?

BOYLE. I was in bed when he stole in like a thief in the night, an' before I knew even what he was thinkin' of, he whipped them from the chair, an' was off like a redshank!

JOXER. An' what, in the name o' God, did he do that for?

BOYLE. What did he do it for? How the hell do I know what he done it for? Jealousy an' spite, I suppose.

JOXER. Did he not say what he done it for?

BOYLE. Amn't I afther tellin' you that he had them whipped up an' was gone before I could open me mouth?

JOXER. That was a very sudden thing to do; there mus' be somethin' behin' it. Did he hear anythin', I wondher?

189 **redshank** backcountryman, proverbially fast and elusive

BOYLE. Did he hear anythin'?—you talk very queer, Joxer—what could he hear?

JOXER. About you not gettin' the money, in some way or t'other?

BOYLE. An' what ud prevent me from gettin' th' money?

JOXER. That's jus' what I was thinkin'—what ud prevent you from gettin' the money—nothin', as far as I can see.

BOYLE [*looking round for bottle of stout with an exclamation*]. Aw, holy God!

JOXER. What's up, Jack?

BOYLE. He must have afther lifted the bottle o' stout that Juno left on the table!

JOXER [*horrified*]. Ah, no, ah, no! He wouldn't be afther doin' that, now.

BOYLE. An' who done it then? Juno left a bottle o' stout here, an' it's gone—it didn't walk, did it?

JOXER. Oh, that's shockin'; ah, man's inhumanity to man makes countless thousands mourn!

MRS. MADIGAN [*appearing at the door*]. I hope I'm not disturbin' you in any discussion on your forthcomin' legacy—if I may use the word—an' that you'll let me have a barny for a minute or two with you, Mr. Boyle.

BOYLE [*uneasily*]. To be sure, Mrs. Madigan—an oul' friend's always welcome.

JOXER. Come in the evenin', come in th' mornin'; come when you're assed, or come without warnin', Mrs. Madigan.

BOYLE. Sit down, Mrs. Madigan.

MRS. MADIGAN [*ominously*]. Th' few words I have to say can be said standin'. Puttin' aside all formularies, I suppose you remember me lendin' you some time ago three poun's that I raised on blankets an' furniture in me uncle's?

BOYLE. I remember it well. I have it recorded in me book—three poun's five shillin's from Maisie Madigan, raised on articles pawned; an', item: fourpence, given to make up the price of a pint, on th' principle that no bird ever flew on wan wing; all to be repaid at par, when the ship comes home.

MRS. MADIGAN. Well, ever since I shoved in the blankets I've been perishing with th' cowld, an' I've decided, if I'll be too hot in th' nex' world aself, I'm not goin' to be too cowld in this wan; an' con-

217 **barny** talk

sequently, I want me three poun's, if you please.

BOYLE. This is a very sudden demand, Mrs. Madigan, an' can't be met; but I'm willin' to give you a receipt in full, in full.

MRS. MADIGAN. Come on, out with th' money, an' don't be jack-actin'.

BOYLE. You can't get blood out of a turnip, can you?

MRS. MADIGAN [*rushing over and shaking him*]. Gimme me money, y'oul' reprobate, or I'll shake the worth of it out of you!

BOYLE. Ey, houl' on, there; houl' on, there! You'll wait for your money now, me lassie!

MRS. MADIGAN [*looking around the room and seeing the gramophone*]. I'll wait for it, will I? Well, I'll not wait long; if I can't get th' cash, I'll get th' worth of it. [*She catches up the gramophone.*]

BOYLE. Ey, ey, there, where'r you goin' with that?

MRS. MADIGAN. I'm goin' to th' pawn to get me three quid five shillin's; I'll bring you th' ticket, an' then you can do what you like, me bucko.

BOYLE. You can't touch that, you can't touch that! It's not my property, an' it's not ped for yet!

MRS. MADIGAN. So much th' betther. It'll be an ayse to me conscience, for I'm takin' what doesn't belong to you. You're not goin' to be swankin' it like a paycock with Maisie Madigan's money—I'll pull some o' the gorgeous feathers out o' your tail!

[*She goes off with the gramophone.*]

BOYLE. What's th' world comin' to at all? I ass you, Joxer Daly, is there any morality left anywhere?

JOXER. I wouldn't ha' believed it, only I seen it with me own two eyes. I didn't think Maisie Madigan was that sort of a woman; she has either a sup taken, or she's heard somethin'.

BOYLE. Heard somethin'—about what, if it's not any harm to ass you?

JOXER. She must ha' heard some rumour or other that you weren't goin' to get th' money.

BOYLE. Who says I'm not goin' to get th' money?

JOXER. Sure, I know—I was only sayin'.

BOYLE. Only sayin' what?

JOXER. Nothin'.

BOYLE. You were goin' to say somethin', don't be a twisther.

273 **twisther** liar

JOXER [*angrily*]. Who's a twisther?

BOYLE. Why don't you speak your mind, then?

JOXER. You never twisted yourself—no, you wouldn't know how!

BOYLE. Did you ever know me to twist; did you ever know me to twist?

JOXER [*fiercely*]. Did you ever do anythin' else! Sure, you can't believe a word that comes out o' your mouth.

BOYLE. Here, get out, ower o' this; I always knew you were a prognosticator an' a procrastinator!

JOXER [*going out as* JOHNNY *comes in*]. The anchor's weighed, farewell, re . . . mem . . . ber . . . me. Jacky Boyle, Esquire, infernal rogue an' damned liar!

JOHNNY. Joxer an' you at it agen?—when are you goin' to have a little respect for yourself, an' not be always makin' a show of us all?

BOYLE. Are you goin' to lecture me now?

JOHNNY. Is mother back from the doctor yet, with Mary?

[MRS. BOYLE *enters; it is apparent from the serious look on her face that something has happened. She takes off her hat and coat without a word and puts them by. She then sits down near the fire, and there is a few moments' pause.*]

BOYLE. Well, what did the doctor say about Mary?

MRS. BOYLE [*in an earnest manner and with suppressed agitation*]. Sit down here, Jack; I've something to say to you . . . about Mary.

BOYLE [*awed by her manner*]. About . . . Mary?

MRS. BOYLE. Close that door there and sit down here.

BOYLE [*closing the door*]. More throuble in our native land, is it? [*He sits down.*] Well, what is it?

MRS. BOYLE. It's about Mary.

BOYLE. Well, what about Mary—there's nothin' wrong with her, is there?

MRS. BOYLE. I'm sorry to say there's a gradle wrong with her.

BOYLE. A gradle wrong with her! [*peevishly*] First Johnny an' now Mary; is the whole house goin' to become an hospital! It's not consumption, is it?

MRS. BOYLE. No . . . it's not consumption . . . it's worse.

JOHNNY. Worse! Well, we'll have to get her into some place ower this, there's no one here to mind her.

MRS. BOYLE. We'll all have to mind her now. You might as well know now, Johnny, as another time. [*to* BOYLE] D'ye you know what the doctor said to me about her, Jack?

BOYLE. How ud I know—I wasn't there, was I?

MRS. BOYLE. He told me to get her married at wanst.

BOYLE. Married at wanst! An' why did he say the like o' that?

MRS. BOYLE. Because Mary's goin' to have a baby in a short time.

BOYLE. Goin' to have a baby!—my God, what'll Bentham say when he hears that?

MRS. BOYLE. Are you blind, man, that you can't see that it was Bentham that has done this wrong to her?

BOYLE [*passionately*]. Then he'll marry her, he'll have to marry her!

MRS. BOYLE. You know he's gone to England, an' God knows where he is now.

BOYLE. I'll folley him, I'll folley him, an' bring him back, an' make him do her justice. The scoundrel, I might ha' known what he was, with his yogees an' his prawna!

MRS. BOYLE. We'll have to keep it quiet till we see what we can do.

BOYLE. Oh, isn't this a nice thing to come on top o' me, an' the state I'm in! A pretty show I'll be to Joxer an' to that oul' wan, Madigan! Amn't I afther goin' through enough without havin' to go through this!

MRS. BOYLE. What you an' I'll have to go through'll be nothin' to what poor Mary'll have to go through; for you an' me is middlin' old, an' most of our years is spent; but Mary'll have maybe forty years to face an' handle, an' every wan of them'll be tainted with a bitther memory.

BOYLE. Where is she? Where is she till I tell her off? I'm tellin' you when I'm done with her she'll be a sorry girl!

MRS. BOYLE. I left her in me sisther's till I came to speak to you. You'll say nothin' to her, Jack; ever since she left school she's earned her living', an' your fatherly care never throubled the poor girl.

BOYLE. Gwan, take her part agen her father! But I'll let you see whether I'll say nothin' to her or no! Her an' her readin'! That's more o' th' blasted nonsense that has the house fallin' down on top of us! What did th' likes of her, born in a tenement house, want with readin'? Her readin's afther bringin' her to a nice pass—oh, it's madnin', madnin', madnin'!

MRS. BOYLE. When she comes back say nothin' to her, Jack, or she'll leave this place.

BOYLE. Leave this place! Ay, she'll leave this place, an' quick too!

MRS. BOYLE. If Mary goes, I'll go with her.

BOYLE. Well, go with her! Well, go, th' pair o' yous! I lived before I seen yous, an' I can live when yous are gone. Isn't this a nice thing to come rollin' in on top o' me afther all your prayin' to St. Anthony an' The Little Flower. An' she's a child o' Mary, too—I wonder what'll the nuns think of her now? An' it'll be bellows'd all over th' disthrict before you could say Jack Robinson; an' whenever I'm seen they'll whisper, "That's th' father of Mary Boyle that had th' kid be th' swank she used to go with; d'ye know, d'ye know?" To be sure they'll know—more about it than I will meself!

JOHNNY. She should be dhriven out o' th' house she's brought disgrace on!

MRS. BOYLE. Hush, you, Johnny. We needn't let it be bellows'd all over the place; all we've got to do is to leave this place quietly an' go somewhere where we're not known, an' nobody'll be the wiser.

BOYLE. You're talkin' like a two-year-oul', woman. Where'll we get a place ou' o' this?—places aren't that easily got.

MRS. BOYLE. But, Jack, when we get the money . . .

BOYLE. Money—what money?

MRS. BOYLE. Why, oul' Ellison's money, of course.

BOYLE. There's no money comin' from oul' Ellison, or any one else. Since you heard of wan trouble, you might as well hear of another. There's no money comin' to us at all—the Will's a wash out!

MRS. BOYLE. What are you sayin', man—no money?

JOHNNY. How could it be a wash out?

BOYLE. The boyo that's afther doin' it to Mary done it to me as well. The thick made out the Will wrong; he said in th' Will, only first cousin an' second cousin, instead of mentionin' our names, an' now any one that thinks he's a first cousin or second cousin t'oul' Ellison can claim the money as well as me, an' they're springin' up in hundreds, an' comin' from America an' Australia, thinkin' to get their whack out of it, while all the time the lawyers is gobblin' it up, till there's not as much as ud buy a stockin' for your lovely daughter's baby!

MRS. BOYLE. I don't believe it, I don't believe it, I don't believe it!

JOHNNY. Why did you nothin' about this before?

MRS. BOYLE. You're not serious, Jack; you're not serious!

BOYLE. I'm tellin' you the scholar, Bentham, made a banjax o' th' Will; instead o' sayin', "th' rest o' me property to be divided between me first cousin, Jack Boyle, an' me second cousin, Mick Finnegan, o' Santhry," he writ down only, "me first an' second cousins," an' the world an' his wife are afther th' property now.

MRS. BOYLE. Now, I know why Bentham left poor Mary in th' lurch; I can see it all now—oh, is there not even a middlin' honest man left in th' world?

JOHNNY [*to* BOYLE]. An' you let us run into debt, an' you borreyed money from everybody to fill yourself with beer! An' now, you tell us the whole thing's a wash out! Oh, if it's thrue, I'm done with you, for you're worse than me sisther Mary!

BOYLE. You hole your tongue, d'ye hear? I'll not take any lip from you. Go an' get Bentham if you want satisfaction for all that's afther happenin' us.

JOHNNY. I won't hole me tongue, I won't hole me tongue! I'll tell you what I think of you, father an' all as you are . . . you . . .

MRS. BOYLE. Johnny, Johnny, Johnny, for God's sake, be quiet!

JOHNNY. I'll not be quiet, I'll not be quiet; he's a nice father, isn't he? Is it any wondher Mary went asthray, when . . .

MRS. BOYLE. Johnny, Johnny, for my sake be quiet—for your mother's sake!

BOYLE. I'm goin' out now to have a few dhrinks with th' last few makes I have, an' tell that lassie o' yours not to be here when I come back; for if I lay me eyes on her, I'll lay me han's on her, an' if I lay me han's on her, I won't be accountable for me actions!

399 **banjax** hodgepodge

JOHNNY. Take care somebody doesn't lay his han's on you—y'oul' . . .

MRS. BOYLE. Johnny, Johnny!

BOYLE [*at door, about to go out*]. Oh, a nice son, an' a nicer daughter, I have. [*calling loudly upstairs*] Joxer, Joxer, are you there?

JOXER [*from a distance*]. I'm here, More . . . ee . . . aar . . . i . . . tee!

BOYLE. I'm goin' down to Foley's—are you comin'?

JOXER. Come with you? With that sweet call me heart is stirred; I'm only waiting for the word, an' I'll be with you, like a bird!

[BOYLE *and* JOXER *pass the door going out.*]

JOHNNY [*throwing himself on the bed*]. I've a nice sisther, an' a nice father, there's no bettin' on it. I wish to God a bullet or a bomb had whipped me ou' o' this long ago! Not one o' yous, not one o' yous, have any thought for me!

MRS. BOYLE [*with passionate remonstrance*]. If you don't whisht, Johnny, you'll drive me mad. Who has kep' th' home together for the past few years—only me. An' who'll have to bear th' biggest part o' this throuble but me—but whinin' an' whingin' isn't going to do any good.

JOHNNY. You're to blame yourself for a gradle of it—givin' him his own way in everything, an' never assin' to check him, no matther what he done. Why didn't you look afther th' money? why . . .

[*There is a knock at the door;* MRS. BOYLE *opens it;* JOHNNY *rises on his elbow to look and listen; two men enter.*]

FIRST MAN. We've been sent up be th' Manager of the Hibernian Furnishing Co., Mrs. Boyle, to take back the furniture that was got a while ago.

MRS. BOYLE. Yous'll touch nothin' here—how do I know who yous are?

FIRST MAN [*showing a paper*]. There's the ordher, ma'am. [*Reading.*] A chest o' drawers, a table, wan easy an' two ordinary chairs; wan mirror; wan chestherfield divan, an' a wardrobe an' two vases. [*to his comrade*] Come on, Bill, it's afther knockin' off time already.

JOHNNY. For God's sake, mother, run down to Foley's an' bring father back, or we'll be left without a stick.

[*The men carry out the table.*]

MRS. BOYLE. What good would it be? You heard what he said before he went out.

JOHNNY. Can't you thry? He ought to be here, an' the like of this goin' on.

[MRS. BOYLE *puts a shawl around her, as* MARY *enters.*]

MARY. What's up, mother? I met men carryin' away the table, an' everybody's talking about us not gettin' the money after all.

MRS. BOYLE. Everythin's gone wrong, Mary, everythin'. We're not gettin' a penny out o' the Will, not a penny—I'll tell you all when I come back; I'm goin' for your father. [*She runs out.*]

JOHNNY [*to* MARY, *who has sat down by the fire*]. It's a wondher you're not ashamed to show your face here, afther what has happened.

[JERRY *enters slowly; there is a look of earnest hope on his face. He looks at* MARY *for a few moments.*]

JERRY [*softly*]. Mary! [MARY *does not answer.*] Mary, I want to speak to you for a few moments, may I?

[MARY *remains silent;* JOHNNY *goes slowly into room on left.*]

JERRY. Your mother has told me everything, Mary, and I have come to you. . . . I have come to tell you, Mary, that my love for you is greater and deeper than ever. . . .

MARY [*with a sob*]. Oh, Jerry, Jerry, say no more; all that is over now; anything like that is impossible now!

JERRY. Impossible? Why do you talk like that, Mary?

MARY. After all that has happened.

JERRY. What does it matter what has happened? We are young enough to be able to forget all those things. [*He catches her hand.*] Mary, Mary, I am pleading for your love. With Labour, Mary, humanity is above everything; we are the Leaders in the fight for a new life. I want to forget Bentham, I want to forget that you left me—even for a while.

MARY. Oh, Jerry, Jerry, you haven't the bitter word of scorn for me after all.

JERRY [*passionately*]. Scorn! I love you, love you, Mary!

MARY [*rising, and looking him in the eyes*]. Even though . . .

JERRY. Even though you threw me over for another man; even though you gave me many a bitter word!

MARY. Yes, yes, I know; but you love me, even though . . . even though . . . I'm . . . goin' . . . goin' . . . [*He looks at her questioningly, and fear gathers in his eyes.*] Ah, I was thinkin' so. . . . You don't know everything!

JERRY [*poignantly*]. Surely to God, Mary, you don't mean that . . . that . . . that . . .

MARY. Now you know all, Jerry; now you know all!

JERRY. My God, Mary, have you fallen as low as that?

MARY. Yes, Jerry, as you say, I have fallen as low as that.

JERRY. I didn't mean it that way, Mary . . . it came on me so sudden, that I didn't mind what I was sayin'. . . . I never expected this—your mother never told me. . . . I'm sorry . . . God knows, I'm sorry for you, Mary.

MARY. Let us say no more, Jerry; I don't blame you for thinkin' it's terrible. . . . I suppose it is. . . . Everybody'll think the same. . . . It's only as I expected—your humanity is just as narrow as the humanity of the others.

JERRY. I'm sorry, all the same. . . . I shouldn't have troubled you. . . . I wouldn't if I'd known . . . if I can do anything for you . . . Mary . . . I will. [*He turns to go, and halts at the door.*]

MARY. Do you remember, Jerry, the verses you read when you gave the lecture in the Socialist Rooms some time ago, on Humanity's Strife with Nature?

JERRY. The verses—no; I don't remember them.

MARY. I do. They're runnin' in me head now—

An' we felt the power that fashion'd
All the lovely things we saw,
That created all the murmur
Of an everlasting law,
Was a hand of force an' beauty,
With an eagle's tearin' claw.

Then we saw our globe of beauty
Was an ugly thing as well,
A hymn divine whose chorus
Was an agonizin' yell;

Like the story of a demon,
That an angel had to tell.

Like a glowin' picture by a
Hand unsteady, brought to ruin;
Like her craters, if their deadness
Could give life unto the moon;
Like the agonizing horror
Of a violin out of tune.

[*There is a pause, and* DEVINE *goes slowly out.*]

JOHNNY [*returning*]. Is he gone?

MARY. Yes.

[*The two men re-enter.*]

FIRST MAN. We can't wait any longer for t'oul' fella—sorry, Miss, but we have to live as well as th' nex' man.

[*They carry out some things.*]

JOHNNY. Oh, isn't this terrible! . . . I suppose you told him everything . . . couldn't you have waited for a few days . . . he'd have stopped th' takin' of the things, if you'd kep' your mouth shut. Are you burnin' to tell every one of the shame you've brought on us?

MARY [*snatching up her hat and coat*]. Oh, this is unbearable!

[*She rushes out.*]

FIRST MAN [*re-entering*]. We'll take the chest o' drawers next—it's the heaviest.

[*The votive light flickers for a moment, and goes out.*]

JOHNNY [*in a cry of fear*]. Mother o' God, the light's afther goin' out!

FIRST MAN. You put the win' up me the way you bawled that time. The oil's all gone, that's all.

JOHNNY [*with an agonizing cry*]. Mother o' God, there's a shot I'm afther gettin'!

FIRST MAN. What's wrong with you, man? Is it a fit you're takin'?

JOHNNY. I'm afther feelin' a pain in me breast, like the tearin' by of a bullet!

FIRST MAN. He's goin' mad—it's a wondher they'd leave a chap like that here be himself.

[*Two* IRREGULARS *enter swiftly; they carry revolvers; one goes over to* JOHNNY; *the other covers the two furniture men.*]

FIRST IRREGULAR [*to the men, quietly and incisively*]. Who are you—what are yous doin' here—quick!

FIRST MAN. Removin' furniture that's not paid for.

FIRST IRREGULAR. Get over to the other end of the room an' turn your faces to the wall—quick.

[*The two men turn their faces to the wall, with their hands up.*]

SECOND IRREGULAR [*to* JOHNNY]. Come on, Sean Boyle, you're wanted; some of us have a word to say to you.

JOHNNY. I'm sick, I can't—what do you want with me?

SECOND IRREGULAR. Come on, come on; we've a distance to go, an' haven't much time—come on.

JOHNNY. I'm an oul' comrade—yous wouldn't shoot an oul' comrade.

SECOND IRREGULAR. Poor Tancred was an oul' comrade o' yours, but you didn't think o' that when you gave him away to the gang that sent him to his grave. But we've no time to waste; come on—here, Dermot, ketch his arm. [*to* JOHNNY] Have you your beads?

JOHNNY. Me beads! Why do you ass me that, why do you ass me that?

SECOND IRREGULAR. Go on, go on, march!

JOHNNY. Are yous goin' to do in a comrade—look at me arm, I lost it for Ireland.

SECOND IRREGULAR. Commandant Tancred lost his life for Ireland.

JOHNNY. Sacred Heart of Jesus, have mercy on me! Mother o' God, pray for me—be with me now in the agonies o' death! . . . Hail, Mary, full o' grace . . . the Lord is . . . with Thee.

[*They drag out* JOHNNY BOYLE, *and the curtain falls. When it rises again the most of the furniture is gone.* MARY *and* MRS. BOYLE, *one on each side, are sitting in a darkened room, by the fire; it is an hour later.*]

MRS. BOYLE. I'll not wait much longer . . . what did they bring him away in the mothor for? Nugent says he thinks they had guns . . . is me throubles never goin' to be over? . . . If anything ud happen to poor Johnny, I think I'd lose me mind . . . I'll go to the Police Station, surely they ought to be able to do somethin'.

580 **Sean** John. The nationalistic Irregulars prefer the Gaelic form of the name.

590 **beads** Rosary

[*Below is heard the sound of voices.*]

MRS. BOYLE. Whisht, is that something? Maybe, it's your father, though when I left him in Foley's he was hardly able to lift his head. Whisht!

[*A knock at the door, and the voice of* MRS. MADIGAN, *speaking very softly:* Mrs. Boyle, Mrs. Boyle. MRS. BOYLE *opens the door.*]

MRS. MADIGAN. Oh, Mrs. Boyle, God an' His Blessed Mother be with you this night!

MRS. BOYLE [*calmly*]. What is it, Mrs. Madigan? It's Johnny—something about Johnny.

MRS. MADIGAN. God send it's not. God send it's not Johnny!

MRS. BOYLE. Don't keep me waitin', Mrs. Madigan; I've gone through so much lately that I feel able for anything.

MRS. MADIGAN. Two polismen below wantin' you.

MRS. BOYLE. Wantin' me; an' why do they want me?

MRS. MADIGAN. Some poor fella's been found, an' they think it's, it's . . .

MRS. BOYLE. Johnny, Johnny!

MARY [*with her arms round her mother*]. Oh, mother, mother, me poor, darlin' mother.

MRS. BOYLE. Hush, hush, darlin'; you'll shortly have your own throuble to bear [*to* MRS. MADIGAN] An' why do the polis think it's Johnny, Mrs. Madigan?

MRS. MADIGAN. Because one o' the doctors knew him when he was attendin' with his poor arm.

MRS. BOYLE. Oh, it's thrue, then; it's Johnny, it's me son, me own son!

MARY. Oh, it's thrue, it's thrue what Jerry Devine says—there isn't a God, there isn't a God; if there was He wouldn't let these things happen!

MRS. BOYLE. Mary, Mary, you mustn't say them things. We'll want all the help we can get from God an' His Blessed Mother now! These things have nothin' to do with the Will o' God. Ah, what can God do agen the stupidity o' men!

MRS. MADIGAN. The polis want you to go with them to the hospital to see the poor body—they're waitin' below.

MRS. BOYLE. We'll go. Come, Mary, an' we'll never come back here agen. Let your father furrage for himself now; I've done all

I could an' it was all no use—he'll be hopeless till the end of his days. I've got a little room in me sisther's where we'll stop till your throuble is over, an' then we'll work together for the sake of the baby.

MARY. My poor little child that'll have no father!

MRS. BOYLE. It'll have what's far betther—it'll have two mothers.

[*A rough voice shouting from below:*]

Are yous goin' to keep us waitin' for yous all night?

MRS. MADIGAN [*going to the door, and shouting down*]. Take your hour, there, take your hour! If yous are in such a hurry, skip off, then, for nobody wants you here—if they did yous wouldn't be found. For you're the same as yous were undher the British Government—never where yous are wanted! As far as I can see, the Polis as Polis, in this city, is Null an' Void!

MRS. BOYLE. We'll go, Mary, we'll go; you to see your poor dead brother, an' me to see me poor dead son!

MARY. I dhread it, mother, I dhread it!

MRS. BOYLE. I forgot, Mary, I forgot; your poor oul' selfish mother was only thinkin' of herself. No, no, you mustn't come—it wouldn't be good for you. You go on to me sisther's an' I'll face th' ordeal meself. Maybe I didn't feel sorry enough for Mrs. Tancred when her poor son was found as Johnny's been found now—because he was a Die-hard! Ah, why didn't I remember that then he wasn't a Die-hard or a Stater, but only a poor dead son! It's well I remember all that she said—an' it's my turn to say it now: What was the pain I suffered, Johnny, bringin' you into the world to carry you to your cradle to the pains I'll suffer carryin' you out o' the world to bring you to your grave! Mother o' God, Mother o' God, have pity on us all! Blessed Virgin, where were you when me darlin' son was riddled with bullets, when me darlin' son was riddled with bullets? Sacred Heart o' Jesus, take away our hearts o' stone, and give us hearts o' flesh! Take away this murdherin' hate, an' give us Thine own eternal love!

[*They all go slowly out. There is a pause; then a sound of shuffling steps on the stairs outside. The door opens and* BOYLE *and* JOXER, *both of them very drunk, enter.*]

BOYLE. I'm able to go no farther. . . . Two polis, ey . . . what were they doin' here, I wondher? . . . Up to no good, anyhow

. . . an' Juno an' that lovely daughter o' mine with them. [*taking a sixpence from his pocket and looking at it*] Wan single, solithary tanner left out of all I borreyed. . . . [*He lets it fall.*] The last o' the Mohicans. . . . The blinds is down, Joxer, the blinds is down!

JOXER [*walking unsteadily across the room, and anchoring at the bed*]. Put all . . . your throubles . . . in your oul' kit bag . . . an' smile . . . smile . . . smile!

BOYLE. The counthry'll have to steady itself . . . it's goin' . . . to hell. . . . Where'r all . . . the chairs . . . gone to . . . steady itself, Joxer. . . . Chairs'll . . . have to . . . steady themselves. . . . No matther . . . what any one may . . . say . . . Irelan's sober . . . is Irelan' . . . free.

JOXER [*stretching himself on the bed*]. Chains . . . an' . . . slaveree . . . that's a darlin' motto . . . a daaarlin' . . . motto!

BOYLE. If th' worst comes . . . to th' worse . . . I can join a . . . flyin' . . . column. . . . I done . . . me bit . . . in Easther Week . . . had no business . . . to . . . be . . . there . . . but Captain Boyle's Captain Boyle!

JOXER. Breathes there a man with soul . . . so . . . de . . . ad . . . this . . . me . . . o . . . wn, me nat . . . ive l . . . an'!

BOYLE [*subsiding into a sitting posture on the floor*]. Commandant Kelly died . . . in them . . . arms . . . Joxer. . . . Tell me Volunteer Butties . . . says he . . . that . . . I died for . . . Irelan'!

JOXER. D'jever rade Willie . . . Reilly . . . an' his . . . own . . . Colleen . . . Bawn? It's a darlin' story, a daarlin' story!

BOYLE. I'm telling you . . . Joxer . . . th' whole worl's . . . in a terr . . . ible state o' . . . chassis!

THE CURTAIN FALLS

701 **flyin' column** detachment of Irregulars

FEDERICO GARCIA LORCA
1898–1936

THE HOUSE OF BERNARDA ALBA

1936

LORCA'S MATRIARCH STANDS CONSCIOUSLY for social order, for the tradition which gives a community its foundation, and for the unwritten codes in which a society incorporates its values. Such codes govern the lives of men and women everywhere, restraining their anarchic impulses and guiding them toward a reconciliation of personal and social needs. They regulate the parents' duties, the child's freedom, the attitudes held toward education, authority, and justice. Perhaps most significantly, they control the relations between the sexes, channeling into courtship, marriage, and the creation of the family an urge which might spend itself in idle promiscuity.

When Bernarda arranges Angustias' marriage, she obeys and enforces the code of her community as she does in rebuffing Martirio's suitor and in restraining Adela. Something, however, has gone wrong. The code no longer suits the needs that gave it being. It has turned hollow, external. "I don't pry into anyone's heart," says Bernarda, "but I want to put up a good front." A good front may well be the perversion of a good life, and Bernarda herself has turned pathologically rigid. With her husband's death she assumes a man's place and becomes governor of her family—but less governor than tyrant. No longer does she strive to accommodate her children's desires to the needs of society; she opposes the desires themselves. She hates the flesh for the rebellious will within it, hates her daughters for the hunger that is theirs. "Hot coals in the place where she sinned!" she screams at the end of Act II, and in that cry her negation is proclaimed. She would literally burn out the source of life.

The home, which should be a miniature of a well-ordered society, turns under Bernarda's tyranny into a prison, its white walls gleaming down in ironic purity on the dying souls within. For eight years of unfelt mourning they will desperately embroider their hope-chest linens, tasting the truth of Amelia's conviction that "to be born a woman's the worst punishment." They will torment one another out of sisterly affection corroded to jealousy. Each in her own fashion will seize at any promise of redemption. Angustias, the power of love withering within her, reaches doubtfully toward a face that "seems to fade away." In the desperation of fantasy fulfillment, Martirio steals Pepe's picture. And Adela, who has "seen death under this roof" and who feels the fire of life in her legs and mouth, resolves to find freedom though she wear "the crown of thorns that belongs to the mistress of a married man."

What one finds in this prison, one finds in the village—in all the villages, Lorca implies, of Spain—for when the code becomes tyrannical, the inhibited will turns corrupt. Hence the prostitution to which Poncia's mother surrendered and the venomous hypocrisy with which Poncia inflames the prurience of the daughters. Hence the rape of Paca la Roseta, which the men discuss with superb impropriety at the funeral of Bernarda's husband. Every whisper sifting through the prison bars tells of flesh escaping into license or succumbing to mortification. Adelaida's "sweetheart doesn't let her go out even to the front doorstep. Before, she was gay. Now, not even powder on her face." And whether the flesh escapes or succumbs, the end is the denial of life. Act II ends with infanticide, Act III with suicide.

In the background the reapers sing their lyric of love, the stallion's hooves explode against his prison walls, and the mad grandmother croons her lullaby, "Little lamb, child of mine, Let's go to the shore of the sea . . . Let's go to the palms at Bethlehem's gate." But maternal love is dead. The sea is far from the hot plains of the riverless village. And the gate of Bethlehem is farther yet. The Church, its representative, is indeed near, as its bells proclaim, but it seems not to enter in any redemptive way into the lives of the villagers.

THE HOUSE OF BERNARDA ALBA / *LORCA*

A DRAMA ABOUT WOMEN IN THE VILLAGES OF SPAIN

TRANSLATED BY

JAMES GRAHAM-LUJÁN AND RICHARD L. O'CONNELL

Characters

BERNARDA	*age 60*
MARIA JOSEFA	*Bernarda's mother, age 80*
ANGUSTIAS	*Bernarda's daughter, age 39*
MAGDALENA	*Bernarda's daughter, age 30*
AMELIA	*Bernarda's daughter, age 27*
MARTIRIO	*Bernarda's daughter, age 24*
ADELA	*Bernarda's daughter, age 20*
A MAID	*age 50*
LA PONCIA	*a maid, age 60*
PRUDENCIA	*age 50*
WOMEN IN MOURNING	

The writer states that these Three Acts are intended as a photographic document.

ACT I

A very white room in Bernarda Alba's house. The walls are white. There are arched doorways with jute curtains tied back with tassels and ruffles. Wicker chairs. On the walls, pictures of unlikely landscapes full of nymphs or legendary kings.

It is summer. A great brooding silence fills the stage. It is empty when the curtain rises. Bells can be heard tolling outside.

FIRST SERVANT [*entering*]. The tolling of those bells hits me right between the eyes.

PONCIA. [*She enters, eating bread and sausage.*] More than two hours of mumbo jumbo. Priests are here from all the towns. The church looks beautiful. At the first responsory for the dead, Magdalena fainted.

FIRST SERVANT. She's the one who's left most alone.

PONCIA. She's the only one who loved her father. Ay! Thank God we're alone for a little. I came over to eat.

FIRST SERVANT. If Bernarda sees you . . . !

PONCIA. She's not eating today so she'd just as soon we'd all die of hunger! Domineering old tyrant! But she'll be fooled! I opened the sausage crock.

FIRST SERVANT [*with an anxious sadness*]. Couldn't you give me some for my little girl, Poncia?

PONCIA. Go ahead! And take a fistful of peas too. She won't know the difference today.

VOICE [*within*]. Bernarda!

PONCIA. There's the grandmother! Isn't she locked up tight?

FIRST SERVANT. Two turns of the key.

PONCIA. You'd better put the cross-bar up too. She's got the fingers of a lock-picker!

VOICE [*within*]. Bernarda!

PONCIA [*shouting*]. She's coming! [*to* THE SERVANT]. Clean everything up good. If Bernarda doesn't find things shining, she'll pull out the few hairs I have left.

SERVANT. What a woman!

PONCIA. Tyrant over everyone around her. She's perfectly capable of sitting on your heart and watching you die for a whole year without turning off that cold little smile she wears on her wicked face. Scrub, scrub those dishes!

SERVANT. I've got blood on my hands from so much polishing of everything.

PONCIA. She's the cleanest, she's the decentest, she's the highest everything! A good rest her poor husband's earned!

[*The bells stop.*]

SERVANT. Did all the relatives come?

PONCIA. Just hers. His people hate her. They came to see him dead and make the sign of the cross over him; that's all.

SERVANT. Are there enough chairs?

PONCIA. More than enough. Let them sit on the floor. When Bernarda's father died people stopped coming under this roof. She doesn't want them to see her in her "domain." Curse her!

SERVANT. She's been good to you.

PONCIA. Thirty years washing her sheets. Thirty years eating her leftovers. Nights of watching when she had a cough. Whole days peeking through a crack in the shutters to spy on the neighbors and carry her the tale. Life without secrets one from the other. But in spite of that—curse her! May the "pain of the piercing nail" strike her in the eyes.

SERVANT. Poncia!

PONCIA. But I'm a good watchdog! I bark when I'm told and bite beggars' heels when she sics me on 'em. My sons work in her fields —both of them already married, but one of these days I'll have enough.

SERVANT. And then . . . ?

PONCIA. Then I'll lock myself up in a room with her and spit in her face—a whole year. "Bernarda, here's for this, that and the other!" Till I leave her—just like a lizard the boys have squashed. For that's what she is—she and her whole family! Not that I envy her her life. Five girls are left her, five ugly daughters—not counting Angustias the eldest, by her first husband, who has money—the rest of them, plenty of eyelets to embroider, plenty of linen petticoats, but bread and grapes when it comes to inheritance.

SERVANT. Well, *I'd* like to have what they've got!

PONCIA. All we have is our hands and a hole in God's earth.

SERVANT. And that's the only earth they'll ever leave to us—to us who have nothing!

56 **"pain of the piercing nail"** Translators' quotation marks seem designed to point out that Lorca's word for 'nail' is the word commonly used for the nails of the cross.

68–71 **daughters . . . inheritance** i.e., of the five daughters only Angustias has a dowry.

PONCIA [*at the cupboard*]. This glass has some specks.

SERVANT. Neither soap nor rag will take them off.

[*The bells toll.*]

PONCIA. The last prayer! I'm going over and listen. I certainly like the way our priest sings. In the Pater Noster his voice went up, and up—like a pitcher filling with water little by little. Of course, at the end his voice cracked, but it's glorious to hear it. No, there never was anybody like the old Sacristan—Tronchapinos. At my mother's Mass, may she rest in peace, he sang. The walls shook—and when he said "Amen," it was as if a wolf had come into the church. [*imitating him*] A-a-a-a-men! [*She starts coughing.*]

SERVANT. Watch out—you'll strain your windpipe!

PONCIA. I'd rather strain something else!

[*Goes out laughing.*]

[THE SERVANT *scrubs. The bells toll.*]

SERVANT [*imitating the bells*]. Dong, dong, dong. Dong, dong, dong. May God forgive him!

BEGGAR WOMAN [*at the door, with a little girl*]. Blesséd be God!

SERVANT. Dong, dong, dong. I hope he waits many years for us! Dong, dong, dong.

BEGGAR [*loudly, a little annoyed*]. Blesséd be God!

SERVANT [*annoyed*]. Forever and ever!

BEGGAR. I came for the scraps.

[*The bells stop tolling.*]

SERVANT. You can go right out the way you came in. Today's scraps are for me.

BEGGAR. But you have somebody to take care of you—and my little girl and I are all alone!

SERVANT. Dogs are alone too, and they live.

BEGGAR. They always give them to me.

SERVANT. Get out of here! Who let you in anyway? You've already tracked up the place. [THE BEGGAR WOMAN *and* LITTLE GIRL *leave.* THE SERVANT *goes on scrubbing.*] Floors finished with oil, cupboards, pedestals, iron beds—but us servants, we can suffer in silence—and live in mud huts with a plate and a spoon. I hope someday not a one will be left to tell it. [*The bells sound again.*] Yes, yes—ring away. Let them put you in a coffin with gold inlay and brocade to carry it on—you're no less dead than I'll be, so take what's coming to you, Antonio María Benavides—stiff in your broadcloth suit and your high boots—take what's coming to you! You'll never again lift my skirts behind the corral door!

[*From the rear door, two by two, women in mourning with large shawls and black skirts and fans, begin to enter. They come in slowly until the stage is full.*]

SERVANT [*breaking into a wail*]. Oh, Antonio María Benavides, now you'll never see these walls, nor break bread in this house again! I'm the one who loved you most of all your servants. [*pulling her hair*] *Must* I live on after you've gone? Must I go on living?

[*The two hundred women finish coming in, and Bernarda and her five daughters enter.* BERNARDA *leans on a cane.*]

BERNARDA [*to* THE SERVANT]. Silence!

SERVANT [*weeping*]. Bernarda!

BERNARDA. Less shrieking and more work. You should have had all this cleaner for the wake. Get out. This isn't your place.

[THE SERVANT *goes off crying.*]

The poor are like animals—they seem to be made of different stuff.

FIRST WOMAN. The poor feel their sorrows too.

BERNARDA. But they forget them in front of a plateful of peas.

FIRST GIRL [*timidly*]. Eating is necessary for living.

BERNARDA. At your age one doesn't talk in front of older people.

WOMAN. Be quiet, child.

BERNARDA. I've never taken lessons from anyone. Sit down. Magdalena, don't cry. If you want to cry, get under your bed. Do you hear me?

SECOND WOMAN [*to* BERNARDA]. Have you started to work the fields?

BERNARDA. Yesterday.

THIRD WOMAN. The sun comes down like lead.

FIRST WOMAN. I haven't known heat like this for years.

[*Pause. They all fan themselves.*]

BERNARDA. Is the lemonade ready?

PONCIA. Yes, Bernarda.

[*She brings in a large tray full of little white jars which she distributes.*]

BERNARDA. Give the men some.

PONCIA. They're already drinking in the patio.

BERNARDA. Let them get out the way they came in. I don't want them walking through here.

A GIRL [*to* ANGUSTIAS]. Pepe el Romano was with the men during the service.

ANGUSTIAS. There he was.

BERNARDA. His mother was there. She saw his mother. Neither she nor I saw Pepe . . .

GIRL. I thought . . .

BERNARDA. The one who *was* there was Darajalí, the widower. Very close to your Aunt. We all of us saw him.

SECOND WOMAN [*aside, in a low voice*]. Wicked, worse than wicked woman!

THIRD WOMAN. A tongue like a knife!

BERNARDA. Women in church shouldn't look at any man but the priest—and him only because he wears skirts. To turn your head is to be looking for the warmth of corduroy.

FIRST WOMAN. Sanctimonious old snake!

PONCIA [*between her teeth*]. Itching for a man's warmth.

BERNARDA [*beating with her cane on the floor*]. Blesséd be God!

ALL [*crossing themselves*]. Forever blesséd and praised.

BERNARDA. Rest in peace with holy company at your head.

ALL. Rest in peace!

BERNARDA. With the Angel Saint Michael, and his sword of justice.

ALL. Rest in peace!

BERNARDA. With the key that opens, and the hand that locks.

ALL. Rest in peace!

BERNARDA. With the most blesséd, and the little lights of the field.

ALL. Rest in peace!

BERNARDA. With our holy charity, and all souls on land and sea.

ALL. Rest in peace!

BERNARDA. Grant rest to your servant, Antonio María Benavides, and give him the crown of your blesséd glory.

171 **Blesséd be God!** The passage which follows is a pastiche of ritual and folk phrases.

ALL. Amen.

BERNARDA. [*She rises and chants.*] Requiem aeternam donat eis domine.

ALL [*standing and chanting in the Gregorian fashion*]. Et lux perpetua luce ab eis.

[*They cross themselves.*]

FIRST WOMAN. May you have health to pray for his soul.

[*They start filing out.*]

THIRD WOMAN. You won't lack loaves of hot bread.

SECOND WOMAN. Nor a roof for your daughters.

[*They are all filing in front of* BERNARDA *and going out.* ANGUSTIAS *leaves by the door to the patio.*]

FOURTH WOMAN. May you go on enjoying your wedding wheat.

PONCIA. [*She enters, carrying a money bag.*] From the men—this bag of money for Masses.

BERNARDA. Thank them—and let them have a glass of brandy.

GIRL [*to* MAGDALENA]. Magdalena . . .

BERNARDA [*to* MAGDALENA, *who is starting to cry*]. Sh-h-h-h! [*She beats with her cane on the floor.*]

[*All the women have gone out.*]

BERNARDA [*to the women who have just left*]. Go back to your houses and criticize everything you've seen! I hope it'll be many years before you pass under the archway of my door again.

PONCIA. You've nothing to complain about. The whole town came.

BERNARDA. Yes, to fill my house with the sweat from their wraps and the poison of their tongues.

AMELIA. Mother, don't talk like that.

BERNARDA. What other way is there to talk about this curséd village with no river—this village full of wells where you drink water always fearful it's been poisoned?

PONCIA. Look what they've done to the floor!

BERNARDA. As though a herd of goats had passed through. [PONCIA *cleans the floor.*] Adela, give me a fan.

189–92 **Requiem . . . luce ab eis** Bernarda and her visitors garble a refrain from the Offices for the Dead. The original means, "Grant them eternal rest, O Lord. And let the everlasting light shine upon them."

ADELA. Take this one. [*She gives her a round fan with green and red flowers.*]

BERNARDA [*throwing the fan on the floor*]. Is that the fan to give to a widow? Give me a black one and learn to respect your father's memory.

MARTIRIO. Take mine.

BERNARDA. And you?

MARTIRIO. I'm not hot.

BERNARDA. Well, look for another, because you'll need it. For the eight years of mourning, not a breath of air will get in this house from the street. We'll act as if we'd sealed up doors and windows with bricks. That's what happened in my father's house—and in my grandfather s house. Meantime, you can all start embroidering your hope-chest linens. I have twenty bolts of linen in the chest from which to cut sheets and coverlets. Magdalena can embroider them.

MAGDALENA. It's all the same to me.

ADELA [*sourly*]. If you don't want to embroider them—they can go without. That way yours will look better.

MAGDALENA. Neither mine nor yours. I know I'm not going to marry. I'd rather carry sacks to the mill. Anything except sit here day after day in this dark room.

BERNARDA. That's what a woman is for.

MAGDALENA. Cursed be all women.

BERNARDA. In this house you'll do what I order. You can't run with the story to your father any more. Needle and thread for women. Whiplash and mules for men. That's the way it has to be for people who have certain obligations.

[ADELA *goes out.*]

VOICE. Bernarda! Let me out!

BERNARDA [*calling*]. Let her out now!

[THE FIRST SERVANT *enters.*]

FIRST SERVANT. I had a hard time holding her. In spite of her eighty years, your mother's strong as an oak.

BERNARDA. It runs in the family. My grandfather was the same way.

SERVANT. Several times during the wake I had to cover her

mouth with an empty sack because she wanted to shout out to you to give her dishwater to drink at least, and some dogmeat, which is what she says you feed her.

MARTIRIO. She's mean!

BERNARDA [*to* SERVANT]. Let her get some fresh air in the patio.

SERVANT. She took her rings and the amethyst earrings out of the box, put them on, and told me she wants to get married.

[*The daughters laugh.*]

BERNARDA. Go with her and be careful she doesn't get near the well.

SERVANT. You don't need to be afraid she'll jump in.

BERNARDA. It's not that– but the neighbors can see her there from their windows.

[THE SERVANT *leaves.*]

MARTIRIO. We'll go change our clothes.

BERNARDA. Yes, but don't take the 'kerchiefs from your heads.

[ADELA *enters.*]

And Angustias?

ADELA [*meaningfully*]. I saw her looking out through the cracks of the back door. The men had just gone.

BERNARDA. And you, what were *you* doing at the door?

ADELA. I went there to see if the hens had laid.

BERNARDA. But the men had already gone!

ADELA [*meaningfully*]. A group of them were still standing outside.

BERNARDA [*furiously*]. Angustias! Angustias!

ANGUSTIAS [*entering*]. Did you want something?

BERNARDA. For what—and at whom—were you looking?

ANGUSTIAS. Nobody.

BERNARDA. Is it decent for a woman of your class to be running after a man the day of her father's funeral? Answer me! Whom were you looking at?

[*Pause.*]

ANGUSTIAS. I . . .

BERNARDA. Yes, you!

ANGUSTIAS. Nobody.

BERNARDA. Soft! Honeytongue! [*She strikes her.*]

PONCIA [*running to her*]. Bernarda, calm down! [*She holds her.* ANGUSTIAS *weeps.*]

BERNARDA. Get out of here, all of you!

[*They all go out.*]

PONCIA. She did it not realizing what she was doing—although it's bad, of course. It really disgusted me to see her sneak along to the patio. Then she stood at the window listening to the men's talk which, as usual, was not the sort one should listen to.

BERNARDA. That's what they come to funerals for. [*with curiosity*] What were they talking about?

PONCIA. They were talking about Paca la Roseta. Last night they tied her husband up in a stall, stuck her on a horse behind the saddle, and carried her away to the depths of the olive grove.

BERNARDA. And what did she do?

PONCIA. She? She was just as happy—they say her breasts were exposed and Maximiliano held on to her as if he were playing a guitar. Terrible!

BERNARDA. And what happened?

PONCIA. What had to happen. They came back almost at daybreak. Paca la Roseta with her hair loose and a wreath of flowers on her head.

BERNARDA. She's the only bad woman we have in the village.

PONCIA. Because she's not from here. She's from far away. And those who went with her are the sons of outsiders too. The men from here aren't up to a thing like that.

BERNARDA. No, but they like to see it, and talk about it, and suck their fingers over it.

PONCIA. They were saying a lot more things.

BERNARDA [*looking from side to side with a certain fear*]. What things?

PONCIA. I'm ashamed to talk about them.

BERNARDA. And my daughter heard them?

PONCIA. Of course!

BERNARDA. That one takes after her Aunts: white and mealy-mouthed and casting sheep's eyes at any little barber's compliment. Oh, what one has to go through and put up with so people will be decent and not too wild!

PONCIA. It's just that your daughters are of an age when they ought to have husbands. Mighty little trouble they give you. Angustias must be much more than thirty now.

BERNARDA. Exactly thirty-nine.

PONCIA. Imagine. And she's never had a beau . . .

BERNARDA [*furiously*]. None of them has ever had a beau and they've never needed one! They get along very well.

PONCIA. I didn't mean to offend you.

BERNARDA. For a hundred miles around there's no one good enough to come near them. The men in this town are not of their class. Do you want me to turn them over to the first shepherd?

PONCIA. You should have moved to another town.

BERNARDA. That's it. To sell them!

PONCIA. No, Bernarda, to change. . . . Of course, any place else, they'd be the poor ones.

BERNARDA. Hold your tormenting tongue!

PONCIA. One can't even talk to you. Do we, or do we not share secrets?

BERNARDA. We do not. You're a servant and I pay you. Nothing more.

PONCIA. But . . .

SERVANT [*entering*]. Don Arturo's here. He's come to see about dividing the inheritance.

BERNARDA. Let's go. [*to* THE SERVANT] You start whitewashing the patio. [*to* LA PONCIA] And you start putting all the dead man's clothes away in the chest.

PONCIA. We could give away some of the things.

BERNARDA. Nothing—not a button even! Not even the cloth we covered his face with.

[*She goes out slowly, leaning on her cane. At the door she turns to look at the two servants. They go out. She leaves.*]

[AMELIA *and* MARTIRIO *enter.*]

AMELIA. Did you take the medicine?

MARTIRIO. For all the good it'll do me.

AMELIA. But you took it?

MARTIRIO. I do things without any faith, but like clockwork.

AMELIA. Since the new doctor came you look livelier.

MARTIRIO. I feel the same.

AMELIA. Did you notice? Adelaida wasn't at the funeral.

MARTIRIO. I know. Her sweetheart doesn't let her go out even to the front doorstep. Before, she was gay. Now, not even powder on her face.

AMELIA. These days a girl doesn't know whether to have a beau or not.

MARTIRIO. It's all the same.

AMELIA. The whole trouble is all these wagging tongues that won't let us live. Adelaida has probably had a bad time.

MARTIRIO. She's afraid of our mother. Mother is the only one who knows the story of Adelaida's father and where he got his lands. Everytime she comes here, Mother twists the knife in the wound. Her father killed his first wife's husband in Cuba so he could marry her himself. Then he left her there and went off with another woman who already had one daughter, and then he took up with this other girl, Adelaida's mother, and married her after his second wife died insane.

AMELIA. But why isn't a man like that put in jail?

MARTIRIO. Because men help each other cover up things like that and no one's able to tell on them.

AMELIA. But Adelaida's not to blame for any of that.

MARTIRIO. No. But history repeats itself. I can see that everything is a terrible repetition. And she'll have the same fate as her mother and grandmother—both of them wife to the man who fathered her.

AMELIA. What an awful thing!

MARTIRIO. It's better never to look at a man. I've been afraid of them since I was a little girl. I'd see them in the yard, yoking the oxen and lifting grain sacks, shouting and stamping, and I was always afraid to grow up for fear one of them would suddenly take me in his arms. God has made me weak and ugly and has definitely put such things away from me.

AMELIA. Don't say that! Enrique Humanas was after you and he liked you.

MARTIRIO. That was just people's ideas! One time I stood in my nightgown at the window until daybreak because he let me know through his shepherd's little girl that he was going to come, and he didn't. It was all just talk. Then he married someone else who had more money than I.

AMELIA. And ugly as the devil.

MARTIRIO. What do men care about ugliness? All they care about is lands, yokes of oxen, and a submissive bitch who'll feed them.

AMELIA. Ay!

[MAGDALENA *enters.*]

MAGDALENA. What are you doing?

MARTIRIO. Just here.

AMELIA. And you?

MAGDALENA. I've been going through all the rooms. Just to walk a little, and look at Grandmother's needlepoint pictures—the little woolen dog, and the black man wrestling with the lion—which we liked so much when we were children. Those were happier times. A wedding lasted ten days and evil tongues weren't in style. Today people are more refined. Brides wear white veils, just as in the cities, and we drink bottled wine, but we rot inside because of what people might say.

MARTIRIO. Lord knows what went on then!

AMELIA [*to* MAGDALENA]. One of your shoelaces has come untied.

MAGDALENA. What of it?

AMELIA. You'll step on it and fall.

MAGDALENA. One less!

MARTIRIO. And Adela?

MAGDALENA. Ah! She put on the green dress she made to wear for her birthday, went out to the yard, and began shouting: "Chickens! Chickens, look at me!" I had to laugh.

AMELIA. If Mother had only seen her!

MAGDALENA. Poor little thing! She's the youngest one of us and still has her illusions. I'd give something to see her happy.

[*Pause.* ANGUSTIAS *crosses the stage, carrying some towels.*]

ANGUSTIAS. What time is it?

MAGDALENA. It must be twelve.

ANGUSTIAS. So late?

AMELIA. It's about to strike.

[ANGUSTIAS *goes out.*]

MAGDALENA [*meaningfully*]. Do you know what? [*pointing after* ANGUSTIAS]

AMELIA. No.

MAGDALENA. Come on!

MARTIRIO. I don't know what you're talking about!

MAGDALENA. Both of you know it better than I do, always with your heads together, like two little sheep, but not letting anybody else in on it. I mean about Pepe el Romano!

MARTIRIO. Ah!

MAGDALENA [*mocking her*]. Ah! The whole town's talking about it. Pepe el Romano is coming to marry Angustias. Last night he was walking around the house and I think he's going to send a declaration soon.

MARTIRIO. I'm glad. He's a good man.

AMELIA. Me too. Angustias is well off.

MAGDALENA. Neither one of you is glad.

MARTIRIO. Magdalena! What do you mean?

MAGDALENA. If he were coming because of Angustias' looks, for Angustias as a woman, I'd be glad too, but he's coming for her money. Even though Angustias is our sister, we're her family here and we know she's old and sickly, and always has been the least attractive one of us! Because if she looked like a dressed-up stick at twenty, what can she look like now, now that she's forty?

MARTIRIO. Don't talk like that. Luck comes to the one who least expects it.

AMELIA. But Magdalena's right after all! Angustias has all her father's money; she's the only rich one in the house and that's why, now that Father's dead and the money will be divided, they're coming for her.

MAGDALENA. Pepe el Romano is twenty-five years old and the best looking man around here. The natural thing would be for him to be after you, Amelia, or our Adela, who's twenty—not looking for the least likely one in this house, a woman who, like her father, talks through her nose.

MARTIRIO. Maybe he likes that!

MAGDALENA. I've never been able to bear your hypocrisy.

MARTIRIO. Heavens!

[ADELA *enters.*]

MAGDALENA. Did the chickens see you?

ADELA. What did you want me to do?

AMELIA. If Mother sees you, she'll drag you by your hair!

ADELA. I had a lot of illusions about this dress. I'd planned to put it on the day we were going to eat watermelons at the well. There wouldn't have been another like it.

MARTIRIO. It's a lovely dress.

ADELA. And one that looks very good on me. It's the best thing Magdalena's ever cut.

MAGDALENA. And the chickens, what did they say to you?

ADELA. They presented me with a few fleas that riddled my legs.

[*They laugh.*]

MARTIRIO. What you can do is dye it black.

MAGDALENA. The best thing you can do is give it to Angustias for her wedding with Pepe el Romano.

ADELA [*with hidden emotion*]. But Pepe el Romano . . .

AMELIA. Haven't you heard about it?

ADELA. No.

MAGDALENA. Well, now you know!

ADELA. But it can't be!

MAGDALENA. Money can do anything.

ADELA. Is that why she went out after the funeral and stood looking through the door? [*Pause.*] And that man would . . .

MAGDALENA. Would do anything.

[*Pause.*]

MARTIRIO. What are you thinking, Adela?

ADELA. I'm thinking that this mourning has caught me at the worst moment of my life for me to bear it.

MAGDALENA. You'll get used to it.

ADELA [*bursting out, crying with rage*]. I will not get used to it! I can't be locked up. I don't want my skin to look like yours. I don't want my skin's whiteness lost in these rooms. Tomorrow I'm going to put on my green dress and go walking in the streets. I want to go out!

[THE FIRST SERVANT *enters.*]

MAGDALENA [*in a tone of authority*]. Adela!

SERVANT. The poor thing! How she misses her father. . . .

[*She goes out.*]

MARTIRIO. Hush!

AMELIA. What happens to one will happen to all of us.

[ADELA *grows calm.*]

MAGDALENA. The servant almost heard you.

SERVANT [*entering*]. Pepe el Romano is coming along at the end of the street.

[AMELIA, MARTIRIO *and* MAGDALENA *run hurriedly.*].

MAGDALENA. Let's go see him!

[*They leave rapidly.*]

SERVANT [*to* ADELA]. Aren't you going?

ADELA. It's nothing to me.

SERVANT. Since he has to turn the corner, you'll see him better from the window of your room.

[THE SERVANT *goes out.* ADELA *is left on the stage, standing doubtfully; after a moment, she also leaves rapidly, going toward her room.* BERNARDA *and* LA PONCIA *come in.*]

BERNARDA. Damned portions and shares.

PONCIA. What a lot of money is left to Angustias!

BERNARDA. Yes.

PONCIA. And for the others, considerably less.

BERNARDA. You've told me that three times now, when you know I don't want it mentioned! Considerably less; a lot less! Don't remind me any more.

[ANGUSTIAS *comes in, her face heavily made up.*]

Angustias!

ANGUSTIAS. Mother.

BERNARDA. Have you dared to powder your face? Have you dared to wash your face on the day of your father's death?

ANGUSTIAS. He wasn't my father. Mine died a long time ago. Have you forgotten that already?

BERNARDA. You owe more to this man, father of your sisters, than to your own. Thanks to him, your fortune is intact.

ANGUSTIAS. We'll have to see about that first!

BERNARDA. Even out of decency! Out of respect!

ANGUSTIAS. Let me go out, Mother!

BERNARDA. Let you go out? After I've taken that powder off your face, I will. Spineless! Painted hussy! Just like your Aunts! [*She removes the powder violently with her handkerchief.*] Now get out!

PONCIA. Bernarda, don't be so hateful!

BERNARDA. Even though my mother is crazy, I still have my five senses and I know what I'm doing.

[*They all enter.*]

MAGDALENA. What's going on here?

BERNARDA. Nothing's "going on here"!

MAGDALENA [*to* ANGUSTIAS]. If you're fighting over the inheritance, you're the richest one and can hang on to it all.

ANGUSTIAS. Keep your tongue in your pocketbook!

BERNARDA [*beating on the floor*]. Don't fool yourselves into thinking you'll sway me. Until I go out of this house feet first I'll give the orders for myself and for you!

[*Voices are heard and* MARIA JOSEFA, BERNARDA'S *mother, enters. She is very old and has decked out her head and breast with flowers.*]

MARIA JOSEFA. Bernarda, where is my mantilla? Nothing, nothing of what I own will be for any of you. Not my rings nor my black moiré dress. Because not a one of you is going to marry—not a one. Bernarda, give me my necklace of pearls.

BERNARDA [*to* THE SERVANT]. Why did you let her get in here?

SERVANT [*trembling*]. She got away from me!

MARIA JOSEFA. I ran away because I want to marry—I want to get married to a beautiful manly man from the shore of the sea. Because here the men run from women.

BERNARDA. Hush, hush, Mother!

MARIA JOSEFA. No, no—I won't hush. I don't want to see these single women, longing for marriage, turning their hearts to dust; and I want to go to my home town. Bernarda, I want a man to get married to and be happy with!

BERNARDA. Lock her up!

MARIA JOSEFA. Let me go out, Bernarda!

[THE SERVANT *seizes* MARIA JOSEFA.]

BERNARDA. Help her, all of you!

[*They all grab the old woman.*]

MARIA JOSEFA. I want to get away from here! Bernarda! To get married by the shore of the sea—by the shore of the sea!

QUICK CURTAIN

ACT II

A white room in BERNARDA'S *house. The doors on the left lead to the bedrooms.*

BERNARDA'S DAUGHTERS *are seated on low chairs, sewing.* MAGDALENA *is embroidering.* LA PONCIA *is with them.*

ANGUSTIAS. I've cut the third sheet.

MARTIRIO. That one goes to Amelia.

MAGDALENA. Angustias, shall I put Pepe's initials here too?

ANGUSTIAS [*dryly*]. No.

MAGDALENA [*calling*]. Adela, aren't you coming?

AMELIA. She's probably stretched out on the bed.

PONCIA. Something's wrong with that one. I find her restless, trembling, frightened—as if a lizard were between her breasts.

MARTIRIO. There's nothing, more or less, wrong with her than there is with all of us.

MAGDALENA. All of us except Angustias.

ANGUSTIAS. I feel fine, and anybody who doesn't like it can pop.

MAGDALENA. We all have to admit the nicest things about you are your figure and your tact.

ANGUSTIAS. Fortunately, I'll soon be out of this hell.

MAGDALENA. Maybe you won't get out!

MARTIRIO. Stop this talk!

ANGUSTIAS. Besides, a good dowry is better than dark eyes in one's face!

MAGDALENA. All you say just goes in one ear and out the other.

AMELIA [*to* LA PONCIA]. Open the patio door and see if we can get a bit of a breeze.

[LA PONCIA *opens the door.*]

MARTIRIO. Last night I couldn't sleep because of the heat.

AMELIA. Neither could I.

MAGDALENA. I got up for a bit of air. There was a black storm cloud and a few drops even fell.

PONCIA. It was one in the morning and the earth seemed to give off fire. I got up too. Angustias was still at the window with Pepe.

MAGDALENA [*with irony*]. That late? What time did he leave?

ANGUSTIAS. Why do you ask, if you saw him?

AMELIA. He must have left about one-thirty.

ANGUSTIAS. Yes. How did you know?

AMELIA. I heard him cough and heard his mare's hoofbeats.

PONCIA. But I heard him leave around four.

ANGUSTIAS. It must have been someone else!

PONCIA. No, I'm sure of it!

AMELIA. That's what it seemed to me, too.

MAGDALENA. That's very strange!

[*Pause.*]

PONCIA. Listen, Angustias, what did he say to you the first time he came by your window?

ANGUSTIAS. Nothing. What should he say? Just talked.

MARTIRIO. It's certainly strange that two people who never knew each other should suddenly meet at a window and be engaged.

ANGUSTIAS. Well, I didn't mind.

AMELIA. I'd have felt very strange about it.

ANGUSTIAS. No, because when a man comes to a window he knows, from all the busybodies who come and go and fetch and carry, that he's going to be told "yes."

MARTIRIO. All right, but he'd have to ask you.

ANGUSTIAS. Of course!

AMELIA [*inquisitively*]. And how did he ask you?

ANGUSTIAS. Why, no way:—"You know I'm after you. I need a good, well brought up woman, and that's you—if it's agreeable."

AMELIA. These things embarrass me!

ANGUSTIAS. They embarrass me too, but one has to go through it!

PONCIA. And did he say anything more?

ANGUSTIAS. Yes, he did all the talking.

MARTIRIO. And you?

ANGUSTIAS. I couldn't have said a word. My heart was almost coming out of my mouth. It was the first time I'd ever been alone at night with a man.

MAGDALENA. And such a handsome man.

ANGUSTIAS. He's not bad looking.

PONCIA. Those things happen among people who have an idea how to do things, who talk and say and move their hand. The first time my husband, Evaristo the Short-tailed, came to my window . . . Ha! Ha! Ha!

AMELIA. What happened?

PONCIA. It was very dark. I saw him coming along and as he went by he said, "Good evening." "Good evening," I said. Then we were both silent for more than half an hour. The sweat poured down my body. Then Evaristo got nearer and nearer as if he wanted to squeeze in through the bars and said in a very low voice—"Come here and let me feel you!"

[*They all laugh.* AMELIA *gets up, runs, and looks through the door.*]

AMELIA. Ay, I thought Mother was coming!

MAGDALENA. What she'd have done to us!

[*They go on laughing.*]

AMELIA. Sh-h-h! She'll hear us.

PONCIA. Then he acted very decently. Instead of getting some other idea, he went to raising birds, until he died. You aren't married but it's good for you to know, anyway, that two weeks after the wedding a man gives up the bed for the table, then the table for the tavern, and the woman who doesn't like it can just rot, weeping in a corner.

AMELIA. You liked it.

PONCIA. I learned how to handle him!

MARTIRIO. Is it true that you sometimes hit him?

PONCIA. Yes, and once I almost poked out one of his eyes!

MAGDALENA. All women ought to be like that!

PONCIA. I'm one of your mother's school. One time I don't know what he said to me, and then I killed all his birds—with the pestle!

[*They laugh.*]

MAGDALENA. Adela, child! Don't miss this.

AMELIA. Adela!

[*Pause.*]

MAGDALENA. I'll go see! [*She goes out.*]

PONCIA. That child is sick!

MARTIRIO. Of course. She hardly sleeps!

PONCIA. What *does* she do, then?

MARTIRIO. How do I know what she does?

PONCIA. You probably know better than we do, since you sleep with just a wall between you.

ANGUSTIAS. Envy gnaws on people.

AMELIA. Don't exaggerate.

ANGUSTIAS. I can tell it in her eyes. She's getting the look of a crazy woman.

MARTIRIO. Don't talk about crazy women. This is one place you're not allowed to say that word.

[MAGDALENA *and* ADELA *enter.*]

MAGDALENA. Didn't you say she was asleep?

ADELA. My body aches.

MARTIRIO [*with a hidden meaning*]. Didn't you sleep well last night?

ADELA. Yes.

MARTIRIO. Then?

ADELA [*loudly*]. Leave me alone. Awake or asleep, it's no affair of yours. I'll do whatever I want to with my body.

MARTIRIO. I was just concerned about you!

ADELA. Concerned?—curious! Weren't you sewing? Well, continue! I wish I were invisible so I could pass through a room without being asked where I was going!

SERVANT [*entering*]. Bernarda is calling you. The man with the laces is here.

[*All but* ADELA *and* LA PONCIA *go out, and as* MARTIRIO *leaves, she looks fixedly at* ADELA.]

ADELA. Don't look at me like that! If you want, I'll give you my eyes, for they're younger, and my back to improve that hump you have, but look the other way when I go by.

PONCIA. Adela, she's your sister, and the one who most loves you besides!

ADELA. She follows me everywhere. Sometimes she looks in my room to see if I'm sleeping. She won't let me breathe, and always, "Too bad about that face!" "Too bad about that body! It's going to waste!" But I won't let that happen. My body will be for whomever I choose.

PONCIA [*insinuatingly, in a low voice*]. For Pepe el Romano, no?

ADELA [*frightened*]. What do you mean?

PONCIA. What I said, Adela!

ADELA. Shut up!

PONCIA [*loudly*]. Don't you think I've noticed?

ADELA. Lower your voice!

PONCIA. Then forget what you're thinking about!

ADELA. What do you know?

PONCIA. We old ones can see through walls. Where do you go when you get up at night?

ADELA. I wish you were blind!

PONCIA. But my head and hands are full of eyes, where something like this is concerned. I couldn't possibly guess your intentions. Why did you sit almost naked at your window, and with the light on and the window open, when Pepe passed by the second night he came to talk with your sister?

ADELA. That's not true!

PONCIA. Don't be a child! Leave your sister alone. And if you like Pepe el Romano, keep it to yourself. [ADELA *weeps.*] Besides, who says you can't marry him? Your sister Angustias is sickly. She'll die with her first child. Narrow waisted, old—and out of my experience I can tell you she'll die. Then Pepe will do what all widowers do in these parts: he'll marry the youngest and most beautiful, and that's you. Live on that hope, forget him, anything; but don't go against God's law.

ADELA. Hush!

PONCIA. I won't hush!

ADELA. Mind your own business. Snooper, traitor!

PONCIA. I'm going to stick to you like a shadow!

ADELA. Instead of cleaning the house and then going to bed and praying for the dead, you root around like an old sow about goings on between men and women—so you can drool over them.

PONCIA. I keep watch; so people won't spit when they pass our door.

ADELA. What a tremendous affection you've suddenly conceived for my sister.

PONCIA. I don't have any affection for any of you. I want to live in a decent house. I don't want to be dirtied in my old age!

ADELA. Save your advice. It's already too late. For I'd leap not over you, just a servant, but over my mother to put out this fire I feel in my legs and my mouth. What can you possibly say about me? That I lock myself in my room and will not open the door? That I don't sleep? I'm smarter than you! See if you can catch the hare with your hands.

PONCIA. Don't defy me, Adela, don't defy me! Because I can shout, light lamps, and make bells ring.

ADELA. Bring four thousand yellow flares and set them about the walls of the yard. No one can stop what has to happen.

PONCIA. You like him that much?

ADELA. That much! Looking in his eyes I seem to drink his blood in slowly.

PONCIA. I won't listen to you.

ADELA. Well, you'll have to! I've been afraid of you. But now I'm stronger than you!

[ANGUSTIAS *enters.*]

ANGUSTIAS. Always arguing!

PONCIA. Certainly. She insists that in all this heat I have to go bring her I don't know what from the store.

ANGUSTIAS. Did you buy me the bottle of perfume?

PONCIA. The most expensive one. And the face powder. I put them on the table in your room.

[ANGUSTIAS *goes out.*]

ADELA. And be quiet!

PONCIA. We'll see!

[MARTIRIO *and* AMELIA *enter.*]

MARTIRIO [*to* ADELA]. Did you see the laces?

AMELIA. Angustias', for her wedding sheets, are beautiful.

ADELA [*to* MARTIRIO, *who is carrying some lace*]. And these?

MARTIRIO. They're for me. For a nightgown.

ADELA [*with sarcasm*]. One needs a sense of humor around here!

MARTIRIO [*meaningfully*]. But only for me to look at. I don't have to exhibit myself before anybody.

PONCIA. No one ever sees us in our nightgowns.

MARTIRIO [*meaningfully, looking at* ADELA]. Sometimes they don't! But I love nice underwear. If I were rich, I'd have it made of

Holland Cloth. It's one of the few tastes I've left.

PONCIA. These laces are beautiful for babies' caps and christening gowns. I could never afford them for my own. Now let's see if Angustias will use them for hers. Once she starts having children, they'll keep her running night and day.

MAGDALENA. I don't intend to sew a stitch on them.

AMELIA. And much less bring up some stranger's children. Look how our neighbors across the road are—making sacrifices for four brats.

PONCIA. They're better off than you. There at least they laugh and you can hear them fight.

MARTIRIO. Well, you go work for them, then.

PONCIA. No, fate has sent me to this nunnery!

[*Tiny bells are heard distantly as though through several thicknesses of wall.*]

MAGDALENA. It's the men going back to work.

PONCIA. It was three o'clock a minute ago.

MARTIRIO. With this sun!

ADELA [*sitting down*]. Ay! If only we could go out in the fields too!

MAGDALENA [*sitting down*]. Each class does what it has to!

MARTIRIO [*sitting down*]. That's it!

AMELIA [*sitting down*]. Ay!

PONCIA. There's no happiness like that in the fields right at this time of year. Yesterday morning the reapers arrived. Forty or fifty handsome young men.

MAGDALENA. Where are they from this year?

PONCIA. From far, far away. They came from the mountains! Happy! Like weathered trees! Shouting and throwing stones! Last night a woman who dresses in sequins and dances, with an accordion, arrived, and fifteen of them made a deal with her to take her to the olive grove. I saw them from far away. The one who talked with her was a boy with green eyes—tight knit as a sheaf of wheat.

AMELIA. Really?

ADELA. Are you sure?

PONCIA. Years ago another one of those women came here, and I myself gave my eldest son some money so he could go. Men need things like that.

ADELA. Everything's forgiven *them*.

AMELIA. To be born a woman's the worst possible punishment.

MAGDALENA. Even our eyes aren't our own.

[*A distant song is heard, coming nearer.*]

PONCIA. There they are. They have a beautiful song.

AMELIA. They're going out to reap now.

CHORUS.

The reapers have set out
Looking for ripe wheat;
They'll carry off the hearts
Of any girls they meet.

[*Tambourines and carrañacas are heard. Pause. They all listen in the silence cut by the sun.*]

AMELIA. And they don't mind the sun!

MARTIRIO. They reap through flames.

ADELA. How I'd like to be a reaper so I could come and go as I pleased. Then we could forget what's eating us all.

MARTIRIO. What do you have to forget?

ADELA. Each one of us has something.

MARTIRIO [*intensely*]. Each one!

PONCIA. Quiet! Quiet!

CHORUS [*very distantly*].

Throw wide your doors and windows,
You girls who live in the town.
The reaper asks you for roses
With which to deck his crown.

PONCIA. What a song!

MARTIRIO [*with nostalgia*].

Throw wide your doors and windows,
You girls who live in the town.

ADELA [*passionately*].

The reaper asks you for roses
With which to deck his crown.

[*The song grows more distant.*]

PONCIA. Now they're turning the corner.

ADELA. Let's watch them from the window of my room.

PONCIA. Be careful not to open the shutters too much because they're likely to give them a push to see who's looking.

273 carrañacas noise-makers (?)

[*The three leave.* MARTIRIO *is left sitting on the low chair with her head between her hands.*]

AMELIA [*drawing near her*]. What's wrong with you?

MARTIRIO. The heat makes me feel ill.

AMELIA. And it's no more than that?

MARTIRIO. I was wishing it were November, the rainy days, the frost—anything except this unending summertime.

AMELIA. It'll pass and come again.

MARTIRIO. Naturally. [*Pause.*] What time did you go to sleep last night?

AMELIA. I don't know. I sleep like a log. Why?

MARTIRIO. Nothing. Only I thought I heard someone in the yard.

AMELIA. Yes?

MARTIRIO. Very late.

AMELIA. And weren't you afraid?

MARTIRIO. No. I've heard it other nights.

AMELIA. We'd better watch out! Couldn't it have been the shepherds?

MARTIRIO. The shepherds come at six.

AMELIA. Maybe a young, unbroken mule?

MARTIRIO [*to herself, with double meaning*]. That's it! That's it. An unbroken little mule.

AMELIA. We'll have to set a watch.

MARTIRIO. No. No. Don't say anything. It may be I've just imagined it.

AMELIA. Maybe.

[*Pause.* AMELIA *starts to go.*]

MARTIRIO. Amelia!

AMELIA [*at the door*]. What?

[*Pause.*]

MARTIRIO. Nothing.

[*Pause.*]

AMELIA. Why did you call me?

[*Pause.*]

MARTIRIO. It just came out. I didn't mean to.

[*Pause.*]

AMELIA. Lie down for a little.

ANGUSTIAS. [*She bursts in furiously, in a manner that makes a great contrast with previous silence.*] Where's that picture of Pepe I had under my pillow? Which one of you has it?

MARTIRIO. No one.

AMELIA. You'd think he was a silver St. Bartholomew.

ANGUSTIAS. Where's the picture?

[PONCIA, MAGDALENA *and* ADELA *enter.*]

ADELA. What picture?

ANGUSTIAS. One of you has hidden it on me.

MAGDALENA. Do you have the effrontery to say that?

ANGUSTIAS. I had it in my room, and now it isn't there.

MARTIRIO. But couldn't it have jumped out into the yard at midnight? Pepe likes to walk around in the moonlight.

ANGUSTIAS. Don't joke with me! When he comes I'll tell him.

PONCIA. Don't do that! Because it'll turn up. [*looking at* ADELA]

ANGUSTIAS. I'd like to know which one of you has it.

ADELA [*looking at* MARTIRIO]. Somebody has it! But not me!

MARTIRIO [*with meaning*]. Of course not you!

BERNARDA [*entering, with her cane*]. What scandal is this in my house in the heat's heavy silence? The neighbors must have their ears glued to the walls.

ANGUSTIAS. They've stolen my sweetheart's picture!

BERNARDA [*fiercely*]. Who? Who?

ANGUSTIAS. They have!

BERNARDA. Which one of you? [*Silence.*] Answer me! [*Silence.*] [*to* LA PONCIA] Search their rooms! Look in their beds. This comes of not tying you up with shorter leashes. But I'll teach you now! [*to* ANGUSTIAS] Are you sure?

ANGUSTIAS. Yes.

BERNARDA. Did you look everywhere?

ANGUSTIAS. Yes, Mother.

[*They all stand in an embarrassed silence.*]

BERNARDA. At the end of my life—to make me drink the bitterest poison a mother knows. [*to* PONCIA] Did you find it?

PONCIA. Here it is.

BERNARDA. Where did you find it?

PONCIA. It was . . .

363 **Look in their beds** Poncia goes out, and re-enters at l. 371

BERNARDA. Say it! Don't be afraid.

PONCIA [*wonderingly*]. Between the sheets in Martirio's bed.

BERNARDA [*to* MARTIRIO]. Is that true?

MARTIRIO. It's true.

BERNARDA [*advancing on her, beating her with her cane*]. You'll come to a bad end yet, you hypocrite! Trouble maker!

MARTIRIO [*fiercely*]. Don't hit me, Mother!

BERNARDA. All I want to!

MARTIRIO. If I let you! You hear me? Get back!

PONCIA. Don't be disrespectful to your mother!

ANGUSTIAS [*holding* BERNARDA]. Let her go, please!

BERNARDA. Not even tears in your eyes.

MARTIRIO. I'm not going to cry just to please you.

BERNARDA. Why did you take the picture?

MARTIRIO. Can't I play a joke on my sister? What else would I want it for?

ADELA [*leaping forward, full of jealousy*]. It wasn't a joke! You never liked to play jokes. It was something else bursting in her breast —trying to come out. Admit it openly now.

MARTIRIO. Hush, and don't make me speak; for if I should speak the walls would close together one against the other with shame.

ADELA. An evil tongue never stops inventing lies.

BERNARDA. Adela!

MAGDALENA. You're crazy.

AMELIA. And you stone us all with your evil suspicions.

MARTIRIO. But some others do things more wicked!

ADELA. Until all at once they stand forth stark naked and the river carries them along.

BERNARDA. Spiteful!

ANGUSTIAS. It's not my fault Pepe el Romano chose me!

ADELA. For your money.

ANGUSTIAS. Mother!

BERNARDA. Silence!

MARTIRIO. For your fields and your orchards.

MAGDALENA. That's only fair.

BERNARDA. Silence, I say! I saw the storm coming but I didn't think it'd burst so soon. Oh, what an avalanche of hate you've thrown on my heart! But I'm not old yet—I have five chains for you, and this house my father built, so not even the weeds will know of my desolation. Out of here!

[*They go out.* BERNARDA *sits down desolately.* LA PONCIA *is standing close to the wall.* BERNARDA *recovers herself, and beats on the floor.*]

I'll have to let them feel the weight of my hand! Bernarda, remember your duty!

PONCIA. May I speak?

BERNARDA. Speak. I'm sorry you heard. A stranger is always out of place in a family.

PONCIA. What I've seen, I've seen.

BERNARDA. Angustias must get married right away.

PONCIA. Certainly. We'll have to get her away from here.

BERNARDA. Not her, him!

PONCIA. Of course. He's the one to get away from here. You've thought it all out.

BERNARDA. I'm not thinking. There are things that shouldn't and can't be thought out. I give orders.

PONCIA. And you think he'll be satisfied to go away?

BERNARDA [*rising*]. What are you imagining now?

PONCIA. He will, of course, marry Angustias.

BERNARDA. Speak up! I know you well enough to see that your knife's out for me.

PONCIA. I never knew a warning could be called murder.

BERNARDA. Have you some "warning" for me?

PONCIA. I'm not making any accusations, Bernarda. I'm only telling you to open your eyes and you'll see.

BERNARDA. See what?

PONCIA. You've always been smart, Bernarda. You've seen other people's sins a hundred miles away. Many times I've thought you could read minds. But, your children are your children, and now you're blind.

BERNARDA. Are you talking about Martirio?

PONCIA. Well, yes—about Martirio . . . [*with curiosity*] I wonder why she hid the picture?

BERNARDA [*shielding her daughter*]. After all, she says it was a joke. What else could it be?

PONCIA [*scornfully*]. Do you believe that?

BERNARDA [*sternly*]. I don't merely believe it. It's so!

PONCIA. Enough of this. We're talking about your family. But if we were talking about your neighbor across the way, what would it be?

BERNARDA. Now you're beginning to pull the point of the knife out.

PONCIA [*always cruelly*]. No, Bernarda. Something very grave is happening here. I don't want to put the blame on your shoulders, but you've never given your daughters any freedom. Martirio is lovesick, I don't care what you say. Why didn't you let her marry Enrique Humanas? Why, on the very day he was coming to her window, did you send him a message not to come?

BERNARDA [*loudly*]. I'd do it a thousand times over! My blood won't mingle with the Humanas' while I live! His father was a shepherd.

PONCIA. And you see now what's happening to you with these airs!

BERNARDA. I have them because I can afford to. And you don't have them because you know where you came from!

PONCIA [*with hate*]. Don't remind me! I'm old now. I've always been grateful for your protection.

BERNARDA [*emboldened*]. You don't seem so!

PONCIA [*with hate, behind softness*]. Martirio will forget this.

BERNARDA. And if she doesn't—the worse for her. I don't believe this is that "very grave thing" that's happening here. Nothing's happening here. It's just that you wish it would! And if it should happen one day, you can be sure it won't go beyond these walls.

PONCIA. I'm not so sure of that! There are people in town who can also read hidden thoughts, from afar.

BERNARDA. How you'd like to see me and my daughters on our way to a whorehouse!

PONCIA. No one knows her own destiny!

BERNARDA. I know my destiny! And my daughters! The whorehouse was for a certain woman, already dead. . . .

PONCIA [*fiercely*]. Bernarda, respect the memory of my mother!

BERNARDA. Then don't plague me with your evil thoughts! [*Pause.*]

PONCIA. I'd better stay out of everything.

BERNARDA. That's what you ought to do. Work and keep your mouth shut. The duty of all who work for a living.

PONCIA. But we can't do that. Don't you think it'd be better for Pepe to marry Martirio or . . . yes! . . . Adela?

BERNARDA. No, I *don't* think so.

PONCIA [*with meaning*]. Adela! She's Romano's real sweetheart!

BERNARDA. Things are never the way we want them!

PONCIA. But it's hard work to turn them from their destined course. For Pepe to be with Angustias seems wrong to me—and to other people—and even to the wind. Who knows if they'll get what they want?

BERNARDA. There you go again! Sneaking up on me—giving me bad dreams. But I won't listen to you, because if all you say should come to pass—I'd scratch your face.

PONCIA. Frighten someone else with that.

BERNARDA. Fortunately, my daughters respect me and have never gone against my will!

PONCIA. That's right! But, as soon as they break loose they'll fly to the rooftops!

BERNARDA. And I'll bring them down with stones!

PONCIA. Oh, yes! You were always the bravest one!

BERNARDA. I've always enjoyed a good fight!

PONCIA. But aren't people strange. You should see Angustias' enthusiasm for her lover, at her age! And he seems very smitten too. Yesterday my oldest son told me that when he passed by with the oxen at four-thirty in the morning they were still talking.

BERNARDA. At four-thirty?

ANGUSTIAS [*entering*]. That's a lie!

PONCIA. That's what he told me.

BERNARDA [*to* ANGUSTIAS]. Speak up!

ANGUSTIAS. For more than a week Pepe has been leaving at one. May God strike me dead if I'm lying.

MARTIRIO [*entering*]. I heard him leave at four too.

BERNARDA. But did you see him with your eyes?

MARTIRIO. I didn't want to look out. Don't you talk now through the side window?

ANGUSTIAS. We talk through my bedroom window.

[ADELA *appears at the door.*]

MARTIRIO. Then . . .

BERNARDA. What's going on here?

PONCIA. If you're not careful, you'll find out! At least Pepe was at *one* of your windows—and at four in the morning too!

BERNARDA. Are you sure of that?

PONCIA. You can't be sure of anything in this life!

ADELA. Mother, don't listen to someone who wants us to lose everything we have.

BERNARDA. I know how to take care of myself! If the townspeople want to come bearing false witness against me, they'll run into a stone wall! Don't any of you talk about this! Sometimes other people try to stir up a wave of filth to drown us.

MARTIRIO. I don't like to lie.

PONCIA. So there must be something.

BERNARDA. There won't be anything. I was born to have my eyes always open. Now I'll watch without closing them 'til I die.

ANGUSTIAS. I have the right to know.

BERNARDA. You don't have any right except to obey. No one's going to fetch and carry for me. [*to* LA PONCIA] And don't meddle in our affairs. No one will take a step without my knowing it.

SERVANT [*entering*]. There's a big crowd at the top of the street, and all the neighbors are at their doors!

BERNARDA [*to* PONCIA]. Run see what's happening!

[*The Girls are about to run out.*]

Where are you going? I always knew you for window-watching women and breakers of your mourning. All of you, to the patio!

[*They go out.* BERNARDA *leaves. Distant shouts are heard.* MARTIRIO *and* ADELA *enter and listen, not daring to step farther than the front door.*]

MARTIRIO. You can be thankful I didn't happen to open my mouth.

ADELA. I would have spoken too.

MARTIRIO. And what were you going to say? Wanting isn't doing!

ADELA. I do what I can and what happens to suit me. You've wanted to, but haven't been able.

MARTIRIO. You won't go on very long.

ADELA. I'll have everything!

MARTIRIO. I'll tear you out of his arms!

ADELA [*pleadingly*]. Martirio, let me be!

MARTIRIO. None of us will have him!

ADELA. He wants me for his house!

MARTIRIO. I saw how he embraced you!

ADELA. I didn't want him to. It's as if I were dragged by a rope.

MARTIRIO. I'll see you dead first!

[MAGDALENA *and* ANGUSTIAS *look in. The tumult is increasing.* THE SERVANT *enters with* BERNARDA. PONCIA *also enters from another door.*]

PONCIA. Bernarda!

BERNARDA. What's happening?

PONCIA. Librada's daughter, the unmarried one, had a child and no one knows whose it is!

ADELA. A child?

PONCIA. And to hide her shame she killed it and hid it under the rocks, but the dogs, with more heart than most Christians, dug it out and, as though directed by the hand of God, left it at her door. Now they want to kill her. They're dragging her through the streets—and down the paths and across the olive groves the men are coming, shouting so the fields shake.

BERNARDA. Yes, let them all come with olive whips and hoe handles—let them all come and kill her!

ADELA. No, not to kill her!

MARTIRIO. Yes—and let us go out too!

BERNARDA. And let whoever loses her decency pay for it!

[*Outside a woman's shriek and a great clamor is heard.*]

ADELA. Let her escape! Don't you go out!

MARTIRIO [*looking at* ADELA]. Let her pay what she owes!

BERNARDA [*at the archway*]. Finish her before the guards come! Hot coals in the place where she sinned!

ADELA [*holding her belly*]. No! No!

BERNARDA. Kill her! Kill her!

CURTAIN

ACT III

Four white walls, lightly washed in blue, of the interior patio of BERNARDA ALBA'S *house. The doorways, illumined by the lights inside the rooms, give a tenuous glow to the stage.*

At the center there is a table with a shaded oil lamp about which BERNARDA *and her* DAUGHTERS *are eating.* LA PONCIA *serves them.* PRUDENCIA *sits apart. When the curtain rises, there is a great silence interrupted only by the noise of plates and silverware.*

PRUDENCIA. I'm going. I've made you a long visit. [*She rises.*]

BERNARDA. But wait, Prudencia. We never see one another.

PRUDENCIA. Have they sounded the last call to rosary?

PONCIA. Not yet.

[PRUDENCIA *sits down again.*]

BERNARDA. And your husband, how's he getting on?

PRUDENCIA. The same.

BERNARDA. We never see him either.

PRUDENCIA. You know how he is. Since he quarrelled with his brothers over the inheritance, he hasn't used the front door. He takes a ladder and climbs over the back wall.

BERNARDA. He's a real man! And your daughter?

PRUDENCIA. He's never forgiven her.

BERNARDA. He's right.

PRUDENCIA. I don't know what he told you. I suffer because of it.

BERNARDA. A daughter who's disobedient stops being a daughter and becomes an enemy.

PRUDENCIA. I let water run. The only consolation I've left is to take refuge in the church, but, since I'm losing my sight, I'll have to stop coming so the children won't make fun of me.

[*A heavy blow is heard against the walls.*]

What's that?

BERNARDA. The stallion. He's locked in the stall and he kicks against the wall of the house. [*shouting*] Tether him and take him out in the yard! [*in a lower voice*] He must be too hot.

PRUDENCIA. Are you going to put the new mares to him?

BERNARDA. At daybreak.

PRUDENCIA. You've known how to increase your stock.

BERNARDA. By dint of money and struggling.

PONCIA [*interrupting*]. And she has the best herd in these parts. It's a shame that prices are low.

BERNARDA. Do you want a little cheese and honey?

PRUDENCIA. I have no appetite.

[*The blow is heard again.*]

PONCIA. My God!

PRUDENCIA. It quivered in my chest!

BERNARDA [*rising, furiously*]. Do I have to say things twice? Let him out to roll on the straw. [*Pause. Then, as though speaking to the Stableman*] Well, then lock the mares in the corral, but let him run free or he may kick down the walls. [*She returns to the table and sits again.*] Ay, what a life!

PRUDENCIA. You have to fight like a man.

BERNARDA. That's it.

[ADELA *gets up from the table.*]

Where are you going?

ADELA. For a drink of water.

BERNARDA [*raising her voice*]. Bring a pitcher of cool water. [*to* ADELA] You can sit down.

[ADELA *sits down.*]

PRUDENCIA. And Angustias, when will she get married?

BERNARDA. They're coming to ask for her within three days.

PRUDENCIA. You must be happy.

ANGUSTIAS. Naturally!

AMELIA [*to* MAGDALENA]. You've spilled the salt!

MAGDALENA. You can't possibly have worse luck than you're having.

AMELIA. It always brings bad luck.

BERNARDA. That's enough!

PRUDENCIA [*to* ANGUSTIAS]. Has he given you the ring yet?

ANGUSTIAS. Look at it. [*She holds it out.*]

PRUDENCIA. It's beautiful. Three pearls. In my day, pearls signified tears.

ANGUSTIAS. But things have changed now.

ADELA. I don't think so. Things go on meaning the same. Engagement rings should be diamonds.

PONCIA. The most appropriate.

BERNARDA. With pearls or without them, things are as one proposes.

MARTIRIO. Or as God disposes.

PRUDENCIA. I've been told your furniture is beautiful.

BERNARDA. It cost sixteen thousand *reales.*

PONCIA [*interrupting*]. The best is the wardrobe with the mirror.

PRUDENCIA. I never saw a piece like that.

BERNARDA. We had chests.

PRUDENCIA. The important thing is that everything be for the best.

ADELA. And that you never know.

BERNARDA. There's no reason why it shouldn't be.

[*Bells are heard very distantly.*]

PRUDENCIA. The last call. [*to* ANGUSTIAS] I'll be coming back to have you show me your clothes.

ANGUSTIAS. Whenever you like.

PRUDENCIA. Good evening—God bless you!

BERNARDA. Good-bye, Prudencia.

ALL FIVE DAUGHTERS [*at the same time*]. God go with you!

[*Pause.* PRUDENCIA *goes out.*]

BERNARDA. Well, we've eaten.

[*They rise.*]

ADELA. I'm going to walk as far as the gate to stretch my legs and get a bit of fresh air.

[MAGDALENA *sits down in a low chair and leans against the wall.*]

AMELIA. I'll go with you.

MARTIRIO. I too.

ADELA [*with contained hate*]. I'm not going to get lost!

AMELIA. One needs company at night.

[*They go out.* BERNARDA *sits down.* ANGUSTIAS *is clearing the table.*]

BERNARDA. I've told you once already! I want you to talk to your sister Martirio. What happened about the picture was a joke and you must forget it.

ANGUSTIAS. You know she doesn't like me.

BERNARDA. Each one knows what she thinks inside. I don't pry into anyone's heart, but I want to put up a good front and have family harmony. You understand?

ANGUSTIAS. Yes.

BERNARDA. Then that's settled.

MAGDALENA. [*She is almost asleep.*] Besides, you'll be gone in no time. [*She falls asleep.*]

ANGUSTIAS. Not soon enough for me.

BERNARDA. What time did you stop talking last night?

ANGUSTIAS. Twelve-thirty.

BERNARDA. What does Pepe talk about?

ANGUSTIAS. I find him absent-minded. He always talks to me as though he were thinking of something else. If I ask him what's the matter, he answers—"We men have our worries."

BERNARDA. You shouldn't ask him. And when you're married, even less. Speak if he speaks, and look at him when he looks at you. That way you'll get along.

ANGUSTIAS. But, Mother, I think he's hiding things from me.

BERNARDA. Don't try to find out. Don't ask him, and above all, never let him see you cry.

ANGUSTIAS. I should be happy, but I'm not.

BERNARDA. It's all the same.

ANGUSTIAS. Many nights I watch Pepe very closely through the window bars and he seems to fade away—as though he were hidden in a cloud of dust like those raised by the flocks.

BERNARDA. That's just because you're not strong.

ANGUSTIAS. I hope so!

BERNARDA. Is he coming tonight?

ANGUSTIAS. No, he went into town with his mother.

BERNARDA. Good, we'll get to bed early. Magdalena!

ANGUSTIAS. She's asleep.

[ADELA, MARTIRIO *and* AMELIA *enter.*]

AMELIA. What a dark night!

ADELA. You can't see two steps in front of you.

MARTIRIO. A good night for robbers, for anyone who needs to hide.

ADELA. The stallion was in the middle of the corral. White. Twice as large. Filling all the darkness.

AMELIA. It's true. It was frightening. Like a ghost.

ADELA. The sky has stars as big as fists.

MARTIRIO. This one stared at them till she almost cracked her neck.

ADELA. Don't you like them up there?

MARTIRIO. What goes on over the roof doesn't mean a thing to me. I have my hands full with what happens under it.

ADELA. Well, that's the way it goes with you!

BERNARDA. And it goes the same for you as for her.

ANGUSTIAS. Good night.

ADELA. Are you going to bed now?

ANGUSTIAS. Yes, Pepe isn't coming tonight.

[*She goes out.*]

ADELA. Mother, why, when a star falls or lightning flashes, does one say:

Holy Barbara, blessed on high
May your name be in the sky
With holy water written high?

BERNARDA. The old people know many things we've forgotten.

AMELIA. I close my eyes so I won't see them.

ADELA. Not I. I like to see what's quiet and been quiet for years on end, running with fire.

MARTIRIO. But all that has nothing to do with us.

BERNARDA. And it's better not to think about it.

ADELA. What a beautiful night! I'd like to stay up till very late and enjoy the breeze from the fields.

BERNARDA. But we have to go to bed. Magdalena!

AMELIA. She's just dropped off.

BERNARDA. Magdalena!

MAGDALENA [*annoyed*]. Leave me alone!

BERNARDA. To bed!

MAGDALENA [*rising, in a bad humor*]. You don't give anyone a moment's peace!

[*She goes off grumbling.*]

AMELIA. Good night!

[*She goes out.*]

BERNARDA. You two get along, too.

MARTIRIO. How is it Angustias' sweetheart isn't coming tonight?

BERNARDA. He went on a trip.

MARTIRIO [*looking at* ADELA]. Ah!

ADELA. I'll see you in the morning!

[*She goes out.* MARTIRIO *drinks some water and goes out slowly, looking at the door to the yard.* LA PONCIA *enters.*]

PONCIA. Are you still here?

BERNARDA. Enjoying this quiet and not seeing anywhere the "very grave thing" that's happening here—according to you.

PONCIA. Bernarda, let's not go any further with this.

BERNARDA. In this house there's no question of a yes or a no. My watchfulness can take care of anything.

PONCIA. Nothing's happening outside. That's true, all right. Your daughters act and are as though stuck in a cupboard. But neither you nor anyone else can keep watch inside a person's heart.

BERNARDA. My daughters breathe calmly enough.

PONCIA. That's your business, since you're their mother. I have enough to do just with serving you.

BERNARDA. Yes, you've turned quiet now.

PONCIA. I keep my place—that's all.

BERNARDA. The trouble is you've nothing to talk about. If there were grass in this house, you'd make it your business to put the neighbors' sheep to pasture here.

PONCIA. I hide more than you think.

BERNARDA. Do your sons still see Pepe at four in the morning? Are they still repeating this house's evil litany?

PONCIA. They say nothing.

BERNARDA. Because they can't. Because there's nothing for them to sink their teeth in. And all because my eyes keep constant watch!

PONCIA. Bernarda, I don't want to talk about this because I'm afraid of what you'll do. But don't you feel so safe.

BERNARDA. Very safe!

PONCIA. Who knows, lightning might strike suddenly. Who knows but what all of a sudden, in a rush of blood, your heart might stop.

BERNARDA. Nothing will happen here. I'm on guard now against all your suspicions.

PONCIA. All the better for you.

BERNARDA. Certainly, all the better!

SERVANT [*entering*]. I've just finished with the dishes. Is there anything else, Bernarda?

BERNARDA [*rising*]. Nothing. I'm going to get some rest.

PONCIA. What time do you want me to call you?

BERNARDA. No time. Tonight I intend to sleep well.

[*She goes out.*]

PONCIA. When you're powerless against the sea, it's easier to turn your back on it and not look at it.

SERVANT. She's so proud! She herself pulls the blindfold over her eyes.

PONCIA. I can do nothing. I tried to head things off, but now they frighten me too much. You feel this silence?—in each room there's a thunderstorm—and the day it breaks, it'll sweep all of us along with it. But I've said what I had to say.

SERVANT. Bernarda thinks nothing can stand against her, yet she doesn't know the strength a man has among women alone.

PONCIA. It's not all the fault of Pepe el Romano. It's true last year he was running after Adela; and she was crazy about him—but she ought to keep her place and not lead him on. A man's a man.

SERVANT. And some there are who believe he didn't have to talk many times with Adela.

PONCIA. That's true. [*in a low voice*] And some other things.

SERVANT. I don't know what's going to happen here.

PONCIA. How I'd like to sail across the sea and leave this house, this battleground, behind!

SERVANT. Bernarda's hurrying the wedding and it's possible nothing will happen.

PONCIA. Things have gone much too far already. Adela is set no matter what comes, and the rest of them watch without rest.

SERVANT. Martirio too . . . ?

PONCIA. That one's the worst. She's a pool of poison. She sees El Romano is not for her, and she'd sink the world if it were in her hand to do so.

SERVANT. How bad they all are!

PONCIA. They're women without men, that's all. And in such matters even blood is forgotten. Sh-h-h-h! [*She listens.*]

SERVANT. What's the matter?

PONCIA. [*She rises.*] The dogs are barking.

SERVANT. Someone must have passed by the back door.

[ADELA *enters wearing a white petticoat and corselet.*]

251 **is set** i.e., has made up her mind

PONCIA. Aren't you in bed yet?

ADELA. I want a drink of water. [*She drinks from a glass on the table.*]

PONCIA. I imagined you were asleep.

ADELA. I got thirsty and woke up. Aren't you two going to get some rest?

SERVANT. Soon now.

[ADELA *goes out.*]

PONCIA. Let's go.

SERVANT. We've certainly earned some sleep. Bernarda doesn't let me rest the whole day.

PONCIA. Take the light.

SERVANT. The dogs are going mad.

PONCIA. They're not going to let us sleep.

[*They go out. The stage is left almost dark.* MARIA JOSEFA *enters with a lamb in her arms.*]

MARIA JOSEFA [*singing*].

Little lamb, child of mine,
Let's go to the shore of the sea,
The tiny ant will be at his doorway,
I'll nurse you and give you your bread.
Bernarda, old leopard-face,
And Magdalena, hyena-face,
Little lamb . . .
Rock, rock-a-bye,
Let's go to the palms at Bethlehem's gate.

[*She laughs.*]

Neither you nor I would want to sleep
The door will open by itself
And on the beach we'll go and hide
In a little coral cabin.
Bernarda, old leopard-face,
And Magdalena, hyena-face,
Little lamb . . .
Rock, rock-a-bye,
Let's go to the palms at Bethlehem's gate.

[*She goes off singing.*]

[ADELA *enters. She looks about cautiously and disappears out the door leading to the corral.* MARTIRIO *enters by another door and stands in anguished watchfulness near the center of the stage. She also is in petticoats. She covers herself with a small black scarf.* MARIA JOSEFA *crosses before her.*]

MARTIRIO. Grandmother, where are you going?

MARIA JOSEFA. You are going to open the door for me? Who are you?

MARTIRIO. How did you get out here?

MARIA JOSEFA. I escaped. You, who are you?

MARTIRIO. Go back to bed.

MARIA JOSEFA. You're Martirio. Now I see you. Martirio, face of a martyr. And when are you going to have a baby? I've had this one.

MARTIRIO. Where did you get that lamb?

MARIA JOSEFA. I know it's a lamb. But can't a lamb be a baby? It's better to have a lamb than not to have anything. Old Bernarda, leopard-face, and Magdalena, hyena-face!

MARTIRIO. Don't shout.

MARIA JOSEFA. It's true. Everything's very dark. Just because I have white hair you think I can't have babies, but I can—babies and babies and babies. This baby will have white hair, and I'd have *this* baby, and another, and this *one* other; and with all of us with snow white hair we'll be like the waves—one, then another, and another. Then we'll all sit down and all of us will have white heads, and we'll be seafoam. Why isn't there any seafoam here? Nothing but mourning shrouds here.

MARTIRIO. Hush, hush.

MARIA JOSEFA. When my neighbor had a baby, I'd carry her some chocolate and later she'd bring me some, and so on—always and always and always. You'll have white hair, but your neighbors won't come. Now I have to go away, but I'm afraid the dogs will bite me. Won't you come with me as far as the fields? I don't like fields. I like houses, but open houses, and the neighbor women asleep in their beds with their little tiny tots, and the men outside sitting in their chairs. Pepe el Romano is a giant. All of you love him. But he's going to devour you because you're grains of wheat. No, not grains of wheat. Frogs with no tongues!

MARTIRIO [*angrily*]. Come, off to bed with you. [*She pushes her.*]

MARIA JOSEFA. Yes, but then you'll open the door for me, won't you?

MARTIRIO. Of course.

MARIA JOSEFA [*weeping*].

Little lamb, child of mine,
Let's go to the shore of the sea,
The tiny ant will be at his doorway,
I'll nurse you and give you your bread.

[MARTIRIO *locks the door through which* MARIA JOSEFA *came out and goes to the yard door. There she hesitates, but goes two steps farther.*]

MARTIRIO [*in a low voice*]. Adela! [*Pause. She advances to the door. Then, calling*] Adela!

[ADELA *enters. Her hair is disarranged.*]

ADELA. And what are you looking for me for?

MARTIRIO. Keep away from him.

ADELA. Who are you to tell me that?

MARTIRIO. That's no place for a decent woman.

ADELA. How you wish *you'd* been there!

MARTIRIO [*shouting*]. This is the moment for me to speak. This can't go on.

ADELA. This is just the beginning. I've had strength enough to push myself forward—the spirit and looks you lack. I've seen death under this roof, and gone out to look for what was mine, what belonged to me.

MARTIRIO. That soulless man came for another woman. You pushed yourself in front of him.

ADELA. He came for the money, but his eyes were always on me.

MARTIRIO. I won't allow you to snatch him away. He'll marry Angustias.

ADELA. You know better than I he doesn't love her.

MARTIRIO. I know.

ADELA. You know because you've seen—he loves me, me!

MARTIRIO [*desperately*]. Yes.

ADELA [*close before her*]. He loves me, *me!* He loves me, *me!*

MARTIRIO. Stick me with a knife if you like, but don't tell me that again.

ADELA. That's why you're trying to fix it so I won't go away with him. It makes no difference to you if he puts his arms around a woman he doesn't love. Nor does it to me. He could be a hundred years with Angustias, but for him to have his arms around me seems terrible to you—because you too love him! You love him!

MARTIRIO [*dramatically*]. Yes! Let me say it without hiding my head. Yes! My breast's bitter, bursting like a pomegranate. I love him!

ADELA [*impulsively, hugging her*]. Martirio, Martirio, I'm not to blame!

MARTIRIO. Don't put your arms around me! Don't try to smooth it over. My blood's no longer yours, and even though I try to think of you as a sister, I see you as just another woman. [*She pushes her away.*]

ADELA. There's no way out here. Whoever has to drown—let her drown. Pepe is mine. He'll carry me to the rushes along the river bank. . . .

MARTIRIO. He won't!

ADELA. I can't stand this horrible house after the taste of his mouth. I'll be what he wants me to be. Everybody in the village against me, burning me with their fiery fingers; pursued by those who claim they're decent, and I'll wear, before them all, the crown of thorns that belongs to the mistress of a married man.

MARTIRIO. Hush!

ADELA. Yes, yes. [*in a low voice*] Let's go to bed. Let's let him marry Angustias. I don't care any more, but I'll go off alone to a little house where he'll come to see me whenever he wants, whenever he feels like it.

MARTIRIO. That'll never happen! Not while I have a drop of blood left in my body.

ADELA. Not just weak you, but a wild horse I could force to his knees with just the strength of my little finger.

MARTIRIO. Don't raise that voice of yours to me. It irritates me. I have a heart full of a force so evil that, without my wanting to be, I'm drowned by it.

ADELA. You show us the way to love our sisters. God must have meant to leave me alone in the midst of darkness, because I can see you as I've never seen you before.

[*A whistle is heard and* ADELA *runs toward the door, but* MARTIRIO *gets in front of her.*]

MARTIRIO. Where are you going?

ADELA. Get away from that door!

MARTIRIO. Get by me if you can!

ADELA. Get away!

[*They struggle.*]

MARTIRIO [*shouts*]. Mother! Mother!

ADELA. Let me go!

[BERNARDA *enters. She wears petticoats and a black shawl.*]

BERNARDA. Quiet! Quiet! How poor I am without even a man to help me!

MARTIRIO [*pointing to* ADELA]. She was with him. Look at those skirts covered with straw!

BERNARDA [*going furiously toward* ADELA]. That's the bed of a bad woman!

ADELA [*facing her*]. There'll be an end to prison voices here!

[ADELA *snatches away her mother's cane and breaks it in two.*]

This is what I do with the tyrant's cane. Not another step. No one but Pepe commands me!

[MAGDALENA *enters.*]

MAGDALENA. Adela!

[LA PONCIA *and* ANGUSTIAS *enter.*]

ADELA. I'm his. [*to* ANGUSTIAS] Know that—and go out in the yard and tell him. He'll be master in this house.

ANGUSTIAS. My God!

BERNARDA. The gun! Where's the gun?

[*She rushes out,* MARTIRIO *following.* AMELIA *enters and looks on frightened, leaning her head against the wall.*]

ADELA. No one can hold me back! [*She tries to go out.*]

ANGUSTIAS [*holding her*]. You're not getting out of here with your body's triumph! Thief! Disgrace of this house!

MAGDALENA. Let her go where we'll never see her again!

[*A shot is heard.*]

BERNARDA [*entering*]. Just try looking for him now!

MARTIRIO [*entering*]. That does away with Pepe el Romano.

ADELA. Pepe! My God! Pepe!

[*She runs out.*]

PONCIA. Did you kill him?

MARTIRIO. No. He raced away on his mare!

BERNARDA. It was my fault. A woman can't aim.

MAGDALENA. Then, why did you say . . . ?

MARTIRIO. For her! I'd like to pour a river of blood over her head!

PONCIA. Curse you!

MAGDALENA. Devil!

BERNARDA. Although it's better this way!

[*A thud is heard.*]

Adela! Adela!

PONCIA [*at her door*]. Open this door!

BERNARDA. Open! Don't think the walls will hide your shame!

SERVANT [*entering*]. All the neighbors are up!

BERNARDA [*in a low voice, but like a roar*]. Open! Or I'll knock the door down! [*Pause. Everything is silent.*]

Adela! [*She walks away from the door.*] A hammer!

[LA PONCIA *throws herself against the door. It opens and she goes in. As she enters, she screams and backs out.*]

What is it?

PONCIA. [*She puts her hands to her throat.*] May we never die like that!

[THE SISTERS *fall back.* THE SERVANT *crosses herself.* BERNARDA *screams and goes forward.*]

Don't go in!

BERNARDA. No, not I! Pepe, you're running now, alive, in the darkness, under the trees, but another day you'll fall. Cut her down! My daughter died a virgin. Take her to another room and dress her as though she were a virgin. No one will say anything about this! She died a virgin. Tell them, so that at dawn, the bells will ring twice.

MARTIRIO. A thousand times happy she, who had him.

BERNARDA. And I want no weeping. Death must be looked at face to face. Silence! [*to one daughter*] Be still, I said! [*to another daughter*] Tears when you're alone! We'll drown ourselves in a sea of mourning. She, the youngest daughter of Bernarda Alba, died a virgin. Did you hear me? Silence, silence, I said. Silence!

CURTAIN

JEAN GIRAUDOUX
1882–1944

THE MADWOMAN OF CHAILLOT

1945

TO CALL *The Madwoman of Chaillot* a fantasy is an excellent way to recognize its playfully grotesque characterization and its casual dramatic structure. It is also an excellent way to discount the play as merely fantastic and charmingly trivial, which it is not. This "fantasy," set in "the Spring of next year," was written in Nazi-occupied Paris, and the cheerful consignment of the pointedly non-Germanic villains to a bottomless pit may be taken as a warning to collaborationists, a salute to the French underground resistance movement, and a fervent assurance of eventual liberation. But Giraudoux, who did not live to see his play produced, gave it a wider and more permanent significance.

Like George Orwell's much grimmer fantasy, *Nighteen Eighty-Four, The Madwoman of Chaillot* is an indelible metaphor of our society. The threat posed in the first act remains real. It is nothing short of the dehumanization of humanity. "I tell you, sir," says the President of International Substrate of Paris, Inc., "the only safeguard of order and discipline in the modern world is a standardized worker with interchangeable parts." "What would you rather have in your garden," the Prospector demands, "—an almond tree or an oil well?" To the exploiters and the power-seekers the question is purely rhetorical. But the question persists and is not to be evaded by dividing the world into two camps—"ours," virtuous and free, and "theirs," vicious and enslaved. It is posed no less acutely by the glowing faith that happiness comes packaged in the latest appliance than by the promotion of totalitarian five-year plans.

Giraudoux would rather have the almond tree, and with it the vagabonds, the young lovers, and the madwomen of Paris—humanity with all its vagaries. One measure of his integrity is that he does not treat "the evil ones" as other than human beings, even when they are turning themselves and others into automatons. The President and the Prospector at their most detestable still have imagination and cynical good humor. It is because they remain at least partly human that their self-betrayal can be judged as an unforgiveable betrayal.

In opposing them the mad countess is a model of sanity and benevolence. The riffraff are her steadfast allies, as are all people who innately revere life even when it is silly or humiliating. "To be alive," says the Madwoman, "is to be fortunate." And on that principle she and her companions undertake to save the world. Since "the greedy are stupid," the preparations for exterminating them leave time for the diverting conversations with which civilized people may properly occupy themselves. Giraudoux implies, however, that it is love rather more than conversation that makes civilization worth saving. The young lovers are, quite simply, what civilization is all about. Yet the amiable and happy people themselves cannot save it. It takes someone like the countess, who has suffered and has sympathy and is "mad" enough to try.

The irresistible upsurge of happiness in the final moments of the play is surely unparalleled in modern drama. When the Deaf-Mute speaks, he both echoes and fulfills the words of prophecy: "Then the eyes of the blind shall be opened, and the ears of the deaf unstopped. Then shall the lame man leap as an hart, and the tongue of the dumb sing." Even after the world has been liberated, not everything, of course, can come true. The Countess cannot retrieve the romance of her youth. The passing moment must be cherished as it passes. The revels now are ended, and the routine of living must regain its sway. Has the liberation itself been only a blissful fantasy? The answer is that civilization has been enabled to remain human and redeemable. Very possibly it is a perennial function of the drama, through all the modes of tragedy and comedy, to keep it so.

THE MADWOMAN OF CHAILLOT / *GIRAUDOUX*

TRANSLATED BY MAURICE VALENCY

Characters

THE WAITER	
THE LITTLE MAN	
THE PROSPECTOR	
THE PRESIDENT	
THE BARON	
THERESE	
THE STREET SINGER	
THE FLOWER GIRL	
THE RAGPICKER	
PAULETTE	
THE DEAF-MUTE	
IRMA	
THE SHOELACE PEDDLER	
THE BROKER	
THE STREET JUGGLER	
DR. JADIN	
COUNTESS AURELIA	*Madwoman of Chaillot*
THE DOORMAN	
THE POLICEMAN	
PIERRE	
THE SERGEANT	
THE SEWER-MAN	
MME. CONSTANCE	*Madwoman of Passy*
MLLE. GABRIELLE	*Madwoman of St. Sulpice*
MME. JOSEPHINE	*Madwoman of La Concorde*
THE PRESIDENTS	

THE PROSPECTORS
THE PRESS AGENTS
THE LADIES
THE ADOLPHE BERTAUTS

SCENE. *Paris.*

ACT I

SCENE. *The café terrace at* Chez Francis, *on the Place de l'Alma in Paris. The Alma is in the stately quarter of Paris known as Chaillot, between the Champs Elysées and the Seine, across the river from the Eiffel Tower.*

Chez Francis *has several rows of tables set out under its awning, and, as it is lunch time, a good many of them are occupied. At a table, downstage, a somewhat obvious* BLONDE *with ravishing legs is sipping a vermouth-cassis and trying hard to engage the attention of the* PROSPECTOR, *who sits at an adjacent table taking little sips of water and rolling them over his tongue with the air of a connoisseur. Downstage right, in front of the tables on the sidewalk, is the usual Paris bench, a stout and uncomfortable affair provided by the municipality for the benefit of those who prefer to sit without drinking. A* POLICEMAN *lounges about, keeping the peace without unnecessary exertion.*

TIME. *It is a little before noon in the Spring of next year.*

AT RISE. THE PRESIDENT *and* THE BARON *enter with importance, and are ushered to a front table by* THE WAITER.

THE PRESIDENT. Baron, sit down. This is a historic occasion. It must be properly celebrated. The waiter is going to bring out my special port.

THE BARON. Splendid.

THE PRESIDENT [*offers his cigar case*]. Cigar? My private brand.

THE BARON. Thank you. You know, this all gives me the feeling of one of those enchanted mornings in the *Arabian Nights* when thieves foregather in the market place. Thieves—pashas . . .

[*He sniffs the cigar judiciously, and begins lighting it.*]

THE PRESIDENT [*chuckles*]. Tell me about yourself.

THE BARON. Well, where shall I begin?

[THE STREET SINGER *enters. He takes off a battered black felt with a flourish and begins singing an ancient mazurka.*]

STREET SINGER [*sings*].

Do you hear, Mademoiselle,
Those musicians of hell?

THE PRESIDENT. Waiter! Get rid of that man.

WAITER. He is singing *La Belle Polonaise.*

THE PRESIDENT. I didn't ask for the program. I asked you to get rid of him. [THE WAITER *doesn't budge.* THE SINGER *goes by himself.*] As you were saying, Baron . . . ?

THE BARON. Well, until I was fifty . . . [THE FLOWER GIRL *enters through the café door, center.*] my life was relatively uncomplicated. It consisted of selling off one by one the various estates left me by my father. Three years ago, I parted with my last farm. Two years ago, I lost my last mistress. And now—all that is left me is . . .

THE FLOWER GIRL [*to* THE BARON]. Violets, sir?

THE PRESIDENT. Run along.

[THE FLOWER GIRL *moves on.*]

THE BARON [*staring after her*]. So that, in short, all I have left now is my name.

THE PRESIDENT. Your name is precisely the name we need on our board of directors.

THE BARON [*with an inclination of his head*]. Very flattering.

THE PRESIDENT. You will understand when I tell you that mine has been a very different experience. I came up from the bottom. My mother spent most of her life bent over a washtub in order to send me to school. I'm eternally grateful to her, of course, but I must confess that I no longer remember her face. It was no doubt beautiful —but when I try to recall it, I see only the part she invariably showed me—her rear.

THE BARON. Very touching.

THE PRESIDENT. When I was thrown out of school for the fifth and last time, I decided to find out for myself what makes the world go round. I ran errands for an editor, a movie star, a financier. . . . I began to understand a little what life is. Then, one day, in the subway, I saw a face. . . . My rise in life dates from that day.

THE BARON. Really?

THE PRESIDENT. One look at that face, and I knew. One look at mine, and he knew. And so I made my first thousand—passing a boxful of counterfeit notes. A year later, I saw another such face. It got me a nice berth in the narcotics business. Since then, all I do is to look out for such faces. And now here I am—president of eleven corporations, director of fifty-two companies, and, beginning today, chairman of the board of the international combine in which you have been so good as to accept a post. [THE RAGPICKER *passes, sees something under* THE PRESIDENT'S *table, and stoops to pick it up.*] Looking for something?

THE RAGPICKER. Did you drop this?

THE PRESIDENT. I never drop anything.

THE RAGPICKER. Then this hundred-franc note isn't yours?

THE PRESIDENT. Give it here.

[THE RAGPICKER *gives him the note, and goes out.*]

THE BARON. Are you sure it's yours?

THE PRESIDENT. All hundred-franc notes, Baron, are mine.

THE BARON. Mr. President, there's something I've been wanting to ask you. What exactly is the purpose of our new company? Or is that an indiscreet question . . . ?

THE PRESIDENT. Indiscreet? Not a bit. Merely unusual. As far as I know, you're the first member of a board of directors ever to ask such a question.

THE BARON. Do we plan to exploit a commodity? A utility?

THE PRESIDENT. My dear sir, I haven't the faintest idea.

THE BARON. But if you don't know—who does?

THE PRESIDENT. Nobody. And at the moment, it's becoming just a trifle embarrassing. Yes, my dear Baron, since we are now close business associates, I must confess that for the time being we're in a little trouble.

THE BARON. I was afraid of that. The stock issue isn't going well?

THE PRESIDENT. No, no—on the contrary. The stock issue is

going beautifully. Yesterday morning at ten o'clock we offered 500, 000 shares to the general public. By 10:05 they were all snapped up at par. By 10:20, when the police finally arrived, our offices were a shambles. . . . Windows smashed—doors torn off their hinges—you never saw anything so beautiful in your life! And this morning our stock is being quoted over the counter at 124 with no sellers, and the orders are still pouring in.

THE BARON. But in that case—what is the trouble?

THE PRESIDENT. The trouble is we have a tremendous capital, and not the slightest idea of what to do with it.

THE BARON. You mean all those people are fighting to buy stock in a company that has no object?

THE PRESIDENT. My dear Baron, do you imagine that when a subscriber buys a share of stock, he has any idea of getting behind a counter or digging a ditch? A stock certificate is not a tool, like a shovel, or a commodity, like a pound of cheese. What we sell a customer is not a share in a business, but a view of the Elysian Fields. A financier is a creative artist. Our function is to stimulate the imagination. We are poets!

THE BARON. But in order to stimulate the imagination, don't you need some field of activity?

THE PRESIDENT. Not at all. What you need for that is a name. A name that will stir the pulse like a trumpet call, set the brain awhirl like a movie star, inspire reverence like a cathedral. *United General International Consolidated!* Of course that's been used. That's what a corporation needs.

THE BARON. And do we have such a name?

THE PRESIDENT. So far we have only a blank space. In that blank space a name must be printed. This name must be a masterpiece. And if I seem a little nervous today, it's because—somehow—I've racked my brains, but it hasn't come to me. Oho! Look at that! Just like the answer to a prayer . . . ! [THE BARON *turns and stares in the direction of the prospector.*] You see? There's one. And what a beauty!

THE BARON. You mean that girl?

THE PRESIDENT. No, no, not the girl. That face. You see . . . ? The one that's drinking water.

THE BARON. You call that a face? That's a tombstone.

THE PRESIDENT. It's a milestone. It's a signpost. But is it pointing the way to steel, or wheat, or phosphates? That's what we have to find out. Ah! He sees me. He understands. He will be over.

THE BARON. And when he comes . . . ?

THE PRESIDENT. He will tell me what to do.

THE BARON. You mean business is done this way? You mean, you would trust a stranger with a matter of this importance?

THE PRESIDENT. Baron, I trust neither my wife, nor my daughter, nor my closest friend. My confidential secretary has no idea where I live. But a face like that I would trust with my inmost secrets. Though we have never laid eyes on each other before, that man and I know each other to the depths of our souls. He's no stranger—he's my brother, he's myself. You'll see. He'll be over in a minute. [THE DEAF-MUTE *enters and passes slowly among the tables, placing a small envelope before each customer. He comes to* THE PRESIDENT'S *table.*] What is this anyway? A conspiracy? We don't want your envelopes. Take them away. [THE DEAF-MUTE *makes a short but pointed speech in sign language.*] Waiter, what the devil's he saying?

WAITER. Only Irma understands him.

THE PRESIDENT. Irma? Who's Irma?

WAITER [*calls*]. Irma! It's the waitress inside, sir. Irma!

[IRMA *comes out. She is twenty. She has the face and figure of an angel.*]

IRMA. Yes?

WAITER. These gentlemen would . . .

THE PRESIDENT. Tell this fellow to get out of here, for God's sake! [THE DEAF-MUTE *makes another manual oration.*] What's he trying to say, anyway?

IRMA. He says it's an exceptionally beautiful morning, sir . . .

THE PRESIDENT. Who asked him?

IRMA. But, he says, it was nicer before the gentleman stuck his face in it.

THE PRESIDENT. Call the manager!

[IRMA *shrugs. She goes back into the restaurant.* THE DEAF-MUTE *walks off, left. Meanwhile a* SHOELACE PEDDLER *has arrived.*]

PEDDLER. Shoelaces? Postcards?

THE BARON. I think I could use a shoelace.

THE PRESIDENT. No, no . . .

PEDDLER. Black? Tan?

THE BARON [*showing his shoes*]. What would you recommend?

PEDDLER. Anybody's guess.

THE BARON. Well, give me one of each.

THE PRESIDENT [*putting a hand on the* BARON'S *arm.*] Baron, although I am your chairman, I have no authority over your personal life—none, that is, except to fix the amount of your director's fees, and eventually to assign a motor car for your use. Therefore, I am asking you, as a personal favor to me, not to purchase anything from this fellow.

THE BARON. How can I resist so gracious a request? [THE PEDDLER *shrugs, and passes on.*] But I really don't understand . . . What difference would it make?

THE PRESIDENT. Look here, Baron. Now that you're with us, you must understand that between this irresponsible riffraff and us there is an impenetrable barrier. *We* have no dealings whatever with *them.*

THE BARON. But without us, the poor devil will starve.

THE PRESIDENT. No, he won't. He expects nothing from us. He has a clientele of his own. He sells shoelaces exclusively to those who have no shoes. Just as the necktie peddler sells only to those who wear no shirts. And that's why these street hawkers can afford to be insolent, disrespectful and independent. They don't need us. They have a world of their own. Ah! My broker. Splendid. He's beaming.

[THE BROKER *walks up and grasps* THE PRESIDENT'S *hand with enthusiasm.*]

BROKER. Mr. President! My heartiest congratulations! What a day! What a day!

[THE STREET JUGGLER *appears, right. He removes his coat, folds it carefully, and puts it on the bench. Then he opens a suitcase, from which he extracts a number of colored clubs.*]

THE PRESIDENT [*presenting* THE BROKER]. Baron Tommard, of our Board of Directors. My broker. [THE BROKER *bows. So does* THE JUGGLER. THE BROKER *sits down and signals for a drink.* THE JUGGLER *prepares to juggle.*] What's happened?

BROKER. Listen to this. Ten o'clock this morning. The market opens. [*As he speaks,* THE JUGGLER *provides a visual counterpart to* THE BROKER'S *lines, his clubs rising and falling in rhythm to* THE

BROKER's *words.*] Half million shares issued at par, par value a hundred, quoted on the curb at 124 and we start buying at 126, 127, 129—and it's going up—up—up—[THE JUGGLER's *clubs rise higher and higher.*]—132—133—138—141—141—141—141 . . .

THE BARON. May I ask . . . ?

THE PRESIDENT. No, no—any explanation would only confuse you.

BROKER. Ten forty-five we start selling short on rumors of a Communist plot, market bearish. . . . 141—138—133—132—and it's down—down—down—102—and we start buying back at 93. Eleven o'clock, rumors denied—95—98—101—106—124—141—and by 11:30 we've got it all back—net profit three and a half million francs.

THE PRESIDENT. Classical. Pure. [THE JUGGLER *bows again. A* LITTLE MAN *leans over from a near-by table, listening intently, and trembling with excitement.*] And how many shares do we reserve to each member of the board?

BROKER. Fifty, as agreed.

THE PRESIDENT. Bit stingy, don't you think?

BROKER. All right—three thousand.

THE PRESIDENT. That's a little better. [*to* THE BARON] You get the idea?

THE BARON. I'm beginning to get it.

BROKER. And now we come to the exciting part . . . [THE JUGGLER *prepares to juggle with balls of fire.*] Listen carefully: With 35 percent of our funded capital under Section 32 I buy 50,000 United at 36 which I immediately reconvert into 32,000 National Amalgamated two's preferred which I set up as collateral on 150,000 General Consols which I deposit against a credit of fifteen billion to buy Eastern Hennequin which I immediately turn into Argentine wheat realizing 136 percent of the original investment which naturally accrues as capital gain and not as corporate income thus saving twelve millions in taxes, and at once convert the 25 percent cotton reserve into lignite, and as our people swing into action in London and New York, I beat up the price on greige goods from 26 to 92—114—203—306— [THE JUGGLER *by now is juggling his fireballs in the sky. The balls no longer return to his hands.*] 404 . . .

[THE LITTLE MAN *can stand no more. He rushes over and dumps a sackful of money on the table.*]

LITTLE MAN. Here—take it—please, take it!

BROKER [*frigidly*]. Who is this man? What is this money?

LITTLE MAN. It's my life's savings. Every cent. I put it all in your hands.

BROKER. Can't you see we're busy?

LITTLE MAN. But I beg you . . . It's my only chance . . . Please don't turn me away.

BROKER. Oh, all right. [*He sweeps the money into his pocket.*] Well?

LITTLE MAN. I thought—perhaps you'd give me a little receipt. . . .

THE PRESIDENT. My dear man, people like us don't give receipts for money. We take them.

LITTLE MAN. Oh, pardon. Of course. I was confused. Here it is. [*Scribbles a receipt.*] Thank you—thank you—thank you.

[*He rushes off joyfully.* THE STREET SINGER *reappears.*]

STREET SINGER [*sings*].

Do you hear, Mademoiselle,
Those musicians of hell?

THE PRESIDENT. What, again? Why does he keep repeating those two lines like a parrot?

WAITER. What else can he do? He doesn't know any more and the song's been out of print for years.

THE BARON. Couldn't he sing a song he knows?

WAITER. He likes this one. He hopes if he keeps singing the beginning someone will turn up to teach him the end.

THE PRESIDENT. Tell him to move on. We don't know the song.

[THE PROFESSOR *strolls by, swinging his cane. He overhears.*]

PROFESSOR [*stops and addresses* THE PRESIDENT *politely*]. Nor do I, my dear sir. Nor do I. And yet, I'm in exactly the same predicament. I remember just two lines of my favorite song, as a child. A mazurka also, in case you're interested. . . .

THE PRESIDENT. I'm not.

PROFESSOR. Why is it, I wonder, that one always forgets the words of a mazurka? I suppose they just get lost in that damnable rhythm. All I remember is: [*He sings.*]

From England to Spain
I have drunk, it was bliss . . .

STREET SINGER [*walks over, and picks up the tune*].

Red wine and champagne
And many a kiss.

PROFESSOR. Oh, God! It all comes back to me . . . ! [*He sings.*]

Red lips and white hands I have known
Where the nightingales dwell. . . .

THE PRESIDENT [*holding his hands to his ears*]. Please—please . . .

STREET SINGER.

And to each one I've whispered, "My own,"
And to each one I've murmured: "Farewell."

THE PRESIDENT. Farewell. Farewell.

STREET SINGER, PROFESSOR [*duo*].

But there's one I shall never forget. . . .

THE PRESIDENT. This isn't a café. It's a circus!

[*The two go off, still singing: "There is one that's engraved in my heart."* THE PROSPECTOR *gets up slowly and walks toward* THE PRESIDENT'S *table. He looks down without a word. There is a tense silence.*]

PROSPECTOR. Well?

THE PRESIDENT. I need a name.

PROSPECTOR [*nods, with complete comprehension*]. I need fifty thousand.

THE PRESIDENT. For a corporation.

PROSPECTOR. For a woman.

THE PRESIDENT. Immediately.

PROSPECTOR. Before evening.

THE PRESIDENT. Something . . .

PROSPECTOR. Unusual?

THE PRESIDENT. Something . . .

PROSPECTOR. Provocative?

THE PRESIDENT. Something . . .

PROSPECTOR. Practical.

THE PRESIDENT. Yes.

PROSPECTOR. Fifty thousand. Cash.

THE PRESIDENT. I'm listening.

PROSPECTOR. *International Substrate of Paris, Inc.*

THE PRESIDENT [*snaps his fingers*]. That's it! [*to* THE BROKER] Pay him off. [THE BROKER *pays with* THE LITTLE MAN'S *money.*] Now —what does it mean?

PROSPECTOR. It means what it says. I'm a prospector.

THE PRESIDENT [*rises*]. A prospector! Allow me to shake your hand. Baron, you are in the presence of one of nature's noblemen. Shake his hand. This is Baron Tommard. [*They shake hands.*] It is this man, my dear Baron, who smells out in the bowels of the earth those deposits of metal or liquid on which can be founded the only social unit of which our age is capable—the corporation. Sit down, please. [*They all sit.*] And now that we have a name . . .

PROSPECTOR. You need a property.

THE PRESIDENT. Precisely.

PROSPECTOR. I have one.

THE PRESIDENT. A claim?

PROSPECTOR. Terrific.

THE PRESIDENT. Foreign?

PROSPECTOR. French.

THE BARON. In Indo-China?

BROKER. Morocco?

THE PRESIDENT. In France?

PROSPECTOR [*matter of fact*]. In Paris.

THE PRESIDENT. In Paris? You've been prospecting in Paris?

THE BARON. For women, no doubt.

THE PRESIDENT. For art?

BROKER. For gold?

PROSPECTOR. Oil.

BROKER. He's crazy.

THE PRESIDENT. Sh! He's inspired.

PROSPECTOR. You think I'm crazy. Well, they thought Columbus was crazy.

THE BARON. Oil in Paris?

BROKER. But how is it possible?

PROSPECTOR. It's not only possible. It's certain.

THE PRESIDENT. Tell us.

PROSPECTOR. You don't know, my dear sir, what treasures Paris conceals. Paris is the least prospected place in the world. We've gone over the rest of the planet with a fine-tooth comb. But has anyone ever thought of looking for oil in Paris? Nobody. Before me, that is.

THE PRESIDENT. Genius!

PROSPECTOR. No. Just a practical man. I use my head.

THE BARON. But why has nobody ever thought of this before?

PROSPECTOR. The treasures of the earth, my dear sir, are not easy to find nor to get at. They are invariably guarded by dragons. Doubtless there is some reason for this. For once we've dug out and consumed the internal ballast of the planet, the chances are it will shoot off on some irresponsible tangent and smash itself up in the sky. Well, that's the risk we take. Anyway, that's not my business. A prospector has enough to worry about.

THE BARON. I know—snakes—tarantulas—fleas . . .

PROSPECTOR. Worse than that, sir. Civilization.

THE PRESIDENT. Does that annoy you?

PROSPECTOR. Civilization gets in our way all the time. In the first place, it covers the earth with cities and towns which are damned awkward to dig up when you want to see what's underneath. It's not only the real-estate people—you can always do business with them—it's human sentimentality. How do you do business with that?

THE PRESIDENT. I see what you mean.

PROSPECTOR. They say that where we pass, nothing ever grows again. What of it? Is a park any better than a coal mine? What's a mountain got that a slag pile hasn't? What would you rather have in your garden—an almond tree or an oil well?

THE PRESIDENT. Well . . .

PROSPECTOR. Exactly. But what's the use of arguing with these fools? Imagine the choicest place you ever saw for an excavation, and what do they put there? A playground for children! Civilization!

THE PRESIDENT. Just show us the point where you want to start digging. We'll do the rest. Even if it's in the middle of the Louvre. Where's the oil?

PROSPECTOR. Perhaps you think it's easy to make an accurate fix in an area like Paris where everything conspires to put you off the scent? Women—perfume—flowers—history. You can talk all you like about geology, but an oil deposit, gentlemen, has to be smelled out. I have a good nose. I go further. I have a phenomenal nose. But the minute I get the right whiff—the minute I'm on the scent—a fragrance rises from what I take to be the spiritual deposits of the past—and I'm completely at sea. Now take this very point, for example, this very spot.

THE BARON. You mean—right here in Chaillot?

PROSPECTOR. Right under here.

THE PRESIDENT. Good heavens!

[*He looks under his chair.*]

PROSPECTOR. It's taken me months to locate the spot.

THE BARON. But what in the world makes you think . . . ?

PROSPECTOR. Do you know this place, Baron?

THE BARON. Well, I've been sitting here for thirty years.

PROSPECTOR. Did you ever taste the water?

THE BARON. The water? Good God, no!

PROSPECTOR. It's plain to see that you are no prospector! A prospector, Baron, is addicted to water as a drunkard to wine. Water, gentlemen, is the one substance from which the earth can conceal nothing. It sucks out its innermost secrets and brings them to our very lips. Well—beginning at Notre Dame, where I first caught the scent of oil three months ago, I worked my way across Paris, glassful by glassful, sampling the water, until at last I came to this café. And here—just two days ago—I took a sip. My heart began to thump. Was it possible that I was deceived? I took another, a third, a fourth, a fifth. I was trembling like a leaf. But there was no mistake. Each time that I drank, my taste-buds thrilled to the most exquisite flavor known to a prospector—the flavor of— [*with utmost lyricism*] Petroleum!

THE PRESIDENT. Waiter! Some water and four glasses. Hurry. This round, gentlemen, is on me. And as a toast—I shall propose International Substrate of Paris, Incorporated. [THE WAITER *brings a decanter and the glasses.* THE PRESIDENT *pours out the water amid profound silence. They taste it with the air of connoisseurs savoring something that has never before passed human lips. Then they look at each other doubtfully.* THE PROSPECTOR *pours himself a second glass and drinks it off.*] Well . . .

BROKER. Ye-es . . .

THE BARON. Mm . . .

PROSPECTOR. Get it?

THE BARON. Tastes queer.

PROSPECTOR. That's it. To the unpracticed palate it tastes queer. But to the taste-buds of the expert—ah!

THE BARON. Still, there's one thing I don't quite understand . . .

PROSPECTOR. Yes?

THE BARON. This café doesn't have its own well, does it?

PROSPECTOR. Of course not. This is Paris water.

BROKER. Then why should it taste different here than anywhere else?

PROSPECTOR. Because, my dear sir, the pipes that carry this water pass deep through the earth, and the earth just here is soaked with oil, and this oil permeates the pores of the iron and flavors the water it carries. Ever so little, yes—but quite enough to betray its presence to the sensitive tongue of the specialist.

THE BARON. I see.

PROSPECTOR. I don't say everyone is capable of tasting it. No. But I—I can detect the presence of oil in water that has passed within fifteen miles of a deposit. Under special circumstances, twenty.

THE PRESIDENT. Phenomenal!

PROSPECTOR. And so here I am with the greatest discovery of the age on my hands—but the blasted authorities won't let me drill a single well unless I show them the oil! Now how can I show them the oil unless they let me dig? Completely stymied! Eh?

THE PRESIDENT. What? A man like you?

PROSPECTOR. That's what they think. That's what they want. Have you noticed the strange glamor of the women this morning? And the quality of the sunshine? And this extraordinary convocation of vagabonds buzzing about protectively like bees around a hive? Do you know why it is? Because they know. It's a plot to distract us, to turn us from our purpose. Well, let them try. I know there's oil here. And I'm going to dig it up, even if I . . . [*He smiles.*] Shall I tell you my little plan?

THE PRESIDENT. By all means.

PROSPECTOR. Well . . . For heaven's sake, what's that?

[*At this point,* THE MADWOMAN *enters. She is dressed in the grand fashion of 1885, a taffeta skirt with an immense train—which she has gathered up by means of a clothespin—ancient button shoes, and a hat in the style of Marie Antoinette. She wears a lorgnette on a chain, and an enormous cameo pin at her throat. In her hand she carries a small basket. She walks in with great dignity, extracts a dinner bell from the bosom of her dress, and rings it sharply.* IRMA *appears.*]

COUNTESS. Are my bones ready, Irma?

IRMA. There won't be much today, Countess. We had broilers. Can you wait? While the gentleman inside finishes eating?

COUNTESS. And my gizzard?

IRMA. I'll try to get it away from him.

COUNTESS. If he eats my gizzard, save me the giblets. They will do for the tomcat that lives under the bridge. He likes a few giblets now and again.

IRMA. Yes, Countess.

[IRMA *goes back into the café.* THE COUNTESS *takes a few steps and stops in front of* THE PRESIDENT'S *table. She examines him with undisguised disapproval.*]

THE PRESIDENT. Waiter. Ask that woman to move on.

WAITER. Sorry, sir. This is her café.

THE PRESIDENT. Is she the manager of the café?

WAITER. She's the Madwoman of Chaillot.

THE PRESIDENT. A Madwoman? She's mad?

WAITER. Who says she's mad?

THE PRESIDENT. You just said so yourself.

WAITER. Look, sir. You asked me who she was. And I told you. What's mad about her? She's the Madwoman of Chaillot.

THE PRESIDENT. Call a policeman.

[THE COUNTESS *whistles through her fingers. At once,* THE DOORMAN *runs out of the café. He has three scarves in his hands.*]

COUNTESS. Have you found it? My feather boa?

DOORMAN. Not yet, Countess. Three scarves. But no boa.

COUNTESS. It's five years since I lost it. Surely you've had time to find it.

DOORMAN. Take one of these, Countess. Nobody's claimed them.

COUNTESS. A boa like that doesn't vanish, you know. A feather boa nine feet long!

DOORMAN. How about this blue one?

COUNTESS. With my pink ruffle and my green veil? You're joking! Let me see the yellow. [*She tries it on.*] How does it look?

DOORMAN. Terrific.

[*With a magnificent gesture, she flings the scarf about her, upsetting* THE PRESIDENT'S *glass and drenching his trousers with water. She stalks off without a glance at him.*]

THE PRESIDENT. Waiter! I'm making a complaint.

WAITER. Against whom?

THE PRESIDENT. Against her! Against you! The whole gang of you! That singer! That shoelace peddler! That female lunatic! Or whatever you call her!

THE BARON. Calm yourself, Mr. President. . . .

THE PRESIDENT. I'll do nothing of the sort! Baron, the first thing we have to do is to get rid of these people! Good heavens, look at them! Every size, shape, color and period of history imaginable. It's utter anarchy! I tell you, sir, the only safeguard of order and discipline in the modern world is a standardized worker with interchangeable parts. That would solve the entire problem of management. Here, the manager . . . And there—one composite drudge grunting and sweating all over the world. Just we two. Ah, how beautiful! How easy on the eyes! How restful for the conscience!

THE BARON. Yes, yes—of course.

THE PRESIDENT. Order. Symmetry. Balance. But instead of that, what? Here in Chaillot, the very citadel of management, these insolent phantoms of the past come to beard us with their raffish individualism—with the right of the voiceless to sing, of the dumb to make speech, of trousers to have no seats and bosoms to have dinner bells!

THE BARON. But, after all, do these people matter?

THE PRESIDENT. My dear sir, wherever the poor are happy, and the servants are proud, and the mad are respected, our power is at an end. Look at that. That waiter! That madwoman! That flower girl! Do I get that sort of service? And suppose that I—president of twelve corporations and ten times a millionaire—were to stick a gladiolus in my buttonhole and start yelling— [*He tinkles his spoon in a glass violently, yelling.*] Are my bones ready, Irma?

THE BARON [*reprovingly*]. Mr. President . . .

[*People at the adjoining tables turn and stare with raised eyebrows.* THE WAITER *starts to come over.*]

THE PRESIDENT. You see? Now.

PROSPECTOR. We were discussing my plan.

THE PRESIDENT. Ah yes, your plan. [*He glances in the direction of* THE MADWOMAN'S *table.*] Careful—she's looking at us.

PROSPECTOR. Do you know what a bomb is?

THE PRESIDENT. I'm told they explode.

PROSPECTOR. Exactly. You see that white building across the river. Do you happen to know what that is?

THE PRESIDENT. I do not.

PROSPECTOR. That's the office of the City Architect. That man has stubbornly refused to give me a permit to drill for oil anywhere within the limits of the city of Paris. I've tried everything with him—influence, bribes, threats. He says I'm crazy. And now . . .

THE PRESIDENT. Oh, my God! What is this one trying to sell us? [*A little old man enters left, and doffs his hat politely. He is somewhat ostentatiously respectable—gloved, pomaded, and carefully dressed, with a white handkerchief peeping out of his breast pocket.*]

DR. JADIN. Nothing but health, sir. Or rather the health of the feet. But remember—as the foot goes, so goes the man. May I present myself . . . ? Dr. Gaspard Jadin, French Navy, retired. Former specialist in the extraction of ticks and chiggers. At present specializing in the extraction of bunions and corns. In case of sudden emergency, Martial the waiter will furnish my home address. My office is here, second row, third table, week days, twelve to five. Thank you very much.

[*He sits at his table.*]

WAITER. Your vermouth, Doctor?

DR. JADIN. My vermouth. My vermouths. How are your gallstones today, Martial?

WAITER. Fine. Fine. They rattle like anything.

DR. JADIN. Splendid. [*He spies* THE COUNTESS.] Good morning, Countess. How's the floating kidney? Still afloat? [*She nods graciously*]. Splendid. Splendid. So long as it floats, it can't sink.

THE PRESIDENT. This is impossible! Let's go somewhere else.

PROSPECTOR. No. It's nearly noon.

THE PRESIDENT. Yes. It is. Five to twelve.

PROSPECTOR. In five minutes' time you're going to see that City Architect blown up, building and all—boom!

BROKER. Are you serious?

PROSPECTOR. That imbecile has no one to blame but himself. Yesterday noon, he got my ultimatum—he's had twenty-four hours to think it over. No permit? All right. Within two minutes my agent is going to drop a little package in his coal bin. And three minutes after that, precisely at noon . . .

THE BARON. You prospectors certainly use modern methods.

PROSPECTOR. The method may be modern. But the idea is old. To get at the treasure, it has always been necessary to slay the dragon. I guarantee that after this, the City Architect will be more reasonable. The new one, I mean.

THE PRESIDENT. Don't you think we're sitting a little close for comfort?

PROSPECTOR. Oh no, no. Don't worry. And, above all, don't stare. We may be watched. [*A clock strikes.*] Why, that's noon. Something's wrong! Good God! What's this? [*A* POLICEMAN *staggers in bearing a lifeless body on his shoulders in the manner prescribed as "The Fireman's Lift."*] It's Pierre! My agent! [*He walks over with affected nonchalance.*] I say, Officer, what's that you've got?

POLICEMAN. Drowned man.

[*He puts him down on the bench.*]

WAITER. He's not drowned. His clothes are dry. He's been slugged.

POLICEMAN. Slugged is also correct. He was just jumping off the bridge when I came along and pulled him back. I slugged him, naturally, so he wouldn't drag me under. Life Saving Manual Rule 5: "In cases where there is danger of being dragged under, it is necessary to render the subject unconscious by means of a sharp blow." He's had that.

[*He loosens the clothes and begins applying artificial respiration.*]

PROSPECTOR. The stupid idiot! What the devil did he do with the bomb? That's what comes of employing amateurs!

THE PRESIDENT. You don't think he'll give you away?

PROSPECTOR. Don't worry. [*He walks over to the policeman.*] Say, what do you think you're doing?

POLICEMAN. Lifesaving. Artificial respiration. First aid to the drowning.

PROSPECTOR. But he's not drowning.

POLICEMAN. But he thinks he is.

PROSPECTOR. You'll never bring him round that way, my friend. That's meant for people who drown in water. It's not good at all for those who drown without water.

POLICEMAN. What am I supposed to do? I've just been sworn in.

It's my first day on the beat. I can't afford to get in trouble. I've got to go by the book.

PROSPECTOR. Perfectly simple. Take him back to the bridge where you found him and throw him in. Then you can save his life and you'll get a medal. This way, you'll get fined for slugging an innocent man.

POLICEMAN. What do you mean, innocent? He was just going to jump when I grabbed him.

PROSPECTOR. Have you any proof of that?

POLICEMAN. Well, I saw him.

PROSPECTOR. Written proof? Witnesses?

POLICEMAN. No, but . . .

PROSPECTOR. Then don't waste time arguing. You're in trouble. Quick—before anybody notices—throw him in and dive after him. It's the only way out.

POLICEMAN. But I don't swim.

THE PRESIDENT. You'll learn how on the way down. Before you were born, did you know how to breathe?

POLICEMAN [*convinced*]. All right. Here we go.

[*He starts lifting the body.*]

DR. JADIN. One moment, please. I don't like to interfere, but it's my professional duty to point out that medical science has definitely established the fact of intra-uterine respiration. Consequently, this policeman, even before he was born, knew not only how to breathe but also how to cough, hiccup and belch.

THE PRESIDENT. Suppose he did—how does it concern you?

DR. JADIN. On the other hand, medical science has never established the fact of intra-uterine swimming or diving. Under the circumstances, we are forced to the opinion, Officer, that if you dive in you will probably drown.

POLICEMAN. You think so?

PROSPECTOR. Who asked you for an opinion?

THE PRESIDENT. Pay no attention to that quack, Officer.

DR. JADIN. Quack, sir?

PROSPECTOR. This is not a medical matter. It's a legal problem. The officer has made a grave error. He's new. We're trying to help him.

BROKER. He's probably afraid of the water.

POLICEMAN. Nothing of the sort. Officially, I'm afraid of nothing. But I always follow doctor's orders.

DR. JADIN. You see, Officer, when a child is born . . .

PROSPECTOR. Now, what does he care about when a child is born? He's got a dying man on his hands. . . . Officer, if you want my advice . . .

POLICEMAN. It so happens, I care a lot about when a child is born. It's part of my duty to aid and assist any woman in childbirth or labor.

THE PRESIDENT. Can you imagine!

POLICEMAN. Is it true, Doctor, what they say, that when you have twins, the first born is considered to be the youngest?

DR. JADIN. Quite correct. And what's more, if the twins happen to be born at midnight on December 31st, the older is a whole year younger. He does his military service a year later. That's why you have to keep your eyes open. And that's the reason why a queen always gives birth before witnesses. . . .

POLICEMAN. God! The things a policeman is supposed to know! Doctor, what does it mean if, when I get up in the morning sometimes . . .

PROSPECTOR [*nudging* THE PRESIDENT *meaningfully*]. The old woman . . .

BROKER. Come on, Baron.

THE PRESIDENT. I think we'd better all run along.

PROSPECTOR. Leave him to me.

THE PRESIDENT. I'll see you later.

[THE PRESIDENT *steals off with* THE BROKER *and* THE BARON.]

POLICEMAN [*still in conference with* DR. JADIN]. But what's really worrying me, Doctor, is this—don't you think it's a bit risky for a man to marry after forty-five?

[THE BROKER *runs in breathlessly.*]

BROKER. Officer! Officer!

POLICEMAN. What's the trouble?

BROKER. Quick! Two women are calling for help—on the sidewalk—Avenue Wilson!

POLICEMAN. Two women at once? Standing up or lying down?

BROKER. You'd better go and see. Quick!

PROSPECTOR. You'd better take the Doctor with you.

POLICEMAN. Come along, Doctor, come along. . . . [*pointing to* PIERRE] Tell him to wait till I get back. Come along, Doctor.

[*He runs out,* THE DOCTOR *following.* THE PROSPECTOR *moves over toward* PIERRE, *but* IRMA *crosses in front of him and takes the boy's hand.*]

IRMA. How beautiful he is! Is he dead, Martial?

WAITER [*handing her a pocket mirror*]. Hold this mirror to his mouth. If it clouds over . . .

IRMA. It clouds over.

WAITER. He's alive.

[*He holds out his hand for the mirror.*]

IRMA. Just a sec— [*She rubs it clean and looks at herself intently. Before handing it back, she fixes her hair and applies her lipstick. Meanwhile* THE PROSPECTOR *tries to get around the other side, but* THE COUNTESS' *eagle eye drives him off. He shrugs his shoulders and exits with* THE BARON.] Oh, look—he's opened his eyes!

[PIERRE *opens his eyes, stares intently at* IRMA *and closes them again with the expression of a man who is among the angels.*]

PIERRE [*murmurs*]. Oh! How beautiful!

VOICE [*from within the café*]. Irma!

IRMA. Coming. Coming.

[*She goes in, not without a certain reluctance.* THE COUNTESS *at once takes her place on the bench, and also the young man's hand.* PIERRE *sits up suddenly, and finds himself staring, not at* IRMA, *but into the very peculiar face of* THE COUNTESS. *His expression changes.*]

COUNTESS. You're looking at my iris? Isn't it beautiful?

PIERRE. Very.

[*He drops back, exhausted.*]

COUNTESS. The Sergeant was good enough to say it becomes me. But I no longer trust his taste. Yesterday, the flower girl gave me a lily, and he said it didn't suit me.

PIERRE [*weakly*]. It's beautiful.

COUNTESS. He'll be very happy to know that you agree with him. He's really quite sensitive. [*She calls.*] Sergeant!

PIERRE. No, please—don't call the police.

COUNTESS. But I must. I think I hurt his feelings.

PIERRE. Let me go, Madame.

COUNTESS. No, no. Stay where you are. Sergeant!

[PIERRE *struggles weakly to get up.*]

PIERRE. Please let me go.

COUNTESS. I'll do nothing of the sort. When you let someone go, you never see him again. I let Charlotte Mazumet go. I never saw her again.

PIERRE. Oh, my head.

COUNTESS. I let Adolphe Bertaut go. And I was holding him. And I never saw him again.

PIERRE. Oh, God!

COUNTESS. Except once. Thirty years later. In the market. He had changed a great deal—he didn't know me. He sneaked a melon from right under my nose, the only good one of the year. Ah, here we are. Sergeant!

[*The* POLICE SERGEANT *comes in with importance.*]

SERGEANT. I'm in a hurry, Countess.

COUNTESS. With regard to the iris. This young man agrees with you. He says it suits me.

SERGEANT [*going*]. There's a man drowning in the Seine.

COUNTESS. He's not drowning in the Seine. He's drowning here. Because I'm holding him tight—as I should have held Adolphe Bertaut. But if I let him go, I'm sure he will go and drown in the Seine. He's a lot better looking than Adolphe Bertaut, wouldn't you say?

[PIERRE *sighs deeply.*]

SERGEANT. How would I know?

COUNTESS. I've shown you his photograph. The one with the bicycle.

SERGEANT. Oh, yes. The one with the harelip.

COUNTESS. I've told you a hundred times! Adolphe Bertaut had no harelip. That was a scratch in the negative. [THE SERGEANT *takes out his notebook and pencil.*] What are you doing?

SERGEANT. I am taking down the drowned man's name, given name and date of birth.

COUNTESS. You think that's going to stop him from jumping in the river? Don't be silly, Sergeant. Put that book away and try to console him.

SERGEANT. I should try and console him?

COUNTESS. When people want to die, it is your job as a guardian of the state to speak out in praise of life. Not mine.

SERGEANT. I should speak out in praise of life?

COUNTESS. I assume you have some motive for interfering with people's attempts to kill each other, and rob each other, and run each other over? If you believe that life has some value, tell him what it is. Go on.

SERGEANT. Well, all right. Now look, young man . . .

COUNTESS. His name is Roderick.

PIERRE. My name is not Roderick.

COUNTESS. Yes, it is. It's noon. At noon all men become Roderick.

SERGEANT. Except Adolphe Bertaut.

COUNTESS. In the days of Adolphe Bertaut, we were forced to change the men when we got tired of their names. Nowadays, we're more practical—each hour on the hour all names are automatically changed. The men remain the same. But you're not here to discuss Adolphe Bertaut, Sergeant. You're here to convince the young man that life is worth living.

PIERRE. It isn't.

SERGEANT. Quiet. Now then—what was the idea of jumping off the bridge, anyway?

COUNTESS. The idea was to land in the river. Roderick doesn't seem to be at all confused about that.

SERGEANT. Now how can I convince anybody that life is worth living if you keep interrupting all the time?

COUNTESS. I'll be quiet.

SERGEANT. First of all, Mr. Roderick, you have to realize that suicide is a crime against the state. And why is it a crime against the state? Because every time anybody commits suicide, that means one soldier less for the army, one taxpayer less for the . . .

COUNTESS. Sergeant, isn't there something about life that you really enjoy?

SERGEANT. That I enjoy?

COUNTESS. Well, surely, in all these years, you must have found something worth living for. Some secret pleasure, or passion. Don't blush. Tell him about it.

SERGEANT. Who's blushing? Well, naturally, yes—I have my passions—like everybody else. The fact is, since you ask me—I love—to play—casino. And if the gentleman would like to join me, by and by when I go off duty, we can sit down to a nice little game in the back room with a nice cold glass of beer. If he wants to kill an hour, that is.

COUNTESS. He doesn't want to kill an hour. He wants to kill himself. Well? Is that all the police force has to offer by way of earthly bliss?

SERGEANT. Huh? You mean— [*He jerks a thumb in the direction of the pretty* BLONDE, *who has just been joined by a* BRUNETTE *of the same stamp.*] Paulette?

[*The young man groans.*]

COUNTESS. You're not earning your salary, Sergeant. I defy anybody to stop dying on your account.

SERGEANT. Go ahead, if you can do any better. But you won't find it easy.

COUNTESS. Oh, this is not a desperate case at all. A young man who has just fallen in love with someone who has fallen in love with him!

PIERRE. She hasn't. How could she?

COUNTESS. Oh, yes, she has. She was holding your hand, just as I'm holding it, when all of a sudden . . . Did you ever know Marshal Canrobert's niece?

SERGEANT. How could he know Marshal Canrobert's niece?

COUNTESS. Lots of people knew her—when she was alive. [PIERRE *begins to struggle energetically.*] No, no, Roderick—stop—stop!

SERGEANT. You see? You won't do any better than I did.

COUNTESS. No? Let's bet. I'll bet my iris against one of your gold buttons. Right?—Roderick, I know very well why you tried to drown yourself in the river.

PIERRE. You don't at all.

COUNTESS. It's because that Prospector wanted you to commit a horrible crime.

PIERRE. How did you know that?

COUNTESS. He stole my boa, and now he wants you to kill me.

PIERRE. Not exactly.

COUNTESS. It wouldn't be the first time they've tried it. But I'm not so easy to get rid of, my boy, oh, no . . . Because . . .

[THE DOORMAN *rides in on his bicycle. He winks at* THE SERGEANT, *who has now seated himself while* THE WAITER *serves him a beer.*]

DOORMAN. Take it easy, Sergeant.

SERGEANT. I'm busy saving a drowning man.

COUNTESS. They can't kill me because—I have no desire to die.

PIERRE. You're fortunate.

COUNTESS. To be alive is to be fortunate, Roderick. Of course, in the morning, when you first awake, it does not always seem so very gay. When you take your hair out of the drawer, and your teeth out of the glass, you are apt to feel a little out of place in this world. Especially if you've just been dreaming that you're a little girl on a pony looking for strawberries in the woods. But all you need to feel the call of life once more is a letter in your mail giving you your schedule for the day—your mending, your shopping, that letter to your grandmother that you never seem to get around to. And so, when you've washed your face in rose-water, and powdered it—not with this awful rice-powder they sell nowadays, which does nothing for the skin, but with a cake of pure white starch—and put on your pins, your rings, your brooches, bracelets, earrings and pearls—in short, when you are dressed for your morning coffee—and have had a good look at yourself—not in the glass, naturally—it lies—but in the side of the brass gong that once belonged to Admiral Courbet—then, Roderick, then you're armed, you're strong, you're ready—you can begin again.

[PIERRE *is listening now intently. There are tears in his eyes.*]

PIERRE. Oh, Madame . . . ! Oh, Madame . . . !

COUNTESS. After that, everything is pure delight. First the morning paper. Not, of course, these current sheets full of lies and vulgarity. I always read the *Gaulois,* the issue of March 22, 1903. It's by far the best. It has some delightful scandal, some excellent fashion notes, and, of course, the last-minute bulletin on the death of Leonide Leblanc. She used to live next door, poor woman, and when I learn of her death every morning, it gives me quite a shock. I'd gladly lend you my copy, but it's in tatters.

SERGEANT. Couldn't we find him a copy in some library?

COUNTESS. I doubt it. And so, when you've taken your fruit salts—not in water, naturally—no matter what they say, it's water that gives you gas—but with a bit of spiced cake—then in sunlight or rain, Chaillot calls. It is time to dress for your morning walk. This takes much longer, of course—without a maid, impossible to do it under an hour, what with your corset, corset-cover and drawers all of which lace or button in the back. I asked Madame Lanvin, a while ago, to fit the drawers with zippers. She was quite charming, but she declined. She thought it would spoil the style.

[THE DEAF-MUTE *comes in.*]

WAITER. I know a place where they put zippers on anything.

[THE RAGPICKER *enters.*]

COUNTESS. I think Lanvin knows best. But I really manage very well, Martial. What I do now is, I lace them up in front, then twist them around to the back. It's quite simple, really. Then you choose a lorgnette, and then the usual fruitless search for the feather boa that the Prospector stole—I know it was he: he didn't dare look me in the eye—and then all you need is a rubber band to slip around your parasol—I lost the catch the day I struck the cat that was stalking the pigeon—it was worth it—ah, that day I earned my wages!

THE RAGPICKER. Countess, if you can use it, I found a nice umbrella catch the other day with a cat's eye in it.

COUNTESS. Thank you, Ragpicker. They say these eyes sometimes come to life and fill with tears. I'd be afraid . . .

PIERRE. Go on, Madame, go on . . .

COUNTESS. Ah! So life is beginning to interest you, is it? You see how beautiful it is?

PIERRE. What a fool I've been!

COUNTESS. Then, Roderick, I begin my rounds. I have my cats to feed, my dogs to pet, my plants to water. I have to see what the evil ones are up to in the district—those who hate people, those who hate plants, those who hate animals. I watch them sneaking off in the morning to put on their disguises—to the baths, to the beauty parlors, to the barbers. But they can't deceive me. And when they come out again with blonde hair and false whiskers, to pull up my flowers and poison my dogs, I'm there, and I'm ready. All you have to do to break their power is to cut across their path from the left. That isn't always easy. Vice moves swiftly. But I have a good long stride and I generally manage. . . . Right, my friends? [THE WAITER *and* THE RAGPICKER *nod their heads with evident approval.*] Yes, the flowers have been marvelous this year. And the butcher's dog on the Rue Bizet, in spite of that wretch that tried to poison him, is friskier than ever. . . .

SERGEANT. That dog had better look out. He has no license.

COUNTESS. He doesn't seem to feel the need of one.

THE RAGPICKER. The Duchess de la Rochefoucauld's whippet is getting awfully thin. . . .

COUNTESS. What can I do? She bought that dog full grown from a kennel where they didn't know his right name. A dog without his right name is bound to get thin.

THE RAGPICKER. I've got a friend who knows a lot about dogs—an Arab . . .

COUNTESS. Ask him to call on the Duchess. She receives. Thursdays, five to seven. You see, then, Roderick. That's life. Does it appeal to you now?

PIERRE. It seems marvelous.

COUNTESS. Ah! Sergeant. My button. [THE SERGEANT *gives her his button and goes off. At this point* THE PROSPECTOR *enters.*] That's only the morning. Wait till I tell you about the afternoon!

PROSPECTOR. All right, Pierre. Come along now.

PIERRE. I'm perfectly all right here.

PROSPECTOR. I said, come along now.

PIERRE [*to* THE COUNTESS]. I'd better go, Madame.

COUNTESS. No.

PIERRE. It's no use. Please let go my hand.

PROSPECTOR. Madame, will you oblige me by letting my friend go?

COUNTESS. I will not oblige you in any way.

PROSPECTOR. All right. Then I'll oblige you . . . !

[*He tries to push her away. She catches up a soda water siphon and squirts it in his face.*]

PIERRE. Countess . . .

COUNTESS. Stay where you are. This man isn't going to take you away. In the first place, I shall need you in a few minutes to take me home. I'm all alone here and I'm very easily frightened.

[THE PROSPECTOR *makes a second attempt to drag* PIERRE *away.* THE COUNTESS *cracks him over the skull with the siphon. They join battle.* THE COUNTESS *whistles.* THE DOORMAN *comes, then the other* VAGABONDS, *and lastly the* POLICE SERGEANT.]

PROSPECTOR. Officer! Arrest this woman!

SERGEANT. What's the trouble here?

PROSPECTOR. She refuses to let this man go.

SERGEANT. Why should she?

PROSPECTOR. It's against the law for a woman to detain a man on the street.

IRMA. Suppose it's her son whom she's found again after twenty years?

THE RAGPICKER [*gallantly*]. Or her long-lost brother? The Countess is not so old.

PROSPECTOR. Officer, this is a clear case of disorderly conduct.

[THE DEAF-MUTE *interrupts with frantic signals.*]

COUNTESS. Irma, what is the Deaf-Mute saying?

IRMA [*interpreting*]. The young man is in danger of his life. He mustn't go with him.

PROSPECTOR. What does he know?

IRMA. He knows everything.

PROSPECTOR. Officer, I'll have to take your number.

COUNTESS. Take his number. It's 2133. It adds up to nine. It will bring you luck.

SERGEANT. Countess, between ourselves, what are you holding him for, anyway?

COUNTESS. I'm holding him because it's very pleasant to hold him. I've never really held anybody before, and I'm making the most of it. And because so long as *I* hold him, he's free.

PROSPECTOR. Pierre, I'm giving you fair warning. . . .

COUNTESS. And I'm holding him because Irma wants me to hold him. Because if I let him go, it will break her heart.

IRMA. Oh, Countess!

SERGEANT [*to* THE PROSPECTOR]. All right, you—move on. Nobody's holding you. You're blocking traffic. Move on.

PROSPECTOR [*menacingly*]. I have your number. [*and murderously, to* PIERRE] You'll regret this, Pierre.

[*Exit* PROSPECTOR.]

PIERRE. Thank you, Countess.

COUNTESS. They're blackmailing you, are they? [PIERRE *nods.*] What have you done? Murdered somebody?

PIERRE. No.

COUNTESS. Stolen something?

PIERRE. No.

COUNTESS. What then?

PIERRE. I forged a signature.

COUNTESS. Whose signature?

PIERRE. My father's. To a note.

COUNTESS. And this man has the paper, I suppose?

PIERRE. He promised to tear it up, if I did what he wanted. But I couldn't do it.

COUNTESS. But the man is mad! Does he really want to destroy the whole neighborhood?

PIERRE. He wants to destroy the whole city.

COUNTESS [*laughs*]. Fantastic.

PIERRE. It's not funny, Countess. He can do it. He's mad, but he's powerful, and he has friends. Their machines are already drawn up and waiting. In three months' time you may see the city covered by a forest of derricks and drills.

COUNTESS. But what are they looking for? Have they lost something?

PIERRE. They're looking for oil. They're convinced that Paris is sitting on a lake of oil.

COUNTESS. Suppose it is. What harm does it do?

PIERRE. They want to bring the oil to the surface, Countess.

COUNTESS [*laughs*]. How silly! Is that a reason to destroy a city? What do they want with this oil?

PIERRE. They want to make war, Countess.

COUNTESS. Oh, dear, let's forget about these horrible men. The world is beautiful. It's happy. That's how God made it. No man can change it.

WAITER. Ah, Countess, if you only knew . . .

COUNTESS. If I only knew what?

WAITER. Shall we tell her now? Shall we tell her?

COUNTESS. What is it you are hiding from me?

THE RAGPICKER. Nothing, Countess. It's you who are hiding.

WAITER. You tell her. You've been a pitchman. You can talk.

ALL. Tell her. Tell her. Tell her.

COUNTESS. You're frightening me, my friends. Go on. I'm listening.

THE RAGPICKER. Countess, there was a time when old clothes were as good as new—in fact, they were better. Because when people wore clothes, they gave something to them. You may not believe it, but right this minute, the highest-priced shops in Paris are selling clothes that were thrown away thirty years ago. They're selling them for new. That's how good they were.

COUNTESS. Well?

THE RAGPICKER. Countess, there was a time when garbage was a pleasure. A garbage can was not what it is now. If it smelled a little strange, it was because it was a little confused—there was everything there—sardines, cologne, iodine, roses. An amateur might jump to a wrong conclusion. But to a professional—it was the smell of God's plenty.

COUNTESS. Well?

THE RAGPICKER. Countess, the world has changed.

COUNTESS. Nonsense. How could it change? People are the same, I hope.

THE RAGPICKER. No, Countess. The people are not the same. The people are different. There's been an invasion. An infiltration. From another planet. The world is not beautiful any more. It's not happy.

COUNTESS. Not happy? Is that true? Why didn't you tell me this before?

THE RAGPICKER. Because you live in a dream, Countess. And we don't like to disturb you.

COUNTESS. But how could it have happened?

THE RAGPICKER. Countess, there was a time when you could walk around Paris, and all the people you met were just like yourself. A little cleaner, maybe, or dirtier, perhaps, or angry, or smiling—but you knew them. They were you. Well, Countess, twenty years ago, one day, on the street, I saw a face in the crowd. A face, you might say, without a face. The eyes—empty. The expression—not human. Not a human face. It saw me staring, and when it looked back at me with its gelatine eyes, I shuddered. Because I knew that to make room for this one, one of us must have left the earth. A while after, I saw another.. And another. And since then, I've seen hundreds come in—yes—thousands.

COUNTESS. Describe them to me.

THE RAGPICKER. You've seen them yourself, Countess. Their clothes don't wrinkle. Their hats don't come off. When they talk, they don't look at you. They don't perspire.

COUNTESS. Have they wives? Have they children?

THE RAGPICKER. They buy the models out of shop windows, furs and all. They animate them by a secret process. Then they marry them. Naturally, they don't have children.

COUNTESS. What work do they do?

THE RAGPICKER. They don't do any work. Whenever they meet, they whisper, and then they pass each other thousand-franc notes. You see them standing on the corner by the Stock Exchange. You see them at auctions—in the back. They never raise a finger—they just stand there. In theater lobbies, by the box office—they never go inside. They don't do anything, but wherever you see them, things are not the same. I remember well the time when a cabbage could sell itself just by being a cabbage. Nowadays it's no good being a cabbage—unless you have an agent and pay him a commission. Nothing is free any more to sell itself or give itself away. These days, Countess, every cabbage has its pimp.

COUNTESS. I can't believe that.

THE RAGPICKER. Countess, little by little, the pimps have taken over the world. They don't do anything, they don't make anything—they just stand there and take their cut. It makes a difference. Look at the shopkeepers. Do you ever see one smiling at a customer any more? Certainly not. Their smiles are strictly for the pimps. The butcher has to smile at the meat-pimp, the florist at the rose-pimp, the grocer at the fresh-fruit-and-vegetable pimp. It's all organized down to the slightest detail. A pimp for bird-seed. A pimp for fish-food. That's why the cost of living keeps going up all the time. You buy a glass of beer—it costs twice as much as it used to. Why? 10 percent for the glass-pimp, 10 percent for the beer-pimp, 20 percent for the glass-of-beer-pimp—that's where our money goes. Personally, I prefer the old-fashioned type. Some of those men at least were loved by the women they sold. But what feelings can a pimp arouse in a leg of lamb? Pardon my language, Irma.

COUNTESS. It's all right. She doesn't understand it.

THE RAGPICKER. So now you know, Countess, why the world is no longer happy. We are the last of the free people of the earth. You saw them looking us over today. Tomorrow, the street-singer will start paying the song-pimp, and the garbage-pimp will be after me. I tell you, Countess, we're finished. It's the end of free enterprise in this world!

COUNTESS. Is this true, Roderick?

PIERRE. I'm afraid it's true.

COUNTESS. Did you know about this, Irma?

IRMA. All I know is the Doorman says that faith is dead.

DOORMAN. I've stopped taking bets over the phone.

JUGGLER. The very air is different, Countess. You can't trust it any more. If I throw my torches up too high, they go out.

THE RAGPICKER. The sky-pimp puts them out.

FLOWER GIRL. My flowers don't last over night now. They wilt.

JUGGLER. Have you noticed, the pigeons don't fly any more?

THE RAGPICKER. They can't afford to. They walk.

COUNTESS. They're a lot of fools and so are you! You should have told me at once! How can you bear to live in a world where there is unhappiness? Where a man is not his own master? Are you cowards? All we have to do is to get rid of these men.

PIERRE. How can we get rid of them? They're too strong.

[THE SERGEANT *walks up again.*]

COUNTESS [*smiling*]. The Sergeant will help us.

SERGEANT. Who? Me?

IRMA. There are a great many of them, Countess. The Deaf-Mute knows them all. They employed him once, years ago, because he was deaf. [THE DEAF-MUTE *wigwags a short speech.*] They fired him because he wasn't blind. [*another flash of sign language*] They're all connected like the parts of a machine.

COUNTESS. So much the better. We shall drive the whole machine into a ditch.

SERGEANT. It's not that easy, Countess. You never catch these birds napping. They change before your very eyes. I remember when I was in the detectives . . . You catch a president, pfft! He turns into a trustee. You catch him as trustee, and pfft! he's not a trustee—he's an honorary vice-chairman. You catch a Senator dead to rights: he becomes Minister of Justice. You get after the Minister of Justice—he is Chief of Police. And there you are—no longer in the detectives.

PIERRE. He's right, Countess. They have all the power. And all the money. And they're greedy for more.

COUNTESS. They're greedy? Ah, then, my friends, they're lost. If they're greedy, they're stupid. If they're greedy—don't worry, I know exactly what to do. Roderick, by tonight you will be an honest man. And, Juggler, your torches will stay lit. And your beer will flow freely again, Martial. And the world will be saved. Let's get to work.

THE RAGPICKER. What are you going to do?

COUNTESS. Have you any kerosene in the house, Irma?

IRMA. Yes. Would you like some?

COUNTESS. I want just a little. In a dirty bottle. With a little mud. And some mange-cure, if you have it. [*to* THE DEAF-MUTE] Deaf-Mute! Take a letter. [IRMA *interprets in sign language. To* THE SINGER] Singer, go and find Madame Constance.

[IRMA *and* THE WAITER *go into the café.*]

SINGER. Yes, Countess.

COUNTESS. Ask her to be at my house by two o'clock. I'll be waiting for her in the cellar. You may tell her we have to discuss the future of humanity. That's sure to bring her.

SINGER. Yes, Countess.

COUNTESS. And ask her to bring Mademoiselle Gabrielle and Madame Josephine with her. Do you know how to get in to speak to Madame Constance? You ring twice, and then meow three times like a cat. Do you know how to meow?

SINGER. I'm better at barking.

COUNTESS. Better practise meowing on the way. Incidentally, I think Madame Constance knows all the verses of your mazurka. Remind me to ask her.

SINGER. Yes, Countess. [*Exit.*]

[IRMA *comes in. She is shaking the oily concoction in a little perfume vial, which she now hands* THE COUNTESS.]

IRMA. Here you are, Countess.

COUNTESS. Thanks, Irma. [*She assumes a presidential manner.*] Deaf-Mute! Ready?

[IRMA *interprets in sign language.* THE WAITER *has brought out a portfolio of letter paper and placed it on a table.* THE DEAF-MUTE *sits down before it, and prepares to write.*]

IRMA [*speaking for* THE DEAF-MUTE]. I'm ready.

COUNTESS. My dear Mr.— What's his name?

[IRMA *wigwags the question to* THE DEAF-MUTE, *who answers in the same manner. It is all done so deftly that it is as if* THE DEAF-MUTE *were actually speaking.*]

IRMA. They are all called Mr. President.

COUNTESS. My dear Mr. President: I have personally verified the existence of a spontaneous outcrop of oil in the cellar of Number 21 Rue de Chaillot, which is at present occupied by a dignified person of unstable mentality. [THE COUNTESS *grins knowingly*.] This explains why, fortunately for us, the discovery has so long been kept secret. If you should wish to verify the existence of this outcrop for yourself, you may call at the above address at three P.M. today. I am herewith enclosing a sample so that you may judge the quality and consistency of the crude. Yours very truly. Roderick, can you sign the Prospector's name?

PIERRE. You wish me to?

COUNTESS. One forgery wipes out the other.

[PIERRE *signs the letter.* THE DEAF-MUTE *types the address on an envelope.*]

IRMA. Who is to deliver this?

COUNTESS. The Doorman, of course. On his bicycle. And as soon as you have delivered it, run over to the Prospector's office. Leave word that the President expects to see him at my house at three.

DOORMAN. Yes, Countess.

COUNTESS. I shall leave you now. I have many pressing things to do. Among others, I must press my red gown.

THE RAGPICKER. But this only takes care of two of them, Countess.

COUNTESS. Didn't the Deaf-Mute say they are all connected like the works of a machine?

IRMA. Yes.

COUNTESS. Then, if one comes, the rest will follow. And we shall have them all. My boa, please.

DOORMAN. The one that's stolen, Countess?

COUNTESS. Naturally. The one the Prospector stole.

DOORMAN. It hasn't turned up yet, Countess. But someone has left an ermine collar.

COUNTESS. Real ermine?

DOORMAN. Looks like it.

COUNTESS. Ermine and iris were made for each other. Let me see it.

DOORMAN. Yes, Countess.

[*Exit* DOORMAN.]

COUNTESS. Roderick, you shall escort me. You still look pale. I have some old Chartreuse at home. I always take a glass each year. Last year I forgot. You shall have it.

PIERRE. If there is anything I can do, Countess . . . ?

COUNTESS. There is a great deal you can do. There are all the things that need to be done in a room that no man has been in for twenty years. You can untwist the cord on the blind and let in a little sunshine for a change. You can take the mirror off the wardrobe door, and deliver me once and for all from the old harpy that lives in the mirror. You can let the mouse out of the trap. I'm tired of feeding it. [*to her friends*] Each man to his post. See you later, my friends. [THE DOORMAN *puts the ermine collar around her shoulders.*] Thank you, my boy. It's rabbit. [*One o'clock strikes.*] Your arm, Valentine.

PIERRE. Valentine?

COUNTESS. It's just struck one. At one, all men become Valentine.

PIERRE [*he offers his arm*]. Permit me.

COUNTESS. Or Valentino. It's obviously far from the same, isn't it, Irma? But they have that much choice.

[*She sweeps out majestically with* PIERRE. *The others disperse. All but* IRMA.]

IRMA [*clearing off the table*]. I hate ugliness. I love beauty. I hate meanness. I adore kindness. It may not seem so grand to some to be a waitress in Paris. I love it. A waitress meets all sorts of people. She observes life. I hate to be alone. I love people. But I have never said I love you to a man. Men try to make me say it. They put their arms around me—I pretend I don't see it. They pinch me—I pretend I don't feel it. They kiss me—I pretend I don't know it. They take me out in the evening and make me drink—but I'm careful, I never say it. If they don't like it, they can leave me alone. Because when I say I love you to Him, He will know just by looking in my eyes that many have held me and pinched me and kissed me, but I have never said I love you to anyone in the world before. Never. No. [*Looking off in the direction in which* PIERRE *has gone, she whispers softly:*] I love you.

VOICE [*from within the café*]. Irma!

IRMA. Coming. [*Exit.*]

CURTAIN

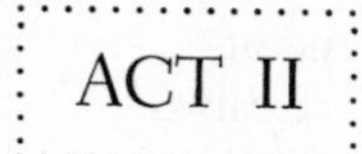

ACT II

SCENE. *The cellar of* THE COUNTESS' *house. An ancient vault set deep in the ground, with walls of solid masonry, part brick and part great ashlars, mossy and sweating. A staircase of medieval pattern is built into the thickness of the wall, and leads up to the street level from a landing halfway down. In the corners of the cellar are piled casks, packing cases, bird-cages, and other odds and ends—the accumulation of centuries—the whole effect utterly fantastic.*

In the center of the vast underground room, some furniture has been arranged to give an impression of a sitting-room of the 1890's. There is a venerable chaise-longue piled with cushions that once were gay, three armchairs, a table with an oil lamp and a bowl of flowers, a shaggy rug. It is two P.M., *the same day.*

AT RISE. THE COUNTESS *is sitting over a bit of mending, in one of the armchairs.* IRMA *appears on the landing and calls down.*

IRMA. Countess! The Sewer Man is here.

COUNTESS. Thank goodness, Irma. Send him down. [THE SEWER MAN *enters. He carries his hip-boots in his hand.*] How do you do, Mr. Sewer Man? [THE SEWER MAN *bows.*] But why do you have your boots in your hand instead of on your feet?

SEWER MAN. Etiquette, Countess. Etiquette.

COUNTESS. How very American! I'm told that Americans nowadays apologize for their gloves if they happen to take one's hand. As if the skin of a human were nicer to touch than the skin of a sheep! And particularly if they have sweaty hands . . . !

SEWER MAN. My feet never sweat, Countess.

COUNTESS. How very nice! But please don't stand on ceremony here. Put your boots on. Put them on.

SEWER MAN [*complying*]. Thanks very much, Countess.

COUNTESS [*while he draws on his boots*]. I'm sure you must have a very poor opinion of the upper world, from what you see of it. The way people throw their filth into your territory is absolutely scandalous! I burn all my refuse, and I scatter the ashes. All I ever throw in the drain is flowers. Did you happen to see a lily float by this morning? Mine. But perhaps you didn't notice?

SEWER MAN. We notice a lot more down there, Countess, than you might think. You'd be surprised the things we notice. There's lots of things come along that were obviously intended for us—little gifts you might call them—sometimes a brand-new shaving brush—sometimes, *The Brothers Karamazov*. . . . Thanks for the lily, Countess. A very sweet thought.

COUNTESS. Tomorrow you shall have this iris. But now, let's come to the point. I have two questions to ask you.

SEWER MAN. Yes, Countess?

COUNTESS. First—and this has nothing to do with our problem—it's just something that has been troubling me. . . . Tell me, is it true that the sewer men of Paris have a king?

SEWER MAN. Oh, now, Countess, that's another of those fairy tales out of the Sunday supplements. It just seems those writers can't keep their minds off the sewers! It fascinates them. They keep thinking of us moving around in our underground canals like gondoliers in Venice, and it sends them into a fever of romance! The things they say about us! They say we have a race of girls down there who never see the light of day! It's completely fantastic! The girls naturally come out—every Christmas and Easter. And orgies by torchlight with gondolas and guitars! With troops of rats that dance as they follow the piper. What nonsense! The rats are not allowed to dance. No, no, no. Of course we have no king. Down in the sewers, you'll find nothing but good Republicans.

COUNTESS. And no queen?

SEWER MAN. No. We may run a beauty contest down there once in a while. Or crown a mermaid Queen of the May. But no queen what you'd call a queen. And, as for these swimming races they talk so much about . . . possibly once in a while—in the summer—in the dog days . . .

COUNTESS. I believe you. I believe you. And now tell me. Do you remember that night I found you here in my cellar—looking very pale and strange—you were half-dead as a matter of fact—and I gave you some brandy . . .

SEWER MAN. Yes, Countess.

COUNTESS. That night you promised if ever I should need it—you would tell me the secret of this room.

SEWER MAN. The secret of the moving stone?

COUNTESS. I need it now.

SEWER MAN. Only the King of the Sewer Men knows this secret.

COUNTESS. I'm sure of it. I know most secrets, of course. As a matter of fact, I have three magic words that will open any door that words can open. I have tried them all—in various tones of voice. They don't seem to work. And this is a matter of life and death.

SEWER MAN. Look, Countess.

[*He locates a brick in the masonry, and pushes it. A huge block of stone slowly pivots and uncovers a trap from which a circular staircase winds into the bowels of the earth.*]

COUNTESS. Good heavens! Where do those stairs lead?

SEWER MAN. Nowhere.

COUNTESS. But they must go somewhere.

SEWER MAN. They just go down.

COUNTESS. Let's go and see.

SEWER MAN. No, Countess. Never again. That time you found me, I had a pretty close shave. I kept going down and around, and down and around for an hour, a year—I don't know. There's no end to it, Countess. Once you start you can't stop. . . . Your head begins to turn—you're lost. No—once you start down, there's no coming up.

COUNTESS. You came up.

SEWER MAN. I—I am a special case. Besides, I had my tools, my ropes. And I stopped in time.

COUNTESS. You could have screamed—shouted.

SEWER MAN. You could fire off a cannon.

COUNTESS. Who could have built a thing like this?

SEWER MAN. Paris is old, you know. Paris is very old.

COUNTESS. You don't suppose, by any chance, there is oil down there?

SEWER MAN. There's only death down there.

COUNTESS. I should have preferred a little oil too—or a vein of gold—or emeralds. You're quite sure there is nothing?

SEWER MAN. Not even rats.

COUNTESS. How does one lower this stone?

SEWER MAN. Simple. To open, you press here. And to close it, you push there. [*He presses the brick. The stone descends.*] Now there's two of us in the world that knows it.

COUNTESS. I won't remember long. Is it all right if I repeat my magic words while I press it?

SEWER MAN. It's bound to help.

[IRMA *enters.*]

IRMA. Countess, Madame Constance and Mademoiselle Gabrielle are here.

COUNTESS. Show them down, Irma. Thank you very much, Mr. Sewer Man.

SEWER MAN. Like that story about the steam laundry that's supposed to be running day and night in my sewer . . . I can assure you . . .

COUNTESS [*edging him toward the door*]. Thank you very much.

SEWER MAN. Pure imagination! They never work nights.

[*He goes off, bowing graciously.*]

[CONSTANCE, *the Madwoman of Passy, and* GABRIELLE, *the Madwoman of St. Sulpice, come down daintily.* CONSTANCE *is all in white. She wears an enormous hat graced with ostrich plumes, and a lavender veil.* GABRIELLE *is costumed with the affected simplicity of the 1880's. She is atrociously made up in a remorseless parody of blushing innocence, and she minces down the stairs with macabre coyness.*]

CONSTANCE. Aurelia! Don't tell us they've found your feather boa?

GABRIELLE. You don't mean Adolphe Bertaut has proposed at last! I knew he would.

COUNTESS. How are you, Constance? [*She shouts.*] How are you, Gabrielle?

GABRIELLE. You needn't shout today, my dear. It's Wednesday. Wednesdays, I hear perfectly.

CONSTANCE. It's Thursday.

GABRIELLE. Oh, dear. Well, never mind. I'm going to make an exception just this once.

CONSTANCE [*to an imaginary dog who has stopped on the landing*].

Come along, Dickie. Come along. And stop barking. What a racket you're making! Come on, darling—we've come to see the longest boa and the handsomest man in Paris. Come on.

COUNTESS. Constance, it's not a question of my boa today. Nor of poor Adolphe. It's a question of the future of the human race.

CONSTANCE. You think it has a future?

COUNTESS. Please don't make silly jokes. Sit down and listen to me. Today we must make a decision which may alter the fate of the world.

CONSTANCE. Couldn't we do it tomorrow? I want to wash my slippers. Now, Dickie—please!

COUNTESS. We haven't a moment to waste. Where is Josephine? Well, we'd best have our tea, and the moment Josephine comes . . .

GABRIELLE. Josephine is sitting on her bench in front of the palace waiting for President Wilson to come out. She says she's sorry, but she positively must see him today.

CONSTANCE. Dickie!

COUNTESS. What a pity! [*She gets the tea things from the side table, pours tea and serves cake and honey.*] I wish she were here to help us. She has a first-class brain.

CONSTANCE. Go ahead, dear. We're listening. [*to* DICKIE] What is it, Dickie? You want to sit in Aunt Aurelia's lap. All right, darling. Go on. Jump, Dickie.

COUNTESS. Constance, we love you, as you know. And we love Dickie. But this is a serious matter. So let's stop being childish for once.

CONSTANCE. And what does that mean, if you please?

COUNTESS. It means Dickie. You know perfectly well that we love him and fuss over him just as if he were still alive. He's a sacred memory and we wouldn't hurt his feelings for the world. But please don't plump him in my lap when I'm settling the future of mankind. His basket is in the corner—he knows where it is, and he can just go and sit in it.

CONSTANCE. So you're against Dickie too! You too!

COUNTESS. Constance! I'm not in the least against Dickie! I adore Dickie. But you know as well as I that Dickie is only a convention with us. It's a beautiful convention—but it doesn't have to bark all the time. Besides, it's you that spoil him. The time you went to visit your niece and left him with me, we got on marvelously together. He didn't bark, he didn't tear things, he didn't even eat. But when you're with him, one can pay attention to nothing else. I'm not going to take Dickie in my lap at a solemn moment like this, no, not for anything in the world. And that's that!

GABRIELLE [*very sweetly*]. Constance, dear, I don't mind taking him in my lap. He loves to sit in my lap, don't you, darling?

CONSTANCE. Kindly stop putting on angelic airs, Gabrielle. I know you very well. You're much too sweet to be sincere. There's plenty of times that I make believe that Dickie is here, when really I've left him home, and you cuddle and pet him just the same.

GABRIELLE. I adore animals.

CONSTANCE. If you adore animals, you shouldn't pet them when they're not there. It's a form of hypocrisy.

COUNTESS. Now, Constance, Gabrielle has as much right as you . . .

CONSTANCE. Gabrielle has no right to do what she does. Do you know what she does? She invites *people* to come to tea with us. *People* whom we know nothing about. *People* who exist only in her imagination.

COUNTESS. You think that's not an existence?

GABRIELLE. I don't invite them at all. They come by themselves. What can I do?

CONSTANCE. You might introduce us.

COUNTESS. If you think they're only imaginary, there's no point in your meeting them, is there?

CONSTANCE. Of course they're imaginary. But who likes to have imaginary people staring at one? Especially strangers.

GABRIELLE. Oh, they're really very nice. . . .

CONSTANCE. Tell me just one thing, Gabrielle—are they here now?

COUNTESS. Am I to be allowed to speak? Or is this going to be the same as the argument about inoculating Josephine's cat, when we didn't get to the subject at all!

CONSTANCE. Never! Never! Never! I'll never give my consent to that. [*to* DICKIE] I'd never do a thing like that to you, Dickie sweet. . . . Oh, no! Oh, no!

[*She begins to weep softly.*]

COUNTESS. Good heavens! Now we have her in tears. What an impossible creature! With the fate of humanity hanging in the balance! All right, all right, stop crying. I'll take him in my lap. Come, Dickie, Dickie.

CONSTANCE. No. He won't go now. Oh, how can you be so cruel? Don't you suppose I know about Dickie? Don't you think I'd rather have him here alive and woolly and frisking around the way he used to? You have your Adolphe, Gabrielle has her birds. But I have only Dickie. Do you think I'd be so silly about him if it wasn't that it's only by pretending that he's here all the time that I get him to come sometimes, really? Next time I won't bring him!

COUNTESS. Now let's not get ourselves worked up over nothing. Come here, Dickie. . . . Irma is going to take you for a nice walk. [*She rings her bell.*] Irma!

[IRMA *appears on the landing.*]

CONSTANCE. No. He doesn't want to go. Besides, I didn't bring him today. So there!

COUNTESS. Very well, then, Irma, make sure the door is locked.

IRMA. Yes, Countess.

[IRMA *exits.*]

CONSTANCE. What do you mean? Why locked? Who's coming?

COUNTESS. If you'd let me get a word in, you'd know by now. A terrible thing has happened. This morning, this very morning, exactly at noon . . .

CONSTANCE [*thrilled*]. Oh, how exciting!

COUNTESS. Be quiet. This morning, exactly at noon, thanks to a young man who'd drowned himself in the Seine . . . Oh, yes, while I think of it—do you know a mazurka called *La Belle Polonaise*?

CONSTANCE. Yes, Aurelia.

COUNTESS. Could you sing it now? This very minute?

CONSTANCE. Yes, Aurelia.

COUNTESS. All of it?

CONSTANCE. Yes, Aurelia. But who's interrupting now, Aurelia?

COUNTESS. You're right. Well, this morning, exactly at noon, I discovered a horrible plot. There is a group of men who intend to tear down the whole city!

CONSTANCE. Is that all?

GABRIELLE. But I don't understand, Aurelia. Why should men

want to tear down the city? It was they themselves who put it up.

COUNTESS. You are so innocent, my poor Gabrielle. There are people in the world who want to destroy everything. They have the fever of destruction. Even when they pretend that they're building, it is only in order to destroy. When they put up a new building, they quietly knock down two old ones. They build cities so that they can destroy the countryside. They destroy space with telephones and time with airplanes. Humanity is now dedicated to the task of universal destruction. I am speaking, of course, primarily of the male sex.

GABRIELLE [*shocked*]. Oh . . . !

CONSTANCE. Aurelia! Must you talk sex in front of Gabrielle?

COUNTESS. There are *two* sexes.

CONSTANCE. Gabrielle is a virgin, Aurelia!

COUNTESS. Oh, she can't be as innocent as all that. She keeps canaries.

GABRIELLE. I think you're being very cruel about men, Aurelia. Men are big and beautiful, and as loyal as dogs. I preferred not to marry, it's true. But I hear excellent reports from friends who have had an opportunity to observe them closely.

COUNTESS. My poor darling! You are still living in a dream. But one day, you will wake up as I have, and then you will see what is happening in the world! The tide has turned, my dear. Men are changing back into beasts. They know it. They no longer try to hide it. There was once such a thing as manners. I remember a time when the hungriest was the one who took the longest to pick up his fork. The one with the broadest grin was the one who needed most to go to the . . . It was such fun to keep them grinning like that for hours. But now they no longer pretend. Just look at them—snuffling their soup like pigs, tearing their meat like tigers, crunching their lettuce like crocodiles! A man doesn't take your hand nowadays. He gives you his paw.

CONSTANCE. Would that trouble you so much if they turned into animals? Personally, I think it's a good idea.

GABRIELLE. Oh, I'd love to see them like that. They'd be sweet.

CONSTANCE. It might be the salvation of the human race.

COUNTESS [*to* CONSTANCE]. You'd make a fine rabbit, wouldn't you?

CONSTANCE. I?

COUNTESS. Naturally. You don't think it's only the men who are changing? You change along with them. Husbands and wives together. We're all one race, you know.

CONSTANCE. You think so? And why would my poor husband have to be a rabbit if he were alive?

COUNTESS. Remember his front teeth? When he nibbled his celery?

CONSTANCE. I'm happy to say, I remember absolutely nothing about him. All I remember on that subject is the time that Father Lacordaire tried to kiss me in the park.

COUNTESS. Yes, yes, of course.

CONSTANCE. And what does that mean, if you please, "Yes, yes, of course?"

COUNTESS. Constance, just this once, look us in the eye and tell us truly—did that really happen or did you read about it in a book?

CONSTANCE. Now I'm being insulted!

COUNTESS. We promise you faithfully that we'll believe it all over again afterwards, won't we, Gabrielle? But tell us the truth this once.

CONSTANCE. How dare you question my memories? Suppose I said your pearls were false!

COUNTESS. They were.

CONSTANCE. I'm not asking what they were. I'm asking what they are. Are they false or are they real?

COUNTESS. Everyone knows that little by little, as one wears pearls, they become real.

CONSTANCE. And isn't it exactly the same with memories?

COUNTESS. Now do not let us waste time. I must go on.

CONSTANCE. I think Gabrielle is perfectly right about men. There are still plenty who haven't changed a bit. There's an old Senator who bows to Gabrielle every day when he passes her in front of the palace. And he takes off his hat each time.

GABRIELLE. That's perfectly true, Aurelia. He's always pushing an empty baby carriage, and he always stops and bows.

COUNTESS. Don't be taken in, Gabrielle. It's all make-believe. And all we can expect from these make-believe men is itself make-believe. They give us facepowder made of stones, sausages made of sawdust, shirts made of glass, stockings made of milk. It's all a vulgar pretense. And if that is the case, imagine what passes, these days, for virtue, sincerity, generosity and love! I warn you, Gabrielle, don't let this Senator with the empty baby carriage pull the wool over your eyes.

GABRIELLE. He's really the soul of courtesy. He seems very correct.

COUNTESS. Those are the worst. Gabrielle, beware! He'll make you put on black riding boots, while he dances the can-can around you, singing God knows what filth at the top of his voice. The very thought makes one's blood run cold!

GABRIELLE. You think that's what he has in mind?

COUNTESS. Of course. Men have lost all sense of decency. They are all equally disgusting. Just look at them in the evening, sitting at their tables in the café, working away in unison with their toothpicks, hour after hour, digging up roast beef, veal, onion . . .

CONSTANCE. They don't harm anyone that way.

COUNTESS. Then why do you barricade your door, and make your friends meow before you let them come up? Incidentally, we must make an interesting sight, Gabrielle and I, yowling together on your doorstep like a couple of tomcats!

CONSTANCE. There's no need at all for you to yowl together. One would be quite enough. And you know perfectly well why I have to do it. It's because there are murderers.

COUNTESS. I don't quite see what prevents murderers from meowing like anybody else. But why are there murderers?

CONSTANCE. Why? Because there are thieves.

COUNTESS. And why are there thieves? Why is there almost nothing but thieves?

CONSTANCE. Because they worship money. Because money is king.

COUNTESS. Ah—now we've come to it. Because we live in the reign of the Golden Calf. Did you realize that, Gabrielle? Men now publicly worship the Golden Calf!

GABRIELLE. How awful! Have the authorities been notified?

COUNTESS. The authorities do it themselves, Gabrielle.

GABRIELLE. Oh! Has anyone talked to the bishop?

COUNTESS. Nowadays only money talks to the bishop. And so you see why I asked you to come here today. The world has gone out of its mind. Unless we do something, humanity is doomed! Constance, have you any suggestions?

CONSTANCE. I know what I always do in a case like this. . . .

COUNTESS. You write to the Prime Minister.

CONSTANCE. He always does what I tell him.

COUNTESS. Does he ever answer your letters?

CONSTANCE. He knows I prefer him not to. It might excite gossip. Besides, I don't always write. Sometimes I wire. The time I told him about the Archbishop's frigidaire, it was by wire. And they sent a new one the very next day.

COUNTESS. There was probably a commission in it for someone. And what do you suggest, Gabrielle?

CONSTANCE. Now, how can she tell you until she's consulted her voices?

GABRIELLE. I could go right home and consult them, and we could meet again after dinner.

COUNTESS. There's no time for that. Besides, your voices are not real voices.

GABRIELLE [*furious*]. How dare you say a thing like that?

COUNTESS. Where do your voices come from? Still from your sewing-machine?

GABRIELLE. Not at all. They've passed into my hot-water bottle. And it's much nicer that way. They don't chatter any more. They gurgle. But they haven't been a bit nice to me lately. Last night they kept telling me to let my canaries out. "Let them out. Let them out. Let them out."

CONSTANCE. Did you?

GABRIELLE. I opened the cage. They wouldn't go.

COUNTESS. I don't call that *voices*. Objects talk—everyone knows that. It's the principle of the phonograph. But to ask a hot-water bottle for advice is silly. What does a hot-water bottle know? No, all we have to consult here is our own judgment.

CONSTANCE. Very well then, tell us what you have decided. Since you're asking our opinion, you've doubtless made up your mind.

COUNTESS. Yes, I've thought the whole thing out. All I really needed to discover was the source of the infection. Today I found it.

CONSTANCE. Where?

COUNTESS. You'll see soon enough. I've baited a trap. In just a few minutes, the rats will be here.

GABRIELLE [*in alarm*]. Rats!

COUNTESS. Don't be alarmed. They're still in human form.

GABRIELLE. Heavens! What are you going to do with them?

COUNTESS. That's just the question. Suppose I get these wicked men all here at once—in my cellar—have I the right to exterminate them?

GABRIELLE. To kill them?

[COUNTESS *nods.*]

CONSTANCE. That's not a question for us. You'll have to ask Father Bridet.

COUNTESS. I have asked him. Yes. One day, in confession, I told him frankly that I had a secret desire to destroy all wicked people. He said: "By all means, my child. And when you're ready to go into action, I'll lend you the jawbone of an ass."

CONSTANCE. That's just talk. You get him to put that in writing.

GABRIELLE. What's your scheme, Aurelia?

COUNTESS. That's a secret.

CONSTANCE. It's not so easy to kill them. Let's say you had a tank full of vitriol all ready for them. You could never get them to walk into it. There's nothing so stubborn as a man when you want him to do something.

COUNTESS. Leave that to me.

CONSTANCE. But if they're killed, they're bound to be missed, and and then we'll be fined. They fine you for every little thing these days.

COUNTESS. They won't be missed.

GABRIELLE. I wish Josephine were here. Her sister's husband was a lawyer. She knows all about these things.

COUNTESS. Do you miss a cold when it's gone? Or the germs that caused it? When the world feels well again, do you think it will regret its illness? No, it will stretch itself joyfully, and it will smile—that's all.

CONSTANCE. Just a moment! Gabrielle, are they here now? Yes or no?

COUNTESS. What's the matter with you now?

CONSTANCE. I'm simply asking Gabrielle if her friends are in the room or not. I have a right to know.

GABRIELLE. I'm not allowed to say.

CONSTANCE. I know very well they are. I'm sure of it. Otherwise you wouldn't be making faces.

COUNTESS. May I ask what difference it makes to you if her friends are in the room?

CONSTANCE. Just this: If they're here, I'm not going to say another word! I'm certainly not going to commit myself in a matter involving the death sentence in the presence of third parties, whether they exist or not.

GABRIELLE. That's not being very nice to my guests, is it?

COUNTESS. Constance, you must be mad! Or are you so stupid as to think that just because we're alone, there's nobody with us? Do you consider us so boring or repulsive that of all the millions of beings, imaginary or otherwise, who are prowling about in space, there's not one who might possibly enjoy spending a little time with us? On the contrary, my dear—my house is full of guests always. They know that here they have a place in the universe where they can come when they're lonely and be sure of a welcome. For my part, I'm delighted to have them.

GABRIELLE. Thank you, Aurelia.

CONSTANCE. You know perfectly well, Aurelia . . .

COUNTESS. I know perfectly well that at this moment the whole universe is listening to us—and that every word we say echoes to the remotest star. To pretend otherwise is the sheerest hypocrisy.

CONSTANCE. Then why do you insult me in front of everybody? I'm not mean. I'm shy. I feel timid about giving an opinion in front of such a crowd. Furthermore, if you think I'm so bad and so stupid, why did you invite me, in the first place?

COUNTESS. I'll tell you. And I'll tell you why, disagreeable as you are, I always give you the biggest piece of cake and my best honey. It's because when you come there's always someone with you—and I don't mean Dickie—I mean someone who resembles you like a sister, only she's young and lovely, and she sits modestly to one side and smiles at me tenderly all the time you're bickering and quarreling, and never says a word. That's the Constance to whom I give the cake that you gobble, and it's because of her that you're here today, and it's her vote that I'm asking you to cast in this crucial moment. And not yours, which is of no importance whatever.

CONSTANCE. I'm leaving.

COUNTESS. Be so good as to sit down. I can't let her go yet.

CONSTANCE [*crossing toward the stairs*]. No. This is too much. I'm taking her with me.

[IRMA *enters.*]

IRMA. Madame Josephine.

COUNTESS. Thank heaven!

GABRIELLE. We're saved.

[JOSEPHINE, *the Madwoman of La Concorde, sweeps in majestically in a get-up somewhere between the regal and the priestly.*]

JOSEPHINE. My dear friends, today once again, I waited for President Wilson—but he didn't come out.

COUNTESS. You'll have to wait quite a while longer before he does. He's been dead since 1924.

JOSEPHINE. I have plenty of time.

COUNTESS. In anyone else, Josephine, these extravagances might seem a little childish. But a person of your judgment doubtless has her reasons for wanting to talk to a man to whom no one would listen when he was alive. We have a legal problem for you. Suppose you had all the world's criminals here in this room. And suppose you had a way of getting rid of them forever. Would you have the right to do it?

JOSEPHINE. Why not?

COUNTESS. Exactly my point.

GABRIELLE. But, Josephine, so many people!

JOSEPHINE. *De minimis non curat lex!* The more there are, the more legal it is. It's impersonal. It's even military. It's the cardinal principle of battle—you get all your enemies in one place, and you kill them all together at one time. Because if you had to track them down one by one in their houses and offices, you'd get tired, and sooner or later you'd stop. I believe your idea is very practical, Aurelia. I can't imagine why we never thought of it before.

GABRIELLE. Well, if you think it's all right to do it . . .

JOSEPHINE. By all means. Your criminals have had a fair trial, I suppose?

COUNTESS. Trial?

JOSEPHINE. Certainly. You can't kill anybody without a trial. That's elementary. "No man shall be deprived of his life, liberty and property without due process of law."

COUNTESS. They deprive us of ours.

JOSEPHINE. That's not the point. You're not accused of anything. Every accused—man, woman or child—has the right to defend himself at the bar of justice. Even animals. Before the Deluge, you will recall, the Lord permitted Noah to speak in defense of his fellow mortals. He evidently stuttered. You know the result. On the other hand, Captain Dreyfus was not only innocent—he was defended by a marvelous orator. The result was precisely the same. So you see, in having a trial, you run no risk whatever.

COUNTESS. But if I give them the slightest cause for suspicion—I'll lose them.

JOSEPHINE. There's a simple procedure prescribed in such cases. You can summon the defendants by calling them three times—mentally, if you like. If they don't appear, the court may designate an attorney who will represent them. This attorney can then argue their case to the court, *in absentia,* and a judgment can then be rendered, *in contumacio.*

COUNTESS. But I don't know any attorneys. And we have only ten minutes.

GABRIELLE. Hurry, Josephine, hurry!

JOSEPHINE. In case of emergency, it is permissible for the court to order the first passer-by to act as attorney for the defense. A defense is like a baptism. Absolutely indispensable, but you don't have to know anything to do it. Ask Irma to get you somebody. Anybody.

COUNTESS. The Deaf-Mute?

JOSEPHINE. Well—that's getting it down a bit fine. That might be questionable on appeal.

COUNTESS [*calls*]. Irma! What about the Police Sergeant?

JOSEPHINE. He won't do. He's under oath to the state.

[IRMA *appears.*]

IRMA. Yes, Countess?

COUNTESS. Who's out there, Irma?

IRMA. All our friends, Countess. There's the Ragpicker and . . .

COUNTESS. Send down the Ragpicker.

CONSTANCE. Do you think it's wise to have all those millionaires represented by a ragpicker?

JOSEPHINE. It's a first-rate choice. Criminals are always represented by their opposites. Murderers, by someone who obviously wouldn't hurt a fly. Rapists, by a member of the League for Decency. Experience shows it's the only way to get an acquittal.

COUNTESS. But we must not have an acquittal. That would mean the end of the world!

JOSEPHINE. Justice is justice, my dear.

[THE RAGPICKER *comes down, with a stately air. Behind him, on the landing, appear the other* VAGABONDS.]

THE RAGPICKER. Greetings, Countess. Greetings, ladies. My most sincere compliments.

COUNTESS. Has Irma told you . . . ?

THE RAGPICKER. She said something about a trial.

COUNTESS. You have been appointed attorney for the defense.

THE RAGPICKER. Terribly flattered, I'm sure.

COUNTESS. You realize, don't you, how much depends on the outcome of this trial?

JOSEPHINE. Do you know the defendants well enough to undertake the case?

THE RAGPICKER. I know them to the bottom of their souls. I go through their garbage every day.

CONSTANCE. And what do you find there?

THE RAGPICKER. Mostly flowers.

GABRIELLE. It's true, you know, the rich are always surrounded with flowers.

CONSTANCE. How beautiful!

COUNTESS. Are you trying to prejudice the court?

THE RAGPICKER. Oh no, Countess, no.

COUNTESS. We want a completely impartial defense.

THE RAGPICKER. Of course, Countess, of course. Permit me to make a suggestion.

COUNTESS. Will you preside, Josephine?

THE RAGPICKER. Instead of speaking as attorney, suppose you let me speak directly as defendant. It will be more convincing, and I can get into it more.

JOSEPHINE. Excellent idea. Motion granted.

COUNTESS. We don't want you to be too convincing, remember.

THE RAGPICKER. Impartial, Countess, impartial.

JOSEPHINE. Well? Have you prepared your case?

THE RAGPICKER. How rich am I?

JOSEPHINE. Millions. Billions.

THE RAGPICKER. How did I get them? Theft? Murder? Embezzlement?

COUNTESS. Most likely.

THE RAGPICKER. Do I have a wife? A mistress?

COUNTESS. Everything.

THE RAGPICKER. All right. I'm ready.

GABRIELLE. Will you have some tea?

THE RAGPICKER. Is that good?

CONSTANCE. Very good for the voice. The Russians drink nothing but tea. And they talk like anything.

THE RAGPICKER. All right. Tea.

JOSEPHINE [*to* THE VAGABONDS]. Come in. Come in. All of you. You may take places. The trial is public. [THE VAGABONDS *dispose themselves on the steps and elsewhere.*] Your bell, if you please, Aurelia.

COUNTESS. But what if I should need to ring for Irma?

JOSEPHINE. Irma will sit here, next to me. If you need her, she can ring for herself. [*to the* POLICE SERGEANT *and the* POLICEMAN] Conduct the accused to the bar. [*The officers conduct* THE RAGPICKER *to a bar improvised with a rocking chair and a packing case marked* FRAGILE. THE RAGPICKER *mounts the box. She rings the bell.*] The court is now in session. [*All sit.*] Counsel for the defense, you may take the oath.

THE RAGPICKER. I swear to tell the truth, the whole truth, and nothing but the truth, so help me God.

JOSEPHINE. Nonsense! You're not a witness. You're an attorney. It's your duty to lie, conceal and distort everything, and slander everybody.

THE RAGPICKER. All right. I swear to lie, conceal and distort everything, and slander everybody.

[JOSEPHINE *rings stridently.*]

JOSEPHINE. Quiet! Begin.

THE RAGPICKER. May it please the honorable, august and elegant Court . . .

JOSEPHINE. Flattery will get you nowhere. That will do. The defense has been heard. Cross-examination.

COUNTESS. Mr. President . . .

THE RAGPICKER [*bowing with dignity*]. Madame.

COUNTESS. Do you know what you are charged with?

THE RAGPICKER. I can't for the life of me imagine. My life is an open book. My ways are known to all. I am a pillar of the church and the sole support of the Opera. My hands are spotless.

COUNTESS. What an atrocious lie! Just look at them!

CONSTANCE. You don't have to insult the man. He's only lying to please you.

COUNTESS. Be quiet, Constance! You don't get the idea at all. [*to* THE RAGPICKER] You are charged with the crime of worshipping money.

THE RAGPICKER. Worshipping money? Me?

JOSEPHINE. Do you plead guilty or not guilty? Which is it?

THE RAGPICKER. Why, Your Honor . . .

JOSEPHINE. Yes or no?

THE RAGPICKER. Yes or no? No! I don't worship money, Countess. Heavens, no! Money worships me. It adores me. It won't let me alone. It's damned embarrassing, I can tell you.

JOSEPHINE. Kindly watch your language.

COUNTESS. Defendant, tell the Court how you came by your money.

THE RAGPICKER. The first time money came to me, I was a mere boy, a little golden-haired child in the bosom of my dear family. It came to me suddenly in the guise of a gold brick which, in my innocence, I picked out of a garbage can one day while playing. I was horrified, as you can imagine. I immediately tried to get rid of it by swapping it for a little rundown one-track railroad which, to my consternation, at once sold itself for a hundred times its value. In a desperate effort to get rid of this money, I began to buy things. I bought the Northern Refineries, the Galeries Lafayette, and the Schneider-Creusot Munition Works. And now I'm stuck with them.

It's a horrible fate—but I'm resigned to it. I don't ask for your sympathy, I don't ask for your pity—all I ask for is a little common human understanding. . . .

[*He begins to cry.*]

COUNTESS. I object. This wretch is trying to play on the emotions of the Court.

JOSEPHINE. The Court has no emotions.

THE RAGPICKER. Everyone knows that the poor have no one but themselves to blame for their poverty. It's only just that they should suffer the consequences. But how is it the fault of the rich if they're rich?

COUNTESS. Dry your tears. You're deceiving nobody. If, as you say, you're ashamed of your money, why is it you hold onto it with such a death-grip?

THE RAGPICKER. Me?

STREET PEDDLER. You never part with a franc!

JUGGLER. You wouldn't even give the poor Deaf-Mute a sou!

THE RAGPICKER. Me, hold onto money? What slander! What injustice! What a thing to say to me in the presence of this honorable, august and elegant Court! I spend all my time trying to spend my money. If I have tan shoes, I buy black ones. If I have a bicycle, I buy a motor car. If I have a wife, I buy . . .

JOSEPHINE [*rings*]. Order!

THE RAGPICKER. I dispatch a plane to Java for a bouquet of flowers. I send a steamer to Egypt for a basket of figs. I send a special representative to New York to fetch me an ice-cream cone. And if it's not just exactly right, back it goes. But no matter what I do, I can't get rid of my money! If I play a hundred to one shot, the horse comes in by twenty lengths. If I throw a diamond in the Seine, it turns up in the trout they serve me for lunch. Ten diamonds—ten trout. Well, now, do you suppose I can get rid of forty millions by giving a sou to a deaf-mute? Is it even worth the effort?

CONSTANCE. He's right.

THE RAGPICKER. Ah! You see, my dear? At last, there is somebody who understands me! Somebody who is not only beautiful, but extraordinarily sensitive and intelligent.

COUNTESS. I object!

JOSEPHINE. Overruled!

THE RAGPICKER. I should be delighted to send you some flowers, Miss—directly I'm acquitted. What flowers do you prefer?

CONSTANCE. Roses.

THE RAGPICKER. You shall have a bale every morning for the next five years. Money means nothing to me.

CONSTANCE. And amaryllis.

THE RAGPICKER. I'll make a note of the name. [*in his best lyrical style*] The lady understands, ladies and gentlemen. The lady is no fool. She's been around and she knows what's what. If I gave the Deaf-Mute a franc, twenty francs, twenty million francs—I still wouldn't make a dent in the forty times a thousand million francs that I'm afflicted with! Right, little lady?

CONSTANCE. Right.

JOSEPHINE. Proceed.

THE RAGPICKER. Like on the Stock Exchange. If *you* buy a stock, it sinks at once like a plummet. But if *I* buy a stock, it turns around and soars like an eagle. If I buy it at 33 . . .

PEDDLER. It goes up to a thousand.

THE RAGPICKER. It goes to twenty thousand! That's how I bought my twelve chateaux, my twenty villas, my 234 farms. That's how I endow the Opera and keep my twelve ballerinas.

FLOWER GIRL. I hope every one of them deceives you every moment of the day!

THE RAGPICKER. How can they deceive me? Suppose they try to deceive me with the male chorus, the general director, the assistant electrician or the English horn—I own them all, body and soul. It would be like deceiving me with my big toe.

CONSTANCE. Don't listen, Gabrielle.

GABRIELLE. Listen to what?

THE RAGPICKER. No. I am incapable of jealousy. I have all the women—or I can have them, which is the same thing. I get the thin ones with caviar—the fat ones with pearls . . .

COUNTESS. So you think there are no women with morals?

THE RAGPICKER. I mix morals with mink—delicious combination. I drip pearls into protests. I adorn resistance with rubies. My touch is jeweled; my smile, a motor car. What woman can withstand me? I lift my little finger—and do they fall?—Like leaves in autumn—like tin cans from a second-story window.

CONSTANCE. That's going a little too far!

COUNTESS. You see where money leads.

THE RAGPICKER. Of course. When you have no money, nobody trusts you, nobody believes you, nobody likes you. Because to have money is to be virtuous, honest, beautiful and witty. And to be without is to be ugly and boring and stupid and useless.

COUNTESS. One last question. Suppose you find this oil you're looking for. What do you propose to do with it?

THE RAGPICKER. I propose to make war! I propose to conquer the world!

COUNTESS. You have heard the defense, such as it is. I demand a verdict of guilty.

THE RAGPICKER. What are you talking about? Guilty? I? I am never guilty!

JOSEPHINE. I order you to keep quiet.

THE RAGPICKER. I am never quiet!

JOSEPHINE. Quiet, in the name of the law!

THE RAGPICKER. I am the law. When I speak, that is the law. When I present my backside, it is etiquette to smile and to apply the lips respectfully. It is more than etiquette—it is a cherished national privilege, guaranteed by the Constitution.

JOSEPHINE. That's contempt of court. The trial is over.

COUNTESS. And the verdict?

ALL. Guilty.

JOSEPHINE. Guilty as charged.

COUNTESS. Then I have full authority to carry out the sentence?

ALL. Yes!

COUNTESS. I can do what I like with them?

ALL. Yes!

COUNTESS. I have the right to exterminate them?

ALL. Yes!

JOSEPHINE. Court adjourned!

COUNTESS [*to* THE RAGPICKER]. Congratulations, Ragpicker. A marvelous defense. Absolutely impartial.

THE RAGPICKER. Had I known a little before, I could have done better. I could have prepared a little speech, like the time I used to sell the Miracle Spot Remover. . . .

JOSEPHINE. No need for that. You did very well, extempore. The likeness was striking and the style reminiscent of Clemenceau. I predict a brilliant future for you. Good-bye, Aurelia. I'll take our little Gabrielle home.

CONSTANCE. I'm going to walk along the river. [*to* DICKIE] Oh! So here you are. And your ear all bloody! Dickie! Have you been fighting again? Oh, dear . . . !

COUNTESS [*to* THE RAGPICKER]. See that she gets home all right, won't you? She loses everything on the way. And in the queerest places. Her prayer book in the butcher shop. And her corset in church.

THE RAGPICKER [*bowing and offering his arm*]. Permit me, Madame.

STREET SINGER. Oh, Countess—my mazurka. Remember?

COUNTESS. Oh, yes, Constance, wait a moment. [*to* THE SINGER] Well? Begin.

SINGER [*sings*].

Do you hear, Mademoiselle,
Those musicians of hell?

CONSTANCE. Why, of course, it's *La Belle Polonaise*. . . . [*She sings.*]

From Poland to France
Comes this marvelous dance,
So gracious,
Audacious,
Will you foot it, perchance?

SINGER. I'm saved!

JOSEPHINE [*reappearing at the head of the stairs*].

Now my arm I entwine
Round these contours divine,
So pure, so impassioned,
Which Cupid has fashioned. . . .

GABRIELLE [*reappearing also, she sings a quartet with the others*].

Come, let's dance the mazurka, that devilish measure,
'Tis a joy that's reserved to the gods for their pleasure—
Let's gallop, let's hop,
With never a stop,
My blonde Polish miss,
Let our heads spin and turn

As the dance-floor we spurn—
There was never such pleasure as this!

[*They all exit, dancing.*]

IRMA. It's time for your afternoon nap.

COUNTESS. But suppose they come, Irma!

IRMA. I'll watch out for them.

COUNTESS. Thank you, Irma. I *am* tired. [*She smiles.*] Did you ever see a trial end more happily in your life?

IRMA. Lie down and close your eyes a moment.

[THE COUNTESS *stretches out on the chaise-longue and shuts her eyes.* IRMA *tiptoes out. In a moment,* PIERRE *comes down softly, the feather boa in his hands. He stands over the chaise-longue, looking tenderly down at the sleeping woman, then kneels beside her and takes her hand.*]

COUNTESS [*without opening her eyes*]. Is it you, Adolphe Bertaut?

PIERRE. It's only Pierre.

COUNTESS. Don't lie to me, Adolphe Bertaut. These are your hands. Why do you complicate things always? Say that it's you.

PIERRE. Yes. It is I.

COUNTESS. Would it cost you so much to call me Aurelia?

PIERRE. It's I, Aurelia.

COUNTESS. Why did you leave me, Adolphe Bertaut? Was she so very lovely, this Georgette of yours?

PIERRE. No. You are a thousand times lovelier.

COUNTESS. But she was clever.

PIERRE. She was stupid.

COUNTESS. It was her soul, then, that drew you? When you looked into her eyes, you saw a vision of heaven, perhaps?

PIERRE. I saw nothing.

COUNTESS. That's how it is with men. They love you because you are beautiful and clever and soulful—and at the first opportunity they leave you for someone who is plain and dull and soulless. But why does it have to be like that, Adolphe Bertaut? Why?

PIERRE. Why, Aurelia?

COUNTESS. I know very well she wasn't rich. Because when I saw you that time at the grocer's, and you snatched the only good melon from right under my nose, your cuffs, my poor friend, were badly frayed. . . .

PIERRE. Yes. She was poor.

COUNTESS. "Was" poor? Is she dead then? If it's because she's dead that you've come back to me—then no. Go away. I will not take their leavings from the dead. I refuse to inherit you. . . .

PIERRE. She's quite well.

COUNTESS. Your hands are still the same, Adolphe Bertaut. Your touch is young and firm. Because it's the only part of you that has stayed with me. The rest of you is pretty far gone, I'm afraid. I can see why you'd rather not come near me when my eyes are open. It's thoughtful of you.

PIERRE. Yes. I've aged.

COUNTESS. Not I. I am young because I haven't had to live down my youth, like you. I have it with me still, as fresh and beautiful as ever. But when you walk now in the park at Colombes with Georgette, I'm sure . . .

PIERRE. There is no longer a park at Colombes.

COUNTESS. Is there a park still at St. Cloud? Is there a park at Versailles? I've never gone back to see. But I think, if they could move, those trees would have walked away in disgust the day you went there with Georgette. . . .

PIERRE. They did. Not many are left.

COUNTESS. You take her also, I suppose, to hear *Denise*?

PIERRE. No one hears *Denise* any more.

COUNTESS. It was on the way home from *Denise,* Adolphe Bertaut, that I first took your arm. Because it was windy and it was late. I have never set foot in that street again. I go the other way round. It's not easy, in the winter, when there's ice. One is quite apt to fall. I often do.

PIERRE. Oh, my darling—forgive me.

COUNTESS. No, never. I will never forgive you. It was very bad taste to take her to the very places where we'd been together.

PIERRE. All the same, I swear, Aurelia . . .

COUNTESS. Don't swear. I know what you did. You gave her the same flowers. You bought her the same chocolates. But has she any left? No. I have all your flowers still. I have twelve chocolates. No, I will never forgive you as long as I live.

PIERRE. I always loved you, Aurelia.

COUNTESS. You "loved" me? Then you too are dead, Adolphe Bertaut?

PIERRE. No. I love you. I shall always love you, Aurelia.

COUNTESS. Yes. I know. That much I've always known. I knew it the moment you went away, Adolphe, and I knew that nothing could ever change it. Georgette is in his arms now—yes. But he loves me. Tonight he's taken Georgette to hear *Denise*—yes. But he loves me. . . . I know it. You never loved her. Do you think I believed for one moment that absurd story about her running off with the osteopath? Of course not. Since you didn't love her, obviously she stayed with you. And, after that, when she came back, and I heard about her going off with the surveyor—I knew that couldn't be true, either. You'll never get rid of her, Adolphe Bertaut—never. Because you don't love her.

PIERRE. I need your pity, Aurelia. I need your love. Don't forget me. . . .

COUNTESS. Farewell, Adolphe Bertaut. Farewell. Let go my hand, and give it to little Pierre. [PIERRE *lets go her hand, and after a moment takes it again.* THE COUNTESS *opens her eyes.*] Pierre? Ah, it's you. Has he gone?

PIERRE. Yes, Countess.

COUNTESS. I didn't hear him go. Oh, he knows how to make a quick exit, that one. [*She see the boa.*] Good heavens! Wherever did you find it?

PIERRE. In the wardrobe, Countess. When I took off the mirror.

COUNTESS. Was there a purple felt shopping bag with it?

PIERRE. Yes, Countess.

COUNTESS. And a little child's sewing box?

PIERRE. No, Countess.

COUNTESS. Oh, they're frightened now. They're trembling for their lives. You see what they're up to? They're quietly putting back all the things they have stolen. I never open that wardrobe, of course, on account of the old woman in the mirror. But I have sharp eyes. I don't need to open it to see what's in it. Up to this morning, that wardrobe was empty. And now—you see? But, dear me, how stupid they are! The one thing I really miss is my little sewing box. It's something they stole from me when I was a child. They haven't put it back? You're quite sure?

PIERRE. What was it like?

COUNTESS. Green cardboard with paper lace and gold stamping.

I got it for Christmas when I was seven. They stole it the very next day. I cried my eyes out every time I thought of it—until I was eight.

PIERRE. It's not there, Countess.

COUNTESS. The thimble was gilt. I swore I'd never use any other. Look at my poor fingers. . . .

PIERRE. They've kept the thimble too.

COUNTESS. Splendid! Then I'm under no obligation to be merciful. Put the boa around my neck, Pierre. I want them to see me wearing it. They'll think it's a real boa.

[IRMA *runs in excitedly.*]

IRMA. Here they come, Countess! You were right—it's a procession. The street is full of limousines and taxis!

COUNTESS. I will receive them. [*As* PIERRE *hesitates to leave her.*] Don't worry. There's nothing to be frightened of. [PIERRE *goes out.*] Irma, did you remember to stir the kerosene into the water?

IRMA. Yes, Countess. Here it is.

COUNTESS [*looking critically at the bottle*]. You might as well pour in what's left of the tea. [IRMA *shakes up the liquid.*] Don't forget, I'm supposed to be deaf. I want to hear what they're thinking.

IRMA. Yes, Countess.

COUNTESS [*putting the finishing touches to her make-up*]. I don't have to be merciful—but, after all, I do want to be just. . . .

[IRMA *goes up to the landing and exits. As soon as she is done,* THE COUNTESS *presses the brick, and the trap door opens. There is a confused sound of auto horns in the street above, and the noise of an approaching crowd.*]

IRMA [*offstage*]. Yes, Mr. President. Come in, Mr. President. You're expected, Mr. President. This way, Mr. President. [THE PRESIDENTS *come down, led by* THE PRESIDENT. *They all look alike, are dressed alike, and all have long cigars.*] The Countess is quite deaf, gentlemen. You'll have to shout. [*She announces.*] The presidents of the boards of directors!

THE PRESIDENT. I had a premonition, Madame, when I saw you this morning, that we should meet again. [THE COUNTESS *smiles vaguely. He continues, a tone louder.*] I want to thank you for your trust. You may place yourself in our hands with complete confidence.

SECOND PRESIDENT. Louder. The old trot can't hear you.

THE PRESIDENT. I have a letter here, Madame, in which . . .

SECOND PRESIDENT. Louder. Louder.

THIRD PRESIDENT [*shouting*]. Is it true that you've located . . . ? [THE COUNTESS *stares at him blankly. He shouts at the top of his voice.*] Oil? [THE COUNTESS *nods with a smile, and points down.* THE PRESIDENT *produces a legal paper and a fountain pen.*] Sign here.

COUNTESS. What is it? I haven't my glasses.

THE PRESIDENT. Your contract.

[*He offers the pen.*]

COUNTESS. Thank you.

SECOND PRESIDENT [*normal voice*]. What is it?

THIRD PRESIDENT. Waiver of all rights. [*He takes it back signed.*] Thank you. [*He hands it to* THE SECOND PRESIDENT.] Witness. [THE SECOND PRESIDENT *witnesses it.* THE PRESIDENT *passes it on to* THE THIRD PRESIDENT.] Notarize. [*The paper is notarized.* THE PRESIDENT *turns to* THE COUNTESS *and shouts.*] My congratulations. And now, Madame– [*He produces a gold brick wrapped in tissue paper.*] If you'll show us the well, this package is yours.

COUNTESS. What is it?

THE PRESIDENT. Pure gold. Twenty-four karat. For you.

COUNTESS. Thank you very much. [*She takes it.*] It's heavy.

SECOND PRESIDENT. Are you going to give her that?

THE PRESIDENT. Don't worry. We'll pick it up again on the way out. [*He shouts at* THE COUNTESS, *pointing at the trap door.*] Is this the way?

COUNTESS. That's the way.

[THE SECOND PRESIDENT *tries to slip in first.* THE PRESIDENT *pulls him back.*]

THE PRESIDENT. Just a minute, Mr. President. After me, if you don't mind. And watch those cigars. It's oil, you know.

[*But as he is about to descend,* THE COUNTESS *steps forward.*]

COUNTESS. Just one moment . . .

THE PRESIDENT. Yes?

COUNTESS. Did any of you happen to bring along a little sewing box?

THE PRESIDENT. Sewing box? [*He pulls back another impatient* PRESIDENT.] Take it easy.

COUNTESS. Or a little gold thimble?

THE PRESIDENT. Not me.

THE PRESIDENTS. Not us.

COUNTESS. What a pity!

THE PRESIDENT. Can we go down now?

COUNTESS. Yes. You may go down now. Watch your step!

[*They hurry down eagerly. When they have quite disappeared,* IRMA *appears on the landing and announces the next echelon.*]

IRMA. Countess, the Prospectors.

COUNTESS. Heavens! Are there more than one?

IRMA. There's a whole delegation.

COUNTESS. Send them down.

[THE PROSPECTOR *comes in, following his nose.*]

IRMA. Come in, please.

THE PROSPECTOR [*sniffing the air like a bloodhound*]. I smell something. . . . Who's that?

IRMA. The Countess. She is very deaf.

THE PROSPECTOR. Good.

[THE PROSPECTORS *also look alike. Sharp clothes, Western hats and long noses. They crowd down the stairs after* THE PROSPECTOR, *sniffing in unison.* THE PROSPECTOR *is especially talented. He casts about on the scent until it leads him to the decanter on the table. He pours himself a glass, drinks it off, and belches with much satisfaction. The others join him at once, and follow his example. They all belch in unison.*]

THE PROSPECTORS. Oil?

THE PROSPECTOR. Oil!

COUNTESS. Oil.

THE PROSPECTOR. Traces? Puddles?

COUNTESS. Pools. Gushers.

SECOND PROSPECTOR. Characteristic odor?

[*He sniffs.*]

THE PROSPECTOR. Chanel Number 5. Nectar! Undoubtedly—the finest—rarest! [*He drinks.*] Sixty gravity crude: straight gasoline! [*to* THE COUNTESS.] How found? By blast? Drill?

COUNTESS. By finger.

THE PROSPECTOR [*whipping out a document*]. Sign here, please.

COUNTESS. What is it?

THE PROSPECTOR. Agreement for dividing the profits . . .

[THE COUNTESS *signs.*]

SECOND PROSPECTOR. [*to* FIRST PROSPECTOR] What is it?

THE PROSPECTOR [*pocketing the paper*]. Application to enter a lunatic asylum. Down there?

COUNTESS. Down there.

[THE PROSPECTORS *go down, sniffing.* IRMA *enters.*]

IRMA. The gentlemen of the press are here.

COUNTESS. The rest of the machine! Show them in.

IRMA. The Public Relations Counsellors! [*They enter, all shapes and sizes, all in blue pin-striped suits and black homburg hats.*] The Countess is very deaf, gentlemen. You'll have to shout!

FIRST PRESS AGENT. You don't say— Delighted to make the acquaintance of so charming and beautiful a lady . . .

SECOND PRESS AGENT. Louder. She can't hear you.

FIRST PRESS AGENT. What a face! [*Shouts.*] Madame, we are the press. You know our power. We fix all values. We set all standards. Your entire future depends on us.

COUNTESS. How do you do?

FIRST PRESS AGENT. What will we charge the old trull? The usual thirty?

SECOND PRESS AGENT. Forty.

THIRD PRESS AGENT. Sixty.

FIRST PRESS AGENT. All right—seventy-five. [*He fills in a form and offers it to* THE COUNTESS.] Sign here, Countess. This contract really gives you a break.

COUNTESS. That is the entrance.

FIRST PRESS AGENT. Entrance to what?

COUNTESS. The oil well.

FIRST PRESS AGENT. Oh, we don't need to see that, Madame.

COUNTESS. Don't need to see it?

FIRST PRESS AGENT. No, no—we don't have to see it to write about it. We can imagine it. An oil well is an oil well. "That's oil we know on earth, and oil we need to know."

[*He bows.*]

COUNTESS. But if you don't see it, how can you be sure the oil is there?

FIRST PRESS AGENT. If it's there, well and good. If it's not, by the time we get through, it will be. You underestimate the creative aspect of our profession, Madame. [THE COUNTESS *shakes her head, handing back the papers.*] I warn you, if you insist on rubbing our noses in this oil, it will cost you 10 percent extra.

COUNTESS. It's worth it.

[*She signs. They cross toward the trapdoor.*]

SECOND PRESS AGENT [*descending*]. You see, Madame, we of the press can refuse a lady nothing.

THIRD PRESS AGENT. Especially, such a lady.

[THIRD PRESS AGENT *starts going down.*]

SECOND PRESS AGENT [*going down; gallantly*]. It's plain to see, Madame, that even fountains of oil have their nymphs. . . . I can use that somewhere. That's copy!

[THE PRESS AGENTS *go down. As he disappears,* THE FIRST PRESS AGENT *steals the gold brick and blows a kiss gallantly to* THE COUNTESS, *who blows one back.*]

[*There is a high-pitched chatter offstage, and* IRMA *comes in, trying hard to hold back* THREE WOMEN *who pay no attention to her whatever. These* WOMEN *are tall, slender, and as soulless as if they were molded of wax. They march down the steps, erect and abstracted like animated window models, but chattering incessantly.*]

IRMA. But, ladies, please—you have no business here—you are not expected. [*to* THE COUNTESS] There are some strange ladies coming. . . .

COUNTESS. Show them in, Irma. [*The* WOMEN *come down, without taking the slightest interest in their surroundings.*] Who are you?

FIRST WOMAN. Madame, we are the most powerful pressure group in the world.

SECOND WOMAN. We are the ultimate dynamic.

THIRD WOMAN. The mainspring of all combinations.

FIRST WOMAN. Nothing succeeds without our assistance. Is that the well, Madame?

COUNTESS. That is the well.

FIRST WOMAN. Put out your cigarettes, girls. We don't want any explosions. Not with my brand-new eyelashes.

[*They go down, still chattering.* THE COUNTESS *crosses to the wall to close the trap. As she does so, there is a commotion on the landing.*]

IRMA. Countess . . .

[*A* MAN *rushes in breathlessly.*]

MAN. Just a minute! Just a minute!

[*He rushes for the trap door.*]

COUNTESS. Wait! Who are you?

MAN. I'm in a hurry. Excuse me. It's my only chance!

[*He rushes down.*]

COUNTESS. But . . . [*But he is gone. She shrugs her shoulders, and presses the brick. The trap closes. She rings the bell for* IRMA.] My gold brick! Why, they've stolen my gold brick! [*She moves toward the trap. It is now closed.*] Well, let them take their god with them.

[IRMA *enters and sees with astonishment that the stage is empty of all but* THE COUNTESS. *Little by little, the scene is suffused with light, faint at first, but increasing as if the very walls were glowing with the quiet radiance of universal joy. Only around the closed trap a shadow lingers.*]

IRMA. But what's happened? They've gone! They've vanished!

COUNTESS. They've evaporated, Irma. They were wicked. Wickedness evaporates.

[PIERRE *enters. He is followed by* THE VAGABONDS, *all of them. The new radiance of the world is now very perceptible. It glows from their faces.*]

PIERRE. Oh, Countess . . . !

WAITER. Countess, everything's changed. Now you can breathe again. Now you can see.

PIERRE. The air is pure. The sky is clear!

IRMA. Life is beautiful again.

THE RAGPICKER [*rushes in*]. Countess—the pigeons! The pigeons are flying!

FLOWER GIRL. They don't have to walk any more.

THE RAGPICKER. They're flying. . . . The air is like crystal. And young grass is sprouting on the pavements.

COUNTESS. Is it possible?

IRMA [*interpreting for* THE DEAF-MUTE]. Now, Juggler, you can throw your fireballs up as high as you please—they won't go out.

SERGEANT. On the street, utter strangers are shaking hands, they don't know why, and offering each other almond bars!

COUNTESS. Oh, my friends . . .

WAITER. Countess, we thank you. . . .

[*They go on talking with happy and animated gestures, but we no longer hear them, for their words blend into a strain of unearthly music which seems to thrill from the uttermost confines of the universe. And out of this music comes a voice.*]

FIRST VOICE. Countess . . .

[*Only* THE COUNTESS *hears it. She turns from the group of* VAGABONDS *in wonder.*]

SECOND VOICE. Countess . . .

THIRD VOICE. Countess . . .

[*As she looks up in rapture,* THE FIRST VOICE *speaks again.*]

FIRST VOICE. Countess, we thank you. We are the friends of animals.

SECOND VOICE. We are the friends of people.

THIRD VOICE. We are the friends of friendship.

FIRST VOICE. You have freed us!

SECOND VOICE. From now on, there will be no hungry cats. . . .

THIRD VOICE. And we shall tell the Duchess her dog's right name!

[THE VOICES *fade off. And now another group of voices is heard.*]

FIRST VOICE. Countess, we thank you. We are the friends of flowers.

SECOND VOICE. From now on, every plant in Paris will be watered. . . .

THIRD VOICE. And the sewers will be fragrant with jasmine!

[*These voices, too, are silent. For an instant, the stage is vibrant with music. Then* THE DEAF-MUTE *speaks, and his voice is the most beautiful of all.*]

DEAF-MUTE. Sadness flies on the wings of the morning, and out of the heart of darkness comes the light.

[*Suddenly a group of figures detaches itself from the shadows. These are exactly similar in face and figure and in dress. They are shabby in the fashion of 1900 and their cuffs are badly frayed. Each bears in his hand a ripe melon.*]

FIRST ADOLPHE BERTAUT. Countess, we thank you. We, too, are freed at last. We are the Adolphe Bertauts of the world.

SECOND ADOLPHE BERTAUT. We are no longer timid.

THIRD ADOLPHE BERTAUT. We are no longer weak.

FIRST ADOLPHE BERTAUT. From this day on, we shall hold fast to what we love. For your sake, henceforth, we shall be handsome, and our cuffs forever immaculate and new. Countess, we bring you this melon and with it our hearts . . . ! [*They all kneel.*] Will you do us the honor to be our wife?

COUNTESS [*sadly*]. Too late! Too late! [*She waves them aside. They take up their melons sadly and vanish. The voices of* THE VAGABONDS *are heard again, and the music dies.*] Too late! Too late!

PIERRE. Too late, Countess?

IRMA. Too late for what?

COUNTESS. I say that it's too late for them. On the twenty-fourth of May, 1881, the most beautiful Easter in the memory of man, it was not too late. And on the fifth of September, 1887, the day they caught the trout and broiled it on the open fire by the brook at Villeneuve, it was not too late. And it was even not too late for them on the twenty-first of August, 1897, the day the Czar visited Paris with his guard. But they did nothing and they said nothing, and now—kiss each other, you two, this very instant!

IRMA. You mean . . . ?

PIERRE. You mean . . . ?

IRMA. But, Countess . . .

COUNTESS. It's three hours since you've met and known and loved each other. Kiss each other quickly. [PIERRE *hesitates.*] Look at him. He hesitates. He trembles. Happiness frightens him. . . . How like a man! Oh, Irma, kiss him, kiss him! If two people who love each other let a single instant wedge itself between them, it grows—it becomes a month, a year, a century; it becomes too late. Kiss him, Irma, kiss him while there is time, or in a moment his hair will be white and there will be another madwoman in Paris! Oh, make her kiss him, all of you! [*They kiss.*] Bravo! Oh, if only you'd had the courage to do that thirty years ago, how different I would be today! Dear Deaf-Mute, be still—your words dazzle our eyes! And Irma is too busy to translate for you. [*They kiss once more.*] Well, there we are. The world is saved. And you see how simple it all was? Nothing is ever so wrong in this world that a sensible woman can't set it right in the course of an afternoon. Only, the next time, don't wait until things begin to look black. The minute you notice anything, tell me at once.

THE RAGPICKER. We will, Countess. We will.

COUNTESS [*puts on her hat. Her tone becomes businesslike*]. Irma. My bones. My gizzard.

IRMA. I have them ready, Countess.

COUNTESS. Good. [*She puts the bones into her basket and starts for the stairs.*] Well, let's get on to more important things. Four o'clock. My poor cats must be starved. What a bore for them if humanity had to be saved every afternoon. They don't think much of it, as it is.

CURTAIN

BERTOLT BRECHT
1898–1956

THE CAUCASIAN CHALK CIRCLE
1946

FROM THE BEGINNING, we have a lively sense that *The Caucasian Chalk Circle* is a literary fiction. The action proper is introduced as a play within a narrative within a play. The narrator continues to interpose himself. The characters are developed to the point where they elicit sympathy but not empathy. And a succession of bizarre episodes engages our interest so fully that we cease to be attuned to psychological depths.

The maintenance of such detachment, or *Verfremdung* as he called it, was a cornerstone of Brecht's artistic creed. He had an unabashedly didactic theory of drama. And, wanting to engage the mind, he sought to inhibit identification, which he conceived as inviting a mindlessly emotional response.

In *The Caucasian Chalk Circle* the message is presented with clarity and animation; in its substance it unites affirmation and disenchantment in a manner characteristic of Brecht. Virtue, the primary source of which seems to be human affection rather than sense of duty, is at length somewhat fortuitously rewarded. The agent of justice is a cowardly and venal man who has paradoxically become the perfect judge because he is too disreputable to have any vested interest, economic or moral. Brecht, though an unrecanting Marxist, clearly did not believe that human values could be programmed. His poetic imagination—as vivid and racy as Voltaire's—asserts its independence of any limited doctrine. Revealing a wholesome if raffish disregard for mere respectability of whatever hue, he borrows traditional tales for his plot and admonishes the exclusive adherents of current ideologies, "Old and new wisdom mix admirably."

From a perspective again broader than that of contemporary ideology, we notice his predilection for comedy, the dramatic mode long described as ethical rather than pathetic. His free-wheeling experiments, which opened new theatrical directions, may be seen in the context of this volume as paths by which he escaped from the confusions of genre vexing the modern stage and returned to a timeless ideal of comic art.

He affirms (*contra* the dramatists of the absurd) that we can contemplate the irrational and arbitrary elements in human life without surrendering our own minds to unintelligibility. *Contra* the existentialists, who keep observing that every man is essentially alone, he points out that for better and for worse we are also social beings. And *contra* all those dramatists both bourgeois and proletarian who would see in the failures of pedestrian men the stuff of tragedy, he delightedly and delightfully descants on the perennial comic theme, "What fools these mortals be!" He unites compassion and humor somewhat in Chekhov's manner, though not in the same proportions. As stylish as Giraudoux, he is perhaps less sentimental. There is not, all in all, a wiser or more humane voice than his in modern drama.

THE CAUCASIAN CHALK CIRCLE : *BRECHT*

TRANSLATED BY ERIC BENTLEY

Characters

OLD MAN	*on the right*
PEASANT WOMAN	*on the right*
YOUNG PEASANT	
A VERY YOUNG WORKER	
OLD MAN	*on the left*
PEASANT WOMAN	*on the left*
AGRICULTURIST KATO	
GIRL TRACTORIST	
WOUNDED SOLDIER	
THE DELEGATE	*from the capital*
THE SINGER	
GEORGI ABASHWILI	*the Governor*
NATELLA	*the Governor's wife*
MICHAEL	*their son*
SHALVA	*an adjutant*
ARSEN KAZBEKI	*a fat prince*
MESSENGER	*from the capital*
NIKO MIKADZE AND	
MIKA LOLADZE	*doctors*
SIMON SHASHAVA	*a soldier*
GRUSHA VASHNADZE	*a kitchen maid*
OLD PEASANT	*with the milk*
CORPORAL AND PRIVATE	
PEASANT AND HIS WIFE	
LAVRENTI VASHNADZE	*Grusha's brother*
ANIKO	*his wife*
PEASANT WOMAN	*for a while Grusha's mother-in-law*

JUSSUP : *her son*
MONK
AZDAK : *village recorder*
SHAUWA : *a policeman*
GRAND DUKE
DOCTOR
INVALID
LIMPING MAN
BLACKMAILER
LUDOVICA
INNKEEPER : *her father-in-law*
STABLEBOY
POOR OLD PEASANT WOMAN
IRAKLI : *her brother-in-law, a bandit*
THREE WEALTHY FARMERS
ILLO SHUBOLADZE AND
SANDRO OBOLADZE : *lawyers*
OLD MARRIED COUPLE
SOLDIERS, SERVANTS, PEASANTS,
BEGGARS, MUSICIANS, MERCHANTS,
NOBLES, AND ARCHITECTS

PROLOGUE

[*Among the ruins of a war-ravaged Caucasian village the* MEMBERS *of two Kolkhoz villages, mostly women and older men, are sitting in a circle, smoking and drinking wine. With them is a* DELEGATE *of the State Reconstruction Commission from Nuka, the capital.*]

PEASANT WOMAN, *left* [*pointing*]. In those hills over there we stopped three Nazi tanks, but the apple orchard was already destroyed.

OLD MAN, *right*. Our beautiful dairy farm; a ruin.

GIRL TRACTORIST. I laid the fire, Comrade.
[*Pause.*]

DELEGATE. Now listen to the report. Delegates from the goat-

Characters: Azdak accent on last syllable.

breeding Kolkhoz "Rosa Luxemburg" have been to Nuka. When Hitler's armies approached, the Kolkhoz had moved its goat herds further east on orders from the authorities. They are now thinking of returning. Their delegates have investigated the village and the land and found a lot of it destroyed. [DELEGATES *on right nod.*] The neighboring fruit-culture Kolkhoz [*to the left*] "Galinsk" is proposing to use the former grazing land of Kolkhoz "Rosa Luxemburg," a valley in which grass doesn't grow very well, for orchards and vineyards. As a delegate of the Reconstruction Commission, I request that the two Kolkhoz villages decide between themselves whether Kolkhoz "Rosa Luxemburg" shall return here or not.

OLD MAN, *right.* First of all, I want to protest against the time limit on discussion. We of Kolkhoz "Rosa Luxemburg" have spent three days and three nights getting here. And now discussion is limited to half a day.

WOUNDED SOLDIER, *left.* Comrade, we haven't as many villages as we used to have. We haven't as many hands. We haven't as much time.

GIRL TRACTORIST. All pleasures have to be rationed. Tobacco is rationed, and wine. Discussion should be rationed.

OLD MAN, *right* [*sighing*]. Death to the fascists! But I will come to the point and explain why we want our valley back. There are a great many reasons, but I'll begin with one of the simplest. Makinä Abakidze, unpack the goat cheese. [PEASANT WOMAN *on the right takes from a basket an enormous cheese wrapped in a cloth. Applause and laughter.*] Help yourselves, Comrades, start in!

OLD MAN, *left* [*suspiciously*]. Is this a way of influencing us?

OLD MAN, *right* [*amid laughter*]. How could it be a way of influencing you, Surab, you valley-thief? Everyone knows you'll take the cheese and the valley, too. [*Laughter.*] All I expect from you is an honest answer. Do you like the cheese?

OLD MAN, *left.* The answer is: yes.

OLD MAN, *right.* Really. [*bitterly*] I ought to have known you know nothing about cheese.

OLD MAN, *left.* Why not? When I tell you I like it?

OLD MAN, *right.* Because you can't like it. Because it's not what it was in the old days. And why not? Because our goats don't like the new grass as they did the old. Cheese is not cheese because grass is not grass, that's the thing. Please put that in your report.

OLD MAN, *left*. But your cheese is excellent.

OLD MAN, *right*. It isn't excellent. It's just passable. The new grazing land is no good, whatever the young people may say. One can't live there. It doesn't even smell of morning in the morning. [*Several people laugh.*]

DELEGATE. Don't mind their laughing: they understand you. Comrades, why does one love one's country? Because the bread tastes better there, the air smells better, voices sound stronger, the sky is higher, the ground is easier to walk on. Isn't that so?

OLD MAN, *right*. The valley has belonged to us from all eternity.

SOLDIER, *left*. What does *that* mean—from all eternity? Nothing belongs to anyone from all eternity. When you were young you didn't even belong to yourself. You belonged to the Kazbeki princes.

OLD MAN, *right*. Doesn't it make a difference, though, what kind of trees stand next to the house you are born in? Or what kind of neighbors you have? Doesn't that make a difference? We want to go back just to have you as our neighbors, valley-thieves! Now you can all laugh again.

OLD MAN, *left* [*laughing*]. Then why don't you listen to what your neighbor, Kato Wachtang, our agriculturist, has to say about the valley?

PEASANT WOMAN, *right*. We've not said all there is to be said about our valley. By no means. Not all the houses are destroyed. As for the dairy farm, at least the foundation wall is still standing.

DELEGATE. You can claim State support—here and there—you know that. I have suggestions here in my pocket.

PEASANT WOMAN, *right*. Comrade Specialist, we haven't come here to bargain. I can't take your cap and hand you another, and say "This one's better." The other one might *be* better, but you *like* yours better.

GIRL TRACTORIST. A piece of land is not a cap—not in our country, Comrade.

DELEGATE. Don't get mad. It's true we have to consider a piece of land as a tool to produce something useful, but it's also true that we must recognize love for a particular piece of land. As far as I'm concerned, I'd like to find out more exactly what you [*to those on the left*] want to do with the valley.

OTHERS. Yes, let Kato speak.

DELEGATE. Comrade Agriculturist!

KATO [*rising; she's in military uniform*]. Comrades, last winter, while we were fighting in these hills here as Partisans, we discussed how, once the Germans were expelled, we could build up our fruit culture to ten times its original size. I've prepared a plan for an irrigation project. By means of a cofferdam on our mountain lake, 300 hectares of unfertile land can be irrigated. Our Kolkhoz could not only cultivate more fruit, but also have vineyards. The project, however, would pay only if the disputed valley of Kolkhoz "Galinsk" were also included. Here are the calculations. [*She hands* DELEGATE *a briefcase.*]

OLD MAN, *right.* Write into a report that our Kolkhoz plans to start a new stud farm.

GIRL TRACTORIST. Comrades, the project was conceived during days and nights when we had to take cover in the mountains. We were often without ammunition for our half-dozen rifles. Even finding a pencil was difficult. [*Applause from both sides.*]

OLD MAN, *right.* Our thanks to the Comrades of Kolkhoz "Galinsk" and all those who've defended our country! [*They shake hands and embrace.*]

PEASANT WOMAN, *left.* In doing this our thought was that our soldiers—both your men and our men—should return to a still more productive homeland.

GIRL TRACTORIST. As the poet Mayakovsky said: "The home of the Soviet people shall also be the home of Reason"!

[*The* DELEGATES *including the* OLD MAN *have got up, and with the* DELEGATE *specified proceed to study the Agriculturist's drawings. Exclamations such as:* "Why is the altitude of all 22 meters?"—"This rock must be blown up"—"Actually, all they need is cement and dynamite"—"They force the water to come down here, that's clever!"]

A VERY YOUNG WORKER, *right* [*to* OLD MAN, *right*]. They're going to irrigate all the fields between the hills, look at that, Aleko!

OLD MAN, *right.* I'm not going to look. I knew the project would be good. I won't have a pistol pointed at me!

DELEGATE. But they only want to point a pencil at you! [*Laughter.*]

OLD MAN, *right* [*gets up gloomily, and walks over to look at the*

113 **Mayakovsky** Vladimir Mayakovsky (1894–1930), Russian poet.

drawings]. These valley-thieves know only too well that we in this country are suckers for machines and projects.

PEASANT WOMAN, *right*. Aleko Bereshwili, you have a weakness for new projects. That's well known.

DELEGATE. What about my report? May I write that you will all support the cession of your old valley in the interests of this project when you get back to your Kolkhoz?

PEASANT WOMAN, *right*. I will. What about you, Aleko?

OLD MAN, *right* [*bent over drawings*]. I suggest that you give us copies of the drawings to take along.

PEASANT WOMAN, *right*. Then we can sit down and eat. Once he has the drawings and he's ready to discuss them, the matter is settled. I know him. And it will be the same with the rest of us.

[DELEGATES *laughingly embrace again*.]

OLD MAN, *left*. Long live the Kolkhoz "Rosa Luxemburg" and much luck to your horse-breeding project!

PEASANT WOMAN, *left*. In honor of the visit of the delegates from Kolkhoz "Rosa Luxemburg" and of the Specialist, the plan is that we all hear a presentation of the Singer Arkadi Tscheidse.

[*Applause*. GIRL TRACTORIST *has gone off to bring the* SINGER.]

PEASANT WOMAN, *right*. Comrades, your entertainment had better be good. It's going to cost us a valley.

PEASANT WOMAN, *left*. Arkadi Tscheidse knows about our discuscussion. He's promised to perform something that has a bearing on the problem.

KATO. We wired to Tiflis three times. The whole thing nearly fell through at the last minute because his driver had a cold.

PEASANT WOMAN, *left*. Arkadi Tscheidse knows 21,000 lines of verse.

OLD MAN, *left*. He's hard to get. You and the Planning Commission should persuade him to come north more often, Comrade.

DELEGATE. We are more interested in economics, I'm afraid.

OLD MAN, *left* [*smiling*]. You arrange the redistribution of vines and tractors, why not songs?

[*Enter the* SINGER *Arkadi Tscheidse, led by* GIRL TRACTORIST. *He is a well-built man of simple manners, accompanied by* FOUR MUSICIANS *with their instruments. The artists are greeted with applause*.]

GIRL TRACTORIST. This is the Comrade Specialist, Arkadi.

[*The* SINGER *greets them all.*]

DELEGATE. Honored to make your acquaintance. I heard about your songs when I was a boy at school. Will it be one of the old legends?

THE SINGER. A very old one. It's called "The Chalk Circle" and comes from the Chinese. But we'll do it, of course, in a changed version. Comrades, it's an honor for me to entertain you after a difficult debate. We hope you will find that the voice of the old poet also sounds well in the shadow of Soviet tractors. It may be a mistake to mix different wines, but old and new wisdom mix admirably. Now I hope we'll get something to eat before the performance begins—it would certainly help.

VOICES. Surely. Everyone into the Club House!

[*While everyone begins to move,* DELEGATE *turns to* GIRL TRACTORIST.]

DELEGATE. I hope it won't take long. I've got to get back tonight.

GIRL TRACTORIST. How long will it last, Arkadi? The Comrade Specialist must get back to Tiflis tonight.

THE SINGER [*casually*]. It's actually two stories. An hour or two.

GIRL TRACTORIST [*confidentially*]. Couldn't you make it shorter?

THE SINGER. No.

VOICE. Arkadi Tscheidse's performance will take place here in the square after the meal.

[*They all go happily to eat.*]

THE NOBLE CHILD

[*As the lights go up, the* SINGER *is seen sitting on the floor, a black sheepskin cloak round his shoulders, and a little, well-thumbed notebook in his hand. A small group of listeners—the* CHORUS*—sits with him. The manner of his recitation makes it clear that he has told his story over and over again. He mechanically fingers the pages, seldom looking at them. With appropriate gestures, he gives the signal for each scene to begin.*]

THE SINGER.

In olden times, in a bloody time,
There ruled in a Caucasian city—

Men called it City of the Damned—
A Governor.
His name was Georgi Abashwili.
He was rich as Croesus
He had a beautiful wife
He had a healthy baby.
No other governor in Grusinia
Had so many horses in his stable
So many beggars on his doorstep
So many soldiers in his service
So many petitioners in his courtyard.
Georgi Abashwili—how shall I describe him to you?
He enjoyed his life.
On the morning of Easter Sunday
The Governor and his family went to church.

[*At the left a large doorway, at the right an even larger gateway.* BEGGARS *and* PETITIONERS *pour from the gateway, holding up thin* CHILDREN, *crutches, and petitions. They are followed by* IRONSHIRTS, *and then, expensively dressed, the* GOVERNOR'S FAMILY.]

BEGGARS AND PETITIONERS. Mercy! Mercy, Your Grace! The taxes are too high.

—I lost my leg in the Persian War, where can I get . . .

—My brother is innocent, Your Grace, a misunderstanding . . .

—The child is starving in my arms!

—Our petition is for our son's discharge from the army, our last remaining son!

—Please, Your Grace, the water inspector takes bribes.

[ONE SERVANT *collects the petitions.* ANOTHER *distributes coins from a purse.* SOLDIERS *push the crowd back, lashing at them with thick leather whips.*]

THE SOLDIER. Get back! Clear the church door!

[*Behind the* GOVERNOR, *his* WIFE, *and the* ADJUTANT, *the* GOVERNOR'S CHILD *is brought through the gateway in an ornate carriage.*]

THE CROWD. The baby!

—I can't see it, don't shove so hard!

—God bless the child, Your Grace!

THE SINGER [*while the crowd is driven back with whips*].
For the first time on that Easter Sunday, the people saw the
Governor's heir.

Two doctors never moved from the noble child, apple of the
Governor's eye.
Even the mighty Prince Kazbeki bows before him at the church
door.

[*A* FAT PRINCE *steps forward and greets the* FAMILY.]

THE FAT PRINCE. Happy Easter, Natella Abashwili! What a day! When it was raining last night, I thought to myself, gloomy holidays! But this morning the sky was gay. I love a gay sky, a simple heart, Natella Abashwili. And little Michael is a governor from head to foot! Tititi! [*He tickles the* CHILD.]

THE GOVERNOR'S WIFE. What do you think, Arsen, at last Georgi has decided to start building the east wing. All those wretched slums are to be torn down to make room for the garden.

THE FAT PRINCE. Good news after so much bad! What's the latest on the war, Brother Georgi? [*The* GOVERNOR *indicates a lack of interest.*] Strategical retreat, I hear. Well, minor reverses are to be expected. Sometimes things go well, sometimes not. Such is war. Doesn't mean a thing, does it?

THE GOVERNOR'S WIFE. He's coughing. Georgi, did you hear? [*She speaks sharply to the* DOCTORS, *two dignified men standing close to the little carriage.*] He's coughing!

THE FIRST DOCTOR [*to the* SECOND]. May I remind you, Niko Mikadze, that I was against the lukewarm bath? [*to the* GOVERNOR'S WIFE] There's been a little error over warming the bath water, Your Grace.

THE SECOND DOCTOR [*equally polite*]. Mika Loladze, I'm afraid I can't agree with you. The temperature of the bath water was exactly what our great, beloved Mishiko Oboladze prescribed. More likely a slight draft during the night, Your Grace.

THE GOVERNOR'S WIFE. But do pay more attention to him. He looks feverish, Georgi.

THE FIRST DOCTOR [*bending over the* CHILD]. No cause for alarm, Your Grace. The bath water will be warmer. It won't occur again.

THE SECOND DOCTOR [*with a venomous glance at the* FIRST]. I won't forget that, my dear Mika Loladze. No cause for concern, Your Grace.

THE FAT PRINCE. Well, well, well! I always say: "A pain in my liver? Then the doctor gets fifty strokes on the soles of his feet." We live in a decadent age. In the old days one said: "Off with his head!"

THE GOVERNOR'S WIFE. Let's go into church. Very likely it's the draft here.

[*The procession of* FAMILY *and* SERVANTS *turns into the doorway. The* FAT PRINCE *follows, but the* GOVERNOR *is kept back by the* ADJUTANT, *a handsome young man. When the crowd of* PETITIONERS *has been driven off, a young dust-stained* RIDER, *his arm in a sling, remains behind.*]

THE ADJUTANT [*pointing at the* RIDER, *who steps forward*]. Won't you hear the messenger from the capital, Your Excellency? He arrived this morning. With confidential papers.

THE GOVERNOR. Not before Service, Shalva. But did you hear Brother Kazbeki wish me a happy Easter? Which is all very well, but I don't believe it did rain last night.

THE ADJUTANT [*nodding*]. We must investigate.

THE GOVERNOR. Yes, at once. Tomorrow.

[*They pass through the doorway. The* RIDER, *who has waited in vain for an audience, turns sharply round and, muttering a curse, goes off. Only one of the palace guards—*SIMON SHASHAVA*—remains at the door.*]

THE SINGER.

The city is still.
Pigeons strut in the church square.
A soldier of the Palace Guard
Is joking with a kitchen maid
As she comes up from the river with a bundle.

[*A girl—*GRUSHA VASHADZE*—comes through the gateway with a bundle made of large green leaves under her arm.*]

SIMON. What, the young lady is not in church? Shirking?

GRUSHA. I was dressed to go. But they needed another goose for the banquet. And they asked me to get it. I know about geese.

SIMON. A goose? [*He feigns suspicion.*] I'd like to see that goose. [GRUSHA *does not understand.*] One must be on one's guard with women. "I only went for a fish," they tell you, but it turns out to be something else.

GRUSHA [*walking resolutely toward him and showing him the goose*]. There! If it isn't a fifteen-pound goose stuffed full of corn, I'll eat the feathers.

SIMON. A queen of a goose! The Governor himself will eat it. So the young lady has been down to the river again?

GRUSHA. Yes, at the poultry farm.

SIMON. Really? At the poultry farm, down by the river . . . not higher up maybe? Near those willows?

GRUSHA. I only go to the willows to wash the linen.

SIMON [*insinuatingly*]. Exactly.

GRUSHA. Exactly what?

SIMON [*winking*]. Exactly that.

GRUSHA. Why shouldn't I wash the linen by the willows?

SIMON [*with exaggerated laughter*]. "Why shouldn't I wash the linen by the willows!" That's good, really good!

GRUSHA. I don't understand the soldier. What's so good about it?

SIMON [*slyly*]. "If something I know someone learns, she'll grow hot and cold by turns!"

GRUSHA. I don't know what I could learn about those willows.

SIMON. Not even if there was a bush opposite? That one could see everything from? Everything that goes on there when a certain person is—"washing linen"?

GRUSHA. What does go on? Won't the soldier say what he means and have done?

SIMON. Something goes on. Something can be seen.

GRUSHA. Could the soldier mean I dip my toes in the water when it's hot? There's nothing else.

SIMON. There's more. Your toes. And more.

GRUSHA. More what? At most my foot?

SIMON. Your foot. And a little more. [*He laughs heartily.*]

GRUSHA [*angrily*]. Simon Shashava, you ought to be ashamed of yourself! To sit in a bush on a hot day and wait till a girl comes and dips her legs in the river! And I bet you bring a friend along too!

[*She runs off.*]

SIMON [*shouting after her*]. I didn't bring any friend along!

[*As the* SINGER *resumes his tale, the* SOLDIER *steps into the doorway as though to listen to the service.*]

THE SINGER.

The city lies still
But why are there armed men?
The Governor's palace is at peace
But why is it a fortress?
And the Governor returned to his palace
And the fortress was a trap

And the goose was plucked and roasted
But the goose was not eaten this time
And noon was no longer the hour to eat:
Noon was the hour to die.

[*From the doorway at the left the* FAT PRINCE *quickly appears, stands still, looks around. Before the gateway at the right* TWO IRONSHIRTS *are squatting and playing dice. The* FAT PRINCE *sees them, walks slowly past, making a sign to them. They rise: one goes through the gateway, the other goes off at the right. Muffled voices are heard from various directions in the rear:* "To your posts!" *The palace is surrounded. The* FAT PRINCE *quickly goes off. Church bells in the distance. Enter, through the doorway, the* GOVERNOR'S FAMILY *and procession, returning from church.*]

THE GOVERNOR'S WIFE [*passing the* ADJUTANT]. It's impossible to live in such a slum. But Georgi, of course, will only build for his little Michael. Never for me! Michael is all! All for Michael!

[*The procession turns into the gateway. Again the* ADJUTANT *lingers behind. He waits. Enter the wounded* RIDER *from the doorway.* TWO IRONSHIRTS *of the Palace Guard have taken up positions by the gateway.*]

THE ADJUTANT [*to the* RIDER]. The Governor does not wish to receive military news before dinner—especially if it's depressing, as I assume. In the afternoon His Excellency will confer with prominent architects. They're coming to dinner too. And here they are! [*Enter* THREE GENTLEMEN *through the doorway.*] Go to the kitchen and eat, my friend. [*As the* RIDER *goes, the* ADJUTANT *greets the* ARCHITECTS.] Gentlemen, His Excellency expects you at dinner. He will devote all his time to you and your great new plans. Come!

ONE OF THE ARCHITECTS. We marvel that His Excellency intends to build. There are disquieting rumors that the war in Persia has taken a turn for the worse.

THE ADJUTANT. All the more reason to build! There's nothing to those rumors anyway. Persia is a long way off, and the garrison here would let itself be hacked to bits for its Governor. [*Noise from the palace. The shrill scream of a woman. Someone is shouting orders. Dumbfounded, the* ADJUTANT *moves toward the gateway. An* IRONSHIRT *steps out, points his lance at him.*] What's this? Put down that lance, you dog.

ONE OF THE ARCHITECTS. It's the Princes! Don't you know the Princes met last night in the capital? And they're against the Grand

Duke and his Governors? Gentlemen, we'd better make ourselves scarce.

[*They rush off. The* ADJUTANT *remains helplessly behind.*]

THE ADJUTANT [*furiously to the Palace Guard*]. Down with those lances! Don't you see the Governor's life is threatened?

[*The* IRONSHIRTS *of the Palace Guard refuse to obey. They stare coldly and indifferently at the* ADJUTANT *and follow the next events without interest.*]

THE SINGER.

O blindness of the great!
They go their way like gods,
Great over bent backs,
Sure of hired fists,
Trusting in the power
Which has lasted so long.
But long is not forever.
O change from age to age!
Thou hope of the people!

[*Enter the* GOVERNOR, *through the gateway, between* TWO SOLDIERS *armed to the teeth. He is in chains. His face is gray.*]

Up, great sir, deign to walk upright!
From your palace the eyes of many foes follow you!
And now you don't need an architect, a carpenter will do.
You won't be moving into a new palace
But into a little hole in the ground.
Look about you once more, blind man!

[*The* ARRESTED MAN *looks round.*]

Does all you had please you?
Between the Easter Mass and the Easter meal
You are walking to a place whence no one returns.

[*The* GOVERNOR *is led off. A horn sounds an alarm. Noise behind the gateway.*]

When the house of a great one collapses
Many little ones are slain.
Those who had no share in the *good* fortunes of the mighty
Often have a share in their *mis*fortunes.
The plunging wagon
Drags the sweating oxen down with it
Into the abyss.

[*The* SERVANTS *come rushing through the gateway in panic.*]

THE SERVANTS [*among themselves*]. The baskets!

—Take them all into the third courtyard! Food for five days!

—The mistress has fainted! Someone must carry her down.

—She must get away.

—What about us? We'll be slaughtered like chickens, as always.

—Goodness, what'll happen? There's bloodshed already in the city, they say.

—Nonsense, the Governor has just been asked to appear at a Princes' meeting. All very correct. Everything'll be ironed out. I heard this on the best authority . . .

[*The* TWO DOCTORS *rush into the courtyard.*]

THE FIRST DOCTOR [*trying to restrain the other*]. Niko Mikadze, it is your duty as a doctor to attend Natella Abashwili.

THE SECOND DOCTOR. My duty! It's yours!

THE FIRST DOCTOR. Whose turn is it to look after the child today, Niko Mikadze, yours or mine?

THE SECOND DOCTOR. Do you really think, Mika Loladze, I'm going to stay a minute longer in this accursed house on that little brat's account? [*They start fighting. All one hears is:* "You neglect your duty!" *and* "Duty, my foot!" *Then the* SECOND DOCTOR *knocks the* FIRST *down.*] Go to hell!

[*Exit.*]

[*Enter the soldier,* SIMON SHASHAVA. *He searches in the crowd for* GRUSHA.]

SIMON. Grusha! There you are at last! What are you going to do?

GRUSHA. Nothing. If worst comes to worst, I've a brother in the mountains. How about you?

SIMON. Forget about me. [*formally again*] Grusha Vashnadze, your wish to know my plans fills me with satisfaction. I've been ordered to accompany Madam Natella Abashwili as her guard.

GRUSHA. But hasn't the Palace Guard mutinied?

SIMON [*seriously*]. That's a fact.

GRUSHA. Isn't it dangerous to go with her?

SIMON. In Tiflis, they say: Isn't the stabbing dangerous for the knife?

GRUSHA. You're not a knife, you're a man, Simon Shashava, what has that woman to do with you?

SIMON. That woman has nothing to do with me. I have my orders, and I go.

GRUSHA. The soldier is pigheaded: he is running into danger for nothing—nothing at all. I must get into the third courtyard, I'm in a hurry.

SIMON. Since we're both in a hurry we shouldn't quarrel. You need time for a good quarrel. May I ask if the young lady still has parents?

GRUSHA. No, just a brother.

SIMON. As time is short—my second question is this: Is the young lady as healthy as a fish in water?

GRUSHA. I may have a pain in the right shoulder once in a while. Otherwise I'm strong enough for my job. No one has complained. So far.

SIMON. That's well known. When it's Easter Sunday, and the question arises who'll run for the goose all the same, she'll be the one. My third question is this: Is the young lady impatient? Does she want apples in winter?

GRUSHA. Impatient? No. But if a man goes to war without any reason and then no message comes—that's bad.

SIMON. A message will come. And now my final question . . .

GRUSHA. Simon Shashava, I must get to the third courtyard at once. My answer is yes.

SIMON [*very embarrassed*]. Haste, they say, is the wind that blows down the scaffolding. But they also say: The rich don't know what haste is. I'm from . . .

GRUSHA. Kutsk.

SIMON. The young lady has been inquiring about me? I'm healthy, I have no dependents, I make ten piasters a month, as paymaster twenty piasters, and I'm asking—very sincerely—for your hand.

GRUSHA. Simon Shashava, it suits me well.

SIMON [*taking from his neck a thin chain with a little cross on it*]. My mother gave me this cross, Grusha Vashnadze. The chain is silver. Please wear it.

GRUSHA. Many thanks, Simon.

SIMON [*hangs it round her neck*]. It would be better to go to the third courtyard now. Or there'll be difficulties. Anyway, I must harness the horses. The young lady will understand?

GRUSHA. Yes, Simon.

[*They stand undecided.*]

SIMON. I'll just take the mistress to the troops that have stayed loyal. When the war's over, I'll be back. In two weeks. Or three. I hope my intended won't get tired, awaiting my return.

GRUSHA.

Simon Shashava, I shall wait for you.
Go calmly into battle, soldier,
The bloody battle, the bitter battle
From which not everyone returns:
When you return I shall be there.
I shall be waiting for you under the green elm
I shall be waiting for you under the bare elm
I shall wait until the last soldier has returned
And longer.
When you come back from the battle
No boots will stand at my door
The pillow beside mine will be empty
And my mouth will be unkissed.
When you return, when you return
You will be able to say: It is just as it was.

SIMON. I thank you, Grusha Vashnadze. And good-bye!

[*He bows low before her. She does the same before him. Then she runs quickly off without looking round. Enter the* ADJUTANT *from the gateway.*]

THE ADJUTANT [*harshly*]. Harness the horses to the carriage! Don't stand there doing nothing, louse!

[SIMON SHASHAVA *stands to attention and goes off.* TWO SERVANTS *crowd from the gateway, bent low under huge trunks. Behind them, supported by her* WOMEN, *stumbles* NATELLA ABASHWILI. *She is followed by a* WOMAN *carrying the* CHILD.]

THE GOVERNOR'S WIFE. I hardly know if my head's still on. Where's Michael? Don't hold him so clumsily. Pile the trunks onto the carriage. No news from the city, Shalva?

THE ADJUTANT. None. All's quiet so far, but there's not a minute to lose. No room for all these trunks in the carriage. Pick out what you need.

[*Exit quickly.*]

THE GOVERNOR'S WIFE. Only essentials! Quick, open the trunks! I'll tell you what I need. [*The trunks are lowered and opened. She points at some brocade dresses.*] The green one! And, of course, the one with the fur trimming. Where are Niko Mikadze and Mika Loladze? I've suddenly got the most terrible migraine again. It always starts in the temples. [*Enter* GRUSHA.] Taking your time, eh? Go and get the hot water bottles this minute! [GRUSHA *runs off, returns later with hot water bottles; the* GOVERNOR'S WIFE *orders her about by signs.*] Don't tear the sleeves.

A YOUNG WOMAN. Pardon, madam, no harm has come to the dress.

THE GOVERNOR'S WIFE. Because I stopped you. I've been watching you for a long time. Nothing in your head but making eyes at Shalva Tzereteli. I'll kill you, you bitch! [*She beats the* YOUNG WOMAN.]

THE ADJUTANT [*appearing in the gateway*]. Please make haste, Natella Abashwili. Firing has broken out in the city.

[*Exit.*]

THE GOVERNOR'S WIFE [*letting go of the* YOUNG WOMAN]. Oh dear, do you think they'll lay hands on us? Why should they? Why? [*She herself begins to rummage in the trunks.*] How's Michael? Asleep?

THE WOMAN WITH THE CHILD. Yes, madam.

THE GOVERNOR'S WIFE. Then put him down a moment and get my little saffron-colored boots from the bedroom. I need them for the green dress. [*The* WOMAN *puts down the* CHILD *and goes off.*] Just look how these things have been packed! No love! No understanding! If you don't give them every order yourself . . . At such moments you realize what kind of servants you have! They gorge themselves at your expense, and never a word of gratitude! I'll remember this.

THE ADJUTANT [*entering, very excited*]. Natella, you must leave at once!

THE GOVERNOR'S WIFE. Why? I've got to take this silver dress—it cost a thousand piasters. And that one there, and where's the wine-colored one?

THE ADJUTANT [*trying to pull her away*]. Riots have broken out! We must leave at once. Where's the baby?

THE GOVERNOR'S WIFE [*calling to the* YOUNG WOMAN *who was holding the baby*]. Maro, get the baby ready! Where on earth are you?

THE ADJUTANT [*leaving*]. We'll probably have to leave the carriage behind and go ahead on horseback.

[*The* GOVERNOR'S WIFE *rummages again among her dresses, throws some onto the heap of chosen clothes, then takes them off again. Noises, drums are heard. The* YOUNG WOMAN *who was beaten creeps away. The sky begins to grow red.*]

THE GOVERNOR'S WIFE [*rummaging desperately*]. I simply cannot find the wine-colored dress. Take the whole pile to the carriage. Where's Asja? And why hasn't Maro come back? Have you all gone crazy?

THE ADJUTANT [*returning*]. Quick! Quick!

THE GOVERNOR'S WIFE [*to the* FIRST WOMAN]. Run! Just throw them into the carriage!

THE ADJUTANT. We're not taking the carriage. And if you don't come now, I'll ride off on my own.

THE GOVERNOR'S WIFE [*as the* FIRST WOMAN *can't carry everything*]. Where's that bitch Asja? [*The* ADJUTANT *pulls her away.*] Maro, bring the baby! [*To the* FIRST WOMAN] Go and look for Masha. No, first take the dresses to the carriage. Such nonsense! I wouldn't dream of going on horseback! [*Turning round, she sees the red sky, and starts back rigid. The fire burns. She is pulled out by the* ADJUTANT. *Shaking, the* FIRST WOMAN *follows with the dresses.*]

MARO [*from the doorway with the boots*]. Madam! [*She sees the trunks and dresses and runs toward the* BABY, *picks it up, and holds it a moment.*] They left it behind, the beasts. [*She hands it to* GRUSHA.] Hold it a moment. [*She runs off, following the* GOVERNOR'S WIFE.]

[*Enter* SERVANTS *from the gateway.*]

THE COOK. Well, so they've actually gone. Without the food wagons, and not a minute too early. It's time for us to clear out.

A GROOM. This'll be an unhealthy neighborhood for quite a while. [*To* ONE OF THE WOMEN] Suliko, take a few blankets and wait for me in the foal stables.

GRUSHA. What have they done with the Governor?

THE GROOM [*gesturing throat cutting*]. Ffffft.

A FAT WOMAN [*seeing the gesture and becoming hysterical*]. Oh dear, oh dear, oh dear, oh dear! Our master Georgi Abashwili! A picture of health he was, at the morning Mass—and now! Oh, take me away, we're all lost, we must die in sin like our master, Georgi Abashwili!

THE OTHER WOMAN [*soothing her*]. Calm down, Nina! You'll be taken to safety. You've never hurt a fly.

THE FAT WOMAN [*being led out*]. Oh dear, oh dear, oh dear! Quick! Let's all get out before they come, before they come!

A YOUNG WOMAN. Nina takes it more to heart than the mistress, that's a fact. They even have to have their weeping done for them.

THE COOK. We'd better get out, all of us.

ANOTHER WOMAN [*glancing back*]. That must be the East Gate burning.

THE YOUNG WOMAN [*seeing the* CHILD *in* GRUSHA'S *arms*]. The baby! What are you doing with it?

GRUSHA. It got left behind.

THE YOUNG WOMAN. She simply left it there. Michael, who was kept out of all the drafts!

[*The* SERVANTS *gather round the* CHILD.]

GRUSHA. He's waking up.

THE GROOM. Better put him down, I tell you. I'd rather not think what'd happen to anybody who was found with that baby.

THE COOK. That's right. Once they get started, they'll kill each other off, whole families at a time. Let's go.

[*Exeunt all but* GRUSHA, *with the* CHILD *on her arm, and* TWO WOMEN.]

THE TWO WOMEN. Didn't you hear? Better put him down.

GRUSHA. The nurse asked me to hold him a moment.

THE OLDER WOMAN. She's not coming back, you simpleton.

THE YOUNGER WOMAN. Keep your hands off it.

THE OLDER WOMAN [*amiably*]. Grusha, you're a good soul, but you're not very bright, and you know it. I tell you, if he had the plague he couldn't be more dangerous.

GRUSHA [*stubbornly*]. He hasn't got the plague. He looks at me! He's human!

THE OLDER WOMAN. Don't look at *him*. You're a fool—the kind that always gets put upon. A person need only say, "Run for the salad, you have the longest legs," and you run. My husband has an ox cart—you can come with us if you hurry! Lord, by now the whole neighborhood must be in flames.

[BOTH WOMEN *leave, sighing. After some hesitation,* GRUSHA *puts the sleeping* CHILD *down, looks at it for a moment, then takes a brocade blanket from the heap of clothes and covers it. Then* BOTH WOMEN *return, dragging bundles.* GRUSHA *starts guiltily away from the* CHILD *and walks a few steps to one side.*]

THE YOUNGER WOMAN. Haven't you packed anything yet? There isn't much time, you know. The Ironshirts will be here from the barracks.

GRUSHA. Coming!

[*She runs through the doorway.* BOTH WOMEN *go to the gateway and wait. The sound of horses is heard. They flee, screaming. Enter the* FAT PRINCE *with drunken* IRONSHIRTS. *One of them carries the Governor's head on a lance.*]

THE FAT PRINCE. Here! In the middle! [ONE SOLDIER *climbs onto the* OTHER'S *back, takes the head, holds it tentatively over the door.*] That's not the middle. Farther to the right. That's it. What I do, my friends, I do well. [*While, with hammer and nail, the* SOLDIER *fastens the head to the wall by its hair*] This morning at the church door I said to Georgi Abashwili: "I love a clear sky." Actually, I prefer the lightning that comes out of a clear sky. Yes, indeed. It's a pity they took the brat along, though, I need him, urgently.

[*Exit with* IRONSHIRTS *through the gateway. Trampling of horses again. Enter* GRUSHA *through the doorway looking cautiously about her. Clearly she has waited for the* IRONSHIRTS *to go. Carrying a bundle, she walks toward the gateway. At the last moment, she turns to see if the* CHILD *is still there. Catching sight of the head over the doorway, she screams. Horrified, she picks up her bundle again, and is about to leave when the* SINGER *starts to speak. She stands rooted to the spot.*]

THE SINGER.

As she was standing between courtyard and gate,
She heard or she thought she heard a low voice calling.
The child called to her,
Not whining, but calling quite sensibly,
Or so it seemed to her.
"Woman," it said, "help me."
And it went on, not whining, but saying quite sensibly:
"Know, woman, he who hears not a cry for help
But passes by with troubled ears will never hear
The gentle call of a lover nor the blackbird at dawn
Nor the happy sigh of the tired grape-picker as the Angelus
rings."

[*She walks a few steps toward the* CHILD *and bends over it.*]

Hearing this she went back for one more look at the child:

Only to sit with him for a moment or two,
Only till someone should come,
His mother, or anyone.

[*Leaning on a trunk, she sits facing the* CHILD.]

Only till she would have to leave, for the danger was too great,
The city was full of flame and crying.

[*The light grows dimmer, as though evening and night were coming on.*]

Fearful is the seductive power of goodness!

[GRUSHA *now settles down to watch over the* CHILD *through the night. Once, she lights a small lamp to look at it. Once, she tucks it in with a coat. From time to time she listens and looks to see whether someone is coming.*]

And she sat with the child a long time,
Till evening came, till night came, till dawn came.
She sat too long, too long she saw
The soft breathing, the small clenched fists,
Till toward morning the seduction was complete
And she rose, and bent down and, sighing, took the child
And carried it away.

[*She does what the* SINGER *says as he describes it.*]

As if it was stolen goods she picked it up.
As if she was a thief she crept away.

THE FLIGHT INTO THE NORTHERN MOUNTAINS

THE SINGER.

When Grusha Vashnadze left the city
On the Grusinian highway
On the way to the Northern Mountains
She sang a song, she bought some milk.

THE CHORUS.

How will this human child escape
The bloodhounds, the trap-setters?
Into the deserted mountains she journeyed
Along the Grusinian highway she journeyed
She sang a song, she bought some milk.

[GRUSHA VASHNADZE *walks on. On her back she carries the* CHILD *in a sack, in one hand is a large stick, in the other a bundle. She sings.*]

The Song of the Four Generals

Four generals
Set out for Iran.
With the first one, war did not agree.
The second never won a victory.
For the third the weather never was right.
For the fourth the men would never fight.
Four generals
And not a single man!
Sosso Robakidse
Went marching to Iran
With him the war did so agree
He soon had won a victory.
For him the weather was always right.
For him the men would always fight.
Sosso Robakidse,
He is our man!

[*A peasant's cottage appears.*]

GRUSHA [*to the* CHILD]. Noontime is meal time. Now we'll sit hopefully in the grass, while the good Grusha goes and buys a little pitcher of milk. [*She lays the* CHILD *down and knocks at the cottage door. An* OLD MAN *opens it.*] Grandfather, could I have a little pitcher of milk? And a corn cake, maybe?

THE OLD MAN. Milk? We have no milk. The soldiers from the city have our goats. Go to the soldiers if you want milk.

GRUSHA. But grandfather, you must have a little pitcher of milk for a baby?

THE OLD MAN. And for a God-bless-you, eh?

GRUSHA. Who said anything about a God-bless-you? [*She shows her purse.*] We'll pay like princes. "Head in the clouds, backside in the water." [*The* PEASANT *goes off, grumbling, for milk.*] How much for the milk?

THE OLD MAN. Three piasters. Milk has gone up.

GRUSHA. Three piasters for this little drop? [*Without a word the* OLD MAN *shuts the door in her face.*] Michael, did you hear that? Three piasters! We can't afford it! [*She goes back, sits down again, and gives the* CHILD *her breast.*] Suck. Think of the three piasters.

There's nothing there, but you *think* you're drinking, and that's something. [*Shaking her head, she sees that the* CHILD *isn't sucking any more. She gets up, walks back to the door, and knocks again.*] Open, grandfather, we'll pay. [*Softly*] May lightning strike you! [*When the* OLD MAN *appears*] I thought it would be half a piaster. But the baby must be fed. How about one piaster for that little drop?

THE OLD MAN. Two.

GRUSHA. Don't shut the door again. [*She fishes a long time in her bag.*] Here are two piasters. The milk better be good. I still have two days' journey ahead of me. It's a murderous business you have here—and sinful, too!

THE OLD MAN. Kill the soldiers if you want milk.

GRUSHA [*giving the* CHILD *some milk*]. This is an expensive joke. Take a sip, Michael, it's a week's pay. Around here they think we earned our mony just sitting around. Oh, Michael, Michael, you're a nice little load for a girl to take on! [*Uneasy, she gets up, puts the* CHILD *on her back, and walks on. The* OLD MAN, *grumbling, picks up the pitcher and looks after her unmoved.*]

THE SINGER.

As Grusha Vashnadze went northward
The Princes' Ironshirts went after her.

THE CHORUS.

How will the barefoot girl escape the Ironshirts,
The bloodhounds, the trap-setters?
They hunt even by night.
Pursuers never tire.
Butchers sleep little.

[TWO IRONSHIRTS *are trudging along the highway.*]

THE CORPORAL. You'll never amount to anything, blockhead, your heart's not in it. Your senior officer sees this in little things. Yesterday, when I made the fat gal, yes, you grabbed her husband as I commanded, and you did kick him in the stomach, at my request, but did not *enjoy* it, like a loyal Private, or were you just doing your duty? I've kept an eye on you blockhead, you're a hollow reed and a tinkling cymbal, you won't get promoted. [*They walk a while in silence.*] Don't think I've forgotten how insubordinate you are, either. Stop limping! I forbid you to limp! You limp because I sold the horses, and I sold the horses because I'd never have got that price again. You limp to show me you don't like marching. I know you. It won't help. You wait. Sing!

THE TWO IRONSHIRTS [*singing*].

Sadly to war I went my way
Leaving my loved one at her door.
My friends will keep her honor safe
Till from the war I'm back once more.

THE CORPORAL. Louder!

THE TWO IRONSHIRTS [*singing*].

When 'neath a headstone I shall be
My love a little earth will bring:
"Here rest the feet that oft would run to me
And here the arms that oft to me would cling."

[*They begin to walk again in silence.*]

THE CORPORAL. A good soldier has his heart and soul in it. When he receives an order, he gets a hard on, and when he drives his lance into the enemy's guts, he comes. [*He shouts for joy.*] He lets himself be torn to bits for his superior officer, and as he lies dying he takes note that his corporal is nodding approval, and that is reward enough, it's his dearest wish. *You* won't get any nod of approval, but you'll croak all right. Christ, how'm I to get my hands on the Governor's bastard with the help of a fool like you! [*They stay on stage behind.*]

THE SINGER.

When Grusha Vashnadze came to the River Sirra
Flight grew too much for her, the helpless child too heavy.
In the cornfields the rosy dawn
Is cold to the sleepless one, only cold.
The gay clatter of the milk cans in the farmyard where the smoke rises
Is only a threat to the fugitive.
She who carries the child feels its weight and little more.

[GRUSHA *stops in front of a farm. A fat* PEASANT WOMAN *is carrying a milk can through the door.* GRUSHA *waits until she has gone in, then approaches the house cautiously.*]

GRUSHA [*to the child*]. Now you've wet yourself again, and you know I've no linen. Michael, this is where we part company. It's far enough from the city. They wouldn't want you *so* much that they'd follow you all *this* way, little good-for-nothing. The peasant woman is kind, and can't you just smell the milk? [*She bends down to lay the* CHILD *on the threshold.*] So farewell, Michael, I'll forget how you kicked me in the back all night to make me walk faster. And you can forget the meager fare—it was meant well. I'd like to have kept you—your nose is so tiny—but it can't be. I'd have shown you your first rabbit, I'd have trained you to keep dry, but now I must turn around. My sweetheart the soldier might be back soon, and suppose he didn't find me? You can't ask that, can you?

[*She creeps up to the door and lays the* CHILD *on the threshold. Then, hiding behind a tree, she waits until the* PEASANT WOMAN *opens the door and sees the bundle.*]

THE PEASANT WOMAN. Good heavens, what's this? Husband!

THE PEASANT. What is it? Let me finish my soup.

THE PEASANT WOMAN [*to the* CHILD]. Where's your mother then? Haven't you got one? It's a boy. Fine linen. He's from a good family, you can see that. And they just leave him on our doorstep. Oh, these are times!

THE PEASANT. If they think we're going to feed it, they're wrong. You can take it to the priest in the village. That's the best we can do.

THE PEASANT WOMAN. What'll the priest do with him? He needs a mother. There, he's waking up. Don't you think we could keep him, though?

THE PEASANT [*shouting*]. No!

THE PEASANT WOMAN. I could lay him in the corner by the armchair. All I need is a crib. I can take him into the fields with me. See him laughing? Husband, we have a roof over our heads. We can do it. Not another word out of you!

[*She carries the* CHILD *into the house. The* PEASANT *follows protesting.* GRUSHA *steps out from behind the tree, laughs, and hurries off in the opposite direction.*]

THE SINGER.

Why so cheerful, making for home?

THE CHORUS.

Because the child has won new parents with a laugh,
Because I'm rid of the little one, I'm cheerful.

THE SINGER.

And why so sad?

THE CHORUS.

Because I'm single and free, I'm sad
Like someone who's been robbed
Someone who's newly poor.

[*She walks for a short while, then meets the* TWO IRONSHIRTS *who point their lances at her.*]

THE CORPORAL. Lady, you are running straight into the arms of the Armed Forces. Where are you coming from? And when? Are you having illicit relations with the enemy? Where is he hiding? What movements is he making in your rear? How about the hills? How about the valleys? How are your stockings held in position? [GRUSHA *stands there frightened.*] Don't be scared, we always stage a retreat, if necessary . . . what, blockhead? I always stage retreats. In that respect at least, I can be relied on. Why are you staring like that at my lance? In the field no soldier drops his lance, that's a rule. Learn it by heart, blockhead. Now, lady, where are you headed?

GRUSHA. To meet my intended, one Simon Shashava, of the Palace Guard in Nuka.

THE CORPORAL. Simon Shashava? Sure, I know him. He gave me the key so I could look you up once in a while. Blockhead, we are getting to be unpopular. We must make her realize we have honorable intentions. Lady, behind apparent frivolity I conceal a serious nature, so let me tell you officially: I want a child from you. [GRUSHA *utters a little scream.*] Blockhead, she understood me. Uh-huh, isn't it a sweet shock? "Then first I must take the noodles out of the oven, Officer. Then first I must change my torn shirt, Colonel." But away with jokes, away with my lance! We are looking for a baby. A baby from a good family. Have you heard of such a baby, from the city, dressed in fine linen, and suddenly turning up here?

GRUSHA. No, I haven't heard a thing. [*Suddenly she turns round and runs back, panic-stricken. The* IRONSHIRTS *glance at each other, then follow her, cursing.*]

THE SINGER.

Run, kind girl! The killers are coming!
Help the helpless babe, helpless girl!
And so she runs!

THE CHORUS.

In the bloodiest times
There are kind people.

[*As* GRUSHA *rushes into the cottage, the* PEASANT WOMAN *is bending over the* CHILD'*s crib.*]

GRUSHA. Hide him. Quick! The Ironshirts are coming! I laid him on your doorstep. But he isn't mine. He's from a good family.

THE PEASANT WOMAN. Who's coming? What Ironshirts?

GRUSHA. Don't ask questions. The Ironshirts that are looking for it.

THE PEASANT WOMAN. They've no business in my house. But I must have a little talk with you, it seems.

GRUSHA. Take off the fine linen. It'll give us away.

THE PEASANT WOMAN. Linen, my foot! In this house I make the decisions! "*You* can't vomit in *my* room!" Why did you abandon it? It's a sin.

GRUSHA [*looking out of the window*]. Look, they're coming out from behind those trees! I shouldn't have run away, it made them angry. Oh, what shall I do?

THE PEASANT WOMAN [*looking out of the window and suddenly starting with fear*]. Gracious! Ironshirts!

GRUSHA. They're after the baby.

THE PEASANT WOMAN. Suppose they come in!

GRUSHA. You mustn't give him to them. Say he's yours.

THE PEASANT WOMAN. Yes.

GRUSHA. They'll run him through if you hand him over.

THE PEASANT WOMAN. But suppose they ask for it? The silver for the harvest is in the house.

GRUSHA. If you let them have him, they'll run him through, right here in this room! You've got to say he's yours!

THE PEASANT WOMAN. Yes. But what if they don't believe me?

GRUSHA. You must be firm.

THE PEASANT WOMAN. They'll burn the roof over our heads.

GRUSHA. That's why you must say he's yours. His name's Michael. But I shouldn't have told you. [*The* PEASANT WOMAN *nods.*] Don't nod like that. And don't tremble—they'll notice.

THE PEASANT WOMAN. Yes.

GRUSHA. And stop saying yes, I can't stand it. [*She shakes the* WOMAN] Don't you have any children?

THE PEASANT WOMAN [*muttering*]. He's in the war.

GRUSHA. Then maybe *he's* an Ironshirt? Do you want *him* to run children through with a lance? You'd bawl him out. "No fooling with lances in my house!" you'd shout, "is that what I've reared you for? Wash your neck before you speak to your mother!"

THE PEASANT WOMAN. That's true, he couldn't get away with anything around here!

GRUSHA. So you'll say he's yours?

THE PEASANT WOMAN. Yes.

GRUSHA. Look! They're coming!

[*There is a knocking at the door. The* WOMEN *don't answer. Enter* IRONSHIRTS. *The* PEASANT WOMAN *bows low.*]

THE CORPORAL. Well, here she is. What did I tell you? What a nose I have! I *smelt* her. Lady, I have a question for you. Why did you run away? What did you think I would do to you? I'll bet it was something dirty. Confess!

GRUSHA [*while the* PEASANT WOMAN *bows again and again*]. I'd left some milk on the stove, and I suddenly remembered it.

THE CORPORAL. Or maybe you imagined I looked at you in a dirty way? Like there could be something between us? A lewd sort of look, know what I mean?

GRUSHA. I didn't see it.

THE CORPORAL. But it's possible, huh? You admit that much. After all, I might be a pig. I'll be frank with you: I could think of all sorts of things if we were alone. [*To the* PEASANT WOMAN] Shouldn't you be busy in the yard? Feeding the hens?

THE PEASANT WOMAN [*falling suddenly to her knees*]. Soldier, I didn't know a thing about it. Please don't burn the roof over our heads.

THE CORPORAL. What are you talking about?

THE PEASANT WOMAN. I had nothing to do with it. She left it on my doorstep, I swear it!

THE CORPORAL [*suddenly seeing the* CHILD *and whistling*]. Ah, so there's a little something in the crib! Blockhead, I smell a thousand piasters. Take the old girl outside and hold on to her. It looks like I have a little cross-examining to do. [*The* PEASANT WOMAN *lets herself be led out by the* PRIVATE, *without a word.*] So, you've *got* the child I wanted from you! [*He walks toward the crib.*]

GRUSHA. Officer, he's mine. He's not the one you're after.

THE CORPORAL. I'll just take a look. [*He bends over the crib.* GRUSHA *looks round in despair.*]

GRUSHA. He's mine! He's mine!

THE CORPORAL. Fine linen!

[GRUSHA *dashes at him to pull him away. He throws her off and again bends over the crib. Again looking round in despair, she sees a log of wood, seizes it, and hits the* CORPORAL *over the head from behind. The* CORPORAL *collapses. She quickly picks up the* CHILD *and rushes off.*]

THE SINGER.

And in her flight from the Ironshirts
After twenty-two days of journeying
At the foot of the Janga-Tu Glacier
Grusha Vashnadze decided to adopt the child.

THE CHORUS.

The helpless girl adopted the helpless child.

[GRUSHA *squats over a half-frozen stream to get the* CHILD *water in the hollow of her hand.*]

GRUSHA.

Since no one else will take you, son,
I must take you.
Since no one else will take you, son,
You must take me.
O black day in a lean, lean year,
The trip was long, the milk was dear,
My legs are tired, my feet are sore:
But I wouldn't be without you any more.
I'll throw your silken shirt away
And dress you in rags and tatters.
I'll wash you, son, and christen you in glacier water.
We'll see it through together.

[*She has taken off the child's fine linen and wrapped it in a rag.*]

THE SINGER.

When Grusha Vashnadze
Pursued by the Ironshirts
Came to the bridge on the glacier
Leading to the villages of the Eastern Slope
She sang the Song of the Rotten Bridge
And risked two lives.

[*A wind has risen. The bridge on the glacier is visible in the dark. One rope is broken and half the bridge is hanging down the abyss.* MERCHANTS, *two men and a woman, stand undecided before the bridge as* GRUSHA *and the* CHILD *arrive.* ONE MAN *is trying to catch the hanging rope with a stick.*]

THE FIRST MAN. Take your time, young woman. You won't get across here anyway.

GRUSHA. But I *have* to get the baby to the east side. To my brother's place.

THE MERCHANT WOMAN. Have to? How d'you mean, "have to"? I have to get there, too—because I have to buy carpets in Atum—carpets a woman had to sell because her husband had to die. But can *I* do what I have to? Can she? Andrei's been fishing for that rope for hours. And I ask you, how are we going to fasten it, even if he gets it up?

THE FIRST MAN [*listening*]. Hush, I think I hear something.

GRUSHA. The bridge isn't quite rotted through. I think I'll try it.

THE MERCHANT WOMAN. *I* wouldn't—if the devil himself were after me. It's suicide.

THE FIRST MAN [*shouting*]. Hi!

GRUSHA. Don't shout! [*To the* MERCHANT WOMAN] Tell him not shout.

THE FIRST MAN. But there's someone down there calling. Maybe they've lost their way.

THE MERCHANT WOMAN. Why shouldn't he shout? Is there something funny about you? Are they after you?

GRUSHA. All right, I'll tell. The Ironshirts are after me. I knocked one down.

THE SECOND MAN. Hide our merchandise! [*The* WOMAN *hides a sack behind a rock.*]

THE FIRST MAN. Why didn't you say so right away? [*To the others*] If they catch her they'll make mincemeat out of her!

GRUSHA. Get out of my way. I've got to cross that bridge.

THE SECOND MAN. You can't. The precipice is two thousand feet deep.

THE FIRST MAN. Even with the rope it'd be no use. We could hold it up with our hands. But then we'd have to do the same for the Ironshirts.

GRUSHA. Go away.

[*There are calls from the distance:* "Hi, up there!"]

THE MERCHANT WOMAN. They're getting near. But you can't take the child on that bridge. It's sure to break. And look!

[GRUSHA *looks down into the abyss. The* IRONSHIRTS *are heard calling again from below.*]

THE SECOND MAN. Two thousand feet!

GRUSHA. But those men are worse.

THE FIRST MAN. You can't do it. Think of the baby. Risk your life but not a child's.

THE SECOND MAN. With the child she's that much heavier!

THE MERCHANT WOMAN. Maybe she's *really* got to get across. Give *me* the baby. I'll hide it. Cross the bridge alone!

GRUSHA. I won't. We belong together. [*To the* CHILD] "Live together, die together." [*She sings.*]

The Song of the Rotten Bridge

Deep is the abyss, son,
I see the weak bridge sway;
But it's not for us, son,
To choose the way.
The way I know
Is the one you must tread,
And all you will eat
Is my bit of bread.
Of every four pieces
You shall have three.
Would that I knew
How big they will be!

Get out of my way, I'll try it without the rope.

THE MERCHANT WOMAN. You are tempting God!

[*There are shouts from below.*]

GRUSHA. Please, throw that stick away, or they'll get the rope and follow me. [*Pressing the* CHILD *to her, she steps onto the swaying bridge. The* MERCHANT WOMAN *screams when it looks as though the bridge is about to collapse. But* GRUSHA *walks on and reaches the far side.*]

THE FIRST MAN. She made it!

THE MERCHANT WOMAN [*who has fallen on her knees and begun to pray, angrily*]. I still think it was a sin.

[*The* IRONSHIRTS *appear; the* CORPORAL'S *head is bandaged.*]

THE CORPORAL. Seen a woman with a child?

THE FIRST MAN [*while the* SECOND MAN *throws the stick into the abyss*]. Yes, there! But the bridge won't carry you!

THE CORPORAL. You'll pay for this, blockhead!

[GRUSHA, *from the far bank, laughs and shows the* CHILD *to the* IRONSHIRTS. *She walks on. The wind blows.*]

GRUSHA [*turning to the* CHILD]. You mustn't be afraid of the wind. He's a poor thing too. He has to push the clouds along and he gets quite cold doing it. [*Snow starts falling.*] And the snow isn't so bad, either, Michael. It covers the little fir trees so they won't die in winter. Let me sing you a little song. [*She sings.*]

The Song of the Child
Your father is a bandit
A harlot the mother who bore you.
Yet honorable men
Shall kneel down before you.
Food to the baby horses
The tiger's son will take.
The mothers will get milk
From the son of the snake.

IN THE NORTHERN MOUNTAINS

THE SINGER.
Seven days the sister, Grusha Vashnadze,
Journeyed across the glacier
And down the slopes she journeyed.
"When I enter my brother's house," she thought,
"He will rise and embrace me."
"Is that you, sister?" he will say,
"I have long expected you.
This is my dear wife,
And this is my farm, come to me by marriage,
With eleven horses and thirty-one cows. Sit down.
Sit down with your child at our table and eat."
The brother's house was in a lovely valley.
When the sister came to the brother,
She was ill from walking.
The brother rose from the table.

[*A* FAT PEASANT COUPLE *rise from the table.* LAVRENTI VASHNADZE *still has a napkin round his neck, as* GRUSHA, *pale and supported by a* SERVANT, *enters with the* CHILD.]

LAVRENTI. Where've *you* come from, Grusha?

GRUSHA [*feebly*]. Across the Janga-Tu Pass, Lavrenti.

THE SERVANT. I found her in front of the hay barn. She has a baby with her.

THE SISTER-IN-LAW. Go and groom the mare.

[*Exit the* SERVANT.]

LAVRENTI. This is my wife Aniko.

THE SISTER-IN-LAW. I thought you were in service in Nuka.

GRUSHA [*barely able to stand*]. Yes, I was.

THE SISTER-IN-LAW. Wasn't it a good job? We were told it was.

GRUSHA. The Governor got killed.

LAVRENTI. Yes, we heard there were riots. Your aunt told us. Remember, Aniko?

THE SISTER-IN-LAW. Here with us, it's very quiet. City people always want something going on. [*She walks toward the door, calling*] Sosso, Sosso, don't take the cake out of the oven yet, d'you hear? Where on earth are you?

[*Exit, calling.*]

LAVRENTI [*quietly, quickly*]. Is there a father? [*As she shakes her head*] I thought not. We must think up something. She's religious.

THE SISTER-IN-LAW [*returning*]. Those servants! [*To* GRUSHA] You have a child.

GRUSHA. It's mine. [*She collapses.* LAVRENTI *rushes to her assistance.*]

THE SISTER-IN-LAW. Heavens, she's ill—what are we going to do?

LAVRENTI [*escorting her to a bench near the stove*]. Sit down, sit. I think it's just weakness, Aniko.

THE SISTER-IN-LAW. As long as it's not scarlet fever!

LAVRENTI. She'd have spots if it was. It's only weakness. Don't worry, Aniko. [*To* GRUSHA] Better, sitting down?

THE SISTER-IN-LAW. Is the child hers?

GRUSHA. Yes, mine.

LAVRENTI. She's on her way to her husband.

THE SISTER-IN-LAW. I see. Your meat's getting cold. [LAVRENTI *sits down and begins to eat.*] Cold food's not good for you, the fat mustn't get cold, you know your stomach's your weak spot. [*To* GRUSHA] If your husband's not in the city, where is he?

LAVRENTI. She got married on the other side of the mountain, she says.

THE SISTER-IN-LAW. On the other side of the mountain. I see. [*She also sits down to eat.*]

GRUSHA. I think I should lie down somewhere, Lavrenti.

THE SISTER-IN-LAW. If it's consumption we'll all get it. [*She goes on cross-examining her.*] Has your husband got a farm?

GRUSHA. He's a soldier.

LAVRENTI. But he's coming into a farm—a small one—from his father.

THE SISTER-IN-LAW. Isn't he in the war? Why not?

GRUSHA [*with effort*]. Yes, he's in the war.

THE SISTER-IN-LAW. Then why d'you want to go to the farm?

LAVRENTI. When he comes back from the war, he'll return to his farm.

THE SISTER-IN-LAW. But you're going there now?

LAVRENTI. Yes, to wait for him.

THE SISTER-IN-LAW [*calling shrilly*]. Sosso, the cake!

GRUSHA [*murmuring feverishly*]. A farm—a soldier—waiting—sit down, eat.

THE SISTER-IN-LAW. It's scarlet fever.

GRUSHA [*starting up*]. Yes, he's got a farm!

LAVRENTI. I think it's just weakness, Aniko. Would you look after the cake yourself, dear?

THE SISTER-IN-LAW. But when will he come back if war's broken out again as people say? [*She waddles off, shouting*] Sosso! Where on earth are you? Sosso!

LAVRENTI [*getting up quickly and going to* GRUSHA]. You'll get a bed in a minute. She has a good heart. But wait till after supper.

GRUSHA [*holding out the* CHILD *to him*]. Take him.

LAVRENTI [*taking it and looking around*]. But you can't stay here long with the child. She's religious, you see. [GRUSHA *collapses.* LAVRENTI *catches her.*]

THE SINGER.

The sister was so ill,
The cowardly brother had to give her shelter.
Summer departed, winter came.
The winter was long, the winter was short,
People mustn't know anything,
Rats mustn't bite,
Spring mustn't come.

[GRUSHA *sits over the weaving loom in a workroom. She and the* CHILD, *who is squatting on the floor, are wrapped in blankets. She sings.*]

The Song of the Center

And the lover started to leave
And his betrothed ran pleading after him
Pleading and weeping, weeping and teaching:
"Dearest mine, dearest mine
When you go to war as now you do
When you fight the foe as soon you will
Don't lead with the front line
And don't push with the rear line
At the front is red fire
In the rear is red smoke
Stay in the war's center
Stay near the standard bearer
The first always die
The last are also hit
Those in the center come home."

Michael, we must be clever. If we make ourselves as small as cockroaches, the sister-in-law will forget we're in the house, and then we can stay till the snow melts.

[*Enter* LAVRENTI. *He sits down beside his* SISTER.]

LAVRENTI. Why are you sitting there muffled up like coachmen, you two? Is it too cold in the room?

GRUSHA [*hastily removing one shawl*]. It's not too cold, Lavrenti.

LAVRENTI. If it's too cold, you shouldn't be sitting here with the child. Aniko would never forgive herself! [*Pause.*] I hope our priest didn't question you about the child?

GRUSHA. He did, but I didn't tell him anything.

LAVRENTI. That's good. I wanted to speak to you about Aniko. She has a good heart but she's very, very sensitive. People need only mention our farm and she's worried. She takes everything hard, you see. One time our milkmaid went to church with a hole in her stocking. Ever since, Aniko has worn two pairs of stockings in church. It's the old family in her. [*He listens.*] Are you sure there are no rats around? If there are rats, you couldn't live here. [*There are sounds as of dripping from the roof.*] What's that, dripping?

GRUSHA. It must be a barrel leaking.

LAVRENTI. Yes, it must be a barrel. You've been here six months, haven't you? Was I talking about Aniko? [*They listen again to the snow melting.*] You can't imagine how worried she gets about your soldier-husband. "Suppose he comes back and can't find her!" she says and lies awake. "He can't come before the spring," I tell her. The dear woman! [*The drops begin to fall faster.*] When d'you think he'll come? What do *you* think? [GRUSHA *is silent.*] Not before the spring, you agree? [GRUSHA *is silent.*] You don't believe he'll come at all? [GRUSHA *is silent.*] But when the spring comes and the snow melts here and on the passes, you can't stay on. They may come and look for you. There's already talk of an illegitimate child. [*The "glockenspiel" of the falling drops has grown faster and steadier.*] Grusha, the snow is melting on the roof. Spring is here.

GRUSHA. Yes.

LAVRENTI [*eagerly*]. I'll tell you what we'll do. You need a place to go, and, because of the child [*he sighs*], you have to have a husband, so people won't talk. Now I've made cautious inquiries to see if we can find you a husband. Grusha, I *have* one. I talked to a peasant woman who has a son. Just the other side of the mountain. A small farm. And she's willing.

GRUSHA. But I *can't* marry! I must wait for Simon Shashava.

LAVRENTI. Of course. That's all been taken care of. You don't need a man in bed—you need a man on paper. And I've found you one. The son of this peasant woman is going to die. Isn't that wonderful? He's at his last gasp. And all in line with our story—a husband from the other side of the mountain! And when you met him he was at the last gasp. So you're a widow. What do you say?

GRUSHA. It's true I could use a document with stamps on it for Michael.

LAVRENTI. Stamps make all the difference. Without something in writing the Shah couldn't prove he's a Shah. And you'll have a place to live.

GRUSHA. How much does the peasant woman want?

LAVRENTI. Four hundred piasters.

GRUSHA. Where will you find it?

LAVRENTI [*guiltily*]. Aniko's milk money.

GRUSHA. No one would know us there. I'll do it.

LAVRENTI [*getting up*]. I'll let the peasant woman know.

[*Quick exit.*]

GRUSHA. Michael, you cause a lot of fuss. I came to you as the pear tree comes to the sparrows. And because a Christian bends down and picks up a crust of bread so nothing will go to waste. Michael, it would have been better had I walked quickly away on that Easter Sunday in Nuka in the second courtyard. Now I *am* a fool.

THE SINGER.

The bridegroom was on his deathbed when the bride arrived.
The bridegroom's mother was waiting at the door, telling her
to hurry.
The bride brought a child along.
The witness hid it during the wedding.

[*On one side the bed. Under the mosquito net lies a very sick* MAN. GRUSHA *is pulled in at a run by her future* MOTHER-IN-LAW. *They are followed by* LAVRENTI *and the* CHILD.]

THE MOTHER-IN-LAW. Quick! Quick! Or he'll die on us before the wedding. [*To* LAVRENTI] I was never told she had a child already.

LAVRENTI. What difference does it make? [*Pointing toward the* DYING MAN] It can't matter to him—in his condition.

THE MOTHER-IN-LAW. To him? But I'll never survive the shame! We are honest people. [*She begins to weep.*] My Jussup doesn't have to marry a girl with a child!

LAVRENTI. All right, make it another two hundred piasters. You'll have it in writing that the farm will go to you: but she'll have the right to live here for two years.

THE MOTHER-IN-LAW [*drying her tears*]. It'll hardly cover the funeral expenses. I hope she'll really lend a hand with the work. And what's happened to the monk? He must have slipped out through the kitchen window. We'll have the whole village on our necks when they hear Jussup's end is come! Oh dear! I'll go get the monk. But he mustn't see the child!

LAVRENTI. I'll take care he doesn't. But why only a monk? Why not a priest?

THE MOTHER-IN-LAW. Oh, he's just as good. I only made one mistake: I paid half his fee in advance. Enough to send him to the tavern. I only hope . . . [*She runs off.*]

LAVRENTI. She saved on the priest, the wretch! Hired a cheap monk.

GRUSHA. You *will* send Simon Shashava to see me if he turns up after all?

LAVRENTI. Yes. [*Pointing at the* SICK MAN] Won't you take a look at him? [GRUSHA, *taking* MICHAEL *to her, shakes her head.*] He's not moving an eyelid. I hope we aren't too late.

[*They listen. On the opposite side enter* NEIGHBORS *who look around and take up positions against the walls, thus forming another wall near the bed, yet leaving an opening so that the bed can be seen. They start murmuring prayers. Enter the* MOTHER-IN-LAW *with a* MONK. *Showing some annoyance and surprise, she bows to the* GUESTS.]

THE MOTHER-IN-LAW. I hope you won't mind waiting a few moments? My son's bride has just arrived from the city. An emergency wedding is about to be celebrated. [*To the* MONK *in the bedroom*] I might have known you couldn't keep your trap shut. [*To* GRUSHA] The wedding can take place at once. Here's the license. Me and the bride's brother [LAVRENTI *tries to hide in the background, after having quietly taken* MICHAEL *back from* GRUSHA. *The* MOTHER-IN-LAW *waves him away*] are the witnesses.

[GRUSHA *has bowed to the* MONK. *They go to the bed. The* MOTHER-IN-LAW *lifts the mosquito net. The* MONK *starts reeling off the marriage ceremony in Latin. Meanwhile, the* MOTHER-IN-LAW *beckons to* LAVRENTI *to get rid of the* CHILD, *but fearing that it will cry he draws its attention to the ceremony.* GRUSHA *glances once at the* CHILD, *and* LAVRENTI *waves the* CHILD's *hand in a greeting.*]

THE MONK. Are you prepared to be a faithful, obedient, and good wife to his man, and to cleave to him until death you do part?

GRUSHA [*looking at the* CHILD]. I am.

THE MONK [*to the* SICK PEASANT]. Are you prepared to be a good and loving husband to your wife until death you do part? [*As the* SICK PEASANT *does not answer, the* MONK *looks inquiringly around.*]

THE MOTHER-IN-LAW. Of course he is! Didn't you hear him say yes?

THE MONK. All right. We declare the marriage contracted! How about extreme unction?

THE MOTHER-IN-LAW. Nothing doing! The wedding cost quite enough. Now I must take care of the mourners. [*To* LAVRENTI] Did we say seven hundred?

LAVRENTI. Six hundred. [*He pays.*] Now I don't want to sit with the guests and get to know people. So farewell, Grusha, and if my widowed sister comes to visit me, she'll get a welcome from my wife, or I'll show my teeth. [*Nods, gives the* CHILD *to* GRUSHA, *and leaves. The* MOURNERS *glance after him without interest.*]

THE MONK. May one ask where this child comes from?

THE MOTHER-IN-LAW. Is there a child? I don't see a child. And you don't see a child either—you understand? Or it may turn out I saw all sorts of things in the tavern! Now come on. [*After* GRUSHA *has put the* CHILD *down and told him to be quiet, they move over left;* GRUSHA *is introduced to the* NEIGHBORS.] This is my daughter-in-law. She arrived just in time to find dear Jussup still alive.

ONE WOMAN. He's been ill now a whole year, hasn't he? When our Vassili was drafted he was there to say good-bye.

ANOTHER WOMAN. Such things are terrible for a farm. The corn all ripe and the farmer in bed! It'll really be a blessing if he doesn't suffer too long, I say.

THE FIRST WOMAN [*confidentially*]. You know why we thought he'd taken to his bed? Because of the draft! And now his end is come!

THE MOTHER-IN-LAW. Sit yourselves down, please! And have some cakes!

[*She beckons to* GRUSHA *and* BOTH WOMEN *go into the bedroom, where they pick up the cake pans off the floor. The* GUESTS, *among them the* MONK, *sit on the floor and begin conversing in subdued voices.*]

ONE PEASANT [*to whom the* MONK *has handed the bottle which he has taken from his soutane*]. There's a child, you say! How can that have happened to Jussup?

A WOMAN. She was certainly lucky to get herself hitched, with him so sick!

THE MOTHER-IN-LAW. They're gossiping already. And wolfing down the funeral cakes at the same time! If he doesn't die today, I'll have to bake some more tomorrow!

GRUSHA. I'll bake them for you.

THE MOTHER-IN-LAW. Yesterday some horsemen rode by, and I went out to see who it was. When I came in again he was lying there like a corpse! So I sent for you. It can't take much longer. [*She listens.*]

THE MONK. Dear wedding and funeral guests! Deeply touched, we stand before a bed of death and marriage. The bride gets a veil; the groom, a shroud: how varied, my children, are the fates of men!

Alas! One man dies and has a roof over his head, and the other is married and the flesh turns to dust from which it was made. Amen.

THE MOTHER-IN-LAW. He's getting his own back. I shouldn't have hired such a cheap one. It's what you'd expect. A more expensive monk would behave himself. In Sura there's one with a real air of sanctity about him, but of course he charges a fortune. A fifty-piaster monk like that has no dignity, and as for piety, just fifty piasters' worth and no more! When I came to get him in the tavern he'd just made a speech, and he was shouting: "The war is over, beware of the peace!" We must go in.

GRUSHA [*giving* MICHAEL *a cake*]. Eat this cake, and keep nice and still, Michael.

[*The* TWO WOMEN *offer cakes to the* GUESTS. *The* DYING MAN *sits up in bed. He puts his head out from under the mosquito net, stares at the* TWO WOMEN, *then sinks back again. The* MONK *takes two bottles from his soutane and offers them to the* PEASANT *beside him. Enter* THREE MUSICIANS *who are greeted with a sly wink by the* MONK.]

THE MOTHER-IN-LAW [*to the* MUSICIANS]. What are you doing here? With instruments?

ONE MUSICIAN. Brother Anastasius here [*pointing at the* MONK] told us there was a wedding on.

THE MOTHER-IN-LAW. What? You brought them? Three more on my neck! Don't you know there's a dying man in the next room?

THE MONK. A very tempting assignment for a musician: something that could be either a subdued Wedding March or a spirited Funeral Dance.

THE MOTHER-IN-LAW. Well, you might as well play. Nobody can stop you eating in any case.

[*The* MUSICIANS *play a potpourri. The* WOMEN *serve cakes.*]

THE MONK. The trumpet sounds like a whining baby. And you, little drum, what have you got to tell the world?

THE DRUNKEN PEASANT [*beside the* MONK, *sings*].

Miss Roundass took the old old man
And said that marriage was the thing
To everyone who met 'er.
She later withdrew from the contract because
Candles are better.

[*The* MOTHER-IN-LAW *throws the* DRUNKEN PEASANT *out. The music stops. The* GUESTS *are embarrassed.*]

THE GUESTS [*loudly*]. Have you heard? The Grand Duke is back! But the Princes are against him.

—They say the Shah of Persia has lent him a great army to restore order in Grusinia.

—But how is that possible? The Shah of Persia is the enemy . . .

—The enemy of Grusinia, you donkey, not the enemy of the Grand Duke!

—In any case, the war's over, so our soldiers are coming back.

[GRUSHA *drops a cake pan.* GUESTS *help her pick up the cake.*]

AN OLD WOMAN [*to* GRUSHA]. Are you feeling bad? It's just excitement about dear Jussup. Sit down and rest a while, my dear. [GRUSHA *staggers.*]

THE GUESTS. Now everything'll be the way it was. Only the taxes'll go up because now we'll have to pay for the war.

GRUSHA [*weakly*]. Did someone say the soldiers are back?

A MAN. I did.

GRUSHA. It can't be true.

THE FIRST MAN [*to a* WOMAN]. Show her the shawl. We bought it from a soldier. It's from Persia.

GRUSHA [*looking at the shawl*]. They are here. [*She gets up, takes a step, kneels down in prayer, takes the silver cross and chain out of her blouse, and kisses it.*]

THE MOTHER-IN-LAW [*while the* GUESTS *silently watch* GRUSHA]. What's the matter with you? Aren't you going to look after our guests? What's all this city nonsense got to do with us?

THE GUESTS [*resuming conversation while* GRUSHA *remains in prayer*]. You can buy Persian saddles from the soldiers too. Though many want crutches in exchange for them.

—The big shots on one side can win a war, the soldiers on both sides lose it.

—Anyway, the war's over. It's something they can't draft you any more.

[*The* DYING MAN *sits bolt upright in bed. He listens.*]

—What we need is two weeks of good weather.

—Our pear trees are hardly bearing a thing this year.

THE MOTHER-IN-LAW [*offering cakes*]. Have some more cakes and welcome! There are more!

[*The* MOTHER-IN-LAW *goes to the bedroom with the empty cake pans. Unaware of the* DYING MAN, *she is bending down to pick up another tray when he begins to talk in a hoarse voice.*]

THE PEASANT. How many more cakes are you going to stuff down their throats? D'you think I can shit money?

[*The* MOTHER-IN-LAW *starts, stares at him aghast, while he climbs out from behind the mosquito net.*]

THE FIRST WOMAN [*talking kindly to* GRUSHA *in the next room*]. Has the young wife got someone at the front?

A MAN. It's good news that they're on their way home, huh?

THE PEASANT. Don't stare at me like that! Where's this wife you've saddled me with?

[*Receiving no answer, he climbs out of bed and in his nightshirt staggers into the other room. Trembling, she follows him with the cake pan.*]

THE GUESTS [*seeing him and shrieking*]. Good God! Jussup!

[*Everyone leaps up in alarm. The* WOMEN *rush to the door.* GRUSHA, *still on her knees, turns round and stares at the* MAN.]

THE PEASANT. A funeral supper! You'd enjoy that, wouldn't you? Get out before I throw you out! [*As the* GUESTS *stampede from the house, gloomily to* GRUSHA] I've upset the apple cart, huh? [*Receiving no answer, he turns round and takes a cake from the pan which his mother is holding.*]

THE SINGER.

O confusion! The wife discovers she has a husband.
By day there's the child, by night there's the husband.
The lover is on his way both day and night.
Husband and wife look at each other.
The bedroom is small.

[*Near the bed the* PEASANT *is sitting in a high wooden bathtub, naked, the* MOTHER-IN-LAW *is pouring water from a pitcher. Opposite* GRUSHA *cowers with* MICHAEL, *who is playing at mending straw mats.*]

THE PEASANT [*to his* MOTHER]. That's her work, not yours. Where's she hiding out now?

THE MOTHER-IN-LAW [*calling*]. Grusha! The peasant wants you!

GRUSHA [*to* MICHAEL]. There are still two holes to mend.

THE PEASANT [*when* GRUSHA *approaches*]. Scrub my back!

GRUSHA. Can't the peasant do it himself?

THE PEASANT. "Can't the peasant do it himself?" Get the brush! To hell with you! Are you the wife here? Or are you a visitor? [*To the* MOTHER-IN-LAW] It's too cold!

THE MOTHER-IN-LAW. I'll run for hot water.

GRUSHA. Let me go.

THE PEASANT. You stay here. [*The* MOTHER-IN-LAW *exits.*] Rub harder. And no shirking. You've seen a naked fellow before. That child didn't come out of thin air.

GRUSHA. The child was not conceived in joy, if that's what the peasant means.

THE PEASANT [*turning and grinning*]. You don't look the type. [GRUSHA *stops scrubbing him, starts back. Enter the* MOTHER-IN-LAW.]

THE PEASANT. A nice thing you've saddled me with! A simpleton for a wife!

THE MOTHER-IN-LAW. She just isn't cooperative.

THE PEASANT. Pour—but go easy! Ow! Go easy, I said. [*To* GRUSHA] Maybe you did something wrong in the city . . . I wouldn't be surprised. Why else should you be here? But I won't talk about that. I've not said a word about the illegitimate object you brought into my house either. But my patience has limits! It's against nature. [*To the* MOTHER-IN-LAW] More! [*To* GRUSHA] And even if your soldier does come back, you're married.

GRUSHA. Yes.

THE PEASANT. But your soldier won't come back. Don't you believe it.

GRUSHA. No.

THE PEASANT. You're cheating me. You're my wife and you're not my wife. Where you lie, nothing lies, and yet no other woman can lie there. When I go to work in the morning I'm tired—when I lie down at night I'm awake as the devil. God has given you sex—and what d'you do? I don't have ten piasters to buy myself a woman in the city. Besides, it's a long way. Woman weeds the fields and opens up her legs, that's what our calendar says. D'you hear?

GRUSHA [*quietly*]. Yes. I didn't mean to cheat you out of it.

THE PEASANT. She didn't mean to cheat me out of it! Pour some more water! [*The* MOTHER-IN-LAW *pours.*] Ow!

THE SINGER.

As she sat by the stream to wash the linen
She saw his image in the water
And his face grew dimmer with the passing moons.
As she raised herself to wring the linen
She heard his voice from the murmuring maple
And his voice grew fainter with the passing moons.
Evasions and sighs grew more numerous,
Tears and sweat flowed.
With the passing moons the child grew up.

[GRUSHA *sits by a stream, dipping linen into the water. In the rear, a few* CHILDREN *are standing.*]

GRUSHA [*to* MICHAEL]. You can play with them, Michael, but don't let them boss you around just because you're the littlest. [MICHAEL *nods and joins the* CHILDREN. *They start playing.*]

THE BIGGEST BOY. Today it's the Heads-Off Game. [*To a* FAT BOY] You're the Prince and you laugh. [*To* MICHAEL] You're the Governor. [*To a* GIRL] You're the Governor's wife and you cry when his head's cut off. And I do the cutting. [*He shows his wooden sword*] With this. First, they lead the Governor into the yard. The Prince walks in front. The Governor's wife comes last.

[*They form a procession. The* FAT BOY *is first and laughs. Then comes* MICHAEL, *then the* BIGGEST BOY, *and then the* GIRL, *who weeps.*]

MICHAEL [*standing still*]. Me cut off head!

THE BIGGEST BOY. That's my job. You're the littlest. The Governor's the easy part. All you do is kneel down and get your head cut off—simple.

MICHAEL. Me want sword!

THE BIGGEST BOY. It's mine! [*He gives him a kick.*]

THE GIRL [*shouting to* GRUSHA]. He won't play his part!

GRUSHA [*laughing*]. Even the little duck is a swimmer, they say.

THE BIGGEST BOY. You can be the Prince if you can laugh. [MICHAEL *shakes his head.*]

THE FAT BOY. I laugh best. Let him cut off the head just once. Then you do it, then me.

[*Reluctantly, the* BIGGEST BOY *hands* MICHAEL *the wooden sword and kneels down. The* FAT BOY *sits down, slaps his thigh, and laughs with all his might. The* GIRL *weeps loudly.* MICHAEL *swings the big sword and "cuts off" the head. In doing so, he topples over.*]

THE BIGGEST BOY. Hey! I'll show you how to cut heads off!

[MICHAEL *runs away. The* CHILDREN *run after him.* GRUSHA *laughs, following them with her eyes. On looking back, she sees* SIMON SHASHAVA *standing on the opposite bank. He wears a shabby uniform.*]

GRUSHA. Simon!

SIMON. Is that Grusha Vashnadze?

GRUSHA. Simon!

SIMON [*formally*]. A good morning to the young lady. I hope she is well.

GRUSHA [*getting up gaily and bowing low*]. A good morning to the soldier. God be thanked he has returned in good health.

SIMON. They found better fish, so they didn't eat me, said the haddock.

GRUSHA. Courage, said the kitchen boy. Good luck, said the hero.

SIMON. How are things here? Was the winter bearable? The neighbor considerate?

GRUSHA. The winter was a trifle rough, the neighbor as usual, Simon.

SIMON. May one ask if a certain person still dips her toes in the water when rinsing the linen?

GRUSHA. The answer is no. Because of the eyes in the bushes.

SIMON. The young lady is speaking of soldiers. Here stands a paymaster.

GRUSHA. A job worth twenty piasters?

SIMON. And lodgings.

GRUSHA [*with tears in her eyes*]. Behind the barracks under the date trees.

SIMON. Yes, there. A certain person has kept her eyes open.

GRUSHA. She has, Simon.

SIMON. And has not forgotten? [GRUSHA *shakes her head.*] So the door is still on its hinges as they say? [GRUSHA *looks at him in silence and shakes her head again.*] What's this? Is anything not as it should be?

GRUSHA. Simon Shashava, I can never return to Nuka. Something has happened.

SIMON. What can have happened?

GRUSHA. For one thing, I knocked an Ironshirt down.

SIMON. Grusha Vashnadze must have had her reasons for that.

GRUSHA. Simon Shashava, I am no longer called what I used to be called.

SIMON [*after a pause*]. I do not understand.

GRUSHA. When do women change their names, Simon? Let me explain. Nothing stands between us. Everything is just as it was. You must believe that.

SIMON. Nothing stands between us and yet there's something?

GRUSHA. How can I explain it so fast and with the stream between us? Couldn't you cross the bridge there?

SIMON. Maybe it's no longer necessary.

GRUSHA. It is very necessary. Come over on this side, Simon. Quick!

SIMON. Does the young lady wish to say someone has come too late?

[GRUSHA *looks up at him in despair, her face streaming with tears.* SIMON *stares before him. He picks up a piece of wood and starts cutting it.*]

THE SINGER.

So many words are said, so many left unsaid.
The soldier has come.
Where he comes from, he does not say.
Hear what he thought and did not say:
"The battle began, gray at dawn, grew bloody at noon.
The first man fell in front of me, the second behind me, the third at my side.
I trod on the first, left the second behind, the third was run through by the captain.
One of my brothers died by steel, the other by smoke.
My neck caught fire, my hands froze in my gloves, my toes in my socks.
I fed on aspen buds, I drank maple juice, I slept on stone, in water."

SIMON. I see a cap in the grass. Is there a little one already?

GRUSHA. There is, Simon. There's no keeping *that* from you. But please don't worry, it is not mine.

SIMON. When the wind once starts to blow, they say, it blows through every cranny. The wife need say no more. [GRUSHA *looks into her lap and is silent.*]

THE SINGER.

There was yearning but there was no waiting.
The oath is broken. Neither could say why.
Hear what she thought but did not say:
"While you fought in the battle, soldier,
The bloody battle, the bitter battle
I found a helpless infant
I had not the heart to destroy him
I had to care for a creature that was lost
I had to stoop for breadcrumbs on the floor
I had to break myself for that which was not mine
That which was other people's.
Someone must help!
For the little tree needs water
The lamb loses its way when the shepherd is asleep
And its cry is unheard!"

SIMON. Give me back the cross I gave you. Better still, throw it in the stream. [*He turns to go.*]

GRUSHA [*getting up*]. Simon Shashava, don't go away! He isn't mine! He isn't mine! [*She hears the* CHILDREN *calling.*] What's the matter, children?

VOICES. Soldiers! And they're taking Michael away!

[GRUSHA *stands aghast as* TWO IRONSHIRTS, *with* MICHAEL *between them, come toward her.*]

ONE OF THE IRONSHIRTS. Are you Grusha? [*She nods.*] Is this your child?

GRUSHA. Yes. [SIMON *goes.*] Simon!

THE IRONSHIRT. We have orders, in the name of the law, to take this child, found in your custody, back to the city. It is suspected that the child is Michael Abashwili, son and heir of the late Governor Georgi Abashwili, and his wife, Natella Abashwili. Here is the document and the seal. [*They lead the* CHILD *away.*]

GRUSHA [*running after them, shouting*]. Leave him here. Please! He's mine!

THE SINGER.

The Ironshirts took the child, the beloved child.
The unhappy girl followed them to the city, the dreaded city.

She who had borne him demanded the child.
She who had raised him faced trial.
Who will decide the case?
To whom will the child be assigned?
Who will the judge be? A good judge? A bad?
The city was in flames.
In the judge's seat sat Azdak.

THE STORY OF THE JUDGE

THE SINGER.
Hear the story of the judge
How he turned judge, how he passed judgment, what kind of judge he was.
On that Easter Sunday of the great revolt, when the Grand Duke was overthrown
And his Governor Abashwili, father of our child, lost his head
The Village Scrivener Azdak found a fugitive in the woods and hid him in his hut.

[AZDAK, *in rags and slightly drunk, is helping an* OLD BEGGAR *into his cottage.*]

AZDAK. Stop snorting, you're not a horse. And it won't do you any good with the police to run like a snotty nose in April. Stand still, I say. [*He catches the* OLD MAN, *who has marched into the cottage as if he'd like to go through the walls.*] Sit down. Feed. Here's a hunk of cheese. [*From under some rags, in a chest, he fishes out some cheese, and the* OLD MAN *greedily begins to eat.*] Haven't eaten in a long time, huh? [*The* OLD MAN *growls.*] Why were you running like that, asshole? The cop wouldn't even have seen you.

THE OLD MAN. Had to! Had to!

AZDAK. Blue funk? [*The* OLD MAN *stares, uncomprehending.*] Cold feet? Panic? Don't lick your chops like a Grand Duke. Or an old sow. I can't stand it. We have to accept respectable stinkers as God made them, but not you! I once heard of a senior judge who farted at a public dinner to show an independent spirit! Watching you eat like that gives me the most awful ideas. Why don't you say something? [*Sharply.*] Show me your hand. Can't you hear? [*The* OLD MAN *slowly puts out his hand.*] White! So you're not a beggar at all! A fraud, a walking swindle! And I'm hiding you from the cops like you were an honest man! Why were you running like that if you're a landowner? For that's what you are. Don't deny it! I see it in your guilty face! [*He gets up.*] Get out! [*The* OLD MAN *looks at him uncertainly.*] What are you waiting for, peasant-flogger?

THE OLD MAN. Pursued. Need undivided attention. Make proposition . . .

AZDAK. Make what? A proposition? Well, if that isn't the height of insolence. He's making me a proposition! The bitten man scratches his fingers bloody, and the leech that's biting him makes him a proposition! Get out, I tell you!

THE OLD MAN. Understand point of view! Persuasion! Pay hundred thousand piasters one night! Yes?

AZDAK. What, you think you can buy me? For a hundred thousand piasters? Let's say a hundred and fifty thousand. Where are they?

THE OLD MAN. Have not them here. Of course. Will be sent. Hope do not doubt.

AZDAK. Doubt very much. Get out!

[*The* OLD MAN *gets up, waddles to the door. A* VOICE *is heard offstage.*]

A VOICE. Azdak!

[*The* OLD MAN *turns, waddles to the opposite corner, stands still.*]

AZDAK [*calling out*]. I'm not in! [*He walks to door.*] So *you're* sniffing around here again, Shauwa?

POLICEMAN SHAUWA [*reproachfully*]. You caught another rabbit, Azdak. And you'd promised me it wouldn't happen again!

AZDAK [*severely*]. Shauwa, don't talk about things you don't understand. The rabbit is a dangerous and destructive beast. It feeds on plants, especially on the species of plants known as weeds. It must therefore be exterminated.

SHAUWA. Azdak, don't be so hard on me. I'll lose my job if I don't arrest you. I know you have a good heart.

AZDAK. I do not have a good heart! How often must I tell you I'm a man of intellect?

SHAUWA [*slyly*]. I know, Azdak. You're a superior person. You say so yourself. I'm just a Christian and an ignoramus. So I ask you: When one of the Prince's rabbits is stolen, and I'm a policeman, what should I do with the offending party?

AZDAK. Shauwa, Shauwa, shame on you. You stand and ask me a question, than which nothing could be more seductive. It's like you were a woman—let's say that bad girl Nunowna, and you showed me your thigh—Nunowna's thigh, that would be—and asked me: "What shall I do with my thigh, it itches?" Is she as innocent as she pretends? Of course not. I catch a rabbit, but you catch a man. Man is made in God's image. Not so a rabbit, you know that. I'm a rabbit-eater, but you're a man-eater, Shauwa. And God will pass judgment on you. Shauwa, go home and repent. No, stop, there's something . . . [*He looks at the* OLD MAN *who stands trembling in the corner.*] No, it's nothing. Go home and repent. [*He slams the door behind* SHAUWA.] Now you're surprised, huh? Surprised I didn't hand you over? I couldn't hand over a bedbug to that animal. It goes against the grain. Now don't tremble because of a cop! So old and still so scared? Finish your cheese, but eat it like a poor man, or else they'll still catch you. Must I even explain how a poor man behaves? [*He pushes him down, and then gives him back the cheese.*] That box is the table. Lay your elbows on the table. Now, encircle the cheese on the plate like it might be snatched from you at any moment—what right have you to be safe, huh?—now, hold your knife like an undersized sickle, and give your cheese a troubled look because, like all beautiful things, it's already fading away. [AZDAK *watches him.*] They're after you, which speaks in your favor, but how can we be sure they're not mistaken about you? In Tiflis one time they hanged a landowner, a Turk, who could prove he quartered his peasants instead of merely cutting them in half, as is the custom, and he squeezed twice the usual amount of taxes out of them, his zeal was above suspicion. And yet they hanged him like a common criminal—because he was a Turk—a thing he couldn't do much about. What injustice! He got onto the gallows by a sheer fluke. In short, I don't trust you.

THE SINGER.

Thus Azdak gave the old beggar a bed,
And learned that old beggar was the old butcher, the Grand Duke himself,
And was ashamed.
He denounced himself and ordered the policeman to take him to Nuka, to court, to be judged.

[*In the court of justice* THREE IRONSHIRTS *sit drinking. From a beam hangs a man in judge's robes. Enter* AZDAK, *in chains, dragging* SHAUWA *behind him.*]

AZDAK [*shouting*]. I've helped the Grand Duke, the Grand Thief, the Grand Butcher, to escape! In the name of justice I ask to be severely judged in public trial!

THE FIRST IRONSHIRT. Who's this queer bird?

SHAUWA. That's our Village Scrivener, Azdak.

AZDAK. I am contemptible! I am a traitor! A branded criminal! Tell them, flatfoot, how I insisted on being tied up and brought to the capital. Because I sheltered the Grand Duke, the Grand Swindler, by mistake. And how I found out afterwards. See the marked man denounce himself! Tell them how I forced you to walk half the night with me to clear the whole thing up.

SHAUWA. And all by threats. That wasn't nice of you, Azdak.

AZDAK. Shut your mouth, Shauwa. You don't understand. A new age is upon us! It'll go thundering over you. You're finished. The police will be wiped out—poof! Everything will be gone into, everything will be brought into the open. The guilty will give themselves up. Why? They couldn't escape the people in any case. [*To* SHAUWA] Tell them how I shouted all along Shoemaker Street [*with big gestures, looking at the* IRONSHIRTS]: "In my ignorance I let the Grand Swindler escape! So tear me to pieces, brothers!" I wanted to get it in first.

THE FIRST IRONSHIRT. And what did your brothers answer?

SHAUWA. They comforted him in Butcher Street, and they laughed themselves sick in Shoemaker Street. That's all.

AZDAK. But with you it's different. I can see you're men of iron. Brothers, where's the judge? I must be tried.

THE FIRST IRONSHIRT [*pointing at the hanged man*]. There's the judge. And please stop "brothering" us. It's rather a sore spot this evening.

AZDAK. "There's the judge." An answer never heard in Grusinia before. Townsman, where's His Excellency the Governor? [*Pointing to the ground*] There's His Excellency, stranger. Where's the Chief Tax Collector? Where's the official Recruiting Officer? The Patriarch? The Chief of Police? There, there, there—all there. Brothers, I expected no less of you.

THE SECOND IRONSHIRT. What? *What* was it you expected, funny man?

AZDAK. What happened in Persia, brother, what happened in Persia?

THE SECOND IRONSHIRT. What did happen in Persia?

AZDAK. Everybody was hanged. Viziers, tax collectors. Everybody. Forty years ago now. My grandfather, a remarkable man by the way, saw it all. For three whole days. Everywhere.

THE SECOND IRONSHIRT. And who ruled when the Vizier was hanged?

AZDAK. A peasant ruled when the Vizier was hanged.

THE SECOND IRONSHIRT. And who commanded the army?

AZDAK. A soldier, a soldier.

THE SECOND IRONSHIRT. And who paid the wages?

AZDAK. A dyer. A dyer paid the wages.

THE SECOND IRONSHIRT. Wasn't it a weaver, maybe?

THE FIRST IRONSHIRT. And why did all this happen, Persian?

AZDAK. Why did all this happen? Must there be a special reason? Why do you scratch yourself, brother? War! Too long a war! And no justice! My grandfather brought back a song that tells how it was. I will sing it for you. With my friend the policeman. [*To* SHAUWA] And hold the rope tight. It's very suitable. [*He sings, with* SHAUWA *holding the rope tight around him.*]

The Song of Injustice in Persia

Why don't our sons bleed any more? Why don't our
daughters weep?
Why do only the slaughterhouse cattle have blood
in their veins?
Why do only the willows shed tears on Lake Urmi?
The king must have a new province, the peasant must
give up his savings.
That the roof of the world might be conquered, the
roof of the cottage is torn down.
Our men are carried to the ends of the earth, so
that great ones can eat at home.
The soldiers kill each other, the marshals salute
each other.
They bite the widow's tax money to see if it's good,
their swords break.

The battle was lost, the helmets were paid for.
Refrain: Is it so? Is it so?

SHAUWA [*refrain*]. Yes, yes, yes, yes, yes it's so.

AZDAK. Want to hear the rest of it? [*The* FIRST IRONSHIRT *nods.*]

THE SECOND IRONSHIRT [*to* SHAUWA]. Did he teach you that song?

SHAUWA. Yes, only my voice isn't very good.

THE SECOND IRONSHIRT. No. [*To* AZDAK] Go on singing.

AZDAK. The second verse is about the peace. [*He sings.*]

The offices are packed, the streets overflow with officials.
The rivers jump their banks and ravage the fields.
Those who cannot let down their own trousers rule countries.
They can't count up to four, but they devour eight courses.
The corn farmers, looking round for buyers, see only the starving.
The weavers go home from their looms in rags.
Refrain: Is it so? Is it so?

SHAUWA [*refrain*]. Yes, yes, yes, yes, yes it's so.

AZDAK.

That's why our sons don't bleed any more, that's why our daughters don't weep.
That's why only the slaughterhouse cattle have blood in their veins,
And only the willows shed tears by Lake Urmi toward morning.

THE FIRST IRONSHIRT. Are you going to sing that song here in town?

AZDAK. Sure. What's wrong with it?

THE FIRST IRONSHIRT. Have you noticed that the sky's getting red? [*Turning round,* AZDAK *sees the sky red with fire.*] It's the people's quarters on the outskirts of town. The carpet weavers have caught the "Persian Sickness," too. And they've been asking if Prince Kazbeki isn't eating too many courses. This morning they strung up the city judge. As for us we beat them to pulp. We were paid one hundred piasters per man, you understand?

AZDAK [*after a pause*]. I understand. [*He glances shyly round and, creeping away, sits down in a corner, his head in his hands.*]

THE IRONSHIRTS [*to each other*]. If there ever was a troublemaker it's him.

—He must've come to the capital to fish in the troubled waters.

SHAUWA. Oh, I don't think he's a really bad character, gentlemen. Steals a few chickens here and there. And maybe a rabbit.

THE SECOND IRONSHIRT [*approaching* AZDAK]. Came to fish in the troubled waters, huh?

AZDAK [*looking up*]. I don't know why I came.

THE SECOND IRONSHIRT. Are you in with the carpet weavers maybe? [AZDAK *shakes his head.*] How about that song?

AZDAK. From my grandfather. A silly and ignorant man.

THE SECOND IRONSHIRT. Right. And how about the dyer who paid the wages?

AZDAK [*muttering*]. That was in Persia.

THE FIRST IRONSHIRT. And this denouncing of yourself? Because you didn't hang the Grand Duke with your own hands?

AZDAK. Didn't I tell you I let him run? [*He creeps farther away and sits on the floor.*]

SHAUWA. I can swear to that: he let him run.

[*The* IRONSHIRTS *burst out laughing and slap* SHAUWA *on the back.* AZDAK *laughs loudest. They slap* AZDAK *too, and unchain him. They all start drinking as the* FAT PRINCE *enters with a* YOUNG MAN.]

THE FIRST IRONSHIRT [*to* AZDAK, *pointing at the* FAT PRINCE]. There's your "new age" for you! [*More laughter.*]

THE FAT PRINCE. Well, my friends, what is there to laugh about? Permit me a serious word. Yesterday morning the Princes of Grusinia overthrew the warmongering government of the Grand Duke and did away with his Governors. Unfortunately the Grand Duke himself escaped. In this fateful hour our carpet weavers, those eternal troublemakers, had the effrontery to stir up a rebellion and hang the universally loved city judge, our dear Illo Orbeliani. Ts— ts— ts. My friends, we need peace, peace, peace in Grusinia! And justice! So I've brought along my dear nephew Bizergan Kazbeki. He'll be the new judge, hm? A very gifted fellow. What do you say? I want your opinion. Let the people decide!

THE SECOND IRONSHIRT. Does this mean *we* elect the judge?

THE FAT PRINCE. Precisely. Let the people propose some very gifted fellow! Confer among yourselves, my friends. [*The* IRONSHIRTS *confer.*] Don't worry, my little fox. The job's yours. And when we catch the Grand Duke we won't have to kiss this rabble's ass any longer.

THE IRONSHIRTS [*among themselves*]. Very funny: they're wetting their pants because they haven't caught the Grand Duke.

—When the outlook isn't so bright, they say: "My friends!" and "Let the people decide!"

—Now he even wants justice for Grusinia! But fun is fun as long as it lasts! [*Pointing at* AZDAK.] *He* knows all about justice. Hey, rascal, would you like this nephew fellow to be the judge?

AZDAK. Are you asking me? You're not asking *me*? !

THE FIRST IRONSHIRT. Why not? Anything for a laugh!

AZDAK. You'd like to test him to the marrow, correct? Have you a criminal on hand? An experienced one? So the candidate can show what he knows?

THE SECOND IRONSHIRT. Let's see. We do have a couple of doctors downstairs. Let's use them.

AZDAK. Oh, no, that's no good, we can't take real criminals till we're sure the judge will be appointed. He may be dumb, but he must be appointed, or the law is violated. And the law is a sensitive organ. It's like the spleen, you musn't hit it—that would be fatal. Of course you can hang those two without violating the law, because there was no judge in the vicinity. But judgment, when pronounced, must be pronounced with absolute gravity—it's all such nonsense. Suppose, for instance, a judge jails a woman—let's say she's stolen a corn cake to feed her child—and this judge isn't wearing his robes—or maybe he's scratching himself while passing sentence and half his body is uncovered—a man's thigh *will* itch once in a while—the sentence this judge passes is a disgrace and the law is violated. In short it would be easier for a judge's robe and a judge's hat to pass judgment than for a man with no robe and no hat. If you don't treat it with respect, the law just disappears on you. Now you don't try out a bottle of wine by offering it to a dog; you'd only lose your wine.

THE FIRST IRONSHIRT. Then what do you suggest, hairsplitter?

AZDAK. I'll be the defendant.

THE FIRST IRONSHIRT. You? [*He bursts out laughing.*]

THE FAT PRINCE. What have you decided?

THE FIRST IRONSHIRT. We've decided to stage a rehearsal. Our friend here will be the defendant. Let the candidate be the judge and sit there.

THE FAT PRINCE. It isn't customary, but why not? [*To the* NEPHEW] A mere formality, my little fox. What have I taught you? Who got there first—the slow runner or the fast?

THE NEPHEW. The silent runner, Uncle Arsen.

[*The* NEPHEW *takes the chair. The* IRONSHIRTS *and the* FAT PRINCE *sit on the steps, Enter* AZDAK, *mimicking the gait of the Grand Duke.*]

AZDAK [*in the Grand Duke's accent*]. Is any here knows me? Am Grand Duke.

THE IRONSHIRTS. *What* is he?

—The Grand Duke. He knows him, too.

—Fine. So get on with the trial.

AZDAK. Listen! Am accused instigating war? Ridiculous! Am saying ridiculous! That enough? If not, have brought lawyers. Believe five hundred. [*He points behind him, pretending to be surrounded by lawyers.*] Requisition all available seats for lawyers! [*The* IRONSHIRTS *laugh; the* FAT PRINCE *joins in.*]

THE NEPHEW [*to the* IRONSHIRTS]. You really wish me to try this case? I find it rather unusual. From the taste angle, I mean.

THE FIRST IRONSHIRT. Let's go!

THE FAT PRINCE [*smiling*]. Let him have it, my little fox!

THE NEPHEW. All right. People of Grusinia versus Grand Duke. Defendant, what have you got to say for yourself?

AZDAK. Plenty. Naturally, have read war lost. Only started on the advice of patriots. Like Uncle Arsen Kazbeki. Call Uncle Arsen as witness.

THE FAT PRINCE [*to the* IRONSHIRTS, *delightedly*]. What a screwball!

THE NEPHEW. Motion rejected. One cannot be arraigned for declaring a war, which every ruler has to do once in a while, but only for running a war badly.

AZDAK. Rubbish! Did not run it at all! Had it run! Had it run by Princes! Naturally, they messed it up.

THE NEPHEW. Do you by any chance deny having been commander-in-chief?

AZDAK. Not at all! Always *was* commander-in-chief. At birth shouted at wet nurse. Was trained drop turds in toilet, grew accustomed to command. Always commanded officials rob my cash box.

Officers flog soldiers only on command. Landowners sleep with peasants' wives only on strictest command. Uncle Arsen here grew his belly at *my* command!

THE IRONSHIRTS [*clapping*]. He's good! Long live the Grand Duke!

THE FAT PRINCE. Answer him, my little fox. I'm with you.

THE NEPHEW. I shall answer him according to the dignity of the law. Defendant, preserve the dignity of the law!

AZDAK. Agreed. Command you proceed with trial!

THE NEPHEW. It is not your place to command me. You claim that the Princes forced you to declare war. How can you claim, then, that they—er—"messed it up"?

AZDAK. Did not send enough people. Embezzled funds. Sent sick horses. During attack, drinking in whorehouse. Call Uncle Arsen as witness.

THE NEPHEW. Are you making the outrageous suggestion that the Princes of this country did not fight?

AZDAK. No. Princes fought. Fought for war contracts.

THE FAT PRINCE [*jumping up*]. That's too much! This man talks like a carpet weaver!

AZDAK. Really? Told nothing but truth.

THE FAT PRINCE. Hang him! Hang him!

THE FIRST IRONSHIRT [*pulling the* PRINCE *down*]. Keep quiet! Go on, Excellency!

THE NEPHEW. Quiet! I now render a verdict: You must be hanged! By the neck! Having lost war!

AZDAK. Young man, seriously advise not fall publicly into jerky clipped speech. Cannot be watchdog if howl like wolf. Got it? If people realize Princes speak same language as Grand Duke, may hang Grand Duke *and Princes,* huh? By the way, must overrule verdict. Reason? War lost, but not for Princes. Princes won their war. Got 3,863,000 piasters for horses not delivered, 8,240,000 piasters for food supplies not produced. Are therefore victors. War lost only for Grusinia, which is not present in this court.

THE FAT PRINCE. I think that will do, my friends. [*To* AZDAK] You can withdraw, funny man. [*To the* IRONSHIRTS] You may now ratify the new judge's appointment, my friends.

THE FIRST IRONSHIRT. Yes, we can. Take down the judge's gown. [ONE IRONSHIRT *climbs on the back of the* OTHER, *pulls the gown off the hanged man.*] [*To the* NEPHEW] Now you run away so the right ass can get on the right chair. [*To* AZDAK] Step forward! Go to the judge's seat! Now sit in it! [AZDAK *steps up, bows, and sits down.*] The judge was always a rascal! Now the rascal shall be a judge! [*The judge's gown is placed round his shoulers, the hat on his head.*] And what a judge!

THE SINGER.

And there was civil war in the land.
The mighty were not safe.
And Azdak was made a judge by the Ironshirts.
And Azdak remained a judge for two years.

THE SINGER AND CHORUS.

When the towns were set afire
And rivers of blood rose higher and higher,
Cockroaches crawled out of every crack.
And the court was full of schemers
And the church of foul blasphemers.
In the judge's cassock sat Azdak.

[AZDAK *sits in the judge's chair, peeling an apple.* SHAUWA *is sweeping out the hall. On one side an* INVALID *in a wheelchair. Opposite, a* YOUNG MAN *accused of blackmail. An* IRONSHIRT *stands guard, holding the Ironshirts' banner.*]

AZDAK. In consideration of the large number of cases, the Court today will hear two cases at a time. Before I open the proceedings, a short announcement—I accept. [*He stretches out his hand. The* BLACKMAILER *is the only one to produce any money. He hands it to* AZDAK.] I reserve the right to punish one of the parties for contempt of court. [*He glances at the* INVALID.] You [*to the* DOCTOR] are a doctor, and you [*to the* INVALID] are bringing a complaint against him. Is the doctor responsible for your condition?

THE INVALID. Yes. I had a stroke on his account.

AZDAK. That would be professional negligence.

THE INVALID. Worse than negligence. I gave this man money for his studies. So far, he hasn't paid me back a cent. It was when I heard he was treating a patient free that I had my stroke.

AZDAK. Rightly. [*To a* LIMPING MAN] And what are *you* doing here?

THE LIMPING MAN. I'm the patient, Your Honor.

AZDAK. He treated your leg for nothing?

THE LIMPING MAN. The wrong leg! My rheumatism was in the left leg, he operated on the right. That's why I limp.

AZDAK. And you were treated free?

THE INVALID. A five-hundred-piaster operation free! For nothing! For a God-bless-you! And I paid for this man's studies! [*To the* DOCTOR] Did they teach you to operate free?

THE DOCTOR. Your Honor, it is the custom to demand the fee before the operation, as the patient is more willing to pay before an operation than after. Which is only human. In the case in question I was convinced, when I started the operation, that my servant had already received the fee. In this I was mistaken.

THE INVALID. He was mistaken! A good doctor doesn't make mistakes! He examines before he operates!

AZDAK. That's right. [*To* SHAUWA] Public Prosecutor, what's the other case about?

SHAUWA [*busily sweeping*]. Blackmail.

THE BLACKMAILER. High Court of Justice, I'm innocent. I only wanted to find out from the landowner concerned if he really *had* raped his niece. He informed me very politely that this was not the case, and gave me the money only so I could pay for my uncle's studies.

AZDAK. Hm. [*To the* DOCTOR] You, on the other hand, can cite no extenuating circumstances for your offense, huh?

THE DOCTOR. Except that to err is human.

AZDAK. And you are aware that in money matters a good doctor is a highly responsible person? I once heard of a doctor who got a thousand piasters for a sprained finger by remarking that sprains have something to do with blood circulation, which after all a less good doctor might have overlooked, and who on another occasion made a real gold mine out of a somewhat disordered gallbladder, he treated it with such loving care. You have no excuse, Doctor. The corn merchant Uxu had his son study medicine to get some knowledge of trade, our medical schools are so good. [*To the* BLACKMAILER] What's the landowner's name?

SHAUWA. He doesn't want it mentioned.

AZDAK. In that case I will pass judgment. The Court considers the blackmail proved. And you [*to the* INVALID] are sentenced to a fine of one thousand piasters. If you have a second stroke, the doctor will have to treat you free. Even if he has to amputate. [*To the* LIMPING MAN] As compensation, you will receive a bottle of rubbing alcohol. [*To the* BLACKMAILER] You are sentenced to hand over half the proceeds of your deal to the Public Prosecutor to keep the landowner's name secret. You are advised, moreover, to study medicine—you seem well suited to that calling. [*To the* DOCTOR] You have perpetrated an unpardonable error in the practice of your profession: you are acquitted. Next cases!

THE SINGER AND CHORUS.

Men won't do much for a shilling.
For a pound they may be willing.
For twenty pounds the verdict's in the sack.
As for the many, all too many,
Those who've only got a penny—
They've one single, sole recourse: Azdak.

[*Enter* AZDAK *from the caravansary on the highroad, followed by an old bearded* INNKEEPER. *The judge's chair is carried by a* STABLEMAN *and* SHAUWA. *An* IRONSHIRT, *with a banner, takes up his position.*]

AZDAK. Put me down. Then we'll get some air, maybe even a good stiff breeze from the lemon grove there. It does justice good to be done in the open: the wind blows her skirts up and you can see what she's got. Shauwa, we've been eating too much. These official journeys are exhausting. [*To the* INNKEEPER] It's a question of your daughter-in-law?

THE INNKEEPER. Your Worship, it's a question of the family honor. I wish to bring an action on behalf of my son, who's away on business on the other side of the mountain. This is the offending stableman, and here's my daughter-in-law.

[*Enter the* DAUGHTER-IN-LAW, *a voluptuous wench. She is veiled.*]

AZDAK [*sitting down*]. I accept. [*Sighing, the* INNKEEPER *hands him some money.*] Good. Now the formalities are disposed of. This is a case of rape?

THE INNKEEPER. Your Honor, I caught the fellow in the act. Ludovica was in the straw on the stable floor.

AZDAK. Quite right, the stable. Lovely horses! I specially liked the little roan.

THE INNKEEPER. The first thing I did, of course, was to question Ludovica. On my son's behalf.

AZDAK [*seriously*]. I said I specially liked the little roan.

THE INNKEEPER [*coldly*]. Really? Ludovica confessed the stableman took her against her will.

AZDAK. Take your veil off, Ludovica. [*She does so.*] Ludovica, you please the Court. Tell us how it happened.

LUDOVICA [*well schooled*]. When I entered the stable to see the new foal the stableman said to me on his own accord: "It's hot today!" and laid his hand on my left breast. I said to him: "Don't do that!" But he continued to handle me indecently, which provoked my anger. Before I realized his sinful intentions, he got much closer. It was all over when my father-in-law entered and accidentally trod on me.

THE INNKEEPER [*explaining*]. On my son's behalf.

AZDAK [*to the* STABLEMAN]. You admit you started it?

THE STABLEMAN. Yes.

AZDAK. Ludovica, you like to eat sweet things?

LUDOVICA. Yes, sunflower seeds!

AZDAK. You like to lie a long time in the bathtub?

LUDOVICA. Half an hour or so.

AZDAK. Public Prosecutor, drop your knife—there—on the ground. [SHAUWA *does so.*] Ludovica, pick up that knife. [LUDOVICA, *swaying her hips, does so.*] See that? [*He points at her.*] The way it moves? The rape is now proven. By eating too much—sweet things, especially—by lying too long in warm water, by laziness and too soft a skin, you have raped that unfortunate man. Think you can run around with a behind like that and get away with it in court? This is a case of intentional assault with a dangerous weapon! You are sentenced to hand over to the Court the little roan which your father liked to ride "on his son's behalf." And now, come with me to the stables, so the Court can inspect the scene of the crime, Ludovica.

THE SINGER AND CHORUS.

When the sharks the sharks devour
Little fishes have their hour.
For a while the load is off their back.
On Grusinia's highways faring
Fixed-up scales of justice bearing
Strode the poor man's magistrate: Azdak.
And he gave to the forsaken
All that from the rich he'd taken.

And a bodyguard of roughnecks was Azdak's.
And our good and evil man, he
Smiled upon Grusinia's Granny.
His emblem was a tear in sealing wax.
All mankind should love each other
But when visiting your brother
Take an ax along and hold it fast.
Not in theory but in practice
Miracles are wrought with axes
And the age of miracles is not past.

[AZDAK'S *judge's chair is in a tavern.* THREE RICH FARMERS *stand before* AZDAK. SHAUWA *brings him wine. In a corner stands an* OLD PEASANT WOMAN. *In the open doorway, and outside, stand* VILLAGERS *looking on. An* IRONSHIRT *stands guard with a banner.*]

AZDAK. The Public Prosecutor has the floor.

SHAUWA. It concerns a cow. For five weeks the defendant has had a cow in her stable, the property of the farmer Suru. She was also found to be in possession of a stolen ham, and a number of cows belonging to Shutoff were killed after he asked the defendant to pay the rent on a piece of land.

THE FARMERS. It's a matter of my ham. Your Honor.
—It's a matter of my cow, Your Honor.
—It's a matter of my land, Your Honor.

AZDAK. Well, Granny, what have *you* got to say to all this?

THE OLD WOMAN. Your Honor, one night toward morning, five weeks ago, there was a knock at my door, and outside stood a bearded man with a cow. "My dear woman," he said, "I am the miracle-working Saint Banditus and because your son has been killed in the war, I bring you this cow as a souvenir. Take good care of it."

THE FARMERS. The robber, Irakli, Your Honor!
—Her brother-in-law, Your Honor!
—The cow-thief!
—The incendiary!
—He must be beheaded!

[*Outside, a woman screams. The* CROWD *grows restless, retreats.*]

[*Enter the* BANDIT *Irakli with a huge ax.*]

THE BANDIT. A very good evening, dear friends! A glass of vodka!

THE FARMERS [*crossing themselves*]. Irakli!

AZDAK. Public Prosecutor, a glass of vodka for our guest. And who are you?

THE BANDIT. I'm a wandering hermit, Your Honor. Thanks for the gracious gift. [*He empties the glass which* SHAUWA *has brought.*] Another!

AZDAK. I am Azdak. [*He gets up and bows. The* BANDIT *also bows.*] The Court welcomes the foreign hermit. Go on with your story, Granny.

THE OLD WOMAN. Your Honor, that first night I didn't yet know Saint Banditus could work miracles, it was only the cow. But one night, a few days later, the farmer's servants came to take the cow away again. Then they turned round in front of my door and went off without the cow. And bumps as big as a fist sprouted on their heads. So I knew that Saint Banditus had changed their hearts and turned them into friendly people.

[*The* BANDIT *roars with laughter.*]

THE FIRST FARMER. I know what changed them.

AZDAK. That's fine. You can tell us later. Continue.

THE OLD WOMAN. Your Honor, the next one to become a good man was the farmer Shutoff—a devil, as everyone knows. But Saint Banditus arranged it so he let me off the rent on the little piece of land.

THE SECOND FARMER. Because my cows were killed in the field.

[*The* BANDIT *laughs.*]

THE OLD WOMAN [*answering* AZDAK'S *sign to continue*]. Then one morning the ham came flying in at my window. It hit me in the small of the back. I'm still lame, Your Honor, look. [*She limps a few steps. The* BANDIT *laughs.*] Your Honor, was there ever a time when a poor old woman could get a ham *without* a miracle?

[*The* BANDIT *starts sobbing.*]

AZDAK [*rising from his chair*]. Granny, that's a question that strikes straight at the Court's heart. Be so kind as to sit here. [*The* OLD WOMAN, *hesitating, sits in the judge's chair.*]

AZDAK [*sits on the floor, glass in hand, reciting*].

Granny
We could almost call you Granny Grusinia
The Woebegone
The Bereaved Mother

Whose sons have gone to war
Receiving the present of a cow
She bursts out crying.
When she is beaten
She remains hopeful.
When she's not beaten
She's surprised.
On us
Who are already damned
May you render a merciful verdict
Granny Grusinia!

[*Bellowing at the* FARMERS] Admit you don't believe in miracles, you atheists! Each of you is sentenced to pay five hundred piasters! For godlessness! Get out! [*The* FARMERS *slink out.*] And you Granny, and you [*to the* BANDIT] pious man, empty a pitcher of wine with the Public Prosecutor and Azdak!

THE SINGER AND CHORUS.

And he broke the rules to save them.
Broken law like bread he gave them,
Brought them to shore upon his crooked back.
At long last the poor and lowly
Had someone who was not too holy
To be bribed by empty hands: Azdak.
For two years it was his pleasure
To give the beasts of prey short measure:
He became a wolf to fight the pack.
From All Hallows to All Hallows
On his chair beside the gallows
Dispensing justice in his fashion sat Azdak.

THE SINGER.

But the era of disorder came to an end.
The Grand Duke returned.
The Governor's wife returned.
A trial was held.
Many died.
The people's quarters burned anew.
And fear seized Azdak.

[AZDAK'S *judge's chair stands again in the court of justice.* AZDAK *sits on the floor, shaving and talking to* SHAUWA. *Noises outside. In the rear the* FAT PRINCE'S *head is carried by on a lance.*]

AZDAK. Shauwa, the days of your slavery are numbered, maybe even the minutes. For a long time now I have held you in the iron curb of reason, and it has torn your mouth till it bleeds. I have lashed you with reasonable arguments, I have manhandled you with logic. You are by nature a weak man, and if one slyly throws an argument in your path, you *have* to snap it up, you can't resist. It is your nature to lick the hand of some superior being. But superior beings can be of very different kinds. And now, with your liberation, you will soon be able to follow your natural inclinations, which are low. You will be able to follow your infallible instinct, which teaches you to plant your fat heel on the faces of men. Gone is the era of confusion and disorder, which I find described in the Song of Chaos. Let us now sing that song together in memory of those terrible days. Sit down and don't do violence to the music. Don't be afraid. It sounds all right. And it has a fine refrain. [*He sings.*]

The Song of Chaos

Sister, hide your face! Brother, take your knife!
The times are out of joint!
Big men are full of complaint
And small men full of joy.
The city says:
"Let us drive the strong ones from our midst!"
Offices are raided. Lists of serfs are destroyed.
They have set Master's nose to the grindstone.
They who lived in the dark have seen the light.
The ebony poor box is broken.
Sesnem wood is sawed up for beds.
Who had no bread have barns full.
Who begged for alms of corn now mete it out.

SHAUWA [*refrain*]. Oh, oh, oh, oh.

AZDAK [*refrain*].

Where are you, General, where are you?
Please, please, please, restore order!

The nobleman's son can no longer be recognized;
The lady's child becomes the son of her slave.

The councilors meet in a shed.
Once, this man was barely allowed to sleep on the wall;
Now, he stretches his limbs in a bed.
Once, this man rowed a boat, now, he owns ships.
Their owner looks for them, but they're his no longer.
Five men are sent on a journey by their master.
"Go yourself," they say, "we have arrived."

SHAUWA [*refrain*]. Oh, oh, oh, oh.

AZDAK [*refrain*].

Where are you, General, where are you?
Please, please, please, restore order!

Yes, so it might have been, had order been neglected much longer. But now the Grand Duke has returned to the capital, and the Persians have lent him an army to restore order with. The suburbs are already aflame. Go and get me the big book I always sit on. [SHAUWA *brings the big book from the judge's chair.* AZDAK *opens it.*] This is the Statute Book and I've always used it, as you can testify. Now I'd better look in this book and see what they can do to me. I've let the down-and-outs get away with murder, and I'll have to pay for it. I helped poverty onto its skinny legs, so they'll hang me for drunkenness. I peeped into the rich man's pocket, which is bad taste. And I can't hide anywhere—everybody knows me because I've helped everybody.

SHAUWA. Someone's coming!

AZDAK [*in panic, he walks trembling to the chair*]. It's the end. And now they'd enjoy seeing what a Great Man I am. I'll deprive them of that pleasure. I'll beg on my knees for mercy. Spittle will slobber down my chin. The fear of death is in me.

[*Enter Natella Abashwili, the* GOVERNOR'S WIFE, *followed by the* ADJUTANT *and an* IRONSHIRT.]

THE GOVERNOR'S WIFE. What sort of a creature is that, Shalva?

AZDAK. A willing one, Your Highness, a man ready to oblige.

THE ADJUTANT. Natella Abashwili, wife of the late Governor, has just returned. She is looking for her two-year-old son, Michael. She has been informed that the child was carried off to the mountains by a former servant.

AZDAK. The child will be brought back, Your Highness, at your service.

THE ADJUTANT. They say that the person in question is passing it off as her own.

AZDAK. She will be beheaded, Your Highness, at your service.

THE ADJUTANT. That is all.

THE GOVERNOR'S WIFE [*leaving*]. I don't like that man.

AZDAK [*following her to door, bowing*]. At your service, Your Highness, it will all be arranged.

THE CHALK CIRCLE

THE SINGER.

Hear now the story of the trial
Concerning Governor Abashwili's child
And the establishing of the true mother
By the famous test of the Chalk Circle.

[*Law court in Nuka.* IRONSHIRTS *lead* MICHAEL *across stage and out at the back.* IRONSHIRTS *hold* GRUSHA *back with their lances under the gateway until the child has been led through. Then she is admitted. She is accompanied by the former Governor's* COOK. *Distant noises and a fire-red sky.*]

GRUSHA [*trying to hide*]. He's brave, he can wash himself now.

THE COOK. You're lucky. It's not a real judge. It's Azdak, a drunk who doesn't know what he's doing. The biggest thieves have got by through him. Because he gets everything mixed up and the rich never offer him big enough bribes, the likes of us sometimes do pretty well.

GRUSHA. I *need* luck right now.

THE COOK. Touch wood. [*She crosses herself.*] I'd better offer up another prayer that the judge may be drunk. [*She prays with motionless lips, while* GRUSHA *looks around, in vain, for the child.*] Why must you hold on to it at any price if it isn't yours? In days like these?

GRUSHA. He's mine. I brought him up.

THE COOK. Have you never thought what'd happen when she came back?

GRUSHA. At first I thought I'd give him to her. Then I thought she wouldn't come back.

THE COOK. And even a borrowed coat keeps a man warm, hm?

[GRUSHA *nods.*] I'll swear to anything for you. You're a decent girl. [*She sees the soldier* SIMON SHASHAVA *approaching.*] You've done wrong by Simon, though. I've been talking with him. He just can't understand.

GRUSHA [*unaware of* SIMON'S *presence*]. Right now I can't be bothered whether he understands or not!

THE COOK. He knows the child isn't yours, but you—married and not free "till death you do part"—he can't understand *that.*

[GRUSHA *sees* SIMON *and greets him.*]

SIMON [*gloomily*]. I wish the lady to know I will swear I am the father of the child.

GRUSHA [*low*]. Thank you, Simon.

SIMON. At the same time I wish the lady to know my hands are not tied—nor are hers.

THE COOK. You needn't have said that. You know she's married.

SIMON. And it needs no rubbing in.

[*Enter an* IRONSHIRT.]

THE IRONSHIRT. Where's the judge? Has anyone seen the judge?

ANOTHER IRONSHIRT [*stepping forward*]. The judge isn't here yet. Nothing but a bed and a pitcher in the whole house!

[*Exeunt* IRONSHIRTS.]

THE COOK. I hope nothing has happened to him. With any other judge you'd have as much chance as a chicken has teeth.

GRUSHA [*who has turned away and covered her face*]. Stand in front of me. I shouldn't have come to Nuka. If I run into the Ironshirt, the one I hit over the head . . .

[*She screams. An* IRONSHIRT *had stopped and, turning his back, had been listening to her. He now wheels around. It is the* CORPORAL, *and he has a huge scar across his face.*]

THE IRONSHIRT [*in the gateway*]. What's the matter, Shotta? Do you know her?

THE CORPORAL [*after staring for some time*]. No.

THE IRONSHIRT. She's the one who stole the Abashwili child, or so they say. If you know anything about it you can make some money, Shotta.

[*Exit the* CORPORAL, *cursing.*]

THE COOK. Was it him? [GRUSHA *nods.*] I think he'll keep his mouth shut, or he'd be admitting he was after the child.

GRUSHA. I'd almost forgotten him.

[*Enter the* GOVERNOR'S WIFE, *followed by the* ADJUTANT *and* TWO LAWYERS.]

THE GOVERNOR'S WIFE. At least there are no common people here, thank God. I can't stand their smell. It always gives me migraine.

THE FIRST LAWYER. Madam, I must ask you to be careful what you say until we have another judge.

THE GOVERNOR'S WIFE. But I didn't say anything, Illo Shuboladze. I love the people with their simple straightforward minds. It's only that their smell brings on my migraine.

THE SECOND LAWYER. There won't be many spectators. The whole population is sitting at home behind locked doors because of the riots on the outskirts of town.

THE GOVERNOR'S WIFE [*looking at* GRUSHA]. Is that the creature?

THE FIRST LAWYER. Please, most gracious Natella Abashwili, abstain from invective until it is certain the Grand Duke has appointed a new judge and we're rid of the present one, who's about the lowest fellow ever seen in judge's gown. Things are all set to move, you see.

[*Enter* IRONSHIRTS *from the courtyard.*]

THE COOK. Her Grace would pull your hair out on the spot if she didn't know Azdak is for the poor. He goes by the face.

[IRONSHIRTS *begin fastening a rope to a beam.* AZDAK, *in chains, is led in, followed by* SHAUWA, *also in chains. The* THREE FARMERS *bring up the rear.*]

AN IRONSHIRT. Trying to run away, were you? [*He strikes* AZDAK.]

ONE FARMER. Off with his judge's gown before we string him up!

[IRONSHIRTS *and* FARMERS *tear off* AZDAK'S *gown. His torn underwear is visible. Then someone kicks him.*]

AN IRONSHIRT [*pushing him into someone else*]. Want a load of justice? Here it is!

[*Accompanied by shouts of* "You take it!" *and* "Let me have him, Brother!" *they throw* AZDAK *back and forth until he collapses. Then he is lifted up and dragged under the noose.*]

THE GOVERNOR'S WIFE [*who, during this "ballgame," has clapped her hands hysterically*]. I disliked that man from the moment I first saw him.

AZDAK [*covered with blood, panting*]. I can't see. Give me a rag.

AN IRONSHIRT. What is it you want to see?

AZDAK. You, you dogs! [*He wipes the blood out of his eyes with his shirt.*] Good morning, dogs! How goes it, dogs! How's the dog world? Does it smell good? Got another boot for me to lick? Are you back at each other's throats, dogs?

[*Accompanied by a* CORPORAL, *a dust-covered* RIDER *enters. He takes some documents from a leather case, looks at them, then interrupts.*]

THE RIDER. Stop! I bring a dispatch from the Grand Duke, containing the latest appointments.

THE CORPORAL [*bellowing*]. Atten–shun!

THE RIDER. Of the new judge it says: "We appoint a man whom we have to thank for saving a life indispensable to the country's welfare–a certain Azdak of Nuka." Which is he?

SHAUWA [*pointing*]. That's him, Your Excellency.

THE CORPORAL [*bellowing*]. What's going on here?

AN IRONSHIRT. I beg to report that His Honor Azdak was already His Honor Azdak, but on these farmers' denunciation was pronounced the Grand Duke's enemy.

THE CORPORAL [*pointing at the* FARMERS]. March them off! [*They are marched off. They bow all the time.*] See to it that His Honor Azdak is exposed to no more violence.

[*Exeunt* RIDER *and* CORPORAL.]

THE COOK [*to* SHAUWA]. She clapped her hands! I hope he saw it!

THE FIRST LAWYER. It's a catastrophe.

[AZDAK *has fainted. Coming to, he is dressed again in judge's robes. He walks, swaying, toward the* IRONSHIRTS.]

AN IRONSHIRT. What does Your Honor desire?

AZDAK. Nothing, fellow dogs, or just an occasional boot to lick. [*To* SHAUWA] I pardon you. [*He is unchained.*] Get me some red wine, the sweet kind. [SHAUWA *stumbles off.*] Get out of here, I've got to judge a case. [*Exeunt* IRONSHIRTS. SHAUWA *returns with a pitcher of wine.* AZDAK *gulps it down.*] Something for my backside. [SHAUWA *brings the Statute Book, puts it on the judge's chair.* AZDAK *sits on it.*] I accept.

[*The* PROSECUTORS, *among whom a worried council has been held, smile with relief. They whisper.*]

THE COOK. Oh dear!

SIMON. A well can't be filled with dew, they say.

THE LAWYERS [*approaching* AZDAK, *who stands up, expectantly*]. A quite ridiculous case, Your Honor. The accused has abducted a child and refuses to hand it over.

AZDAK [*stretching out his hand, glancing at* GRUSHA]. A most attractive person. [*He fingers the money, then sits down, satisfied.*] I declare the proceedings open and demand the whole truth. [*To* GRUSHA] Especially from you.

THE FIRST LAWYER. High Court of Justice! Blood, as the popular saying goes, is thicker than water. This old adage . . .

AZDAK [*interrupting*]. The Court wants to know the lawyers' fee.

THE FIRST LAWYER [*surprised*]. I beg your pardon? [AZDAK, *smiling, rubs his thumb and index finger.*] Oh, I see. Five hundred piasters, Your Honor, to answer the Court's somewhat unusual question.

AZDAK. Did you hear? The question is unusual. I ask it because I listen in quite a different way when I know you're good.

THE FIRST LAWYER [*bowing*]. Thank you, Your Honor. High Court of Justice, of all ties the ties of blood are strongest. Mother and child—is there a more intimate relationship? Can one tear a child from its mother? High Court of Justice, she has conceived it in the holy ecstasies of love. She has carried it in her womb. She has fed it with her blood. She has borne it with pain. High Court of Justice, it has been observed that even the wild tigress, robbed of her young, roams restless through the mountains, shrunk to a shadow. Nature herself . . .

AZDAK [*interrupting, to* GRUSHA]. What's your answer to all this and anything else that lawyer might have to say?

GRUSHA. He's mine.

AZDAK. Is that all? I hope you can prove it. Why should I assign the child to you in any case?

GRUSHA. I brought him up like the priest says "according to my best knowledge and conscience." I always found him something to eat. Most of the time he had a roof over his head. And I went to such trouble for him. I had expenses too. I didn't look out for my own comfort. I brought the child up to be friendly with everyone, and from the beginning taught him to work. As well as he could, that is. He's still very little.

THE FIRST LAWYER. Your Honor, it is significant that the girl herself doesn't claim any tie of blood between her and the child.

AZDAK. The Court takes note of that.

THE FIRST LAWYER. Thank you, Your Honor. And now permit a woman bowed in sorrow—who has already lost her husband and now has also to fear the loss of her child—to address a few words to you. The gracious Natella Abashwili is . . .

THE GOVERNOR'S WIFE [*quietly*]. A most cruel fate, sir, forces me to describe to you the tortures of a bereaved mother's soul, the anxiety, the sleepless nights, the . . .

THE SECOND LAWYER [*bursting out*]. It's outrageous the way this woman is being treated! Her husband's palace is closed to her! The revenue of her estates is blocked, and she is cold-bloodedly told that it's tied to the heir. She can't do a thing without that child. She can't even pay her lawyers! ! [*To the* FIRST LAWYER, *who, desperate about this outburst, makes frantic gestures to keep him from speaking*] Dear Illo Shuboladze, surely it can be divulged now that the Abashwili estates are at stake?

THE FIRST LAWYER. Please, Honored Sandro Oboladze! We agreed . . . [*To* AZDAK] Of course it is correct that the trial will also decide if our noble client can dispose of the Abashwili estates, which are rather extensive. I say "also" advisedly, for in the foreground stands the human tragedy of a mother, as Natella Abashwili very properly explained in the first words of her moving statement. Even if Michael Abashwili were not heir to the estates, he would still be the dearly beloved child of my client.

AZDAK. Stop! The Court is touched by the mention of estates. It's a proof of human feeling.

THE SECOND LAWYER. Thanks, Your Honor. Dear Illo Shuboladze, we can prove in any case that the woman who took the child is not the child's mother. Permit me to lay before the Court the bare facts. High Court of Justice, by an unfortunate chain of circumstances, Michael Abashwili was left behind on that Easter Sunday while his mother was making her escape. Grusha, a palace kitchen maid, was seen with the baby . . .

THE COOK. All her mistress was thinking of was what dresses she'd take along!

THE SECOND LAWYER [*unmoved*]. Nearly a year later Grusha turned up in a mountain village with a baby and there entered into the state of matrimony with . . .

AZDAK. How'd you get to that mountain village?

GRUSHA. On foot, Your Honor. And he was mine.

SIMON. I'm the father, Your Honor.

THE COOK. I used to look after it for them, Your Honor. For five piasters.

THE SECOND LAWYER. This man is engaged to Grusha, High Court of Justice: his testimony is suspect.

AZDAK. Are you the man she married in the mountain village?

SIMON. No, Your Honor, she married a peasant.

AZDAK [*to* GRUSHA]. Why? [*Pointing at* SIMON] Is he no good in bed? Tell the truth.

GRUSHA. We didn't get that far. I married because of the baby. So he'd have a roof over his head. [*Pointing at* SIMON] He was in the war, Your Honor.

AZDAK. And now he wants you back again, huh?

SIMON. I wish to state in evidence . . .

GRUSHA [*angrily*]. I am no longer free, Your Honor.

AZDAK. And the child, you claim, comes from whoring? [GRUSHA *doesn't answer.*] I'm going to ask you a question: What kind of child is he? A ragged little bastard? Or from a good family?

GRUSHA [*angrily*]. He's an ordinary child.

AZDAK. I mean—did he have refined features from the beginning?

GRUSHA. He had a nose on his face.

AZDAK. A very significant comment! It has been said of me that I went out one time and sniffed at a rosebush before rendering a verdict—tricks like that are needed nowadays. Well, I'll make it short, and not listen to any more lies. [*To* GRUSHA] Especially not yours. [*To all the accused*] I can imagine what you've cooked up to cheat me! I know you people. You're swindlers.

GRUSHA [*suddenly*]. I can understand your wanting to cut it short, now I've seen what you accepted!

AZDAK. Shut up! Did I accept anything from you?

GRUSHA [*while the* COOK *tries to restrain her*]. I haven't got anything.

AZDAK. True. Quite true. From starvelings, I never get a thing. I might just as well starve, myself. You want justice, but do you want to pay for it, hm? When you go to a butcher you know you have to pay, but you people go to a judge as if you were off to a funeral supper.

SIMON [*loudly*]. When the horse was shod, the horsefly held out its leg, as the saying is.

AZDAK [*eagerly accepting the challenge*]. Better a treasure in manure than a stone in a mountain stream.

SIMON. A fine day. Let's go fishing, said the angler to the worm.

AZDAK. I'm my own master, said the servant, and cut off his foot.

SIMON. I love you as a father, said the Czar to the peasants, and had the Czarevitch's head chopped off.

AZDAK. A fool's worst enemy is himself.

SIMON. However, a fart has no nose.

AZDAK. Fined ten piasters for indecent language in court! That'll teach you what justice is.

GRUSHA [*furiously*]. A fine kind of justice! You play fast and loose with us because we don't talk as refined as that crowd with their lawyers!

AZDAK. That's true. You people are too dumb. It's only right you should get it in the neck.

GRUSHA. You want to hand the child over to her, and she wouldn't even know how to keep it dry, she's so "refined"! You know about as much about justice as I do!

AZDAK. There's something in that. I'm an ignorant man. Haven't even a decent pair of pants on under this gown. Look! With me, everything goes for food and drink—I was educated in a convent. Incidentally, I'll fine you ten piasters for contempt of court. And you're a very silly girl, to turn me against you, instead of making eyes at me and wiggling your backside a little to keep me in a good temper. Twenty piasters!

GRUSHA. Even if it was thirty, I'd tell you what I think of your justice, you drunken onion! [*Incoherently*] How dare you talk to me like the cracked Isaiah on the church window? As if you were somebody? For you weren't born to this. You weren't born to rap your own mother on the knuckles if she swipes a little bowl of salt someplace. Aren't you ashamed of yourself when you see how I tremble before you? You've made yourself their servant so no one will take their houses from them—houses they had stolen! Since when have houses belonged to the bedbugs? But you're on the watch, or they couldn't drag our men into their wars! You bribetaker! [AZDAK *half gets up, starts beaming. With his little hammer he halfheartedly knocks on the table as if to get silence. As* GRUSHA'*s scolding con-*

tinues, he only beats time with his hammer.] I've no respect for you. No more than for a thief or a bandit with a knife! You can do what you want. You can take the child away from me, a hundred against one, but I tell you one thing: only extortioners should be chosen for a profession like yours, and men who rape children! As punishment! Yes, let *them* sit in judgment on their fellow creatures. It is worse than to hang from the gallows.

AZDAK [*sitting down*]. Now it'll be thirty! And I won't go on squabbling with you—we're not in a tavern. What'd happen to my dignity as a judge? Anyway, I've lost interest in your case. Where's the couple who wanted a divorce? [*To* SHAUWA] Bring 'em in. This case is adjourned for fifteen minutes.

THE FIRST LAWYER [*to the* GOVERNOR'S WIFE]. Even without using the rest of the evidence, Madam, we have the verdict in the bag.

THE COOK [*to* GRUSHA]. You've gone and spoiled your chances with him. You won't get the child now.

THE GOVERNOR'S WIFE. Shalva, my smelling salts!

[*Enter a* VERY OLD COUPLE.]

AZDAK. I accept. [*The* OLD COUPLE *don't understand.*] I hear you want to be divorced. How long have you been together?

THE OLD MAN. Forty years, Your Honor.

AZDAK. And why do you want a divorce?

THE OLD MAN. We don't like each other, Your Honor.

AZDAK. Since when?

THE OLD WOMAN. Oh, from the very beginning, Your Honor.

AZDAK. I'll think about your request and render my verdict when I'm through with the other case. [SHAUWA *leads them back.*] I need the child. [*He beckons* GRUSHA *to him and bends not unkindly toward her.*] I've noticed you have a soft spot for justice. I don't believe he's your child, but if he *were* yours, woman, wouldn't you want him to be rich? You'd only have to say he wasn't yours, and he'd have a palace and many horses in his stable and many beggars on his doorstep and many soldiers in his service and many petitioners in his courtyard, wouldn't he? What do you say—don't you want him to be rich? [GRUSHA *is silent.*]

THE SINGER.

Hear now what the angry girl thought but did not say:
Had he golden shoes to wear
He'd be cruel as a bear.

Evil would his life disgrace.
He'd laugh in my face.
Carrying a heart of flint
Is too troublesome a stint.
Being powerful and bad
Is hard on a lad.
Then let hunger be his foe!
Hungry men and women, no.
Let him fear the darksome night
But not daylight!

AZDAK. I think I understand you, woman.

GRUSHA [*suddenly and loudly*]. I won't give him up. I've raised him, and he knows me.

[*Enter* SHAUWA *with the* CHILD.]

THE GOVERNOR'S WIFE. He's in rags!

GRUSHA. That's not true. But I wasn't given time to put his good shirt on.

THE GOVERNOR'S WIFE. He must have been in pigsty.

GRUSHA [*furiously*]. I'm not a pig, but there are some who are! Where did you leave your baby?

THE GOVERNOR'S WIFE. I'll show you, you vulgar creature! [*She is about to throw herself on* GRUSHA, *but is restrained by her* LAWYERS.] She's a criminal, she must be whipped. Immediately!

THE SECOND LAWYER [*holding his hand over her mouth*]. Natella Abashwili, you promised . . . Your Honor, the plaintiff's nerves . . .

AZDAK. Plaintiff and defendant! The Court has listened to your case, and has come to no decision as to who the real mother is; therefore, I, the judge, am obliged to *choose* a mother for the child. I'll make a test. Shauwa, get a piece of chalk and draw a circle on the floor. [SHAUWA *does so.*] Now place the child in the center. [SHAUWA *puts* MICHAEL, *who smiles at* GRUSHA, *in the center of the circle.*] Stand near the circle, both of you. [*The* GOVERNOR'S WIFE *and* GRUSHA *step up to the circle.*] Now each of you take the child by one hand. [*They do so.*] The true mother is she who can pull the child out of the circle.

THE SECOND LAWYER [*quickly*]. High Court of Justice, I object! The fate of the great Abashwili estates, which are tied to the child, as the heir, should not be made dependent on such a doubtful duel.

In addition, my client does not command the strength of this person, who is accustomed to physical work.

AZDAK. She looks pretty well fed to me. Pull! [*The* GOVERNOR'S WIFE *pulls the* CHILD *out of the circle on her side;* GRUSHA *has let go and stands aghast.*] What's the matter with you? You didn't pull!

GRUSHA. I didn't hold on to him.

THE FIRST LAWYER [*congratulating the* GOVERNOR'S WIFE]. What did I say! The ties of blood!

GRUSHA [*running to* AZDAK]. Your Honor, I take back everything I said against you. I ask your forgiveness. But could I keep him till he can speak all the words? He knows a few.

AZDAK. Don't influence the Court. I bet you only know about twenty words yourself. All right, I'll make the test once more, just to be certain. [*The* TWO WOMEN *take up their positions again.*] Pull! [*Again* GRUSHA *lets go of the* CHILD.]

GRUSHA [*in despair*]. I brought him up! Shall I also tear him to bits? I can't!

AZDAK [*rising*]. And in this manner the Court has established the true mother. [*To* GRUSHA] Take your child and be off. I advise you not to stay in the city with him. [*To the* GOVERNOR'S WIFE] And you disappear before I fine you for fraud. Your estates fall to the city. They'll be converted into a playground for the children. They need one, and I've decided it'll be called after me: Azdak's Garden. [*The* GOVERNOR'S WIFE *has fainted and is carried out by the* LAWYERS *and the* ADJUTANT. GRUSHA *stands motionless.* SHAUWA *leads the* CHILD *toward her.*] Now I'll take off this judge's gown—it's got too hot for me. I'm not cut out for a hero. In token of farewell I invite you all to a little dance in the meadow outside. Oh, I'd almost forgotten something in my excitement . . . to sign the divorce decree. [*Using the judge's chair as a table, he writes something on a piece of paper, and prepares to leave. Dance music has started.*]

SHAUWA [*having read what is on the paper*]. But that's not right. You've not divorced the old people. You've divorced Grusha!

AZDAK. Divorced the wrong couple? What a pity! And I never retract! If I did, how could we keep order in the land? [*To the* OLD COUPLE] I'll invite you to my party instead. You don't mind dancing with each other, do you? [*To* GRUSHA *and* SIMON] I've got forty piasters coming from you.

SIMON [*pulling out his purse*]. Cheap at the price, Your Honor. And many thanks.

AZDAK [*pocketing the cash*]. I'll be needing this.

GRUSHA [*to* MICHAEL]. So we'd better leave the city tonight, Michael? [*To* SIMON] You like him?

SIMON. With my respects, I like him.

GRUSHA. Now I can tell you: I took him because on that Easter Sunday I got engaged to you. So he's a child of love. Michael, let's dance.

[*She dances with* MICHAEL, SIMON *dances with the* COOK, *the* OLD COUPLE *with each other.* AZDAK *stands lost in thought. The dancers soon hide him from view. Occasionally he is seen, but less and less as* MORE COUPLES *join the dance.*]

THE SINGER.

And after that evening Azdak vanished and was never seen again.
The people of Grusinia did not forget him but long remembered
The period of his judging as a brief golden age,
Almost an age of justice.

[ALL THE COUPLES *dance off.* AZDAK *has disappeared.*]

But you, you who have listened to the Story of the Chalk Circle,
Take note what men of old concluded:
That what there is shall go to those who are good for it,
Children to the motherly, that they prosper,
Carts to good drivers, that they be driven well,
The valley to the waterers, that it yield fruit.

END

SAMUEL BECKETT
1906–

ALL THAT FALL, 1957
ACT WITHOUT WORDS I, 1957

IT IS COMMONLY said that Samuel Beckett contemplates the human condition without hope and without faith, representing life as futile and man as impotent. It would be nothing new for a dramatist to ponder how life may be sustained without the support of hope and faith. That vision has entered into the terror and dignity of great tragic drama, whether Sophoclean or Shakespearean. Nor does comedy refuse to recognize some ultimate absurdity in human predicaments. When at the end of *Juno and the Paycock* the two befuddled derelicts judge the whole world to be "in a terrible state o' chassis," the scene is a plangent mingling of the pathetic and the ludicrous. O'Casey there anticipates the quality of tone in Beckett's plays.

Beckett has brought to almost perfect realization a special kind of drama that fuses and also reanimates the traditional comic and tragic modes. His perspective embraces contraries. Whatever appears tragic, spiritual, or even merely decorous in human behavior is seen to be toppling into the rankest commonplace; on the other hand, whatever seems ludicrous, grossly physical, or grotesque has a tone of spiritual desolation, a dying echo of tragic suffering. His most characteristic effect is a sudden and ludicrous deflation or exposure of pretentions (an effect properly known as *bathos*). However, he also sometimes reverses the process, investing the most ordinary event or object with comic nobility. No sentiment is too lofty to be shot down, no fact too mean to be oddly significant.

In *All That Fall* Mrs. Rooney's ejaculations inspired by the death of a hen illustrate Beckett's characteristic manner. Her eulogy, mingling the vulgar and the sentimental, is of course ridiculously inflated:

What a death! One minute picking happy at the dung, on the road, in the sun, with now and then a dust bath, and then—bang!—all her troubles over. [*Pause.*] All the laying and the hatching. [*Pause.*] Just one great squawk and then . . . peace. [*Pause.*] They would have slit her weasand in any case. [*Pause.*]

Absurd. Yet in full context Mrs. Rooney's words are neither purely sentimental nor merely vulgar. The theme of the play is a commonplace, that in the midst of life we are in death. Realized most obviously in the accidental death of a child, it reverberates throughout. At the beginning and the end are allusions to Schubert's "Death and the Maiden," a song in which Death whispers amorously to a dying girl. And there are scores of other similar allusions—for example, to hymns and Biblical texts conventionally associated with funerals, and to the death of Mrs. Rooney's daughter. The flow of time itself, though spanning literally only an hour of a June day, is toward the fall and winter. Given such orchestration of the theme of death, in every key from inanity to horror, Mrs. Rooney's eulogy on a dead hen contributes its odd hilarious solemnity to the changes rung upon the title, *All That Fall.*

That the play was written for radio and is therefore exclusively auditory indicates no limitation of dramatic force. It exploits in addition to verbal meaning the imagined scenes and gestures that sounds powerfully suggest—bird calls, train noises, shuffling feet—and, especially, the pauses, hundreds of momentary silences that feed the imagination. Because its language is both bizarre and exact, punctuated by fertile silences, *All That Fall* possesses an almost preternatural realism. Because it excites the imagination, the whole conveys not a depressing weight of philosophic despair, but an impression of extraordinary and sometimes outrageous liveliness.

Act Without Words, consisting only of stage directions, as purely represents the visual and gestural elements of drama as *All That Fall* represents the auditory. From one viewpoint the "mime" describes a series of sadistically inflicted frustrations; from another it describes a clown's meticulous parody of self-pity. Characteristically, Beckett excludes neither viewpoint. The combination provokes a double vision achieved with the utmost economy and verve. Though without much hope or faith, Beckett brings to the drama a renovation of words and actions through a form and style both traditional and new.

ALL THAT FALL · BECKETT

A PLAY FOR RADIO

Characters

MRS. ROONEY (MADDY)	*a lady in her seventies*
CHRISTY	*a carter*
MR. TYLER	*a retired bill-broker*
MR. SLOCUM	*Clerk of the Racecourse*
TOMMY	*a porter*
MR. BARRELL	*a station-master*
MISS FITT	*a lady in her thirties*
A FEMALE VOICE	
DOLLY	*a small girl*
MR. ROONEY (DAN)	*husband of* MRS. ROONEY, *blind*
JERRY	*a small boy*

[*Rural sounds. Sheep, bird, cow, cock, severally, then together. Silence.* MRS. ROONEY *advances along country road towards railway station. Sound of her dragging feet. Music faint from house by way. "Death and the Maiden." The steps slow down, stop.*]

MRS. ROONEY. Poor woman. All alone in that ruinous old house.

[*Music louder. Silence but for music playing. The steps resume. Music dies.* MRS. ROONEY *murmurs, melody. Her murmur dies. Sound of approaching cartwheels. The cart stops. The steps slow down, stop.*]

MRS. ROONEY. Is that you, Christy?

CHRISTY. It is, Ma'am.

MRS. ROONEY. I thought the hinny was familiar. How is your poor wife?

CHRISTY. No better, Ma'am.

MRS. ROONEY. Your daughter then?

CHRISTY. No worse, Ma'am.

[*Silence.*]

MRS. ROONEY. Why do you halt? [*Pause.*] But why do I halt?

[*Silence.*]

CHRISTY. Nice day for the races, Ma'am.

MRS. ROONEY. No doubt it is. [*Pause.*] But will it hold up? [*Pause. With emotion.*] Will it hold up?

[*Silence.*]

CHRISTY. I suppose you wouldn't——

MRS. ROONEY. Hist! [*Pause.*] Surely to goodness that cannot be the up mail I hear already.

[*Silence. The hinny neighs. Silence.*]

CHRISTY. Damn the mail.

MRS. ROONEY. Oh thank God for that! I could have sworn I heard it, thundering up the track in the far distance. [*Pause.*] So hinnies whinny. Well, it is not surprising.

CHRISTY. I suppose you wouldn't be in need of a small load of dung?

MRS. ROONEY. Dung? What class of dung?

CHRISTY. Stydung.

MRS. ROONEY. Stydung . . . I like your frankness, Christy. [*Pause.*] I'll ask the master. [*Pause.*] Christy.

CHRISTY. Yes, Ma'am.

MRS. ROONEY. Do you find anything . . . bizarre about my way of speaking? [*Pause.*] I do not mean the voice. [*Pause.*] No, I mean the words. [*Pause. More to herself.*] I use none but the simplest words, I hope, and yet I sometimes find my way of speaking very . . . bizarre. [*Pause.*] Mercy! What was that?

CHRISTY. Never mind her, Ma'am, she's very fresh in herself today.

[*Silence.*]

MRS. ROONEY. Dung? What would we want with dung, at our time of life? [*Pause.*] Why are you on your feet down on the road? Why do you not climb up on the crest of your manure and let yourself be carried along? Is it that you have no head for heights?

[*Silence.*]

CHRISTY [*to the hinny*]. Yep! [*Pause. Louder.*] Yep wiyya to hell owwa that!

[*Silence.*]

MRS. ROONEY. She does not move a muscle. [*Pause.*] I too should be getting along, if I do not wish to arrive late at the station. [*Pause.*] But a moment ago she neighed and pawed the ground. And now she refuses to advance. Give her a good welt on the rump. [*Sound of welt. Pause.*] Harder! [*Sound of welt. Pause.*] Well! If someone were to do that for me I should not dally. [*Pause.*] How she gazes at me to be sure, with her great moist cleg-tormented eyes! Perhaps if I were to move on, down the road, out of her field of vision . . . [*Sound of welt.*] No, no, enough! Take her by the snaffle and pull her eyes away from me. Oh this is awful! [*She moves on. Sound of her dragging feet.*] What have I done to deserve all this, what, what? [*Dragging feet.*] So long ago . . . No! No! [*Dragging feet. Quotes.*] "Sigh out a something something tale of things, Done long ago and ill done." [*She halts.*] How can I go on, I cannot. Oh let me just flop down flat on the road like a big fat jelly out of a bowl and never move again! A great big slop thick with grit and dust and flies, they would have to scoop me up with a shovel. [*Pause.*] Heavens, there is that up mail again, what will become of me! [*The dragging steps resume.*] Oh I am just a hysterical old hag, I know, destroyed with sorrow and pining and gentility and church-going and fat and rheumatism and childlessness. [*Pause. Brokenly.*] Minnie! Little Minnie! [*Pause.*] Love, that is all I asked, a little love, daily, twice daily, fifty years of twice daily love like a Paris horse-butcher's regular, what normal woman wants affection? A peck on the jaw at morning, near the ear, and another at evening, peck, peck, till you grow whiskers on you. There is that lovely laburnum again.

[*Dragging feet. Sound of bicycle-bell. It is old* MR. TYLER *coming up behind her on his bicycle, on his way to the station. Squeak of brakes. He slows down and rides abreast of her.*]

MR. TYLER. Mrs. Rooney! Pardon me if I do not doff my cap, I'd fall off. Divine day for the meeting.

MRS. ROONEY. Oh, Mr. Tyler, you startled the life out of me stealing up behind me like that like a deer-stalker! Oh!

MR. TYLER [*playfully*]. I rang my bell, Mrs. Rooney, the moment I sighted you I started tinkling my bell, now don't you deny it.

MRS. ROONEY. Your bell is one thing, Mr. Tyler, and you are another. What news of your poor daughter?

61 **cleg-tormented** tormented by horseflies.

MR. TYLER. Fair, fair. They removed everything, you know, the whole . . . er . . . bag of tricks. Now I am grandchildless.

[*Dragging feet.*]

MRS. ROONEY. Gracious how you wobble! Dismount, for mercy's sake, or ride on.

MR. TYLER. Perhaps if I were to lay my hand lightly on your shoulder, Mrs. Rooney, how would that be? [*Pause.*] Would you permit that?

MRS. ROONEY. No, Mr. Rooney, Mr. Tyler I mean, I am tired of light old hands on my shoulders and other senseless places, sick and tired of them. Heavens, here comes Connolly's van! [*She halts. Sound of motor-van. It approaches, passes with thunderous rattle, recedes.*] Are you all right, Mr. Tyler? [*Pause.*] Where is he? [*Pause.*] Ah there you are! [*The dragging steps resume.*] That was a narrow squeak.

MR. TYLER. I alit in the nick of time.

MRS. ROONEY. It is suicide to be abroad. But what is it to be at home, Mr. Tyler, what is it to be at home? A lingering dissolution. Now we are white with dust from head to foot. I beg your pardon?

MR. TYLER. Nothing, Mrs. Rooney, nothing, I was merely cursing, under my breath, God and man, under my breath, and the wet Saturday afternoon of my conception. My back tire has gone down again. I pumped it hard as iron before I set out. And now I am on the rim.

MRS. ROONEY. Oh what a shame!

MR. TYLER. Now if it were the front I should not so much mind. But the back. The back! The chain! The oil! The grease! The hub! The brakes! The gear! No! It is too much!

[*Dragging steps.*]

MRS. ROONEY. Are we very late, Mr. Tyler? I have not the courage to look at my watch.

MR. TYLER [*bitterly*]. Late! I on my bicycle as I bowled along was already late. Now therefore we are doubly late, trebly, quadrupedly late. Would I had shot by you, without a word.

[*Dragging feet.*]

MRS. ROONEY. Whom are you meeting, Mr. Tyler?

MR. TYLER. Hardy. [*Pause.*] We used to climb together. [*Pause.*] I saved his life once. [*Pause.*] I have not forgotten it.

[*Dragging feet. They stop.*]

MRS. ROONEY. Let us halt a moment and let this vile dust fall back upon the viler worms.

[*Silence. Rural sounds.*]

MR. TYLER. What sky! What light! Ah in spite of all it is a blessed thing to be alive in such weather, and out of hospital.

MRS. ROONEY. Alive?

MR. TYLER. Well half alive shall we say?

MRS. ROONEY. Speak for yourself, Mr. Tyler. I am not half alive nor anything approaching it. [*Pause.*] What are we standing here for? This dust will not settle in our time. And when it does some great roaring machine will come and whirl it all skyhigh again.

MR. TYLER. Well, shall we be getting along in that case?

MRS. ROONEY. No.

MR. TYLER. Come, Mrs. Rooney——

MRS. ROONEY. Go, Mr. Tyler, go on and leave me, listening to the cooing of the ringdoves. [*Cooing.*] If you see my poor blind Dan tell him I was on my way to meet him when it all came over me again, like a flood. Say to him, Your poor wife, she told me to tell you it all came flooding over her again and . . . [*the voice breaks*] . . . she simply went back home . . . straight back home . . .

MR. TYLER. Come, Mrs. Rooney, come, the mail has not yet gone up, just take my free arm and we'll be there with time and to spare.

MRS. ROONEY [*sobbing*]. What? What's all this now? [*Calmer.*] Can't you see I'm in trouble? [*With anger.*] Have you no respect for misery? [*Sobbing.*] Minnie! Little Minnie!

MR. TYLER. Come, Mrs. Rooney, come, the mail has not yet gone up, just take my free arm and we'll be there with time and to spare.

MRS. ROONEY [*brokenly*]. In her forties now she'd be, I don't know, fifty, girding up her lovely little loins, getting ready for the change . . .

MR. TYLER. Come, Mrs. Rooney, come the mail——

MRS. ROONEY [*exploding*]. Will you get along with you, Mr. Rooney, Mr. Tyler I mean, will you get along with you now and cease molesting me? What kind of a country is this where a woman can't weep her heart out on the highways and byways without being tormented by retired bill-brokers! [MR. TYLER *prepares to mount his bicycle.*] Heavens you're not going to ride her flat! [MR. TYLER *mounts.*] You'll tear your tube to ribbons! [MR. TYLER *rides off. Receding sound of bumping bicycle. Silence. Cooing.*] Venus birds!

Billing in the woods all the long summer long. [*Pause.*] Oh cursed corset! If I could let it out, without indecent exposure. Mr. Tyler! Mr. Tyler! Come back and unlace me behind the hedge! [*She laughs wildly, ceases.*] What's wrong with me, what's wrong with me, never tranquil, seething out of my dirty old pelt, out of my skull, oh to be in atoms, in atoms! [*Frenziedly.*] ATOMS! [*Silence. Cooing. Faintly.*] Jesus! [*Pause.*] Jesus!

[*Sound of car coming up behind her. It slows down and draws up beside her, engine running. It is* MR. SLOCUM, *the Clerk of the Racecourse.*]

MR. SLOCUM. Is anything wrong, Mrs. Rooney? You are bent all double. Have you a pain in the stomach?

[*Silence.* MRS. ROONEY *laughs wildly. Finally.*]

MRS. ROONEY. Well if it isn't my old admirer the Clerk of the Course, in his limousine.

MR. SLOCUM. May I offer you a lift, Mrs. Rooney? Are you going in my direction?

MRS. ROONEY. I am, Mr. Slocum, we all are. [*Pause.*] How is your poor mother?

MR. SLOCUM. Thank you, she is fairly comfortable. We manage to keep her out of pain. That is the great thing, Mrs. Rooney, is it not?

MRS. ROONEY. Yes, indeed, Mr. Slocum, that is the great thing, I don't know how you do it. [*Pause. She slaps her cheek violently.*] Ah these wasps!

MR. SLOCUM [*coolly*]. May I then offer you a seat, Madam?

MRS. ROONEY [*with exaggerated enthusiasm*]. Oh that would be heavenly, Mr. Slocum, just simply heavenly. [*Dubiously.*] But would I ever get in, you look very high off the ground today, these new balloon tires I presume. [*Sound of door opening and* MRS. ROONEY *trying to get in.*] Does this roof never come off? No? [*Efforts of* MRS. ROONEY.] No . . . I'll never do it . . . you'll have to get down, Mr. Slocum, and help me from the rear. [*Pause.*] What was that? [*Pause. Aggrieved.*] This is all your suggestion, Mr. Slocum, not mine. Drive on, Sir, drive on.

MR. SLOCUM [*switching off the engine*]. I'm coming, Mrs. Rooney, I'm coming, give me time, I'm as stiff as yourself.

[*Sound of* MR. SLOCUM *extracting himself from driver's seat.*]

MRS. ROONEY. Stiff! Well I like that! And me heaving all over back and front. [*To herself.*] The dry old reprobate!

MR. SLOCUM [*in position behind her*]. Now, Mrs. Rooney, how shall we do this?

MRS. ROONEY. As if I were a bale, Mr. Slocum, don't be afraid. [*Pause. Sounds of effort.*] That's the way! [*Effort.*] Lower! [*Effort.*] Wait! [*Pause.*] No, don't let go! [*Pause.*] Suppose I do get up, will I ever get down?

MR. SLOCUM [*breathing hard*]. You'll get down, Mrs. Rooney, you'll get down. We may not get you up, but I warrant you we'll get you down.

[*He resumes his efforts. Sound of these.*]

MRS. ROONEY. Oh! . . . Lower! . . . Don't be afraid! . . . We're past the age when . . . There! . . . Now! . . . Get your shoulder under it . . . Oh! . . . [*Giggles.*] Oh glory! . . . Up! Up! . . . Ah! . . . I'm in! [*Panting of* MR. SLOCUM. *He slams the door. In a scream.*] My frock! You've nipped my frock! [MR. SLOCUM *opens the door.* MRS. ROONEY *frees her frock.* MR. SLOCUM *slams the door. His violent unintelligible muttering as he walks round to the other door. Tearfully.*] My nice frock! Look what you've done to my nice frock! [MR. SLOCUM *gets into his seat, slams driver's door, presses starter. The engine does not start. He releases starter.*] What will Dan say when he sees me?

MR. SLOCUM. Has he then recovered his sight?

MRS. ROONEY. No, I mean when he knows, what will he say when he feels the hole? [MR. SLOCUM *presses starter. As before. Silence.*] What are you doing, Mr. Slocum?

MR. SLOCUM. Gazing straight before me, Mrs. Rooney, through the windscreen, into the void.

MRS. ROONEY. Start her up, I beseech you, and let us be off. This is awful!

MR. SLOCUM [*dreamily*]. All morning she went like a dream and now she is dead. That is what you get for a good deed. [*Pause. Hopefully.*] Perhaps if I were to to choke her. [*He does so, presses the starter. The engine roars. Roaring to make himself heard.*] She was getting too much air!

[*He throttles down, grinds in his first gear, moves off, changes up in a grinding of gears.*]

MRS. ROONEY [*in anguish*]. Mind the hen! [*Scream of brakes. Squawk of hen.*] Oh, mother, you have squashed her, drive on, drive on! [*The car accelerates. Pause.*] What a death! One minute picking happy at the dung, on the road, in the sun, with now and then a dust bath, and then—bang!—all her troubles over. [*Pause.*] All the laying and the hatching. [*Pause.*] Just one great squawk and then . . . peace. [*Pause.*] They would have slit her weasand in any case. [*Pause.*] Here we are, let me down. [*The car slows down, stops, engine running.* MR. SLOCUM *blows his horn. Pause. Louder. Pause.*] What are you up to now, Mr. Slocum? We are at a standstill, all danger is past and you blow your horn. Now if instead of blowing it now you had blown it at that unfortunate——

[*Horn violently.* TOMMY *the porter appears at top of station steps.*]

MR. SLOCUM [*calling*]. Will you come down, Tommy, and help this lady out, she's stuck. [TOMMY *descends the steps.*] Open the door, Tommy, and ease her out.

[TOMMY *opens the door.*]

TOMMY. Certainly, sir. Nice day for the races, sir. What would you fancy for——

MRS. ROONEY. Don't mind me. Don't take any notice of me. I do not exist. The fact is well known.

MR. SLOCUM. Do as you're asked, Tommy, for the love of God.

TOMMY. Yessir. Now, Mrs. Rooney.

[*He starts pulling her out.*]

MRS. ROONEY. Wait, Tommy, wait now, don't bustle me, just let me wheel round and get my feet to the ground. [*Her efforts to achieve this.*] Now.

TOMMY [*pulling her out*]. Mind your feather, Ma'am. [*Sounds of effort.*] Easy now, easy.

MRS. ROONEY. Wait, for God's sake, you'll have me beheaded.

TOMMY. Crouch down, Mrs. Rooney, crouch down, and get your head in the open.

MRS. ROONEY. Crouch down! At my time of life! This is lunacy!

TOMMY. Press her down, sir.

[*Sounds of combined efforts.*]

MRS. ROONEY. Pity!

TOMMY. Now! She's coming! Straighten up, Ma'am! There!

[MR. SLOCUM *slams the door.*]

MRS. ROONEY. Am I out?

[*The voice of* MR. BARRELL, *the station-master, raised in anger.*]

MR. BARRELL. Tommy! Tommy! Where the hell is he?

[MR. SLOCUM *grinds in his gear.*]

TOMMY [*hurriedly*]. You wouldn't have something for the Ladies Plate, sir. I was given Flash Harry.

MR. SLOCUM [*scornfully*]. Flash Harry! That carthorse!

MR. BARRELL [*at top of steps, roaring*]. Tommy! Blast your bleeding bloody—[*He sees* MRS. ROONEY.] Oh, Mrs. Rooney . . . [MR. SLOCUM *drives away in a grinding of gears.*] Who's that crucifying his gearbox, Tommy?

TOMMY. Old Cissy Slocum.

MRS. ROONEY. Cissy Slocum! That's a nice way to refer to your betters. Cissy Slocum! And you an orphan!

MR. BARRELL [*angrily to* TOMMY]. What are you doing stravaging down here on the public road? This is no place for you at all! Nip up there on the platform now and whip out the truck! Won't the twelve-thirty be on top of us before we can turn round?

TOMMY [*bitterly*]. And that's the thanks you get for a Christian act.

MR. BARRELL [*violently*]. Get on with you now before I report you! [*Slow feet of* TOMMY *climbing steps.*] Do you want me to come down to you with the shovel? [*The feet quicken, recede, cease.*] Ah God forgive me, it's a hard life. [*Pause.*] Well, Mrs. Rooney, it's nice to see you up and about again. You were laid up there a long time.

MRS. ROONEY. Not long enough, Mr. Barrell. [*Pause.*] Would I were still in bed, Mr. Barrell. [*Pause.*] Would I were lying stretched out in my comfortable bed, Mr. Barrell, just wasting slowly, painlessly away, keeping up my strength with arrowroot and calvesfoot jelly, till in the end you wouldn't see me under the blankets any more than a board. [*Pause.*] Oh no coughing or spitting or bleeding or vomiting, just drifting gently down into the higher life, and remembering, remembering . . . [*the voice breaks*] . . . all the silly unhappiness . . . as though . . . it had never happened . . . What did I do with that handkerchief? [*Sound of handkerchief loudly applied.*] How long have you been master of this station now, Mr. Barrell?

MR. BARRELL. Don't ask me, Mrs. Rooney, don't ask me.

MRS. ROONEY. You stepped into your father's shoes, I believe, when he took them off.

MR. BARRELL. Poor Pappy! [*Reverent pause.*] He didn't live long to enjoy his ease.

MRS. ROONEY. I remember him clearly. A small ferrety purple-faced widower, deaf as a doornail, very testy and snappy. [*Pause.*] I suppose you'll be retiring soon yourself, Mr. Barrell, and growing your roses. [*Pause.*] Did I understand you to say the twelve-thirty would soon be upon us?

MR. BARRELL. Those were my words.

MRS. ROONEY. But according to my watch which is more or less right—or was—by the eight o'clock news the time is now coming up to twelve . . . [*pause as she consults her watch*] . . . thirty-six. [*Pause.*] And yet upon the other hand the up mail has not yet gone through. [*Pause.*] Or has it sped by unbeknown to me? [*Pause.*] For there was a moment there, I remember now, I was so plunged in sorrow I wouldn't have heard a steam roller go over me. [*Pause.* MR. BARRELL *turns to go.*] Don't go, Mr. Barrell! [MR. BARRELL *goes. Loud.*] Mr. Barrell! [*Pause. Louder.*] Mr. Barrell!

[MR. BARRELL *comes back.*]

MR. BARRELL [*testily*]. What is it, Mrs. Rooney, I have my work to do.

[*Silence. Sound of wind.*]

MRS. ROONEY. The wind is getting up. [*Pause. Wind.*] The best of the day is over. [*Pause. Wind. Dreamily.*] Soon the rain will begin to fall and go on falling, all afternoon. [MR. BARRELL *goes.*] Then at evening the clouds will part, the setting sun will shine an instant, then sink, behind the hills. [*She realizes* MR. BARRELL *has gone.*] Mr. Barrell! Mr. Barrell! [*Silence.*] I estrange them all. They come towards me, uninvited, bygones bygones, full of kindness, anxious to help . . . [*the voice breaks*] . . . genuinely pleased . . . to see me again . . . looking so well . . . [*Handkerchief.*] A few simple words . . . from my heart . . . and I am all alone . . . once more . . . [*Handkerchief. Vehemently.*] I should not be out at all. I should never leave the grounds! [*Pause.*] Oh there is that Fitt woman, I wonder will she bow to me. [*Sound of* MISS FITT *approaching, humming a hymn. She starts climbing the steps.*] Miss

Fitt! [MISS FITT *halts, stops humming.*] Am I then invisible, Miss Fitt? Is this cretonne so becoming to me that I merge into the masonry? [MISS FITT *descends a step.*] That is right, Miss Fitt, look closely and you will finally distinguish a once female shape.

MISS FITT. Mrs. Rooney! I saw you, but I did not know you.

MRS. ROONEY. Last Sunday we worshipped together. We knelt side by side at the same altar. We drank from the same chalice. Have I so changed since then?

MISS FITT [*shocked*]. Oh but in church, Mrs. Rooney, in church I am alone with my Maker. Are not you? [*Pause.*] Why even the sexton himself, you know, when he takes up the collection, knows it is useless to pause before me. I simply do not see the plate, or bag, whatever it is they use, how could I? [*Pause.*] Why even when all is over and I go out into the sweet fresh air, why even then for the first furlong or so I stumble in a kind of daze as you might say, oblivious to my co-religionists. And they are very kind I must admit—the vast majority—very kind and understanding. They know me now and take no umbrage. There she goes, they say, there goes the dark Miss Fitt, alone with her Maker, take no notice of her. And they step down off the path to avoid my running into them. [*Pause.*] Ah yes, I am distray, very distray, even on week-days. Ask Mother, if you do not believe me. Hetty, she says, when I start eating my doily instead of the thin bread and butter, Hetty, how can you be so distray? [*Sighs.*] I suppose the truth is I am not there, Mrs. Rooney, just not really there at all. I see, hear, smell, and so on, I go through the usual motions, but my heart is not in it, Mrs. Rooney, but heart is in none of it. Left to myself, with no one to check me, I would soon be flown . . . home. [*Pause.*] So if you think I cut you just now, Mrs. Rooney, you do me an injustice. All I saw was a big pale blur, just another big pale blur. [*Pause.*] Is anything amiss, Mrs. Rooney, you do not look normal somehow. So bowed and bent.

MRS. ROONEY [*ruefully*]. Maddy Rooney, née Dunne, the big pale blur. [*Pause.*] You have piercing sight, Miss Fitt, if you only knew it, literally piercing.

[*Pause.*]

MISS FITT. Well . . . is there anything I can do, now that I am here?

MRS. ROONEY. If you would help me up the face of this cliff, Miss Fitt, I have little doubt your Maker would requite you, if no one else.

MISS FITT. Now, now, Mrs. Rooney, don't put your teeth in me. Requite! I make these sacrifices for nothing—or not at all. [*Pause. Sound of her descending steps.*] I take it you want to lean on me, Mrs. Rooney.

MRS. ROONEY. I asked Mr. Barrell to give me his arm, just give me his arm. [*Pause.*] He turned on his heel and strode away.

MISS FITT. Is it my arm you want then? [*Pause. Impatiently.*] Is it my arm you want, Mrs. Rooney, or what is it?

MRS. ROONEY [*exploding*]. Your arm! Any arm! A helping hand! For five seconds! Christ what a planet!

MISS FITT. Really . . . Do you know what it is, Mrs. Rooney, I do not think it is wise of you to be going about at all.

MRS. ROONEY [*violently*]. Come down here, Miss Fitt, and give me your arm, before I scream down the parish!

[*Pause. Wind. Sound of* MISS FITT *descending last steps.*]

MISS FITT [*resignedly*]. Well, I suppose it is the Protestant thing to do.

MRS. ROONEY. Pismires do it for one another. [*Pause.*] I have seen slugs do it. [MISS FITT *proffers her arm.*] No, the other side, my dear, if it's all the same to you, I'm left-handed on top of everything else. [*She takes* MISS FITT's *right arm.*] Heavens, child, you're just a bag of bones, you need building up. [*Sound of her toiling up steps on* MISS FITT's *arm.*] This is worse than the Matterhorn, were you ever up the Matterhorn, Miss Fitt, great honeymoon resort. [*Sound of toiling.*] Why don't they have a handrail? [*Panting.*] Wait till I get some air. [*Pause.*] Don't let me go! [MISS FITT *hums her hymn. After a moment* MRS. ROONEY *joins in with the words.*] . . . the encircling gloo-oom . . . [MISS FITT *stops humming.*] . . . tum tum me on. [*Forte.*] The night is dark and I am far from ho-ome, tum tum——

MISS FITT [*hysterically*]. Stop it, Mrs. Rooney, stop it, or I'll drop you!

MRS. ROONEY. Wasn't it that they sung on the *Lusitania*? Or Rock of Ages? Most touching it must have been. Or was it the *Titanic*?

427 **her hymn** John Henry Newman's "Lead, Kindly Light."

[*Attracted by the noise a group, including* MR. TYLER, MR. BARRELL, *and* TOMMY, *gathers at top of steps.*]

MR. BARRELL. What the——

[*Silence.*]

MR. TYLER. Lovely day for the fixture.

[*Loud titter from* TOMMY *cut short by* MR. BARRELL *with back-handed blow in the stomach. Appropriate noise from* TOMMY.]

FEMALE VOICE [*shrill*]. Oh look, Dolly, look!

DOLLY. What, Mamma?

FEMALE VOICE. They are stuck! [*Cackling laugh.*] They are stuck!

MRS. ROONEY. Now we are the laughing-stock of the twenty-six counties. Or is it thirty-six?

MR. TYLER. That is a nice way to treat your defenseless subordinates, Mr. Barrell, hitting them without warning in the pit of the stomach.

MISS FITT. Has anybody seen my mother?

MR. BARRELL. Who is that?

TOMMY. The dark Miss Fitt.

MR. BARRELL. Where is her face?

MRS. ROONEY. Now, deary, I am ready if you are. [*They toil up remaining steps.*] Stand back, you cads!

[*Shuffle of feet.*]

FEMALE VOICE. Mind yourself, Dolly!

MRS. ROONEY. Thank you, Miss Fitt, thank you, that will do, just prop me up against the wall like a roll of tarpaulin and that will be all, for the moment. [*Pause.*] I am sorry for all this ramdam, Miss Fitt, had I known you were looking for your mother I should not have importuned you, I know what it is.

MR. TYLER [*in marvelling aside*]. Ramdam!

FEMALE VOICE. Come, Dolly darling, let us take up our stand before the first class smokers. Give me your hand and hold me tight, one can be sucked under.

MR. TYLER. You have lost your mother, Miss Fitt?

MISS FITT. Good morning, Mr. Tyler.

MR. TYLER. Good morning, Miss Fitt.

MR. BARRELL. Good morning, Miss Fitt.

MISS FITT. Good morning, Mr. Barrell.

460 **ramdam** rumpus or rampage.

MR. TYLER. You have lost your mother, Miss Fitt?

MISS FITT. She said she would be on the last train.

MRS. ROONEY. Do not imagine, because I am silent, that I am not present, and alive, to all that is going on.

MR. TYLER [*to* MISS FITT]. When you say the last train——

MRS. ROONEY. Do not flatter yourselves for one moment, because I hold aloof, that my sufferings have ceased. No. The entire scene, the hills, the plain, the racecourse with its miles and miles of white rails and three red stands, the pretty little wayside station, even you yourselves, yes, I mean it, and over all the clouding blue, I see it all, I stand here and see it all with eyes . . . [*the voice breaks*] . . . through eyes . . . oh if you had my eyes . . . you would understand . . . the things they have seen . . . and not looked away . . . this is nothing . . . nothing . . . what did I do with that handkerchief?

[*Pause.*]

MR. TYLER [*to* MISS FITT]. When you say the last train—[MRS. ROONEY *blows her nose violently and long*]—when you say the last train, Miss Fitt, I take it you mean the twelve-thirty.

MISS FITT. What else could I mean, Mr. Tyler, what else could I *conceivably* mean?

MR. TYLER. Then you have no cause for anxiety, Miss Fitt, for the twelve-thirty has not yet arrived. Look. [MISS FITT *looks.*] No, up the line. [MISS FITT *looks. Patiently.*] No, Miss Fitt, follow the direction of my index. [MISS FITT *looks.*] There. You see now. The signal. At the bawdy hour of nine. [*In rueful afterthought.*] Or three alas! [MR. BARRELL *stifles a guffaw.*] Thank you, Mr. Barrell.

MISS FITT. But the time is now getting on for——

MR. TYLER [*patiently*]. We all know, Miss Fitt, we all know only too well what the time is now getting on for, and yet the cruel fact remains that the twelve-thirty has not yet arrived.

MISS FITT. Not an accident, I trust! [*Pause.*] Do not tell me she has left the track! [*Pause.*] Oh darling mother! With the fresh sole for lunch!

[*Loud titter from* TOMMY, *checked as before by* MR. BARRELL.]

MR. BARRELL. That's enough old guff out of you. Nip up to the box now and see has Mr. Case anything for me.

[TOMMY *goes.*]

MRS. ROONEY. Poor Dan!

MISS FITT [*in anguish*]. What terrible thing has happened?

MR. TYLER. Now now, Miss Fitt, do not——

MRS. ROONEY [*with vehement sadness*]. Poor Dan!

MR. TYLER. Now now, Miss Fitt, do not give way . . . to despair, all will come right . . . in the end. [*Aside to* MR. BARRELL.] What *is* the situation, Mr. Barrell? Not a collision surely?

MRS. ROONEY [*enthusiastically*]. A collision! Oh that would be wonderful!

MISS FITT [*horrified*]. A collision! I knew it!

MR. TYLER. Come, Miss Fitt, let us move a little up the platform.

MRS. ROONEY. Yes, let us all do that. [*Pause.*] No? [*Pause.*] You have changed your mind? [*Pause.*] I quite agree, we are better here, in the shadow of the waiting-room.

MR. BARRELL. Excuse me a moment.

MRS. ROONEY. Before you slink away, Mr. Barrell, please, a statement of some kind, I insist. Even the slowest train on this brief line is not ten minutes and more behind its scheduled time without good cause, one imagines. [*Pause.*] We all know your station is the best kept of the entire network, but there are times when that is not enough, just not enough. [*Pause.*] Now, Mr. Barrell, leave off chewing your whiskers, we are waiting to hear from you—we the unfortunate ticket-holders' nearest if not dearest.

[*Pause.*]

MR. TYLER [*reasonably*]. I do think we are owed some kind of explanation, Mr. Barrell, if only to set our minds at rest.

MR. BARRELL. I know nothing. All I know is there has been a hitch. All traffic is retarded.

MRS. ROONEY [*derisively*]. Retarded! A hitch! Ah these celibates! Here we are eating our hearts out with anxiety for our loved ones and he calls that a hitch! Those of us like myself with heart and kidney trouble may collapse at any moment and he calls that a hitch! In our ovens the Saturday roast is burning to a shrivel and he calls that——

MR. TYLER. Here comes Tommy, running! I am glad I have been spared to see this.

TOMMY [*excitedly, in the distance*]. She's coming. [*Pause. Nearer.*] She's at the level-crossing!

[*Immediately exaggerated station sounds. Falling signals. Bells. Whistles. Crescendo of train whistle approaching. Sound of train rushing through station.*]

MRS. ROONEY [*above rush of train*]. The up mail! The up mail!

[*The up mail recedes, the down train approaches, enters the station, pulls up with great hissing of steam and clashing of couplings. Noise of passengers descending, doors banging,* MR. BARRELL *shouting "Boghill! Boghill!", etc. Piercingly.*] Dan! . . . Are you all right? . . . Where is he? . . . Dan! . . . Did you see my husband? . . . Dan! . . . [*Noise of station emptying. Guard's whistle. Train departing, receding. Silence.*] He isn't on it! The misery I have endured, to get here, and he isn't on it! . . . Mr. Barrell! . . . Was he not on it? [*Pause.*] Is anything the matter, you look as if you had seen a ghost. [*Pause.*] Tommy! . . . Did you see the master?

TOMMY. He'll be along, Ma'am, Jerry is minding him.

[MR. ROONEY *suddenly appears on platform, advancing on small boy* JERRY'S *arm. He is blind, thumps the ground with his stick and pants incessantly.*]

MRS. ROONEY. Oh, Dan! There you are! [*Her dragging feet as she hastens towards him. She reaches him. They halt.*] Where in the world were you?

MR. ROONEY [*coolly*]. Maddy.

MRS. ROONEY. Where were you all this time?

MR. ROONEY. In the men's.

MRS. ROONEY. Kiss me!

MR. ROONEY. Kiss you? In public? On the platform? Before the boy? Have you taken leave of your senses?

MRS. ROONEY. Jerry wouldn't mind. Would you, Jerry?

JERRY. No, Ma'am.

MRS. ROONEY. How is your poor father?

JERRY. They took him away, Ma'am.

MRS. ROONEY. Then you are all alone?

JERRY. Yes, Ma'am.

MR. ROONEY. Why are you here? You did not notify me.

MRS. ROONEY. I wanted to give you a surprise. For your birthday.

MR. ROONEY. My birthday?

MRS. ROONEY. Don't you remember? I wished you your happy returns in the bathroom.

MR. ROONEY. I did not hear you.

MRS. ROONEY. But I gave you a tie! You have it on!

[*Pause.*]

MR. ROONEY. How old am I now?

MRS. ROONEY. Now never mind about that. Come.

MR. ROONEY. Why did you not cancel the boy? Now we shall have to give him a penny.

MRS. ROONEY [*miserably*]. I forgot! I had such a time getting here! Such horrid nasty people! [*Pause. Pleading.*] Be nice to me, Dan, be nice to me today!

MR. ROONEY. Give the boy a penny.

MRS. ROONEY. Here are two halfpennies, Jerry. Run along now and buy yourself a nice gobstopper.

JERRY. Yes, Ma'am.

MR. ROONEY. Come for me on Monday, if I am still alive.

JERRY. Yessir.

[*He runs off.*]

MR. ROONEY. We could have saved sixpence. We have saved fivepence. [*Pause.*] But at what cost?

[*They move off along platform arm in arm. Dragging feet, panting, thudding stick.*]

MRS. ROONEY. Are you not well?

[*They halt, on* MR. ROONEY'S *initiative.*]

MR. ROONEY. Once and for all, do not ask me to speak and move at the same time. I shall not say this in this life again.

[*They move off. Dragging feet, etc. They halt at top of steps.*]

MRS. ROONEY. Are you not——

MR. ROONEY. Let us get this precipice over.

MRS. ROONEY. Put your arm around me.

MR. ROONEY. Have you been drinking again? [*Pause.*] You are quivering like a blanc-mange. [*Pause.*] Are you in a condition to lead me? [*Pause.*] We shall fall into the ditch.

MRS. ROONEY. Oh, Dan! It will be like old times!

MR. ROONEY. Pull yourself together or I shall send Tommy for the cab. Then instead of having saved sixpence, no, fivepence, we shall have lost . . . [*calculating mumble*] . . . two and three less six one and no plus one one and no plus three one and nine and one ten and three two and one . . . [*normal voice*] two and one, we shall be the poorer to the tune of two and one. [*Pause.*] Curse that sun, it has gone in. What is the day doing?

[*Wind.*]

MRS. ROONEY. Shrouding, shrouding, the best of it is past. [*Pause.*] Soon the first great drops will fall splashing in the dust.

MR. ROONEY. And yet the glass was firm. [*Pause.*] Let us hasten home and sit before the fire. We shall draw the blinds. You will read to me. I think Effie is going to commit adultery with the Major. [*Brief drag of feet.*] Wait! [*Feet cease. Stick tapping at steps.*] I have been up and down these steps five thousand times and still I do not know how many there are. When I think there are six there are four or five or seven or eight and when I remember there are five there are three or four or six or seven and when finally I realize there are seven there are five or six or eight or nine. Sometimes I wonder if they do not change them in the night. [*Pause. Irritably.*] Well? How many do you make them today?

MRS. ROONEY. Do not ask me to count, Dan, not now.

MR. ROONEY. Not count! One of the few satisfactions in life!

MRS. ROONEY. Not steps, Dan, please, I always get them wrong. Then you might fall on your wound and I would have that on my manure-heap on top of everything else. No, just cling to me and all will be well.

[*Confused noise of their descent. Panting, stumbling, ejaculations, curses. Silence.*]

MR. ROONEY. Well! That is what you call well!

MRS. ROONEY. We are down. And little the worse. [*Silence. A donkey brays. Silence.*] That was a true donkey. Its father and mother were donkeys.

[*Silence.*]

MR. ROONEY. Do you know what it is, I think I shall retire.

MRS. ROONEY [*appalled*]. Retire! And live at home? On your grant!

MR. ROONEY. Never tread these cursed steps again. Trudge this hellish road for the last time. Sit at home on the remnants of my bottom counting the hours—till the next meal. [*Pause.*] The very thought puts life in me! Forward, before it dies!

[*They move on. Dragging feet, panting, thudding stick.*]

MRS. ROONEY. Now mind, here is the path . . . Up! . . . Well done! Now we are in safety and a straight run home.

MR. ROONEY [*without halting, between gasps*]. A straight . . . run! . . . She calls that . . . a straight . . . run! . . .

MRS. ROONEY. Hush! Do not speak as you go along, you know it is not good for your coronary. [*Dragging steps, etc.*] Just concentrate on putting one foot before the next or whatever the expression is.

[*Dragging feet, etc.*] That is the way, now we are doing nicely. [*Dragging feet, etc. They suddenly halt, on* MRS. ROONEY'S *initiative.*] Heavens! I knew there was something! With all the excitement! I forgot!

MR. ROONEY [*quietly*]. Good God.

MRS. ROONEY. But you must know, Dan, of course, you were on it. Whatever happened? Tell me!

MR. ROONEY. I have never known anything to happen.

MRS. ROONEY. But you must——

MR. ROONEY [*violently*]. All this stopping and starting again is devilish, devilish! I get a little way on me and begin to be carried along when suddenly you stop dead! Two hundred pounds of unhealthy fat! What possessed you to come out at all? Let go of me!

MRS. ROONEY [*in great agitation*]. No, I must know, we won't stir from here till you tell me. Fifteen minutes late! On a thirty-minute run! It's unheard of!

MR. ROONEY. I know nothing. Let go of me before I shake you off.

MRS. ROONEY. But you must know! You were on it! Was it at the terminus? Did you leave on time? Or was it on the line? [*Pause.*] Did something happen on the line? [*Pause.*] Dan! [*Brokenly.*] Why won't you tell me!

[*Silence. They move off. Dragging feet, etc. They halt. Pause.*]

MR. ROONEY. Poor Maddy! [*Pause. Children's cries.*] What was that?

[*Pause for* MRS. ROONEY *to ascertain.*]

MRS. ROONEY. The Lynch twins jeering at us.

[*Cries.*]

MR. ROONEY. Will they pelt us with mud today, do you suppose?

[*Cries.*]

MRS. ROONEY. Let us turn and face them. [*Cries. They turn. Silence.*] Threaten them with your stick. [*Silence.*] They have run away.

[*Pause.*]

MR. ROONEY. Did you ever wish to kill a child? [*Pause.*] Nip some young doom in the bud. [*Pause.*] Many a time at night, in winter, on the black road home, I nearly attacked the boy. [*Pause.*] Poor Jerry! [*Pause.*] What restrained me then? [*Pause.*] Not fear of man. [*Pause.*] Shall we go on backwards now a little?

MRS. ROONEY. Backwards?

MR. ROONEY. Yes. Or you forwards and I backwards. The perfect pair. Like Dante's damned, with their faces arsy-versy. Our tears will water our bottoms.

MRS. ROONEY. What is the matter, Dan? Are you not well?

MR. ROONEY. Well! Did you ever know me to be well? The day you met me I should have been in bed. The day you proposed to me the doctors gave me up. You knew that, did you not? The night you married me they came for me with an ambulance. You have not forgotten that, I suppose? [*Pause.*] No, I cannot be said to be well. But I am no worse. Indeed I am better than I was. The loss of my sight was a great fillip. If I could go deaf and dumb I think I might pant on to be a hundred. Or have I done so? [*Pause.*] Was I a hundred today? [*Pause.*] Am I a hundred, Maddy?

[*Silence.*]

MRS. ROONEY. All is still. No living soul in sight. There is no one to ask. The world is feeding. The wind—[*brief wind*]—scarcely stirs the leaves and the birds—[*brief chirp*]—are tired singing. The cows—[*brief moo*]—and sheep—[*brief baa*]—ruminate in silence. The dogs [*brief bark*]—are hushed and the hens—[*brief cackle*]—sprawl torpid in the dust. We are alone. There is no one to ask.

[*Silence.*]

MR. ROONEY [*clearing his throat, narrative tone*]. We drew out on the tick of time, I can vouch for that. I was——

MRS. ROONEY. How can you vouch for it?

MR. ROONEY [*normal tone, angrily*]. I can vouch for it, I tell you! Do you want my relation or don't you? [*Pause. Narrative tone.*] On the tick of time. I had the compartment to myself, as usual. At least I hope so, for I made no attempt to restrain myself. My mind—[*Normal tone.*] But why do we not sit down somewhere? Are we afraid we should never rise again?

MRS. ROONEY. Sit down on what?

MR. ROONEY. On a bench, for example.

MRS. ROONEY. There is no bench.

MR. ROONEY. Then on a bank, let us sink down upon a bank.

MRS. ROONEY. There is no bank.

MR. ROONEY. Then we cannot. [*Pause.*] I dream of other roads, in other lands. Of another home, another—[*he hesitates*]—another home. [*Pause.*] What was I trying to say?

MRS. ROONEY. Something about your mind.

MR. ROONEY [*startled*]. My mind? Are you sure? [*Pause. Incredulous.*] My mind? . . . [*Pause.*] Ah yes. [*Narrative tone.*] Alone in the compartment my mind began to work, as so often after office hours, on the way home, in the train, to the lilt of the bogeys. Your season-ticket, I said, costs you twelve pounds a year and you earn, on an average, seven and six a day, that is to say barely enough to keep you alive and twitching with the help of food, drink, tobacco and periodicals until you finally reach home and fall into bed. Add to this—or subtract from it—rent, stationery, various subscriptions, tramfares to and fro, light and heat, permits and licences, hairtrims and shaves, tips to escorts, upkeep of premises and appearances, and a thousand unspecifiable sundries, and it is clear that by lying at home in bed, day and night, winter and summer, with a change of pyjamas once a fortnight, you would add very considerably to your income. Business, I said—[*A cry. Pause. Again. Normal tone.*] Did I hear a cry?

MRS. ROONEY. Mrs. Tully I fancy. Her poor husband is in constant pain and beats her unmercifully.

[*Silence.*]

MR. ROONEY. That was a short knock. [*Pause.*] What was I trying to get at?

MRS. ROONEY. Business.

MR. ROONEY. Ah yes, business. [*Narrative tone.*] Business, old man, I said, retire from business, it has retired from you. [*Normal tone.*] One has these moments of lucidity.

MRS. ROONEY. I feel very cold and weak.

MR. ROONEY [*narrative tone*]. On the other hand, I said, there are the horrors of home life, the dusting, sweeping, airing, scrubbing, waxing, waning, washing, mangling, drying, mowing, clipping, raking, rolling, scuffling, shovelling, grinding, tearing, pounding, banging and slamming. And the brats, the happy little healthy little howling neighbours' brats. Of all this and much more the week-end, the Saturday intermission and then the day of rest, have given you some idea. But what must it be like on a working-day? A Wednesday? A Friday! What must it be like on a Friday! And I fell to thinking of my silent, backstreet, basement office, with its obliterated plate, rest-couch and velvet hangings, and what it means to be buried there alive, if only from ten to five, with convenient to the one hand a bottle of light pale ale and to the other a long ice-cold fillet of hake.

Nothing, I said, not even fully certified death, can ever take the place of that. It was then I noticed we were at a standstill. [*Pause. Normal tone. Irritably.*] Why are you hanging out of me like that? Have you swooned away?

MRS. ROONEY. I feel very cold and faint. The wind—[*whistling wind*]—is whistling through my summer frock as if I had nothing on over my bloomers. I have had no solid food since my elevenses.

MR. ROONEY. You have ceased to care. I speak—and you listen to the wind.

MRS. ROONEY. No no, I am agog, tell me all, then we shall press on and never pause, never pause, till we come safe to haven.

[*Pause.*]

MR. ROONEY. Never pause . . . safe to haven . . . Do you know, Maddy, sometimes one would think you were struggling with a dead language.

MRS. ROONEY. Yes indeed, Dan, I know full well what you mean, I often have that feeling, it is unspeakably excruciating.

MR. ROONEY. I confess I have it sometimes myself, when I happen to overhear what I am saying.

MRS. ROONEY. Well, you know, it will be dead in time, just like our own poor dear Gaelic, there is that to be said.

[*Urgent baa.*]

MR. ROONEY [*startled*]. Good God!

MRS. ROONEY. Oh the pretty little woolly lamb, crying to suck its mother! Theirs has not changed, since Arcady.

[*Pause.*]

MR. ROONEY. Where was I in my composition?

MRS. ROONEY. At a standstill.

MR. ROONEY. Ah yes. [*Clears his throat. Narrative tone.*] I concluded naturally that we had entered a station and would soon be on our way again, and I sat on, without misgiving. Not a sound. Things are very dull today, I said, nobody getting down, nobody getting on. Then as time flew by and nothing happened I realized my error. We had not entered a station.

MRS. ROONEY. Did you not spring up and poke your head out of the window?

MR. ROONEY. What good would that have done me?

792 **elevenses** a light mid-morning meal.

MRS. ROONEY. Why to call out to be told what was amiss.

MR. ROONEY. I did not care what was amiss. No, I just sat on, saying, If this train were never to move again I should not greatly mind. Then gradually a—how shall I say—a growing desire to—er—you know—welled up within me. Nervous probably. In fact now I am sure. You know, the feeling of being confined.

MRS. ROONEY. Yes yes, I have been through that.

MR. ROONEY. If we sit here much longer, I said, I really do not know what I shall do. I got up and paced to and fro between the seats, like a caged beast.

MRS. ROONEY. That is a help sometimes.

MR. ROONEY. After what seemed an eternity we simply moved off. And the next thing was Barrell bawling the abhorred name. I got down and Jerry led me to the men's, or Fir as they call it now, from Vir Viris I suppose, the V becoming F, in accordance with Grimm's Law. [*Pause.*] The rest you know. [*Pause.*] You say nothing? [*Pause.*] Say something, Maddy. Say you believe me.

MRS. ROONEY. I remember once attending a lecture by one of these new mind doctors, I forget what you call them. He spoke——

MR. ROONEY. A lunatic specialist?

MRS. ROONEY. No no, just the troubled mind. I was hoping he might shed a little light on my lifelong preoccupation with horses' buttocks.

MR. ROONEY. A neurologist.

MRS. ROONEY. No no, just mental distress, the name will come back to me in the night. I remember his telling us the story of a little girl, very strange and unhappy in her ways, and how he treated her unsuccessfully over a period of years and was finally obliged to give up the case. He could find nothing wrong with her, he said. The only thing wrong with her as far as he could see was that she was dying. And she did in fact die, shortly after he washed his hands of her.

MR. ROONEY. Well? What is there so wonderful about that?

MRS. ROONEY. No, it was just something he said, and the way he said it, that have haunted me ever since.

MR. ROONEY. You lie awake at night, tossing to and fro and brooding on it.

MRS. ROONEY. On it and other . . . wretchedness. [*Pause.*] When he had done with the little girl he stood there motionless for some time, quite two minutes I should say, looking down at his table. Then he suddenly raised his head and exclaimed, as if he had had a revelation, The trouble with her was she had never been really born! [*Pause.*] He spoke throughout without notes. [*Pause.*] I left before the end.

MR. ROONEY. Nothing about your buttocks? [MRS. ROONEY *weeps. In affectionate remonstrance.*] Maddy!

MRS. ROONEY. There is nothing to be done for those people!

MR. ROONEY. For which is there? [*Pause.*] That does not sound right somehow. [*Pause.*] What way am I facing?

MRS. ROONEY. What?

MR. ROONEY. I have forgotten what way I am facing.

MRS. ROONEY. You have turned aside and are bowed down over the ditch.

MR. ROONEY. There is a dead dog down there.

MRS. ROONEY. No no, just the rotting leaves.

MR. ROONEY. In June? Rotting leaves in June?

MRS. ROONEY. Yes, dear, from last year, and from the year before last, and from the year before that again. [*Silence. Rainy wind. They move on. Dragging steps, etc.*] There is that lovely laburnum again. Poor thing, it is losing all its tassels. [*Dragging steps, etc.*] There are the first drops. [*Rain. Dragging feet, etc.*] Golden drizzle. [*Dragging steps, etc.*] Do not mind me, dear, I am just talking to myself. [*Rain heavier. Dragging steps, etc.*] Can hinnies procreate, I wonder?

[*They halt.*]

MR. ROONEY. Say that again.

MRS. ROONEY. Come on, dear, don't mind me, we are getting drenched.

MR. ROONEY [*forcibly*]. Can what what?

MRS. ROONEY. Hinnies procreate. [*Silence.*] You know, hinnies, or jinnies, aren't they barren, or sterile, or whatever it is? [*Pause.*] It wasn't an ass's colt at all, you know, I asked the Regius Professor.

[*Pause.*]

MR. ROONEY. He should know.

MRS. ROONEY. Yes, it was a hinny, he rode into Jerusalem or wherever it was on a hinny. [*Pause.*] That must mean something.

893 **an ass's colt** on which Jesus rode into Jerusalem on Palm Sunday; see Matthew 21:2–8.

[*Pause.*] It's like the sparrows, than many of which we are of more value, they weren't sparrows at all.

MR. ROONEY. Than many of which! . . . You exaggerate, Maddy.

MRS. ROONEY [*with emotion*]. They weren't sparrows at all!

MR. ROONEY. Does that put our price up?

[*Silence. They move on. Wind and rain. Dragging feet, etc. They halt.*]

MRS. ROONEY. Do you want some dung? [*Silence. They move on. Wind and rain, etc. They halt.*] Why do you stop? Do you want to say something?

MR. ROONEY. No.

MRS. ROONEY. Then why do you stop?

MR. ROONEY. It is easier.

MRS. ROONEY. Are you very wet?

MR. ROONEY. To the buff.

MRS. ROONEY. The buff?

MR. ROONEY. The buff. From buffalo.

MRS. ROONEY. We shall hang up all our things in the hot-cupboard and get into our dressing-gowns. [*Pause.*] Put your arm round me. [*Pause.*] Be nice to me! [*Pause. Gratefully.*] Ah, Dan! [*They move on. Wind and rain. Dragging feet, etc. Faintly same music as before. They halt. Music clearer. Silence but for music playing. Music dies.*] All day the same old record. All alone in that great empty house. She must be a very old woman now.

MR. ROONEY [*indistinctly*]. Death and the Maiden.

[*Silence.*]

MRS. ROONEY. You are crying. [*Pause.*] Are you crying?

MR. ROONEY [*violently*]. Yes! [*They move on. Wind and rain. Dragging feet, etc. They halt. They move on. Wind and rain. Dragging feet, etc. They halt.*] Who is the preacher tomorrow? The incumbent?

MRS. ROONEY. No.

MR. ROONEY. Thank God for that. Who?

MRS. ROONEY. Hardy.

MR. ROONEY. "How to be Happy though Married"?

MRS. ROONEY. No no, he died, you remember. No connexion.

MR. ROONEY. Has he announced his text?

MRS. ROONEY. "The Lord upholdeth all that fall and raiseth up all those that be bowed down." [*Silence. They join in wild laughter.*

They move on. Wind and rain. Dragging feet, etc.] Hold me tighter, Dan! [*Pause.*] Oh yes!

[*They halt.*]

MR. ROONEY. I hear something behind us.

[*Pause.*]

MRS. ROONEY. It looks like Jerry [*Pause.*] It is Jerry.

[*Sound of* JERRY's *running steps approaching. He halts beside them, panting.*]

JERRY [*panting*]. You dropped——

MRS. ROONEY. Take your time, my little man, you will burst a blood-vessel.

JERRY [*panting*]. You dropped something, sir. Mr. Barrell told me to run after you.

MRS. ROONEY. Show. [*She takes the object.*] What is it? [*She examines it.*] What is this thing, Dan?

MR. ROONEY. Perhaps it is not mine at all.

JERRY. Mr. Barrell said it was, sir.

MRS. ROONEY. It looks like a kind of ball. And yet it is not a ball.

MR. ROONEY. Give it to me.

MRS. ROONEY [*giving it*]. What *is* it, Dan?

MR. ROONEY. It is a thing I carry about with me.

MRS. ROONEY. Yes, but what——

MR. ROONEY [*violently*]. It is a thing I carry about with me!

[*Silence.* MRS. ROONEY *looks for a penny.*]

MRS. ROONEY. I have no small money. Have you?

MR. ROONEY. I have none of any kind.

MRS. ROONEY. We are out of change, Jerry. Remind Mr. Rooney on Monday and he will give you a penny for your pains.

JERRY. Yes, Ma'am.

MR. ROONEY. If I am alive.

JERRY. Yessir.

[JERRY *starts running back towards the station.*]

MRS. ROONEY. Jerry! [JERRY *halts.*] Did you hear what the hitch was? [*Pause.*] Did you hear what kept the train so late?

MR. ROONEY. How would he have heard? Come on.

MRS. ROONEY. What was it, Jerry?

JERRY. It was a——

MR. ROONEY. Leave the boy alone, he knows nothing! Come on!

MRS. ROONEY. What was it, Jerry?

JERRY. It was a little child, Ma'am.

[MR. ROONEY *groans.*]

MRS. ROONEY. What do you mean, it was a little child?

JERRY. It was a little child fell out of the carriage, Ma'am. [*Pause.*] On to the line, Ma'am. [*Pause.*] Under the wheels, Ma'am.

[*Silence.* JERRY *runs off. His steps die away. Tempest of wind and rain. It abates. They move on. Dragging steps, etc. They halt. Tempest of wind and rain.*]

END

ACT WITHOUT WORDS I : *BECKETT*

A MIME FOR ONE PLAYER

TRANSLATED FROM THE FRENCH BY THE AUTHOR

Desert. Dazzling light.

The man is flung backwards on stage from right wing. He falls, gets up immediately, dusts himself, turns aside, reflects.

Whistle from right wing.

He reflects, goes out right.

Immediately flung back on stage he falls, gets up immediately, dusts himself, turns aside, reflects.

Whistle from left wing.

He reflects, goes out left.

Immediately flung back on stage he falls, gets up immediately, dusts himself, turns aside, reflects.

Whistle from left wing.

He reflects, goes towards left wing, hesitates, thinks better of it, halts, turns aside, reflects.

A little tree descends from flies, lands. It has a single bough some three yards from ground and at its summit a meager tuft of palms casting at its foot a circle of shadow.

He continues to reflect.

Whistle from above.

He turns, sees tree, reflects, goes to it, sits down in its shadow, looks at his hands.

A pair of tailor's scissors descends from flies, comes to rest before tree, a yard from ground.

He continues to look at his hands.

Whistle from above.

He looks up, sees scissors, takes them and starts to trim his nails.

The palms close like a parasol, the shadow disappears.

He drops scissors, reflects.

A tiny carafe, to which is attached a huge label inscribed WATER, descends from flies, comes to rest some three yards from ground.

He continues to reflect.

Whistle from above.

He looks up, sees carafe, reflects, gets up, goes and stands under it, tries in vain to reach it, renounces, turns aside, reflects.

A big cube descends from flies, lands.

He continues to reflect.

Whistle from above.

He turns, sees cube, looks at it, at carafe, reflects, goes to cube, takes it up, carries it over and sets it down under carafe, tests its stability, gets up on it, tries in vain to reach carafe, renounces, gets down, carries cube back to its place, turns aside, reflects.

A second smaller cube descends from flies, lands.

He continues to reflect.

Whistle from above.

He turns, sees second cube, looks at it, at carafe, goes to second cube, takes it up, carries it over and sets it down under carafe, tests its stability, gets up on it, tries in vain to reach carafe, renounces, gets down, takes up second cube to carry it back to its place, hesitates, thinks better of it, sets it down, goes to big cube, takes it up, carries it over and puts it on small one, tests their stability, gets up on them, the cubes collapse, he falls, gets up immediately, brushes himself, reflects.

He takes up small cube, puts it on big one, tests their stability, gets up on them and is about to reach carafe when it is pulled up a little way and comes to rest beyond his reach.

He gets down, reflects, carries cubes back to their place, one by one, turns aside, reflects.

A third still smaller cube descends from flies, lands.

He continues to reflect.

Whistle from above.

He turns, sees third cube, looks at it, reflects, turns aside, reflects.

The third cube is pulled up and disappears in flies.

Beside carafe a rope descends from flies, with knots to facilitate ascent.

He continues to reflect.

Whistle from above.

He turns, sees rope, reflects, goes to it, climbs up it and is about to reach carafe when rope is let out and deposits him back on ground.

He reflects, looks around for scissors, sees them, goes and picks them up, returns to rope and starts to cut it with scissors.

The rope is pulled up, lifts him off ground, he hangs on, succeeds in cutting rope, falls back on ground, drops scissors, falls, gets up again immediately, brushes himself, reflects.

The rope is pulled up quickly and disappears in flies.

With length of rope in his possession he makes a lasso with which he tries to lasso carafe.

The carafe is pulled up quickly and disappears in flies.

He turns aside, reflects.

He goes with lasso in his hand to tree, looks at bough, turns and looks at cubes, looks again at bough, drops lasso, goes to cubes, takes up small one, carries it over and sets it down under bough, goes back for big one, takes it up and carries it over under bough, makes to put it on small one, hesitates, thinks better of it, sets it down, takes up small one and puts it on big one, tests their stability, turns aside and stoops to pick up lasso.

The bough folds down against trunk.

He straightens up with lasso in his hand, turns and sees what has happened.

He drops lasso, turns aside, reflects.

He carries back cubes to their place, one by one, goes back for lasso, carries it over to cubes and lays it in a neat coil on small one.

He turns aside, reflects.

Whistle from right wing.

He reflects, goes out right.

Immediately flung back on stage he falls, gets up immediately, brushes himself, turns aside, reflects.

Whistle from left wing.

He does not move.

He looks at his hands, looks around for scissors, sees them, goes and picks them up, starts to trim his nails, stops, reflects, runs his finger along blade of scissors, goes and lays them on small cube, turns aside, opens his collar, frees his neck and fingers it.

The small cube is pulled up and disappears in flies, carrying away rope and scissors.

He turns to take scissors, sees what has happened.

He turns aside, reflects.

He goes and sits down on big cube.

The big cube is pulled from under him. He falls. The big cube is pulled up and disappears in flies.

He remains lying on his side, his face towards auditorium, staring before him.

The carafe descends from flies and comes to rest a few feet from his body.

He does not move.

Whistle from above.

He does not move.

The carafe descends further, dangles and plays about his face.

He does not move.

The carafe is pulled up and disappears in flies.

The bough returns to horizontal, the palms open, the shadow returns.

Whistle from above.

He does not move.

The tree is pulled up and disappears in flies.

He looks at his hands.

END